The Complete
SPEAKERS
SOURCEBOOK

Also by Eleanor Doan . . .

A Child's Treasury of Verse

The Complete
SPEAKERS
SOURCEBOOK

8,000
Illustrations &
Quotations for
Every Occasion

ELEANOR DOAN

ZondervanPublishingHouse
Grand Rapids, Michigan

A Division of HarperCollinsPublishers

The Complete Speakers Sourcebook
Copyright © 1996 by Zondervan Publishing House

Speakers Sourcebook
Copyright © 1960 by The Zondervan Corporation. Renewed 1988
by the Zondervan Corporation.

Speakers Sourcebook II
Copyright © 1988 by Zondervan Publishing House

Requests for information should be addressed to:

🏛 ZondervanPublishingHouse
Grand Rapids, Michigan 49530

Library of Congress Cataloging-in-Publication Data

Speaker's Sourcebook of 4,000 illustrations, quotations, sayings, anecdotes, poems, attention
   getters, sentence sermons
      The Complete Speakers Sourcebook : 8,000 illustrations and quotations for every
occasion / [compiled by] Eleanor Doan.
      p. cm.
   First work originally published: The speaker's sourcebook of 4,000 illustrations, quota-
tions, sayings, anecdotes, poems, attention getters, sentence sermons. Grand Rapids, Mich. :
Zondervan, 1960. Second work originally published : Speakers sourcebook II. Grand Rapids,
MI : Ministry Resources Library, 1989.
      Includes index.
      ISBN: 0-310-20951-X
      1. Quotations, English. I. Doan, Eleanor Lloyd, 1914– . II. Speakers sourcebook II.
III. Title.
PN6081.S7218   1996
808.88 ' 2–dc 20   95-52385
                                                                                    CIP

This edition printed on acid-free paper and meets the American National Standards Institute Z39.48 standard.

Printed in the United States of America

96 97 98 99 00 01 02 03 / ❖ DH / 10 9 8 7 6 5 4 3 2

Dedicated to

My Father, who unknowingly started me on this series
of books, and

My Mother, whose help with the first book inspired
continuance with this volume
and with grateful appreciation to

Jackie McGregor for invaluable assistance in classifying and checking materials,

Helena Wiebe for her faithful help in typing, recheck-
ing contents, and finalizing copy,

and to many others whose names I do not know, but
whose contributions are invaluable.

OUNCES OF ILLUSTRATION . . .

Everyone at one time or another searches frantically for an attention-getter whether it be an adage, anecdote, illustration, maxim or poem. He is firmly convinced of this truth: "An ounce of illustration is worth a ton of talk." The problem, however, is where to find this "ounce of illustration" in a hurry. Have you found this to be true? If so, this book is your answer.

Attention-getters are many and varied (see the helpful glossary) and success in using them depends upon our understanding their purpose. The words "attention-getters" are self-explanatory. However, besides attracting attention, they are used for the purposes of clinching a truth and giving light. The late Philip E. Howard, Sr., former publisher of *The Sunday School Times*, has given us this fine counsel: "Every good illustration throws light. Every good illustration gives additional light."

Every good illustration gives additional light in an unexpected way. Mr. Howard then summarizes: "An illustration should be opened just as a Christmas package is opened in the home. The tighter the string, the tighter the expectancy, particularly if you can't tell from the shape of the box what is in it."

Every consideration possible should be given to the careful use of attention-getters. They should always be in good taste and should be evaluated as to fitness of subject and range of understanding of audience. Proper timing also is important, as is appropriate telling or expression. Among considerations are two don'ts: (1) Don't antagonize your audience, and (2) don't imitate another person. Never use illustrations for the purpose of telling something interesting or clever. They are helpers only.

"How and where can I find attention-getters?" is a frequently asked question. The answer to the "how" is constant alertness and searching. The answer to "where" is twofold: life itself and reading.

Life about us overflows with resources for stories, illustrations, axioms and anecdotes. Talk with people; pry into their experiences and listen with a pencil in hand. Children will come forth with rare gems of wisdom and unpredictable answers. Teachers will share unusual classroom conversations and experiences. Missionaries will tell thrilling stories for all ages. Parents and neighbors can be more helpful than we realize. Firsthand life experience is indeed an important source of help.

Reading is the second source of real help. Read carefully; read widely. Read missionary papers, biographies, magazines, newspapers. Current news is the best reflector of current life so read with alertness for items which will furnish illustrations. If possible, read with a pair of scissors in hand.

Always keep a little notebook and pencil in your pocket or purse and be prepared to jot down any apt saying, story or illustrative information which you hear or read. Do not trust to memory.

A further question you may ask concerning the gathering of attention-getters is, "How and where should I keep all this material?" Keeping material is as important as gathering it but unfortunately it is usually just kept without any thought as to where or how.

Most everyone has a "Fibber McGee" notebook or desk drawer full of clippings, poetry and similar "things" he wants to keep because someday he will use them. When he does, he looks in the notebook or drawer, shakes his head and says, "Now, where did I put that story or quotation?" Of course he doesn't find it and doesn't use it. But he goes on saving it and hundreds of others, believing that "One of these days I'll sort things out."

Has this ever happened to you? Perhaps you don't have a notebook or drawer, but have assorted boxes under the bed, a spindle in the back of a cupboard or sheaves of papers in assorted envelopes. How can you convert this chaos into an organized handbook? I Corinthians 14:40 gives the answer: "Let all things be done decently and in order."

Have a purpose for saving what you save. Save only what materials you know will be useful to you.

Know where to put what you save. Have a place to put clippings and notes as they accumulate. Decide the method of keeping materials which will best suit your needs. Mark the items as they are saved. Paste materials in notebooks, the size depending upon items saved. The most popular type is a loose-leaf style notebook in which an alphabetizer has been placed. Don't let materials accumulate. Put them into notebooks as soon as possible after they are collected.

Classify what you save. Provide a "table of contents" for each notebook. Keep classification simple and functional. (The index of this book is an example of a practical pattern to follow). Don't serve a system; make it serve you.

The topical method of compiling this book is for the purpose of making it a handbook — usable for innumerable occasions.

In addition to using this book for written or verbal purposes, use it:
1. As a source of quotes for church papers, calendars, bulletin boards.
2. For teacher training poster ideas.
3. For selecting club, class and organization mottoes.
4. For youth bulletins, papers and calendars. Feature in a "Quote Korner" or "Gems of Wisdom" box — it will do more for young people than a ton of talk.

Adapted from *A Little Kit of Teachers' Tools* by Philip E. Howard, Sr., Philadelphia, Pennsylvania, *The Sunday School Times*. Used by permission.

A HELPFUL GLOSSARY . . .

ADAGE — A saying of long established authority and universal appreciation.

ANECDOTE — A brief narrative of curious interest, usually biographical.

APHORISM — A pithy sentence stating a general truth or sentiment or doctrinal truth.

AXIOM — A statement of self-evident truth taken for granted.

CLICHE — A trite or hackneyed expression.

DICTUM — An authoritative statement or dogmatic principle.

ILLUSTRATION — A brief narrative to elucidate a point.

MAXIM — A precept sanctioned by experience and relating especially to the practical concerns of life.

MOTTO — A maxim.

PROVERB — An adage couched, usually, in a homely and vividly concrete phrase.

QUIP — A witty outburst or saying.

SAYING — Any brief current or habitual expression; an axiom.

STORY — An anecdote.

SPEAKERS
SOURCEBOOK

A

Ability

When our capabilities are of God, we are never incapable.

———•———

It is not ability that God wants, but usability.

———•———

There is a great deal of unmapped country within us.   GEORGE ELIOT

———•———

Many people have ability, but lack stability.

———•———

Absence, Absent, Absentee

If absence makes the heart grow fonder, how some people must *love* Sunday school and church.

———•———

Absent pupils cannot be reached by absent callers.

———•———

Absence makes the heart go wander.

———•———

Absent today, lost tomorrow.

———•———

We have a little grievance:
  We just don't think it's fair
That children come to Sunday school
  But their parents are not there.
Can it be they do not care to hear
  That story old and sweet?
Are they too wise and dignified
  To sit at Jesus' feet?   P.A.S.S. News

———•———

The Absentee

"Someone is absent," the Shepherd said,
  As over my class book He bent His head;
"For several Sundays absent, too,
  So tell Me, teacher, what did you do?"

"I didn't call as perhaps I should,
  I wrote some cards, but they did no good,
I've never heard and she never came,
  So I decided to drop her name."

He answered gravely, "A flock was mine,
  A hundred — no, there were ninety and nine;
For one was lost in the dark and cold;
  So I sought that sheep which had left the fold.

"The path was stony and edged with thorns;
  My feet were wounded, and bruised and torn,
But I kept on seeking, nor counted the cost;
  And, oh, the joy when I found the lost!"

Thus spake the Shepherd in tender tone,
  I looked and lo — I was alone,
But God a vision had sent to me,
  To show His will toward the absentee.
                              AUTHOR UNKNOWN

———•———

The Board of Absentees

We are the Board of Absentees;
We attend our church about as we please;
We judge it will run of itself, you know,
And, Sundays, we're just too tired to go!

We are the Board of Absentees;
At business meetings our chance we seize
To tell exactly how things should be run,
But we lift not a finger to get them done.

We are the Board of Absentees;
We like our drive in the morning breeze;
Of course the budget should all be paid,
"But privately now, I'm in the red."

We are the Board of Absentees;
Men and women of all degrees;
"Shall we give up the church? O never, never!"
"Shall we go today?" Well, scarcely ever!

We look for a world far better than this,
A world of peace and of moderate bliss,
A day of right through the Seven Seas—
Just now we're the Board of Absentees!
                    The Christian Register

They won't miss me, said the mother as she repeatedly left her children for rounds of teas and parties. The devil did not "miss" the children either.

They won't miss me, said the soldier as he went A.W.O.L. But he spent thirty days in the guard house after that.

They won't miss me, said the sentry as he slipped away from duty. But the enemy surprised and massacred his comrades that very night.

They won't miss me, said the man on the assembly line, as he slipped away without permission. But the airplane crashed and killed his brother for the lack of a single part.

They won't miss me, said the Christian worker as he shed his responsibilities in a day of crisis, and then he wondered why his country gave way to softness and demoralization.

They won't miss me, said the church member as he omitted worship one Sunday, and then another, for trivial reasons, and then wondered why he no longer enjoyed a victorious Christian life. *The Baptist Outlook*

Private Interpretation of Scripture

I will come into Thy house in the multitude of Thy mercy —
except in summer.
The Lord is in His holy temple —
except in summer.
One thing have I desired of the Lord, that I will seek after;
That I may dwell in the house of the Lord all the days of my life —
except in summer.
God is known in her palaces for a refuge —
except in summer.
How amiable are Thy tabernacles —
except in summer.
My soul longeth, even fainteth for the courts of the Lord —
except in summer.
Preach the word; be instant in season and out of season —
except in summer.

Not forsaking the assembling of ourselves together —
except in summer.
They continued steadfastly in the apostles' doctrine and fellowship,
And in breaking of bread and in prayers —
except in summer.

Accidents

One day a young man had an accident — he was struck with a thought.

Accidents don't just happen; they are caused!

"Did you hear about the terrible accident down town today?" the boy asked.
"No," his friend answered. "What was it?"
"Well, a streetcar ran over a peanut and killed two kernels."

Accomplish, Accomplishment

You can get anything done if you don't care who gets the credit.

Between the great things we cannot do and the little things we will not do, the danger is that we will do nothing. H. G. WEAVER

The reward of a thing well done is to have done it. RALPH WALDO EMERSON

The world is blessed most by men who do things, and not by those who merely talk about them. JAMES OLIVER

The great doing of little things makes the great life. EUGENIA PRICE

If the mountain won't come to Mohammed, Mohammed will come to the mountain.

Those who would bring great things to pass must rise early. MATTHEW HENRY

Specialize in doing what you can't.

There is no right way to do a wrong thing.

————◆————

Zacchaeus had short legs, but he outran the crowd when Jesus passed through town.

Short legs will get you there as fast as long legs if you know how to use them. DR. BOB JONES, SR.

————◆————

Do the best you can
with what you've got,
where you are.

————◆————

He does most in God's great world who does his best in his own little world. THOMAS JEFFERSON

————◆————

If what you did yesterday still looks big to you, you haven't done much today. *The Sunday School*

————◆————

If I cannot do great things,
I can do small things in a great way. J. F. CLARKE

————◆————

Unless a man undertakes more than he possibly can do he will never do all that he can. HENRY DRUMMOND

————◆————

Free peoples can escape being mastered by others only by being able to master themselves. THEODORE ROOSEVELT

————◆————

If people knew how hard I have had to work to gain my mastery, it would not seem wonderful at all. MICHELANGELO

————◆————

God will not look you over for medals, degrees or diplomas, but for scars.

————◆————

What most folks need is an alarm clock that will ring when it's time for them to rise to the occasion.

————◆————

An engine of one-cat power running all the time is more effective than an engine of forty-horse power standing idle. *The Sunday School*

————◆————

No gains without pains. BENJAMIN FRANKLIN

The fellow who "does it now" has time to do something else while the other fellow is "still thinking about it."

————◆————

Go as far as you can see, and when you get there you will see farther. ORISON SWEET MARDEN

————◆————

The Pessimist says, "It can't be done."
The Optimist says, "It can be done."
The Peptimist says, "I just did it."

————◆————

The greatest things in the world have been done by those who systematized their work and organized their time. ORISON SWEET MARDEN

————◆————

Nobody don't never get nothing for nothing nowhere, no time, nohow. *American Proverb*

————◆————

I divide the world in three classes —
the few who make things happen,
the many who watch things happen,
the overwhelming majority who have
no notion of what happens. NICHOLAS MURRAY BUTLER

————◆————

Footprints in the sands of time were not made sitting down.

————◆————

Accountability

The most frightening fact we have to face: ". . . every one of us shall give account of himself to God." Romans 14:12.

————◆————

Accuracy

Accuracy is better than speed.

————◆————

Accuse, Accuser

A ready accuser may be a self-excuser.

————◆————

He that accuses all mankind of corruption ought to remember that he is sure to convict only one. EDMUND BURKE

————◆————

Let us be excusers rather than accusers.

————◆————

Clean your fingers before you point at my spots. BENJAMIN FRANKLIN

Adult

When adults act like children, they're silly.

When children act like adults, they're delinquent. *The Kernel*

———♦———

All adults ought to have at least one job before anyone has more than one job.

———♦———

Adverse, Adversity

God develops spiritual power in our lives through pressure of hard places.

———♦———

When any calamity has been suffered, the first thing to be remembered is, how much has been escaped. SAMUEL JOHNSON

———♦———

God sometimes puts us in the dark to prove to us that He is light.

———♦———

Adversity

To the thorns of life I'm more indebted
Than am I to the roses sweet;
They will not let me lie inactive
While round me there are tasks to meet.
They spur me on to nobler action,
Nor long allow me quiet ease,
But keep on pricking at my conscience —
And often drive me to my knees. RUTH SMELTZER

———♦———

God gets His best soldiers out of the highlands of affliction.

———♦———

The school of affliction graduates rare scholars.

———♦———

Our Heavenly Father never takes anything from His children unless He means to give them something better. GEORGE MUELLER

———♦———

To bear other people's afflictions, everyone has courage and enough to spare. BENJAMIN FRANKLIN

———♦———

If God sends us on stony paths He will provide us with strong shoes. ALEXANDER MACLAREN

My Web of Life

No chance has brought this ill to me;
'Tis God's sweet will, so let it be,
He seeth what I cannot see.
There is a need be for each pain;
And He will one day make it plain
That earthly loss is heavenly gain.
Like as a piece of tapestry
Viewed from the back appears to be
But tangled threads mixed hopelessly;
But in the front a picture fair
Rewards the worker for his care,
Proving his skill and patience rare.
Thou art the workman, I the frame;
Lord, for the glory of Thy name
Perfect Thine image on the same. ANONYMOUS

———♦———

If men can be found faithful in hard places they can be trusted in high places.

———♦———

Trial is the school of trust.

———♦———

God pounds you in your soft spots until you toughen up. PAUL WHITE

———♦———

God promises a safe landing but not a calm passage. *Bulgarian Proverb*

———♦———

The diamond cannot be polished without friction, nor the man perfected without trials. *Chinese Proverb*

———♦———

The brook would lose its song if you removed the rocks. FRED BECK

———♦———

Advertise

Advertise

A lion met a tiger
    As they drew beside a pool,
Said the tiger, "Tell me why
    You're roaring like a fool."
"That's not foolish," said the lion
    With a twinkle in his eyes.
"They call me king of all beasts
    Because I advertise."
A rabbit heard them talking
    And ran home like a streak;
He thought he'd try the lion's plan,
    But his roar was just a squeak.

A fox came to investigate —
Had luncheon in the woods,
So when you advertise, my friend,
Be sure you've got the goods.
Exchange

———✦———

The little city boy was on his first real vacation with this father. The two were hiking in the mountains when his daddy pointed out a brilliant rainbow.

"It sure is pretty," said the youngster. "What's it advertising?"

———✦———

Advice

Advice is seldom welcome; and those who want it the most always like it the least. LORD CHESTERFIELD

———✦———

To profit from good advice requires more wisdom than to give it. CHURTON COLLINS

———✦———

Advice is like snow; the softer it falls the longer it dwells upon, and the deeper it sinks into the mind. SAMUEL COLERIDGE

———✦———

Correct your own mistakes by avoiding those of others.

———✦———

Ill customs and bad advice are seldom forgotten. BENJAMIN FRANKLIN

———✦———

Two things in life I've had and ample: Good advice and bad example.

———✦———

He that won't be counseled can't be helped. BENJAMIN FRANKLIN

———✦———

It is safer to hear and take counsel than to give it.

———✦———

The best counsel I can give is the advice a friend wrote to a young man who had just been promoted: "Keep on doing what it took to get started." JOHN L. MC CAFFERY, *International Harvester*

———✦———

Bride: "How can I keep my wedding ring clean?"

Mother: "Soak gently in dishwater three times a day!"

Timely Advice

If you are *impatient,* sit down quietly and talk with Job.

If you are just a little *strong-headed,* go and see Moses.

If you are getting *weak-kneed,* take a good look at Elijah.

If there is *no song in your heart,* listen to David.

If you are a *policy man,* read Daniel.

If your *faith is below par,* read Paul.

If you are getting *lazy,* watch James.

If you are *losing sight of the future,* climb up the stairs of Revelation and get a glimpse of the promised land. CHARLES E. FULLER

———✦———

Keep your eye on the ball, your shoulder to the wheel, and your ear to the ground . . . now try to work in that position.

———✦———

Two young children built a clubhouse in their yard. On the wall, in childish lettering is a list of club rules. No. 1 rule reads:

Nobody act big,
Nobody act small,
Everybody act medium.
Voice of Youth

———✦———

Fear less, hope more;
Eat less, chew more;
Whine less, breathe more;
Talk less, say more;
Hate less, love more;
And all good things will be yours.
Swedish Proverb

———✦———

Don't Let Yourself

WORRY when you are doing your best.

HURRY when success depends upon accuracy.

THINK evil of a friend until you have the facts.

BELIEVE a thing is impossible without trying it.

WASTE time on peevish and peeving matters.

IMAGINE that good intentions are a satisfying excuse.

HARBOR bitterness in your soul toward God or man. *Christ for World Messenger*

Don't Let This Happen to You

There was a man who lived by the side of the road and sold hot dogs.

He was hard of hearing so he had no radio.

He had trouble with his eyes so he read no newspapers.

But he sold good hot dogs.

He put up signs on the highway telling how good they were.

He stood on the side of the road and cried, "Buy a hot dog, Mister?"

And people bought his hot dogs.

He increased his meat and bun orders.

He bought a bigger stove to take care of his trade.

He finally got his son home from college to help out.

But then something happened.

His son said, "Father, haven't you been listening to the radio?

"Haven't you been reading the newspaper?

"There's a big recession on.

"The European situation is terrible.

"The Domestic situation is worse."

Whereupon the father thought, "Well, my son's been to college, he reads the papers and he listens to the radio, and he ought to know."

So the father cut down his meat and bun orders, took down his signs, and no longer bothered to stand out on the highway to sell his hot dogs.

His sales fell overnight.

"You're right, son," the father said to the boy.

"We certainly are in the middle of a big recession."

———◆———

No vice is so bad as advice.
MARIE DRESSLER

———◆———

Lucky men need no counsel.
H. G. BOHN

———◆———

If your head is wax, don't walk in the sun.
BENJAMIN FRANKLIN

———◆———

Age

Age is a quality of the mind.

———◆———

Gray hairs are death's blossoms.

Nobody knows the age of the human race, but all agree that it is old enough to know better.
ANONYMOUS

———◆———

Let your age be measured by spiritual progress.
Eternity

———◆———

We live in an age which thinks being lost in the woods is a new freedom.

———◆———

This generation plays everything but safe.
FRED BECK

———◆———

The Golden Age was never the present age.
BENJAMIN FRANKLIN

———◆———

The best thing to save for old age is yourself.
National Motorist

———◆———

One has to grow older to become more tolerant.
GOETHE

———◆———

As soon as you feel too old to do a thing, do it.
MARGARET DELAND

———◆———

A man who celebrated his fiftieth wedding anniversary recently, says, "A man is always as young as he feels but seldom as important."

———◆———

A great many people who are worried about adding years to their life should try adding life to their years.

———◆———

An old young man will be a young old man.
BENJAMIN FRANKLIN

———◆———

I Shall Not Mind

I shall not mind
  The whiteness of my hair,
Or that slow steps falter
  On the stair,
Or that young friends hurry
  As they pass,
Or what strange image
  Greets me in the glass —
If I can feel,
  As roots feel in the sod,
That I am growing old to bloom
  Before the face of God.
AUTHOR UNKNOWN

Forty is the old age of youth, fifty is the youth of old age. VICTOR HUGO

———◆———

Do not resent growing old. Think how much you'd resent being denied the privilege.

———◆———

At 20 years of age the will reigns;
At 30 the wit;
At 40 the judgment. BENJAMIN FRANKLIN

———◆———

The six ages of man:
Beef broth,
Ground steak,
Sirloin,
Filet mignon,
Ground steak,
Beef broth.

———◆———

Who at twenty knows nothing,
At thirty does nothing,
At forty has nothing. *Italian Proverb*

———◆———

How to Grow Old

If you want to be an old man long before your time,
Never fool with poetry, never make a rhyme.
Never play with children, never skip the rope,
Never have a good time blowing bubble soap.
Never go a fishing, never pass the ball,
Never ramble in the woods in summer or in fall.
Never lift your eyes to God, keep 'em looking down,
Never wear a pleasant smile, always wear a frown.
Never take your time to eat, always overstuff,
Never have the sense to know when you've had enough. ALEX RENNIE

———◆———

A birthday is the one time that every woman wants her past forgotten and her present remembered.

———◆———

Grecian ladies counted their age from their marriage, not from their birth. HOMER

No woman should ever be quite accurate about her age. It looks so calculating. OSCAR WILDE

———◆———

Most women not only respect old age, they approach it with extreme caution.

———◆———

When one woman was asked her age she said, "I'm as old as my nose and a little older than my teeth."

———◆———

Alexandre Dumas, in answer to the question, "How do you grow old so gracefully?" replied, "Madam, I give all my time to it."

———◆———

When you begin to notice what a jolly time the young people are having, you're getting old.

———◆———

Middle age is when you're just as young as ever, but it takes a lot more effort. HAL CHADWICK

———◆———

Definition of B-29: What women in their middle forties wish they could again.

———◆———

The longest period in a woman's life is the 10 years between the time she is 39 and 40.

———◆———

Four

Four is too big for his breeches,
Knows infinitely more than his mother,
Four is matinee idol
To two-and-a-half, his brother.

Four is a lyric composer,
Raconteur extraordinaire,
Four gets away with murder,
Out of line, and into hair.

Where Four is, there dirt is also,
And nails and lengths of twine,
Four is Mr. Fix-it
And all of his tools are mine.

Four barges into everything
(Hearts, too) without a knock
Four will be five on the twelfth of July
And I wish I could stop the clock.
ELISE GIBBS *in Reader's Digest*

If you want to know how old a woman is, ask her sister-in-law.

EDGAR W. HOWE

———◆———

A historian says that women used cosmetics in the Middle Ages. They still use cosmetics in the middle ages.

———◆———

Seven Ages of Woman

The infant
The little girl,
The miss.
The young woman,
The young woman,
The young woman,
The young woman.

———◆———

Man's life means
Tender teens,
Teachable twenties,
Tireless thirties,
Fiery forties,
Forceful fifties,
Serious sixties,
Sacred seventies,
Aching eighties,
Shortening breath,
Death,
The Sod,
God.

———◆———

You may be old at 40 and young at 80; but you are genuinely old at any age if:
You feel old;
You feel you have learned all there is to learn;
You find yourself saying, "I'm too old to do that";
You feel tomorrow holds no promise;
You take no interest in the activities of youth;
You would rather talk than listen;
You long for the "good old days" feeling they were the best.

Minnesota State Medical Association

———◆———

Old age is the time when men pay more attention to their food than they do to the waitresses.

ALBERT FLETCHER, *Southern Reporter*

An old-timer is one who remembers when we counted our blessings instead of our calories.

National Motorist

———◆———

Altar

Altars

A man I know has made an altar
Of his factory bench.
And one has turned the counter of his store
Into a place of sacrifice and holy ministry.
Another still has changed his office desk
Into a pulpit desk, from which to speak and write,
Transforming commonplace affairs
Into the business of the King.

A Martha in our midst has made
Her kitchen table a communion table,
A postman makes his daily round
A walk in the temple of God . . .
To all of these each daily happening
Has come to be a whisper from the lips of God,
Each separate task a listening post,
And every common circumstance a wayside shrine.

EDGAR FRANK

———◆———

A family altar leads to an altered life.

The Friendly Messenger

———◆———

The family altar which does not alter the family is not a good family altar.

———◆———

Evening Is Best

I like the evening best
 When children say their prayers.
When little tousled towheads
 Stumble up the stairs.
I like the birds' soft twitter.
 The friendly sounds of night;
A hearth where cherry driftwood
 Throws a ruddy light.

HARRIET MARKHAM GILL

———◆———

Ambition

If your pet ambition doesn't mean a "hard row to hoe," it may not have a future worth digging for.

Better to say, "This one thing I do," than to dabble in forty.

It is a sin to do less than your best. DR. BOB JONES, SR.

I rise early because no day is long enough for a day's work. JUSTICE BRANDEIS

You draw nothing out of the bank of life except what you deposit in it.

A winner never quits and a quitter never wins.

Nothing is humbler than ambition when it is about to climb. BENJAMIN FRANKLIN

From a little spark may burst a mighty flame. DANTE

Stand still and silently watch the world go by — and it will.

There is always room at the top because many of those who get there go to sleep and roll off. National Motorist

Achievement can be no greater than the plans you make.

After a junior high school class toured the White House, the teacher asked each student to write impressions of the visit. One boy wrote: "I was especially glad to have this opportunity to visit my future home."

Ancestors

It is the general rule, that all superior men inherit the elements of superiority from their mothers. NICHELET

We used to do things for posterity, but now we do things for ourselves and leave the bill to posterity. Lutheran Education

As I understand it, heredity is what a man believes in until his son begins to act like a delinquent. Presbyterian Life

No person can have in-laws without being one. DR. ALICE SOWERS

A rich relative is described as "the kin we love to touch."

It is a poor tribute to our forefathers to camp where they fell.

Relatives are like sweet potatoes, the best part is under the ground.

Angels

In reviewing the story of Jacob's dream, a Sunday school teacher asked the class, "Why did the angels use the ladder when they had wings?"

One bright pupil quickly replied, "Because they were molting."

Little Hugh had been fascinated about the sermon he had heard on angels. As he was telling a friend about it they got into an argument. The little friend insisted that all angels had wings, but Hugh disagreed.

"It isn't true," insisted Hugh. "Our preacher says that some of them are strangers in underwares."

Anger

The prudent man does not let his temper boil over lest he get into hot water.

Anger is a stone cast into a wasp's nest. Malabar Proverb

Anger is just one letter short of Danger.

Anger manages everything badly. STATIUS

Anger is never without a reason, but seldom with a good one. BENJAMIN FRANKLIN

A husband's wrath spoils the best broth.

Two people ought not to get angry at the same time.

———◆———

Anger is a wind which blows out the lamp of the mind.

———◆———

Animals

One day as we were driving through the country, my small son David spoke up excitedly saying, "Oh, Mother, look at the cow's popsicle." I looked over in a field and saw a cow calmly licking a large block of salt which was placed on a small post on the ground.

HELEN MAC MILLAN in *Christian Home*

———◆———

Me? Owl

In friendship, a rift
Occurs when they've written:
"We're sending a gift
To your children — a kitten."

———◆———

The postman stared doubtfully at the formidable looking animal lying on the doorstep. "What kind of dog is that?" he asked the little old lady.

"I don't rightly know," she said. "My brother sent it from Africa."

"Well," the postman hesitated, "it's the oddest looking dog I've ever seen."

The prim lady nodded her head. "You should have seen it before I cut its mane off."

———◆———

A little boy and his daddy were looking at a litter of puppies, planning to buy one, and the daddy asked the boy which one he wanted. The lad pointed to a pup whose tail was wagging furiously and said, "That one with the happy ending." *Presbyterian Life*

———◆———

Zoo's Who A-B-C

Alligator, beetle, porcupine, whale,
Bobolink, panther, dragonfly, snail,
Crocodile, monkey, buffalo, hare,
Dromedary, leopard, mud turtle, bear,
Elephant, badger, pelican, ox,
Flying fish, reindeer, anaconda, fox,
Guinea pig, dolphin, antelope, goose,
Hummingbird, weasel, pickerel, moose,
Ibex, rhinoceros, owl, kangaroo,
Jackal, opossum, toad, cockatoo,
Kingfisher, peacock, anteater, bat,
Lizard, ichneumon, honeybee, rat,
Mockingbird, camel, grasshopper, mouse,
Nightingale, spider, cuttlefish, grouse,
Ocelot, pheasant, wolverine, auk,
Periwinkle, ermine, katydid, hawk,
Quail, hippopotamus, armadillo, moth,
Rattlesnake, lion, woodpecker, sloth,
Salamander, goldfish, angleworm, dog,
Tiger, flamingo, scorpion, frog,
Unicorn, ostrich, nautilus, mole,
Viper, gorilla, basilisk, sole,
Whippoorwill, beaver, centipede, fawn,
Xantho, canary, pollywog, swan,
Yellowhammer, eagle, hyena, lark,
Zebra, chameleon, butterfly, shark.

HENRY KNIGHT

———◆———

A kindergarten-age lad was deeply grieved because his tiger cat had just died. His mother helped the boy put the cat in a box and bury it. Some weeks later the lad came running into the house excitedly, urging his mother to go outside with him and look up into the tree. Looking down at the boy and his mother was a tiger cat a little larger than the one that had died, but marked the same way.

"There he is, Mommy," the boy said. "See? I planted Tiger and he just growed up."

———◆———

One Sunday afternoon a family was driving out in the country. The children were telling about the Bible story they had heard in Sunday school that morning — David and the giant. Suddenly little Sally interrupted the conversation and pointed to some Holstein cows. "There's some of those Philistines now!"

———◆———

Anxiety

Mistrust the man who finds everything good, the man who finds everything evil, and, still more, the man who is indifferent to everything. LAVATER

The most anxious man in a prison is the governor. GEORGE BERNARD SHAW

The beginning of anxiety is the end of faith, and the beginning of true faith is the end of anxiety. GEORGE MUELLER

The crosses which we make for ourselves by a restless anxiety as to the future are not crosses which come from God.

Anxiety is a word of unbelief or unreasoning dread. We have no right to allow it. Full faith in God puts it to rest. HORACE BUSHNELL

Anxiety is like the rust of life, destroying its brightness and weakening its power. A childlike and abiding trust in Providence is its best preventive and remedy.

Appearance

A long face and a broad mind are rarely found under the same hat.

A dear old Quaker lady, distinguished for her youthful appearance, was asked what she used to preserve her charms. She replied sweetly, "I used for the lips, truth; for the voice, prayer; for the eyes, pity; for the hand, charity; for the figure, uprightness; and for the heart, love." JERRY FLEISHMAN

Young Charles, age four, came in for his midmorning glass of fruit juice. It was a warm morning and he had been playing hard. Also, because he liked the treat he had come for, he was juice-conscious.

"Mother," he said, "would you wipe my face with a wet cloth? It is sort of sticky."

"What did you get on it, dear?" his mother asked as she reached for the washcloth.

"Nothin'," he replied in his slow western drawl, "it's just face juice." *Christian Home*

Application

"Grandma," asked a youngster, "were you once a little girl like me?"

"Yes, dear."

"Then," continued the child, "I suppose you know how it feels to get an ice cream cone when you don't expect it."

One day little Jane was seated alone at a small table while her parents sat with their guests at the large table. This greatly displeased Jane. Before eating, Jane's parents thought it would be nice for Jane to be included in the group although she was seated separately, so father asked her to say the blessing. This was her prayer: "Lord, I thank Thee for this table in the presence of mine enemies. Amen."

During the observance of Animal Week the fourth graders told about their kindness to pets. Asked what he had done, one little boy said, "I kicked a boy for kicking his dog."

The teacher told the children they could take turns telling a brief story about something exciting. After listening to a few more lengthy stories, Bobby arose, bowed politely and said, "Help!"

To live is not to learn, but to apply. LEGOUVE

Appreciate, Appreciation

It's better to appreciate things you don't have than to have things you don't appreciate.

If you cannot have everything, make the best of everything you have.

Next to excellence is the appreciation of it. THACKERAY

The chance for appreciation is much increased by being the child of an appreciator. RALPH WALDO EMERSON

23

Argue

Two boys were fighting and the one on the bottom was yelling. At last the mother of the boy on top came out and called her son. He hit the boy on the bottom a few more times and then spit in his eye. The mother said to him when he got up, "Why do you fight all the time? It must be the devil in you."

After a little thought the boy replied, "It may be the devil in me that makes me hit, but spitting in that guy's eye was my own idea."

———◆———

Too many sound arguments are all sound.

———◆———

It is better to debate a question without settling it than to settle it without debate. JOUBERT

———◆———

To win an argument is to lose a friend.

———◆———

A family jar is no good for preserving the peace.

———◆———

It is a lot easier to get the best of an argument than it is to prove you are right.

———◆———

Many a long dispute among Divines may thus be abridged: It is so: It is not so: It is so: It is not so. BENJAMIN FRANKLIN

———◆———

Some people are so constituted that they would rather lose a friend than an argument. Be yourself, simple, honest and unpretending, and you will enjoy through life the respect and love of friends. SHERMAN

———◆———

When nobody disagrees with you, you can assure yourself that you are exceptionally brilliant. Or else you're the boss.

———◆———

The springs of human conflict cannot be eradicated through institutions, but only through the reform of the individual human being. GENERAL DOUGLAS MAC ARTHUR

To disagree is one thing; to be disagreeable is another.

———◆———

Arithmetic

I was trying to teach arithmetic reasoning when I asked, "If you know the price of seven hats, how would you find the cost of one?"

"Ask the clerk," replied one 10-year-old. ETHEL FISCHER in NEA Journal

———◆———

Teacher asked Wally how he would divide 10 potatoes equally among 20 people. Wally promptly replied, "I'd mash them."

———◆———

Add to the pleasure of others.
Subtract from another's unhappiness.
Multiply the pleasures of others.
Divide the good things that come your way.

———◆———

Attendance

Simply stopping the leaks in Sunday school attendance would more than triple the number of new members.

———◆———

Little is accomplished if we lose pupils out the back door as fast as we bring them in at the front.

———◆———

Announcing a special meeting the minister said, "Come early if you hope to get a back seat."

———◆———

A minister, out driving, passed a track where a horse race was in progress. His six-year-old son gazed from the window at the crowded stadium. "Oh, Daddy," he exclaimed, "all the pews are filled!" *Together*

———◆———

I see in your church convention that you discussed the subject, "How to Get People to Attend Church." I have never heard a single address at a farmer's convention on how to get the cattle to come to the rack. We spend our time discussing the best kind of feed. *The Baptist Outlook*

Little Johnny came home from Sunday school and told his mother that if he missed three Sundays in a row, teacher would throw him into the furnace. The horrified mother telephoned the teacher at once. "What I said was," the calm teacher explained, "that if any child missed three Sundays in a row, he would be dropped from the register." *Presbyterian Life*

When a man refuses to attend church any day in the week, he is a "Seven Day Absentist."

This Means U!

We cannot spell S U nday without U
We cannot spell ch U rch without U
We cannot spell cens U s without U
We cannot spell s U ccess without U
Our church needs U to help
We are counting on U.
The Sunday School Builder

Ten Reasons for Attending Sunday School

1. From the Standpoint of Godliness:
It teaches the Bible — which is the basis of our faith in God — and leads to Christ as personal Saviour and Lord.
2. From the Standpoint of Education:
It trains the mind and heart along the lines of things eternal.
3. From the Social Standpoint:
It enables one to enjoy the friendship and fellowship of genuine Christians.
4. From the Standpoint of Personality:
It helps to develop the Christian character necessary to face life's problems victoriously.
5. From the Standpoint of Character:
It is the chief aim of the Sunday school to teach us to be examples of the believer in word and deed.
6. From the Standpoint of Interest:
It presents interesting programs for our delight and culture.
7. From the Standpoint of Family:
It has a class for every age, and the whole family can go together and profit by its teaching.

8. From the Standpoint of Service:
It affords simple opportunity to serve God and the Church in activities that are not open elsewhere.
9. From the Standpoint of Immortality:
It turns our eyes heavenward and makes us realize that we must prepare for a life beyond the mortal grave.
10. From the Practical Standpoint:
The hour or so spent in Sunday school each Sunday could not be expended more profitably.
National S.S. Association and Greater Chicago S.S. Association

Attention

The true art of memory is the art of attention. SAMUEL JOHNSON

One Sunday morning a man entered the church and sat down near the front with his hat on. Noting the man, one of the ushers spoke to him, asking him if he knew he forgot to remove his hat.
"Yes," the man replied, "I realize I have my hat on. I've been coming to this church for two months and this is the only way I could get anyone to speak to me."

"But, Sir, that's the wrong way to spell *paint*," said the apprentice to his employer.
"Yes, I know," rejoined the other, "but I have a reason for spelling it that way."
He then explained that when he wrote the usual "Wet Paint" sign, passers-by paid little heed and often ruined their clothes, but "Wet Pent" would catch their attention, and while they might laugh at the ignorance of the painter, they remembered to keep away from danger.

Residents of a little village were perturbed because motorists sped through their town at dangerously high speeds, paying no attention to the neat "Drive Slowly" sign posted at the entrance. Finally they dragged a badly wrecked car to the spot and added to the sign the words, "This Might Happen to You." The effect was tremendous.

Even a Sunday school superintendent or teacher might find his suggestions more effective if stated in some unusual way. *The Sunday School*

Attitude

Often attitudes are kindled in the flame of others' convictions. LOIS E. LE BAR

———♦———

It's not the outlook, but the uplook that counts.

———♦———

They conquer who believe they can.

———♦———

It is your actions and attitude when you are on your own that reflect what you really are. MARTIN VANBEE

———♦———

We should be slower to think that the man at his worst is the real man, and certain that the better we are ourselves the less likely is he to be at his worst in our company. JAMES M. BARRIE

———♦———

The best answer to self-consciousness is God-consciousness. F. B. MEYER

———♦———

The person who always looks down his nose gets the wrong slant.

———♦———

The attitude of the individual determines the attitude of the group.

———♦———

Don't go around with a chip on your shoulder, people might think it came off your head. *Changing Times*

Automobile

The part of the automobile that causes the most accidents is the nut that holds the steering wheel.

———♦———

The difference between the driver of a new automobile and the owner of a new automobile is 24 monthly payments. *Glendale News Press*

———♦———

Car sickness is that feeling you get every month when the payment falls due. *American Weiser, Idaho*

———♦———

A smart aleck stopped at the garage and asked a mechanic: "How do you tell how much horsepower a car has?"

The mechanic replied: "Lift the hood and count the plugs."

———♦———

A station wagon is something city folks buy when they move to the country so the country folks will know they're from the city. *Glendale News Press*

———♦———

Station attendant to beautiful young driver whose new car had two wrinkled fenders: "How much mileage do you get per fender?"

———♦———

Traffic officer to motorist: "The highway sign '90' means the route number, not the speed limit."

———♦———

If you want to live to see ninety, don't look for it on the automobile speedometer.

B

Baby, Babies

The great events of this world are not battles and earthquakes and hurricanes. The great events of this world are babies. They are earthquakes and hurricanes.

Young Father: "In your sermon this morning you spoke about a baby being a new wave on the ocean of life."

Minister: "That's right."

Young Father: "Don't you think a fresh squall would have been nearer the truth?"

We haven't all had the good fortune to be ladies; we haven't all been generals, or poets, or statesmen; but when the toast works down to the babies, we stand on common ground. MARK TWAIN

———◆———

A Baby

That which makes the home happier,
Love stronger,
Patience greater
Hands busier,
Nights longer,
Days shorter,
Purses lighter,
Clothes shabbier,
The past forgotten,
The future brighter. MARION LAWRENCE

———◆———

Think not that he is all too young to teach,
His little heart will like a magnet reach
And touch the truth for which you have no speech. FROEBEL

———◆———

A baby is the little rivet in the bonds of matrimony.

———◆———

Sign on a church's crib room: "Bawl Room."

———◆———

Infancy conforms to nobody; all conform to it.

———◆———

Baby Shoes

Often tiny baby feet,
Tired from their play,
Kick off scuffed-up little shoes
At the close of day.
And often tired mothers
Find them lying there,
And over them send up to God
This fervent, whispered prayer:
"God, guide his every footstep
In paths where Thou has stood;
God, make him brave; God, make him strong;
And please, God, make him good!"
And every man must walk a path,
And every man must choose;
But some forget their mother's prayers
Over their baby shoes.
MARY HOLMES in The War Cry

It's marvelous how the cry of a little baby in the still of the night evokes wonder. Usually you wonder which one of you will get up. *Changing Times*

———◆———

Bachelor

A bachelor is one who didn't make the same mistake once.

———◆———

A bachelor is a man who has cheated some woman out of a divorce.

———◆———

"I could marry any girl I please," said the young man, "but I don't please any."

———◆———

A bachelor is a man who can have a girl on his knees without having her on his hands.

———◆———

A bachelor never gets over the idea that he is a thing of beauty and a boy forever. HELEN ROWLAND

———◆———

Baptism

A minister was baptizing a six-year-old boy and repeated his name with a "Junior" after it. Instantly he was interrupted in a voice loud enough to fill the great sanctuary.

"It's the third," said the lad, "I'm named after my father and my grandfather, and I have to carry on in their honor, my mother says, but just call me 'Butch,' will you, huh?"

———◆———

A Presbyterian and a Baptist minister were discussing baptism. After a beautiful dissertation on the subject by the Baptist minister, the Presbyterian minister asked if the Baptist considered a person baptized if he were immersed in water up to his chin. "No," said the Baptist.

"Is he considered baptized if he is immersed up to his nose?" asked the Presbyterian.

Again the Baptist's answer was "No."

"Well, if you immerse him up to his eyebrows do you consider him baptized?" queried the Presbyterian.

27

"You don't seem to understand," said the Baptist. "He must be immersed completely in water — until his head is covered."

"That's what I've been trying to tell you all along," said the Presbyterian, "it's only a little water on the top of the head that counts."

Beauty

Beauty is as beauty does.

———◆———

The best part of beauty is that which no picture can express.

FRANCIS BACON

———◆———

Beauty is only skin deep — but oh, what skin!

———◆———

A woman deserves no credit for her beauty at sixteen but beauty of sixty is her own soul's doing.   ANONYMOUS

———◆———

Beauty belongs to beauty.

———◆———

A plain face is often surprisingly beautiful by reason of an inner light.

HENRY E. WALBERY

———◆———

What is beautiful is good, and who is good will soon also be beautiful.

SAPPHO

———◆———

Beginnings

A teakettle singing on the stove was the beginning of the steam engine.

A shirt waving on a clothesline was the beginning of a balloon, the forerunner of the Graf Zeppelin.

A spider web strung across a garden path suggested the suspension bridge.

A lantern swinging in a tower was the beginning of the pendulum.

An apple falling from a tree was the cause of discovering the law of gravitation.   Reville

———◆———

Behavior

If you are bent on having a fling, don't forget it carries a sting.

———◆———

Always put off until tomorrow the things you should not do today.

It is not so important to be active, but to be effective.

Six-year-old Bobby's report card showed excellent marks except in deportment.

"Bobby," said his mother, "the teacher has a note attached that says you were a little boisterous."

"Well, what did you expect," bristled Bobby. "Did you think I'd be a little girlsterous?"   National Parent Teacher

———◆———

You Tell on Yourself

You tell on yourself by the friends you seek,
By the very manner in which you speak,
By the way you employ your leisure time,
By the use you make of dollar and dime.
You tell what you are by the things you wear
By the spirit in which you burdens bear,
By the kind of things at which you laugh,
By the records you play on the phonograph,
You tell what you are by the way you walk,
By the things of which you delight to talk,
By the manner in which you bear defeat,
By so simple a thing as how you eat.
By the books you choose from the well-filled shelf:
In these ways and more, you tell on yourself.
So, there's really no particle of sense,
In an effort to keep up false pretense.

Selected

———◆———

Always do right. This will gratify some people and astonish the rest.

MARK TWAIN

———◆———

Many a child is spoiled because you can't spank two grandmothers.

Town Journal

———◆———

The man who sows wild oats away from home usually raises cain at home.

Conduct is three-fourths of character, but habits are nine-tenths of conduct. We know character by habits.

———◆———

People may doubt what you say, but they will always believe what you do.

———◆———

What you are speaks so loudly that men cannot hear what you say.

EMERSON

———◆———

It is far better to do well than to say well.

———◆———

All the beautiful sentiments in the world weigh less than a single lovely action. JAMES RUSSELL LOWELL

———◆———

There probably isn't a business in America that hasn't one or more practices that irritate the public and are not really essential to the business. All our practices need constant examination and appraisal by one whose first precept is that every company action must promote good will and not bad feeling.

KEITH S. MC HUGH

———◆———

Never explain your actions. Your friends don't need it and your enemies won't believe you anyway.

———◆———

A fond mother asked her four-year-old son what the nursery school had taught the pupils that day. Replied the youngster, "They taught the kids who hit, not to hit; and the ones who don't hit, to hit back." Parents' Magazine

Belief, Believe, Believers

More persons, on the whole, are humbugged by believing in nothing, than by believing too much.

P. T. BARNUM

———◆———

Believe that you have a thing and you have it.

———◆———

It wasn't Dunninger, but some other mental wizard, who remarked: "Tell me what you believe and I'll tell you what you'll achieve."

What you believe is what you are.

NATHANIEL OLSON

———◆———

Brethren, be great believers. Little faith will bring your souls to heaven, but great faith will bring heaven to your souls. SPURGEON

———◆———

Belief is a truth held in the mind. Faith is a fire in the heart.

JOSEPH FORT NEWTON

———◆———

A good question for an atheist is to serve him a fine dinner, and then ask him if he believes there is a cook.

———◆———

Atheism can never be an institution. It is destitution.

———◆———

Unbelief is not a problem of the intellect but of the will.

———◆———

Believers are not hired servants, supporting themselves by their own work, but children maintained at their Father's expense. HORATIUS BONAR

———◆———

Bible

Seven Wonders of the Word:

1. The wonder of its formation — the way in which it grew is one of the mysteries of time.
2. The wonder of its unification — a library of 66 books, yet one book.
3. The wonder of its age — most ancient of all books.
4. The wonder of its sale — best seller of any book.
5. The wonder of its interest — only book in world read by all classes.
6. The wonder of its language — written largely by uneducated men, yet the best from a literary standpoint.
7. The wonder of its preservation—the most hated of all books, yet it continues to exist. "The word of our God shall stand for ever."

———◆———

While a minister was packing his suitcase he found a little room in it. "So," he told a friend, "there is still enough room for me to pack a guide-

BIBLE

book, a lamp, a mirror, a telescope, a book of poems, a number of biographies, a bundle of old letters, a hymn book, a sharp sword, a small library of 30 volumes."

When the friend looked at the small space for all this he asked, "How can you manage all that in the space you have?"

"That is easy," said his friend, "for the Bible contains all of these things."

Gospel Herald

How to Handle the Bible

Get everything out of it,
Do not read anything into it,
Let nothing remain unread in it.

J. A. BENGEL

Seven Wonderful Things in the Bible

1. Peter's hook — to bring up fish.
2. David's crook — to guide the sheep.
3. Gideon's torch — to light the dark places.
4. Moses' rod — to overcome.
5. David's sling — to prostrate giant foes.
6. Brazen serpent — to cure bite of world's snakes.
7. Paul's armor — to be our protection.

Bible Cake

1 cup butter (Judges 5:25)
3½ cups flour (I Kings 4:22)
3 cups sugar (Jeremiah 6:20)
2 cups raisins (I Samuel 30:12)
2 cups figs (I Samuel 30:12)
1 cup water (Genesis 24:17)
1 cup almonds (Genesis 43:11)
6 eggs (Isaiah 10:14)
1 tsp. honey (Exodus 16:31)
pinch of salt (Leviticus 2:13)
2 tsp. baking powder (I Corinthians 5:6)
spice to taste (I Kings 10:10)

Follow Solomon's advice for making good boys and girls and you will have a good cake (Proverbs 23:14).

PICKERING

The most desirable time to read the Bible is as often as possible.

Know the Bible in your mind,
Keep it in your heart;
Live it in your life,
Share it with the world.

Bible Society Record

The Books of the Bible

In *Genesis* the world was made by God's creative hand;
In *Exodus* the Hebrews marched to gain the Promised Land;
Leviticus contains the law, holy, and just and good.
Numbers records the tribes enrolled — all sons of Abraham's blood.
Moses in *Deuteronomy*, records God's mighty deeds;
Brave *Joshua* into Canaan's land the host of Israel leads.
In *Judges* their rebellion oft provokes the Lord to smite.
But *Ruth* records the faith of one well pleasing in His sight,
In First and Second *Samuel* of Jesse's son we read.
Ten Tribes in First and Second *Kings* revolted from his seed.
The First and Second *Chronicles* see Judah captive made:
But *Ezra* leads a remnant back by princely Cyrus' aid.
The city wall of Zion, *Nehemiah* builds again,
While *Esther* saves her people from the plots of wicked men.
In *Job* we read how faith will live beneath affliction's rod,
And David's *Psalms* are precious songs to every child of God.
The *Proverbs* like a goodly string of choicest pearls appear,
Ecclesiastes teaches man how vain are all things here.
The mystic *Song of Solomon* exalts sweet Sharon's Rose;
Whilst Christ the Saviour and the King, the "rapt *Isaiah*" shows.
The warning *Jeremiah* apostate Israel scorns;
His plaintive *Lamentations* their awful downfall mourns.

30

Ezekiel tells in wondrous words of
dazzling mysteries;
While kings and empires yet to come,
Daniel in vision sees.
Of judgment and of mercy, *Hosea* loves
to tell;
Joel describes the blessed days when
God with man shall dwell.
Among Tekoa's herdsmen *Amos* re-
ceived his call;
While *Obadiah* prophesies of Edom's
final fall.
Jonah enshrines a wondrous type of
Christ, our risen Lord,
Micah pronounces Judah lost—lost, but
again restored.
Nahum declares on Nineveh just judg-
ment shall be poured.
A view of Chaldea's coming doom
Habakkuk's visions give;
Next *Zephaniah* warns the Jews to turn,
repent, and live;
Haggai wrote to those who saw the
Temple built again,
And *Zechariah* prophesied of Christ's
triumphant reign.
Malachi was the last who touched the
high prophetic cord;
Its final notes sublimely show the com-
ing of the Lord.

Matthew and *Mark* and *Luke* and *John*
the Holy Gospel wrote,
Describing how the Saviour died — His
life, and all He taught;
Acts proves how God the apostles
owned with signs in every place.
St. Paul, in *Romans*, teaches us how
man is saved by grace.
The apostle, in *Corinthians*, instructs,
exhorts, reproves,
Galatians shows that faith in Christ
alone the Father loves.
Ephesians and *Philippians* tell what
Christians ought to be:
Colossians bids us live to God and for
eternity.
In *Thessalonians* we are taught the
Lord will come from heaven.
In *Timothy* and *Titus*, a bishop's rule
is given.
Philemon marks a Christian's love,
which only Christians know.

Hebrews reveals the Gospel prefigured
by the Law.
James teaches without holiness faith
is but vain and dead.
St. Peter points the narrow way in
which the saints are led.
John in his three epistles on love delights to dwell.
St. Jude gives awful warning of judgment, wrath and hell;
The *Revelation* prophesies of that tremendous day
When Christ — and Christ alone — shall
be the trembling sinner's stay.

AUTHOR UNKNOWN

The Twelve Apostles

Of all the Twelve Apostles,
The Gospels give the names;
First, Andrew, John, and Peter,
Bartholomew and James,
Matthew, and Simon, Thomas,
Were friends both tried and true.
Then Philip, James and Thaddeus,
The traitor Judas, too.
They followed Christ the Master
O'er mountain, shore, and sea,
Samaria, Judea, Perea, Galilee.

AUTHOR UNKNOWN

Bible First Aid Kit

If you find yourself in *sudden trouble
or sorrow*, apply instantly Hebrews
12:5-11 and saturate your heart in
Psalm 23.
If you have *slipped down* and hurt
yourself, Psalm 91 will be found to
greatly benefit.
When that *lonely feeling* steals over the
heart, a good stimulant will be found
in Matthew 11:28-30.
Should you be suffering from *loss of
memory* and cannot call to mind your
blessings, try a good dose of Psalm
103.
In time of *failing strength* and courage, two or three applications of I
John 5:13-15 will be found beneficial.
Whenever you find that *bitter taste* in
your mouth and cannot speak lovingly of others, take a good draught

BIBLE

of I Corinthians 13 and Psalm
34:12, 13.
Some days when your *faith is weak* try
the tonic found in Hebrews 11.

———◆———

The Bible contains
The mind of God.
The state of man.
The way of salvation.
The doom of sinners.
The happiness of believers.
Light to direct you.
Food to support you.
Comfort to cheer you.

It is
The traveler's map.
The pilgrim's staff.
The pilot's compass.
The soldier's sword.
The Christian's charter.
A mine of wealth.
A paradise of glory.
A river of pleasure.

Its doctrines are holy.
Its precepts are binding.
Its histories are true.
Its decisions are immutable.
Christ is its grand subject.
Our good its design.
The glory of God its end.

Read it to be wise.
Believe it to be safe.
Practice it to be holy.

Read it slowly, frequently, prayerfully.

It should
Fill the memory.
Rule the heart.
Guide the feet.

It is given you in life,
Will be opened at the Judgment,
And be remembered for ever.

It involves the highest responsibility,
Will reward the greatest labor,
Condemn all who trifle with its
sacred contents.

It is "the Word of our God which
shall stand for ever." AUTHOR UNKNOWN

The longest telegraphic message ever
dispatched was in May, 1881. It carried 180,000 words. It was printed in
full that day by the *Chicago Times*,
which gave space for the four gospels
complete, the Acts and the Epistle to
the Romans. "A triumph of publicity,"
was the verdict of the press. All this
was done because the Revised Version
of the New Testament in English was
on sale that day. In New York 33,000
copies were sold within twenty-four
hours.

———◆———

How to Defend the Bible

I am the Bible.
I am God's wonderful library.
I am always — and above all — the
Truth.
To the weary pilgrim, I am a good
strong Staff.
To the one who sits in black gloom,
I am the glorious Light.
To those who stoop beneath heavy
burdens, I am sweet Rest.
To him who has lost his way, I am a
safe Guide.
To those who have been hurt by sin,
I am healing Balm.
To the discouraged, I whisper a glad
message of Hope.
To those who are distressed by the
storms of life, I am an Anchor, sure
and steadfast.
To those who suffer in lonely solitude,
I am as a cool, soft Hand resting
upon a fevered brow.
Oh, child of man, to best defend me,
just *use me!*   *Selected*

———◆———

The Bible

Century follows century — there it
stands.
Empires rise and fall and are forgotten
— there it stands.
Dynasty succeeds dynasty — there it
stands.
Kings are crowned and uncrowned —
there it stands.
Despised and torn to pieces — there it
stands.

Storms of hate swirl about it — there it stands.
Atheists rail against it — there it stands.
Profane, prayerless punsters caricature it — there it stands.
Unbelief abandons it — there it stands.
Thunderbolts of wrath smite it — there it stands.
The flames are kindled about it — there it stands.   *Selected*

———◆———

The Bible is one of the solid facts of Christianity.
What it is, is not affected by what men think of it.
Changing opinions about the Bible do not change the Bible.
Whatever the Bible was, the Bible is.
And what it is, it has always been.
It is not men's thoughts about the Bible that judge it.
It is the Bible which judges men and their thoughts.
It has nothing to fear but ignorance and neglect.
And the church need have no other fear on its account.
The Bible will take care of itself if . . . *the church will distribute it and get it read.*   ROBERT E. SPEER

———◆———

Yet It Lives

Generation follows generation — yet it lives.
Nations rise and fall — yet it lives.
Kings, dictators, presidents come and go — yet it lives.
Hated, despised, cursed — yet it lives.
Doubted, suspected, criticized — yet it lives.
Condemned by atheists — yet it lives.
Scoffed at by scorners — yet it lives.
Exaggerated by fanatics — yet it lives.
Misconstrued and misstated — yet it lives.
Ranted and raved about — yet it lives.
Its inspiration denied — yet it lives.

Yet it lives — as a lamp to our feet.
Yet it lives — as a light to our path.
Yet it lives — as the gate to heaven.

Yet it lives — as a standard for childhood.
Yet it lives — as a guide for youth.
Yet it lives — as an inspiration for the matured.
Yet it lives — as a comfort for the aged.
Yet it lives — as food for the hungry.
Yet it lives — as water for the thirsty.
Yet it lives — as rest for the weary.
Yet it lives — as light for the heathen.
Yet it lives — as salvation for the sinner.
Yet it lives — as grace for the Christian.

To know it is to love it.
To love it is to accept it.
To accept it means life eternal.
AUTHOR UNKNOWN, *from Gideon Magazine*

———◆———

The Ten Commandments in Rhyme

1. Thou no gods shalt have but me.
2. Before no idol bend the knee.
3. Take not the name of God in vain.
4. Dare not the Sabbath day profane.
5. Give to thy parents honor due.
6. Take heed that thou no murder do.
7. Abstain from words and deeds unclean.
8. Steal not, for thou by God art seen.
9. Tell not a willful lie, nor love it.
10. What is thy neighbor's do not covet.
AUTHOR UNKNOWN

———◆———

The Message of the Bible

The Bible is concerned only incidentally with the history of Israel or a system of ethics. The Bible is primarily concerned with the story of redemption of God as it is in Jesus Christ. If you read the Scriptures and miss the story of salvation, you have missed its message and meaning. There have been those who have gone through the Bible and traced the story of Jesus:
In Genesis He is the Seed of the Woman.
In Exodus He is the Passover Lamb.
In Leviticus He is the Atoning Sacrifice.
In Numbers He is the Smitten Rock.
In Deuteronomy He is the Prophet.

In Joshua He is the Captain of the Lord's hosts.

In Judges He is the Deliverer.

In Ruth He is the Heavenly Kinsman.

In the six books of Kings He is the Promised King.

In Nehemiah He is the Restorer of the nation.

In Esther He is the Advocate.

In Job He is my Redeemer.

In Psalms He is my All and in All.

In Proverbs He is my Pattern.

In Ecclesiastes He is my Goal.

In the Song of Solomon He is my Satisfier.

In the prophets He is the Coming Prince of Peace.

In the Gospels He is Christ coming to seek and to save.

In Acts He is Christ risen.

In the Epistles He is Christ at the Father's right hand.

In the Revelation He is Christ returning and reigning.   BILLY GRAHAM

———◆———

How to Read the Bible

Read the Bible, not as a newspaper, but as a home letter.

If a cluster of heavenly fruit hangs within reach, gather it.

If a promise lies upon the page as a blank check, cash it.

If a prayer is recorded, appropriate it, and launch it as a feathered arrow from the bow of your desire.

If an example of holiness gleams before you, ask God to do as much for you.

If the truth is revealed in all its intrinsic splendor, entreat that its brilliance may ever irradiate the hemisphere of your life.   F. B. MEYER

———◆———

Read Your Bible

1. Slowly, with mind alert.
2. Carefully and with prayer.
3. Expectantly and with anticipation.
4. In a spirit of enjoyment.
5. Eager to respond inwardly.
6. Seeking a personal message.
7. Repeating aloud verses which strike fire.
8. Keeping a definite time each day for reading.
9. Copying out a key verse to carry with you for re-reading through the day.   *Selected*

———◆———

How to Make the Best Use of the Bible

Read it *through.*

Pray it *in.*

Work it *out.*

Note it *down.*

Pass it *on.*   PICKERING

———◆———

The Whole Bible Contains

The mind of God.

The state of man.

The doom of sinners.

The happiness of believers.

Its doctrines are holy.

Its precepts are binding.

Its histories are true.

Its decisions are immutable.

———◆———

My Bible and I

We've traveled together, my Bible and I,
Through all kinds of weather, with smile or with sigh!
In sorrow or sunshine, in tempest or calm!
Thy friendship unchanging, my lamp and my psalm.

We've traveled together, my Bible and I,
When life had grown weary and death e'en was nigh!
But all through the darkness of mist or of wrong,
I found there a solace, a prayer and a song.

So now who shall part us, my Bible and I?
Shall isms or schisms or "new lights" who try?
Shall shadow or substance or stone for good bread
Supplant thy sound wisdom, give folly instead?

Oh, no, my dear Bible, exponent of light!
Thou sword of the Spirit, put error to flight!
And still through life's journey, until my last sigh,
We'll travel together, my Bible and I.
Selected

———

Believe it or not: Edgar G. Watts of North Hollywood, California, age 84, read the Bible from cover to cover 161 times. He had the use of only one eye for 55 years.

———

My Bible

Though the cover is worn,
And the pages are torn,
   And though places bear traces of tears,
Yet more precious than gold
Is the Book worn and old,
   That can shatter and scatter my fears.

When I prayerfully look
In the precious old Book,
   As my eyes scan the pages I see
Many tokens of love
From the Father above,
   Who is nearest and dearest to me.

This old Book is my guide,
'Tis a friend by my side,
   It will lighten and brighten my way;
And each promise I find
Soothes and gladdens my mind
   As I read it and heed it today.
AUTHOR UNKNOWN

———

Read It Through

I supposed I knew my Bible,
   Reading piecemeal, hit or miss,
Now a bit of John or Matthew,
   Now a snatch of Genesis;
Certain chapters of Isaiah,
   Certain Psalms (the twenty-third),
Twelfth of Romans, first of Proverbs,
   Yes, I thought I knew the Word.
But I found a thorough reading
   Was a different thing to do,
And the way was unfamiliar
   When I read the Bible through.

You who like to play at Bible,
   Dip and dabble here and there,
Just before you kneel a-weary,
   And yawn out a hurried prayer;
You who treat the Crown of Writing
   As you treat no other book —
Just a paragraph disjointed,
   Just a crude, impatient look —
Try a worthier procedure,
   Try a broad and steady view —
You will kneel in very rapture
   When you read the Bible through.
AMOS R. WELLS

———

My Bible

My Bible is not true in spots,
   But true in every sense;
True in its tittles and its jots,
   True in each verb and tense;
True when it speaks of heaven's joy,
   True when it warns of hell;
Its truth is gold without alloy —
   Its source a Springing Well.
KEITH BROOKS

———

My Neighbor's Bible

I am my neighbor's Bible
   He reads me when we meet;
Today he reads me in my home —
   Tomorrow, in the street.
He may be a relative or friend,
   Or slight acquaintance be;
He may not even know my name,
   Yet he is reading me.
And pray, who is this neighbor,
   Who reads me day by day,
To learn if I am living right,
   And walking as I pray?

Oh, he is with me always,
   To criticize or blame;
So worldly wise in his own eyes,
   And "Sinner" is his name.
Dear Christian friends and brothers,
   If we could only know
How faithfully the world records
   Just what we say and do;
Oh, we would write our record plain,
   And come in time to see
Our worldly neighbor won to Christ
   While reading you and me.
The Herald of Light

The Bible

The charter of all true liberty.
The forerunner of civilization.
The moulder of institutions and governments.
The fashioner of law.
The secret of national progress.
The guide of history.
The ornament and mainspring of literature.
The friend of science.
The inspiration of philosophies.
The textbook of ethics.
The light of intellect.
The answer to the deepest human heart hungerings.
The soul of all strong heart life.
The illuminator of darkness.
The foe of superstition.
The enemy of oppression.
The uprooter of sin.
The regulator of all high and worthy standards.
The comfort in sorrow.
The strength in weakness.
The pathway in perplexity.
The escape from temptation.
The steadier in the day of power.
The embodiment of all lofty ideals.
The begetter of life.
The promise of the future.
The star of death's night.
The revealer of God.
The guide and hope and inspiration of man. BISHOP ANDERSON

What Great Men Have Said about the Bible

MATTHEW ARNOLD — To the Bible men will return because they cannot do without it. The true God is and must be preeminently the God of the Bible, the eternal who makes for righteousness from whom Jesus came forth, and whose spirit governs the course of humanity.

NAPOLEON BONAPARTE—The Bible contains a complete series of facts and of historical men, to explain time and eternity, such as no other religion has to offer . . . What happiness that Book procures for those who believe it! What marvels those admire there who reflect upon it!

WILLIAM E. GLADSTONE — There is but one question of the hour: how to bring the truths of God's Word into vital contact with the minds and hearts of all classes of people.

GOETHE — (The universal and most highly cultivated of poets) I consider the Gospels to be thoroughly genuine; for in them there is the effective reflection of a sublimity which emanated from the Person of Christ; and this is as Divine as ever the Divine appeared on earth.

ULYSSES S. GRANT — Hold fast to the Bible as the sheet anchor of your liberties; write its precepts on your heart and practice them in your lives. To the influence of this Book we are indebted for the progress made, and to this we must look as our guide in the future.

HORACE GREELEY — It is impossible to mentally or socially enslave a Bible-reading people.

PATRICK HENRY — This is a Book worth all other books which were ever printed.

HERBERT HOOVER — We are indebted to the Book of books for our ideals and institutions. Their preservation rests in adhering to its principles.

The study of the Bible is a rich post-graduate course in the richest library of human experience.

J. EDGAR HOOVER — Inspiration has been the keynote of America's phenomenal growth. Inspiration has been the backbone of America's greatness. Inspiration has been the difference between defeat and victory in America's wars. And this inspiration has come from faith in God, faith in the teachings of the Sermon on the Mount, and faith in the belief that the Holy Bible is the inspired Word of God.

Reading the Holy Bible within the family circle is more important today than ever before. It draws the family together into a more closely knit unit. It gives each member a faith to live by.

As a small boy I sat at my mother's knee while she read the Bible to me and explained the meaning with the stories as we went along. It served to make the bond of faith between us much stronger. Then, there were those wonderful nights when my father would gather the family around him and read aloud verses from the Bible. This led to family discussions which were interesting, lively and informative. These wonderful sessions left me with an imprint of the power of faith and the power of prayer which has sustained me in trying moments throughout my entire life.

ANDREW JACKSON — The Bible is the rock on which our republic rests.

THOMAS JEFFERSON — The Bible is the cornerstone of liberty.

SIR WILLIAM JONES—The Bible contains more true sensibility, more exquisite beauty, more pure morality, more important history, and finer strains of poetry and eloquence, than can be collected from all other books in whatever age or language they may be written.

ROBERT E. LEE — The Bible is a book in comparison with which all others are of minor importance. In all my perplexities and distress the Bible never failed to give me light and strength.

ABRAHAM LINCOLN — In regard to the great Book, I have only to say that it is the best gift which God has given to man.

WILLIAM MCKINLEY — The more profoundly we study this wonderful Book and the more closely we observe its divine precepts, the better citizens we will become and the higher will be the destiny of our nation.

WILLIAM LYON PHELPS (Called the most beloved professor in America — of Yale University) — I thoroughly believe in university education for both men and women, but I believe a knowledge of the Bible without a college course is more valuable than a college course without the Bible.

JEAN JACQUES ROUSSEAU — The majesty of the Scriptures strikes me with admiration, as the purity of the Gospel has its influence on my heart. Pursue the works of our philosophers with all their pomp of diction, how mean, how contemptible are they, compared with the Scriptures.

GEORGE WASHINGTON — It is impossible rightly to govern the world without God and the Bible.

DANIEL WEBSTER — There is no solid basis for civilization but in the Word of God.

If we abide by the principles taught in the Bible, our country will go on prospering and to prosper.

I make it a practice to read the Bible through once every year.

WOODROW WILSON — A man has deprived himself of the best there is in the world who has deprived himself of this, a knowledge of the Bible.

When you have read the Bible, you will know that it is the Word of God, because you will have found it the key to your own heart, your own happiness, and your own duty.

———◆———

The Christian who is careless in Bible reading is careless in Christian living.
MAX REICH

———◆———

I have read many books, but the Bible reads me.

———◆———

The reason people are down on the Bible is that they're not up on the Bible.
WILLIAM W. AYER

———◆———

The Bible needs less defense and more practice.

———◆———

God's mirror reveals but never cleanses.

The Bible does not need to be re-written, but reread.

———♦———

For top performance we must refuel daily from the Word.

———♦———

The Bible is an international manifesto.

———♦———

The Ten Commandments and the multiplication table are in no danger of being outmoded.

———♦———

The Bible sure throws a lot of light on the Bible commentaries.   BARNHOUSE

———♦———

Study the Bible to be wise; believe it to be safe; practice it to be holy.

———♦———

Be not miserable about what may happen tomorrow. The same everlasting Father, who cares for you today, will care for you tomorrow and every day. Either He will shield you from suffering or He will give you unfailing strength to bear it.   FRANCIS DE SALES

———♦———

Don't think the Bible is dry inside because it is dusty on the outside.

———♦———

Slip of the tongue by the pastor: "I am well-reversed in the Scriptures."

———♦———

England has two books, the Bible and Shakespeare. England made Shakespeare but the Bible made England.   VICTOR HUGO

———♦———

A young man, after hearing a discussion as to various versions of the Bible, declared, "I prefer my mother's version to any other. She translated it into the language of daily life."

———♦———

A skeptic in London recently said, in speaking of the Bible, that it was quite impossible in these days to believe in any book whose author was unknown. A Christian asked him if the compiler of the multiplication table was known. "No," he answered.

"Then, of course, you do not believe in it?"

"Oh, yes, I believe in it because it works well," replied the skeptic.

"So does the Bible," was the rejoinder, and the skeptic had no answer to make.

———♦———

A lady was mailing a gift of a Bible to a relative. The postal clerk examined the heavy package and inquired if it contained anything breakable. "Nothing," the lady told him, "but the Ten Commandments."

———♦———

When a rich Chinese man came home from a visit to England, he proudly showed his friends a powerful microscope he had bought. But one day he looked at a tiny bit of his dinner rice under the microscope.

Horrors! He saw that tiny living creatures actually crawled all over it. And part of his religion was to eat no animal life.

What did he do? He loved rice. So he simply smashed the microscope!

Foolish, you say? Yes, but no more foolish than the person who rejects the Bible when he sees some things the Bible reveals. "For the word of God . . . is a discerner of the thoughts and intents of the heart" (Hebrews 4:12).   *Sunday School Journal*

———♦———

An infidel said, "There is one thing that mars all the pleasures of my life."

"Indeed!" replied his friend. "What is that?"

He answered, "I am afraid the Bible is true. If I could know for certain that death is an eternal sleep, I should be happy; my joy would be complete! But here is the thorn that stings me. This is the word that pierces my very soul — if the Bible is true, I am lost forever."

———♦———

Some years ago in Italy a missionary lady offered a Bible to a stonemason who was building a wall. He did not want the Bible but finally accepted it. When the lady left the man removed a stone from the wall and placed the Bible in a hollow space.

He then continued building the wall around it, laughing to think how he had fooled her. Not many years after this there was an earthquake which caused many buildings and walls to fall. One dangerous wall was still standing and the workmen were tapping it to make it fall. "Perhaps there is a treasure there," one worker said as he moved part of the stones. There, in the hollow place where the mason had placed the Bible several years before, the workman found the "treasure." He took it home and read it, and was led to love it and to serve God. Indeed he had found a great treasure.

———◆———

We come back laden from our quest
To find that all the sages said
Is in the Book our Mothers read.
WHITTIER

———◆———

Today man sees all his hopes and aspirations crumbling before him. He is perplexed and knows not whither he is drifting. But he must realize that the Bible is his refuge, and the rallying point for all humanity. It is here man will find the solution of his present difficulties and guidance for his future action, and unless he accepts with clear conscience the Bible and its great message, he cannot hope for salvation. For my part, I glory in the Bible.
HAILE SELASSIE, Emperor of Ethiopia

———◆———

Bible (and Children)

Johnny volunteered to review the story of Noah and the Ark for the Sunday school class. "All the animals went into Noah's ark two by two," he said, "except the worms they went in the apples."

———◆———

"What were the names of Noah's three sons, Tommy?" asked his Sunday school teacher.

"I can't remember them exactly," Tommy replied, "but I think one was called Bacon."

"What Bible story did you hear in Sunday school today?" a mother asked Junior.

"Oh, we heard the loafing story," Junior replied.

"Well, that's one I never heard," said the mother. "Tell me about it."

So, Junior told her: "Somebody loafs and fishes."

———◆———

Child: "Mother, what number is this hair I pulled out?"

Mother: "Child, I don't know."

Child: "Well, the Bible says that the hairs of your head are all numbered."
Sunday School Journal

———◆———

The Sunday school teacher asked a little girl if she knew who Matthew was. The answer was no. The teacher then asked if she knew who John was. Again the answer was "no." Finally the teacher asked if she knew who Peter was.

She answered: "I think he was a rabbit."

———◆———

Her Sunday school teacher asked a ten-year-old how Solomon happened to be so wise. "Because," she answered, after due meditation, "he had so many wives to advise him."

———◆———

Charles was telling his friend John about the mystery writing he had learned about in Sunday school.

"It was in the story of Daniel," Charles said. "And a finger wrote some words on the wall of the palace. The king must not have behaved in church as the message was for him."

"What was the message?" asked John.

Happily Charles told him: "Meany, meany, tickle the parson!"

———◆———

One day the Sunday school teacher gave the children a written review of the lesson. Subject: Noah. Laboriously Alfred wrote, but only briefly. He handed in his paper and the teacher read his paper. "You say that Noah went fishing while he was in the ark," commented the teacher, "but gave up after only five minutes. Why did he do that, Alfred?"

"Because," came the prompt reply, "Noah didn't have but two worms."

———♦———

"Joseph was the boy who never had a cold neck," the boy told his mother when she quizzed him about the Sunday school lesson.

"How do you know that?" mother asked.

"Because," replied the lad, "Joseph had a coat of many collars."

———♦———

At a midnight watch service the pastor was conducting a Bible quiz. He asked the question, "Who are the three Johns in the Scriptures?"

One eager ten-year-old volunteered the answer: "First, Second and Third John."

———♦———

During a review one Sunday the teacher asked if the class knew who the twin boys were in the Bible.

"That's easy," said Charles. "First and Second Samuel."

———♦———

After the teacher had told her class they could draw a picture of the Bible story she had told them, she went around to see what the children had done. She noticed that little Sherry hadn't drawn a Bible picture at all, so asked the child to tell the class about her picture.

"This is a car. The man in the front seat is God. The people in the back seat are Adam and Eve. God is driving them out of the Garden of Eden."

———♦———

On another occasion when the teacher let the children "draw" the Bible story they had heard, one little boy drew the picture of an airplane with a pilot in the front seat. The passengers were a man, woman and baby. When asked to tell about his picture, he said:

"This is Pontius the pilot taking Mary and Joseph and Baby Jesus on a flight out of Egypt."

Blessings

To get the blessing we must do the work.

———♦———

Don't count your blessings without praising the Blesser.

———♦———

The private and personal blessings we enjoy, the blessings of immunity, safeguard, liberty, and integrity, deserve the thanksgiving of a whole life.
JEREMY TAYLOR

———♦———

Not only count your blessings, but consider their source. *Eternity*

———♦———

Blood

His blood for my fault;
His robe for my blame.

———♦———

Moody said: "The blood alone makes us safe; the Word alone makes us sure."

———♦———

Boast, Brag, Bluff

Self-brag is half scandal.

———♦———

The man who bragged that he was self-made loved to worship his creator.

———♦———

Nothing in the world is more haughty than a man of moderate capacity when once raised to power. WESSENBURG

———♦———

A show-off never fails to be shown up in a show down.

———♦———

Folks with a lot of brass are seldom polished. PHILIP W. BEMIS

———♦———

A bully's greatest fall is when he stumbles over his own bluff.

———♦———

Great talkers are little doers.
FRANKLIN

———♦———

When a youth was giving himself airs in the theatre and saying, "I am wise for I have talked with many wise men," Epictetus replied, "I too have conversed with many rich men, yet I am not rich."

6

Any party which takes credit for the rain must not be surprised if its opponents blame it for the drought.

DWIGHT W. MORROW

———◆———

He that knows, and knows that he knows, doesn't have to blow and blow.

———◆———

The man who has a right to boast doesn't have to.

———◆———

A Boston salesman visited Texas and heard one particular Texan boasting about heroes of the Alamo who, almost alone, held off whole armies.

"I don't think you ever had anyone so brave around Boston," challenged the Texan.

"Did you ever hear of Paul Revere?" asked the Bostonian.

"Paul Revere?" said the Texan. "Isn't that the guy who ran for help?"

———◆———

Books

Never lend books — no one ever returns them. The only books I have in my library are those people have lent me.

ANATOLE FRANCE

———◆———

Bad books are fountains of vice.

———◆———

Classic: A book which people praise and don't read.

MARK TWAIN

———◆———

Use books as bees use flowers.

———◆———

They borrow books they will not buy.
They have no ethics or religions;
I wish some kind Burbankian guy
Could cross my books with homing pigeons.

CAROLYN WELLS

———◆———

Who Gives a Book

He who gives a man a book
Gives that man a sweeping look
Through its pages
Down the ages;

Gives that man a ship to sail
Where the far adventures hail
Down the sea
Of destiny!

Gives that man a vision wide
As the skies where stars abide,
Anchored in
The love of him;

Gives that man great dreams to dream,
Sun-lit ways that glint and gleam,
Where the sages
Tramp the ages.

WILLIAM L. STIDGER

———◆———

To a friend who visited Mark Twain, the great man explained the clutter of books on the floor and chairs, "You see, I can't borrow shelves, too."

———◆———

Some books leave us free and some books make us free.

EMERSON

———◆———

Books are but waste paper, unless we spend in action the wisdom we get from thought.

BULWER

———◆———

If religious books are not widely circulated among the masses in this country and the people do not become religious, I do not know what is to become of us as a nation. And the thought is one to cause solemn reflection on the part of every patriot and Christian. If the truth be not diffused, error will be; if God and His Word are not known and received, the devil and his works will gain the ascendancy; if the evangelical volume does not reach every hamlet, the pages of corrupt and licentious literature will.

DANIEL WEBSTER

———◆———

Books and study are merely the steps of the ladder by which one climbs to the summit; as soon as a step has been advanced, he leaves it behind. The majority of mankind, however, who study to fill their memory with facts, do not use the steps of the ladder to mount upward, but take them off and lay them on their shoulders in order that they may take them along, delighting in the weight of the burden they are carrying. They ever remain below because they carry what should carry them.

SCHOPENHAUER

41

A rare volume is a borrowed book that comes back.

———◆———

Books

Books! Books! Books!
And we thank Thee, God
For the gift of them;
And the lift of them;
   For the gleam in them
   And the dream in them;
For the things they teach
And the souls they reach!
   For the maze of them
   And the blaze of them;
For the ways they open to us
And the rays that they shoot through us.

Books! Books! Books!
And we thank Thee, God
For the light in them;
For the might in them;
   For the urge in them;
   And the surge in them;
For the souls they wake
And the paths they break;
   For the gong in them
   And the song in them;
For the throngs of folks they bring to us
And the songs of hope they sing to us!
    WILLIAM L. STIDGER

———◆———

Books are friendly things. Do not count as wasted the hours spent in selecting them.   JOHNSON

———◆———

Don't sell your books and keep your diplomas. Sell your diplomas — if you can get anyone to buy them — and keep your books.   WALTER PITKIN

———◆———

Boss

The fellow who doesn't need a boss is often the one selected to be one.
Christlife Magazine

———◆———

The boss was pointing out to his secretary several errors she had made during the day, when she interrupted with, "Mr. Jones, it's two minutes past five and you're annoying me on my own time."

Men who complain that the boss is dumb would be out of a job if he were any smarter.

———◆———

If the boss practiced what he preaches, he'd work himself to death.

———◆———

The man who delegates authority must forego the luxury of blowing his top.

———◆———

Boy, Boys

The way to keep a boy out of hot water is to put soap in it.

———◆———

Sons are the anchors of a mother's life.   SOPHOCLES

———◆———

Fishing Boy

A little lean boy with a freckled nose
And a fishing pole and two bandaged toes
With his tousled hair looking like ripened wheat
"Tippy-toed" through the back door on kitten-quick feet
And made a beeline for the cookie jar,
In each of his blue eyes a little blue star,
For he knew so exactly what waited for him
When he poked crawfish fingers across the jar's rim.
Round cookies crusted with raisins and spice
Were his favorite kind, and Grandma was nice,
For she left the jar filled for a boy going fishing
And low on the shelf so he needn't stand wishing!   ANABEL ARMOUR

———◆———

Jimmy

He is just ten years old.
He is made up of the following ingredients:
  Noise, energy, imagination, curiosity and hunger.
He is the "cute little fellow down the street,"

"That spoiled imp next door," or "My
    son,"
Depending upon who you are.
He is something to be kept, fed, clothed,
    healthy, happy and out of trouble.
BUT . . .
He is something else, too.
He is tomorrow.
He is the future we are working for:
He is part of the world's most impor-
    tant generation.
Our generation must love them and
    win them.
His generation will determine whether
    it was worth doing.
He is one of the most important people
    in history.
SO . . .
Anyone who influences his life is also
    a mighty important person.
                              P.A.A.S News

Only a Boy

His trousers are torn, rolled up to the
    knee;
A hole in his shirt which he caught on
    a tree;
But I see a soul for whom Jesus has
    died,
Clothed in His righteousness, pressed
    to His side.

I see not labor and hours of prayer
Spent for that freckled-faced naughty
    boy there,
But I see a Saviour with arms open
    wide,
Waiting in heaven to take him inside.

I see not freckles, but man fully grown,
A heart filled with God's Word I've
    carefully sown,
A life speaking forth for the Saviour
    each day,
O Lord, for this boy I most earnestly
    pray.

I see not his mischief, but energy bent,
Put to the task where the Lord wants
    it spent;
O God, make this lively, mischievous
    boy
A power for Thee, to Thy heart great
    joy.   MILDRED MORNINGSTAR

The Christian parents' problem is to
keep the life of the boy normal — and
yet steer him into Christian channels.
                    Sunday School Journal

A Boy

Nobody knows what a boy is worth,
    A boy at his work or play,
A boy who whistles around the place,
    Or laughs in an artless way.

Nobody knows what a boy is worth,
    And the world must wait and see,
For every man in an honored place,
    Is a boy that used to be.

Nobody knows what a boy is worth,
    A boy with his face aglow,
For hid in his heart there are secrets
    deep
Not even the wisest know.

Nobody knows what a boy is worth,
    A boy with his bare, white feet;
So have a smile and a kindly word,
    For every boy you meet.
                              AUTHOR UNKNOWN

Build

Man builds for a century; the Christian builds for eternity.

Too low they build who build beneath the stars.   EDWARD YOUNG

Building a Temple

A builder builded a temple,
He wrought it with grace and skill:
Pillars and groins and arches
All fashioned to work his will.
Men said, as they saw its beauty,
"It shall never know decay,
Great is thy skill, O builder,
Thy fame shall endure for aye."

A teacher builded a temple
With loving and infinite care,
Planning each arch with patience,
Laying each stone with prayer.
None praised her unceasing efforts,
None knew of her wondrous plan;
For the temple the teacher builded
Was unseen by the eyes of men.

Gone is the builder's temple,
Crumbled into the dust;
Low lies each stately pillar,
Food for consuming rust.
But the temple the teacher builded
Will last while the ages roll,
For that beautiful unseen temple
Is the child's immortal soul.

THOMAS CURTIS CLARK

Business

A lot of people never get interested in a thing until they find it is none of their business.

A shady business never yields a sunny life.

Drive thy business, or it will drive thee. BENJAMIN FRANKLIN

Business circles should be on the square.

An institution is the lengthened shadow of an individual.

Your chief competition is yourself.

A scissors grinder is the only person whose business is good when things are dull.

The public business of the nation is the private business of every citizen.

The things most people want to know about are usually none of their business.

GEORGE BERNARD SHAW

The man who minds his own business usually has a good one.

Sign on the window of a men's clothing store that went bankrupt after three months in business: "Opened by Mistake."

Running a business without advertising is the same thing as winking at a girl in the dark. You know what you're doing, but she doesn't.

Some years ago a harness dealer had a customer who picked out a fancy saddle for his pony and said, "I'll take it. Please charge it."

After the customer had left, the proprietor asked his bookkeeper to charge the customer with the purchase.

"To whom?" asked the bookkeeper.

"Don't *you* know him?" replied the proprietor. "No," answered the bookkeeper.

"Well," said the proprietor, "only twelve men have ponies in town — send them all a bill." The bookkeeper did. Three of them paid.

WILLIAM WACHER, *The Rotarian*

Business Daffynitions

To expedite: this means to confound confusion with commotion.

Under consideration: This means never heard of it.

Reliable source: the guy you just met.

Informed source: the guy who told the guy you just met.

Unimpeachable source: the guy who started the rumor originally.

We are making a survey: we need more time to think of an answer.

Will advise, in due course: if we figure it out, we'll let you know.

AUTHOR UNKNOWN

Busy

Some of the busiest people in the world are only picking up the beans they spilled.

It isn't enough just to be busy. What are you busy about?

The surest way to get a job done is to give it to a busy man. He'll have his secretary do it.

Keep busy! It's the cheapest kind of medicine there is on this earth, and one of the best. Don't allow yourself to become upset by the small things that come your way; life is too short to be little! Think and act cheerfully, and you will feel cheerful. Cooperate with the inevitable.

A man never gets too busy to attend his own funeral.

———◆———

A man who is too busy for God is too busy.

———◆———

It is very significant that in every recorded instance the Apostles were busy at their daily work when the Master called them.

Peter and Andrew were fishing;

James and John were mending their nets;

Matthew was sitting at the receipt of custom.

God never visits an idle or unserviceable life.   DAVID SMITH

———◆———

Rush hour: That hour during which traffic is almost at a standstill.

If We Are . . .

too busy to read a book that promises to widen our horizons;
too busy to keep our friendships in good repair;
too busy to maintain a consistent devotional life;
too busy to keep warm, vital loves of our fireside burning;
too busy to conserve our health in the interest of our highest efficiency;
too busy to cultivate the sense of a personal acquaintance with God;
too busy to spend one hour during the week in worship;
too busy to expose ourselves each day to beauty;
too busy to cultivate souls . . .
Then we are indeed *too busy.*   *Selected*

C

Capital

Capital is what you and I have saved out of yesterday's wages.

———◆———

The strongest objection socialists and communists have against capital is that they don't have any.

Caution

It is better to build a fence around the top of the precipice before the child goes over than it is to build a hospital at the bottom of it.   GYPSY SMITH

———◆———

Sign on a Texas farm fence: Hunters! Don't shoot anything that doesn't move. It may be my hired man.

———◆———

In a discreet man's mouth a public thing is private.   BENJAMIN FRANKLIN

———◆———

To a quick question, give a slow answer.   *Italian Proverb*

It is better to be careful a thousand times than killed once.

———◆———

Watch Your Can'ts and Can's

If you would have some worthwhile plans,
You've got to watch your "can'ts" and "can's."
You can't aim low and then rise high;
You can't succeed if you don't try;
You can't go wrong and come out right;
You can't love sin and walk in light;
You can't throw time and means away
And live sublime from day to day.

You can be great if you'll be good
And do God's will as all men should.
You can ascend life's upward road,
Although you bear a heavy load;
You can be honest, truthful, clean,
By turning from the low and mean;
You can uplift the souls of men
By words and deed, or by your pen.

So, watch your "can'ts" and watch your
"can's"
And watch your walks and watch your
stands,
And watch the way you talk and act
And do not take the false for fact;
And watch indeed the way you take,
And watch the things that mar or make;
For life is great to every man
Who lives to do the best he can.

The Wesleyan Youth

You will be careful,
If you are wise,
How you touch men's religion,
Or credit, or eyes.

BENJAMIN FRANKLIN

Challenge

Be thankful if you have a job a little
harder than you like. A razor cannot
be sharpened on a piece of velvet.

Unless we can and do constantly
seek and find ways and means to do
a better job; unless we accept the challenge of the changing times; we have
no right to survive and we shall not
survive.

CHESTER O. FISCHER

Tackle more than you can do —
Then do it!
Bite off more than you can chew —
Then chew it!
Hitch your wagon to a star,
Keep your seat, and there you are!

AUTHOR UNKNOWN

Don't try to think why you can't.
Think how you can.

It can't be done,
It never has been done;
Therefore I will do it.

Change

We are never two minutes the same,
and still we never change one bit from
what we are.   ANATOLE FRANCE

Character

Your character is what God knows
you to be. Your reputation is what
men think you are.   DR. BOB JONES, SR.

Character is what you are in the
dark.   DWIGHT L. MOODY

Strong foundations are necessary for
a towering structure.

You can sell out character but you
can't purchase it.

More knowledge may be gained of
a man's real character by a short conversation with one of his servants than
from a formal and studied narrative,
begun with his pedigree and ended
with his funeral.   SAMUEL JOHNSON

What you are tomorrow, you are
becoming today.

To be worth anything, character
must be capable of standing firm upon
its feet in the world of daily work,
temptation and trial; and able to bear
the wear and tear of actual life. Clois-
tered virtues do not count for much.

SAMUEL SMILES

Hardship makes character.

Thought creates character.

ANNE BESANT

You don't make your character in a
crisis; you exhibit it.

OREN ARNOLD, *Presbyterian Life*

If men speak ill of you, live so that
no one will believe them.

You are what you have been becoming.

Much may be known of a man's
character by what excites his laughter.

GOETHE

When the ceiling of a man's life is
lower than the heavens, he needs more
room for character expansion.

Every man has in himself a continent of undiscovered character. Happy is he who acts the Columbus to his own soul. SIR J. STEVENS

The test of your character is what you would do if you knew no one would ever know. DR. BOB JONES, SR.

Character is made by many acts; it may be lost by a single one.

What thou art in the sight of God, that thou truly art. THOMAS A' KEMPIS

You can borrow brains, but you cannot borrow character. DR. BOB JONES, SR.

Character is like a tree and reputation like its shadow. The shadow is what we think of it: the tree is the real thing. ABRAHAM LINCOLN

What we like determines what we are, and is the sign of what we are; and to teach taste is inevitably to form character. JOHN RUSKIN

The strength of a nation lies in the character of its citizens.

It is easier and better to build boys than to repair men.

Character is made by what you stand for; reputation by what you fall for. ROBERT QUILLEN

A man's strength of character may be measured by his ability to control his temper, instead of letting his temper control him. J. SHERMAN WALLACE

Every human being is intended to have a character of his own; to be what no other is, and to do what no other can do. WILLIAM ELLERY CHANNING

Charity

Music Lover: "I'm sorry that other engagements prevent my attending your charity concert, but I shall be with you in spirit."

Solicitor: "That's fine! Where would you like your spirit to sit? We have tickets for a half dollar, a dollar, and two dollars."

Let us grant that charity begins at home, but only selfishness will stay there.

Charity gives itself rich; covetousness hoards itself poor. German Proverb

He who has conferred a kindness should be silent, he who has received one should speak of it. SENECA

It is not enough to help the feeble up, but to support him after. SHAKESPEARE

A philanthropist is one who gives it away when he should be giving it back.

Charm

Charm, which means the power to effect work without employing brute force, is indispensable to women. Charm is a woman's strength just as strength is a man's charm. HAVELOCK ELLIS

Charm is the ability to make someone else think that both of you are pretty wonderful.

Cheer, Cheerful, Cheerfulness

I shall feel until I die a desire to increase the stock of harmless cheerfulness. CHARLES DICKENS

Wondrous is the strength of cheerfulness, and its power of endurance — the cheerful man will do more in the same time, will do it better, will persevere in it longer, than the sad or sullen. CARLYLE

The cheerful live longest in years and afterwards in our regards.

Cheerfulness is the window-cleaner of the mind.

47

What sunshine is to flowers, smiles are to humanity. They are but trifles, to be sure, but scattered along life's pathway, the good they do is inconceivable.

ADDISON

Child, Childish, Childlike, Children

We should consider not so much what the child is today as what he may become tomorrow.

———◆———

Today's unchurched child is tomorrow's criminal.

J. EDGAR HOOVER

———◆———

Train up a child in the way he should go and go that way yourself.

———◆———

A child is your second chance.

———◆———

A little child is the only true democrat.

HARRIET BEECHER STOWE

———◆———

A child that is loved has many names.

Hungarian Proverb

———◆———

Give me the children until they are seven and anyone may have them afterwards.

XAVIER

———◆———

People who handle other peoples' money are required to account for every cent. Are children less valuable?

———◆———

Jesus put a child in the midst; many churches put him in the basement.

———◆———

If you want a garden of good fruit, get the trees young.

———◆———

If children grew up according to early indications, we would have nothing but geniuses.

GOETHE

———◆———

Kindly interest will do more to attract children than stately majesty.

THEO. G. STELZER

———◆———

If we paid no more attention to our plants than we have to our children, we would now be living in a jungle of weeds.

Our children are the only earthly possessions we can take with us to glory.

———◆———

Child by child we build our nation.

Prize-winning Slogan

———◆———

The more children's fingerprints in a home, the fewer on police records.

———◆———

The family next door went stork mad; they have eleven children.

———◆———

Children are natural mimics — they act like their parents in spite of every attempt to teach them good manners.

———◆———

While men believe in the possibilities of children being religious, they are largely failing to make them so, because they are offering them not a child's but a man's religion — men's forms of truth and men's forms of experience.

PHILLIPS BROOKS

———◆———

A boy is a noise with some dirt on it.

———◆———

Are All the Children In?

I think oftimes as the night draws nigh
Of an old house on the hill,
Of a yard all wide and blossom-starred
Where the children played at will.
And when the night at last came down,
Hushing the merry din,
Mother would look around and ask,
"Are all the children in?"

'Tis many and many a year since then,
And the old house on the hill
No longer echoes to childish feet,
And the yard is still, so still.
But I see it all as the shadows creep,
And though many the years have been,
Even now, I can hear my mother ask,
"Are all the children in?"

I wonder if, when the shadows fall
On the last short, earthly day,
When we say goodbye to the world outside,
All tired with our childish play,
When we step out into that Other Land

Where mother so long has been,
Will we hear her ask, as we did of old,
"Are all the children in?"

And I wonder, too, what the Lord will
    say,
To us older children of His,
Have we cared for the lambs? Have we
    showed them the fold?
A privilege joyful it is.
And I wonder, too, what our answers
    will be,
When His loving questions begin:
"Have you heeded My voice? Have
    you told of My love?
Have you brought My children in?"

AUTHOR UNKNOWN; *last verse by*
MARION BISHOP BOWER

————◆————

Childhood is like a mirror which re-
flects in afterlife the images presented
to it.   SAMUEL SMILES

————◆————

Nothing is too good for the child.
GOETHE

————◆————

Good manners require a great deal
of time, as does a wise treatment of
children.   EMERSON

————◆————

Children are poor men's riches.

————◆————

Let every father and mother realize
that when their child is three years of
age, they have done more than half
they will ever do for its character.
HORACE BUSHNELL

————◆————

Young Things

Give me the bending of the frail and
    fragile stalk,
Give me the tending of the babe that
    learns to walk;
Give me the training of the slim and
    slender vine,
Give me the guiding of the colt that
    learns the line.
Give me the young things, and future
    years will show
All the good care brings, as they shall
    older grow.
LALIA MITCHELL THORNTON, *The Banner*

————◆————

There's nothing thirstier than a child
who has just gone to bed.

The kind of person your child is going to be, he is already becoming.
Heart-to-Heart Program

————◆————

Those who educate children well
are more to be honored than they who
produce them; for these only gave
them life, those the art of living well.
ARISTOTLE

————◆————

There's only one pretty child in the
world, and every mother has it.
Cheshire Proverb

————◆————

Every child born into the world is a
new thought of God, an ever-fresh
and radiant possibility.
KATE DOUGLAS WIGGIN

————◆————

It is said that the eighteenth century
discovered the man, the nineteenth
century discovered the woman, and the
twentieth century discovered the child.
Now that he is discovered, let's train
him!

————◆————

Recipe for Preserving Children

1 large grassy field
6 children
3 small dogs
A narrow strip of brook with pebbles
Flowers
A deep blue sky

Mix the children with the dogs and
empty into the field, stirring continuously. Sprinkle the field with the deep
blue sky and bake it in a hot sun.
When the children are well browned
they may be removed. They will be
found right for setting away to cool in
a bathtub.   *Childhood Education*

————◆————

Recipe for Raising Children

Love — Oceans of it.
Self Respect — Give generous portions.
Cultural Advantages — Plenty of the
    best available.
Music }
Laughter } Use generously for seasoning
Play }
Money — Scant and sparingly.
Religion — Use judiciously to thicken;
    makes the best foundation.

CHILDREN

Susannah's Rules for Rearing Children

Susannah Wesley, mother of nineteen, didn't go to textbooks for her theories on child guidance. Though two hundred years old, her rules are still valid today for teaching a child to be obedient and to "cry softly."

1. Allow no eating between meals.
2. Put all children in bed by eight o'clock.
3. Require them to take medicine without complaining.
4. Subdue self-will in a child and thus work together with God to save his soul.
5. Teach each one to pray as soon as he can speak.
6. Require all to be still during family worship.
7. Give them nothing that they cry for, and only that which they ask for politely.
8. To prevent lying, punish no fault which is first confessed and repented of.
9. Never allow a sinful act to go unpunished.
10. Never punish a child twice for a single offense.
11. Commend and reward good behavior.
12. Any attempt to please, even if poorly performed, should be commended.
13. Preserve property rights, even in the smallest matters.
14. Strictly observe all promises.
15. Require no daughter to work before she can read well.
16. Teach children to fear the rod.

Home Life

————◆————

Passing the Buck

The college professor says:
"Such rawness in a student is a shame,
But high school preparation is to blame."
The high school teacher remarks:
"From such youth I should be spared;
They send them up so unprepared."
The elementary school teacher observes:

"A cover for the dunce's stool,
Why was he ever sent to school?"
The kindergarten teacher whispers:
"Never such lack of training did I see!
What kind of person must the mother be?"
The mother replies:
"Poor child, but he is not to blame;
His father's folks were all the same."

GLENN SEELEY, *The Teacher's Treasure Chest*

————◆————

Portrait in Three Lines

Small boy tracing.
Mom erasing
Wall defacing.

IRENE S. SHOEMAKER

————◆————

Some would gather money
Along the path of life.
Some would gather roses
And rest from worldly strife,
But I would gather children
From among the thorns of sin;
I would seek a golden curl
And a freckled, toothless grin.

For money cannot enter
In that land of endless day,
And the roses that are gathered
Soon will wilt along the way.
But, oh, the laughing children,
As I cross the Sunset Sea
And the gates swing wide to heaven,
I can take them in with me.

AUTHOR UNKNOWN

————◆————

Child of the Age

His mind's a flying saucery,
His room a satelloid.
His words are from a glossary
An Einstein would avoid.

He's quite adept in rocketry.
He knows the names of stars.
He's forsworn Davy Crockettry
To plan a trip to Mars.

He boldly deals in distancy.
Fine spacemanship's his mark,
With just one inconsistency —
He's frightened of the dark.

MARY MARGARET MILBRATH in
The Wall Street Journal

Children in Church

The little children in each pew are like
  enchanted flowers.
They nod and sway — and yet, they
  plan — across the quiet hours.
And some of them drift into sleep,
  against a mother's breast,
And some of them, in singing hymns,
  find stimulating rest!
Their parents smile and sometimes nod,
  above each curly head,
But, oh, they listen carefully as lesson
  texts are read —
And feeling fingers touch their own,
  like drifting butterflies,
They peer, with heightened tenderness,
  into each other's eyes.
MARGARET SANGSTER

An angel passed in his onward flight,
With a seed of love and truth and light,
And cried, O where shall the seed be
  sown —
That it yield most fruit when fully
  grown?
The Saviour heard and He said, as He
  smiled,
Place it for Me in the heart of a child.
ANONYMOUS

The Soul of a Child

The soul of a child is the loveliest
  flower
  That grows in the garden of God.
Its climb is from weakness to knowl-
  edge and power,
  To the sky from the clay and the
  clod.
To beauty and sweetness it grows un-
  der care,
  Neglected, 'tis ragged and wild.
'Tis a plant that is tender, but won-
  drously rare,
  The sweet, wistful soul of a child.

Be tender, O gardener, and give it its
  share
Of moisture, of warmth, and of light,
And let it not lack for the painstaking
  care,
  To protect it from frost and from
  blight.

A glad day will come when its bloom
  shall unfold,
It will seem that an angel has smiled,
Reflecting a beauty and sweetness un-
  told
In the sensitive soul of a child.
AUTHOR UNKNOWN

Who Wants the Boys and Girls?

God wants the boys, the merry, merry
  boys,
The noisy boys, the funny boys,
  The thoughtless boys;
God wants the boys with all their joys,
That He as gold may make them pure,
And teach them trials to endure;
  His heroes brave, He'd have them
  be,
  Fighting for truth and purity.
  God wants the boys!
God wants the happy-hearted girls,
The loving girls, the best of girls,
  The worst of girls;
God wants to make the girls His pearls,
And so reflect His holy face,
And bring to mind His wondrous grace,
  That beautiful the world may be,
  And filled with love and purity,
  God wants the girls! AUTHOR UNKNOWN

An American couple decided to send
a playpen to a friend in Northern Canada on the arrival of her fourth child.
"Thank you so much for the·pen,"
she wrote. "It is wonderful — I sit in it
every afternoon and read. The children can't get near me."

A five-year-old girl was asked by the
minister how many children there were
in her family.
She replied, "Seven."
The minister observed that so many
children must cost a lot.
"Oh, no," the child replied. "We
don't buy 'em, we raise 'em."
Together

A woman never stops to consider
how very uninteresting her children
would be if they were some other
woman's.
ROBERT C. EDWARDS

51

Heart of a Child

Whatever you write on the heart of a
child
No water can wash away.
The sand may be shifted when billows
are wild
And the efforts of time may decay.
Some stories may perish, some songs
be forgot
But this graven record—time changes
it not.
Whatever you write on the heart of a
child,
A story of gladness or care
That heaven has blessed or earth has
defiled,
Will linger unchangeably there.

Selected

———◆———

Three-year-old Bobby didn't like the
routine of being scrubbed, especially
when soap was applied.

"Bobby, don't you want to be nice
and clean?" his mother asked.

"Sure," replied Bobby, "but can't you
just dust me?"

———◆———

Choice, Choose

The granddaughter of Aaron Burr
had gone to an evangelistic service
and given her heart to Christ. That
evening she came to her grandfather
and asked him why he didn't do the
same. His story was a sad one. He
told her that when he was fifteen
years old he had gone to an evangelistic service and walked out without
giving his heart to Christ. Out under
the stars he looked up toward the
heavens and said, "God, if you don't
bother me, I'll never bother you."

"Honey," he told his little granddaughter, "God kept His part of the
bargain. He's never bothered me. Now
it is too late."

———◆———

Little choices determine habit;
Habit carves and molds character
Which makes the big decisions.

———◆———

Choose: the attainment of man or
the atonement of Christ.   *This Day*

God always gives His best to those
who leave the choice with Him.

———◆———

Choice, not chance, determines human destiny.

———◆———

Christ

Jesus lived that He might die and
died that we might live!

———◆———

If Christ stays, sin goes; if sin stays,
Christ goes.

———◆———

Nature forms us; sin deforms us;
school informs us; but only Christ
transforms us.

———◆———

Christ is no law-giver, but a life-
giver.   LUTHER

———◆———

Christ's limitless resources meet endless needs.

———◆———

Christ is the great central fact in
the world's history; to Him everything
looks forward or backward.   SPURGEON

———◆———

Try the ways of being good, and you
will fail; but try the way of Christ and
you will succeed.   MATTHEW ARNOLD

———◆———

If Socrates would enter the room, we
should rise and do him honor. But if
Jesus Christ came into the room, we
should fall down on our knees and worship Him.   NAPOLEON

———◆———

Jesus Christ forgave voluntarily; He
died vicariously; He arose visibly, and
He lives victoriously.   JIM E. STARK

———◆———

The Lord Jesus Christ loves to reveal
Himself to those who dare to take the
bleak side of the hill with Him.
This Day

———◆———

The only person who ever lived before He was born is Jesus Christ.

———◆———

When Jesus Christ has you for anything, then you have Him for everything.   FLEECE

52

Life of Christ
Virgin Birth
Virtuous Life
Vicarious Death
Victorious Resurrection
Visible Return

———◆———

When I'm on top of the mountain,
He's the bright and morning star.
When I'm on the side of the mountain,
He is the Rose of Sharon.
When I'm in the valley,
He's the lily of the valley.

———◆———

If Christ is the Way, why waste time traveling some other way?

———◆———

Christ sends none away empty but those who are full of themselves.

———◆———

I Met the Master Face to Face

I had walked life's way with an easy tread,
Had followed where comforts and pleasures led,
Until one day in a quiet place
I met the Master face to face.

With station and rank and wealth for my goal,
Much thought for my body but none for my soul,
I had entered to win in Life's mad race,
When I met the Master face to face.

I met Him and knew Him and blushed to see
That His eyes full of sorrow were fixed on me,
And I faltered and fell at His feet that day
While my castles melted and vanished away.

Melted and vanished, and in their place,
Naught else did I see but the Master's face;
And I cried aloud, "Oh, make me meet
To follow the steps of Thy wounded feet."

My thought is now for the souls of men;
I have lost my life to find it again,
E'er since one day in a quiet place
I met the Master face to face.
                    AUTHOR UNKNOWN

———◆———

Christ is all-sufficient. For the
ARTIST He is the altogether lovely — Song of Solomon 5:16.
ARCHITECT He is the chief cornerstone — I Peter 2:6.
ASTRONOMER He is the sun of righteousness — Malachi 4:2.
BAKER He is the living bread — John 6:51.
BANKER He is the unsearchable riches — Ephesians 3:8.
BUILDER He is the sure foundation — Isaiah 28:16; I Corinthians 3:11.
CARPENTER He is the door — John 10:9.
EDITOR He is good tidings of great joy — Luke 2:10.
ELECTRICIAN He is the light of the world John 8:12.
FARMER He is sower and the Lord of the harvest — Matthew 13:37; Luke 10:2.
FLORIST He is the rose of Sharon and the lily of the valley — Song of Solomon 2:1.
JEWELER He is the living precious stone — I Peter 2:4.
LAWYER He is the counselor, lawgiver and advocate—Isaiah 9:6; I John 2:1.
LABORER He is the giver of rest — Matthew 11:28.   SOURCE UNKNOWN

———◆———

The Touch of the Master's Hand

It was battered and scarred, and the auctioneer
Thought it scarcely worth the while,
To waste much time on the old violin,
But he held it up with a smile.

"What am I bid for this old violin?
Who will start the bidding for me?
A dollar, a dollar, who'll make it two?
Two dollars, and who'll make it three?

"Three dollars once, three dollars twice,
Going for three," but no;

From the back of the room a gray haired man
Came forward and took up the bow.

Then wiping the dust from the old violin,
And tightening up all the strings,
He played a melody pure and sweet,
As sweet as the angels sing.

The music ceased and the auctioneer
With a voice that was quiet and low
Said, "What am I bid for the old violin?"
And he held it up with the bow.

"A thousand dollars, and who'll make it two?
Two thousand, and who'll make it three?
Three thousand once, three thousand twice,
Going, and gone," said he.

The people cheered, but some of them said,
"We do not quite understand,
What changed its worth?" Came the reply,
"The touch of the master's hand."

And many a man with his life out of tune,
And battered and scarred with sin,
Is auctioned cheap to a thoughtless crowd,
Much like the old violin.

A mess of pottage, a glass of wine,
A game, and he shuffles along;
He's going once, and he's going twice,
He's going and almost gone.

But the Master comes, and the thoughtless crowd
Never can quite understand
The worth of the soul, and the change that is wrought
By the touch of the Master's hand.
MYRA BROOKS WELCH

———◆———

He who receives scars for Christ here will wear stars with Christ there.

Christian, Christianity*

A Christian . . .
is a mind through which Christ thinks.
is a heart through which Christ lives.
is a voice through which Christ speaks.
is a hand through which Christ helps.
F. A. NOBLE

———◆———

The Scriptures give four names to Christians:
saints, for their holiness.
believers, for their faith.
brethren, for their love.
disciples, for their knowledge.

———◆———

Two marks of a Christian: giving and forgiving.

There are those who are *truly* Christians but not *wholly,* and if not *wholly,* then not *holy.*

———◆———

Only entirely devoted Christians are entirely happy Christians.

———◆———

Nine per cent of the world's population speak English, but ninety per cent of the Christians speak English.
BOB THOMPSON

———◆———

A Christian is anyone in whom Christ lives.
EUGENIA PRICE

———◆———

A real Christian is a person who can give his pet parrot to the town gossip.
BILLY GRAHAM

———◆———

Going to church doesn't make you a Christian any more than going to a garage makes you an automobile.
BILLY SUNDAY

———◆———

The devil is willing for a person to confess Christianity as long as he does not practice it.
The Defender

———◆———

A thirty per cent Christian cannot be a hundred per cent American.

———◆———

A Christian is a man who knows how to acquire without cheating, how to lose without regret, and how to give without hesitation.

*Also Christian Growth, Christian Life, Christian Living.

Some Christians are childish and not childlike.

God needs Christians who are separators and not mixers.

The Christian who sells out to Christ is always unsatisfied but NOT dissatisfied. EUGENIA PRICE

A Christian, like a candle, must keep cool and burn at the same time. MERV ROSELL

The Christian is the freest of all, slave to none. LUTHER

A Christian should not be a question mark for God, but an exclamation point! VANCE HAVNER

If your Christianity won't work where you are, it won't work anywhere. VANCE HAVNER

A Christian is a blot or a blessing, a blank he cannot be. *This Day*

Christianity is the one place where surrender brings victory.

Christianity begins where religion ends — with the resurrection.

Christianity is not a religion, it is a relationship. DR. THIEME

A lot of Christians are like wheelbarrows — not good unless pushed.
Some are like canoes — they need to be paddled.
Some are like kites — if you don't keep a string on them, they fly away.
Some are like footballs — you can't tell which way they will bounce next.
Some are like balloons — full of wind and ready to blow up.
Some are like trailers — they have to be pulled.
Some are like neon lights — they keep going on and off.
Some are like a good watch — open face, pure gold, quietly busy and full of good works. *Slovak Courier*

It is not that Christianity fails, but the Christian. ELD

There are but two great dangers for Christianity: that it should become localized, and that it should become institutionalized. ARNOLD OLSON

He who shall introduce into public affairs the principles of primitive Christianity will revolutionize the world. BENJAMIN FRANKLIN

The Christian faith offers
Peace in war,
Comfort in sorrow,
Strength in weakness,
Light in darkness. WALTER A. MAIER

Christianity is like the seafaring life — a smooth sea never made a good sailor.

An Old Question

Question: Can I be a Christian without joining the church?
Answer: Yes, it is possible. It is something like being:
A student who will not go to school.
A soldier who will not join an army.
A citizen who does not pay taxes or vote.
A salesman with no customers.
An explorer with no base camp.
A seaman on a ship without a crew.
A business man on a deserted island.
An author without readers.
A tuba player without an orchestra.
A parent without a family.
A football player without a team.
A politician who is a hermit.
A scientist who does not share his findings.
A bee without a hive. *Wesleyan Christian Advocate*

I envy not the twelve,
Nearer to me is He;
The life He once lived here on earth,
He lives again in me.

Christian growth comes not by pouring in, but by giving out.

55

CHRISTIANITY

Definition of a Christian

He has a mind and he knows it.
He has a will and shows it.
He sees his way and goes it.
He draws a line and toes it.
He has a chance, and takes it,
A friendly hand and shakes it,
A rule, and never breaks it,
If there's no time, he makes it.
He loves the truth, stands by it,
Never, ever tries to shy it,
Whoever may deny it,
Or openly defy it.
He hears a lie and slays it.
He owes a debt and pays it.
And, as I have heard him praise it,
He knows the game and plays it.
He sees the path Christ trod
And grips the hand of God.

ANONYMOUS *from UEA*

———◆———

There are too many Christians hunting for the things that are IN Christ.

EUGENIA PRICE

———◆———

God wants spiritual fruit, not religious nuts.

ETHEL WILCOX

———◆———

God is not looking for ornamental but fruit-bearing Christians.

HAROLD W. ERICKSON

———◆———

The state of life in a tree is shown by the fruit.

HAROLD W. ERICKSON

———◆———

Dying men have said, "I am sorry I have been an atheist, infidel, agnostic, skeptic, or sinner," but no man ever said on his deathbed, "I am sorry I have lived a Christian life."

DR. BOB JONES, SR.

———◆———

You can tell the metal of a Christian when he rubs against the world. The right kind will shine.

———◆———

The straight and narrow way has the lowest accident rate.

———◆———

On the "straight and narrow" road, traffic is all one way.

———◆———

It is not hard to live a Christian life; it is impossible.

There is only one thing to do about anything and that is the right thing.

DR. BOB JONES, SR.

———◆———

A holy life has a voice. It speaks when the tongue is silent, and is either a constant attraction or a perpetual reproof.

HINTON

———◆———

You and God make a majority in your community.

DR. BOB JONES, SR.

———◆———

You can't be religious without religion. You can't be a Christian without Christ. You can't deliver the goods unless you have the goods to deliver. Quit trying to pump water out of a dry well.

DR. BOB JONES, SR.

———◆———

Live the Christian Life!
Men will admire you,
Women will respect you,
Little children will love you and
God will crown your life with success.
And when the twilight of your life mingles with the purpling dawn of eternity
Men will speak your name with honor
And baptize your grave with tears,
As God attunes for you the evening chimes.

BILLY SUNDAY

———◆———

We get no deeper into Christ than we allow Him to get into us.

DR. JOWETT

———◆———

No man is high-born until he is born from on high.

DR. BOB JONES, SR.

———◆———

He who walks with God will never be late to his spiritual meals.

———◆———

The Christian life is not a search for God, but a response to Him.

Eternity

———◆———

If you will give God your heart He will comb the kinks out of your head.

DR. BOB JONES, SR.

———◆———

Christianity helps us to face the music, even when we don't like the tune.

PHILLIPS BROOKS

My Neighbor's Bible

I am my neighbor's Bible
He reads me when we meet;
He reads me in my home —
Tomorrow, in the street.
  He may be my relative or friend,
  Or slight acquaintance be;
He may not even know my name
Yet he is reading me.
       Youth on the March News

———◆———

His Best

God has His best things for the few
  Who dare to stand the test.
He has His second choice for those
  Who will not have His best.

———◆———   ANONYMOUS

A rather pompous-looking deacon was endeavoring to impress on a class of young boys the importance of living the Christian life.

"Why do people call me a Christian?" the dignitary asked, standing very erect and beaming down upon them.

A moment's pause, then one youngster said: "It may be because they don't know you." *Ladies' Home Journal*

———◆———

A buoy is fastened securely to a rock at the bottom of the sea. The waves splash around it; it floats serenely in its appointed place. The tide rises and falls; it is still there. The Atlantic rollers come racing toward it; it mounts them one by one and rides upon them as they roll past. The tempest descends, the billows rush upon the little buoy, and for a moment it is submerged. But immediately it rises to the surface and is in its place again, unmoved and unharmed.

What a picture of the conquering life! What a power and a privilege for a soul to be able thus to rise lightly above every opponent, every vexation, never to sink into discontentment, never to be overwhelmed with fear and doubt, always to be on top of the fretful sea of life! *S.S. Chronicle*

Little Things

A holy Christian life is made up of a number of small things:
  Little words, not eloquent sermons;
  Little deeds, not miracles of battle
  Or one great, heroic deed of martyrdom;
The little constant sunbeam, not the lightning.

The avoidance of little evils,
  Little inconsistencies, little weaknesses,
  Little follies and indiscretions,
  And little indulgences of the flesh make up
The beauty of a holy life.   ANDREW BONAR

———◆———

Not in Vain

To talk with God
No breath is lost —
  Talk on!
To walk with God
No strength is lost —
  Walk on!
To wait on God
No time is lost —
  Wait on!   AUTHOR UNKNOWN

———◆———

Christmas

The Night After Christmas

'Twas the night after Christmas,
When all through the house
Not a creature was stirring,
But a hungry gray mouse.
The stockings all empty
On the floor had been flung,
The toys were abandoned,
No carols were sung.
The children were snuggled
All close in their beds,
Held there while Dad
Applied ice to their heads.
And Mama in her kerchief
And I in my cap retired
After midnight to catch
A short nap. When out on the street
There arose such a fuss,
We knew in a moment

It was Dr. Pill's bus.
It rattled and clattered
Like coal in the clink,
His motor was smoking,
His lights on the blink.
His horn had a voice
Like a sledgehammer's blow,
And his four wheels were chugging
Through the new-fallen snow.
He was making his regular
Christmas night call
To check on our pulses,
Our tummies, and all.
As he came up the stairway,
His eyes twinkled bright,
But when our groans reached him,
He cried out "Good Night!"
He bent to his bag,
And the chain 'cross his belly
Shook as he searched
For his old menthol jelly.
He ransacked his satchel
For cough syrup and pills
And enough Analgesique
To cure all our ills.
With a smile on his face,
A quick jerk of his head,
He plastered and pasted
And put all to bed.
He turned on his heel
And cut out the light.
He put on his earmuffs
And pulled out of sight.
We heard him exclaim,
Ere he left us that night,
"Now keep under cover,
Pipe down, and sleep tight!"

RUTH SCOTT HUBBARD, *This Day*

———◆———

The Christmas spirit that goes out with the dried-up Christmas tree is just as worthless. FRED BECK

———◆———

An older sister was trying to motivate her younger brother to good behavior. "If you are not better, Santa Claus will not stop and see you next week," she told the four-year-old. "He'll pass right over this house."

"What?" said the tot. "Won't he even stop for you?"

Christmas living is the best kind of Christmas giving. VAN DYKE

———◆———

Some children, all in their early school years, got out of line while putting on a Christmas pageant in church. It was disconcerting.

Thirteen of them were to walk across the stage, each carrying a letter-bearing placard. All together — if they were in correct order and in line — spelled: B-E-T-H-L-E-H-E-M S-T-A-R.

But the "star" bearers got turned around and went in backwards, so to speak, spelling out: B-E-T-H-L-E-H-E-M R-A-T-S! *Kuna, Idaho*

———◆———

Little Janie was being taught that it was the proper thing to do to write a "thank-you" letter to those persons who sent her gifts at Christmas. She seemed to do pretty well until it came to Aunt Martha's gift. Finally she finished her note which read: "Thank you for your Christmas present. I always wanted a pin-cushion, although not very much."

———◆———

If you hitch your wagon to a star, be sure it is the Star of Bethlehem.

———◆———

The first Christmas that little Linda learned to read she was allowed to distribute the family gifts on Christmas eve. According to the family custom, the one who distributed the gifts could open the first package. After all the gifts were distributed with loving care, Linda kept looking and looking around the tree and among its branches. Finally father asked, "What are you looking for, dear?"

To which Linda replied, "I thought Christmas was Jesus' birthday and I was just wondering where His present is. I guess everyone forgot Him. Did they, Daddy?"

———◆———

Church (Attendance, Membership, etc.)

God puts the church in the world; Satan puts the world into the church.

If the church aims to hit sin it should pull the trigger. c. GRANT

————◆————

If you want the church to go on, go to church.

————◆————

The church is not made up of people who are better than the rest, but of people who want to become better than they are.

————◆————

Church membership is a poor substitute for real Christianity.

————◆————

Too many church members are starched and ironed but not washed. VANCE HAVNER

————◆————

The church cannot remain evangelical in faith unless it remains evangelistic.

————◆————

An ounce of church is worth a pound of police court.

————◆————

The church is fairly well supplied with conductors. It shows a shortage of engineers, but an over supply of brakemen.

————◆————

Any church which is satisfied to hold her own is on the way to the cemetery. This Day

————◆————

What the church of God needs is men who will talk less and work more. GYPSY SMITH

————◆————

There is a hotter place than the church in summer. Christian Parent

————◆————

I am your church. Without you I am nothing. If you fail to make an investment in me, I cannot materialize. Invest in me or I will die.

————◆————

The church must not spend her strength in trifles — in trifles she becomes anemic. JOWETT

————◆————

Too many well-meaning people wait for the hearse to bring them to church. Presbyterian Life

————◆————

The glory of the local church is that it is not local. This Day

The church service is not a convention to which a family should merely send a delegate.

————◆————

Most churches are full of well-fed saints who need spiritual exercise.

————◆————

The church is not a dormitory, it is a workshop.

————◆————

The quickest way to get a church on its feet is to get it on its knees. WILLIAM WARD AYER

————◆————

The bell calls others to church, but itself never minds the sermon. BENJAMIN FRANKLIN

————◆————

When church services are over, your service begins. This Day

————◆————

Many folks think that what a church has is for everyone else.

————◆————

Church Definitions

Pillars — worship regularly, giving time and money.

Supporters — give time and money if they like the minister and treasurer.

Leaners — use the church for funerals, baptisms and marriages but give no time or money to support it.

Working Leaners — work, but do not give money.

Specials — help and give occasionally for something that appeals to them.

Annuals, or *Easter-Birds* — dress up, look serious and go to church on Easter.

Sponges — take all blessings and benefits, even the sacrament, but give no money to support the church.

Tramps — go from church to church, but support none.

Gossips — talk freely about everyone except the Lord Jesus.

Scrappers — take offense, criticize and fight.

Orphans — are children sent by parents who do not set them an example.

Backsliders—go back and walk no more with Jesus (John 6:66). St. Phillips Society

Some pillars in the church are really nothing but caterpillars.

———♦———

Mr. Lazybones

Died — of spiritual inertia — Samuel Lazybones, Esq., on the fourteenth. The immediate cause of death was paralysis of the spine, induced by long absence from church. His last words were: "A little more sleep, a little more slumber, a little more folding of the hands to sleep." He was a prominent member of the Ancient Order of Adhesive Recalcitrants, and a large concourse of the order, in full regalia, followed his remains. The chaplain delivered an 'eloquent eulogy and said he had "passed on to rest." *Western Recorder*

———♦———

Recently a blase TV audience was startled into thought when someone read a letter from a girl on the topic: "Why I Go to Church.'" She said: "I go to church every Sunday so when they carry me in one day, the Lord won't turn and ask, 'Who is it?' " *This Day*

———♦———

The congregation in one church grew so small that when the minister said, "Dearly beloved," the maiden lady thought he was proposing.

———♦———

The following notice was displayed outside a church:

CH ? ? CH

What is missing? *F. DODDS*

———♦———

Come to Church

1. Come.
2. Come early.
3. Come with your entire family.
4. Take a place near the front.
5. Be devout.
6. Be considerate of the comfort of others.
7. Be kind to strangers — they are the guests of the church.
8. Give a good offering, cheerfully.
9. Never rush for the door after the benediction. *Selected*

Why People Go to Church

Some go to church to take a walk;
Some go to church to laugh and talk;
Some go there to meet a friend;
Some go there their time to spend;
Some go there to meet a lover;
Some go there a fault to cover;
Some go there for speculation;
Some go there for observation;
Some go there to doze and nod;
The wise go there to worship God.
Gospel Herald

———♦———

The retiring usher was instructing his youthful successor in the details of his office. "And remember, my boy, that we have nothing but good, kind Christians in this church — until you try to put someone else in their pew."

———♦———

This is the way the church sometimes looks to the pastor when he goes into the pulpit! The pastor would just as soon preach to a woodpile as to empty benches. He does not find one single bit of inspiration in all the vacant pews!

(Back seats only usually filled)

HOWEVERTHISISREAL-
LYTHEWAYTHECHURCH
OUGHTTOLOOKATEVERY
SERVICE.ANDITWILLIF
EACHONEDOESHISPART
BYCOMINGHIMSELFAND
BRINGINGAFRIENDOR
NEIGHBORORRELATIVE!
THEBESTWAYONEARTH
TO"PEPUP"ANDINSPIRE
THEPREACHERISTOHIDE
ALLTHEEMPTYBENCH-
ESINTHECHURCHWITH
PEOPLEEVERYWEEK.

———♦———

Why Should We Go to Church?

1. Because going to church prepares us for the responsibilities of the week.
2. Because going to church rekindles our spiritual fires.

3. Because going to church affords us the opportunity of expressing our thanks.
4. Because going to church gives us companionship with other believers.
5. Because going to church makes our lives witnesses of our faith.
6. Because going to church enables us to worship God.

———◆———

Lord, what a change within us one short hour
Spent in thy presence will prevail to make!
What heavy burdens from our bosoms take,
What parched grounds revive as with a shower!
We kneel, and all around us seems to lower;
We rise, and all, the distant and the near,
Stands forth a sunny outline brave and clear;
We kneel, how weak! We rise, how full of power!

RICHARD CHEVENIX TRENCH, *Prayer*

———◆———

I Am Your Church

I am brick, stone, metal, mortar and lath.
I am sanctuary, pews, hymnals, chancel and lectern.
I am classroom, furniture, Bibles, literature, and religious art.
I am boys and girls learning to think, work and play.
I am youth seeking inspiration and guidance.
I am young couples planning to establish a Christian home.
I am the repository of a man's spiritual heritage.
I am the bearer of the evangel of Christ.
I am the custodian of your deepest hopes.
In me there is love and truth, inspiration and instruction, joy and pleasure, help and strength.
In a chaotic and troubled world I hold the answer to its greatest need.

In me there is promise for tomorrow.
In my fellowship you shall find peace.
Whatever else you neglect, do not neglect me.

AUTHOR UNKNOWN

———◆———

If There Were No Churches

If there were no churches there would be:
No church fellowship!
No Sunday schools!
No prayer meetings!
No Christian homes!
No "salt of the earth"!
No "light of the world"!
No gospel preached to lost sinners!
No missionaries sent to the foreign fields!
No "body of Christ" in the world!
No rapture and wedding day of the church to look for!
No training courses for the youth of the land!
No family altars!
No preachers to visit the sad and lonely homes!
No prayers for sinners!
No moral training for boys and girls!
No Christian colleges!
No love for the lost sinner!

AUTHOR UNKNOWN

———◆———

I Am Your Church Office

I feel neglected.
When you are planning to move, you notify every magazine to which you subscribe. You notify all your friends, but you fail to notify me. I am your church office, I feel neglected.
When your class plans to have a meeting, you notify all the members, but fail to tell me. Sometimes you plan to have a meeting in the church, and still you fail to let me know. Sometimes it almost embarrasses me, because I have promised the room you want to use to another group. You see, I am your church office — I feel neglected.
When a member of your family is ill, you seem to manage to call all your friends, except me. I like to know all

our people who are ill, so why don't you call me? I am your church office. I feel neglected!

Christ for the World Messenger

———◆———

Too many board members are just bored members.   ELD

———◆———

The Early Christian Church — a Model Church

It was:

Happy — "had rest," Acts 9:31.
Healthy — "edified" and "walking."
Humble — "in the fear of the Lord."
Holy — "comforted" of the Holy Ghost.
Hearty — multiplied.

———◆———

Pastor Jones in our church had been paying five-year-old Tommy Brown ten cents a week to keep his grandfather awake during the sermon. Last week Tommy didn't deliver, and that night Pastor Jones jumped him. "I know, sir," explained the lad, "but Grandfather pays me fifteen cents to let him sleep."   *Presbyterian Life*

———◆———

"Johnny, do you know when your church was founded?" asked the pastor.
"Founded?" asked Johnny. "I didn't know it was losted!"

———◆———

Family at Church

Hand in hand, in Sunday dress,
  Parents with their children go,
Asking God their lives to bless,
  Wanting all His love to know.

At the church door families meet,
  Chatting as the spire bells chime,
Telling all upon the street
  Once again it's worship time.

By the pew the father stands,
  Joining them when still are they.
Then, eyes closed and folded hands,
  All together kneel to pray.

Earth has glorious scenes to see;
  Near and far is beauty rare.
But no fairer sight can be
  Than a family joined in prayer.

EDGAR A. GUEST

Some Who Do Not Go to Church

Mr. Speeds will clean his auto,
  Mr. Spurs will groom his horse,
Mr. Gadds will go to Coney,
  With the little Gadds, of course,
Mr. Flite will put carbolic
  On his homing pigeon's perch,
Mr. Weeds will mow his bluegrass,
  Mr. Jones will go to church.

Mr. Cleet will drive a golf ball,
  Mr. Tiller steer his boat,
Mr. Popper, on his cycle,
  Round and round the state will mote.
Mr. Swatt will watch a ball game,
  Mr. Stake and sons will search
Through the bosky woods for mushrooms,
  Mr. Wilks will go to church.

Do you ask me what's the matter?
  Do you wonder what is wrong?
When the nation turns from worship,
  Sermon, prayer and sacred song?
Why do people rush for pleasure,
  Leave religion in the lurch?
Why prefer a padded auto
  To the cushioned pew in church?

Reader, well I know the answer,
  But if I should speak aloud
What I think is the real reason,
  It would queer me with the crowd.
You'll be popular, dear reader,
  When you wield the critic's birch;
You'll be safely in the fashion
  If you blame things on the church.

ANONYMOUS, from *The World's Best Loved Poems*

———◆———

Church Member's Beatitudes

Blessed is he who will not strain at a drizzle and swallow a downpour.

Blessed is he who tries a little harder when all around say: "It cannot be done."

Blessed is he whose program contains a prayer meeting night.

Blessed is the church leader who is not pessimistic.

Blessed is he who loves the church before his business.

Blessed is he who can walk as fast to a religious service as to town.

Blessed is he who invites people to church and comes along himself.

Blessed are those who never gossip about the faults of the church but work to make it better.

Dead Weight

I've been a dead weight many years,
Around the church's neck.
I've let the others carry me
And always pay the check.
I've had my name upon the rolls,
For years and years gone by;
I've criticized and grumbled, too;
Nothing could satisfy.

I've been a dead weight long enough
Upon the church's back,
Beginning now, I'm going to take
A wholly different track.
I'm going to pray and pay and work;
And carry loads instead;
And not have others carry me
Like people do the dead. ANONYMOUS

Ten Commandments for Church-Goers

1. Thou shalt recognize that church-going is a fine art which demands the best preparation of which thou art capable.
2. Thou shalt go to church regularly, for a prescription cannot do thee much good nor be effective if taken only once a year.
3. Thou shalt get in condition for Sunday by refraining from late hours and activities that clash with the will of God during the week, especially on Saturday night.
4. Thou shalt go to church in a relaxed state of body and mind, for the absence of tension is a primary requisite to successful worship.
5. Thou shalt remember that worship in church is not a gloomy exercise, therefore go in a spirit of enjoyment, radiant and happy to enjoy thy religion.
6. Thou shalt sit relaxed in thy pew, for the power of God cannot come to thy personality when thou art rigid and full of tensions.
7. Thou shalt not bring thy problems to church, for six days are sufficient for thee to think upon thy problems, but the church service giveth thee a supreme opportunity to let the peace of God bring thee insight for thy intellectual processes.
8. Thou shalt not bring ill will to church, for the flow of spiritual power is effectively blocked by harboring a grudge against thy neighbor.
9. Thou shalt practice the art of spiritual contemplation by the daily use of Scripture reading and prayer so that thou be not a stranger to the God whose Presence thou canst enter in the sanctuary.
10. Thou shalt go to church expectantly, for great things have happened to those who worship in spirit and truth — and the spiritual miracle can happen unto thee according to thy faith. BENJAMIN F. SWARTZ

I Am a Church Member

BECAUSE if no one belonged to church there would be no church to point men to God and heaven.

BECAUSE I cannot ignore my spiritual nature. My soul culture is as necessary as my physical culture.

BECAUSE it benefits me, and enables me to undergird home and democracy with Christianity.

BECAUSE here I can transfer my personal allegiance to Christ in altruistic actions.

BECAUSE others are watching me, and I dare not set an example which will keep them from church.

BECAUSE I need the strength that comes from worship and fellowship with other Christians.

BECAUSE no matter how much I do for Christ it is but little compared with what He did for me.
New Jersey Baptist Bulletin

———♦———

One day the telephone rang in the clergyman's office of the Washington church which President Franklin Roosevelt attended. An eager voice inquired, "Do you expect the President to be in church Sunday?"

"That," answered the clergyman, "I cannot promise. But we expect God to be there and we fancy that should be incentive enough for a reasonably large attendance." *Together*

———♦———

Circumstances

If our circumstances find us in God, we shall find God in all our circumstances.

———♦———

It's not the circumstance that matters, it's your reaction to it.

———♦———

Don't look to God through your circumstances, look at your circumstances through God.

———♦———

Civilization

Unless our civilization is redeemed spiritually, it cannot endure materially.
WOODROW WILSON

———♦———

There is no solid basis for civilization but in the Word of God. DANIEL WEBSTER

———♦———

What a civilization! The poor man worries over his next meal and the rich man over his last one.

———♦———

Honesty is not only the best policy, but it is the foundation of civilization.

———♦———

A Los Angeles teacher training her class in the use of proverbs said, "Cleanliness is next to what?"

A little boy exclaimed, feelingly, "Impossible!" *Christian Herald*

Clothing

The latest thing in men's clothing today is women.

———♦———

Women who claim they haven't a thing to wear usually need their husband's closets to keep it in. *Town Journal*

———♦———

I have never seen a badly dressed woman who was agreeable and good-humored. HONORE DE BALZAC

———♦———

Joe College wrote home and asked his father to send him $100 to buy a suit of clothes. Dad wrote a prompt reply and enclosed $50 with this advice, "Join a fraternity."

———♦———

Comfort

God does not comfort us that we may be comfortable but that we may be comforters. ALEXANDER NOWELL

———♦———

It is such a comfort to drop the tangles of life into God's hands and leave them there. C. E. COWMAN

———♦———

The only comfort that counts is the comfort that results when we do something about the things that make us all uncomfortable. HAROLD W. RUOPP

———♦———

Would you live with ease,
Do what you ought,
Not what you please.
BENJAMIN FRANKLIN

———♦———

"Mama, when is God going to send us a blanket?" asked seven-year-old Caryl one day.

"Why do you think God is going to send us a blanket?" asked her mother.

"Because," replied the young daughter, "our Sunday school teacher said that God promised a comforter when Jesus went back to heaven. And Jesus has been in heaven a long time."

———♦———

A little girl came home from a neighbor's house where her little friend had died.

"Why did you go?" questioned her father.

"To comfort her mother," replied the child.

"What could you do to comfort her?" the father continued.

"I climbed into her lap and cried with her," answered the child.   *Selected*

Howard Maxwell of Los Angeles had a four-year-old daughter, Melinda, who had acquired a fixation for "The Three Little Pigs" and demanded that he read it to her night after night. Mr. Maxwell, pleased with himself, tape-recorded the story. When Melinda next asked for it, he simply switched on the playback. This worked for a couple of nights, but then one evening Melinda pushed the storybook at her father. "Now honey," he said, "you know how to turn on the recorder."

"Yes," said Melinda, "but I can't sit on its lap."
GENE SHERMAN in Los Angeles Times

Committee

To be effective, a committee should be made up of three persons. But to get anything done, one member should be sick, another absent.
Chadwick, Illinois Review

A committee is a group that keeps minutes but wastes hours.

A committee of five usually consists of the man who does the work, three others to pat him on the back, and one to bring in a minority report.
Fort Worth Record-Telegram

Blessed is the man who will work on a committee of which he wanted to be chairman.

A committee is a group of people who individually can do nothing and who collectively decide nothing can be done.

A conference is a way of postponing a decision.

Common Sense

Nothing astonishes men so much as common sense and plain dealing.
RALPH WALDO EMERSON

Fads come and go; good sense goes on forever.

Common sense is not so common.
VOLTAIRE

Horse sense naturally dwells in a stable mind.

Common sense is genius in homespun.   *A. N. WHITEHEAD*

It is better to be saved by a lighthouse than by a lifeboat. *ERNEST J. KUNSCH*

"Dad, what do they mean when they say a fellow has horse sense?"
"He can say, 'nay,' son."

Always keep the head cool and the feet warm.

Better go home and make a net than dive into a pool after fish. *Chinese Proverb*

We hardly find any persons of good sense save those who agree with us.
LA ROCHEFOUCAULD

Communism

Communism is the devil's imitation of Christianity.   *A. W. TOZER*

Compassion

Compassion will cure more sins than condemnation.   *H. W. BEECHER*

We cannot heal the wounds we do not feel.   *S. R. SMALLEY*

Compensation

It's what we weave in this world that we shall wear in the next.
BISHOP TAYLOR SMITH

All too often it's a man's own weaknesses that overpower his strength.

65

There's a payday for every day — even for the fellow who merely labors under a delusion. *Lutheran Education*

———◆———

Cheat me once
Shame for you;
Cheat me twice,
Shame for me.
Scottish Proverb

———◆———

Complain

Nagging isn't horse sense.

———◆———

I had no shoes, and I murmured, till I met a man who had no feet.

———◆———

Park your grouch outside.

———◆———

When you feel dog-tired at night, it may be because you growled all day.

———◆———

Compliment

It is ten to one that when someone slaps you on the back he is trying to make you cough up something.

———◆———

A pat on the back is all right provided it is administered early enough, hard enough and low enough.

———◆———

The best way to compliment your wife is frequently. *Changing Times*

———◆———

Compliments are like perfume to be inhaled but not swallowed.
CHARLES CLARK MUNN

———◆———

Try praising your wife, even if it does frighten her at first. BILLY SUNDAY

———◆———

Talk to a man about himself and he will listen for hours. DISRAELI

———◆———

The art of praising is the beginning of the fine art of pleasing.

———◆———

The same man cannot be both friend and flatterer. BENJAMIN FRANKLIN

———◆———

A little flattery, now and then, makes husbands out of single men.

Many a man thinks he is being "cultivated" when he's only being trimmed like a Christmas tree. *Lutheran Education*

———◆———

Approve not of him who commends all you say. BENJAMIN FRANKLIN

———◆———

A flatterer never seems absurd; the flattered always takes his word.
BENJAMIN FRANKLIN

———◆———

A woman noted for her remarkably ugly face was calling on the minister's wife when the little boy of the house blurted out, "You sure are ugly!"

The horrified mother chided him.

The boy was apologetic. "I only meant it for a joke," he said.

Without thinking, his mother replied, "Well, dear, how much better the joke would have been had you said, 'How pretty you are!'" *Together*

———◆———

Conceit

People say that he's a self-made man who loves his creator.

———◆———

A man wrapped up in himself is a pretty small bundle.

———◆———

Conceit is incompatible with understanding. TOLSTOY

———◆———

Self-love is often rather arrogant than blind; it does not hide our faults from ourselves, but persuades us that they escape the notice of others.
SAMUEL JOHNSON

———◆———

The person who sings his own praises is quite likely to be a soloist.
The Valve World

———◆———

The bigger a man's head gets the easier it is to fill his shoes.

———◆———

We know more bad things about ourselves than does anyone else, yet no one thinks so highly of us as we do of ourselves. FRANZ V. SCHOENTHAN

———◆———

One type of inflation is the most dangerous of all — an inflated ego.

Conceited men often seem a harmless kind of men, who by an overweening self-respect relieve others from the duty of respecting them at all.

HENRY WARD BEECHER

———◆———

A snob is a person who wants to know only the ones who don't want to know him.

———◆———

Even the conceited bore has one striking virtue — he seldom talks about other people.

———◆———

The world tolerates conceit from those who are successful, but not from anyone else.

JOHN BLAKE

———◆———

Forget the "I" stuff. Learn to say "you" and to take the other person's interest into consideration.

———◆———

Confess, Confession

A man should never be ashamed to own he has been wrong, which is but saying in other words, that he is wiser today than he was yesterday.

ALEXANDER POPE

———◆———

The confession of evil works is the first beginning of good works.

ST. AUGUSTINE

———◆———

Confession of sin puts the soul under the blessing of God.

———◆———

How we love to confess the sins of others.

———◆———

Last night my little boy confessed to me
Some childish wrong;
And kneeling at my knee
He prayed with tears —
"Dear God, make me a man
Like Daddy — wise and strong.
I know You can."
Then while he slept
I knelt beside his bed,
Confessed my sins,
And prayed with low-bowed head,
"O God, make me a child
Like my child here —
Pure, guileless,
Trusting Thee with faith sincere."

AUTHOR UNKNOWN

Confidence

Confidence is the thing that enables you to eat blackberry jam on a picnic without looking to see if the seeds move.

———◆———

Optimist: One who finds an opportunity in every difficulty.
Pessimist: One who finds a difficulty in every opportunity.

———◆———

If you lose confidence in yourself that makes the vote unanimous.

———◆———

I have held many things in my hands, and I have lost them all; but whatever I have placed in God's hands, that I still possess.

MARTIN LUTHER

———◆———

Confidence and enthusiasm are the great sales producer.

———◆———

It's great to believe in oneself, but don't be too easily convinced.

———◆———

They conquer who believe they can. He has not learned the lesson of life who does not each day surmount a fear.

EMERSON

———◆———

Conscience

When you have a fight with your conscience and get licked, you win.

Nuggets

———◆———

A clear conscience is a will of brass.

———◆———

There is no pillow so soft as a clear conscience.

French Proverb

———◆———

Small boy's definition of conscience: "Something that makes you tell your mother before your sister does."

National Motorist

———◆———

Conscience doesn't keep you from doing anything; it just keeps you from enjoying it.

———◆———

The testimony of a good conscience is worth more than a dozen character witnesses.

A man's first care should be to avoid the reproaches of his own heart; his next to escape the censures of the world.

ADDISON

---◆---

A quiet conscience sleeps in thunder, but rest and guilt live far asunder.

BENJAMIN FRANKLIN

---◆---

The best preacher is the heart; the best teacher is time; the best book is the world; the best friend is God.

Talmud

---◆---

E'er you remark another's sin, bid your own conscience look within.

BENJAMIN FRANKLIN

---◆---

"Oh, yes," said the Indian, "I know what my conscience is. It is a little three-cornered thing in here," he laid his hand on his heart, "that stands still when I am good; but when I am bad it turns round, and the corners hurt very much. But if I keep on doing wrong, by-and-by the corners wear off and it doesn't hurt any more."

J. ELLIS, *Weapons for Workers*

---◆---

The teacher had given her English class a test. As the teacher began to read off the correct answers, one of the boys changed an answer further down on the paper. This troubled him as he thought the teacher might think he had changed the answer she had just given. He raised his hand and asked what he should do about changing answers after the teacher started reading the correct ones.

"Let your conscience be your guide," the teacher told him.

The boy scratched his head and seemed so puzzled that the teacher asked him what was the matter.

"My conscience can't make up its mind," the boy replied.

---◆---

Consecrate, Consecration

Christ will not take 70 per cent, 90 per cent or 99 per cent. He wants our all.

BILLY GRAHAM

The Lord doesn't want the first place in my life, He wants all of my life.

HOWARD AMERDING

---◆---

"Will you please tell me in a word," said a Christian woman to a minister, "what your idea of consecration is?" Holding out a blank sheet of paper the pastor replied, "It is to sign your name at the bottom of this blank sheet, and let God fill it in as He wills."

---◆---

The greatness of a man's power is the measure of his surrender.

WILLIAM BOOTH

---◆---

It is not a question of who or what you are, but whether God controls you.

DR. J. WILBUR CHAPMAN

---◆---

Surrender

Let me hold lightly
Things of this earth;
Transient treasures,
What are they worth?
Moths can corrupt them,
Rust can decay;
All their bright beauty
Fades in a day.
Let me hold lightly
Temporal things,
I, who am deathless,
I, who wear wings!
Let me hold fast, Lord,
Things of the skies,
Quicken my vision,
Open my eyes!
Show me Thy riches,
Glory and grace,
Boundless as time is,
Endless as space!
Let me hold lightly
Things that are mine —
Lord, Thou hast giv'n me
All that is Thine!

MARTHA SNELL NICHOLSON

---◆---

Dr. Mason of Burma once wanted a teacher to visit and labor among a warlike tribe and asked his converted boatman if he would go. He told him that as a teacher he would receive only four rupees per month whereas as boatman he was then receiving fifteen rupees.

After praying over the matter, the boatman returned to the doctor and the following conversation occurred:

"Well, Shapon," said the doctor, "what have you decided? Will you go for four rupees a month?"

"No, teacher," replied Shapon, "I will not go for four rupees a month but I will go for Christ."

Selected

———◆———

The Man with a Consecrated Car

He couldn't speak before a crowd;
　He couldn't teach a class;
But when he came to Sunday school
　He brought the folks "en masse."
He couldn't sing to save his life,
　In public couldn't pray,
But always his "jalopy"
　Was crammed on each Lord's Day.

Although he could not sing,
　Nor teach, nor lead in prayer,
He listened well and had a smile
　And he was always there
With all the others whom he brought,
　Who lived both near and far,
And God's work prospered — for he had
　A consecrated car.

AUTHOR UNKNOWN

———◆———

"Use Me"

A beautiful tree stood among many others on a lovely hillside, its stem dark and glossy, its beautiful feathery branches gently quivering in the evening breeze.

As we admired it we became conscious of a gentle rustling of the leaves, and a low murmur was heard: "You think me beautiful and admire my graceful branches, but I have nothing of which to boast; all I have I owe to the loving care of my Master. He planted me in this fruitful hill where my roots, reaching down and dwelling in hidden springs, continually drink of their life-giving water, receiving nourishment, beauty and strength for my whole being.

"The characters on my stem are cut into my very being. The process was painful, but it was my Master's own hand that used the knife, and when the work was finished, with joy I recognized His own name on my stem! Then I knew that He loved me and wanted the world to know I belonged to Him!"

Even as the tree was speaking, the Master Himself stood there. In His hand He held a sharp axe. "I have need of thee," He said. "Art thou willing to give thyself to Me?"

"Master," replied the tree, "I am all Thine own but what use can such as I be to Thee?"

"I need thee," said the Master, "to take My living water to some dry, parched places where there is none."

"But Master, how can I do this? What have I to give to others?"

The Master's voice grew wondrously tender as He replied, "I can use thee if thou art willing. I would fain cut thee down and lop off all thy branches, leaving thee naked and bare; then I would take thee right away from this thy home and carry thee out alone on the far hillside where there will be none to whisper lovingly to thee — only grass and a tangled growth of briers and weeds. Yes, and I would use the painful knife to cut away within thy heart all barriers till there is a free channel for My living water to flow through thee. Thy beauty will be gone; henceforth no one will look on thee and admire thy freshness and grace, but many, many thirsty souls will stoop and drink of the life-giving stream which will reach them so freely through thee. They may give thee no thought, but will they not bless thy Master who has given them His water of life through thee? Art thou willing for this, my tree?"

And the tree replied, "Take and use me as Thou wilt, my Master, if only Thou canst thus bring living water to thirsty souls!"

Adapted from B. E. NEWCOMBE

Content, Contentment

Contentment often serves as a brake on the wheels of progress. God has the correct formula: "Godliness with contentment is great gain."

———✦———

To be content with what we possess is the greatest of all riches.

———✦———

Content makes poor men rich; discontent makes rich men poor.

BENJAMIN FRANKLIN

———✦———

Our idea of a contented man is the one, if any, who enjoys the scenery along the detour.

———✦———

A man from Texas said that he came from the greatest state in the world — the state of contentment.

———✦———

Content is wealth, the riches of the mind; and happy is he who can such riches find.

JOHN DRYDEN

———✦———

Conversion

I found that I was not only converted, but I was invaded.

EUGENIA PRICE

———✦———

Small boy: "Dad, what is a religious traitor?"
Father: "A man who leaves our church and joins another."
Boy: "And what is a man who leaves his church and joins ours?"
Father: "A convert, son, a convert."

Together

———✦———

Convict, Conviction

You cannot sell anything you do not believe in.

———✦———

It's always easier to arrive at a firm conviction about a problem after you know what the boss thinks.

———✦———

The strength of a country is the strength of its religious convictions.

CALVIN COOLIDGE

Cook

About the only thing the modern girl can cook as well as her mother is some man's goose.

———✦———

Mother to teenager thinking about marriage: "Now in getting a meal, what is the first and most important thing?"
Daughter: "Find the can opener."

———✦———

Most brides' cooking is a sacrifice: all burnt offerings.

———✦———

As is the cook, so is the kitchen.

———✦———

Cooperate, Cooperation

The mule can't kick and pull at the same time; neither can a church member.

———✦———

The fellow who is pulling the oars usually hasn't time to rock the boat.

———✦———

It's not the way he kicks, but the way he pulls, that makes a mule useful.

———✦———

You can employ men and hire hands to work for you, but you must win their hearts to have them work with you.

TIORIO

Cost

Beware of little expenses; a small leak will sink a great ship.

BENJAMIN FRANKLIN

———✦———

The best is always the cheapest.

———✦———

When you have to swallow your own medicine, the spoon seems very large.

———✦———

One father was complaining in the presence of another father of the fact that his son was costing him so much. He had to have money for clothes, books, carfare, lunch, etc. It was a burden.
The other father remarked, "My son does not cost me a dollar. I wish I could spend something on him."

"Why doesn't your son cost you?" asked the first father.

"Because," replied the second father, "we lost him a few months ago."

———◆———

Cost of Following God

It cost Abraham the willingness to yield his only son.

It cost Esther the risk of her life.

It cost Daniel being cast into the den of lions.

It cost Shadrach, Meshach and Abednego being put in a fiery furnace.

It cost Stephen death by stoning.

It cost Peter a martyr's death.

It cost Jesus His life.

Does it cost you anything?   *Challenge*

Courage, Courageous

To see what is right, and not to do it, is want of courage.   CONFUCIUS

———◆———

It is human to stand with the crowd. It is divine to stand alone.

———◆———

Any coward can praise Christ, but it takes a courageous man to follow Him.

———◆———

It takes more courage to face grins than to face guns.

———◆———

Courage is holding on five minutes longer.

———◆———

Those who act faithfully act bravely.

———◆———

Nothing is difficult to the brave.

———◆———

Every time we lose courage, we lose several days of our life.
          MAURICE MAETERLINCK

———◆———

Keep your chin up, but don't stick it out.   *KVP Philosopher*

———◆———

The companion virtue of courage is patience.

———◆———

No man in the world has more courage than the man who can stop after he has eaten one peanut.
          CHANNING POLLOCK

The man who lacks courage to start, made a finish already.

———◆———

Heroism is the soul's high privilege, and the ranks of those who wear it nobly are always bigger than we know.
          Youth's Companion

———◆———

One man with courage makes a majority.   ANDREW JACKSON

Have courage for the great sorrows of life, and patience for the small ones. And when you have laboriously accomplished your daily task, go to sleep in peace. God is awake.   VICTOR HUGO

———◆———

Courage is the standing army of the soul which keeps it from conquest, pillage and slavery.   HENRY VAN DYKE

———◆———

Courage is knowing what not to fear.
          SOCRATES

———◆———

God moves in a mysterious way
His wonders to perform
And plants His footsteps in the sea
And rides upon the storm.

Ye fearful saints, fresh courage take,
The clouds ye so much dread
Are big with mercy and shall break
With blessings on your head.
          WILLIAM COWPER

———◆———

Courteous, Courtesy

Nothing costs so little and goes so far as courtesy.

———◆———

Courtesy is contagious.

———◆———

I am a little thing with a big meaning.

I help everyone.

I unlock doors, open hearts, banish prejudice;

I create friendship and good will.

I inspire respect and admiration.

I violate no law.

I cost nothing. Many have praised me; none have condemned me.

I am pleasing to those of high and low degree.

I am useful every moment.

I am courtesy!   ANONYMOUS

71

Courtesy opens every gate and doesn't cost a cent.

———————

Hail the small sweet courtesies of life, for smooth do they make the road of it.   LAURENCE STERNE

———————

Courtesy is a coin that will pass at par in any nation.

———————

Life is short, but there is always time for courtesy.   EMERSON

———————

Courtesy can be understood in any language.   ELD

———————

Chivalry is a man's inclination to defend a woman against every man but himself.

———————

This is the final test of a gentleman: his respect for those who can be of no possible service to him.
                    WILLIAM LYON PHELPS

———————

Coward

Most people are color blind — they think they are blue when they are only yellow.

———————

There are no proofs of cowardice.
                    LAURENCE STERNE

———————

The only thing worse than a quitter is the man who is afraid to begin.

———————

The coward never started and the weak died along the way.

———————

Create, Creation, Creative

The world God made was a beautiful world. The ugliness in it is man's own idea.

———————

All This and More

God made the sunlight, but it cannot laugh,
God made the moonbeams, but they cannot smile;
God made the stars, but they cannot play;

God made the endearing fawn, but it cannot sing;
God made the birds, but they cannot hold the heart;
God made music, but it cannot love.
So, God made you, my child.
                    DORCAS S. MILLER *in Gospel Herald*

———————

While reviewing a Sunday school lesson on the creation story, the teacher asked one junior boy how God created the world.

"With His left hand," replied the boy.

"Why do you say that God created the world with His left hand?" asked the teacher.

"Because," the boy explained, "the Bible says that Jesus is seated at the right hand of God."

———————

The kindergarten teacher asked the children what story they would like to hear. Most of the children agreed that they would like to hear about "How God Made the Beautiful World." And so the teacher began and captivated every small child in the room.

"Then God made the lovely sky," she went on, "and for the nighttime He made it dark. And he put the beautiful twinkly stars up in the sky to wink at us and to shine ever so brightly. Then God took some green cheese and made a very beautiful moon and placed it in the nighttime sky with the stars."

At this point one little girl waved her hand so wildly that the teacher asked her what she wanted.

"Well," replied the child, "that part of the story is not true. God made the sun and the moon and the stars on the fourth day and He never made no cows till the fifth day!"

———————

A small girl who lived in a remote section of the country was receiving her first Bible instruction at the hands of her elderly grandmother, and the old lady was reading the child the story of the creation. After the story had been finished the little girl seemed lost in thought.

"Well, dear," said the grandmother, "what do you think of it?"

"Oh, I love it. It's so exciting," exclaimed the youngster. "You never know what God is going to do next!"

Creeds

A Child's Creed

I believe in God above;
I believe in Jesus' love;
I believe His Spirit, too,
Comes to teach me what to do;
I believe that I must be
True and good, dear Lord, like Thee.

A Creed for Everyone

SILENCE when your words would hurt.
PATIENCE when your neighbor's curt.
DEAFNESS when the scandal flows.
THOUGHTFULNESS for others' woes.
PROMPTNESS when stern duty calls.
COURAGE when misfortune falls.
Enos Magazine

Crime, Criminal

Some people do not think it is a sin to commit a crime, only to be found out is wrong.

The cure of crime is not the electric chair, but the high chair.
J. EDGAR HOOVER

Following the lines of least resistance makes men and rivers crooked.
RALPH PIERCE

If it is a crime to make a counterfeit dollar, it is ten thousand times worse to make a counterfeit man. **LINCOLN**

Criminals are home-grown.
J. EDGAR HOOVER

Critic, Criticism, Criticize

Constructive criticism is when I criticize you. Destructive criticism is when you criticize me.

You can't make a hit in this world by knocking the other fellow.

You shouldn't criticize your wife's judgment . . . look who she married.

Did you ever notice that a knocker is always outside of the door?

Throwing mud at a good man only soils your own hands.

The person who always sweeps before his neighbor's door has never seriously examined his own doorstep.

It is well to remember that mansions in the sky cannot be built out of the mud thrown at others. *Evangelist*

If someone belittles you, he is only trying to cut you down to his size.

Some men put anti-knock into their automobiles, when they ought to be taking it themselves.

Analyze yourself first — before you criticize another.

Knockers belong on a door, not in church.

Keep a fair-sized cemetery in your back yard, in which to bury the faults of your friends. **BEECHER**

If it is painful for you to criticize your friends, you are safe in doing it. But if you take pleasure in it, that's the time to hold your tongue.

The stones the critics hurl with harsh intent, a man may use to build his monument. **ARTHUR GUTTERMAN**

No man can justly censure or condemn another, because indeed no man truly knows another. **SIR THOMAS BROWNE**

The critic is a person who has you write it, sing it, play it, paint it, or carve it as he would — if he could!

CRITIC

I criticize by creation; not by finding fault. CICERO

———

Soiling another will never make one's self clean. TENNYSON

———

Children have more need of models than critics. JOUBERT

———

A statue has never been set up to a critic.

———

If people speak ill of you, live so that no one will believe them. PLATO

———

To avoid criticism
say nothing,
do nothing,
be nothing!

———

Search thy own heart; what paineth thee in others in thyself may be. J. G. WHITTIER

———

The trouble with most of us is that we would rather be ruined by praise than saved with criticism. *Lutheran Education*

———

When It's the Other Fellow

Have you ever noticed?

When the other fellow acts a certain way, he is "ill-tempered"; when you do it, it's "nerves."

When the other fellow is set in his ways, he's "obstinate"; when you are it is just "firmness."

When the other fellow doesn't like your friends, he's "prejudiced"; when you don't like his, you are simply showing that you are a good judge of human nature.

When the other fellow tries to treat someone especially well, he is a "flatterer"; when you try the same thing you are using "tact."

When the other fellow takes time to do things, he is "dead slow"; when you do it, you are "deliberate."

When the other fellow spends a lot he is a "spendthrift"; when you do, you are "generous."

When the other fellow holds too tight to his money, he is "close"; when you do, you are "prudent."

When the other fellow dresses extra well, he's a "dude"; when you do, it is simply "a duty one owes to society."

When the other fellow runs great risks in business, he is "foolhardy"; when you do, you are a "great financier."

When the other fellow says what he thinks, he is "spiteful"; when you do, you are "frank."

———

Take a Walk Around Yourself

When you're criticizing others,
And are finding here and there
A fault or two to speak of,
Or a weakness you can tear;
When you're blaming someone's meanness
Or accusing some of self,
It's time that you went out
To take a walk around yourself.

There's a lot of human failures
In the average of us all,
And lots of grave shortcomings
In the short ones and the tall;
But when we think of evils
Men should lay upon the shelves
It's time that we all went out
To take a walk around ourselves.

We need so oft in this life
This balancing set of scales
Thus seeing how much in us wins
And how much in us fails;
But before you judge another,
Just to lay him on the shelf,
It would be a splendid plan
To take a walk around yourself. *Cincinnati Bulletin*

———

Think Twice

Should you feel inclined to censure
Faults you may in others view,
Ask your own heart, ere you venture,
If that has not failings, too.

Let not friendly vows be broken;
Rather strive a friend to gain;
Many a word in anger spoken
Finds its passage home again.

Do not, then, in idle pleasure,
Trifle with a brother's fame,
Guard it as a valued treasure,
Sacred as your own good name.

Do not form opinions blindly,
Hastiness to trouble tends;
Those of whom we thought unkindly
Oft become our warmest friends.

AUTHOR UNKNOWN

Cross

Christ did not bear the cross — He used it.

———

We do not need culture, but we need Calvary.

VANCE HAVNER

———

The cross is God's plus sign to a needy world.

———

The Tree

Some people touch a tree and find but
    wood to feed a fire;
Yet, carpenters can feel a floor or sense
    a soaring spire. . . .
The sculptor looks upon its trunk and
    carvings fill the air,
While others come and see the hearts
    which lovers whittled there. . . .

The farmer reaches for its fruit; the
    traveler seeks its shade;
The boy can see a raft of logs on
    streams of flowing jade. . . .
The outdoorsman will think of crafts
    to blunt an ocean's rage;
The pharmacist will see its roots; the
    publisher a page. . . .

The bird finds one beloved branch;
    but mothers see the beds
Wherein at nightfall, they will tuck
    their precious heads. . . .
The artist grasps the golden flame that
    leaves of autumn toss,
And some, whose souls are deep as
    time, can see a Savior's cross.

FRANK H. KEITH

———

The cross is the only ladder high enough to touch heaven's threshold.

G. D. BOARDMAN

After crosses and losses, men grow humbler and wiser.

BENJAMIN FRANKLIN

———

Taking up your cross is carrying whatever you find is given you to carry as well and stoutly as you can without making faces or calling people to come and look at you. All you have to do is to keep your back straight and not think of what is on it — above all do not boast of what is on it.

JOHN RUSKIN

———

Crowd (also see Courage)

Those who follow the crowd are quickly lost in it.

ANONYMOUS

———

Curiosity, Curious

Curiosity killed a cat; satisfaction brought it back.

———

The things most people want to know about are usually none of their business.

GEORGE BERNARD SHAW

———

Curiosity is one of the most permanent and certain characteristics of a vigorous intellect.

———

If you tell the average man there are 278,805,732,168 stars in the universe, he will believe you. But if a sign says, "Fresh Paint" he has to make a personal investigation.

Daily Telegraph, Bluefield, Va.

———

Customer

Take time to make friends before trying to make customers.

ELMER WHEELER

———

The seller of liquor is the only man who is ashamed of his best customers.

HERBERT W. THOMSON

———

The Name Means the Same

The lawyer calls him a client.
The doctor calls him a patient.
The hotel calls him a guest.

The editor calls him a subscriber.
The broadcaster calls him a listener-viewer.
The cooperative calls him a patron.
The retailer calls him a shopper.
The educator calls him a student.
The manufacturer calls him a dealer.
The politician calls him a constituent.
The banker calls him a depositor-borrower.
The sports promoter calls him a fan.
The railroad-airlines calls him a passenger.
The minister calls him a parishioner.

You may give a professional name to the person who buys your product or service, but no matter what you call him, he is always the customer.

Sales Management

Research

Research in the retail field has turned up some startling facts and figures. Of each 100 customers

15 are lost the 1st year, leaving 85.
13 are lost the 2nd year, leaving 72.
11 are lost the 3rd year, leaving 61.
9 are lost the 4th year, leaving 52.
8 are lost the 5th year, leaving 44.
7 are lost the 6th year, leaving 37.
6 are lost the 7th year, leaving 31.
5 are lost the 8th year, leaving 26.
4 are lost the 9th year, leaving 22.
3 are lost the 10th year, leaving 19.

Eighty per cent are lost over a ten-year period. Lost customers can be replaced with new customers, at a national average cost of $20.00 each. And a lot of them can be brought back if you are willing to make the effort and take the time necessary. *Advertising Age*

D

Dark, Darkness

There is not enough darkness in the whole world to put out the light of a single candle. *The Sunday School*

Don't curse the darkness — light a candle. *Chinese Proverb*

Dead, Death

It is given unto all men once to die — after that the writeup. CARL N. WARREN

Fear not death; for the sooner we die, the longer shall we be immortal.

We understand death for the first time when He puts His hand upon one whom we love. MME. DE STAEL

While some friends were talking about death, one old lady said, "I am not looking for the undertaker, but for the uptaker."

Fruit is not borne by doing, but by dying.

For every person who is dead and doesn't know it, there are ten living and don't know it.

When Robert Ingersoll died, the printed notice of his funeral said, "There will be no singing."

More people commit suicide with a fork than with any other weapon.

Francis of Assisi, hoeing his garden, was asked what he would do if he were suddenly to learn that he was to die at sunset that day. He said, "I would finish hoeing my garden."

If you would not be forgotten as soon as you are dead, either write things worth reading or do things worth writing. BENJAMIN FRANKLIN

When a man dies he clutches in his hands only that which he has given away in his lifetime. ROUSSEAU

———◆———

When death comes to me it will find me busy, unless I am asleep. If I thought I was going to die tomorrow, I should nevertheless plant a tree to-day. STEPHEN GIRARD

———◆———

Die when I may, I want it said of me by those who knew me best, that I always plucked a thistle and planted a flower where I thought a flower would grow. ABRAHAM LINCOLN

———◆———

It was a truly human tombstone which bore the inscription, "I expected this, but not just yet."

———◆———

Death takes no bribes. BENJAMIN FRANKLIN

———◆———

They were burying a rather unsavory character who had never been near a place of worship in his life. The services were being conducted by a minister who had never heard of him.

Carried away by the occasion, he poured on praise for the departed man. After ten minutes of describing the late lamented as a father, husband and boss, the widow, whose expression had grown more and more puzzled, nudged her son and whispered:

"Go up there and make sure it's Papa." *National Motorist*

———◆———

At the last moment, a minister was asked to preach a funeral sermon for another minister who had suddenly become ill.

Realizing he had forgotten to ask if the deceased had been a man or woman, he frantically tried to catch a mourner's eye. Finally succeeding, he pointed to the casket and whispered, "Brother or sister?"

"Cousin," came the faint reply. *Together*

Debt

The surest way to have the world beat a path to your door is to owe everyone money.

———◆———

Out of debt, out of danger.

———◆———

If you are in debt, someone owns part of you.

———◆———

Men in debt are often stoned.

———◆———

Creditors have better memories than debtors. BENJAMIN FRANKLIN

———◆———

No one can live without being a debtor; no one should live without being a creditor. N. J. PANIN

———◆———

Industry pays debts, despair increases them.

———◆———

Decide, Decision

Decision determines destiny. Eternity — where?

———◆———

Some people decide to be saved at the eleventh hour, and die at ten-thirty.

———◆———

Our decisions must be based on what's right, not who is right.

———◆———

Sunday morning test: Auto or ought to?

———◆———

Learn to say "no!" It will be of more use to you than to be able to read Latin. CHARLES H. SPURGEON

———◆———

History is made whenever you make a decision.

———◆———

One day a farmer hired a man. He asked him to paint the barn. He estimated it would take three days — the man did it in one day. Then he asked him to cut up a pile of wood. He estimated that would take four days — the man did it in one day. Then he asked the man to sort a pile of potatoes. He wanted them divided into three groups: one pile that he could

77

use for seed potatoes; one pile that he could use to sell; one pile to use to feed the hogs. He estimated that he would do that in one day. At the end of the day he went to see the man to see how he had done and found three little groups. He hadn't even started on the pile. He asked what was wrong and the man said, "I can work, but I can't make decisions."

Deeds

Deeds are better than words.

———◆———

To remind a man of the good turns you have done him is very much like a reproach. DEMOSTHENES

Some men are known by their deeds, others by their mortgages.

———◆———

Well done is better than well said. BENJAMIN FRANKLIN

———◆———

Sometimes when I consider what tremendous consequences come from little things — a chance word, a tap on the shoulder, or a penny dropped on a newsstand — I am tempted to think . . . there are no little things. BRUCE BARTON

———◆———

Defeat

If you think you are beaten, you are;
If you think you dare not, you don't,
If you'd like to win but you think you can't
It's almost a cinch you won't.

If you think you'll lose, you're lost,
For out of the world we find
Success begins with a fellow's will
It's all in the state of mind.

If you think you're outclassed, you are;
You've got to think high to rise
You've got to be sure of yourself before
You can ever win a prize.

Life's battles don't always go
To stronger or faster men
But soon or late the man who wins
Is the one who thinks he can.
AUTHOR UNKNOWN

Defeated

I meant to study all the week
And very carefully prepare.
I meant to kneel — yes, every day
And bear each pupil up in prayer.
But I was weary and I found
So many things that I must do —
Important things that could not wait —
The week was gone before I knew.

I meant to visit several homes,
And mail some cards to absentees
To let them know that they were missed,
For such a word is sure to please,
And often brings them quickly back.
But somehow every day went by,
And not a single card I sent.
And now I ask, "Why didn't I?"

So this morning when I rose
I tried to study while I ate.
I briefly read my quarterly,
And hurried out, five minutes late.
I found them singing, and I dropped
Breathless, ashamed, into my seat,
For I intended to be there
That I the earliest child might greet.

Time for the lessons, and a group
Of eager voices beg their turn
To quote by heart the memory verse
Which I, alas, forgot to learn.
And so I stumbled through the hour,
And built with stubble, hay, and wood —
Instead of gold and precious stones
And silver, as His servants should.

"Go feed my lambs," was His command,
And shall I hope for them to live
On little morsels such as this,
When mighty feasts are mine to give?
"Forgive me, Lord, that I should treat
Thy Word in such a shameful way,
And may I never stand again
Defeated, as I've done today."
AUTHOR UNKNOWN

———◆———

Defeat comes not so much from physical effects, as from a state of mind which makes men reduce or cease from their efforts.
GEN. CHARLES P. SUMMERALL

You are never defeated unless you defeat yourself.

Definitions

Amateur Carpenter — A carpenter who resembles lightning. He never strikes twice in the same place.

Ambiguity — is like a blind man looking in a dark room for a black cat that isn't there.

Baby Sitter — Someone you pay to watch your television set while your kids cry themselves to sleep.

Bore — One who talks about himself while you want to talk about yourself.

Candor — What a woman thinks about another woman's gown. Tact is what she says about it.
The Cynic's Dictionary

Celebrity — The advantage of being known to people who don't know you.
CHAMFORT

Coordinator — One who can bring organized chaos out of regimented confusion.

Depression — A period when you can't spend money you don't have.

Draw — The result of a battle between a dentist and a patient.

Electrician — A man who wires for money.

Homiletics — The studying of sanctified salesmanship.

Hospital—A place where people who are run down wind up.

Individual — A person with the rough edges still showing.

Nuisance — Is the right person in the wrong place.

Office Filing — Is an orderly system of misplacing important papers.

Pattern — Is a picture of what the story is going to be.

Penury — Wages of the pen.
WILLIAM DEAN HOWELLS

Perfume Counter — Where people talk scents.
Changing Times

Perfectionist — One who takes great pains and gives them to other people.
Changing Times

Public Officials — The trustees of the people.
GROVER CLEVELAND

Steam — Water turning crazy with the heat.

Upper Crust — A few crumbs held together with a little dough.

Waitress — A girl who thinks money grows on trays.
Whitehall Wisconsin Times

Deliberate

He who hesitates is lost.

Act in haste, repent at leisure.

That done with deliberation is done quickly enough, and better; what is made in haste is unmade as quickly.

Delinquent

There would be less juvenile delinquency if parents led the way instead of pointing to it.

We wonder sometimes whether the conversion of so many woodsheds into garages hasn't had something to do with the alarming increase of juvenile delinquencies.
ROY G. ROBINSON, *The Sunday School*

Teenager: "Mother, where did you learn all the things you tell me not to do?"

Prisons are a monument to neglected youth.

———◆———

Juvenile delinquents are other people's children.

———◆———

Most children who get classified as delinquents come from homes that have failed. It is their parents who are delinquent – either too poor to care for the child, or mentally or morally deficient, or have criminal tendencies themselves. Parents fail by neglect, ignorance, and unwillingness or inability to direct their children. They don't want to, they don't know how, or they can't – because of poverty, hopelessness, or some other cause.

1954 Annual Report, St. Louis Police Dept.

———◆———

If we can keep our adolescents in Sunday school, we will close our courts and fill our churches.

———◆———

Ninety per cent of most youth problems are adult. DR. LOUIS EVANS

———◆———

Adult Delinquency

Fathers and mothers, listen to me!
   Who is to blame for delinquency –
You or your untrained girl or boy
   Who turned to crime in search of joy?

Do you delight in obeying God?
   And train your child with reproof and rod?
Or does he grow from a babe to youth,
   Devoid of the knowledge of Christian truth?

Do you take your children to Sunday school
   To learn of God and the Golden Rule?
Or are they sent to a picture show
   Where most delinquent children go?

They learn of crime and of sinful lust,
   But not of Christ whom they ought to trust.
They learn to lie and to steal and kill
   But not to love and to do God's will.

Who is to blame – you or the child,
   If he turns to crime and becomes defiled?
Who should go to the prison cell,
   The rope or the chair, and a burning hell?

God is your Judge in heaven above,
   He bids you repent and in His grace and love
To turn from your careless, wicked way,
   And to start to study His Word and pray.

Forsake the world and the social whirl,
   And go to church with your boy and girl,
O parents, pause and listen to me,
   For *you* are the cause of delinquency!
DWIGHT C. RITCHIE

———◆———

Democracy, Democratic

Democracy means not "I am as good as you are," but "You are as good as I am." PARKER

———◆———

Democracy becomes a government of bullies tempered by editors. EMERSON

———◆———

Rule of the majority in America has been successful only to the extent that the majority has constantly recognized the rights of the minority.

———◆———

A democratic country: a place where people say what they think without thinking.

———◆———

A democracy is a country in which everyone has an equal right to feel superior to the other fellow.

———◆———

Denominations

The Salvation Army picks a man up.
The Baptists washes him up.
The Methodists warm him up.
The Episcopalian introduces him to society.

———◆———

Our denominational fences should be low enough to permit us to shake hands.

Depend, Dependence, Dependent

Dependence is a poor trade to follow.

———

The sturdy oak is just an acorn that held its ground!

———

God depends upon our dependence upon Him.

———

Shipwrecked on God!

Shipwrecked on God! of all else forsaken,
All hope of help from every source has fled.
'Tis then and only then we find the Rock
Beneath us that wrecked our keel and stranded
Us on God. Shipwrecked on God! 'Tis not till
Then we know Him. 'Tis not till then we trust
Him to the uttermost. 'Tis not till then
We prove Him all sufficient and feed upon
His bread alone. Release thy hold of all
That binds thee to another; let shore-lines
Go, and dare the swelling tide; it will but
Bear thee safely into heaven, and land
Thee safe upon the Rock, shipwrecked on God.

Shipwrecked on God! O blessed place of safety.
Shipwrecked on God! No greater place of rest.
Shipwrecked on God! All shore-lines broke asunder
With nothing left in all the universe but God.
Shipwrecked on God! Then face to face we see
Him, with naught between to dim the vision
Of His Love. 'Tis then we learn the secret
Of Redemption, when we have nothing left

In earth or heaven — but God. Shipwrecked on God!
'Tis then we learn to know Him, as heart meets
Heart in unison of love; then no more
Twain, but married to another — He whom
God gave from out the bosom of His Love.
Shipwrecked on God! 'Tis not till then we vanish.
'Tis not till then we find we're hid with Christ in God,

And cease from all our trying and our struggling,
To find at last that Christ is all in all.
Shipwrecked on God! No land in sight to flee
To, where height and depth cannot be reached or
Length or breadth be spanned; we sink into the
Mighty sea of God's Own fullness, to find
That nothing else remains — but Him, the Christ of God.
Shipwrecked on God! With naught but Christ remaining,
I find Him Life and Breath, Environment —
Yea, all! I've ceased from all my trying and
My toiling; I've entered into rest to
Toil no more. He lives His Life while I abide
Within Him, and now "For me to live is Christ" forevermore.

CECILIA M. BARTON

———

Desire

'Tis easier to suppress the first desire than to satisfy all that follows it.

BENJAMIN FRANKLIN

———

Life is a continuous struggle to keep one's earning capacity up to one's yearning capacity.

———

If you get what you wanted, you'll be fortunate. If you want what you get, you'll be happy.

Many a man has been led astray by following his own inclinations.

———◆———

Essentials

Give me work to do;
Give me health;
Give me joy in simple things.
Give me an eye for beauty,
A tongue for truth,
A heart that loves,
A mind that reasons,
A sympathy that understands;
Give me neither malice nor envy,
But a true kindness
And a noble common sense.
At the close of each day
Give me a book,
And a friend with whom
I can be silent.   AUTHOR UNKNOWN

———◆———

Destination, Destiny

The future destiny of the child is always the work of the mother.
                                           NAPOLEON

———◆———

Methods of locomotion have improved greatly in recent years, but places to go remain about the same.
                                           DON HEROLD

———◆———

Sad Story

The curfew tolls the knell of parting day,
A line of cars winds slowly o'er the lea.
A hiker plods his absent-minded way,
And leaves the world quite unexpectedly.   AUTHOR UNKNOWN

———◆———

Choice, not chance, determines human destiny.

———◆———

Determination, Determine

Satisfy your want and wish power by overcoming your can't and won't power with can and will power.
                                    WM. J. H. BOETCHER

———◆———

When it is definitely settled that a thing can't be done, watch someone do it.

Nothing turns out right unless someone makes it his job to see that it does.

———◆———

Attempt great things for God; expect great things from God.   WILLIAM CAREY

———◆———

Our grand business is not to see what lies dimly at a distance, but to do what lies clearly at hand.

———◆———

The woman who is determined to be respected can be so in the midst of an army of soldiers.

———◆———

You

All that stands between your goal
And the deeds you hope to do,
And the dreams which stir your restless soul —
Is you!

The way is rough and the way is long,
And the end is hid from view,
But the one to say if you shall be strong —
Is you!   *Mac-Sim-Ology*

———◆———

It is not life that counts but the fortitude you bring to it.
                                    JOHN GALSWORTHY

———◆———

If you have plenty of push you will not be bothered by a pull.

———◆———

When you get to the end of your rope, tie a knot and hang on.

———◆———

Determination

I am only one, but I am one;
I cannot do everything,
But I can do something,
What I can do I ought to do,
And what I ought to do
By God's grace I will do.
                                    Listen

———◆———

The man who, when given a letter to Garcia, quietly takes the missive, without asking any idiotic questions, and with no lurking intention of chucking it into the nearest sewer, or of doing aught else but deliver it, never gets "laid off" nor has to go on strike for higher wages. Civilization is one long, anxious search for just such individuals. Anything such a man asks shall be granted; his kind is so rare that no employer can afford to let him go. He is wanted in every city, town and village — in every office, shop and store and factory. The world cries out for such; he is needed and needed badly — the man who can "carry a message to Garcia."   ELBERT HUBBARD

———◆———

Behold the turtle. He makes progress only when he sticks his neck out.   JAMES BRYANT CONANT

———◆———

You cannot prevent the birds from flying overhead but you can prevent them from making a nest in your hair.

———◆———

Some people will never be convinced that they are on the right course until they have explored all the wrong ones.   *Lutheran Education*

———◆———

Among the students of one of our well-known colleges some years ago was a young man who was obliged to walk with crutches. He was a stumbling, homely sort of human being but he was a genius for intelligence, friendliness and optimism.

During his four years in college, this crippled young man won many scholastic honors. During all that time his friends, out of consideration and respect, refrained from questioning him about the cause of his deformity but one day his pal made bold to ask him the fateful question.

"Infantile paralysis," was the brief answer.

"Then, tell me," said the friend, "with a misfortune like that, how could you face the world so confidently and without bitterness?"

The young man's eyes smiled and he tapped his chest with his hand. "Oh," he replied, "you see, it never touched my heart."   *The Message*

Be the Best of Whatever You Are

If you can't be a pine on the top of the hill,
Be a scrub in the valley — but be
The best little scrub by the side of the rill;
Be a bush if you can't be a tree.

If you can't be a bush, be a bit of the grass,
And some highway happier make;
If you can't be a muskie then just be a bass —
But the liveliest bass in the lake!

We can't all be captains, we've got to be crew,
There's something for all of us here,
There's big work to do and there's lesser to do,
And the task we must do is the near.

If you can't be a highway, then just be a trail,
If you can't be the sun, be a star;
It isn't by size that you win or you fail —
Be the best of whatever you are!   DOUGLAS MALLOCH

———◆———

A pound of determination is worth a ton of repentance.

———◆———

Devil

The devil's meal is all bran.

———◆———

Idleness is the devil's workshop.

———◆———

The devil comes because the house is empty.

———◆———

Satan contests every soul that accepts Christ as Saviour.   GORDON VAN ROOY

———◆———

Devil or Jesus

DEVIL	JESUS
EVIL wrought	EFFECTED on
VILE temptation	Calvary
and	SALVATION for
ILL brought	UNDONE
LYING still.	SINNERS.

Matthew 4:1-11; 6:24

83

When the devil calls, let Jesus answer the door.

———◆———

The devil has no happy old men.

———◆———

The old idea that children must sow their wild oats and go to the devil before they can come to Christ is contrary to Christian experience, is not warranted by Scripture and is not in accord with the teachings of Jesus.
SENSABAUGH

———◆———

Two boys were walking home from Sunday school. They had had a lesson that morning on the devil.

"What do you think of this devil business?" one boy asked the other.

"Well," the other boy replied, "you know how Santa Claus turned out — it is either your mother or your dad."

———◆———

The little girl couldn't quite remember the correct words of the memory verse, "Resist the devil and he will flee from you," but she got the idea. Her version: "Tell the devil to get out and he's got to go!"

———◆———

The devil's best work is done by many who claim to love the Lord.

———◆———

The devil is never too busy to rock the cradle of a sleeping backslider.

———◆———

Devotion

Devotional life, like muscle, develops with exercise.

———◆———

If we do not come apart, we will come apart.

———◆———

When you are so devoted to doing what is right that you press straight on and disregard what men are saying about you, there is the triumph of moral courage.
PHILLIPS BROOKS

———◆———

Difficult, Difficulty

Good manners and soft words have brought many a difficult thing to pass.
AESOP

Difficulties are stepping stones to success.

———◆———

There are three things difficult: to keep a secret, to suffer an injury, to use leisure.
VOLTAIRE

———◆———

Some folks look to God through their difficulties;
Some look at their difficulties through God.

———◆———

The people we have the most trouble with is ourselves.

———◆———

All things are difficult before they are easy.

———◆———

Difficulties are things that show what men are.
EPICTETUS

———◆———

Difficulties are God's errands; and when we are sent upon them we should esteem it a proof of God's confidence as a compliment from Him.
HENRY WARD BEECHER

———◆———

Most of the shadows of life are caused by standing in our own sunshine.
EMERSON

———◆———

Often the thrill of life comes from the difficult work well done.

———◆———

It Is Hard

To forget
To apologize
To save money
To be unselfish
To avoid mistakes
To keep out of a rut
To begin all over again
To make the best of all things
To keep your temper at all times
To think first and act afterwards
To maintain a high standard
To keep on keeping on
To shoulder blame
To be charitable
To admit error
To take advice
To forgive
But it pays!

The greater the difficulty, the more glory in surmounting it. Skillful pilots gain their reputation from storms and tempests. EPICURUS

Diplomat

A diplomat is a person who remembers a woman's birthday but forgets her age.

Disappoint, Disappointments

Life's disappointments are veiled love's appointments. C. A. FOX

Disappointments should be cremated and not embalmed.

We can praise our Heavenly Father that sorrows and disappointments are not meant to disfigure but to transform us.

The most disappointed people in the world are those who get just exactly what is coming to them and no more.

Blessed is he that expects nothing, for he shall never be disappointed.

Discipline

Depend upon divine displacement rather than self-discipline. DR. ROBERT B. MUNGER

Discipline: Before you flare up at your child's faults, take time to count ten . . . ten of your own.

The handwriting on the wall usually means someone's going to get a spanking.

God is more interested in making us what He wants us to be than giving us what we ought to have. WALTER L. WILSON

Teacher: "This is the fifth time this week that I have had to punish you. What have you to say, Charles?"
Charles: "I'm glad it's Friday!"

Today's dilemma: "Everything in the modern home is controlled with a switch except the child."

A teacher left her class one day and on returning found all the children sitting in profound silence with their arms folded. She was not only surprised at such silence, but bewildered and asked for an explanation. A little girl arose and said:
"Teacher, you told us one day if you ever left the class room and came back and found all of us sitting perfectly silent, you would drop dead."

A switch in time saves crime. ROY B. NEWELL

When a mother was disciplining her small boy, he begged, "Don't say 'must,' Mother. It makes me feel 'won't' all over."

When the archaeologists were digging in the ruins of Nineveh they came upon a library of plaques containing the laws of the realm. One of the laws reads, in effect, that anyone guilty of neglect would be held responsible for the result of his neglect. . . . If you fail to teach your child to obey, if you fail to teach him to respect the property rights of others, *you and not he* are responsible for the result of your neglect. WILLIAM TAIT, *Is It Juvenile or Adult Delinquency*

Three-year-old Bobby insisted in standing up in his highchair although mother had admonished him to remain seated then emphasized her admonishment by twice reseating him. After the third time little Bobby remained seated but looked at his mother searchingly and said, "Mommy, I'm still standing up inside."

Discourage, Discouragement

Ten rules for getting rid of the blues: Go out and do something for someone else — and repeat it nine times. *Selected*

85

DISCOURAGEMENT

One cause for depression in people is hunger for appreciation.

Church Management

———♦———

You can tell how big a man is by observing how much it takes to discourage him.

———♦———

Don't despair. Even the sun has a sinking spell every night, but it rises again in the morning.

———♦———

Keep Scrappin'

When you're sick and you think, What's the use?
And you're tired, discouraged, afraid;
And you keep asking why they don't let you die
And forget the mistakes you have made;
When you're chuck full of pain and you're tired of the game,
And you want to get out of it all —
That's the time to begin to stick out your chin
And fight with your back to the wall!

When you've done all you can to scrap like a man
But you can't keep your head up much more;
And the end of the bout leaves you all down and out,
Bleeding, and reeling, and sore;
When you've prayed all along for the sound of the gong
To ring for the fight to stop —
Just keep on your feet and smile at defeat;
That's the real way to come out on top!

When you're tired of hard knocks and you're right on the rocks,
And nobody lends you a hand;
When none of your schemes, the best of your dreams,
Turn out in the way you'd planned,
And you've lost all your grit and you're ready to quit
For life's just a failure for you,
Why, start in again and see if all men
Don't call you a man through and through.

AUTHOR UNKNOWN

The One Who Stubbed His Toe

Did you ever meet a youngster who had been an' stubbed his toe,
An' was settin' by the roadside, just a-cryin' soft and low,
A-holdin' of his dusty foot, so hard and brown and bare,
Tryin' to keep from his eyes the tears a-gatherin' there?
You hear him sort o' sobbin' like, an' sniffin' of his nose;
You stop and pat him on the head an' try to ease his woes,
You treat him sort o' kind like, an' the first thing that you know,
He's up and off a-smilin' — clean forgot he's stubbed his toe.

Now, 'long the road of life you'll find a fellow goin' slow,
An' like as not he's some poor man who's been and stubbed his toe;
He was makin' swimmin' headway till he bumped into a stone,
An' his friends kept hurryin' onward an' left him there alone;
He's not sobbin', he's not sniffin', he's just too old for cries,
But he's grievin' just as earnest, if it only comes in sighs.
An' it does a lot of good sometimes to go a little slow,
An' speak a word of comfort to the man who stubbed his toe.

Today, you're bright and happy in the world's sunlight and glow,
An' tomorrow you're a-freezin' and trudgin' thro the snow,
The time you think you've got the world the tightest in your grip
Is the very time you'll find that you're the likeliest to slip.
So it does a lot o' good sometimes to go a little slow,
An' speak a word o' comfort to the man who's stubbed his toe.

AUTHOR UNKNOWN

———♦———

Do not get discouraged; it may be the last key in the bunch that opens the door.

STANAIFER

86

The surest way to petrify the human heart is to awaken feelings and give it nothing to do.

———✦———

Depression, gloom, pessimism, despair, discouragement — these slay ten human beings to every one murdered by typhoid, influenza, diabetes, or pneumonia. If tuberculosis is the great white plague, fear is the great black plague. Be cheerful! DR. FRANK CRANE

Discover, Discovery

Discover

I cannot invent
New things,
Like the airships
Which sail
On silver wings;
But today
A wonderful thought
In the dawn was given,
And the stripes on my robe,
Shining from wear,
Were suddenly fair,
Bright with a light.
Falling from Heaven —
Gold and silver and bronze
Light from the windows of Heaven.
And the thought
Was this:
That a secret plan
Is hid in my hand,
That my hand is big
Big.
Because of this plan.
That God,
Who dwells in my hand,
Knows this secret plan
Of the things He will do for the world.
Using my hand! TOYOHIKO KAGAWA

———✦———

Disposition

All the world's a camera; look pleasant, please!

———✦———

A smile doesn't look good on some faces but a kind disposition wins friends everywhere.

Half of the secret of getting along with people is consideration of their views; the other half is tolerance in one's own views. DAVID FRAHMAN

———✦———

Uneasy lies the head that wears the frown.

———✦———

Sour godliness is the devil's religion. JOHN WESLEY

———✦———

When dressing, don't forget to put on a smile.

———✦———

If not actually disgruntled, he was far from being gruntled. P. G. WODEHOUSE

———✦———

It's easy to smile when someone cares.

———✦———

All people smile in the same language.

———✦———

Who can tell by computation,
The true value of a smile;
You'll save many a situation,
E'en though humble be your station;
By the simple application
	Of a *smile*. PETER AULD

———✦———

Let Us Smile

The thing that goes the farthest toward
	Making life worthwhile,
That costs the least and does the most,
	Is just a pleasant smile.
The smile that bubbles from a heart
	That loves its fellow men,
Will drive away the clouds of gloom,
	And coax the sun again;
It's full of worth and goodness, too,
	With manly kindness blent,
It's worth a million dollars, and
	It doesn't cost a cent.

There is no room for sadness
	When we see a cheery smile
It always has the same good look —
	It's never out of style;
It nerves us on to try again
	When failure makes us blue,
The dimples of encouragement
	Are good for me and you;

It pays a higher interest
  For it is merely lent,
It's worth a million dollars and
  It doesn't cost a cent. AUTHOR UNKNOWN

Divorce

Why divorce? What is needed is not a change *of* partners but a change *in* partners. *Family Altar Crusader*

Divorce is the hash made from domestic scraps.

Doctor

He's the best physician that knows the worthlessness of the most medicines.

God heals and the doctor takes the fee. BENJAMIN FRANKLIN

Zeke has finally figured out what the doctor's scribbling means on a prescription blank. He says it is a message for the druggist saying: "I got my $5.00, now he's all yours." *Glendale News Press*

Those Medics

If you're fat or if you're thin,
If your toes are turning in,
If you've bunions on your shin —
  It's your tonsils!

If your hair is falling out
If you're suffering from the gout,
If you're getting far too stout
  It's your adenoids!

If your dome is turning gray,
And you can't eat bales of hay,
If you're failing day by day —
  It's your teeth!

Pain in thumb, or ache in toe,
When to "Doc" you sadly go,
He will say his little piece —
  "Tonsils, adenoids, or your teeth!"
    AUTHOR UNKNOWN

Doubt

Doubt sees the obstacles;
Faith sees the way.
Doubt sees the darkest night,

Faith sees the day!
Doubt dreads to take a step;
Faith soars on high,
Doubt questions, "Who believes?"
Faith answers, "I!" *The Good News*

When in doubt, don't.

Dreams

Dreams are as true today as they were a hundred years ago. *Dutch Proverb*

It isn't a bad thing to be a dreamer, provided you are awake when you dream.

Some people find life an empty dream because they put nothing into it.

Don't part with your illusions.
When they are gone you may still exist,
But you cease to live. SWIFT

You have to stay awake to make dreams come true.

Drive, Driver, Driving

His fuel was rich,
His speed was high;
He parked in a ditch
To let the curve go by.

Some people drive as though determined that no accident will be prevented if they can help it.

Perhaps

If you can drive a car when all about you
  The homeward rush is on at five o'clock,
And know you're right when all the family doubt you,
  And red lights flag you down at every block.
If you can trust your instinct to inform you
  Which way the guy in front intended to turn,

Though he hasn't given any sign to
warn you
Excepting that his stop light starts
to burn;
If you're content to drive the speed
that's safest.
Regardless of the speed by law allowed,
And, knowing you are good, can still
give credit
To those who are with greater skill
endowed;
If you can use your horn and not
abuse it
When those in front are creeping
like a snail —
The boulevard is yours, to have and
use it.
And what is more, you may keep
out of jail! AUTHOR UNKNOWN

Sing While You Drive

At 45 miles per hour, sing:
"Highways Are Happy Ways."

At 55 miles per hour, sing:
"I'm But a Stranger Here, Heaven
Is My Home."

At 65 miles per hour, sing:
"When the Roll Is Called Up Yonder,
I'll Be There."

At 85 miles per hour, sing:
"Lord, I'm Coming Home."

Two motorists met on a street too
narrow for both cars to pass.
"I'll never back up for an idiot,"
yelled one driver.
"That's all right," said the other
shifting into reverse, "I always do."

When you feel that the motorist
ahead of you is proceeding at a snail's
pace, check your speedometer. A snail's
pace, according to the University of
Maryland scientist, is .000363005 miles
per hour. *Executive Digest*

If you drink, don't drive; if you
drive, don't drink.

A tree is something that will stand
by the side of the road for fifty years
and then suddenly jump in front of a
woman driver.

The biggest problems for the road
safety campaigns are the urban, subur-
ban and bourbon drivers.
  Record, Treynor, Iowa

Reckless automobile driving arouses
the suspicion that much of the horse
sense of the good old days was possessed by the horse. ANONYMOUS

Natives who beat drums to beat off
evil spirits are objects of scorn to smart
American motorists who blow horns to
break up traffic jams. *National Motorist*

Duty

Duty makes us do things well, but
love makes us do them beautifully.
  PHILLIPS BROOKS

He who is false to present duty
breaks a thread in the loom, and will
find the flaw when he may have forgotten the cause. H. W. BEECHER

Count your obligations,
Name them one by one,
And it will surprise you
What the Lord wants done!

The duty of the many should not be
the task of the few.

Duty is not beneficial because it is
commanded, but it is commanded because it is beneficial. BENJAMIN FRANKLIN

A sense of duty pursues us ever. It
is omnipresent, like the Deity.

For duty must be done; the rule applies to everyone. W. S. GILBERT

E

Easter

The great Easter truth is not that we are to live newly after death — that is not the great thing — but that we are to be new here and now by the power of the resurrection; not so much that we are to live forever as that we are to, and may, live nobly now because we are to live forever.   PHILLIPS BROOKS

———◆———

Christ died for you but you can live for Him.

———◆———

The value of Easter Sunday attendance cannot be evaluated until attendance is taken the following Sunday.

———◆———

Let us place more emphasis on the Easter heart than the Easter hat.

———◆———

The empty tomb proves Christianity, but an empty church denies it.

———◆———

The stone at Jesus' tomb was a pebble to the Rock of Ages inside.   FRED BECK

———◆———

The kindergarten-age child came home from Sunday school Easter Sunday and told his mother he could understand about Christ but not about the roses and asked his mother, "Why was Christ a rose?"

———◆———

Eat, Eating

Hunger is good kitchen meat.

———◆———

Hunger is the best sauce.

———◆———

A good dinner is better than a fine coat.

———◆———

The old-fashioned housewife's menus were carefully thought out. The modern housewife's are carefully thawed out.   *Changing Times*

More people commit suicide with a fork than any other weapon.

———◆———

One first grade class in public school was marching past the room of another first grade class where the children were singing a prayer song with their heads bowed and hands clasped. As the children marched on past the room and to the cafeteria one boy said to his teacher, "I know why they were praying. They were hoping they wouldn't have spinach today."

———◆———

I eat my peas with honey,
I've done so all my life,
It makes the peas taste funny,
But it keeps them on my knife.

———◆———

Someone has said that the writer of Psalm 91 must have been speaking at a luncheon club when he wrote about the "Destruction that wasteth at noon day." Perhaps he referred to banquets when he spoke of "The pestilence that walketh in darkness."
CHARLES F. BANNING in *Church Management*

———◆———

Diet for Every Man

Jam — for car conductors.
Cereals — for novelists.
Mincemeat — for autoists.
Beets — for policemen.
Pie — for printers.
Corn — for chiropodists.
Starch — for henpecked husbands.
Gumdrops — for dentists.
Taffy — for after-dinner speakers.
Dough — for insurance company presidents.   ANONYMOUS

———◆———

"Tommy," said the teacher, "can you tell us what is meant by nutritious food?"

"Yes'm," said Tommy, "it's food what ain't got no taste to it."

Young Charles, age four, came in for his midmorning glass of fruit juice. It was a warm morning and he had been playing hard. Also, because of the treat he had come for, he was very juice-conscious.

"Mother," he said, "would you wipe my face with a wet cloth? It is sort of sticky."

"What did you get on it, dear?" his mother asked as she reached for the washcloth.

"Nothin'," he replied in his slow western drawl, "it's just face juice."

F. M. MORTON *in Christian Home*

———✦———

Parsley is the food you push aside to see what is under it.

PAUL H. GILBERT, *Seattle Times*

———✦———

The new minister was a bachelor, and when he helped himself to the biscuits for the third time he looked across the table at the hostess' small daughter. She was staring at him with round eyes.

"I don't often have such a good supper as this, my dear," he told her.

"We don't either," said the little girl. "I'm glad you came."

MRS. J. C. FRY *in Together*

———✦———

Summer advice to all eaters: If you are thin, don't eat fast. If you are fat, don't eat. Fast!   *Presbyterian Life*

———✦———

Diner: "What sort of bird is this?"
Waiter: "It's a wood pigeon, sir."
Diner: "I thought so. Get me a saw."

———✦———

On eating an apple
And finding inside
A hole deeply burrowed
But unoccupied,
Don't pity yourself
As you frantically squirm,
But think of the worry
You've given the worm.

WILLIAM W. PRATT

———✦———

'Twas in a restaurant they met,
Brave Romeo and Juliet;
He had no dough to pay his debt,
So Romeo'd what Juli 'et.

To lengthen thy life, lessen thy meals.

BENJAMIN FRANKLIN

———✦———

Eat to live, and do not live to eat.

BENJAMIN FRANKLIN

———✦———

Rare: The way you get a steak when you order it well-done.

EVAN ESAR, *Comic Dictionary*

———✦———

Diet: Something to take the starch out of you.   *Pathfinder*

———✦———

Sandwich Spread: What you get from eating between meals.

EARL WILSON

———✦———

Army Food: The spoils of war.

Hudson Newsletter

———✦———

Economics, Economy

In the family as in the state the best source of wealth is economy.

———✦———

With economy few need be poor.

———✦———

Economy is the household mint.

———✦———

An economist reports that Jones is having a tough time keeping up with himself.

———✦———

An economist is a man who plans something which should be done with the money someone else made.

———✦———

Some men's idea of practicing economy is to preach it daily to their wives.

———✦———

He that buys by the penny, maintains not only himself, but other people.   BENJAMIN FRANKLIN

———✦———

Someone has said our economic situation is one where this generation pays the debts of the last generation by issuing bonds for the next generation.   *This Day*

Education

Education is learning a lot about how little you know.

Degrees

M.A. for master of action
D.D. for a doctor of doing
M.A. for a missionary artist
B.A. for a bachelor assimilator

———♦———

By the time a child is seven he has received three-fourths of his basic education.

———♦———

A college student in his four years does not make proportionately a fraction of the progress the well-trained infant does in his first two years.

ERNEST M. LIGNON

———♦———

A child educated only at school is an uneducated child.

SANTAYANA

———♦———

Never let your studies interfere with your education.

———♦———

Once I was a tadpole a-beginning to begin,
Next I was a toad-frog with my tail tucked in,
Then I was a monkey in a banyan tree.
But look at me now, I'm a Ph.D.

———♦———

It takes diplomacy to get a diploma.

———♦———

A college education never hurt anyone who was willing to learn something afterwards.

———♦———

The thing that surprises a college man the most when he gets out into the world is how much uneducated people know that he doesn't know.

———♦———

Young people can go to college now and pay later. Like Pop always said, you have to give a lot of credit to a fellow who wants to get ahead.

Changing Times

———♦———

A young man who had just received his degree from college rushed out and said, "Here I am, world; I have my A.B."

The world replied: "Sit down, son, and I'll teach you the rest of the alphabet."

Some men go to college to learn to express their ignorance in scientific terms.

———♦———

The time education rings up a score is when you can't spell round the kids anymore.

PAT CUNNINGHAM in *Christian Home*

———♦———

To educate a man in mind and not in morals is to educate a menace to society.

THEODORE ROOSEVELT

———♦———

Perhaps the most valuable result of all education is the ability to make yourself do the thing you have to do when it has to be done, whether you like it or not.

HUXLEY

———♦———

Secular education can make men clever, but it cannot make them good.

———♦———

All who have meditated on the art of governing mankind have been convinced that the fate of empires depends on the education of youth.

ARISTOTLE

———♦———

By education I mean that training in excellence from youth upward which makes a man passionately desire to be a perfect citizen, and teaches him to rule, and to obey, with justice. This is the only education which deserves the name. That other sort of training which aims at acquiring wealth or bodily strength is not worthy to be called education at all.

PLATO

———♦———

It now costs more to amuse a child than it once did to educate his father.

———♦———

Education should include knowledge of what to do with it.

———♦———

'Tis education forms the common mind:
Just as the twig is bent, the tree's inclined.

POPE

———♦———

Education does not mean teaching people to know what they do not know; it means teaching them to behave as they do not behave.

MARK TWAIN

The heart of education is the education of the heart.

———◆———

Education is the mirror of society.

ELD

To *look* is one thing. To *see* what you look at is another. To *understand* what you see is a third. To *learn* from what you understand is still something else. But *to act* on what you learn is what really matters. *Educator's Dispatch*

———◆———

Three steps in Christian education:
To know
To will
To do.

———◆———

It is said that Protestant boys and girls receive 52 hours of religious instruction a year; Jewish boys and girls receive 325 hours of religious instruction a year and Roman Catholics receive 200 hours a year. Due to tardiness, untrained Sunday school teachers, absences, poor lesson materials and surroundings it is said that even the 52 hours of instruction actually only average about 17 hours per year. *Selected*

———◆———

When the farmer boy explained to another about the special speaker at his church he puzzled over the letters Ph.D. after the speaker's name. Then he explained that it meant "Post-hole digger."

———◆———

Father: "I'm worried about your being at the bottom of the class."
Son: "Don't worry, Pop, they teach the same stuff at both ends."

———◆———

"Oh, I know a few things!" exclaimed the haughty senior.
"Well, you haven't anything on me," retorted the freshman confidently; "I guess I know as few things as anyone."

———◆———

"Why were you kept in after school?" the father asked his son.
"I didn't know where the Azores were," replied the son.
"In the future," said father, "just remember where you put your things."

Effort

There is a great distance between "said" and "done."

———◆———

The top is reached by topping yesterday's effort.

———◆———

The mode by which the inevitable comes to pass is effort. JUSTICE HOLMES

———◆———

Those who try to do something and fail are infinitely better than those who try to do nothing and succeed at it.

———◆———

Little Janie was trying to dress herself.
"Mother," she said after a long period of effort, "I guess you'll have to button my dress. The buttons are behind and I'm in front." *National Motorist*

———◆———

Ego, Egotism

Egotism has been described as just a case of mistaken nonentity. *Toastmaster*

———◆———

A high brow is a person educated beyond his own intelligence.
Ladies' Home Journal

———◆———

The egotist is an I specialist.

———◆———

You can always tell an egotist, but unfortunately you can't tell him much.

———◆———

An egotist is one who thinks that if he hadn't been born, people would wonder why. *Changing Times*

———◆———

When a man is wrapped up in himself, he makes a pretty small package.
JOHN RUSKIN

———◆———

Big shots are usually small shots who kept on shooting.

———◆———

Employ, Employer, Employment

The following notice was posted in a Chicago store in 1858:
This store will be open from 6 a.m. to 9 p.m. the year round.

On arrival each morning, store must be swept, counters, shelves, and showcases dusted. Lamps must be trimmed, pens made, a pail of water and a bucket of coal brought in before breakfast.

The employee who is in the habit of smoking Spanish cigars, being shaved at the barber's, going to dances and other places of amusement, will surely give his employer reason to be suspicious of his integrity.

Each employee must pay not less than $5.00 per year to the church and must attend Sunday school regularly.

Men employees are given one evening a week for courting, and two if they go to prayer meeting.

After 14 hours of work, leisure hours should be spent mostly in reading.

———◆———

Thomas Jefferson said in hiring men that he considered these three items:
1. Is he honest?
2. Will he work?
3. Is he loyal?

———◆———

Encourage, Encouragement

Each time we meet, you always say
　Some word of praise that makes me gay.
You see some hidden, struggling trait,
　Encourage it and make it great.
Tight-fisted little buds of good
　Bloom large because you said they would.
A glad, mad music in me sings;
　My soul sprouts tiny flaming wings.
My day takes on a brand-new zest.
　Your gift of praising brings my best,
Revives my spirit, flings it high;
　For God loves praise, and so do I.
AUTHOR UNKNOWN

———◆———

God keeps his choicest cordials for our deepest faintings.　C. E. COWMAN

———◆———

The blue of heaven is larger than the clouds.

———◆———

Correction can help, but encouragement can help far more.

There is no high hill but beside some deep valley. There is no birth without a pang.　DAN CRAWFORD

———◆———

The Sermon on the Mount can lift us out of the Valley of Depression.

———◆———

Correction does much, but encouragement does more. Encouragement coming after censure is the sun after a shower.　J. WOLFGANG GOETHE

———◆———

"What I need most," wrote Emerson, "is something to make me do what I can." One of the most rewarding experiences you can ever have is to be that "something" for someone — to be the catalyst that dispels inertia and brings out the best in someone you know. The thing that brings out the best in most people is encouragement, and you — no matter what your circumstances are — can provide those around you with this precious morale plasma. Think encouraging thoughts, speak encouraging words, and, most important of all, adopt an air of confident expectancy toward those you are trying to help. Be genuinely interested, let your attitude be more eloquent than your words. In this way, you can be, in truth, a "best" friend. There is no happiness quite comparable to the happiness you can earn in this way.
Whatsoever Things

———◆———

There's Hope for the Rest of Us

Napoleon was number forty-two in his class. (Wonder who the forty-one were ahead of him?)

Sir Isaac Newton was next to the lowest in his form. He failed in geometry because he didn't do his problems according to the book.

George Eliot learned to read with great difficulty, giving no promise of brilliance in her youth.

James Russell Lowell was suspended from Harvard for complete indolence.

Oliver Goldsmith was at the bottom of his class.

James Watt was the butt of jokes by his schoolmates.

Endurance, Endure

The battle against evil is difficult, not so much because of the action required, but because of the endurance necessary to achieve victory.

———

Flowers that last have deep roots and bloom late. Things that endure grow slowly.

———

If there is anything that cannot bear free thought, let it crack.
WENDELL PHILLIPS

———

When some people yell for tolerance, what they really want is special privilege. *Garner (Iowa) Leader*

Enemies, Enemy

Speak well of your enemies. You made them.

———

My enemies are my friends who don't know me.

———

If we would read the secret history of our enemies, we would find in each man's life a sorrow and suffering enough to disarm all hostility.
LONGFELLOW

———

The only satisfactory way to make people do things is to make them want to do them. Enemies are never truly conquered until their friendship is won. WILFERD PETERSON

———

Love your enemies, for they tell you your faults. BENJAMIN FRANKLIN

———

Love your enemy — it will drive him nuts.

Enthusiasm

Enthusiasm is the best protection in any situation. Wholeheartedness is contagious. Give yourself, if you wish to get others. DAVID SEABURY, *Good Business*

———

You cannot kindle a fire in any other heart until it is burning within your own. ANONYMOUS

In order to do great things, one must be enthusiastic. DE ROUVROY

———

The worst bankrupt in the world is the man who has lost his enthusiasm.

———

Enthusiasm is unmistakable evidence that you're in love with your work.

———

Enthusiasm is the fever of reason.

———

When a man is enthusiastic about hard work, the chances are that he's an employer. HAL CHADWICK

———

We act as though comfort and luxury were the chief requirements of life, when all that we need to make us really happy is something to be enthusiastic about. CHARLES KINGSLEY

———

If you can give your son only one gift, let it be enthusiasm. BRUCE BARTON

———

Enthusiasm is the genius of sincerity, and truth accomplishes no victories without it. BULWER-LYTTON

Environment

You can take a boy out of the country but you can't take the country out of the boy.

———

God is not interested in changing environment but in renewing men.
MALCOLM R. CRONK

Epitaphs

It is said that on the tomb of Confucius are the words, "He taught for 10,000 years."
On your tomb can it be said, "He taught for eternity"?

———

The marks on the grave of a guide who died while climbing the Alps were: "He died climbing." On the tomb of a Christian astronomer were these words (by his partner): "We have gazed too long at the stars together to be afraid of the night."

Here is the original epitaph of Benjamin Franklin:

> The body of B. Franklin
> Printer
> Like the cover of an old book
> Its contents torn out
> And stript of its lettering and gilding
> Lies here food for worms.
> But the work shall not be wholly lost
> For it will, as he believes, appear
> once more
> In a new and more perfect edition
> Corrected and amended
> By the Author.

Even a tombstone will say good things about a fellow when he is down.

Better a little "taffy" while they are living than so much "epitaphy" when they're dead.

These words are on the grave of a scientist who died at the age of 85: "He died learning."

Live so that the man who carves your epitaph on the tombstone won't feel like a prevaricator.

Epitaph on a grave: "All dressed up and no place to go."

This man died at 30; he was buried at 70.

Original inscription on tombstone:
> Remember, friend, when passing by,
> As you are now, so once was I.
> As I am now, soon you will be,
> Prepare for death and follow me.

Added comment to inscription:
> To follow you I'm not content.
> Until I know which way you went.

Error

A man should never be ashamed to own he has been in the wrong, which is but saying, in other words, that he is wiser today than he was yesterday.   ALEXANDER POPE

Eternal, Eternal Life, Eternity

Eternal life begins with salvation.

Join thyself to the eternal God, and thou shalt be eternal.   AUGUSTINE

He who provides for this life, but takes no care for eternity, is wise for a moment, but a fool forever.   TILLOTSON

He who has no vision of eternity will never get a true hold of time.   CARLYLE

There is only one way to get ready for immortality, and that is to love this life and live it as bravely and faithfully and cheerfully as we can.

HENRY VAN DYKE

Over the triple doorway of the Cathedral of Milan there are three inscriptions spanning the splendid arches. Over one is carved a beautiful wreath of roses, and underneath is the legend, "All that pleases is but for a moment." Over the other is sculptured a cross, and these are the words beneath: "All that troubles is but for a moment." But underneath the great central entrance in the main aisle is the inscription, "That only is important which is eternal."

Ethics

A four-way test of business ethics:
1. Is it the truth?
2. Is it fair to all concerned?
3. Will it build goodwill and better friendships?
4. Will it be beneficial to all concerned?

"Ethics," the man told his son, "is vital to everyday living. For example, today an old friend paid me back a loan with a new hundred-dollar bill. As he was leaving I discovered he'd given me two bills stuck together. Immediately a question of ethics arose: Should I tell your mother?"

Evangelism, Evangelistic

Before reaching the uttermost we must keep Jerusalem uppermost in mind.

———♦———

We have a Samaria vision but only a Jerusalem zeal.

———♦———

You can't emphasize the Bible unless you have pupils.

———♦———

You say you don't believe in magnifying numbers and perhaps that's why you don't have them.

———♦———

Personal evangelism is a collision of souls. In the Book of Acts the Christians went after souls and got them.

———♦———

When a child is old enough to knowingly sin he is old enough to savingly believe.

———♦———

It is easier to win an entire family than it is to win them as individuals.
HARRY DENMAN

———♦———

Reach all you can, teach all you reach, win all you teach, train all you win, enlist all you train.

———♦———

The monument I want after I am dead is a monument with two legs going around the world — a saved sinner telling about the salvation of Jesus Christ.
D. L. MOODY

———♦———

The Lord, our gentle shepherd, stands,
With all engaging charms,
Hark! how He calls the tender lambs,
And folds them in His arms.

"Permit them to approach," He cries,
"Nor scorn their humble name,
For 'twas to bless such souls as these
The Lord of angels came."

We bring them, Lord, in thankful hands,
And yield them up to Thee;
Joyful that we ourselves are Thine;
Thine let our offspring be. *Selected*

We never move people until we are moved.

———♦———

The only ladder to heaven is the cross.

———♦———

The only thing a man can really gain before he dies is heaven.

———♦———

Evil

No man is justified in doing evil on the grounds of expediency.
THEODORE ROOSEVELT

———♦———

For evil to triumph, it is only necessary for good men to do nothing.
EDMUND BURKE

———♦———

Some of your hurts you have cured,
And the sharpest you still have survived,
But what torments of grief you endured
From evils which never arrived.
EMERSON

———♦———

Exaggerate, Exaggeration

A fish is an underwater creature that grows fastest between the time it is caught and the time the fisherman describes it to his friends.

———♦———

A woman approached evangelist Billy Sunday after one of his sermons and asked pensively, "I wonder if you can help me? I have a terrible habit of exaggeration."

"Certainly, madam," replied Sunday. "Just call it lying!"

———♦———

Example

There is just one way to bring up a child in the way he should go and that is to travel that way yourself.
ABRAHAM LINCOLN

———♦———

One example is worth a thousand precepts.

———♦———

How many people have made you homesick to know God?

97

The Little Chap

A careful man I ought to be –
A little fellow follows me.
I do not dare to go astray,
For fear he'll go the selfsame way.

I cannot once escape his eyes.
What'er he sees me do, he tries.
Like me, he says he's going to be –
The little chap who follows me.

He thinks that I am good and fine,
Believes in every word of mine.
Wrong steps by me he must not see –
The little fellow who follows me.

I must remember as I go,
Through summer's sun and winter's
snow,
I'm building for the years to be,
The little chap who follows me.

ANONYMOUS

———

Men who won't read the Bible will
read "living epistles."

———

I'd rather see a sermon, than hear one
any day;
I'd rather one should walk with me,
than merely show the way;
The eye's a better pupil, and more willing than the ear,
Fine counsel is confusing but example's always clear.
And best of all the preachers, are the
men who live their creeds,
For to see good put in action is what
everybody needs.
I soon can learn to do it, if you'll let
me see it done;
I can see your hands in action, but
your tongue too fast may run.
And the lectures you deliver may be
very fine and true;
But I'd rather get my lesson by observing what you do;
For I may not understand you and the
high advice you give.
But there's no misunderstanding how
you act and how you live.

EDGAR A. GUEST

———

Children you teach are now becoming what you are going to be.

A good example is worth a thousand
sermons.

———

Of all commentaries upon the Scriptures, good examples are the best and
liveliest.   JOHN DONNE

———

A pint of example is worth a gallon
of advice.

———

An ounce of practice is worth a
pound of preach.

———

"When I was a little child," the
sergeant sweetly addressed his men
at the end of an exhaustive hour of
drill, "I had a set of wooden soldiers.
There was a poor little boy in the
neighborhood and after I had been
to Sunday school one day and listened
to a stirring talk on the beauties of
charity, I was soft enough to give them
to him. Then I wanted them back
and cried, but my mother said: 'Don't
cry, Johnnie; some day you'll get your
wooden soldiers back.'

"And believe me, you lop-sided, mut-
ton-headed, goofus-brained set of cer-
tified rolling pins, that day has come!"

———

There are four classes of men:
1. He who knows not, and knows
   not he knows not,
   He is a fool; shun him.
2. He who knows not, and knows
   he knows not,
   He is simple, teach him.
3. He who knows, and knows not
   he knows,
   He is asleep; waken him.
4. He who knows, and knows he
   knows,
   He is wise; follow him.

AUTHOR UNKNOWN

———

Excuse, Excuses

Let us be excusers rather than accusers.

———

The man who is good for excuses
is good for nothing else.

BENJAMIN FRANKLIN

———

The worst buy is an alibi.

98

Then there were the two Sunday fishermen who heard bells ringing in the distance. One said, contritely, "You know, Sam, we really ought to be in church." Sam re-baited his hook and answered, "Well, I couldn't go, anyway. My wife is sick."
Presbyterian Life

You may often make excuses for another, never to yourself.
PUBLILIUS SYRUS

Executive

An executive is one who makes an immediate decision and is sometimes right.

It is a safer thing any time to fol-a man's advice rather than his example.
JOSH BILLINGS

A consultant is an executive who can't find another job.   HENRY W. PLATT

The man who delegates authority must forego the luxury of blowing his top.   *Nation's Business*

He that multiplieth the doers is greater than he that doeth the work.
JOHN R. MOTT

They that govern the most make the least noise.

A good executive is simply a man who can set up an organization that can run efficiently without him.

Experience

Experience is not what happens to a man; it is what a man does with what happens to him.   HUXLEY

One thorn of experience is worth a whole wilderness of warning.   LOWELL

Experience may not be worth what it costs, but I can't seem to get it for any less.   *Presbyterian Life*

Experience is the mother of science.

Past experience should be a guide post, not a hitching post.

There is no free tuition in the school of experience.

Experience is what you get while you are looking for something else.

There are no vacations from the school of experience.

Experience keeps a dear school, yet fools will learn in no other.
BENJAMIN FRANKLIN

Experience is a good teacher but it is very costly.

Expert

An expert is any little spurt away from home.

An expert is a little drip under pressure.

An expert is one smart enough to tell you how to run your own business but too smart to start one of his own.

An expert — a big shot — small caliber, big bore.

1st neighbor: "My husband is an efficiency expert in a large office."
2nd neighbor: "What does an efficiency expert do?"
1st neighbor: "Well, if we women did it, they'd call it nagging."

Express, Expression

Of all the things you wear, your expression is the most important.

As soon as you move one step up from the bottom, your effectiveness depends on your ability to reach others through the spoken or written word. This ability to express oneself is perhaps the most important of all skills a man can possess.
PETER BRUCKNER *in Fortune*

F

Facts

An eminent English editor said, "Opinion is free, but facts are sacred."

————◆————

Facts do not change; feelings do.

————◆————

You can tell how many seeds are in an apple, but you cannot tell how many apples are in a seed.

————◆————

The modern 7-inch-long lead pencil can draw a line 35 miles in length; it can write an average of 45,000 words; and it can take an average of 17 sharpenings.

————◆————

An ounce of fact means more than a ton of argument. MARTIN VANBEE

————◆————

There are 44,379,000 children under 14 living in homes where both parents are of the same faith, and 4,148,000 in homes where there is a mixed marriage or where one partner has "no religion."

————◆————

Eighty per cent of the heads of the science departments of the great universities of the United States say grace at the table in their homes. This was the observation of an eminent scientist from New Zealand who visited these United States scientists during his six months tour of scientific institutions here.

————◆————

Fail, Failure

Life's greatest failure is failing to be true to the best you know.

————◆————

One seldom meets a man who fails at doing what he likes to do.

————◆————

It isn't that we fail when we try, but that we fail to try! DR. HENRIETTA C. MEARS

Our greatest glory consists not in never failing, but in rising every time we do fail.

————◆————

Failure can become a weight or it can give you wings.

————◆————

Failure is the only thing that can be achieved without much effort.

————◆————

Failure is the line of least persistence. STEPHANIE MARTINO

————◆————

It is no disgrace to fail when trying. The one time you don't want to fail is the last time you try. CHARLES F. KETTERING

————◆————

You can achieve one very important thing without effort — failure.

————◆————

Formula for failure: Try to please everyone. HERBERT BAYARD SWOPE

————◆————

No man ever fails until he fails on the inside.

————◆————

The world of failure is divided north and south by lines of lassitude, east and west by lines of loungitude.

————◆————

Some of the "room at the top" is created by the men who go to sleep there and fall off.

————◆————

It is at night that the astronomers discover new worlds. It is often in the night of failure that men discover the light of a new hope.

————◆————

Most failures begin in failure to try.

————◆————

We need to teach the highly educated person that it is not a disgrace to fail and that he must analyze every failure to find its cause. He must learn how to fail intelligently, for failing is one of the greatest arts in the world. CHARLES F. KETTERING

———◆———

Failure is only the opportunity to begin again, more intelligently. HENRY FORD

Faith, Faithful, Faithfulness

The greatest victories are the victories of faith. It is not so much what we can do that counts, but what we can trust God to do.

———◆———

Faith in God sees the invisible, believes the incredible, and receives the impossible.

———◆———

"Daddy, may I have a cat?" kindergarten-age Peggy asked her father.

"Yes," replied her father, "but not until we move into a larger home."

"Daddy, may I have two cats?" asked the eager little girl.

"Yes, you may have two cats, or three or four cats if you wish," he answered, sure that the family would not be moving. But the inevitable happened and the family moved into a spacious home with an over-sized yard. Daddy had forgotten about the promised cats, but not Peggy. And she kept pressing her father, who made excuses. Peggy, however, was hopeful and believed the day would come when she could have a cat, or two or three . . . but one night she decided to change her prayer. Instead of praying that she would soon have the promised cat, she said, "Thank You, God, for sending me a cat."

"Peggy, why did you say that to God?" her older sister asked her when putting her to bed.

"Well," the little miss replied, "I thought that if I thanked God He would be embarrassed and send the cats."

The next day Peggy was playing out in the back yard and chanced to go into the tool shed. There she found an old mother cat and a litter of baby kittens. Of course no one in the family knew about the cat family or when the mother cat chose her home, but Peggy maintained it was a good thing she had embarrassed God!

———◆———

One day a man went running and puffing into the railroad station to catch a train, but missed it. He looked at his watch and said, "Watch, I had a lot of faith in you." A friend overheard him and said, "Don't you know that faith without works is dead?"

———◆———

The steps of faith fall on the seeming void and find rock beneath. JOHN GREENLEAF WHITTIER

———◆———

Faith is belief in action.

———◆———

You will never learn faith in comfortable surroundings. A. B. SIMPSON

———◆———

Faith honors God;
God honors faith.

———◆———

Faith is a lively, richless confidence in God. MARTIN LUTHER

———◆———

F - orsaking
A - ll
I
T - ake
H - im

———◆———

Religious faith is not a final goal to be reached, but a highway to be traveled.

———◆———

Living without faith is like driving in the fog.

———◆———

Faith is the one great moving force which we can neither weigh in the balance nor test in the crucible. SIR WILLIAM OSLER

———◆———

Faith is the pencil of the soul that pictures heavenly things. T. BURBRIDGE

———◆———

A little boy was crossing the ocean with his father, who was captain of the ship, when they ran into a storm. The waves tossed the ship about like a cork and everyone was stricken with fear. But the boy sat still, with his eyes directed toward a certain spot.

He sat there quite unperturbed as the ship was being dashed about by the waves. Someone asked him if he were not afraid, and he answered:

"I have my eye on that little window, and through that window I can see the bridge, and on that bridge is my father. My father is the captain of the ship, and he has taken it through many storms."

———♦———

Faith is to believe what we do not see, and the reward of this faith is to see what we believe. ST. AUGUSTINE

———♦———

The Christian faith offers peace in war, comfort in sorrow, strength in weakness, and light in darkness. WALTER A. MAIER

———♦———

Faith is the link that binds our nothingness to almightiness.

———♦———

Faith either removes mountains or tunnels through.

———♦———

Faith that is sure of God is the only faith there is. OSWALD CHAMBERS

———♦———

Faith contains belief, but belief is not the whole of faith. Eternity

———♦———

There are a thousand ways of pleasing God, but not one without faith.

———♦———

Small faith may take you to heaven but great faith may bring heaven to you.

———♦———

Faith ends where worry begins and worry ends where faith begins.

———♦———

Faith, like light, should always be simple and unbending; while love, like warmth, should beam forth on every side, and bend to every necessity of our brethren. LUTHER

———♦———

While reason is puzzling herself about the mystery, faith is turning into her daily bread and feeding on it thankfully in her heart of hearts. F. D. HUNTINGTON

I cannot explain the wind, but I can hoist a sail.

———♦———

The most precious things are near at hand, without money and without price. All that I have ever had, may be yours by stretching forth your hand and taking it. JOHN BURROUGHS

———♦———

Faith does not demand miracles but often accomplishes them.

———♦———

Credit is applied faith.

———♦———

When faithfulness is most difficult, it is most necessary.

———♦———

Faith is what made the little girl take an umbrella to a prayer meeting called especially to pray for rain. Grownups wore sun glasses.

———♦———

Faith's answer to the question "How?" is one word, "God!"

———♦———

Faith does not eliminate foresight.

———♦———

Fame

Fame and fortune never got any man to heaven.

———♦———

The man who wakes up and finds himself famous hasn't been asleep.

———♦———

No one ever traveled the road to fame on a pass.

———♦———

Family

The family that prays together, stays together.

———♦———

A family jar is no good for preserving the peace!

———♦———

There is just as much authority in the family today as there ever was — only now the children exercise it.

———♦———

He that has no fools, knaves nor beggars in his family must have been begot by a flash of lightning THOMAS FULLER

The family is like a book,
The children are the leaves,
The parents are the covers
That protective beauty gives.
At first the pages of the book
Are blank and purely fair,
But time soon writes its memories
And paints its pictures there.
Love is the little golden clasp
That bindeth up the trust.
Oh, break it not, lest all the leaves
Shall scatter and be lost.
AUTHOR UNKNOWN

Every family tree has some sap in it.

Fanatic, Fanaticism

Fanaticism is redoubling your effort when you have forgotten your aim.

Father

My Dad

He couldn't speak before a crowd;
He couldn't teach a class;
But when he came to Sunday school
He brought the folks en masse.

He couldn't sing to save his life,
In public couldn't pray;
But always his jalopy was just
Crammed on each Lord's day.

And although he couldn't sing,
Nor teach, nor lead in prayer,
He listened well, he had a smile,
And he was always there
With all the others whom he brought
Who lived both far and near —
And God's work prospered, for
I had a consecrated dad.   Selected

Fatigue

Fatigue is the devil's best weapon.

Fault, Faults

I see no fault that I might not have committed myself.   GOETHE

Next time you are tempted to pick out the faults in your brother, take time to count ten — ten of your own.

Faults are thick when love is thin.

The greatest fault is to be conscious of none.   CARLYLE

Blaming your faults on your nature does not change the nature of your faults.   ANONYMOUS

You can bear your own faults, why not a fault in your wife?
BENJAMIN FRANKLIN

Wink at small faults — remember thou hast great ones.   BENJAMIN FRANKLIN

Make sure that however good you may be, you have some faults; that however dull you may be, you can find out what they are; and that however slight they may be, you had better make some patient effort to get rid of them.

How few there are who have courage enough to own their faults, or resolution enough to mend them!
BENJAMIN FRANKLIN

Women's faults are many,
Men have only two:
Everything they say, everything they do.

When you are looking for faults to correct, look in the mirror.

Favors

Any person who accepts favors from others is placing a mortgage on his peace of mind.

Fear

If you fear that people will know, don't do it.

Nothing in life is to be feared, it is only to be understood.

Keep your fears to yourself, but share your courage with others.
ROBERT LOUIS STEVENSON

Fear always springs from ignorance.

EMERSON

———♦———

Fear of failure is the father of failure.

———♦———

Fear is unbelief parading in disguise.

———♦———

Don't be afraid of the day you have never seen. English Proverb

———♦———

"He lies there that never feared the face of man," so mused the Regent Morton over the open grave of John Knox. To fear God and to fear nothing else in God's universe — this, indeed, is to be a man. JOHN ROADMENDER

———♦———

Feelings

It is with feelings as with waters, the shallow murmur, but the deep are dumb. RALEIGH

———♦———

We often dislike a people not for what they are but for what we are.

ANONYMOUS

———♦———

Someone asked Luther, "Do you feel sure that you have been forgiven?"
He answered, "No, but I'm as sure as there's a God in heaven."

———♦———

For feelings come, and feelings go,
And feelings are deceiving,
My warrant is the Word of God
Naught else is worth believing.

Selected

———♦———

Emotion rises out of truth; emotionalism is poured on to it.

———♦———

Fellowship

Fellowship with God means warfare with the world. CHARLES E. FULLER

———♦———

Most Christians do not have fellowship with God; they have fellowship with each other about God.

PARIS REIDHEAD

———♦———

Fire

It is not enough to light a fire; you must put fuel on it.

Flag

We all love that flag. It gladdens the heart of the old and the young, and it shelters us all. Wherever it is raised, on land or sea, at home or in our distant possessions, it always stands for liberty and humanity; and wherever it is assaulted the whole nation rises up to defend it. WILLIAM MC KINLEY

———♦———

A flag neglected means flagging patriotism.

———♦———

Flowers

It is better to bring a cheap bouquet
To a living friend this very day,
Than a bushel of roses,
To lay on his casket when he's dead.

AUTHOR UNKNOWN

———♦———

The church-nursery school teacher had placed a lovely bouquet of daffodils on a table in the nursery room. When little Sandra came into the room she was fascinated by the flowers and said to her teacher, "Aren't these pretty telephones God made? I think I'll call God up and say, 'Thank you for the pretty flowers.'"

———♦———

Fool, Fools, Fooling

Oh what a tangled web we weave
When first we practice to deceive.

———♦———

Who has deceived thee so oft as thyself. BENJAMIN FRANKLIN

———♦———

It is never wise to argue with a fool. Bystanders don't know which is which.

———♦———

All are not fools that look so.

———♦———

Any fool can criticize, condemn and complain — and generally does.

———♦———

A fool tells us what he will do; a boaster what he has done; the wise man does it and says nothing.

———♦———

You can't fool all the people all the time. Some of them are fooling you.

A magician was sailing the Pacific right after World War II, entertaining the passengers. With each amazing feat of magic, a parrot, who perched on his shoulder would squawk, "Faker, faker." No matter what the magician did, rabbits out of hats, vanishing bird cage and all, he would repeatedly cry, "Faker, faker." The magician and parrot became bitter enemies. Finally the magician promised that he would do a trick that would out-Houdini Houdini. The night came, the wand was waved, the "woofle dust" was sprinkled. At that minute the ship hit a floating mine, which blew the ship to pieces. The next morning, on a make-shift life raft, the parrot was perched at one end, the magician at the other. Finally the parrot hopped over and said, "O.K. Buddy, you win, but what did you do with the ship?"

The family of fools is ancient.
BENJAMIN FRANKLIN

Fools are never uneasy. Stupidity is without anxiety.
GOETHE

Forget

What a grand world this would be if we could forget our troubles as easily as we forget our blessings.
Tips

Always remember to forget
The things that made you sad,
But never forget to remember
The things that made you glad.

If you were busy being true
To what you knew you ought to do,
You'd be so busy you'd forget
The blunders of the folks you met.
ANONYMOUS

"Did you forget your memory verse, Johnny?" the teacher asked when he did not say it.
"Oh, no," replied Johnny. "I didn't learn it. I can't forget what I didn't learn."

Forgive, Forgiveness

Christ can forgive any trespass. He can overlook none.

Pardon others often, thyself seldom.

He who forgives ends the quarrel.

He who cannot forgive others breaks the bridge over which he must pass himself.
GEORGE HERBERT

It is usually easier to forgive an enemy than a friend.

Doing an injury puts you below your enemy;
Revenging one makes you but even with him;
Forgiving it sets you above him.
BENJAMIN FRANKLIN

They never pardon who commit the wrong.
JOHN DRYDEN

Forgiveness is man's deepest need and highest achievement.
HORACE BUSHNELL

Forgive and forget. When you bury a mad dog, don't leave his tail above the ground.
SPURGEON

Forgiveness is more than the remission of penalty; it should mean the restoration of a broken fellowship.

Fortune

Fortune does not so much change men as it unmasks them.

It is no use to wait for your ship to come in, unless you have sent one out.
Belgian Proverb

As pride increases, fortune declines.
BENJAMIN FRANKLIN

He that waits upon fortune is never sure of a dinner.
BENJAMIN FRANKLIN

105

Free, Freedom

Freedom is not a question of doing as we like but doing as we ought.

————◆————

You should never wear your best trousers when you go out to fight for freedom and truth. HENRIK IBSEN

————◆————

Freedom is only a word until you have been close to losing it.

————◆————

Freedom is not worth having if it does not include the freedom to make mistakes. GANDHI

————◆————

The greatest glory of a freeborn people is to transmit that freedom to their children. WILLIAM HARVARD

————◆————

Freedom of religion does not mean freedom from religion. N. Y. Supreme Court

————◆————

In a free country there is much clamor with little suffering; in a despotic state there is little complaint but much suffering. CARNOT

————◆————

There are two freedoms — the false, where a man is free to do what he likes; the true, where a man is free to do what he ought. CHARLES KINGSLEY

————◆————

Friends, Friendship

A friend is someone who will make us do what we can when we are saying we can't. EMERSON

————◆————

There are three faithful friends — an old wife, an old dog and ready money. BENJAMIN FRANKLIN

————◆————

Friendship is a disinterested commerce between equals. OLIVER GOLDSMITH

————◆————

The only way to have a friend is to be one. EMERSON

————◆————

There's happiness in little things,
There's joy in passing pleasure.
But friendships are, from year to year,
The best of all life's treasure.

Every friend lost pushes you one step closer to the brink of character bankruptcy.

————◆————

God evidently does not intend us all to be rich, or powerful or great, but He does intend us all to be friends. EMERSON

————◆————

Lord Brooke was so delighted with the friendship of Sir Philip Sydney that he ordered to be engraved upon his tomb nothing but this — "Here lies the friend of Sir Philip Sydney."

————◆————

An open foe may prove a curse; but a pretended friend is worse. BENJAMIN FRANKLIN

————◆————

He that lieth down with dogs, shall rise up with fleas. BENJAMIN FRANKLIN

————◆————

Friendships cemented together with sin do not hold.

————◆————

The best way to keep your friends is not to give them away.

————◆————

Friendship is a responsibility, not an opportunity.

————◆————

Most of us are so busy trying to get something else that we can't enjoy what we have. Friendly Thoughts

————◆————

I do with my friends as I do with books. I would have them where I can find them but seldom use them. RALPH WALDO EMERSON

————◆————

Friendship increases by visiting friends, but by visiting seldom. BENJAMIN FRANKLIN

————◆————

True friendship is a plant of slow growth, and must undergo and withstand the shocks of adversity before it is entitled to the appellation. GEORGE WASHINGTON

————◆————

Happy is the house that shelters a friend. RALPH WALDO EMERSON

————◆————

Be slow in choosing a friend, slower in changing. BENJAMIN FRANKLIN

The only safe and sure way to destroy an enemy is to make him your friend.

———+———

The quickest way to wipe out friendship is to sponge on it.

———+———

Life has no blessing like a prudent friend.

———+———

The wisest man I have ever known once said to me, "Nine out of every ten people improve on acquaintance," and I have found his words true.

FRANK SWINNERTON

———+———

A brother may not be a friend, but a friend will always be a brother.

BENJAMIN FRANKLIN

———+———

The higher style we demand of friendship, the less easy to establish it with flesh and blood.

RALPH WALDO EMERSON

———+———

If you were another person would you like to be a friend of yours?

———+———

Friendship does not mean knowing all about a person. It is knowing him.

DR. HENRIETTA C. MEARS

———+———

Ever notice how a dog wins friends and influences people without reading books?

Vidette, Iuka, Miss.

———+———

Do good to thy friend to keep him, to thy enemy to gain him.

BENJAMIN FRANKLIN

———+———

If a man does not make new acquaintances as he passes through life, he will soon find himself left alone. A man should keep his friendships in constant repair.

JOHNSON

———+———

A true friend unbosoms freely, advises justly, assists readily, adventures boldly, takes all patiently, defends courageously, and continues a friend unchangeable.

WILLIAM PENN

———+———

When befriended, remember it; when you befriend, forget it.

BENJAMIN FRANKLIN

Friendship is a treasure ship anyone can launch.

———+———

Oh, the comfort, the inexpressible comfort of feeling safe with a person; having neither to weigh thoughts nor measure words, but to pour them all out, just as they are, chaff and grain together, knowing that a faithful hand will take and sift them, keep what is worth keeping, and then, with the breath of kindness, blow the rest away.

GEORGE ELIOT

———+———

Cultivate the qualities you desire in a friend because someone is looking for you as their friend.

———+———

I never considered a difference of opinion in politics, in religion, in philosophy, as cause for withdrawing from a friend.

THOMAS JEFFERSON

———+———

A thirteen-year-old girl's definition: A friend is one in front of whom you can be your own true self.

———+———

Friendship cannot live without ceremony, nor without civility.

BENJAMIN FRANKLIN

———+———

A friend is a present you give yourself by being friendly.

Home Life

———+———

It's a Funny Thing But True

It's a funny thing but true,
The folks you don't like, don't like you.
I don't know why this should be so
But just the same I always know,
That when I'm sour, friends are few,
When I'm friendly, folks are, too.
I sometimes get up in the morn,
Awishin' I was never born,
And then I make cross remarks, a few,
And then my family wishes, too,
That I had gone some other place,
But then I change my little tune,
And sing and smile,
And then the folks around me sing
    and smile.
I guess 'twas catching all the while.
It's a funny thing but true,
The folks you like, they sure like you!

AUTHOR UNKNOWN

I know I've never told you
In the hurried rush of days
How much your friendship helps me
In a thousand little ways;
But you've played such a part
In all I do or try to be,
I want to tell you thank you
For being friends with me. ANONYMOUS

———◆———

You can make more friends in two months by becoming interested in other people than you can in two years by trying to get other people interested in you. DALE CARNEGIE

———◆———

Abraham Lincoln was once taken to task by an associate for his attitude toward his enemies: "Why do you try to make friends of them? You should try to destroy them."

Lincoln replied gently, "Am I not destroying my enemies when I make them my friends?"

———◆———

We do not make friends
 As we do houses,
But discover them
 As we do the arbutus,
Under the leaves of our lives,
Concealed in our experience.
RADER

If you are an archer,
 And friendship your date,
Take aim very carefully —
 Don't pierce the wrong heart.

For friendship misplaced
 Is bound to bring sorrow;
Perhaps not today,
 But most surely tomorrow.

———◆———

Friends

The joy of being friends is just
A simple code of faith and trust,
A homey comradeship that stays
The threatened fear of darker days;
The kind of faith that brings to light
The good, the beautiful, and bright;
And best and blest, and true and rare —
Is having friends who love and care!
AUTHOR UNKNOWN

———◆———

Future

The best thing about the future is that it comes only one day at a time.

———◆———

My interest is in the future because I am going to spend the rest of my life there. CHARLES F. KETTERING

G

Genius

It is necessary to be almost a genius to make a good husband. BALZAC

———◆———

Doing easily what others find difficult is talent; doing what is impossible is genius. AMIEL

———◆———

Common sense is instinct, and enough of it is genius. G. B. SHAW

———◆———

Genius without education is like silver in the mine. FRANKLIN

———◆———

Genius is only the power of making continuous effort. ELBERT HUBBARD

We'd have a generation of geniuses if all our children were as brilliant in school and as well-behaved at home as we parents think we remember being.

———◆———

A genius is a man seen driving his own car when his son and daughter are home from college. *Town Journal*

———◆———

If we are to have genius we must put up with the inconvenience of genius, a thing the world will never do; it wants geniuses, but would like them just like other people. GEORGE MOORE

Girls

A little girl is many things . . .
To Grandma, she's an angel,
To Daddy, she's a flirt,
To the boy next door, she's an awful
  pest
With her face all covered with dirt.
To Mommy she is all these things
And a miniature woman, too,
But they don't suspect for a minute . . .
What their little girl is to you. . . .
To you, her teacher, a little girl is a
sponge soaking up knowledge. In her
you see the promise of a bright future
which you have the chance to help
mold. If she's selfish, you teach her to
share; if she fibs, you teach her truth.
If she is insecure, you do your best to
give her confidence. Through her Sunday school work you discover talents
seldom recognized or understood by
her parents. These you encourage and
develop to the satisfaction of you both.
To you, little girls and little boys are
individuals, and you give them many
attentions above and beyond the cur-
ricular call of duty. AUTHOR UNKNOWN

A girl who knows all the answers has
been asked all the questions.

The Taking Girl

She took my hand in sheltered nooks,
She took my candy and my books,
She took the lustrous wrap of fur,
She took those gloves I bought for her,
She took my words of love and care,
She took my flowers, rich and rare,
She took my ring with tender smile,
She took my time for quite a while,
She took my kisses, maid so shy —
She took, I must confess, my eye,
She took whatever I would buy,
And then she took the other guy!

Give, Giving, Gifts

Every gift, though it be small, is in
reality great if given with affection.
PINDAR

Who gives himself, with his alms, feeds
  three,
Himself, his hungering neighbor, and
  Me. *The Vision of Sir Launfal*

Old Deacon Horner, sat in a corner
As the contribution box passed by;
Sweetly content, he dropped in a cent,
And said, "What a good churchman
  am I."

A gift is never lost; only what is
selfishly kept impoverishes.

When God sends the dawn, he sends
it for all. CERVANTES

The most expensive gift is the gift
of gab.

Be not niggardly of what costs thee
nothing, as courtesy, counsel and countenance. BENJAMIN FRANKLIN

Generosity does not come naturally;
it must be taught.

Treasure in heaven is laid up only
as treasure on earth is laid down.

The Greatest Gift — John 3:16

GOD . . . . The Greatest Lover
SO LOVED . . . . The Greatest Degree
THE WORLD . . . . The Greatest Company
THAT HE GAVE . . . . . . The Greatest Act
HIS ONLY
  BEGOTTEN SON . . . . The Greatest Gift
THAT WHO-
  SOEVER . . . The Greatest Opportunity
BELIEVETH . . . . The Greatest Simplicity
IN HIM . . . . . . The Greatest Attraction
SHOULD NOT
  PERISH . . . . The Greatest Promise
BUT . . . . The Greatest Difference
HAVE . . . . The Greatest Certainty
EVERLASTING
  LIFE . . . . The Greatest Possession

The hand that gives, gathers.

Give what you have; to someone it
may be better than you dare to think.
LONGFELLOW

GIVING

Our Heavenly Father never takes anything from His children unless He means to give them something better.
GEORGE MUELLER

———♦———

Some Christians give to the Lord's work weekly; others just give weakly.

———♦———

To whom much is given, much is expected.

———♦———

The minister of a small church believed some practical joker was joshing him as I.O.U.'s began to appear in the collection plate. But one Sunday night weeks later the collection included an envelope containing bills equal to the total of the I.O.U.'s.

After that, the parson could hardly wait to see what amount the anonymous doner had promised. The range in contributions was from five to fifteen dollars — apparently based on what the donor thought the sermon to be worth — for there came a Sunday when the collection plate brought a note reading, "U.O. Me $5."
Pathfinder

———♦———

A government income tax inspector visited a clergyman and expressed a desire to see his church. The clergyman beamed with pleasure at the request. Afterwards he asked the inspector what he thought of it.

"Frankly, I'm a bit disappointed," said the government man. "After looking at the income tax returns of your parishioners and the fine gifts they claim to your church, I had come to the conclusion that the aisles must be paved with gold."

———♦———

There are three kinds of givers — the flint, the sponge and the honeycomb.

To get anything out of a flint you must hammer it. And then you get only chips and sparks.

To get water out of a sponge you must squeeze it, and the more you use pressure, the more you will get.

But the honeycomb just overflows with its own sweetness.
The Evangel

Whatever is offered to the Lord, broken in His hands, and given to the multitude, is sufficient for the need.
V. RAYMOND EDMAN

———♦———

You may give without loving, but you can't love without giving.

———♦———

The Lord takes notice, not only of what we give, but of what we have left.

———♦———

Think It Over:

God made the sun — it gives.
God made the moon — it gives.
God made the stars — they give.
God made the air — it gives.
God made the clouds — they give.
God made the earth — it gives.
God made the sea — it gives.
God made the trees — they give.
God made the flowers — they give.
God made the fowls — they give.
God made the beasts — they give.
God made the Plan — He gives.
God made man — He . . .? *Selected*

———♦———

Do your givin'
While you're livin'
Then you're knowin'
Where it's goin'.

———♦———

There is more power in the open hand than in the clenched fist.
HERBERT N. CASSON

———♦———

Some people give according to their means and others according to their meanness.

———♦———

Once there was a Christian, he had a pious look.
His consecration was complete, except his pocketbook.
He'd put a nickel in the plate,
Then with might and main,
He'd sing, "When we asunder part, it gives us inward pain."
He dropped a nickel in the plate, meekly raised his eyes
Glad the weekly rent was paid for a mansion in the skies.
Western Messenger

Don't give till it hurts: Give a little more . . . give till it feels good.

———◆———

You can't outgive God.

———◆———

You cannot get without giving.

———◆———

A lady was filling a box for India when a child brought her a penny. With it the lady bought a tract to put in the box. The tract was at length given to a Burmese chief, and it led him to Christ. The chief told the story of his Saviour and his great happiness to his friends. They also believed, and cast away their idols. A church was built there. A missionary was sent, and fifteen hundred were converted from heathenism. All of these wonderful changes were the result of that little seed.   SOURCE UNKNOWN

———◆———

Give a penny and hear it squeal
Give a quarter and hear it speak
But if you'd hear a real live holler
Drop on the plate a silver dollar.

———◆———

A steward in a church asked a member for a contribution, and the member said that he didn't have any money to give. The steward said, "Brother, we only have two kinds of members in our church. Those who give to the church and those the church gives to . . . and right now we'll start helping you."

Result: The steward got a sizable donation.

———◆———

Don't give from the top of your purse but from the bottom of your heart.

———◆———

A pig was lamenting his lack of popularity. He complained to the cow that people were always talking about the cow's gentleness and kind eyes, whereas his name was used as an insult. The pig admitted that the cow gave milk and cream, but maintained that pigs gave more. "Why," the animal complained, "we pigs give bacon and ham and bristles and people even pickle our feet. I don't see why you cows are esteemed so much more."

The cow thought awhile and said gently: "Maybe it's because we give while we're still living."

———◆———

The best thing to give . . .
to your enemy is forgiveness;
to an opponent, tolerance;
to a friend, your heart;
to your child, a good example;
to a father, deference;
to your mother, conduct that will
make her proud of you;
to yourself, respect;
to all men, charity.   LORD BALFOUR

———◆———

Wife to husband on Christmas morning: "You angel! Just what I need to exchange for just what I wanted."

———◆———

Do you know what the buffalo on the nickel said to the offering plate? "I need a little green stuff to feed on."

———◆———

A small boy observed his mother put a penny on the offering plate at the morning service. On the way home from church, she freely criticized the poor sermon they had heard. "But, Mother," said the boy, "what could you expect for a penny?"

———◆———

If you train up a child to give pennies, when he is old he will not depart from it.

———◆———

May God forbid that we should present our gifts and withhold ourselves.

———◆———

Minister to congregation: "This morning we will worship the Lord in silent prayer, followed by a silent offering. It will fall even more silently if you fold it."

———◆———

When the collection plate was passed, the little old lady began fumbling in her purse. The nearer the ushers approached, the more frantically she searched her bag. Finally, noticing her plight, the little boy sitting nearby slid over and nudged her.

"Here lady," he told her. "You take my dime. I can hide under the seat."

Together

———◆———

While a minister was announcing that a missionary offering would be taken, one man in the congregation said he would not give because he did not believe in missions.

"All right then," said the minister, "take some of the offering out of the plate because it is for the heathen."

———◆———

A practical demonstration of love for God needs to be made by way of the collection plate.

———◆———

To Pledge or Not to Pledge

To pledge or not to pledge —
That is the question.
Whether 'tis nobler in a man
To take the Gospel free
And let another foot the bill,
Or sign a pledge and pay toward
Church expense!
To give, to pay — aye, there's the rub,
To pay —
When on the free-pew plan a man
May have
A sitting free and take the Gospel, too,
As though he paid, and none be aught
The wiser
Save the church committee who —
Most honorable men — can keep a secret!
"To err is human," and human, too, to buy
At cheapest rate. I'll take the Gospel so!
For others do the same — a common rule!
I'm wise; I'll wait, not work —
I'll pray, not pay,
And let the other fellow foot the bills,
And so I'll get the Gospel free,
You see!

AUTHOR UNKNOWN

Goals

Knowing what our goal is and desiring to reach it doesn't bring us closer to it. Doing something does!   ELD

———◆———

For finding the best in life:
Go!
Keep going!
Help someone else to go!

———◆———

Are you a pilgrim or a vagrant? A pilgrim is one who is traveling to a certain place. A vagrant is a mere stroller, with no settled purpose or goal.   T. C. INNES

———◆———

Education teaches a student good marksmanship before he takes aim at his goal in life.

———◆———

Set your goal high. You may not reach it, but you'll put on muscle climbing toward it.

———◆———

You must have long-range goals to keep you from being frustrated by short-range failures.   CHARLES C. NOBLE

———◆———

There is only one way of seeing things rightly, and that is seeing the whole of them.   JOHN RUSKIN

———◆———

Aim at the unattainable so that your work will have an ideal direction even though it never achieves perfection.   EMERSON

———◆———

One of the best marksmen in the country was passing through a small town and everywhere he saw evidence of amazing shooting. On trees, on walls, on fences, and on barns were countless targets with a bullet hole in the exact center of the bull's-eye. So the man sought out the person responsible for this great marksmanship.

"This is the most wonderful shooting I have ever seen," the man said. "How in the world did you do it?"

"Easy as pie," replied the marksman, "I shot first and drew the circles afterwards."

National Motorist

You don't hit anything unless you aim at it.

———♦———

There are two words we ought to keep in mind: today and that day.

———♦———

Our objectives are not set on what we have done, they are not set on what we would like to do; they are set on what we ought to do.

———♦———

If we could first know where we are, and whither we are tending, we could better judge what to do and how to do it. ABRAHAM LINCOLN

———♦———

It may be a long way to a goal, but it is never far to the next step toward the goal.

———♦———

The first two letters of the word goal spell GO. ELD

———♦———

The great thing in this world is not so much where we stand as in what direction we are moving.
OLIVER WENDELL HOLMES

———♦———

Men, like tacks, are useful if they have good heads and are pointed in the right direction.

———♦———

If you haven't figured out where you are going, you're lost before you start.

———♦———

God

Reach up as far as you can, and God will reach down all the way.
BISHOP VINCENT

———♦———

It is easier for God to do a difficult thing than an easy thing.

———♦———

I have lived a long time and the longer I live the more convincing proofs I see that God governs in the affairs of men. BENJAMIN FRANKLIN

———♦———

"Tell me," said a philosopher, "where is God?"
"First tell me," said the other, "where He is not." ANONYMOUS

We must accept the existence of a Creator in order to accept our American way of life because He is the source of our Freedom. If there is no God then the Communists are right. If there's a God, the American way is right. *American Childhood*

———♦———

God must first do something *for* us and *in* us, before He can do something *through* us.

———♦———

When God measures men He puts the tape around the heart, not the head.

———♦———

We are all dangerous folk without God's controlling hand. W. W. AYER

———♦———

God can do without us, but we cannot do without Him.

———♦———

All God's giants have been weak men who did great things for God because they reckoned on His being with them. J. HUDSON TAYLOR

———♦———

God has given us a will to choose His will. DR. HENRIETTA C. MEARS

———♦———

The Lord's choice is always choice.

———♦———

Even as you can't outrun God when you dodge His will, it is equally impossible to outrun His care when you are in His will. CAL GUY, *The Teacher*

———♦———

The most important thing in the world is not to know the Lord's will but to know the Lord. WALLACE BOYS

———♦———

God's way becomes plain when we walk in it. *This Day*

———♦———

The mystery of godliness is God humbling Himself to become man. The mystery of iniquity is man exalting himself to become God. A. J. GORDON

———♦———

God can give Himself to us only in the measure in which we give ourselves to Him.

Sour godliness is the devil's religion.

JOHN WESLEY

———◆———

Unless there is within us that which is above us, we shall soon yield to that which is about us.　PETER FORSYTHE

———◆———

God is the answer . . .

When you have sinned and need forgiveness;
When you are about to make a decision;
When you feel ill toward another;
When you think you are better than other people;
When your home is at the point of breaking;
When your marriage begins to waver;
When your children begin to lose respect for you;
When you want to live a life of triumph and joy — for here and hereafter.　*Bethel Methodist Church News*

———◆———

A theological school instructor shared a seat with a small boy on a shuttle train. The boy was holding a Sunday school book.

"Do you go to Sunday school, my boy?" asked the man in a friendly way.

"Yes, sir."

"Tell me, my boy," continued the man, thinking to have some fun with the lad, "tell me where God is, and I'll give you an apple."

The boy looked up sharply at the man and promptly replied, "I will give you a whole barrel of apples if you tell me where He is not."

———◆———

A man met a boy on a country road with a basket of bread on his arm. "What have you in that basket, my boy?" asked the man.

"Bread, sir."

"Where did you get that bread?"

"From the baker, sir."

"And where did he get the flour?" asked the man.

"From the farmer, sir."

"And where did the farmer get the flour?" continued the man.

"From seed, sir."

"And where did he get the seed?" persisted the man.

The boy paused, then exclaimed in an awe-struck voice, "From God, sir!"

Yes, behind each loaf of bread is God!

———◆———

God's Way

God moves in a mysterious way,
　His wonders to perform;
He plants His footsteps in the sea,
　And rides upon the storm.

Deep in unfathomable mines
　Of never-failing skill,
He treasures up His bright designs
　And works His sov'reign will.

Ye fearful saints, fresh courage take,
　The clouds ye so much dread
Are big with mercy, and shall break
　In blessing on your head.

Judge not the Lord by feeble sense,
　But trust Him for His grace;
Behind a frowning providence
　He hides a smiling face.

His purposes will ripen fast,
　Unfolding every hour;
The bud may have a bitter taste,
　But sweet will be the flower.

Blind unbelief is sure to err,
　And scan His work in vain;
God is His own interpreter,
　And He will make it plain.

COWPER, 1779

———◆———

Good, Good Will, Good Works

Do all the good you can,
By all the means you can,
In all the ways you can,
In all the places you can,
At all the times you can,
To all the people you can,
As long as ever you can.

JOHN WESLEY

———◆———

The value of our good is not measured by what it costs us but by the amount of good it does the one concerned.

If "God" is taken out of "good" nothing (o) is left.

What is serving God?
'Tis doing good to man.

There is so much good in the worst of us,
And so much bad in the best of us,
That it ill becomes any of us
To find fault with the rest of us.

The man who tries to keep a book account of the good he does never does enough good to pay for the binding of the book. WILLIAM JENNINGS BRYAN

I'd rather be a good man than a brilliant man. HAROLD L. LUNDQUIST

When you are good to others you are always best to yourself.

Little Things

Little drops of water, little grains of sand,
Make the mighty ocean and the pleasant land;
So the little moments, humble though they be,
Make the mighty ages of eternity.

So our little errors lead the soul away
From the path of virtue, far in sin to stray.
Little deeds of kindness, little words of love,
Help to make earth happy like the heaven above. JULIA FLETCHER CARNEY

I shall pass through this world but once. Any good therefore that I can do or any kindness that I can show to any human being, let me do it now. Let me not defer or neglect it, for I shall not pass this way again.

Worth, true worth, rarely needs a megaphone to announce its presence. There are no arrows pointing the way to the sun.

Good, the more communicated, the more abundant grows. MILTON

Goodness consists not in the outward things we do, but in the inward things we are. To be good is the great thing. E. H. CHAPIN

You are expected to make good—not to make excuses.

He who stops being better stops being good. OLIVER CROMWELL

Somehow, the better we are, the better the people are that we meet.

Good, better, best;
Never let it rest
Till your good is better,
And your better best. *Old Maxim*

Good will is the one and only asset that competition cannot understand or destroy. MARSHALL FIELD

The most precious thing anyone can have is the good will of others. It is something as fragile as an orchid—and as beautiful. As precious as a gold nugget and as hard to find. As powerful as a great turbine and as hard to build—as wonderful as youth and as hard to keep. AMOS PARISH

Spurgeon once said that one might better try to sail the Atlantic in a paper boat, than try to get to heaven on good works.

The best minds that accept Christianity as a divinely inspired system believe that the great end of the Gospel is not merely the saving, but the educating of men's souls, the creating within them of holy disposition, the subduing of egotistical pretentions, and the perpetual enhancing of the desire that the will of God—a will synonymous with goodness and truth—may be done on earth. GEORGE ELIOT

Gospel

That the Gospel is to be
  opposed is inevitable —
    disbelieved is to be expected —
But that it should be made
  dull is intolerable!   GERALD KENNEDY

———♦———

The Gospel breaks hard hearts and heals broken hearts.

———♦———

The good news is that God meets us where we are, because we cannot rise to where He would have us be.

———♦———

Christ came, not to preach the Gospel, but that there might be a Gospel to preach.   DR. GRIFFETH THOMAS

———♦———

The Gospel According to You

There's a sweet old story translated for men,
But writ in the long, long ago,
The Gospel according to Mark, Luke and John
Of Christ and His mission below.

Men read and admire the Gospel of Christ,
With its love so unfailing and true;
But what do they say, and what do they think,
Of the gospel "according to you"?

'Tis a wonderful story, that gospel of love,
As it shines in the Christ life divine;
And, oh, that its truth might be told again
In the story of your life and mine!

Unselfishness mirrors in every scene;
Love blossoms on every sod;
And back from its vision the heart comes to tell
The wonderful goodness of God.

You are writing each day a letter to men;
Take care that the writing is true;
'Tis the only gospel that some men will read —
That gospel according to you.
   AUTHOR UNKNOWN

G - lad Tidings
O - ffer Pardon
S - alvation
P - eace
E - ternal Life
L - asting Joy

———♦———

Run, John, and live! the Law commands,
Yet gives me neither legs nor hands.
A better note the Gospel brings,
It bids me fly — and gives me wings.

———♦———

There is only one Gospel. It is for the whole man, his family, his community, his neighbor, his nation, his world.   HERBERT GEZORK

———♦———

It is not nearly so important that we send sputniks around the globe as that we should send the message of Christ around the world.
   The Sunday Bulletin

———♦———

Another version of
The Gospel According to You

"You are our epistle, written in our hearts, known and read of all men."

The Gospels of Matthew, Mark, Luke and John,
Are read by more than a few,
But the one that is most read and commented on
Is the gospel according to *you.*

You are writing a gospel, a chapter each day
By things that you do and words that you say,
Men read what you write, whether faithless or true.
Say, what is the gospel according to *you?*

Do men read His truth and His love in your life,
Or has yours been too full of malice and strife?
Does your life speak of evil, or does it ring true?
Say, what is the gospel according to *you?*
   AUTHOR UNKNOWN

You can't spell Gospel without Go.
Nor Pray without Pay, you know.
But if we put them together and pray
and pay
The Gospel will go to lands far away.
The Tower of St. Paul

Gossip

Gossip is the art of saying nothing and leaving nothing unsaid.

———◆———

A great many people, like cats, lick themselves with their tongues.

———◆———

It is well to remember that mansions in the sky cannot be built out of the mud thrown at others. *Evangelist*

———◆———

Gossiping and lying go hand in hand.

———◆———

A little girl explained that the teacher had said: "Go into all the world and preach the gossip."

———◆———

A gossip is a person with a keen sense of rumor.

———◆———

Gossip is like mud thrown against a clean wall; it may not stick, but it leaves a mark.

———◆———

If you say nothing, no one will repeat it.

———◆———

It's easier to float a rumor than to sink one!

———◆———

The Shady Dozen

"I heard. . . ."
"They say. . . ."
"Everybody says. . . ."
"Have you heard . . .?"
"Did you hear . . .?"
"Isn't it awful . . .?"
"People say. . . ."
"Did you ever . . .?"
"Somebody said . . ."
"Would you think . . .?"
"Don't say I told you . . ."
"Oh, I think it is terrible. . . ."
The Outlook

When it comes to spreading gossip it seems that the female of the species is much faster than the mail.
Glendale News Press

———◆———

The difference between gossip and news is whether you hear it or tell it.

———◆———

Four preachers met for a friendly gathering. During the conversation one preacher said, "Our people come to us and pour out their hearts, confess certain sins and needs. Let's do the same. Confession is good for the soul." In due time they agreed. One confessed he liked to go to the movies, and would sneak off when away from his church. The second confessed to liking to smoke cigars, and the third one confessed to liking to play cards. When they came to the fourth one, he wouldn't confess. The others pressed him, saying, "Come now, we confessed ours, what is your secret sin or vice?" Finally he answered, "It is gossiping and I can hardly wait to get out of here."

———◆———

I Know Something Good About You

Wouldn't this old world be better
If the folks we met would say,
"I know something good about you!"
And then treat us just that way?

Wouldn't it be fine and dandy,
If each handclasp, warm and true,
Carried with it this assurance,
"I know something good about you?"

Wouldn't life be lots more happy,
If the good that's in us all
Were the only thing about us
That folks bothered to recall?

Wouldn't life be lots more happy,
If we praised the good we see?
For there's such a lot of goodness
In the worst of you and me.

Wouldn't it be nice to practice
That fine way of thinking, too;
You know something good about me;
I know something good about you?
ANONYMOUS

117

Government

In rivers and bad governments, the lightest things swim at the top.

BENJAMIN FRANKLIN

Government is impossible where moral character is wanting.

While just government protects all in their religious rites, true religion affords government its surest support.

GEORGE WASHINGTON

Accepting government aid is like taking drugs — pleasant at first, habit-forming later, damning at last.

W. W. WARD

It used to be that when you said a man had gone to his everlasting rest, it didn't mean he had landed a job with the government.

Grace

The higher a man is in grace, the lower he will be in his own esteem.

SPURGEON

Graduation

A father, attending his son's graduation exercises from college, was heard to remark, "Well, I worked my way through college, and now I have just finished working my son's way through."

The Watchman Examiner

Graduation Means:

G - oing forward
R - eady to
A - ccept God's will —
D - etermined to
U - nderstand His Word —
A - lert to
T - emptations —
I - nterested in
O - thers
N - ever forgetting that Christ is my helper.

ELD

All that stands between the graduate and the top of the ladder is the ladder.

Great, Greatness

Greatness stands on a precipice.

To be great is to be misunderstood.

A great man is great until he finds it out; then he is a danger and a nuisance.

Great men are known by their deeds — the rest of us by our mortgages.

The great man is the man who does a thing for the first time.

ALEXANDER SMITH

There never was any heart truly great and gracious that was not also tender and compassionate.

SOUTH

No man is small who does a small job in a great way.

I will expect great things from God, and I will attempt great things for God.

WILLIAM CAREY

The Greatest of All

My greatest loss, to lose my soul.
My greatest gain, Christ as my Saviour.
My greatest object, to glorify God.
My greatest price, a crown of glory.
My greatest work, to win souls for Christ.
My greatest joy, the joy of God's salvation.
My greatest inheritance, heaven and its glories.
My greatest neglect, the neglect of so great salvation.
My greatest crime, to reject Christ the only Saviour.
My greatest privilege, power to become a child of God.
My greatest bargain, to lose all things to win Christ.
My greatest profit, godliness in this life and that to come.
My greatest peace, the peace that passeth understanding.
My greatest knowledge, to know God and Jesus Christ whom He hath sent.

AUTHOR UNKNOWN

There is in every man something greater than he had begun to dream of. Men are nobler than they think themselves. PHILLIPS BROOKS

———✦———

Go as far as you can see, and when you get there you will see farther.

———✦———

The greatest things in the world have been done by those who systematized their work and organized their time. ORISON SWEET MARDEN

———✦———

Grow, Growth

To grow tall spiritually, a man first must learn to kneel.

———✦———

As we grow better we meet better people. ELBERT HUBBARD

———✦———

When Longfellow was well along in years, his head as white as snow, but his cheeks as red as a rose, an ardent admirer asked him how it was that he was able to keep so vigorous and write so beautifully. Pointing to a blooming apple tree nearby, he replied: "That apple tree is very old, but I never saw prettier blossoms upon it than those it now bears. The tree grows a little new wood every year, and I suppose it is out of that new wood that those blossoms come. Like the apple tree, I try to grow a little new wood every year." And what Longfellow did, we all ought to do.

———✦———

Guide, Guidance

If God has called you, don't look over your shoulder to see who is following you.

———✦———

When God shuts and bolts the door, don't try to get in through the window.

———✦———

If you would have God's guidance, you must listen as well as talk to the guide. ELD

———✦———

I know not the way God leads me, but well do I know my Guide. MARTIN LUTHER

Guilt, Guilty

Guilt is always suspicious.

H

Habit, Habits

We Cannot

Sow bad habits and reap a good character;

Sow jealousy and hatred and reap love and friendship;

Sow dissipation and reap a healthy body;

Sow deception and reap confidence;

Sow cowardice and reap courage;

Sow neglect of the Bible and reap a well-guided life. AUTHOR UNKNOWN

———✦———

It is easier to prevent bad habits than to break them.

———✦———

Choose the best life, habits will make it pleasant.

Every bad habit acquired by a person actually places a chattel mortgage on his personality.

———✦———

Habits shape personality — encourage the Sunday school habit.

———✦———

One good way to break a bad habit: drop it! C. GRANT

———✦———

Happy, Happiness

Happiness is beneficial for the body but it is grief that develops the power of the mind. MARCEL PROUST

———✦———

Those who bring sunshine into the lives of others cannot keep it from themselves. J. M. BARRIE

The first steps to happiness are the church steps.

———◆———

Happiness is found not in reward but in honorable effort.

———◆———

"You should do something every day to make other people happy," one person said to another, "even if it's only to leave them alone."

———◆———

To be happy at home is the ultimate result of all ambition. SAMUEL JOHNSON

———◆———

Folks are generally as happy as they make up their minds to be. ABRAHAM LINCOLN

———◆———

Rules for Happiness

Something to do,
Some one to love,
Something to hope for. KANT

———◆———

The happiness of your life depends upon the character of your thoughts. MARCUS AURELIUS

———◆———

Some people bring happiness wherever they go; others whenever they go.

———◆———

Happiness is a butterfly, which when pursued is always just beyond your grasp, but which if you will sit down quietly will light upon you. HAWTHORNE

———◆———

To be happy with a man you must understand him a lot and love him a little. To be happy with a woman you must love her a lot and not try to understand her at all. HELEN ROWLAND

———◆———

Happiness is not the end of life; character is. H. W. BEECHER

———◆———

Rule for Happiness

1 cup filled to overflowing with
Industry
Concentration
Enthusiasm
1 pinch of spice
1 pinch of sand
Served with sauce of smiles.

The Constitution guarantees only the right to the pursuit of happiness and not the ability to catch it.

———◆———

Happiness is in the heart, not in the circumstances.

———◆———

An effort made for the happiness of others lifts us above ourselves. Happiness isn't so much a matter of position as it is of disposition. Many a train of thought is just a string of empties.

———◆———

The days that make us happy make us wise. JOHN MASEFIELD

———◆———

Many persons have a wrong idea about what constitutes true happiness. It is not attained through self-gratifications, but through fidelity to a worthy purpose. HELEN KELLER

———◆———

Happiness consists in being happy with what we have got and with what we haven't got. SPURGEON

———◆———

You cannot build your happiness on someone else's unhappiness.

———◆———

Plant Happiness

First plant five rows of peas:
Perseverance,
Presence,
Preparation,
Promptness,
Purity.
Next plant three rows of squash:
Squash gossip,
Squash criticism and
Squash indifference.
Then five rows of lettuce:
Let us be faithful to duty.
Let us be unselfish and loyal.
Let us be true to our own obligations.
Let us love one another.
No garden is complete without turnips:
Turn up for important meetings.
Turn up with a smile.
Turn up with new ideas.
Turn up with determination to make everything count for something good and worthwhile. AUTHOR UNKNOWN

Happiness has no reason. It is not to be found in the facts of our lives, but in the color of the light by which we look at the facts.

Society is so interwoven that no individual can attain real happiness alone.

Be Happy

Life is too short to be sad in,
To carry a grouch or be mad in,
'Tis made to be happy and glad in,
So let us be friends and be happy!

Friends are too scarce to be sore at,
To gloom and to glower and roar at,
They're made to be loved and not
    "swore at,"
So let us be friends and be happy!

Love is the store we should lay in,
Love is the coin we should pay in,
Love is the language to pray in,
So fill up with love and be happy.
CLARA COLBURN WOUTERS

Happiness is no easy matter; 'tis very hard to find it within ourselves, and impossible to find it anywhere else.
CHAMFORT

After all, it is not what is around us, but what is in us; not what we have, but what we are, that makes us really happy.
GEIKE

God evidently does not intend us all to be rich, or powerful, or great, but He does intend us all to be friends.
EMERSON

If you make children happy now, you will make them happy twenty years hence by the memory of it.
KATE DOUGLAS WIGGIN

Happiness can be built only on virtue, and must of necessity have truth for its foundation.
COLERIDGE

No human being can come into this world without increasing or diminishing the sum total of human happiness.
ELIHU BURRETT

If our lives are in harmony with the world, they are out of harmony with God.
WENDELL P. LOVELESS

You can be happy by yourself but you can be happier with someone else.

Labor and trouble one can always get through alone, but it takes two to be glad.
IBSEN

It's the counterfeit of happiness that costs the most.

True happiness comes from the knowledge that we are some use in this world.

The office of government is not to confer happiness but to give men opportunity to work out happiness for themselves.
WILLIAM ELLERY CHANNING

The story is told of a king who had an unhappy little son. The prince had everything he could wish for — pony, toys, even a yacht to sail in the lake. Still he was unhappy.

One day the king consulted a wise old man about his son. The old man took a piece of paper and wrote on it some words in invisible ink. He told the king to hold the paper between his eyes and a lighted candle that night and he would be able to read the words.

That night the king lit a candle and held the paper before it. Here was the message:

"The secret of true happiness is to do a little kindness to someone every day."

Where Is Happiness?

Not in unbelief — Voltaire was an infidel of the most pronounced type. He wrote: "I wish I had never been born."

Not in pleasure — Lord Byron lived a life of pleasure, if anyone did. He wrote: "The worm, the canker and the grief are mine alone."

Not in money—Jay Gould, the American millionaire, had plenty of that.

When dying, he said: "I suppose I am the most miserable man on earth."

Not in possession and fame — Lord Beaconsfield enjoyed more than his share of both. He wrote: "Youth is a mistake, manhood a struggle, old age a regret."

Not in military glory — Alexander the Great conquered the known world of his day. Having done so, he wept in his tent, because, as he said, "There are no more worlds to conquer."

Where, then, is happiness found? The answer is simple: "In Christ alone." He said: "I will see you again and your heart shall rejoice, and your joy no man taketh from you" (John 16:22).   MARCARTNEY

Some years ago a newspaper offered a prize for the best definition of "money." Out of hundreds who competed, the winner submitted the following:

"Money is a universal provider of everything but happiness; and a passport everywhere but to heaven."

Harmony

There is a unique harmony in the Bible. Compare, for example, the first two and the last two chapters:
In GENESIS the earth is created;
In REVELATION it passes away.
In GENESIS the sun and moon appear;
In REVELATION there is no need of the sun or moon.
In GENESIS there is a garden, the home of a man;
In REVELATION there is a city, the home of the nations.
In GENESIS we are introduced to Satan;
In REVELATION we see his doom.
In GENESIS we hear the first sob and see the first tear;
In REVELATION we read: "God shall wipe away all tears from their eyes."
In GENESIS the curse is pronounced;
In REVELATION we read: "There shall be no more curse."   *Selected*

Haste, Hurry

Haste makes waste.
                BENJAMIN FRANKLIN

Why is it that people who don't know whether they are coming or going are usually in such a big hurry to get there?

He that riseth late, must trot all day, and shall scarce overtake his business at night.   BENJAMIN FRANKLIN

Haste Is Waste

No doubt a nervous speed or hurry
Can bring about a senseless worry
That grows into a fretful flurry
For haste.

Whoever dashes yon and hither
May watch his cherished plans all wither
And find that any kind of dither
Is waste.
                MARJORIE LINDSEY BREWER,
                The Baptist Standard

Hate

It is better to take many injuries than to give one.   BENJAMIN FRANKLIN

Health

Without health all men are poor.

Health is better than wealth.

Prayer for Health

Lord, look with pity on my pain,
And soon my strength restore,
And grant me life and health again,
To serve Thee evermore.
                AUTHOR UNKNOWN

Heart, Hearts

A merry heart goes all the day, a sad tires in a mile.   SHAKESPEARE

The head has not heard until the heart has listened.

A new heart creates a new life.

The world is shrinking faster than the human heart is expanding.

MARION F. MOORHEAD

————◆————

Carve your name on hearts and not on marble.

C. H. SPURGEON

————◆————

In vacation Bible school little four-year-old Mary insisted on placing her hand on the top of her head while the group said the pledge to the American flag. When her teacher asked her why she did this she replied:

"Well, that's where my heart is. Mother always put her hand on the top of my head and says, 'Bless your little heart, Mary.' "

————◆————

Little Susan, four years old, returned from Sunday school with her offering money.

"Why didn't you give your money in the offering today, dear?" her mother asked.

"Because our teacher told us that if we love Jesus He comes and lives in our hearts. And you told me never to put money in my mouth. So I didn't know what to do. If I gave my money to Jesus I would have to swallow it."

————◆————

Heathen

Heathenness is all ungodliness.

————◆————

Heaven

You can't get into heaven by naturalization papers.

————◆————

God may not give us an easy journey to the Promised Land, but He will give us a safe one.

BONAR

————◆————

When we go to heaven we will go heart-first, not head-first.

————◆————

When traveling by plane, the minister said, "If I go down, I go up."

————◆————

A little boy, caught in mischief, was asked by his mother: "How do you expect to get into heaven?"

He thought a minute, and then said:

"Well, I'll just run in and out and keep slamming the door till they say, 'For goodness' sake, come in or stay out,' then I'll go in."

Christian Herald

————◆————

It is our main business in this world to secure an interest in the next.

————◆————

If you are seated in heavenly places, sit still.

————◆————

"And," concluded the Sunday school teacher, "If you are a good boy, Tommy, you will go to heaven and have a crown of gold on your head."

"Not me!" said Tommy, "I had one of those things put on a tooth once."

————◆————

A Man May Go to Heaven

Without health,
  Without wealth,
    Without fame,
      Without a great name,
        Without learning,
          Without big earning,
            Without culture,
              Without beauty,
                Without friends.
Without 10,000 other things.
  But he can
    Never go to heaven
      Without Christ.

PHA

————◆————

"How is your wife?" the man asked a friend he hadn't seen for years.

"She's in heaven," replied the friend.

"Oh, I'm sorry." Then he realized that was not the thing to say, so he added, "I mean, I'm glad." And that was even worse. He finally came out with, "Well, I'm surprised."

Christian Herald

————◆————

A big advertising man had a small daughter who came home from Sunday school one day carrying a bundle of pamphlets and cards.

"And what do you have there?" asked the man.

"Oh, nothing much," answered the little girl. "Just some ads about heaven."

A preacher was asked if a man who learned to play a cornet on Sunday would go to heaven. The preacher's cryptic reply was: "I don't see why he shouldn't . . . but . . ." after a pause, "I doubt whether the man next door will."

Hell

It does not require a decision to go to hell.

A true fear of hell has sent many a soul to heaven.

Help, Helpful

For a web begun, God sends thread.
Italian Proverb

Help thyself and heaven will help thee.

Where God's finger points, there God's hand will make the way.

A candle loses nothing by lighting another candle. ANONYMOUS

Consider

Is anybody happier
  Because you passed his way?
Does anyone remember
  That you spoke to him today?
This day is almost over,
  And its toiling time is through;
Is there anyone to utter now,
  A friendly word for you?

Can you say tonight in passing,
  With the day that slipped so fast,
That you helped a single person,
  Of the many that you passed?
Is a single heart rejoicing,
  Over what you did or said?
Does one whose hopes were fading
  Now with courage look ahead?

Did you waste the day, or lose it?
Was it well or poorly spent?
Did you leave a trail of kindness,
Or a scar of discontent? ANONYMOUS

Bearing one another's burdens is different from bearing down on them.

There is no exercise better for the heart than reaching down and lifting people up. JOHN ANDREW HOLMER

A mother was telling her six-year-old son about the Golden Rule. "Always remember," she said, "that we are here to help others."

The youngster mulled this over for a minute and then asked, "Well, what are the others here for?" *Christian Herald*

God helps them that help themselves.
BENJAMIN FRANKLIN

Life is short and we have never too much time for gladdening the hearts of those who are traveling the dark journey with us. *Amiel's Journal*

One day a teacher asked her first-graders what they did to help at home. They took turns giving such answers as "dry dishes," "feed the dog," and "make my bed." She noticed that Johnny hadn't spoken, so she asked him to tell what he did.

After hesitating a moment, he replied, "Mostly I stay out of the way." *The Instructor*

History

The worst thing about history is that every time it repeats itself the price goes up. *Pillar in Coronet*

It is only world history that repeats itself. Your private history is repeated by the neighbors.

Christ is the great central fact in the world's history; to Him everything looks forward or backward.
CHARLES E. SPURGEON

In the last four thousand years of history, there have been but 268 years entirely free of war. *Coronet*

A great man does not make his place in history. He finds it and fills it.
FRANK NELSON

———◆———

The highways of history are strewn with the wreckage of nations that forgot God.

———◆———

Holy, Holiness

Holiness is wholeness — the whole of Christ in the whole life.

———◆———

Holiness vanishes when you talk about it, but becomes gloriously conspicuous when you live it.

———◆———

A holy life has a voice. It speaks when the tongue is silent, and is either a constant attraction or a perpetual reproof.
HINTON

———◆———

Holy Spirit

He who has the Holy Spirit in his heart and the Scripture in his hands has all he needs.
ALEXANDER MACLAREN

———◆———

My human best filled with the Holy Spirit makes a good motto.
Sunday School Journal

———◆———

No one wants to see an old barn, but everyone likes to see the old barn burn.
DR. HENRIETTA C. MEARS

———◆———

The Holy Spirit is God at work.
D. L. MOODY

———◆———

The Fruits of the Spirit

In newspaper English, Galatians 5: 22, 23 would read something like this: "The fruit of the Spirit is an affectionate, lovable disposition, a radiant spirit and a cheerful temper, a tranquil mind and a quiet manner, a forbearing patience in provoking circumstances and with trying people, a sympathetic insight and tactful helpfulness, generous judgment and a big-souled charity, loyalty and reliableness under all circumstances, humility that forgets self in the joy of others, in all things self-mastered and self-controlled, which is the final mark of perfecting."

Home

Home should 'be more than a filling station.
DR. W. W. AYER

———◆———

It takes a hundred men to make an encampment, but one woman can make a home.

———◆———

Be it ever so humble, nobody stays home.

———◆———

Home is where the mortgage is.

———◆———

Home Blessing
Bless our home,
  Our lives, our friends
With love that, Lord,
  On Thee depends.   Amen.

———◆———

Recipe for a Happy Home

To 3 cups of love and 2 cups of understanding add 4 teaspoons of courtesy and 2 teaspoons each of thoughtfulness and helpfulness. Sift together thoroughly, then stir in an equal amount of work and play. Add 3 teaspoons of responsibility. Season to taste with study and culture, then fold in a generous amount of worship. Place in a pan well greased with security and lined with respect for personality. Sprinkle lightly with a sense of humor. Allow to set in an atmosphere of democratic planning and of mutual sharing. Bake in a moderate oven. When well done, remove and top with a thick coating of Christian teachings. Serve on a platter of friendliness garnished with smiles.
PAULINE AND LEONARD MILLER

Dry bread at home is better than roast meat abroad.

———◆———

Home — the place where the great are small and the small are great.

———◆———

The home can be the strongest ally of the Sunday school or its greatest enemy, depending on the parents.

———◆———

Only the home can found a state.
JOSEPH COOK

125

What a Real Home Is

A Real Home is a gymnasium. The ideal of a healthy body is the first one to give a child.

A Real Home is a lighthouse. A lighthouse reveals the breakers ahead and shows a clear way past them.

A Real Home is a playground. Beware of the house where you "dassn't frolic" — there mischief is brewing for someone.

A Real Home is a workshop. Pity the boy without a kit of tools or the girl without a sewing basket. They haven't learned the fun of doing things — and there is no fun like that.

A Real Home is a forum. Honest, open discussion of life's great problems belongs originally in the family circle.

A Real Home is a secret society. Loyalty to one's family should mean keeping silent on family matters — just this and nothing more.

A Real Home is a health resort. Mothers are the natural physicians.

A Real Home is a cooperative league. Households flourish where the interests of each is made the interest of all.

A Real Home is a business concern. Order is a housewife's hobby. But order without system is a harness without the horse.

A Real Home is a haven of refuge. The world does this for us all: it makes us hunger for a loving sympathy and a calming, soothing touch.

A Real Home is a temple of worship.

EDWARD PURINTON, *Covenanter Witness*

————◆————

Home

"What makes a home?"
I asked my little boy.
And this is what he said,
"You, Mother,
And when Father comes,
Our table set all shiny,
And my bed,
And, Mother, I think it's home,
Because we love each other."
You who are old and wise,
What would you say
If you were asked the question?
Tell me, pray
Thus simply as a little child, we learn
A home is made from love.
Warm as the golden hearthfire on the floor,
A table and a lamp for light,
And smooth white beds at night —
Only the old sweet fundamental things.
And long ago I learned —
Home may be near, home may be far,
But it is anywhere that love
And a few plain household treasures are.

AUTHOR UNKNOWN

————◆————

Little Alice was allowed to sit in her mother's place at the dinner table one evening when her mother was absent. Her slightly older brother, resenting the arrangement, sneered, "So you're the mother tonight. All right, how much is two times seven?"

Without a moment's hesitation, Alice replied nonchalantly, "I'm busy. Ask your father."

Teens

————◆————

Recipe for a Home

Half a cup of friendship
And a cup of thoughtfulness,
Creamed together with a pinch
Of powdered tenderness.

Very lightly beaten
In a bowl of loyalty,
With a cup of faith, and one of hope,
And one of charity.

Be sure to add a spoonful each
Of gaiety-that-sings.
And also the ability
To-laugh-at-little-things.

Moisten with the sudden tears
Of heartfelt sympathy;
Bake in a good-natured pan
And serve repeatedly.

Christian Home

————◆————

Honest, Honesty

Honesty is the best policy, especially when you want to borrow your policy.

————◆————

The whole art of government consists in the art of being honest.

THOMAS JEFFERSON

It matters not what you do —
Make a nation or a shoe;
For he who does an honest thing
In God's pure sight is ranked a king.
JOHN PARNELL

————◆————

The badge of honesty is simplicity.

————◆————

It is often surprising to find what heights may be obtained merely by remaining on the level.

————◆————

When a man gets in the straight way, he finds there is no room for crooked dealings. *The Presbyterian*

————◆————

An honest man will receive neither money nor praise that is not his due.
BENJAMIN FRANKLIN

————◆————

Hope

Get a Transfer

If you are on a gloomy line,
Get a transfer.
If you're inclined to fret and pine,
Get a transfer.
Get off the track of Doubt and Gloom,
Get on a Sunshine Train, there's room.
Get a transfer.
If you are on the Worry Train,
Get a transfer.
You must not stay there and complain;
Get a transfer.
The Cheerful Cars are passing through,
And there is lots of room for you,
Get a transfer.
If you are on the Grouchy Track,
Get a transfer.
Just take a Happy Special back,
Get a transfer.
Jump on the train and pull the rope,
That lands you at the Station Hope,
Get a transfer. *Canadian Baptist*

————◆————

Hope is as cheap as despair.

————◆————

Living on hope is a slim diet.

————◆————

We promise according to our hopes, and perform according to our fears.
LA ROCHEFOUCAULD

When hope is alive, the night is less dark; the solitude less deep, fear less acute.

————◆————

Hospitality

Hospitality should have no other nature than love. DR. HENRIETTA C. MEARS

————◆————

Human, Humanity, Human Nature

After all, there is but one race — humanity. GEORGE MOORE

————◆————

Who lives for humanity must be content to lose himself.
O. B. FROTHINGHAM

————◆————

Human nature is the same all over the world; but its operations are so varied by education and habit that one must see it in all its dresses.
LORD CHESTERFIELD

————◆————

Humble, Humility

Only if man strikes rock bottom in the sense of his own nothingness will he strike the Rock of Ages.

————◆————

If we do not learn humility, we will learn humiliation.

————◆————

The only way up is down on your knees.

————◆————

Meekness is not weakness, but strength harnessed for service.

————◆————

The smaller we are the more room God has.

————◆————

I believe the first test of a truly great man is his humility. JOHN RUSKIN

————◆————

To be humble to superiors is duty, to equals courtesy, to inferiors nobleness. BENJAMIN FRANKLIN

————◆————

It is no humility for a man to think less of himself than he ought, though it might rather puzzle him to do that.
SPURGEON

127

A mountain shames a molehill until both are humbled by the stars.

———♦——— AUTHOR UNKNOWN

Humility is to make a right estimate of oneself.

———♦——— SPURGEON

Humility is such a frail and delicate thing that he who dares to think that he has it, proves by that single thought that he has it not. IVAN O. MILLER

———♦———

Nothing sets a person so much out of the devil's reach as humility.

JONATHAN EDWARDS

———♦———

The humblest citizen of all the land, when clad in the armor of a righteous cause, is stronger than all the hosts of error. WILLIAM JENNINGS BRYAN

The dogmas of the quiet past are inadequate to the stormy present. The occasion is piled high with difficulty, so we must rise with the occasion. As our case is new, so we must think anew and act anew. We must disenthrall ourselves. ABRAHAM LINCOLN, 1862

———♦———

Humor

A good thing to have up your sleeve is a funny-bone.

———♦———

Asked to define "medieval," a college freshman wrote, "partly bad."

———♦———

Funny?

As soon as day begins to dawn
The meadow lark starts singing.
As soon as evening comes a star —
The angel's lamp starts swinging.
As soon as I am in the tub
The telephone starts ringing!

———♦———

Student Boners

Scalped potatoes are a tasty dish.
Chicken is the most wildly eaten food in America.
Pyrenees are tombs the Egyptians are buried in.
The three departments of government are Alaska, Maryland, Greece.

Bribery is having more than one wife.
Strategy is the studying of the moon and stars.
A plebiscite is a trader or rat, as you might call him.
The duties of a squire are to take care of a knight's armor.
Louis Pasteur discovered germs and apple cider. NEA Journal

———♦———

From School Examinations!

Poise is the way a Dutchman says boys.
Esquinox is a wild animal that lives in the Arctic.
Rabbi is plural for rabbit.
Copernicus invented the cornucopia.
Etiquette teaches us how to be polite without trying to remember to be.
In the stone age all the men were ossified.
The climax of a story is where it says it is to be continued.
Prohibition means a very dry state to be in.
Buttress is a butler's wife.
A gulf is a dent in a continent.
Conservation means doing without things we need.
If Ponce de Leon hadn't died before he found the fountain of youth, he wouldn't have died.

———♦———

Whatever trouble Adam had,
No man in days of yore
Could say, when Adam cracked a joke,
"I've heard that one before."

———♦———

Husband

"If you were to lose your husband," the insurance salesman asked the young housewife, "what would you get?"

She thought for a moment, then: "A parakeet."

———♦———

I should like to see any kind of a man, distinguishable from a gorilla, that some good and even pretty woman could not shape a husband out of.

OLIVER WENDELL HOLMES

One of a husband's tougher problems in life is getting back some of his take-home pay after he takes it home.

———◆———

Husband to wife: "Did you see that pretty girl smile at me?"
Wife: "That's nothing, the first time I saw you I laughed out loud."

———◆———

Irate husband: "Light bill, water bill, gas bill, milk bill — you've got to quit this wild spending!"

Hypocrisy, Hypocrite

Don't stay away from church because there are so many hypocrites; there is always room for one more.

———◆———

Certainly there are hypocrites in the church, for any church is but a gathering of sinful people. And what better place for us to be? *Presbyterian Life*

———◆———

The devil is helped most by the inconsistent Christian.

I

Idea, Ideas

Getting an idea should be like sitting on a pin; it should make you jump up and do something. SIMPSON

———◆———

The reason that so many good ideas die is that they cannot stand solitary confinement.

———◆———

Ideas are funny things, they do not work unless you do.

———◆———

Many ideas grow better when transplanted into another mind than in the one where they sprang up. OLIVER WENDELL HOLMES

———◆———

Some folks entertain ideas; others work them.

———◆———

Ideas rule life and in the long run shape the ages.

———◆———

There is something inevitable about an idea whose hour has struck. GOETHE

———◆———

You have to hatch ideas, and then hitch them. EMERSON

———◆———

The man who is set in his ways doesn't hatch new ideas.

———◆———

No big ideas ever came from swelled heads!

Ideas are like weapons. Men possess thoughts, but ideas possess men. MAX LERNER

———◆———

He who wishes to fulfill his mission in the world must be a man of one idea that is one of the great overmastering purposes, overshadowing all his aims, and guiding and controlling his entire life. BATES

Ideal, Ideals

Those who live on a mountain have a longer day than those who live in a valley.

Idle, Idleness

Business may be troublesome, but idleness is pernicious.

———◆———

Busybodies never have anything to do.

———◆———

Idle folks take the most pains.

———◆———

Be always ashamed to catch thyself idle. BENJAMIN FRANKLIN

———◆———

Too much idleness, I have observed, fills up a man's time much more completely, and leaves him less his own master, than any sort of employment whatsoever. EDMUND BURKE

The idler does not waste time; he merely wastes himself. *The Defender*

Idolatry, Idols

When God comes in the idols tumble down.

Ignorance, Ignorant

To be conscious that you are ignorant is a great step to knowledge.

Seems like people who know the least know it mighty fluently.
Lutheran Education

The man who cheapens himself in public is sure to be marked down by his neighbors.

One of the speakers at a church conference was haranguing against higher education and the universities. He closed his speech with pious gratitude that he had never been corrupted by contact with learning and college.

The next speaker was an erudite bishop. He peered at the anti-education man and then rumbled, "Do I understand that Mr. Dobson is thankful for his ignorance?"

"Well, yes," was the answer. "You can put it that way if you like."

The bishop beamed at his solemn audience and when he spoke his voice was like a benediction. "All I have to say," he intoned, "is that this man has a great deal, a very great deal to be thankful for." *Coronet*

Ill, Illness

A cold is both positive and negative. Sometimes the eyes have it, sometimes the nose.

Many people who review their illness are really giving an organ recital.

Wife to husband sick in bed: "It's a sympathy card from your secretary to me."

I enjoy convalescence. It is the part that makes the illness worthwhile.
G. B. SHAW

A disease known is half cured.

Diseases are taxes on pleasure.

Illustrations

One illustration is worth a ton of chalk.

Illustrations in a story are like sunshine streaming through a window.

Never state a fact if you can bring the fact to life with an illustration.

Illustrate, but don't illustrate the obvious.

We needs must illustrate the greater by the analogy of the less, but your illustration must not belittle you the theme.

"I want you to look at this picture," said the Sunday school teacher. "It illustrates today's lesson. Lot was told to take his daughters and wife, and flee out of Sodom. Here are Lot and his daughters, with his wife just behind them. There is Sodom in the background. Does anyone have any questions about the picture?"

Came a voice from the back of the room: "Where is the flea?" *Together*

Teaching a Sunday school class without the use of illustrations to explain the lesson is like building a house with no windows to let the light in. The well-constructed house has both walls and windows — walls for strength and protection, and windows for light. And is not good teaching something like building a house?

Who would build a house without windows? And who would build a house with all windows? Both windows and walls are needed in every house. In much the same way teaching needs the solid structure of Biblical truths to provide for the safety and salvation of young lives as well as selected illustrations and stories which emphasize and illumine those truths.

W. G. MONTGOMERY in *Sunday School World*

Imagination, Imagine

What is now proved was once only imagined. WILLIAM BLAKE

Solitude is as needful to the imagination as society is wholesome for the character. JAMES RUSSELL LOWELL

Do not let work divorce itself from imagination.

Grandmother saw Billy running around the house slapping himself and asked him why.

"Well," said Billy, "I just got so tired of walking that I thought I'd ride my horse for a while."

Unless a man constantly keeps a partition between his imagination and his facts, he is in danger of becoming just an ordinary liar.

Imitate, Imitation

Don't worry because a rival imitates you. As long as he follows in your tracks he can't pass you.

The young heroes, aged 10 to 14, were being honored for rescuing a comrade who had fallen through the ice. "Did you think of the idea of forming a human chain, or did you learn that in Scout work?" they were asked.

"Oh, that," piped one. "I saw it in a comic book."

A devoted father (who was a Sunday school superintendent) asked his young son, "What are you going to be when you grow up?"

The admiring son, without hesitation answered, "I'm going to be a Sunday school superintendent."

There is much difference between imitating a good man, and counterfeiting him. BENJAMIN FRANKLIN

Important

Important Things

The things that count are never weighed on scales
Nor measured by the dollar's gruesome face;
They are the friendly smile that never fails,
The handclasp that no bribery can replace.
The things that count are not of mansion size,
Nor lined with jeweled satin nor brocade;
They are the simple trust in children's eyes
And prayer that helps the person who has prayed.
The things that count are courage in distress
And hope that shines as brightly as a star
And vision and humility that bless
With God's true plan all living things that are.
These are the things that have the deepest worth;
These are the most important things on earth. MARY O'CONNOR

How often we place the thing of major importance upon the side track while the secondary consideration goes thundering through on the main line.

Let us not major on minor things.

It's nice to be important, but it's important to be nice.

Impossible

Only an all-powerful God can do the impossible with the impossible. ELD

The difficult we do immediately, the impossible takes a little longer — this is a good motto for any business.

131

When God is going to do something wonderful He begins with a difficulty; if He is going to do something very wonderful, he begins with an impossibility!

Impress, Impressions

"Don't write there," said one to a lad who was writing with a diamond pin on a pane of glass in the window of a hotel.

"Why?" the boy inquired.

"Because you can't rub it out."

Glass may be destroyed but the human soul is immortal. What about impressions made on the minds and hearts of boys and girls? They, too, are indelible. *Sunday School Journal*

Improve, Improvement

By improving yourself is the world made better.

Americans seem to have an excess of everything except parking space and religion. Is this an improvement of things?

The biggest room in the world is the room for improvement.

If you are still breathing, you can improve.

Where we cannot invent we can at least improve.

Inaction, Inertia

Iron rusts from disuse; stagnant water loses its purity, and in cold weather becomes frozen; even so does inaction sap the vigors of the mind.
LEONARDO DA VINCI

Indifference, Indifferent

The crude and physical agony of the Cross was nothing compared to the indifference of the crowd on Main Street as they "passed by."
ALLAN KNIGHT CHALMERS

When . . .

When parents use movies and television sets for baby sitters, regardless of the nature of pictures and programs . . .

When workers come to church meetings only if there is nothing else to do . . .

When people feel no responsibility for the welfare of others besides those in their own families . . .

When workers do not fill places of service at the church and do not explain their absence to leaders . . .

When parents leave little children in the care of others while they make money for luxuries . . .

When workers are unwilling to spend three hours a week preparing to teach Bible truths in the Sunday school . . .

When people use Sundays to mow lawns, fish, play baseball, and attend the movies . . .

When parents give much time to their own social life and little to good times with their children . . .

When workers do not keep their promises to boys and girls . . .

When people prefer to live where church people will not "bother them" . . .

Then . . . it must be time for a moral awakening in America!
The Sunday School Builder

Even if you are on the right track you will get run over if you just sit there. *Rays of Sunshine*

How to Kill a Sunday School

Attend only when convenient;

Arrive late when you do go;

Grumble about having to go;

Criticize the officers and teachers before your family and friends;

Decline to take any office, do it grudgingly and neglect it often;

Avoid all meetings of officers and teachers;

Neglect your records and reports, considering them unnecessary;

Be disinterested and sleepy throughout the teaching period;

Appear relieved when the session is over;

Be icily dignified and distant toward strangers;

Let outsiders feel that you belong and they don't;

Show as little enthusiasm as possible with any new venture;

Never cooperate with new workers or their plans and methods;

If teaching, be impatient and distant with your scholars;

Don't let the children of your Sunday school get the idea you love them;

Regard the teachers of your children as upstarts or busybodies;

Be free to show your distrust or disapproval of them when they call;

Never introduce your pastor or Sunday school superintendent to your friends or neighbors;

Don't let it be known what Sunday school you attend; it might be humiliating to have them go, too.

On no account support it with your money;

Never make sacrifices to see it go;

Squelch every effort to beautify grounds or Sunday school rooms;

Grumble habitually because your Sunday school is dying out.

ALICE LYONS DYER *in*
The Sunday School Worker

————◆————

Influence

The only way in which one human being can properly attempt to influence another is by encouraging him to think for himself, instead of endeavoring to instill ready-made opinions into his head. SIR LESLIE STEPHEN

————◆————

The serene, silent beauty of a holy life is the most powerful influence in the world, next to the might of God.

PASCAL

————◆————

In the footprints on the sands of time some people leave only the marks of a heel.

The rocking chair used by a hymn-singing mother has more power to rid the world of evil than the electric chair used by a justice meeting state.

C. EARL COOPER

————◆————

Plastic Clay

I took a piece of plastic clay,
And idly fashioned it one day,
And as my fingers pressed it still,
It bent and yielded to my will.

I came again when days were past;
The bit of clay was hard at last.
The form I gave it still it bore,
But I could change that form no more.

I took a piece of living clay
And gently formed it day by day
And molded it with power and art —
A young child's soft and yielded heart.

I came again when years were gone;
He was a man I looked upon.
The early imprint still he bore,
But I could change him then no more.

AUTHOR UNKNOWN

————◆————

My Influence

My life shall touch a dozen lives before this day is done,
Leave countless marks for good or ill ere sets the evening sun,
This is the wish I always wish, the prayer I always pray;
Lord, may my life help other lives it touches by the way. Selected

————◆————

The Things I Do

The things I do,
The things I say,
Will lead some person
Aright or astray.
So the things we do
Should be the best,
And the things we say
Should be to bless.

CAL STARGEL *in This Day*

————◆————

Inform

Seek information from the experienced. CICERO

133

Never awake me when you have good news to announce, because, with good news, nothing presses; but when you have bad news, arouse me immediately, for then there is not an instant to be lost. NAPOLEON

Ingenuity

A young mother was worried about her nine-year-old son. No matter how much she scolded, he kept running round with his shirt tails flapping. On the other hand, her neighbor had four boys, and each one of them always wore his shirt neatly tucked in. Finally the young mother asked her neighbor to tell her the secret.

"Oh, it's simple," she replied. "I just take all their shirts and sew an edging of lace around the bottom."

C. VICTORY in *The Evangel*

Inspiration

Sometimes the best inspiration is born of desperation.

Inspiration in presentation is perspiration in preparation.

Intellect, Intelligence

The intelligent person is one who has learned how to choose wisely and therefore has a sense of values, a purpose in life and a sense of direction.

J. MARTIN KLOTSCHE

Intentions

Good intentions never saved anyone.

The road to hell is paved with good intentions.

Unless one is a genius, it is best to aim at being intelligible. A. HOPE

The smallest deed is better than the grandest intention. *Sunday School Counselor*

Good intentions and good eggs soon spoil unless they soon hatch.

Interest

The whole secret of life is to be interested in one thing profoundly, and in a thousand things well.

HUGH WALPOLE

Interpretation

The great religions express the second great commandment, "Thou shalt love thy neighbor as thyself," thus:

Christianity: All things whatsoever ye would that men should do to you, do ye even so to them; for this is the law and the prophets.

Judaism: What is hateful to you, do not to your fellow men. That is the entire law; all the rest is commentary.

Buddhism: Hurt not others in ways that you yourself would find hurtful.

Islam: No one of you is a believer until he desires for his brother that which he desires for himself.

Brahmanism: This is the sum of duty: Do nought unto others which would cause you pain if done to you.

Confucianism: Is there one maxim which ought to be acted upon throughout one's whole life? Surely it is the maxim of loving-kindness: Do not unto others what you would not have them do unto you.

Taoism: Regard your neighbor's gain as your own gain, and your neighbor's loss as your own loss.

Zoroastrianism: That nature alone is good which refrains from doing unto others whatsoever is not good for itself.

Many young stage and screen hopefuls are under the impression that to become a star they have to stay out late at night.

At a missionary meeting some young people were discussing the text, "Ye are the salt of the earth." One suggestion after another was made as to the meaning of "salt" in this verse. "Salt imparts a desirable flavor," said one. "Salt preserves from decay," another suggested.

Then at last a Chinese Christian girl spoke out of an experience none of the others had. "Salt creates thirst," she said, and there was a sudden hush in the room. Everyone was thinking, "Have I ever made anyone thirsty for the Lord Jesus Christ?"

——•——

Intolerance

He that will have none but a perfect brother must resign himself to remain brotherless. *Italian Proverb*

Invitation

God put a crook in your arm to hook into another fellow's and bring him to church.

——•——

Come unto Me

(Matthew 11:28)

C - stands for Children
O - stands for Old People
M - stands for Middle-aged People
E - stands for Everybody.
The Christian Parent

——•——

Irritation

Irritation in the heart of a believer is always an invitation to the devil to stand by.

J

Jealousy

Suspicion and jealousy never did help any man in any situation.
ABRAHAM LINCOLN

——•——

Moral indignation is jealousy with a halo. H. G. WELLS

——•——

Stones and sticks are thrown only at fruit-bearing trees. SAADI

——•——

Jew

The Jew

Scattered by God's avenging hand,
Afflicted and forlorn,
Sad wanderers from their pleasant land,
Do Judah's children mourn;
And e'en in Christian countries, few
Breathe thoughts of pity for the Jew.

Yet listen, Gentile, do you love
The Bible's precious page?
Then let your heart with kindness move
To Israel's heritage;
Who traced those lines of love for you?
Each sacred writer was a Jew.

And then as years and ages passed,
And nations rose and fell,
Though clouds and darkness oft were cast
O'er captive Israel
The oracles of God for you
Were kept in safety by the Jew.

And when the great Redeemer came
For guilty man to bleed,
He did not take an angel's name;
No, born of Abraham's seed,
Jesus, who gave His life for you —
The gentle Saviour — was a Jew.

And though His own received Him not,
And turned in pride away,
Whence is the Gentile's happier lot?
Are you more just than they?
No! God in pity turned to you —
Have you no pity for the Jew?

Go, then, and bend your knee to pray
For Israel's ancient race;
Ask the dear Saviour every day
To call them by His grace.
Go, for a debt of love is due
From Christian Gentiles to the Jew.
AUTHOR UNKNOWN

135

Job

Do not pray for an easy task. Pray to be stronger.

———◆———

Don't worry about the job you don't like — someone else will soon have it.

———◆———

The best job insurance is work well done.

———◆———

Nothing turns out right unless someone makes it his job to see that it does.

———◆———

If you aspire to the assignment of big jobs, be faithful in the performance of little ones.

———◆———

Times are always hard for those who seek soft jobs.

———◆———

Looking for a soft job is the job of a soft man.

———◆———

When you make your job important, it will return the favor.

———◆———

Always ask, "Isn't there some better way to do it?"

———◆———

You won't ever get started if you wait for all the conditions to be "just right."

———◆———

If you paddle your own canoe, there's no one to rock the boat.

Joy

Joy shared is joy doubled.

———◆———

Joy is multiplied as it is divided with others.

———◆———

Mirth is never good without God.

———◆———

So rejoice that you can rejoice over your rejoicing.

———◆———

Joy is more divine than sorrow, for joy is bread and sorrow is medicine.
                                H. W. BEECHER

———◆———

Joys are our wings; sorrows our spurs.   RICHTER

I Have Found Joy

I have found such joy in simple
    things —
A plain clean room, a nut-brown loaf
    of bread,
A cup of milk, a kettle as it sings,
And in a leaf-flecked square upon a
    floor,
Where yellow sunlight glimmers
    through a door.

I have found such joy in things that fill
My quiet days, — a curtain's blowing
    grace,
A growing-plant upon a window sill,
A rose fresh-cut and placed within a
    vase,
A table cleared, a lamp beside a chair,
And books I long have loved beside
    me there.

———◆———

If life seems full of struggle, it is also full of joy. Trouble is temporary; happiness is eternal.   CHARLES M. SHELDON

———◆———

Grief can take care of itself, but to get the full value of joy, we must have somebody to divide it with.   MARK TWAIN

———◆———

Judge, Judgment, Justice
See also Accuse, Criticize

Judge not thy friend until thou standest in his place.   RABBI HILLEL

———◆———

The judgments of our fellow men serve as weights to hold us.

———◆———

Judge not without knowledge, nor without necessity and never without charity.   ———◆———

'Tis with our judgments as our
    watches, none
Go just alike, yet each believes
    his own.   ———◆———   ALEXANDER POPE

In giving your judgment, give it boldly and with decision, but never give a reason for it; your judgment, nine times out of ten, will be right, because it is founded on experience; but your reason will probably be wrong, being only an afterthought.
                        GEORGE WHITEFIELD

Too often we judge ourselves by our motives; others by their actions.

———+———

Do Not Judge Too Hard

Pray do not find fault with the man
    that limps —
Or stumbles along the road, unless
    you have worn the shoes he
    wears —
Or struggled beneath his load.
There may be tacks in his shoes that
    hurt, though hidden from view,
Or the burdens he bears placed on
    your back —
Might cause you to stumble, too.

Don't sneer at the man who is down
    today —
Unless you have felt the blow that
    caused his fall,
Or felt the pain that only the fallen
    know.

You may be strong, but still the blows
    that were his,
If dealt to you in the selfsame way
    at the selfsame time —
Might cause you to stagger, too.

Don't be too hard on the man who sins,
    Or pelt him with words or a stone,
    unless you are sure, doubly sure,
That you have not sins of your own.

For you know perhaps if the tempter's
    voice
Should whisper as soft to you as it
    did to him when he went astray,
'Twould cause you to falter, too.
             AUTHOR UNKNOWN

———+———

Justice is truth in action.
             JOSEPH JOUBERT

———+———

My great concern is not whether God is on our side; my great concern is to be on God's side.   ABRAHAM LINCOLN

K

Kindness

Kindness has converted more sinners than zeal, eloquence, or learning.
        DR. HENRIETTA C. MEARS

———+———

Kindness gives birth to kindness.
        SOPHOCLES

———+———

Don't expect to enjoy life if you keep your milk of human kindness all bottled up.

———+———

Kindness is the golden chain by which society is bound together.
        GOETHE

———+———

Forbearance should be cultivated till your heart yields a fine crop of it. Pray for a short memory as to all unkindness.   SPURGEON

———+———

To give pleasure to a single heart by a single kind act is better than a thousand head-bowings in prayer.
        SAADI

So many gods, so many creeds,

———+———

Seeds of Kindness

If you have a friend worth loving,
    Love him. Yes, and let him know
That you love him, ere life's evening
    Tinge his brow with sunset glow.
Why should good words ne'er be said
Of a friend — till he is dead?

If you hear a song that thrills you,
    Sung by any child of song,
Praise it. Do not let the singer
    Wait deserved praises long.
Why should one who thrills your heart
Lack the joy you may impart?

If you hear a prayer that moves you
    By its humble, pleading tone,
Join it. Do not let the seeker
    Bow before his God alone.
Why should not your brother share
The strength of "two or three" in
    prayer?

If you see the hot tears falling
From a brother's weeping eyes
Share them. And by kindly sharing
Own your kinship in the skies.
Why should anyone be glad
When another's heart is sad?
AUTHOR UNKNOWN

———◆———

One can pay back the loan of gold, but one dies forever in debt to those who are kind.   *Malayan Proverb*

———◆———

Two things stand like stone:
Kindness in another's troubles;
Courage in one's own.   LORD DEWAR

———◆———

So many paths that wind and wind;
When just the art of being kind
Is all this sad world needs.
ELLA WHEELER WILCOX

———◆———

He who has conferred a kindness should be silent; he who has received one should speak of it.   SENECA

———◆———

There is no debt so heavy to a grateful mind as a debt of kindness unpaid.
STERNE

———◆———

Forget and Remember

Forget each kindness that you do
As soon as you have done it,
Forget the praise that falls on you
The moment you have won it;
Forget the slander that you hear
Before you can repeat it;
Forget each slight, each spite, each sneer,
Wherever you may meet it.
Remember every kindness done
To you, whate'er its measure;
Remember praise by others won
And pass it on with pleasure;
Remember those who lend you aid
And be a grateful debtor;
Remember every promise made
And keep it to the letter.   ANONYMOUS

———◆———

Knowledge

Knowledge is not what the pupil remembers but what he cannot forget.

What is meant by "knowledge of the world" is simply an acquaintance with the infirmities of men.   DICKENS

———◆———

Half knowledge is worse than ignorance.

———◆———

Knowledge and timber should not be used until they are seasoned.
OLIVER WENDELL HOLMES

———◆———

Nice 'Twould Be

How nice 'twould be if knowledge grew
On bushes as the berries do;
Then we would plant our spelling seed
And gather all the words we need!
And sums from off the slates we'd wipe
And wait for figures to be ripe,
And go into the field and pick
Whole bushels of arithmetic!

Or, if we wished to learn Chinese
We'd just go out and shake the trees,
And grammar, then in all our towns
Would grow with proper verbs and nouns;
And in the garden there would be
Great bunches of geography,
And all the passersby would stop
And marvel at the knowledge crop.
AUTHOR UNKNOWN

———◆———

It is in knowledge as in swimming; he who flounders and splashes on the surface makes more noise and attracts more attention than the pearl diver who quietly dives in quest of treasures at the bottom.   WASHINGTON IRVING

———◆———

Knowledge is power only if a man knows what facts not to bother about.
ROBERT LYND

———◆———

Whoever requires a knowledge and does not use it is like one who plows but does not sow.   SAADI

———◆———

Knowledge humbleth the great man, astonishes the common man, puffeth up the little man.

He who knows, and knows he knows —
He is wise — follow him.
He who knows, and knows not he knows —
He is asleep — wake him.
He who knows not, and knows not he knows not —

He is a fool — shun him.
He who knows not, and knows he knows not —,
He is a child — teach him.

Arabian Proverb

As for me, all I know is that I know nothing. SOCRATES

L

Labor

The greatest labor saving device today is tomorrow.

Labor disgraces no man: unfortunately man occasionally disgraces labor. ULYSSES S. GRANT

Set it down as a fact to which there are no exceptions, that we must labor for all that we have, and nothing is worth possessing or offering to others, which costs us nothing. *The Sunday School*

Language

The six sweetest phrases in the American language:

I love you.
Dinner is served.
All is forgiven.
Sleep until noon.
Keep the change.
Here's that five.

The art of saying appropriate words in a kindly way is one that never goes out of fashion, never ceases to please and is within the reach of the humblest. F. W. FABER

The common faults of American language are an ambition of effect, a want of simplicity and a turgid abuse of terms. JAMES FENIMORE COOPER

Language, like linen, looks best when it is clean.

A lad in Boston, rather small for his age, worked in an office as an errand boy. One day his employers were chaffing him a little about being so small and said, "You will never amount to much; you are too small."

The lad looked at them and said, "Well, I can do something which none of you four men can do."

"What is it?" they asked.

"I don't know that I should tell you," he replied.

They were eager to know and urged him to tell them what he could do that none of them was able to do.

"I can keep from swearing," said the little fellow.

That ended the conversation. *The Sign*

If we put the word "but" after God, there is paralysis. When the word is put before God it is power.

The story is told of Gordon Maxwell, missionary to India, that when he asked a Hindu scholar to teach him the language, the Hindu replied:

"No Sahib, I will not teach you my language. You would make me a Christian."

Gordon Maxwell replied, "You misunderstand me. I am simply asking you to teach me your language."

Again the Hindu responded, "No, Sahib, I will not teach you. No man can live with you and not become a Christian." *Selected*

Kathy tripped over a block. "I always knowed that was going to happen," she remarked to her teacher.

"I always knew it was going to happen," the teacher corrected.

"Oh!" Kathy exclaimed in delighted surprise at the coincidence. "You always knowed it, too?" NEA Journal

The Funniest Language

We'll begin with box, the plural is boxes;
But the plural of ox should be oxen, not oxes;
One fowl is a goose, but two are called geese
But the plural of mouse should never be meese;
You may find a lone mouse or a whole nest of mice
But the plural of house is houses, not hice;
If the plural of man is always called men,
Why shouldn't the plural of pan be called pen?
The cows in the plural may be called cows, or kine;
But a bow, if repeated, is never called bine.
And the plural of vow is vows, never vine.
If I speak of a foot you show me two feet
And I give you a boot, would a pair be called beet?
If one is a tooth and a whole set are teeth
Why shouldn't the plural of booth be called beeth?
If the singular's this and the plural is these
Should the plural of a kiss ever be written keese?
And the one may be that, and the two may be those
Yet hat in the plural would never be hose.
And the plural of cat is cats and not cose.
We speak of brother and also of brethren

But the way we say mother, we never say methren.
Then the masculine pronouns are his, he and him,
But imagine the feminine, she, shis and shim!
So the English, I think you will agree
Is the funniest language you ever did see. AUTHOR UNKNOWN

Laugh, Laughter

Laugh

Build for yourself a strong box,
  Fashion each part with care;
Fit it with hasp and padlock,
  Put all your troubles there.
Hide therein all your failures,
  And each bitter cup you quaff,
Lock all your heartaches within it
  Then — sit on the lid and laugh!

Tell no one of its contents;
  Never its secrets share;
Drop in your cares and worries,
  Keep them forever there,
Hide them from sight so completely,
  The world will never dream half.
Fasten the top down securely,
  Then — sit on the lid and laugh! ANONYMOUS

Laugh and the world laughs with you, complain and you live alone.

A woman without a laugh in her is the greatest bore in existence. WILLIAM THACKERAY

A laugh is worth a hundred groans in any market. LAMB

Whether laughter is healthful or not depends on the size of the fellow you're laughing at!

Laughing is the sensation of feeling good all over, and showing it principally in one spot. JOSH BILLINGS

Laughter is wholesome. God is not so dull as some people make out. Did He not make the kitten to chase its tail? HEINRICH HEINE

We never stop laughing because we are old. We grow old because we stop laughing.

———◆———

He who laughs last laughs best.

———◆———

I am persuaded that every time a man smiles, but much more when he laughs, it adds something to this fragment of life. STERNE

Law, Lawyer

The Law was broken in the people's hearts before it was broken by Moses' hand.

———◆———

There are 35 million laws and no improvement on the Ten Commandments.

———◆———

The laws of God are to be obeyed, not debated.

———◆———

The state that tolerates disrespect for any law breeds defiance to all law.

———◆———

Lawyer: "When I was a boy, my highest ambition was to be a pirate."
Client: "Congratulations."

———◆———

God works wonders now and then;
Behold! a lawyer, an honest man.
BENJAMIN FRANKLIN

———◆———

Layman

The Layman's Beatitudes

Blessed is the man whose calendar contains prayer meeting nights.
Blessed is the man who does not remain away from church because it rains.
Blessed is the man who can stay over an hour in a church service.
Blessed is the man who loves the Lord's work with his pocketbook as well as his heart.
Blessed is the man whose watch keeps church time as well as business time.
Blessed is the man who leaves the back pew for the late comers.
Blessed is the man who does not have a summer "lay-off" from his religion.
Sunday School Digest

It's the Layman

Leave it only to the pastors, and soon the church will die;
Leave it to the womenfolk, the young will pass it by.
For the church is all that lifts us from the coarse and selfish mob,
And the church that is to prosper needs the layman on the job.
Now a layman has his business, and a layman has his joys,
But he also has the training of all our girls and boys;
And I wonder how he'd like it if there were no churches here,
And he had to raise his children in a godless atmosphere.
It's the church's special function to uphold the finer things,
To teach that way of living from which all that's noble springs;
But the pastor can't do it singlehanded and alone,
For the laymen of the country are the church's buildingstones.
When you see a church that's empty, though its doors are open wide,
It's not the church that's dying — it's the laymen who have died.
It's not just by song or sermon that the church's work is done,
It's the laymen of the country who for God must carry on. EDGAR A. GUEST

———◆———

Laziness, Lazy

While some are standing on the promises, others just sit on the premises.

———◆———

A lazy man is good for two things: good for nothing and no good.

———◆———

Experience has taught us that laziness may get a man a good day's rest, but in time it will cost him dearly.
Church Management

———◆———

Doctor: "To be quite candid with you, your trouble is just laziness."
Patient: "Yes, doctor, I know, but what is a scientific name for it? I've got to report to my wife."

Father told his little son that he couldn't go to church because he was suffering from a severe case of voluntary inertia.

"I bet you aren't," the little boy answered, "I bet you're just lazy."

———◆———

Many want to learn the "tricks of the trade" without the trouble of learning the trade.

———◆———

There are lazy minds as well as lazy bodies.   BENJAMIN FRANKLIN

———◆———

We are as lazy as our circumstances permit us to be.

———◆———

An indolent man is just a dead one who can't be legally buried.

———◆———

Leader, Leadership

A Born Leader

I'm paid to be a foreman.
My job is leading men.
My boss thinks I'm a natural,
But if I am, why then,
I wish someone would tell me
Why snow-swept walks I clean,
When in the house sit two grown sons
Who made the football team.
                              AUTHOR UNKNOWN

———◆———

A leader is an ordinary person with extraordinary determination.
                              Southwestern Advocate

———◆———

The mob has many heads, but no brains.

———◆———

Followers will never go any further than their leader.

———◆———

Of a good leader,
When his task is finished, his goal
    achieved,
They will say,
"We did this ourselves."   LAO-TSE

———◆———

A leader is anyone who has two characteristics: First he is going someplace; second he is able to persuade other people to go with him.
                              W. H. COWLEY

Those who participate also contribute.

———◆———

Don't beg men to serve, stimulate them.

———◆———

He who leads without leading others to lead is no leader.

———◆———

Leaders are servers.

———◆———

Be an opener of doors for such as come after thee, and do not try to make the universe a blind alley.
                       RALPH WALDO EMERSON

———◆———

A man who wants to lead the orchestra must turn his back on the crowd.

———◆———

A leader sees three things: what ought to be done, what can be done, and how to do it.

———◆———

A good leader never does anything he can give someone else the privilege of doing.

———◆———

What America Needs

A leader like Moses, who refused to be called the son of Pharaoh's daughter, but was willing to go with God.

Army generals like Joshua, who knew God and could pray and shout things to pass rather than blow them to pieces with atomic energy.

A food administrator like Joseph, who knew God and had the answer to famine.

Preachers like Peter, who would not be afraid to look people in the eye and say, "Repent or perish," and denounce their personal as well as national sins.

Mothers like Hannah, who would pray for a child that she might give him to God, rather than women who are delinquent mothers of delinquent children.

Children like Samuel, who would talk to God in the night hours.

Physicians like Luke, who could care for physical needs and introduce their patients to Jesus Christ who is a specialist in spiritual trouble.

A God like Israel's, instead of the "dollar god," the "entertainment god," and the "auto god."

A Saviour like Jesus, who could and would save from the uttermost to the uttermost. *Quo Vadis, from UEA*

―――♦―――

Christ the Leader

L - oving   Hebrews 2:10
Because He has made the way at such a cost.

E - ssential   Philippians 4:19
Cannot do without Him.

A - bsolute   John 21:22
Must let Him lead altogether.

D - ivine   John 14:6
He knows the way.

E - xcellent   Psalm 23:2, 3
Good company, and He cannot err.

R - eady   Isaiah 48:17
But only becomes ours when we accept Him.

―――♦―――

Learn, Learning

To live is not to learn, but to apply. LEGOUVE

―――♦―――

If you would turn the best schoolmaster out of your life, fail to learn from your mistakes.

―――♦―――

You can't learn much by listening to yourself all the time. *National Motorist*

―――♦―――

We learn only what we accept for our living. DR. WM. HEARD KIRKPATRICK

―――♦―――

Supposing is good, but finding out is better. MARK TWAIN

―――♦―――

Learn from the mistakes of others — you can't live long enough to make them all yourself.

―――♦―――

It's what you learn after you know it all that counts. WILLARD GRIFFIN

―――♦―――

They can't call you an old dog as long as you're learning new tricks.

The great trouble with most men is that those who have been educated become uneducated just as soon as they stop inquiring and investigating life and its problems for themselves. NEWTON D. BAKER

―――♦―――

Yearn to learn.

―――♦―――

And one student told the teacher that an adjective is a word, phrase, or clause that mortifies a noun or pronoun. *NEA Journal*

―――♦―――

The wise man studies others so that he can learn from their mistakes and at their expense.

―――♦―――

Anyone who stops learning is old, whether this happens at twenty or eighty. Anyone who keeps on learning not only remains young but becomes increasingly valuable. *Bible News Flashes*

―――♦―――

Someone has figured out that the peak years of mental activity must be between the ages of four and eighteen.
At four we know all the questions.
At eighteen we know all the answers.

―――♦―――

I can neither eat for you nor learn for you. RALPH W. HOUSE

―――♦―――

Legal

It is easier to make certain things legal than to make them legitimate. S. R. N. CHAMFORT

―――♦―――

Leisure

Leisure is the time you spend on jobs you don't get paid for. *Changing Times*

―――♦―――

Lesson

His Last Regrets

(With apologies to
Clement Clark Moore)

'Twas on Monday before Sunday and all through his head
Not an idea was stirring, not even a thread

Of thought for the Sunday school lesson to learn
To teach those ten boys with ambition to burn.

And Tuesday came on with a decided ambition
To study the lesson, his soul to condition.

And Wednesday slipped by with no preparation
And Thursday escaped with the same consternation.

Now Friday was here and still there was time
To get at his lesson by six fifty-nine.

But Amos 'n Andy his thoughts did envelope
And left him no time the lesson to develop.

But Saturday is free from manual care
To leave him full time his lesson to prepare.

No foolin', he'll get at his lesson tomorrow
And end the glad day with no inward sorrow.

But the day was too filled with un-thought-of-chores –
The flivver to polish and other such lures
That evening came on with no preparation
To teach those ten boys 'gainst worldly temptations.

He'll wait till that evening when all through the house
Not a creature'll be stirring, not even a mouse,
His mind will be clear from annoying confusion
And the lesson he'll learn with the Spirit's infusion.

The supper now ended, the day's labor past,
He'll get at his lesson to prepare it at last
As soon as he glances at the headlines all through
To end up with Dagwood and Palooka, too.

But the day was too strenuous, the supper too good:
He soon fell asleep with no likelihood
Of getting his lesson those "rascals" to teach
He'd try it tomorrow – his achievement to reach.

'Twas the hour before Sunday school when all through the house
Every creature was stirring, yes, even the mouse.
With full desperation he studied in vain
His thoughts to collect and the lesson to gain.

'Twas five minutes to ten and all through his heart
Condemnation was stirring in every part
The school now is over and all his week's flare
Ended up in confusion and perfect despair.

A. L. BROWN, in Sunday School Journal

———✦———

One college student to another: "Never let your lessons interfere with your education."

———✦———

Liberty

God grants liberty only to those who love it, and are always ready to guard and defend it.

DANIEL WEBSTER

———✦———

Your personal liberty ends where my nose begins.

———✦———

Liberty has never come from the government. . . . The history of liberty is the history of the limitations of governmental power, not the increase of it.

WOODROW WILSON

———✦———

They that can give up essential liberty to obtain a little temporary safety deserve neither liberty nor safety.

BENJAMIN FRANKLIN

———✦———

God grant that not only a love of liberty but a thorough knowledge of the rights of men may pervade all the nations of the earth, so that a philosopher may set his foot anywhere on its surface and say, "This is my country."

BENJAMIN FRANKLIN

———♦———

Library

A man's library consists of all the books he has that no one wants to borrow.

———♦———

A sparrow sat on a window sill
And shook his head in doubt
He wondered where those book worms
     were
He'd heard so much about.

———♦———

Lie, Lying

One lie begets another.

———♦———

You can get to the ends of the earth by lying, but you'll never get back.

Russian Proverb

———♦———

Sin has many tools, but a lie is a handle that fits them all.

———♦———

Those who are given to white lies soon become color blind.

———♦———

No man has a good enough memory to be a successful liar.   LINCOLN

———♦———

It is easy to tell one lie, but hard to tell just one.

———♦———

A lie has no legs to support itself — it requires other lies.

———♦———

He who approves a white lie will find the shade growing darker.

———♦———

A lie stands on one leg, truth on two.

BENJAMIN FRANKLIN

———♦———

Mrs. Brown was shocked to learn that Junior had told a lie. Taking the youngster aside for a heart-to-heart talk, she graphically explained the consequences of falsehood:
"A tall black man with red fiery eyes and two sharp horns grabs little boys who tell lies and carries them off at night. He takes them to Mars where they have to work in a dark canyon for fifty years! Now," she concluded, satisfied, "you won't tell a lie again, will you, dear?"
"No, Mom," replied Junior gravely. "You tell better ones."   F. G. KERNAN

———♦———

Life

What Is Life?
Life is what we make it,
Sweet or bitter,
Hot or cold;
As water slaking thirst,
We take it;
Life is either ashes, or pure gold.
The Old Shoemaker

———♦———

It is such a comfort to drop the tangles of life into God's hands and leave them there.

———♦———

Jesus never taught men how to make a living. He taught men how to live.

DR. BOB JONES, SR.

———♦———

Life makes one demand on every living organism; namely, that it come to terms with the situation it confronts, realizing there are two ways to meet a situation. Sometimes you can change the situation; other times you must change yourself.

———♦———

If place I choose, or place I shun,
     My soul is satisfied with none;
But when Thy will directs my way,
     'Tis equal joy to go or stay.

———♦———

However mean your life is, meet it and live it, do not shun it and call it hard names. It is not so bad as you are. The faultfinder will find faults even in Paradise. Love your life, poor as it is.   HENRY DAVID THOREAU

———♦———

Life, like a mirror, never gives back more than we put into it.

———♦———

In the Orient, living is substituted for efficiency and a cup of tea for on-the-dot punctuality.

145

Life bores only when it has no purpose.

————◆————

Three Anchors of Life —
1. I believe God.
2. I belong to God.
3. I serve God.

————◆————

Life is no looseleaf book; each page that is turned remains intact with all that we have penned, and when we've turned the last there is no refill.

FRED BECK

————◆————

Since life is so short, let's make it broader.

————◆————

When young men are beginning life, the most important period, it is often said, is that in which their habits are formed. That is a very important period. But the period in which the ideas of the young are formed and adopted is more important still. For the ideal with which you go forth determines the nature, so far as you are concerned, of everything you meet.

H. W. BEECHER

————◆————

What is put into the first of life is put into all of life.

J. M. PACE

————◆————

Life is a one-way street and we are not coming back.

————◆————

We do not need a new leaf to turn over but a new life to receive.

————◆————

If life is a grind, use it to sharpen your wits.

————◆————

Outline of Life

Tender Teens
 Teachable Twenties
  Tireless Thirties
   Fiery Forties
    Forceful Fifties
     Serious Sixties
      Sacred Seventies
       Aching Eighties
        . . . shortening breath.
        Death,
        Sod . . .
        God.

A handful of good life is worth a bushel of learning.

GEORGE HERBERT

————◆————

A useless life is only an early death.

GOETHE

————◆————

The great use of life is to spend it for something that will outlast it.

WILLIAM JAMES

————◆————

Let God have your life; He can do more with it than you can.

D. L. MOODY

————◆————

The Secret of a Happy Life

The secret of a happy life
Is an industrious hand,
Which gladness finds in earnest work
For noble purpose planned.
It leaves no time for idle fears,
Thoughts morbid or depressed,
But cheerfully it does its part
And leaves to Heaven the rest.

The secret of a happy life
Is in a loving heart
Whose good-will flows to all its kind,
To all would joy impart.
It shares in others' weal and woe;
Is not with self engrossed.
The richest and the happiest heart
Is his who loves the most.

The secret of a happy life
Is a believing soul
Serenely trusting in the power
Which animates the whole.
On earnest, upright, loving lives
Heavens' choicest blessings fall;
The Christ of God within the soul
The crowning joy of all.

CHARLES WENDTE

————◆————

Key Words to Life

1 - 20 years — learning
20 - 30 years — ladies
30 - 40 years — living
40 - 50 years — liberty
50 - 60 years — leisure
60 - 70 years — living

————◆————

There has never yet been a man in our history who led a life of ease whose name is worth remembering.

THEODORE ROOSEVELT

The first years of man's need make provision for the last. SAMUEL JOHNSON

———♦———

Do not take life too seriously; you will never get out of it alive. ELBERT HUBBARD

———♦———

Enjoy your life without comparing it with that of others. MARQUIS DE CONDORCET

———♦———

Calmly, see the mystic Weaver
  Throw His shuttle to and fro:
'Mid the noise and wild confusion,
  Well the Weaver seems to know
What each motion and commotion,
  What each fusion and confusion
In the grand result will show.

———♦———

Beware of the easy road — it always leads down.

———♦———

Life is not salvage to be saved out of the world, but an investment to be used in the world.

———♦———

Life — What Is It?

(James 4:14)

Life Is a Mystery.
  Life itself is thus. Our earthly life, likewise, is often mysterious.
Life Is a Gracious Gift from God.
  There is nothing we count more precious than life.
Life Is a Race.
  It involves preparation, struggle and reward.
Life Is a Journey.
  This speaks of observations, experiences and destination.
Life Is Uncertain.
  This is true as to its content, as well as its length.
Life Is Brief.
  It is like a vapor, the flower, the grass, etc.
Life Is Eternal.
  Death does not end all. ANONYMOUS

———♦———

It is not doing the thing we like, but liking the thing we have to do that makes life happy. GOETHE

Life is a story in volumes three,
  The Past
  The Present
  The Yet-to-be
The first is finished and laid away,
The second we're reading day by day,
The third and last of volume three
  Is locked from sight;
  God keeps the key!

———♦———

Take care of your life and the Lord will take care of your death. GEORGE WHITEFIELD

———♦———

Life is not a cup to be drained, but a measure to be filled.

———♦———

A Bible and a newspaper in every house, a good school in every district — all studied and appreciated as they merit — are the principal support of virtue, morality and civil liberty. BENJAMIN FRANKLIN

———♦———

Life with Christ is an endless hope; without Him a hopeless end.

———♦———

Only God can live a holy life in sinful flesh. GORDON

———♦———

The latter part of a wise man's life is taken up in curing all of the follies, prejudices and false opinions he had contracted in the former. JONATHAN SWIFT

———♦———

Do not despise your situation. In it you must act, suffer and conquer. From every point on earth we are equally near to heaven and the infinite. AMIEL

———♦———

In life, as in driving, there is nothing wrong with wanting to get ahead, but it's not considered good form to blow your horn while passing. *National Motorist*

———♦———

Certainly life expectancy is increasing. Nowadays you can expect anything.

———♦———

Life does not require us to make good; it asks only that we give our best on each new level of experience. HAROLD W. RUOPP

Things That Count

Not what we have, but what we use;
 Not what we see, but what we choose.
These are the things that mar or bless
 The sum of human happiness.

The things near by, not things afar;
 Not what we seem, but what we are.
These are the things that make or break
 That give the heart its joy or ache.

Not what seems fair, but what is true;
 Not what we dream, but the good we do,
These are the things that shine like gems,
 Like stars in fortune's diadems.

Not what we take, but what we give;
 Not as we pray, but as we live,
These are the things that make for peace,
 Both now and after time shall cease.

A Garden We All Can Plant

Four rows of peas:
 Patience,
 Perseverance,
 Promise to win others,
 Prayer.
Three rows of lettuce:
 Let us be unselfish,
 Let us love,
 Let us tithe.
One row of squash:
 Squash indifference.
Four rows of turnips:
 Turn up for church,
 Turn up regularly,
 Turn up to help,
 Turn up with determination.
 AUTHOR UNKNOWN

A holy life will produce the deepest impression. Lighthouses blow no horns; they only shine. D. L. MOODY

Life is a fragment, a moment between two eternities, influenced by all that has preceded, and to influence all that follows. W. E. CHANNING

Life is too short to be little. DISRAELI

Light

Harry Lauter once talked about the man in England who went around with a light on a long pole to light the gas lamps along the street. The man couldn't be seen at the end of the pole but he left a light in the darkness.

The Lord Jesus didn't say, "Let your light so twinkle" — but let it "shine!"

The light that shines the farthest shines brightest at home.

The class had been told about the prodigious rate at which light travels. "Just think," said the teacher, "of light coming to us from the sun at the rate of all those thousands of miles a second. Isn't it wonderful?"

"Not so very," said one lad. "It's downhill all the way!"

Liquor (Alcohol, Temperance)

See Who I Am

I am the greatest criminal in history.
I have killed more men than have fallen in all the wars of the world.
I have turned men into brutes.
I have made millions of homes unhappy.
I have transformed many ambitious youths into hopeless parasites.
I made smooth the downward path for countless millions.
I destroy the weak and weaken the strong.
I make the wise man a fool and trample the fool into his folly.
I ensnare the innocent.
The abandoned wife knows me, the hungry children know me.
The parents, whose child has bowed their gray heads in sorrow, know me.
I have ruined millions and shall try to ruin millions more.
I am alcohol. H. W. GIBSON in Young Pilgrim

148

Statistics show that 10,000 people are killed by liquor where only one is killed by a mad dog; yet we shoot the dog and license the liquor. What sense is there to this? *Bible Crusaders News*

———♦———

The liquor traffic would destroy the church if it could, and the church could destroy the liquor traffic if it would. *National Voice*

———♦———

The last man hired, the first man fired — the man who drinks. *Poster of U. S. Steel Corp.*

———♦———

There are more old drunkards than old doctors. BENJAMIN FRANKLIN

———♦———

The most valued thing in the world is the human brain, and the worst enemy of the brain in modern society is beverage alcohol. DR. GEORGE A. LITTLE

———♦———

A hangover is something to occupy a head that wasn't used the night before.

———♦———

Dignity can't be preserved in alcohol.

———♦———

When wine enters, wisdom goes abroad.

———♦———

To put alcohol in the human brain is like putting sand in the bearing of an engine. THOMAS A. EDISON

———♦———

He is a fool who puts into his mouth that which takes away his brains.

———♦———

Booze builds business up — for the undertaker.

———♦———

Drink is the mother of want and the nurse of crime. LORD BROUGHMAN, 1830

———♦———

First the man takes a drink,
Then the drink takes a drink,
Then the drink takes the man.
Japanese Proverb

———♦———

The tavern keeper likes the drunkard, but he does not want him for a son-in-law. *Greek Primer*

Drink does not drown care, but waters it, and makes it grow faster. BENJAMIN FRANKLIN

———♦———

Better shun the bait than struggle in the snare. DRYDEN

———♦———

William Penn was once advising a drunkard to give up his habit of drinking intoxicating liquors.

"Can you tell me how to do it?" the man asked.

"Yes, friend," Penn replied. "It is just as easy as to open thy hand."

"Convince me of that," the drunkard explained, "and I will promise upon my honor to do as you tell me."

"Well, my friend, when thou findest any vessel of intoxicating liquor in thy hand, open the hand that contains it before it reaches thy mouth, and thou wilt never be drunk again."

This plain advice so delighted the drunkard that he straightway proceeded to follow it.

———♦———

Drunkenness, that worst of evils, makes some men fools, some beasts, some devils. BENJAMIN FRANKLIN

———♦———

The tavern keeper is the only business man who is ashamed of his customers.

———♦———

Sir William Osler, the famed physician, was examining a patient who was a heavy drinker.

"You'll have to cut out alcohol," ordered Osler.

"But, doctor," protested the other, "I've heard it said that alcohol makes people do things better."

"Nonsense," said Osler, "it only makes them less ashamed of doing them poorly." *Listen*

———♦———

Said the glass of beer to the bottle of gin, "I'm not much of a mathematician, but I can
Add to a man's nervous troubles;
Subtract cash from his pocketbook;
Multiply his aches and pains;
Divide his property with liquor sellers, so that

149

Fractions only remain for him. Moreover, I
Take interest from his work, and
Discount his chances for health and
success."

AUTHOR UNKNOWN

——◆——

Listen

Listening is fifty per cent of our
education.

——◆——

A good listener is not only popular
everywhere, but after a while he knows
something.

WILSON MIZNER

——◆——

Always listen to the opinions of
others. It probably won't do you any
good but it will them.

——◆——

A pair of good ears will drink dry a
hundred tongues.

BENJAMIN FRANKLIN

——◆——

If you want your wife to listen, talk
to another woman.

——◆——

Little Things

Little Things

Only a little shriveled seed –
It might be a flower or grass or weed;
Only a box of earth on the edge
Of a narrow, dusty window-ledge;
Only a few scant summer showers;
Only a few clear, shining hours –
That was all. Yet God could make
Out of these for a sick child's sake,
A blossom-wonder as fair and sweet
As ever broke at an angel's feet
Only a life of barren pain,
Wet with sorrowful tears for rain;
Warmed sometimes by a wandering
gleam
Of joy that seemed but a happy dream.
A life as common and brown and bare
As the box of earth in the window
there;
Yet it bore at last the precious bloom
Of a perfect soul in a narrow room –
Pure as the snowy leaves that fold
Over the flower's heart of gold.

HENRY VAN DYKE

Little Things

Oh, it's just the little, homely things,
The unobtrusive, friendly things,
The "Won't-you-let-me-help-you" things
That make the pathway light.
And it's just the jolly, joking things,
The "Laugh-with-me-it's-funny" things,
The "Never-mind-the-trouble" things
That make our world seem bright.

For all the countless, famous things,
The wondrous, record-breaking things,
Those "Never-can-be-equalled" things
That all the papers cite,
Can't match the little, human things,
The "Just-because-I-like-you" things,
Those "Oh-it's-simply-nothing" things,
That make us happy, quite.

So here's to all the little things,
The every-day-encountered things,
The "Smile-and-face-your-trouble"
things,
"Trust God to put it right,"
The "Done-and-then-forgotten" things,
The "Can't-you-see-I-love-you" things,
The hearty "I-am-with-you!" things
That make life worth the fight.

EVA M. HINCKLEY

——◆——

Live, Living

The world owes you a living only
when you have earned it.

——◆——

You can make a good living yet live
a poor life.

——◆——

If we teach a child nothing about
right living we have no reason to complain if he goes wrong. It is not his
fault, it is our neglect.

——◆——

Too much of our living is resolution-
ary and not revolutionary.

——◆——

Live the Gospel first! Tell about it
afterwards!

——◆——

Free to know, free to do – this is
living!

——◆——

A living dog is better than a dead
lion.

Right living will keep you out of jail, but not out of hell; only Christ can do that.

Too many persons live in imitation of Christ instead of in identification with Him. VANCE HAVNER

Work determines what we get out of living; giving determines what we put into living.

The Christian dies to live. D. L. MOODY

Jesus perfectly lived what he perfectly taught. HERMAN H. HORNE

Live among men as if God beheld you; speak to God as if men were listening. SENECA

I live every day as if this were the first day I had ever seen and the last I was going to see. WILLIAM LYON PHELPS

You have not lived a perfect day, even though you have earned your money, unless you have done something for someone who will never be able to repay you. ANONYMOUS

A Negro lady was testifying in court in behalf of her husband and admitted during the questioning that he never worked and she had to support him.

"Why do you live with such a trifling husband?" she was asked.

"Well, it am dis way, I makes de livin' and he makes de livin' worthwhile."

Let us endeavor so to live that when we come to die even the undertaker will be sorry. MARK TWAIN

He that would live in peace and ease
Must not speak all he knows nor judge
all he sees. BENJAMIN FRANKLIN

Life would be a perpetual flea hunt if a man were obliged to run down all the innuendos, inveracities, insinuations and misrepresentations which are uttered against him. H. W. BEECHER

He Truly Lives

Who has a work he can respect.
Who has found a cause he would die for.
Who has a faith that supports him in the days of difficulty.
Who has great causes to live for, regardless of what he has to live on.
Who has great ideas to keep him company in lonely hours.

Your town will be a delightful place to live in if you are a delightful person to live beside. *O'Brannons Between Calls*

There are two things needed in these days: first, for rich men to find out how poor men live; and second, for poor men to know how rich men work. E. ATKINSON

It is better to live for Christ than to wish you had.

This country will not be a really good place for any of us to live in if it is not a really good place for all of us to live in. THEODORE ROOSEVELT

The philosopher says to live and learn but some people just live.

According to doctors, you will live much longer if you give up everything that makes you want to.

Live as if you expected to live a hundred years, but might die tomorrow. ANN LEE

To live the resurrection life in Christ is to lead many to believe in Christ as the resurrection and the life.

Part of the world is living on borrowed time while the rest of it is living on borrowed money.

We will never have life taken in high seriousness by all people unless the best people repudiate shallow and superficial ways of living.

We can always live on less when we have more to live for.

S. STEPHEN MC KENNY

———◆———

Let all live as they would die.

GEORGE HERBERT

———◆———

A good description of modern living: "A senseless whirl which has been spelled in three words — hurry, worry, bury."

Moody Monthly

———◆———

When life seems just a dreary grind,
　And things seem fated to annoy,
Say something nice to someone else
And watch the world light up with
　joy.

AUTHOR UNKNOWN

———◆———

The way you teach is very important, and what you teach is even more important, but how you live is most important.

———◆———

To live well in the quiet routine of life; to fill a little space because God wills it; to go on cheerfully with a petty round of little duties, little avocations; to smile for the joy of others when the heart is aching — who does this, his works will follow him. He may not be a hero to the world, but he is one of God's heroes.

AUTHOR UNKNOWN

———◆———

Livelihood

Don't believe the world owes you a living; the world owes nothing — it was here first.

ROBERT J. BURDETTE

———◆———

Loaf

A sign on the bus station window read, "If you have nothing to do, don't do it around this window."

———◆———

The Bible promises no loaves to the loafer.

———◆———

Father to son: "I can tell that you are going to become a baker by your loaf."

Loneliness, Lonely

Alone I sit
And sip my tea;
I dream of you
Eternally.

It's been so long
Since you were here . . .
Do you sip tea
Alone, my dear?

ELIZABETH WILDT

———◆———

If we spend our life building walls around our private preserves, what right have we to complain if we're lonely?

———◆———

Loneliness is not so much a matter of isolation as of insulation.

HAROLD W. RUOPP

———◆———

People are lonely because they build walls instead of bridges.

J. F. NEWTON

———◆———

It is better to be alone than in bad company.

———◆———

When alone, guard your thoughts; in the family, guard your temper; in company, guard your words.

———◆———

Last summer Jim spent his first week away from home at a summer camp. He was not much of a letter writer, but one day I did receive a card from him. All it said was:
"Dear Mom,
"There are 50 boys here this week but I sure wish there were only 49. Jim."

The Instructor

———◆———

Alone with a book by a fire — that's
　swell.
Alone on the dunes — there's a certain
　spell to that.
Or alone is a pleasant way to go for a
　walk on a stormy day.
It's thrilling alone, with the reins in
　hand
And to be alone, with some work is
　grand.
Alone in a mist, with a moon — that's
　magic.
Alone on a Saturday night — that's
　tragic.

MARGARET ENGLEMAN

Look

Some people never look up until they are flat on their back.

Seven Looks

LOOK BACK — Remember God's
goodness . . . . I Kings 8:56
LOOK UP — In praise. . . . Psalm 103:1
LOOK DOWN — In humility;
in caution. . . . . . . I Corinthians 10:12
LOOK FORWARD—In confidence;
in hope . . . . II Timothy 1:12
LOOK WITHIN — Daily,
thoroughly . . . . Psalm 19:14
LOOK AROUND —
Be vigilant . . . . Hebrews 12:15
LOOK UNTO JESUS . . . . Isaiah 45:22

Lord

If Christ is not Lord of all, He is not Lord at all.

Where the Lord Is

The Lord is *before* His people —
Micah 2:13; John 10:4
The Lord is *behind* His people —
Psalm 139:5
The Lord is *above* His people —
Deuteronomy 33:12; Psalm 63:7; 91:1
The Lord is *beneath* His people —
Deuteronomy 32:11;
Isaiah 40:11; 46:4
The Lord is *around* His people —
Psalm 125:2; 139:3
The Lord is *with* His people —
Numbers 23:21; Matthew 1:23; 28:20
The Lord is in the *midst* of His
people — Isaiah 12:6; Zephaniah 3:17

Lose, Loses

He who loses money loses much; he who loses a friend loses more; but he who loses his spirit loses all.

Love, Love of Christ, Lovers

Love is like the measles, worse if it comes late in life.

Love at first sight never happens before breakfast.

"Yes, Robert, amo is the Latin word meaning 'I love you.' Now what word suggests its opposite?"
"Reno," replied Robert.
The Watchman Examiner

Love is a funny thing,
It's just like a lizard.
It curls up round your heart
And jumps in your gizzard!

Love is like an onion
We taste it with delight
But when it's gone, we wonder
What ever made us bite.

The lasting love knot is tied with just one beau.

The magic of first love is our ignorance that it can ever end. DISRAELI

It is hard to express love with a clenched fist.

Love is swell.
It's so enticing,
It's orange jell,
It's strawberry icing,
It's chocolate russe,
It's roasted goose,
It's ham on rye,
It's banana pie.
Love's all good things without a question,
In other words — it's indigestion!

To My Ever Present Temptation

I have tried to love you lightly
But without success;
To love you very little
And never to excess.
I have sought to love you wisely
But this I cannot do,
For all my vows are shattered
Each time I look at you.
AUTHOR UNKNOWN

They who love are but one step from heaven. JAMES RUSSELL LOWELL

153

LOVE

Remember, we were enjoined only to love our neighbor. We don't have to agree with all his silly ideas.

———♦———

We love according to the way people treat us. EUGENIA PRICE

———♦———

Love never asks how much must I do, but how much can I do. FREDERICK A. AGAR, *Royal Service*

———♦———

There are more people who wish to be loved than there are willing to love. CHAMFORT

———♦———

Interest will begin a hard work. Grit will continue it. But only love makes a man endure to the end.

———♦———

God purposes that we should love Him — not just the things He gives us. *Eternity*

———♦———

The cat and the love you give away always come back to you.

———♦———

Lovers remember everything.

———♦———

Love gives everything, but only to lovers. BALZAC

———♦———

An old man used to go about selling little boxes of cement which could mend all family jars and even broken hearts.

Some only laughed at him, but those who purchased one of the little boxes for a cent or so found a small piece of paper inside. On it was written the word *Love*. What a sure cure for family jars and broken hearts.

———♦———

Children need love, especially when they do not deserve it. HAROLD S. HULBERT

———♦———

Love and a toothache have many cures, but none infallible, except possession and dispossession. BENJAMIN FRANKLIN

———♦———

To love the whole world
For me is no chore;
My only real problem's
My neighbor next door.
C. W. VANDERBERGH

So long as we love, we serve; so long as we are loved by others I would almost say that we are indispensable; and no man is useless while he has a friend. ROBERT LOUIS STEVENSON

———♦———

We must love men ere they will seem worthy of our love. SHAKESPEARE

———♦———

The love that unites Christians is stronger than the differences that divide them.

———♦———

Human beings must be known to be loved; but divine things must be loved to be known. PASCAL

———♦———

If there is a tug-of-war, let the rope be the love of God.

———♦———

Love Is . . .

Slow to suspect — quick to trust,
Slow to condemn — quick to justify,
Slow to offend — quick to defend,
Slow to expose — quick to shield,
Slow to reprimand—quick to forbear,
Slow to belittle—quick to appreciate,
Slow to demand — quick to give,
Slow to provoke — quick to help,
Slow to resent — quick to forgive.
AUTHOR UNKNOWN

———♦———

God's love for us is not a love that always exempts us from trials, but rather, a love that sees us through trials.

———♦———

God is the source of love.
Christ is the proof of love.
Service is the expression of love.
Boldness is the outcome of love.

———♦———

Love is not getting, but giving; not a wild dream of pleasure and a madness of desire — oh, no — love is not that! It is goodness and honor, and peace and pure living — yes, love is that and is the best thing in the world, and the thing that lives longest. VAN DYKE

———♦———

The fact that you have never experienced the love of God does not prove it doesn't exist. EVERT MORGAN

One's love for God is equal to the love one has for the man he loves least.

JOHN J. HUGO

———✦———

When Hudson Taylor was staying in the home of a friend on one occasion, his host asked him, "But are you always conscious of abiding in Christ?"

"While sleeping last night," replied Mr. Taylor, "did I cease to abide in your home because I was unconscious of the fact? We should never be conscious of not abiding in Christ."

———✦———

A little four-year-old boy didn't want to eat the peas his mother had put on his plate.

"If you don't eat these, Bobby, you will have to leave the table," his mother said.

Whereupon Bobby left the table. After a time mother went to look for him and found him in the bathroom.

He had climbed upon a stool and was looking into the mirror. Tears were streaming down his face but he was looking at himself and singing, *"Jesus Loves Me."*

———✦———

Walking down the street one day a lady noticed a little girl leaving the church by herself. When the child passed her, the lady inquired where she had been.

"In there," replied the little girl, pointing to the church.

"And what were you doing in there?" the woman asked.

"Praying," was the prompt reply.

Thinking the child was probably bothered with some problem the lady inquired, "What were you praying for, dear?"

"Nothing," the child replied. "I was just loving Jesus."

M

Magnanimous

Let us be excusers rather than accusers.

———✦———

Write injuries in dust, benefits in marble.

BENJAMIN FRANKLIN

———✦———

Don't look for the flaws as you go
  through life,
And even if you find them,
Be wise and kind and somewhat blind,
And look for the good behind them.

AUTHOR UNKNOWN

———✦———

Any fool can find fault but it takes a man with a great heart to discover the good in others and speak of that good.

———✦———

Have a deaf ear for unkind remarks about others, and a blind eye to the trivial faults of your brethren.

WALTER SCOTT

Seven Things You Never Regret

Showing kindness to an aged person.
Destroying a letter written in anger.
Offering the apology that saves a
  friendship.
Stopping a scandal that was wrecking
  a reputation.
Helping a boy find himself.
Taking time to show your mother consideration.
Accepting the judgment of God on any
  question.

ROY L. SMITH

———✦———

Try

To be so young that nothing can disturb your peace of mind.
To talk health, happiness and prosperity to every person you meet.
To make all your friends feel that there is something in them.
To look on the sunny side of every-

thing and make your optimism come true.

To think only of the best, to work only for the best and to expect only the best.

To be just as enthusiastic about success for others as you are about your own.

To forget the mistakes of the past and press onward to greater achievements in the future.

To wear a cheerful countenance at all times and to have a smile ready for every living creature you meet.

To give so much time to the improvement of yourself that you have no time to criticize others.

To be too large for worry, too noble for anger, too strong for fear and too happy to permit the presence of trouble. *The Rustler*

Maiden

A certain congregation had dwindled in size so much that when the minister said "Dearly Beloved," the maiden lady in the front row thought he was proposing.

———◆———

The maiden lady, chairman of a school organization, was outlining the program for the coming year. "Our basic need," she said, "is a man."

———◆———

Under the bunch of mistletoe,
The homely maiden stands,
And stands, and stands, and stands, and stands,
And stands, and stands, and stands.

———◆———

Manager

A manager is a "glue man" who can hold a good team together and give it leadership, direction and esprit de corps.

———◆———

Man, Manhood, Men

The man wears the pants in the family, but the woman provides the suspenders.

Many a man thinks he's being cultivated when he's only being trimmed.

———◆———

"There are two kinds of men who never amount to very much," Cyrus H. K. Curtis remarked one day to his associate, Edward Bok.

"And what kinds are those?" inquired Bok.

"Those who cannot do what they are told," replied the famous publisher, "and those who can do nothing else."
Sunday School Journal

———◆———

Unknown Man

Oh, unknown man, whose rib I am,
Why don't you come for me?
A lonely, homesick rib I am
That would with others be.
I want to wed — There, now, 'tis said!
(I won't deny and fib) —
I want my man to come at once
And claim his rib!

Some men have thought that I'd be theirs,
But only for a bit;
We found out soon it wouldn't do:
We didn't seem to fit.
There's just one place
The only space
I'll fit (I will not fib) —
I want that man to come at once
And claim his rib!

Oh, don't you sometimes feel a lack,
A new rib needed there?
It's I! Do come and get me soon
Before I have gray hair!
Come, get me, dear!
I'm homesick here!
I want (and I'll not fib) —
I want my man to come at once
And claim his rib. AUTHOR UNKNOWN

———◆———

The Noblest Man

The happiest man that you can know
Is one who daily lives above
The plane where sordidness can grow,
And breathes the atmosphere of love

When ill will bides within a heart,
It brews a venom with a sting
More harmful than a poisoned dart,
And not the least of good will bring.

Revenge and lust and greed are foes
More deadly than the rapier's thrust,
And enmity brings naught but woes
That wisest men cannot adjust.

The noblest man is one who will
Not harbor evil in his breast,
But fits it for love's domicile
That every joy may be his guest.

REV. WILLIAM JAMES ROBINSON

Measure of a Man

Not — how did he die?
But — how did he live?
Not — what did he gain?
But — what did he give?
These are the units
To measure the worth
Of a man as a man
Regardless of birth.

Not — what was his station?
But — had he a heart?
And how did he play
His God-given part?
Was he ever ready
With a word of good cheer,
To bring back a smile,
To banish a tear?

Not — what was his church?
Nor — what was his creed?
But — had he befriended
Those really in need?
Not — what did the sketch
In the newspapers say?
But — how many were sorry
When he passed away?

AUTHOR UNKNOWN

Men will always be what the women make them; if, therefore, you would have men great and virtuous, impress upon the minds of women what greatness and virtue are. ROUSSEAU

Some men depend entirely upon themselves. Others marry.

Man was made before woman, and perhaps the reason was to give him time to think up some answers to her first questions. Glendale News Press

Average man: one who has had unusual expenses every month of his life — but expects none next month.

It may be a man's world, but we'll give you odds that it's in his wife's name. Glendale News Press

Manners

The test of good manners is to be able to put up pleasantly with bad ones. WENDELL WILKIE

A bird in the hand is bad table manners. National Motorist

The society of woman is the foundation of good manners. GOETHE

Manners are the happy ways of doing things.

No amount of manner can make up for matter when making a speech.

Manners is the ability to say, "No, thank you," when you're still hungry.

Marriage

Slippery ice — very thin;
Pretty girl — tumbled in.
Saw a fellow on the bank;
Gave a shriek — then she sank.
Boy on hand — heard her shout;
Jumped right in — pulled her out.
Now he's hers — very nice,
But she had to break the ice.

Success in marriage consists not only in finding the right mate, but also in being the right mate.

A man and his wife were getting along just fine — until the other day when she decided to return home.

157

MARRIAGE

There'd be less fuss in married life
  If husbands would extend
The selfsame courtesy to a wife
  That they do to an average friend;
Or even a little less
  Would be o.k., I guess.
                    W. E. FARBSTEIN

———◆———

"Doctors say that married men live longer than bachelors," the young miss said to the bachelor.

"Well, I've heard that, too," he replied, "but my married friends claim that it only seems longer."

———◆———

The sum which two married people owe to one another defies calculation. It is an infinite debt, which can only be discharged through all eternity.
                    GOETHE

———◆———

It might be said that a wedding ring is a sort of tourniquet which is worn on a girl's left hand to stop her circulation.

———◆———

Usher, passing collection plate at church wedding: "Yes, ma'am, it is unusual, but the father of the bride requested it."

———◆———

When it comes to such activity as painting a room or pruning a tree, I've learned my wife's editorial "we" means ME!

———◆———

After man came woman and she has been after him ever since.

———◆———

When the late Mr. and Mrs. Henry Ford celebrated their golden wedding anniversary, a reporter asked them, "To what do you attribute your 50 years of successful married life?"

"The formula," said Ford, "is the same formula I have always used in making cars — just stick to one model."

———◆———

A man never realizes his insignificance until he gets married.
                    Town Journal

———◆———

Marriage begins when you sink in his arms and ends with your arms in the sink.

"How come you never married?"

"It was like this. I kept looking for an ideal woman."

"And you never found her?"

"Oh, sure, but just my luck — she was looking for the ideal man."

———◆———

Keep thy eyes wide open before marriage, and half shut afterwards.
                    BENJAMIN FRANKLIN

———◆———

The average wife remembers when and where she got married. What escapes her is why.

———◆———

A neighbor's four-year-old daughter confided to me one day: "When I grow up I'm going to marry Danny."

I asked her why she was going to marry the boy next door and she replied seriously: "I have to. I'm not allowed to cross the street where the other boys live."
                    The Instructor

———◆———

It seems that Rusty misunderstood what the preacher said at his uncle's wedding, because later he was overheard re-enacting it in play, "Rosemary, do you take this man for your awful wedded husband?"
                    Presbyterian Life

———◆———

"Where have you been the last three hours?" demanded the minister's wife, annoyed.

"I met Mrs. Jones on the street and asked how her married daughter was getting along," sighed the weary pastor, "so she told me."

———◆———

Muddle at home make husbands roam.

———◆———

Yawn: Nature's provision for letting married men open their mouths.

———◆———

Doing housework for ten dollars a week is domestic service — but doing it for nothing is matrimony.

———◆———

Marriage is like a cafeteria, you can look over all the dishes, then choose one and pay later.

The sea of matrimony is filled with hardships.

———♦———

It takes two to make a marriage — a single girl and an anxious mother.

———♦———

The way to fight a wife is with your hat — grab it and run.

———♦———

Jack: "Do you tell your wife everything?"

Jim: "No, what she doesn't know won't hurt me."

———♦———

A man always chases a woman until she catches him.

———♦———

Honeymoon: The period between "I do" and "You'd better."

———♦———

"We've been married a year and never quarreled. If a difference of opinion arises and I'm right, my husband gives in."

"And what if he's right?"

"That has never occurred."

———♦———

"John is two-thirds married," said his sister to a friend.

"How's that?"

"Well, he's willing and the preacher is willing."

———♦———

Mature, Maturity

Few Christians ever grow up. They merely change their play things.

———♦———

A Maturity I.Q. Check-up

1. A mature person does not take himself too seriously — his job, yes!
2. A mature person keeps himself alert in mind.
3. A mature person does not always "view with alarm" every adverse situation that arises.
4. A mature person is too big to be little.
5. A mature person has faith in himself which becomes stronger as it is fortified by his faith in God.
6. A mature person never feels too great to do the little things and never too proud to do the humble things.
7. A mature person never accepts either success or failure in themselves as permanent.
8. A mature person never accepts any one of his moods as permanent.
9. A mature person is one who is able to control his impulses.
10. A mature person is not afraid to make mistakes.   LEONARD WEDEL

———♦———

So far in the history of the world, there have never been enough mature people in the right places.
GEORGE CHISHOLM

———♦———

You are young only once, but you can stay immature indefinitely.
R & R Magazine

———♦———

Maxims

Three things most difficult:
To keep a secret.
To forget an injury.
To make good use of leisure.   CHILD

———♦———

Early to bed and early to rise,
Makes a man healthy, wealthy and wise.   BENJAMIN FRANKLIN

———♦———

Modern version of the above:
Late to bed and early to rise
Makes a man baggy under the eyes.

———♦———

Four New England Maxims:
Eat it up.
Wear it out.
Make it do.
Do without.
Quoted by CALVIN COOLIDGE

———♦———

Meditation

Meditation is mental mastication.

———♦———

Every factor of the Bible is meant to be a factor of life.

Meditation — thinking with a view of doing.

————◆————

A Moment with Him

We mutter and sputter,
We fume and we spurt;
We mumble and grumble,
Our feelings get hurt;
We can't understand things,
Our vision grows dim,
When all that we need is
A moment with Him.   *Selected*

————◆————

Meet, Meeting

The pastor noticed a man who came way down front for service.

Afterwards the pastor spoke to the man and asked, "How was it that you came and sat right in front, being a stranger here?"

"Oh," said the man, "I'm a bus driver and I just came to see how you get everyone to the rear of the building."

————◆————

A model meeting:
Participated in by everybody;
Monopolized by nobody;
Where everybody is somebody.

————◆————

After a speaker had wearied the Sunday school assembly he asked, "What shall I say next?"

A small boy near the front answered promptly: "Say amen and sit down."

————◆————

Memory

Memory is the receptacle and sheath of all knowledge.   CICERO

————◆————

Memory is the sheath in which the sword of the Lord is kept.

————◆————

One of the best uses of memory is to remember to forget the unpleasant things.

————◆————

Don't worry if you start losing your memory. Just forget about it.

Many complain of their memory, few of their judgment.   BENJAMIN FRANKLIN

Memory alone is a poor substitute for thought.

————◆————

"Say the Bible words, 'God is Love,' after me," the kindergarten teacher asked her class.

And so, in unison they said, "God is love after me."

————◆————

Mental

Jumping at conclusions is not nearly as good a mental exercise as digging for facts.

————◆————

Fog is exceedingly dangerous to drive in, especially if it's mental.
    Presbyterian Life

————◆————

Ten Rules for Mental Health

1. I will mind my own business and not gossip.
2. I will not wear my feelings on my sleeve or be so sensitive that I look for personal offenses or slights.
3. I will wear a smile. When I am gloomy, I will go away and hide rather than inflict myself on others.
4. I will be considerate of others.
5. I will not be headstrong.
6. I will play the game of life on the square.
7. I will hold my temper and each night ask God to forgive me as I have forgiven my neighbors.
8. I will face the world each morning with confidence, determined to be as happy and brave as I can.
9. I will move into battle for a worthy cause.
10. I will not be too egotistical to pray.
    Milwaukee Road Magazine

————◆————

Mercy

Blessed are the merciful for they shall obtain mercy.

————◆————

Teach me to feel another's woe
To hide the fault I see;
That mercy I to others show,
That mercy show to me.   *Selected*

God's wrath comes by measure; His mercy without measure.

———◆———

The quality of mercy is not strained;
It droppeth as the gentle rain from heaven
Upon the place beneath: it is twice blest;
It blesseth him that gives and him that takes:
'Tis mightiest in the mightiest; it becomes
The throned monarch better than his crown.   SHAKESPEARE

Methods

Be sure your method is modern but your message old-fashioned.

———◆———

An old-fashioned faith with modern methods makes your teaching effective.

———◆———

Mind

The human mind is the greatest tramp in the universe. Some of you are in China right now!   WM. M. RUNYAN

———◆———

The neurotic builds castles in the sky. The psychotic lives in them. The psychiatrist collects the rent.

———◆———

The worth of the mind consisteth not in going high, but in marching orderly.   MICHEL DE MONTAIGNE

———◆———

Some minds are like concrete — thoroughly mixed and permanently set.

———◆———

"Closed for Repairs" should be posted on a lot of open minds.

———◆———

In the scale of destinies, brawn will never weigh so much as brain.

———◆———

Minds are like parachutes — they only function when open.   LORD DEWAR

———◆———

The easiest way to get a reputation for possessing a superior mind is to nod approval and let the other fellow do all the talking.

Cobwebs form in the unused human attic.

———◆———

The greatest undeveloped territory in the world lies under your hat.

———◆———

I have a photographic memory. My brain is just like a negative — all it needs is developing.

———◆———

One day a young man had an accident: He was struck with a thought.

———◆———

You can lead a horse to water but you can't make him think.

———◆———

Think, do not guess.

———◆———

There's nothing more useless than a train of thought which carries no freight.   BILLY B. VAN

———◆———

The brain is no stronger than its weakest think.

———◆———

Give your mind to Christ that you may be guided by His wisdom.
                                        Eternity

———◆———

Sometimes when a person thinks his mind is getting broader, it is just his conscience stretching.   Tid-Bits

———◆———

Keep God's love in your mind as well as your heart.

———◆———

The one thing worse than a vacant mind is one filled with spiteful thoughts.

———◆———

Many men boast of an open mind when it really is only a blank space.

———◆———

When the tongue is making 1200 revolutions a minute, the brain must be in neutral.

———◆———

It wouldn't be so bad to let one's mind go blank if one always remembered to turn off the sound.

———◆———

Man's mind, stretched to a new idea, never goes back to its original dimensions.   OLIVER WENDELL HOLMES

People sometimes grow so broad-minded that their thinking gets shallow.

———◆———

Little minds are wounded too much by little things; great minds see all, and are not even hurt. LA ROCHEFOUCAULD

———◆———

A man cannot think constantly of himself without being discouraged. DAVID GRAYSON

———◆———

It takes a strong mind to hold an unruly tongue.

———◆———

Quiet minds cannot be perplexed or frightened, but go on in fortune or misfortune at their own private pace, like a clock during a thunderstorm. ROBERT LOUIS STEVENSON

———◆———

Vacant lots and vacant minds usually become dumping grounds for rubbish.

———◆———

The absent-minded professor called his biology class to order shortly after the lunch hour.

"Our special work this afternoon," he said, "will be cutting up and inspecting the inward workings of a frog. I have a dead frog here in my pocket to be used as a specimen."

He reached into his pocket and pulled out a paper sack, shook its contents on the table and out rolled a nice looking ham sandwich. The professor looked at it, perplexed, scratched his head and muttered:

"That's funny; I distinctly remember eating my lunch." *Selected*

———◆———

Minister

A burglar had entered a poor minister's house at midnight, but was disturbed by the awakening of the occupant of the room he was in.

Drawing his weapon, he said, "If you stir you are a dead man. I'm hunting for your money."

"Let me get up and turn on the light," said the minister, "and I'll hunt with you."

A strong and faithful pulpit is no mean safeguard to a nation's life.

———◆———

The former minister and his wife decided to attend the church social of his previous parish.

The new minister greeted his predecessor heartily. "I'm very pleased to see you," he said, "and this must be your most charming wife?"

"This," the other replied, "is my only wife."

———◆———

It may be that you don't like your minister. Then here is a tested prescription by which you can get rid of him:

1. Look him straight in the eye when he's preaching, and maybe say "amen" occasionally. The man will preach himself to death in a short time.

2. Start paying him whatever he is worth. Having been on starvation wages for years, he'll promptly eat himself to death.

3. Shake hands with him, tell him he's doing a good job. He'll work himself to death.

4. Rededicate your own life to God and ask the minister to give you some church work to do. Very likely he'll keel over with heart failure.

5. If all else fails, this one is certain to succeed — get your congregation to unite in prayer for him. He will soon be so effective that some larger church will take him off your hands. *Presbyterian Life*

———◆———

The church elders in the little New Hampshire town had voted to keep their minister in spite of his radical tendencies. A visitor to the village, knowing their extremely narrow beliefs, commended one of the elders for having taken such a broad view.

"Broad view, nonsense!" retorted the elder. "We all know the dominie has dangerous ideas, but we'd rather have him here." The elder winked a shrewd eye. "If he wasn't here, he'd be somewhere else. *There* people might listen to him." *Coronet*

Johnny and the Ministry

My folks is Methodists, and so
When conference comes our way, you
    know,
Or some big meetin' is in town
That brings a lot of preachers 'round,
Why, Mother opens wide the door
And entertains a few — or more —
            Of preachers.

And don't I like to see 'em come?
I tell you what, we're goin' some
When we have chicken twice a day,
And fruit that Mother's put away
For winter — jam and preserves!
She sure gets reckless when she serves
            The preachers.

And I can't help a-thinkin' — well,
When I set there and hear 'em tell
About the boys *they* used to be,
Just little chaps like Joe and me,
And had to milk, and chop the wood —
That they must find it mighty good,
            Bein' preachers.

And then they sometimes want to know
If I don't think I'd like to go
To Afriky as soon's I can,
And help to save my fellowman;
But I don't 'spress no special haste,
'Cause cann'bals has an awful taste
            For preachers.

I'd whole lot ruther, when I'm grown,
Just be a preacher here at home.
There's drawbacks even then, of course,
Some things is better, and some worse,
But when they go a-visitin', why,
There's allus chicken and pumpkin pie
            For preachers.
                    FRANCES POINDEXTER

------♦------

Miracles

A sixth grade girl's definition of a miracle: "Something extraordinary that happens without any strings attached."

------♦------

Miracles

There are those who doubt the story
Of the fishes and the bread —
I have watched a daffodil lifting
From its cheerless winter bed.

There are those who say that Jesus
Never walked upon the sea —
I have learned to hear the willows
Whispering strange things to me.
"Lazarus," some wise folks tell me,
"Was not dead, when Jesus came!"
I have watched the spring returning
In a green and fragrant flame.
                    AUTHOR UNKNOWN

------♦------

Misfortune

The greatest misfortune of all is not to be able to bear misfortune. *Bias*

------♦------

Misquotes, Misconceptions

The Lord is my shepherd, I can do what I want.

------♦------

"He anointeth my head with coal oil," said the little boy when quoting the twenty-third Psalm.

------♦------

Three boys about four years of age were displaying a new toy. One boy said, "Let's see your gun."
The other said, "It's not a gun, it's a pistol!"
Our four-year-old daughter added, "I know what a pistol is! Our minister talks about one every Sunday."
                    Christian Parent

------♦------

A junior high school student wrote about the "writ of hideous corpus" in an examination.
Another junior high student quoted thus from the Declaration of Independence: ". . . Every man should be divided equal." *NEA Journal*

------♦------

Missionary, Missions

Visions without work is visionary; work without vision is mercenary; together they are missionary.

------♦------

A true missionary is God's man in God's place, doing God's work in God's way for God's glory.

------♦------

The one calling not overcrowded is the missionary calling.

MISSIONARY

The Missionary's Equipment

A life yielded to God and controlled by His Spirit.

A restful trust in God for the supply of all needs.

A sympathetic spirit and a willingness to take a lowly place.

Tact in dealing with men and adaptability toward circumstances.

Zeal in service and steadfastness in discouragement.

Love for communion with God and for the study of His Word.

Some experience and blessing in the Lord's work at home.

A healthy body and a vigorous mind.

HUDSON TAYLOR

A worthy vicar in a rural parish waxed eloquent in the interest of foreign missions one Sunday, and was surprised on entering the village shop during the week to be greeted with marked coldness by the woman who kept it.

On asking the cause, the good woman produced a half crown from a drawer, and throwing it down before him, said:

"I marked that coin and put it in the plate last Sunday, and here it is back in my shop. I know well them poor Africans never got the money!"

An African pastor asked missionaries leaving on furlough to "tell our friends in America that we do not have refrigerators and other modern contrivances. Tell them that we could even dispense with automobiles, but tell them we cannot do without the Gospel of the Son of God."

The Lordship of Jesus Christ is the first step in missions.   J. ALLEN BLAIR

The missionary enterprise is not the church's afterthought; it is Christ's forethought.   HENRY VAN DYKE

A New Hebrides chieftain sat peacefully reading the Bible, when he was interrupted by a French trader.

"Bah," he said in French. "Why are you reading the Bible? I suppose the missionaries have got hold of you, you poor fool. Throw it away! The Bible never did anyone any good."

Replied the chieftain, calmly, "If it weren't for this Bible, you'd be in my kettle there by now!"   Selected

Out of fifty who offer their lives for missionary service, only twelve do anything; four go to the field and only one returns a second time.

The missionary can know that he has been sent, that he is safe and that he is supplied by God.   ALAN REDPATH

Where there is one who does not know Jesus Christ there is a mission field.   Eternity

What are the churches for but to make missionaries?

What is education for but to train them?

What is commerce for but to carry them?

What is money for but to send them?

What is life itself for but to fulfill the purpose
of Missions!
the enthroning of Jesus
in the hearts of men?
AUGUSTUS H. STRONG

I Believe in Missions

Because the greatest mission ever known was when God sent His only begotten Son into the world to save it.

Because the world will never be brought to Christ until men bring Christ to the world.

Because Jesus Himself taught us that missions was the only way to make disciples.

Because I am a disobedient lover of Jesus if I do not obey His command when He said . . . "Go."

Because if salvation means everything

164

to me, I cannot be happy unless I share it with others.

Because a Christian who does not believe in missions always gets narrow and loses his world vision.

Because the missionary is the greatest hope of the world in its present historical crises.   CHARLES M. SHELDON

———◆———

Bessie's mother gave her a quarter just as the minister came to call.

"Ah, Bessie," the pastor said, "I see you have a shiny new coin. Why don't you give to the missions?"

"I thought about that," the girl answered, "But I think I'll buy a soda and let the druggist give it to the missions."
    Together

———◆———

Mistake, Mistakes

With mistakes, like a lot of other things, it isn't the initial cost — it's the upkeep.

———◆———

To err is human, but if the eraser wears out before the pencil, you're overdoing it a bit.   *National Motorist*

———◆———

To err is human, to forgive is divine.   POPE

———◆———

He who never made a mistake never made anything.

———◆———

Everyone is liable to make mistakes, but fools practice them.

———◆———

To err is human, to repent divine; to persist devilish.

———◆———

The man who never makes a mistake probably gets his salary from one who does.   *Trailer Talk*

———◆———

When a fellow makes the same mistake twice he's got to own up to carelessness or cussedness.   G. H. LORIMER

———◆———

Money

Riches may have wings all right, but all I ever see is the tail feathers.

That money talks I will agree.
It always says good-by to me.
    ALAN DORSEY

———◆———

A fool and his money are welcome everywhere.

———◆———

The one person you have to watch if you're going to save money is yourself.

———◆———

A man whom others called poor, but who had just enough fortune to support himself, went about the country in the simplest way, studying and enjoying the life and beauty of it.

He once talked with a great millionaire who was engaged in business, working at it daily, and getting richer each week. The poor man said to the millionaire, "I am a richer man than you are."

"How do you figure that?" asked the millionaire.

"Why," he replied, "I have as much money as I want, and you haven't."
    Sunday School Chronicle

———◆———

"How do you manage to get money from your husband?"

"It's easy. I just say I'm going back to mother and he hands me the fare."

———◆———

Today, after you make money, you have to hire an accountant to explain how you did it.

———◆———

Money is a good servant, but a poor master.   BONHOURS

———◆———

It is known that Lincoln had no great admiration for mere financial success. "Financial success," he once said, "is purely metallic. The man who gains it has four metallic attributes: gold in his palm, silver on his tongue, brass in his face, and iron in his heart!"
    This Day

———◆———

The proper use of money is the only advantage there is in having it.

———◆———

Money is made round to slip through your fingers.   EDWIN L. BROOKS

165

MONEY

Spend less than you earn and you'll never be in debt. *Amish Proverb*

———◆———

A farmer once went to hear John Wesley preach. The great leader was dealing with the question of money, and was examining it under three divisions.

His first thought was. "Get all you can."

The farmer nudged his neighbor and said: "That man has got something in him; it is admirable preaching!"

Wesley reached his second thought. "Save all you can."

The farmer became quite excited. "Was there ever anything like this!" he said. The preacher denounced thriftlessness and waste, and the farmer rubbed his hand as he thought, *all this have I been taught from my youth up.* What with getting and with hoarding, it seemed to him that "salvation" had come to his house.

But Wesley went on to his third thought which was, "Give all you can."

"Oh, dear," exclaimed the farmer, "he's gone and spoiled it all!"

Getting without giving makes only stagnant pools of men and women.

———◆———

Take care of your pennies — and the dollars will take care of your heirs and their lawyers.

———◆———

A beggar will never be bankrupt.

———◆———

Not only will a man rob God, but he will take an income tax deduction on it.

———◆———

A fool and his money are soon parted.

———◆———

There are no pockets in a shroud. ELD

———◆———

If you want dough do what the word says, "Do."

———◆———

I have learned that money is not the measure of a man, but it is often the means of finding out how small he is. OSWALD J. SMITH

It is better to have your bank in heaven than to have your heaven in a bank.

———◆———

A six-year-old went into a bank and asked to see the president. A courteous clerk showed her into his private office. She explained that her girls' club was raising money for a new club house and would he please contribute?

The banker laid a dollar and a dime on the desk and said, "Take your choice, Miss."

She picked up the dime and said, "My mother always taught me to take the smallest piece." Picking up the dollar bill also, she added: "But so I won't lose this dime, I'll take this piece of paper to wrap it up in." *National Motorist*

———◆———

Dollars go farther when accompanied by sense.

———◆———

Mr. Average American spends only 5c a day for religious and welfare causes. In contrast to this nickel, each day he spends 9c for tobacco, 15c for alcoholic beverages, 22c for recreation, 58c for transportation including foreign travel, 59c for taxes, $1.12 for food and $2.30 for other household expenses such as rent, clothing, savings, medical and miscellaneous expense. *Southern Baptist Handbook*

———◆———

Money talks all right; but in these days a dollar doesn't have enough cents to say anything worthwhile.

———◆———

He who works only for money seldom gets far.

———◆———

A fool and his money are soon petted.

———◆———

When your outgo exceeds your income, your upkeep is your downfall. *Executive Digest*

———◆———

The Scotchman sent an indignant letter to the editor of the newspaper. He said that if any more stories about stingy Scotchmen appeared in the columns, he was going to stop borrowing the paper.

Hard work is the yeast that raises the dough.

———•———

When it comes to money, enough is enough — no man can enjoy more.

ROBERT SOUTHEY

———•———

One reason why it's hard to save money is that our neighbors are always buying something we can't afford.

———•———

People are funny; they spend money they don't have, to buy things they don't need, to impress folks they don't like.

———•———

A banker is a man who will loan you money if you prove to him you don't need it.

———•———

If money is your only hope for independence, you will never have it. The only real security that a man can have in this world is a reserve of knowledge, experience and ability.

HENRY FORD

———•———

Budget: a system of reminding yourself that you can't afford the kind of living you've grown accustomed to.

Changing Times

———•———

A small boy came home from Sunday school and began emptying his pockets of money — pennies, nickels and dimes — while his parents gasped.

"Where did you get all that money?" The youngster replied, "At Sunday school. They've got bowls of it."

San Antonio Express

———•———

The younger generation will learn the value of money when it begins paying off our debts.

———•———

$1.00 spent for lunch lasts five hours.
$1.00 spent for a necktie lasts five weeks.
$1.00 spent for a cap lasts five months.
$1.00 spent for an auto lasts five years.
$1.00 spent for a railroad lasts five decades.
$1.00 spent in God's service lasts for eternity.

ROGER W. BABSON

Some people are in debt because they spend all their neighbors think they make.

———•———

In the old days a man who saved money was a miser; nowadays he's a wonder.

ANONYMOUS

———•———

If you would lose a troublesome visitor, lend him money.

FRANKLIN

———•———

A London paper offered a prize for the best definition of money. This was the winning answer:

Money is an instrument that can buy you everything but happiness and pay your fare to every place but heaven.

———•———

How America Spends Her Dollars

Gambling ...... 30 Billion Dollars
Crime .... 20 Billion Dollars
Alcoholic
    Beverages .... 9.05 Billion Dollars
Tobacco ....5,373 Billion Dollars
Religious and
    Welfare ......3,356 Billion Dollars
Dog Food ..... 175 Million Dollars
Foreign Missions 130 Million Dollars

The Evangel

———•———

Money is that which, having not, we want; having, want more; having more, want more still; and the more we get the less contented we are.

———•———

Money in the Bible

A farthing would equal one and one-half cents.

A gerah would be worth about three cents.

A shekel of gold would equal eight dollars.

A shekel of silver would equal about fifty cents.

A mite would be less than a quarter of a cent.

A piece of silver or a penny would equal thirteen cents.

A talent of gold would equal thirteen hundred dollars.

Money, like flowing water, when it becomes stagnant, is less useful.

———◆———

Money isn't everything . . . but it's way ahead of whatever is in second place.

———◆———

Money and time are the heaviest burdens of life, and the unhappiest of all mortals are those who have more of either than they know how to use.   JOHNSON

Mother

God could not be everywhere, and so He made mothers.   *Jewish Proverb*

———◆———

Heaven is at the feet of mothers.   *Persian Proverb*

———◆———

An ounce of mother is worth a pound of clergy.   *Spanish Proverb*

———◆———

Mother is the name for God in the lips and hearts of little children.   WILLIAM MAKEPEACE THACKERAY

———◆———

He who takes the child by the hand takes mother by the heart.   *Danish Proverb*

———◆———

I think it must somewhere be written, that the virtues of the mothers shall be visited on their children as well as the sins of the fathers.   DICKENS

———◆———

The sweetest face in all the world to me,
Set in a frame of shining golden hair,
With eyes whose language is fidelity;
This is my mother. Is she not most fair?   MAY RILEY SMITH

———◆———

An old-timer is one who can remember when a baby sitter was called mother.

———◆———

It is easy to pick out the children whose mothers are good housekeepers; they are usually found in other yards.

———◆———

I don't think there are enough devils in hell to take a young person from the arms of a godly mother.   BILLY SUNDAY

Where there is a mother in the home, matters speed well.   A. B. ALCOTT

———◆———

The mother's heart is the child's schoolroom.   HENRY WARD BEECHER

———◆———

Men are what their mothers make them.   EMERSON

———◆———

The sweetest sounds to mortals given
Are heard in mother, home and heaven.   WILLIAM GOLDSMITH BROWN

———◆———

The future destiny of the child is always the work of the mother.   NAPOLEON BONAPARTE

———◆———

All that I am or hope to be, I owe to my angel mother.   ABRAHAM LINCOLN

———◆———

You may have tangible wealth untold;
Caskets of jewels and coffers of gold;
Richer than I you can never be —
I had a mother who read to me.   STRICKLAND GILLILAN

———◆———

Oh, the comfort, the inexpressible comfort of feeling safe with a person, having neither to weigh thoughts nor measure words, but pour them all right out just as they are, chaff and grain together, knowing that a faithful hand will take and sift them, keep what is worth keeping and then with the breath of kindness blow the rest away. This is mother.   *Selected*

———◆———

Most of all the other beautiful things in life come by twos and threes, by dozens and hundreds. Plenty of roses, stars, sunsets, rainbows, brothers, and sisters, aunts and cousins, but only one mother in the whole world.   KATE DOUGLAS WIGGIN

———◆———

Men and women frequently forget each other, but everyone remembers mother.   JEROME PAINE BATES

———◆———

Of all the men I have known, I cannot recall one whose mother did her level best for him when he was little, who did not turn out well when he grew up.   FRANCES PARKINSON KEYES

She could not paint, nor write, nor
    rhyme
Her footprints on the sands of time,
As some distinguished women do;
    Just simple things of life she knew —
Like tucking little folks in bed,
    Or soothing someone's aching head.

She was no singer, neither blessed
    With any special loveliness
To win applause and passing fame;
    No headlines ever blazed her name.
But, oh, she was a shining light
    To all her loved ones, day and night!

Her home her kingdom, she its queen;
    Her reign was faithful, honest, clean,
Impartial, loving, just, to each
    And every one she sought to teach.
Her name? Of course, there is no other
In all the world so sweet — just
    Mother!   MAY ALLREAD BAKER

———◆———

A mother is the only person on earth
who can divide her love among ten
children and each child still have all
her love.

———◆———

Mother

The noblest thoughts my soul can
    claim,
The holiest words my tongue can
    frame,
Unworthy are to praise the name
    More sacred than all other.
An infant, when her love first came —
A man, I find it just the same;
Reverently I breath her name,
    The blessed name of mother.
    GEORGE GRIFFITH FETTER

———◆———

To Mother — At Set of Sun

As once you stroked my thin and silver
    hair
    So I stroke yours now at the set of
    sun.
I watch your tottering mind, its day's
    work done,
    As once you watched with forward-
    looking care
My tottering feet. I love you as I
    should.

Stay with me; lean on me; I'll make
    no sign.
I was your child, and now time makes
    you mine.
Stay with me yet a while at home,
    and do me good.   AUTHOR UNKNOWN

———◆———

Motive

Many a good thing is done with a
wrong motive.

———◆———

The noblest motive is the public
good.

———◆———

Music

A father had taken his small son to
church. The boy sat and listened attentively without saying a word until
the clergyman announced, "We will now
sing hymn two hundred and twenty-
two: 'Ten Thousand Times Ten Thousand,' two hundred and twenty-two."
    The puzzled boy nudged his father.
"Daddy, we don't have to work this
out, do we?"

———◆———

I must have lots of music in me as
none of it ever came out.

———◆———

A violinist is one who is up to his
ear in music.

———◆———

Music Lessons:
    Sometimes B sharp
    Never B flat
    Always B natural

———◆———

A little girl was standing between
her parents during a hymn so they gave
her an open hymnal. After looking it
over carefully, she handed it back with
this comment: "No pictures; all advertising."   Together

———◆———

The leading soloist in the church
cantata was unable to get a baby sitter. So she had to drag her reluctant
young son to every practice session.
Finally, completely bored with the reiterated musical expression, he rebelled
and insisted on remaining at home.

MUSIC

The singer acknowledged his flowery introduction by saying: "I sing for my own amazement."

———◆———

"But, darling," the young mother remonstrated, "you should learn to enjoy church music. Why, the angels sing around God's throne all day long!"

"Well," said the child, "I just can't see how God can stand it."

Watchman Examiner

———◆———

The young pastor was quite long-winded one night talking to the young people. After nearly an hour he suddenly stopped, smiled and asked, "What hymn shall we sing?"

One boy called out, appropriately, "Revive Us Again."

———◆———

A child who went to Sunday school for the first time came home and told her father that she learned the train song — "Lead Us Not into Penn Station." Later her father learned that the children had sung a prayer hymn, "Lead Us Not into Temptation."

———◆———

A loyal minister's wife sang in the choir to bolster its membership. One Sunday the father of an eight-year-old in the congregation asked the child if he knew the minister's wife.

"Oh, yes," came the reply, "she's one of the chorus girls."

Together

———◆———

After the little girl returned from Sunday school where she had learned the song, "Jesus Wants Me for a Sunbeam," she sang the song to her mother and then, seriously, asked her: "Mother, why does Jesus need me for a mixmaster?"

———◆———

The fine symphony orchestra from the big city had played in a small New England town, the first experience of the kind for many of the inhabitants. Next day some of the old-timers gathered around the stove in the general store and expressed their opinions. The comment of one of the oldest inhabitants was: "All I got to say is — it was an awful long way to bring that big bass drum only to bang it once."

———◆———

"Has your husband a good ear for music?"

"I'm afraid not. He seems to think that everything he hears in church is a lullaby."

———◆———

The little girl was happily humming a hymn as she dusted the furniture to help her mother.

"Mommie, will I be dusting God's chair when I get to heaven, the way the hymn says?" she asked.

Mother looked up with surprise. "Which hymn, honey?"

"And dust around the throne," her little girl quoted. It took a while before the mother learned that she was quoting a line from the hymn "Marching to Zion," "and thus surround the throne." *Adapted*

———◆———

Bill: "Since when did you stop singing in the choir?"

Charlie: "Since the Sunday I was absent, and everyone thought the organ had been tuned!"

———◆———

Confusion was created by a church bulletin which read: Text for today, "Thou Shalt Not Steal." The choir will sing, "Steal Away, Steal Away."

———◆———

A third-grade Sunday school teacher asked her students to list their favorite hymns. One little girl looked up in surprise, blushed, then scribbled, "Peter and Tom."

———◆———

A little five-year-old girl had been attending the church kindergarten. Each day before the children were dismissed, the teacher had them sing the Doxology, which the little five-year-old loved to sing, but in her own words: "Praise God from whom all blessings flow, Praise Him all creatures, here we go!"

Christian Parent

At a banquet in the Russian capital during World War II, United States Chamber of Commerce President Eric Johnston and Author William L. White listened to their hosts sing Russian songs. Then the Russians requested their guests to sing an American song.

Johnston and White consulted for a few moments and responded with the only song they both remembered — "Jesus Wants Me for a Sunbeam."

Sunday School Digest

There are many interesting versions of hymn titles, according to children who do not understand the words. Here are a few most interesting ones:

"The Cross-Eyed Bear" for "Jesus, I Thy Cross Would Bear."

"Bringing in the Sheets" for "Bringing in the Sheaves."

"He Carrots for You" for "He Careth for You."

N

Name

If your name is to live at all, it is much better to have it live in people's hearts than only in their brains.

HOLMES

———◆———

Your name is something you have that everyone else uses more than you do.

———◆———

If I had been named according to the life I have lived my first name would be "Ima" and my last name "Mess."

———◆———

Some folks have trouble naming a new baby. Others have rich relatives.

Times, Thief River Falls, Minn.

———◆———

Nation

National honor is national property of the highest value.   JAMES MONROE

———◆———

The government is us; we are the government, you and I.

THEODORE ROOSEVELT

———◆———

Nature

Nature's Message

There is a God, all nature cries,
I see it in the painted skies.
I see it in the flow'ring spring,
I hear it when the birdlings sing.

I see it in the flowing main,
I see it in the falling rain,
I see it stamped on hail and snow,
I see it when the streamlets flow.
I see it in the clouds that soar,
I hear it when the thunders roar.
I see it when the morning shines,
I see it when the day declines,
I see it in the morning height,
I see it in the smallest mite,
I see it everywhere abroad.
I feel — I know — there is a God.

AUTHOR UNKNOWN

Outdoors

I like to get out in the open,
    Outdoors, 'neath the blue of the sky
Away from the hustle,
    The turmoil and bustle —
And let all my worries go by!
    I like to lie down on a hillside
And loaf in the shade of the trees —
    Not planning and scheming,
    But dozing and dreaming,
Caressed by the fan of the breeze!

And soothing to me is the quiet,
    And restful is each gentle sound —
The chirp of the cricket,
    A bird in a thicket,
Or twigs falling down to the ground.
    I seem far away from my troubles,
As there I recline on the sod,
    Beneath the Great Ceiling —
And I have the feeling
Outdoors, that I'm closer to God.

CHARLES S. KINNISON

Dogwood Is Barking

The crocuses are crowing
    The southern zephyrs blowing;
The nectarines are necking by the sea;
    The cat-tails cater-wauling;
The cauliflowers calling
    And spring is springing up along the lea.

The yellow cowslip's slipping;
    The catnip starts a nipping,
And the saps along the street begin to stir;
    You know that spring is springing
When the bluebell's bells are ringing,
    And the pussywillow buds begin to purr.

JUDGE

——◆——

He who lives after nature shall never be poor.

——◆——

Need

To know the need is to sow the seed.

——◆——

He looks most that longs most.

——◆——

The tragedy of our generation is that there are untold millions still untold.

——◆——

God can't meet your need until you feel your need.

——◆——

Place your needs up against His riches and they will soon disappear.

Eternity

Neglect

Miss Meant-to has a comrade
And her name is Didn't-do.
Have you ever chanced to meet them,
Did they ever call on you?
These two girls now live together
In the house of Never-win,
And I'm told that it is haunted
By the ghost of Might-have-been.

The Sunday School Journal

——◆——

The Cost of Neglecting One Boy

Ex-governor Dickinson, of the state of Michigan, told the following story.

A young lad, the son of a business-man, walked up to his busy father and said, "Dad, if you do not send me off to a state institution today, I am going to commit suicide tonight." This was startling to a father who had been making money, looking after public interests, but neglecting his own offspring. The young lad went on to relate that he was socially diseased. And it is appalling when we learn that millions of our American youth are in the same condition today.

Mr. Dickinson said that the business-man's son was sent off to a state institution for treatment. In a year he came back home thinking he was cured. But God says that the sins of the fathers are visited unto the children of the third and fourth generation of them that hate Him. Whatever a boy sows in his early life, he shall reap in later years.

This lad married a beautiful young girl. Their first and only child was a son. The mother died in childbirth. The young diseased father went over and looked at a half-blind idiotic baby. He exclaimed, "It is more than I can bear." He picked up a revolver, went outside the bedroom and took his own life.

The baby lived. In later years he stood in a long line in Buffalo, New York, to shake the hand of President William McKinley. When his turn came, he stretched out one hand to the President, drew a revolver with the other hand, and out went the life of William McKinley.

It was not long until this young man was brought to justice. He was sentenced to die. And one of the saddest sights on earth is to see a young man awaiting his day of execution! What a pity that the state has to take the life of any young man or woman as penalty for a crime.

The ex-governor said that five tragedies resulted from the failure of the church and state to save one boy.

First, there was the premature death of a young mother. She paid the pen-

172

alty of the sins of another by losing her life.

Second, there was the birth of a baby, born with inherited criminal tendencies.

Third, there was the suicide of the young father.

Fourth, there was the tragic death of President William McKinley, a Christian statesman.

Fifth, there was the execution of a young man who had been neglected in his formative years, and who knew nothing but a life of crime and degradation and shame.

It was costly business to fail to save Leon Czolgosz. Five tragedies came out of this one lad's sin. And it may be that the boy at your door, or just around the corner from your home or church, will commit a crime which will shock the state and nation if he is not won to the Sunday school and to Christ.   *Sunday School Digest*

——◆——

Neighbor

Love Thy Neighbor

Let me be a little kinder;
Let me be a little blinder
To the faults of those about me;
    Let me praise a little more.

Let me be, when I am weary,
Just a little bit more cheery;
Let me serve a little better
    Those whom I am striving for.

Let me be a little braver
When temptation bids me waver;
Let me strive a little harder
    To be all that I should be.

Let me be a little meeker,
With the brother who is weaker,
Let me think more of my neighbor
And a little less of me.
                    AUTHOR UNKNOWN

——◆——

I love the path my neighbor made
Across the grass up to my door;
My lawn that once was smoothly green,
Is now much dearer than before.
                    WILLIAM A. WOFFORD

Talk About Your Neighbors

Let us talk about our neighbors;
Talk of them where'er we go;
Talk about our friend and brother,
And of everyone we know.
Let us talk about our kindred,
Spread the news both near and far,
Till the whole town hears the story
Of what splendid folks they are.

Let us talk about our neighbors;
Of the kindly deeds they do;
Of the little acts of kindness
Which they do for me — for you.
Tell about the hours of watching
Through the night with you in pain;
Of the words of cheer and courage
When your struggles all seem vain.

Let us talk about our neighbors,
In the home or at our work,
Where the conversation's cheerful
Or where germs of envy lurk.
Let us talk about our neighbors,
But let's be as neighbors should —
Let's not talk about their failures —
Let us tell of something good.
                    AUTHOR UNKNOWN

——◆——

Every man's neighbor is his mirror.

——◆——

Love your neighbor, yet don't pull down your hedge.   BENJAMIN FRANKLIN

——◆——

New Year

Happy New Year

H - ear God's Word.......Isaiah 55:3
A - nswer God's Call..Matthew 11:28
P - ardon Receive.....Nehemiah 9:17
P - eace Possess ....Romans 15:33
Y - ield to God..........Romans 6:13

N - o Condemnation ......Romans 8:1
E - ternal Life Is a Gift...Romans 6:23
W - alk Uprightly ......Ephesians 5:2

Y - outh Is the Time for
    Service ....Ecclesiastes 12:1
E - arly Seek God.........Psalm 63:1
A - ttend to God's
    Word.............Numbers 12:6a
R - ejoice in the Lord..Philippians 4:4

NEW YEAR

Another year is but another call from God
To do some deed undone and duty we forgot;
To think some wider thought of man and good.
To see and love with kindlier eyes and warmer heart.
Until acquainted more with Him and keener-eyed to sense the need of man
We serve with larger sacrifice and readier hand our kind.

———◆———

This Year Is Yours

God built and launched this year for you,
Upon the bridge you stand;
It's your ship, your own ship,
And you are in command.
Just what the twelve months' trip will do
Rests wholly, solely, friend with you,
Your log book kept from day to day —
My friend, what will it show?
The log will tell, like guiding star
The sort of captain that you are.
For weal or woe, this year is yours;
Your ship is on life's sea, your acts
As captain must decide
Which ever it will be.
So now, in starting on your trip,
We ask God to help you sail your ship.

EMMA MARTINDALE

———◆———

Another Year

Another year! The future path lies hidden;
And shadows seem to fall across the way.
Press on! a light before thee shineth
Yet more and more unto the perfect day.

Another year! The days are growing evil,
And Satan's threat'nings dark forebodings send.
Fear not! thy Lord hath surely spoken,
"Lo I am with you . . . even to the end."

Another year! the land is parched and thirsty;
Our souls are faint — low droops the precious grain.
Plead on! Elijah's God will answer,
And pour, in mighty floods, the latter rain.

Another year! we wait with eager longing;
The hour is late — midnight comes on apace.
Look up! Redemption's day is dawning;
Perhaps this year we'll see the Bridegroom's face.

MARGARET ARMSTRONG

———◆———

Good-by, Old Year!

Good-by, Old Year! Before you go
Into oblivion's starless night —
With recording book — of wrong and right,
With broken vows and words of hate;
Kind deeds, forgot — until too late —
Bless and forgive me, e'er you go.

New Year, with gladness you arrive —
And with radiant torch new trails you blaze —
To fresh endeavor and better days.
Weak faith make strong, with strength to win —
Amid temptations, nor with sin.
New Year, oh, keep that faith alive.

M.R.W. in Southern Churchman

———◆———

The New Year

A flower unblown; a book unread;
A tree with fruit unharvested;
A path untrod; a house whose rooms
Lack yet the heart's divine perfumes;
A landscape whose wide border lies
In silent shade 'neath silent skies;
A wondrous fountain yet unsealed;
A casket with its gifts concealed—
This is the year that for you waits
Beyond tomorrow's mystic gates.

HORATIO NELSON POWERS

———◆———

The path into the New Year is aglow with opportunity to work for Christ.

174

Facing the New Year

We pledge ourselves
To follow through the coming year
The light which God gives us;
The light of Truth, wherever it may lead;
The light of Freedom, revealing new opportunities for individual development and social service:
The light of Faith, opening new visions of the better world to be;
The light of Love, daily binding brother to brother and man to God in ever closer bonds of friendship and affection.
Guided by this light,
We shall go forward to the work of another year with steadfastness and confidence. AUTHOR UNKNOWN

———

No one ever regarded the first of January with indifference. CHARLES LAMB

———

The New Year!

The New Year like a book lies before me;
On its cover two words, "My Life," I see.
I open the covers and look between —
Each page is empty, no words can be seen,
For I am a writer, I hold the pen
That'll fill these pages to be read by men.
Just what kind of book will my book be,
My life written there for others to see,
Each day a page written, one by one —
Will it be worthwhile when finished and done?
Lord, help me keep these pages clean and fair
By living the life I'd have written there. GERTRUDE LAURA GAST

———

The first thing that's broken after Christmas is a New Year's resolution.

———

Noise

"Breaking through the sound barrier" is an expression that applies to aviation, and not to a man trying to make himself heard on the telephone while Cub Pack No. 21 meets in the next room.

———

Now

Just Now

Never mind about tomorrow —
It always is today;
Yesterday has vanished.
Wherever, none can say.
Each minute must be guarded —
Make worth the while somehow;
There are no other moments;
It's always, Just Now.

Just now is the hour that's golden,
The moment to defend.
Just now is without beginning;
Just now can never end.
Then never mind tomorrow —
'Tis today you must enjoy
With all that's true and noble;
And the time for this is —
Now! AUTHOR UNKNOWN

O

Obedience, Obey

It is a great deal easier to do that which God gives us to do, no matter how hard it is, than to face the responsibilities of not doing it. DR. J. R. MILLER

Obedience is the fruit of faith; patience the bloom on the fruit. CHRISTINA ROSSETTI

———

Obedience to law is the largest liberty.

Let thy child's first lesson be obedience, and the second will be what thou wilt.   BENJAMIN FRANKLIN

A child has to learn obedience in the home or he will never learn obedience to the Heavenly Father.   DR. BOB SMITH

He that cannot obey, cannot command.   BENJAMIN FRANKLIN

Resistance to tyrants is obedience to God.   JEFFERSON

Offend

When anyone has offended me, I try to raise my soul so high that the offense cannot reach me.

Omnipotence

A Sunday school teacher was examining her pupils after a series of lessons on God's omnipotence. She asked, "Is there anything God can't do?"
There was silence. Finally, one lad held up his hand. The teacher, disappointed that the lesson's point had been missed, asked resignedly, "Well, just what is it that God can't do?"
"Well," replied the boy, "He can't please everybody."   *Together*

Opinion

What young America thinks of Christ today determines our nation's tomorrow.

People who are so sure they know where the younger generation is going should try to remember where it came from.

Often the fellow who hits the nail right on the head is driving it in the wrong direction.

Many people think they are broadminded just because they are too lazy to form an opinion.

Opinion is free, facts are scarce.

Everyone all over the world takes a wife's estimate into account in forming an opinion of a man.   BALZAC

In a discussion, the difficulty lies, not in being able to defend your opinion, but to know it.   ANDRE MAUROIS

Opinions are a luxury.

The man who never alters his opinion is like standing water, and breeds reptiles of the mind.   BLAKE

My idea of an agreeable person is a person who agrees with me.   DISRAELI

Man is a creature who has to argue down another man's opinion before he can believe in his own.

God cares nothing about public opinion. The voice of the people is rarely, if ever, the voice of God.   W. W. AYER

"Public opinion" is what some people think most people are thinking.

Public opinion is just private opinion that makes enough noise to attract attention.

A well-informed person is one who has opinions just like yours.

Opportunity

The measure of your responsibility is the measure of your opportunity.
DR. BOB JONES, SR.

Opportunities like millstones may drown you or grind your corn.

God's best gift to us is not things, but opportunities.

The doors of opportunity are marked "push."

We don't need more opportunities, we should take advantage of the opportunities we have.

I have known God to use people who never had a chance, but I have never known God to use a person who has had a chance and will not take it.
DR. BOB JONES, SR.

———♦———

Greater opportunity is the reward of past accomplishment.

———♦———

If you want to open the door of opportunity, push.

———♦———

Don't wait for opportunity to come; it's already here.

———♦———

Sometimes opportunity drops into a lap, but the lap must be where opportunity is.

———♦———

Opportunity sometimes comes dressed in overalls.

———♦———

Opportunity is often lost by deliberation.

———♦———

With every opportunity comes the weight of responsibility.

———♦———

People are so anxious to talk about closed doors that they forget the open doors. CHR. CHRISTIANSEN

———♦———

A closed door is not a call to inactivity, but a leading into a new field of service. CHR. CHRISTIANSEN

———♦———

When you dismiss an opportunity you miss success.

———♦———

High privileges prompt us to high living.

———♦———

A Dutch farmer in South Africa used to sit on a stone ridge that crossed his farm and mourn over the sterility of his land. He was only too happy to sell it for $25,000. But the man who bought the farm opened a gold mine right under the rocky ridge where the farmer used to sit and pity himself.

———♦———

Striking while the iron is hot is all right but don't strike while the head is hot.

Opportunity never knocks at the door of a knocker.

———♦———

My Opportunity

My opportunity! Dear Lord, I do not ask
That Thou shouldst give me some high work of Thine.
Some noble calling, or some wondrous task —
Give me a little hand to hold in mine.

I do not ask that I should ever stand
Among the wise, the worthy, or the great;
I only ask that softly, hand in hand,
A child and I may enter at the gate.

Give me a little child to point the way
Over the strange, sweet path that leads to Thee;
Give me a little voice to teach to pray;
Give me two shining eyes Thy face to see.

The only crown I ask, dear Lord, to wear,
Is this: that I may teach a little child
How beautiful, oh, how divinely fair,
Is Thy dear face, so loving, sweet and mild!

I do not ask for more than this,
My opportunity! 'Tis standing at my door;
What sorrow if this blessing I should miss!
A little child! What should I ask for more?
MARION C. CRAIG

———♦———

There is no security on this earth. There is only opportunity.
DOUGLAS MAC ARTHUR

———♦———

The stairs of opportunity
Are sometimes hard to climb;
And that can only be well done
By one step at a time.
But he who would go to the top
Ne'er sits down and despairs;
Instead of staring up the steps
He just steps up the stairs.
AUTHOR UNKNOWN

177

Opposition

Hardship and opposition are the native soil of manhood and self-reliance. NEAL

—— ♦ ——

Optimism, Optimist

Optimism is what the teakettle has — up to its neck in hot water, it keeps on singing.

—— ♦ ——

An optimist is a man who thinks he can find some big strawberries in the bottom of the box.

—— ♦ ——

Optimism is the content of small men in high places. F. SCOTT FITZGERALD

—— ♦ ——

Opportunity does not batter a door off its hinges when it knocks.

—— ♦ ——

There is a new definition of an optimist and a pessimist. The optimist says, "A year from now we will all be begging."
The pessimist asks, "From whom?"

—— ♦ ——

An optimist sees windows as something to let light shine through; a pessimist sees them as something that gets dirty.

—— ♦ ——

The optimist is wrong as often as the pessimist is, but he has a lot more fun.

—— ♦ ——

Two frogs fell into a deep cream bowl,
One was an optimistic soul,
But the other took the gloomy view,
"We shall drown," he cried without more ado!
So with a last despairing cry,
He flung up his legs and he said, "Good-by!"
Quoth the other frog with a merry grin,
"I can't get out, but I won't give in,
I'll just swim around till my strength is spent,
Then will I die the more content!"
Bravely he swam till it would seem,
His struggles began to churn the cream!
On the top of the butter at last he stopped,
And out of the bowl he gaily hopped!
What is the moral? 'Tis easily found:
If you can't hop out, keep swimming round! AUTHOR UNKNOWN

—— ♦ ——

Organization, Organize

If effort is organized, accomplishment follows.

—— ♦ ——

A boy can usually find as many reasons for harboring a stray dog as a man can find for keeping up his membership in some useless organizations.

—— ♦ ——

Original, Originality

The merit of originality is not novelty, it is sincerity. The believing man is the original man; he believes for himself, not for another. CARLYLE

—— ♦ ——

The more originality you have in yourself, the more you see in others. PASCAL

—— ♦ ——

Others

If you are looking for Christ in folks you will not be dwelling on their faults. CHARLES E. FULLER

—— ♦ ——

There is no loving others without living for others.

—— ♦ ——

Others

Lord, help me to live from day to day
In such a self-forgetful way
That even when I kneel to pray
My prayer shall be for — others.

Help me in all the work I do
To ever be sincere and true
And know that all I'd do for you
Must needs be done for — others.

Let "Self" be crucified and slain
And buried deep; and all in vain
May efforts be to rise again
Unless to live for — others.

And when my work on earth is done
And my new work in heaven's begun
May I forget the crown I've won
While thinking still of — *others*.

Others, Lord, yes, others
  Let this my motto be,
Help me to live for others
  That I may live like Thee.

C. D. MEIGS

———◆———

To keep in the middle of the road
one must be able to see both sides.

Outlook

To look around is to be distressed.
To look within is to be depressed.
To look to God is to be blessed.

AUTHOR UNKNOWN

———◆———

Look at self and be disappointed.
Look at others and be discouraged.
Look at Christ and be satisfied.

P

Paraphrases

If

If you can trust when everyone about
    you
  Is doubting Him, proclaiming Him
    untrue,
If you can hope in Christ though all
    forsake you
  And say 'tis not the thing for you to
    do;
If you can wait on God, nor wish to
    hurry,
  Or, being greatly used, keep humble
    still,
Or if you're tested, cater not to worry
  And yet remain within His sovereign
    will;
If you can say 'tis well when sorrow
    greets you
  And death has taken those you hold
    most dear,
If you can smile when adverse trials
    meet you
  And be content e'en though your
    lot be drear;
If you can be reviled and never mur-
    mur,
  Or being tempted not give way to
    sin;
If you can fight for right and stand
    the firmer,
  Or lose the battle when you ought
    to win;

If you can really long for His appear-
    ing,
  And therefore set your heart on
    things above;
If you can speak for Christ in spite
    of sneering,
  Or to the most unlovely one show
    love;
If you hear, hear the call of God to
    labor,
  And answer "yes," in yieldingness
    and trust,
And go to tell the story of the Saviour
  To the souls in darkness o'er the
    desert's dust;
If you can pray when Satan's darts are
    strongest
  And take the road of faith instead
    of sight,
Or walk with God, e'en though His
    way be longest,
  And swerve not to the left or to the
    right;
If you desire Himself alone to fill you,
  For Him alone you care to live and
    be;
Then 'tis not you, but Christ that
    dwelleth in you,
  And that, O child of God, is Victory.

GRACE REYNOLDS

———◆———

The Seaman's Psalm

The Lord is my Pilot; I shall not
drift. He lighteth me across the dark

179

waters; He steereth me in the deep channels; He keepeth my log.

He guideth me by the star of holiness for His name's sake. Yea, though I sail 'mid the thunders and the tempests of life, I shall dread no danger; for Thou art near me; Thy love and Thy care, they shelter me.

Thou preparest a harbor before me in the homeland of eternity; Thou anointest the waters with oil; my ship rideth calmly.

Surely sunlight and starlight shall favor me on the voyage I take, and I will rest in the port of my God forever.

CAPTAIN J. ROGERS

———◆———

Modernistic Version of Psalm 23

(Suggested after reading much of the present-day jargon of life and morals, by those who have forsaken God as their Good Shepherd, and now darken counsel by words without knowledge.)

The unseen Infinite is the source of my motivation, and I shall not want personality. He maketh me to experience true self-expression and to attempt new projects in the psychology of adolescence. He restoreth the right complex to my introvert soul. He leadeth me into a preface to morals for goodness' sake! Yea, though I peregrinate through the present depression, exuberant health gives me a stiff upper lip. I grin and bear my fate. Good luck is always with me. Its creative impulse and the pep of my *élan vital* comfort me. Surely normal behaviorism and carefully controlled altruism will follow me until the jig is up, and then (properly cremated) I shall dwell in a marble urn forever. DR. SAMUEL M. ZWEMER

———◆———

The Teacher's Psalm

The Lord is my helper, I shall not fear in guiding these pupils.

He leadeth me into the Holy of Holies before I prepare this lesson.

He leadeth me to the heart of the truth and prepareth the minds of the pupils for the truth.

He giveth me a vision of the immortality of these lives.

He leadeth me to see the sacredness of teaching His Book.

Yea, tho' I become discouraged and despair at times, yet shall I lift up my head, for His promises cannot fail me.

His Word will not return to Him void, and my faith undimmed shall burn through all the coming years.

Thou walketh before me that the seed planted shall grow.

Thou shalt stand by my side on Sunday and speak through these lips so that these pupils feel the nearness of God.

Thou shalt cause each broken effort to gather sheaves through unnumbered years. My joy is full when I know that every effort in Thy Name shall abide forever.

Surely Thy love and watch care shall be with me every day of my life and someday I shall live with those who turn many to righteousness forever and ever. ROSALEE MILES APPLEBY

———◆———

Understanding

A Paraphrase of I Corinthians 13

Though I teach with the skill of the finest teachers (leaders), and have not understanding,

I am become only a clever speaker and a charming entertainer,

And though I understand all techniques and all methods,

And though I have much training,

So that I feel quite competent

But have no understanding of the way my pupils think,

It is not enough.

And if I spend many hours in lesson preparation,

And become tense and nervous with the strain,

But have no understanding of the personal problems of my pupils,

It is still not enough.

The understanding teacher is very patient, very kind;
Is not shocked when young people bring him their confidences;
does not gossip;
is not easily discouraged;
does not behave himself in ways that are unworthy;
But is at all times a living example to his students of the good way of life of which he speaks.

Understanding never fails.
But whether there be materials,
they shall become obsolete;
Whether there be methods,
they shall be outmoded;
Whether there be techniques,
they shall be abandoned;
For we know only a little
and can pass on to our children only a little.

But when we have understanding,
then all our efforts will become creative
And our influence will live forever in the lives of our pupils.
When I was a child
I spoke with immaturity,
My emotions were uncontrolled
And I behaved childishly
But now that I am an adult,
I must face life as it is,
With courage and understanding.

And now abideth
skill,
devotion,
understanding,
these three,
and the greatest of these is understanding.
ELOUISE RIVINIUS

Blessed Is the Church

Blessed is the church which has a concern for the children of the community, for it will find a way to minister to them and to their homes.
Blessed is the church which provides a comfortable, attractive place for children, for it is the most evident sign that the church counts them important.
Blessed is the church that has teachers who respect children, and have warm, friendly ways, for children want to do and be their best in their presence.
Blessed is the church that provides the best teaching materials for its children, for good work is more easily done with good tools.
Blessed is the church that helps its teachers improve their skill in teaching, for the effectiveness of their work shall surely show in the lives of children.
Blessed is the church whose teachers are wise and genuinely Christian, for children will try to be like them.
Blessed is the church that, when all manner of needs and difficulties press in upon it, still provides an adequate program for children, for they shall love this church, and determine to be a part of its fellowship all of their lives. *The Messenger*

Parents

To Parents

"I'll lend you for a little time
A child of mine," He said,
"For you to love the while she lives
And mourn for when she's dead.
I cannot promise she will stay,
Since all from life return,
But there are lessons taught down there
I want this child to learn.
I've looked the wide world over
In my search for teachers true,
And from the throngs that crowd life's lanes
I have selected you.
Now, will you give her all your love,
Nor think the labor vain,
Nor hate me when I come to call
To take her back again?"
AUTHOR UNKNOWN

181

PARENTS

The parent's life is the child's copybook.

———♦———

One father said, "When it comes to being a godly Christian counselor to my boy, I either skid or skidoo."

———♦———

The influence of the parent surpasses the influence of the pastor, the superintendent, the Sunday school teacher, the public school teacher or any other person.

———♦———

If, for Parents

If you can stay the spanking hand
And truly say you understand;
If you can keep your savoir-faire
When your offspring's in your hair;
If you can quietly listen to
The cute things others' children do;
And when the neighbors' kids are naughty
And their parents cold and haughty
Blame your little "innocence,"
If you do not take offence;
And if you find you're in position
To keep a sunny disposition
When Junior's friends daub him with paint
— You're no parent — you're a saint!
                              ALICE DUCH

———♦———

Parents wonder why the streams are bitter when they themselves have poisoned the fountain.   JOHN LOCKE

———♦———

Ye parents hear what Jesus taught
When little ones to Him were brought;
Forbid them not, but heed My plea
And suffer them to come to Me.

Obey your Lord and let His truth
Be taught your children in their youth
That they in church and school may dwell
And learn their Saviour's praise to tell.

For if you love Him as you ought,
To Christ your children will be brought.
If thus you place them in His care,
You and your household well shall fare.   LUDWIG HELMBOLD, 1596

A parent is no sooner through worrying about the scratches children put on the furniture than he has to begin worrying about the ones they put on the car.   ANONYMOUS

———♦———

A Mother's Prayer

I wash the dirt from little feet,
  And as I wash I pray,
"Lord, keep them ever pure and true
  To walk the narrow way."
I wash the dirt from little hands,
  And earnestly I ask,
"Lord, may they ever yielded be
  To do the humblest task."
I wash the dirt from little knees,
  And pray, "Lord, may they be
The place where victories are won,
  And orders sought from Thee."
I scrub the clothes that soil so soon,
  And pray, "Lord, may her dress
Throughout eternal ages be
  Thy robe of righteousness."

E'er many hours shall pass, I know
  I'll wash these hands again;
And there'll be dirt upon her dress
  Before the day shall end,
But as she journeys on through life
  And learns of want and pain,
Lord, keep her precious little heart
  Cleansed from all sin and stain;
For soap and water cannot reach
  Where Thou alone canst see
Her hands and feet, these I can wash—
  I trust her heart to Thee.   B. RYBERG

———♦———

For Parents Only

THINKING that three hours of any movie are harmless for the child, but that two hours of Church and Sunday school are too much for his nervous system is just bad thinking.

GIVING him a nickel for the collection and fifty cents for the movie not only shows a parent's sense of value, but is also not likely to produce a giver.

LETTING him watch and listen to several hours of TV thrillers a day with no time for one short prayer and a few Bible verses is criminal unbalance.

BEING careful that Junior has his weekday lessons, and caring not that he knows not his Sunday school lesson makes for spiritual illiteracy.

SAYING that a child must make his own decisions as to whether or not he should go to church, or as to what church, is shirking parental responsibility.

WHEN FATHER spends Sunday morning in mowing the lawn, cleaning the garden, or playing golf, his sons are left to walk alone.

WHEN PARENTS idle away Sunday morning in reading the paper or listening to the radio or TV while brother and sister are sent by themselves to church, something happens to the children's evaluation of church attendance. *Selected*

———◆———

C — Cheerful, courageous, a churchgoer, converts others.

H — Hopeful, honest, helpful, hospitable, humble.

R — Reverent, responsible, righteous, reliable.

I — Industrious, informed, inspiring.

S — Sincere, slow to anger, shares with others, serene.

T — Tolerant, temperate, thankful, trustworthy.

I — Instrument for good, increasing in grace.

A — Alert, appreciative.

N — Neighborly, never coveting or gossiping.

P — Patient, practical, participates in children's activities.

A — Appreciative, affectionate, approachable,

R — Religious, reasonable, relaxed.

E — Enthusiastic, even-tempered.

N — Neighborly, never breaks a promise.

T — Tolerant, tactful, temperate in all things. *Selected*

Hands

My hand is large and his is small,
And there is nothing on earth at all
More important than the task
That lies ahead of me. I ask
For wisdom, Lord, that I may lead
This child aright; his every need
Depends on me. Be Thou my guide
That I, in walking by his side,
May choose the right paths for his feet.
The days are swift, the years are fleet,
Make me alert in deed and word
As we go forward, blessed Lord:
His precious clinging hand in mine,
With always, Lord, my hand in Thine.
GRACE NOLL CROWELL

———◆———

Past

We live in the present
We dream of the future,
But we learn eternal truths from the past.
MADAME CHIANG KAI-SHEK

———◆———

Patience, Patient

Patience is like a mosquito sitting on the bed of an anemic person who is waiting for a blood transfusion.

———◆———

Be patient! God always uses the yielded life — but in His own way.

———◆———

To hold one's ground calmly and steadfastly often requires more courage than to attack.

———◆———

We must be a patient people
  With children,
  With parents,
  With administrators,
  With ourselves.
Watching with a quiet, anxious breath,
Listening with a still, magnetic ear,
Living with a slow, emerging self.
Guided by the values we hold dear,
While following a planned and charted course,
To find the time in every day "to do the right,
As God would have us see the right" to do.
JANET EATON

183

Try Him Once More

Some years ago in a manufacturing town of Scotland a young lady applied to the superintendent of a Sunday school for a class. At his suggestion she gathered a class of poor boys. The superintendent told them to come to his house during the week and he would get them each a new suit of clothes. They came, and each was nicely fitted out.

The worst and most unpromising boy in the class was a lad named Bob. After two or three Sundays he was missing and the teacher went out to hunt him up. She found that his new clothes were torn and dirty, but she invited him back to the school, and he came. The superintendent gave him a second new suit, but, after attending once or twice, Bob was again absent. Once again she sought him out, only to find that the second suit had gone the way of the first.

"I am utterly discouraged with Bob," she said, when she reported the case to the superintendent, "and I must give him up."

"Please don't do that," the superintendent replied. "I can't but hope there is something good in Bob. Try him once more. I'll give him a third suit if he'll promise to attend regularly."

Bob did promise, and received his third new suit. He attended regularly after that, and became interested in the school. He became an earnest and persevering seeker after Jesus, and found Him. He joined the church. He was made a teacher. He studied for the ministry. The end of the story is that this discouraging boy—forlorn, ragged, runaway Bob — became Robert Morrison, the great missionary to China who translated the Bible into the Chinese language, and by so doing, opened the kingdom of heaven to the teeming millions of that vast country. *Selected*

———◆———

The most useful virtue is patience.
JOHN DEWEY

———◆———

Patience is a plaster for all sores.

Whoever is out of patience is out of possession of his soul. Men must not turn bees and kill themselves in stinging others.

———◆———

After several hours of fishing the little girl suddenly threw down her pole and cried, "I quit!"

"What's the matter?" her father asked her.

"Nothing," said the child, "except I can't seem to get waited on."

———◆———

Patience is a virtue,
Possess it if you can,
Seldom in a woman,
Never in a man!

———◆———

He that can have patience can have what he will. BENJAMIN FRANKLIN

———◆———

Patriotic, Patriotism

Patriotic men do not shrink from danger when conscience points the path.

———◆———

Peace

Where there is no peace, there is no feast.

———◆———

From prudence peace; from peace abundance.

———◆———

Peace is not made at the council tables, or by treaties, but in the hearts of men. HERBERT HOOVER

———◆———

We lose the peace of years when we hunt after the rapture of moments.
BULWER

———◆———

Peace comes only from loving, from mutual self-sacrifice and self-forgetfulness. Few today have humility or wisdom enough to know the world's deep need of love. We are too much possessed by national and racial and cultural pride. HORACE W. B. DONEGAN, D.D.

———◆———

He that would live in peace and at ease, must not speak all he knows, nor judge all he sees. BENJAMIN FRANKLIN

Peace rules the day when Christ rules the mind.

———

The peace of God passeth all understanding and misunderstanding. *Eternity*

———

No one is fool enough to choose war instead of peace. For in peace sons bury fathers, but in war fathers bury sons. HERODOTUS

———

Hidden Treasures

There is a calm the poor in spirit know,
That softens sorrow, and that sweetens woe;
There is a peace that dwells within the breast,
When all without is stormy and distressed:
There is light that gilds the darkest hour.
When dangers thicken and when tempests lower,
That calm, to faith and hope and love is given,
That peace remains when all beside is riven.
That light shines down to man direct from heaven. *From the Latin*

———

Lord, make me an instrument of thy peace!
Where there is hatred . . . let me sow love.
Where there is injury . . . pardon.
Where there is doubt . . . faith.
Where there is despair . . . hope.
Where there is darkness . . . light.
Where there is sadness . . . joy.
O Divine Master, grant that I may not so much seek
To be consoled . . . as to console,
To be understood . . . as to understand,
To be loved . . . as to love.
For,
It is in giving . . . that we receive,
It is in pardoning . . . that we are pardoned,
It is in dying . . . that we are born to eternal life. SAINT FRANCIS OF ASSISI

Rest is not a hallowed feeling that comes over us in church; it is the repose of a heart set deep in God. HENRY DRUMMOND

———

Peace dwells only in the soul.

———

Pentecost

Pentecost was only a few drops of the coming shower.

———

People

Some folks we click with, some folks we cross with. Love is manifested when we love those who cross us. TED KUMMERFELD

———

Of course it takes all kinds of people to make a world. But a lot of them won't help.

———

People respond to you like you treat them.

———

People are funny; they spend money they don't have, to buy things they don't need, to impress people they don't like.

———

We do not love people so much for the good they have done us, as for the good we have done them. TOLSTOY

———

Whatever you may be sure of, be sure of this, that you are dreadfully like other people. OLIVER WENDELL HOLMES

———

We get from people what we give;
We find in them what we bring;
We discover that the changes in them are really changes in ourselves.

———

There are three kinds of people in the world:
the wills,
the won'ts,
the can'ts.
The first accomplish everything;
The second approve everything;
The third fail in everything. *Electric Magazine*

Which Are You?

The bones in the body are two hundred or more,
But in sorting out people, we need only four:

Wishbone People

They hope for, they long for, they wish for and sigh;
They want things to come, but aren't willing to try.

Funnybone People

They laugh, grin and giggle, smile, twinkle the eye;
If work is a joke, sure, they'll give it a try.

Jawbone People

They scold, jaw and sputter, they froth, rave and cry,
They're long on the talk, but they're short on the try.

Backbone People

They strike from the shoulder, they never say die;
They're winners in life — for they know how to try. *First Free Footnotes*

———♦———

Persecute, Persecution

People aren't persecuted for doing wrong but for doing right.

———♦———

Perseverance, Persevere, Persist, Persistence

School Teacher: "Johnny, can you tell me the difference between perseverance and obstinacy?"
Johnny: "One is a strong will and the other is a strong won't."

———♦———

The best place to find a helpin' hand is at the end of your own arm.

———♦———

Everyone has his superstitions. One of mine has always been when I started to go anywhere, or to do anything, never to turn back or to stop until the thing intended was accomplished.
ULYSSES S. GRANT

———♦———

Don't wait to see what happens — take hold and make it happen.

Teacher (lecturing on perseverance): "He drove straight to his goal. He looked neither to the right nor to the left, but pressed forward, moved by a definite purpose. Neither friend nor foe could delay him, nor turn him from his course. All who crossed his path did so at their own peril. What would you call such a man?"
Graduate: "A truck driver!"

———♦———

If you are not afraid to face the music, you may someday lead the band. *Spuk Tidings*

———♦———

It is better to stumble toward a better life than not to take any steps at all. *Church Management*

———♦———

Even if you are on the right track, you will get run over if you just sit there. *The Journeyman Barker*

———♦———

There is always water if you bore deep enough.

———♦———

Faint heart never won fair lady, nor escaped one either.

———♦———

The line between failure and success is so fine that we scarcely know when we pass it — so fine that we are often on the line and we do not know it.

———♦———

The only way to make a "come back" is to go on.

———♦———

Nothing in the world, including talent, genius and education, can take the place of persistence.

———♦———

The man who removed the mountain began by carrying away small stones. *Chinese Proverb*

———♦———

It's the daily grind which gives you the edge.

———♦———

Don't Quit

When things go wrong, as they sometimes will,
When the road you're trudging seems all up hill,

When the funds are low and the debts
are high,
And you want to smile, but you have
to sigh,
When care is pressing you down a bit,
Rest, if you must — but don't you quit.

Life is queer with its twists and turns,
As every one of us sometimes learns,
And many a failure turns about
When he might have won had he
stuck it out;
Don't give up, though the pace seems
slow —
You might succeed with another blow.

Often the goal is nearer than
It seems to a faint and faltering man,
Often the struggler has given up
When he might have captured the
victor's cup,
And he learned too late, when the
night slipped down,
How close he was to the golden crown.

Success is failure turned inside out —
The silver tint of the clouds of doubt —
And you never can tell how close you
are,
It may be near when it seems afar;
So stick to the fight when you're hard-
est hit —
It's when things seem worst that you
mustn't quit.   AUTHOR UNKNOWN

Don't Give Up!

I've taught a class for many years;
Borne many burdens — toiled through
tears
But folks don't notice me a bit;
I'm so discouraged — I'll just quit.

Sometime ago I joined the choir
That many folks I might inspire;
But folks don't seem moved a bit
And I won't stand it. I'll just quit.

I've led young people day and night
And sacrificed to lead them right.
But folks won't help me out a bit,
And I'm so tired, I think I'll quit.

Christ's cause is hindered everywhere
And folks are dying in despair.
The reason why? Just think a bit;
The Church is full of folks who quit.
    AUTHOR UNKNOWN

Personality

The personality should give wings to
thoughts.

Why be difficult when with a little
more effort you could be impossible?

The contact of every human personality is for a divine purpose.

On his second trip to see the doctor
about an illness, the doctor asked Mose,
"How do you feel?"
"Exuberatin'," Mose said. "I took all
dat subscription you give me and it
went through my whol' personality."

Personality has the power to open
many doors but character must keep
them open.   *Megiddo Message*

The power to purpose in the heart
is the spinal column of personality and
the measure of manhood.

Blessed is the man who has a skin
of the right thickness. He can work
happily in spite of enemies and friends.
    HENRY T. BAILEY

Perspective

Write it on your heart that every day
is the best day of the year.
    RALPH WALDO EMERSON

A father reading his paper came
across a map of the world. He clipped
it out, cut it into pieces, and told his
small son to put the world together.
After a while the boy called, "I've done
it!"
His father marveled, "As quick as
this? How did you do it?"
The son said, "I turned it over and
on the back was a picture of a man. I
put the man together — and the world
was right!"   AUTHOR UNKNOWN

The blue of heaven is larger than the cloud.　　　E. B. BROWNING

———◆———

To be honest, to be kind, to earn a little and to spend a little less;
To make, upon the whole, a family happier for his presence;
To renounce when that shall be necessary and not be embittered;
To keep a few friends but these without capitulation — above all, on the same condition to keep friends with himself —
There is a task for all that a man has of fortitude and delicacy.
　　　ROBERT LOUIS STEVENSON

———◆———

Persuade, Persuasion

Few are open to conviction, but the majority of men are open to persuasion.　　　GOETHE

———◆———

Would you persuade, speak of interest, not of reason.　　　BENJAMIN FRANKLIN

———◆———

Pessimism, Pessimist

A pessimist is a person who suffers seasickness during the entire journey of life.

———◆———

A pessimist is a person who blows out the candle to see how dark it is.

———◆———

A fellow who says it can't be done is likely to be interrupted by someone doing it.

———◆———

The pessimist says, "If I don't try, I can't fail." The optimist says, "If I don't try, I can't win."

———◆———

A pessimist says: "I don't think it can be done."
An optimist says: "I'm sure there is a way."
A peptimist says: "I just did it."

———◆———

'Twixt optimist and pessimist
The difference is droll:
The optimist sees the doughnut,
While the pessimist sees the hole.

A farmer was watching the men fire a locomotive. "They'll never make her go," he said.
But they did. As he watched it move, the farmer said, "They'll never make her stop."

———◆———

A pessimist is a man who financed an optimist.

———◆———

The Pessimist's Creed

What's the use of sunshine? Only blinds your eyes.
What's the use of knowledge? Only makes you wise.
What's the use of smiling? Wrinkles up your face.
What's the use of flowers? Clutter up the place.
What's the use of eating? Nothing — only taste.
What's the use of hustling? Haste is only waste.
What's the use of music? Just a lot of noise.
What's the use of loving? Only for the joys.
What's the use of singing? Only makes you glad.
What's the use of goodness when the whole world's bad?
What's the use of health? You might as well be sick.
What's the use of doing anything but kick?　　　AUTHOR UNKNOWN

———◆———

Petty

Do not make a business of the trivial: to convert petty annoyances into matters of importance is to become seriously involved over nothing.

———◆———

Philosophy

A philosopher says we are not what we think we are; we are what we think. Well, then, if we are what we think, what we think we are, we are, are we not — or are we?
　　　AUTHOR UNKNOWN

Philosophy is a study which enables a man to be unhappy more intelligently.

———◆———

Philosophy: a system of thinking about things which enables one to be quite happy, or hopping mad, about the whole mess.

———◆———

Plagues

The four greatest scourges of mankind have been drink, war, pestilence and famine—and strong drink has been more destructive than war, pestilence and famine combined.   WM. E. GLADSTONE

———◆———

Plan, Planning

Plan your work! Work your plan!

———◆———

Plan in marble if you would work in stone.

———◆———

If God is your partner, make your plans large.

———◆———

Nothing of importance is ever done without a plan.

———◆———

I try to have no plans the failure of which would greatly annoy me. Half the unhappiness in the world is due to the failure of plans which were never reasonable, and often impossible.   EDGAR WATSON HOWE

———◆———

Plan for today as well as for tomorrow.

———◆———

He Has a Plan for Me

I to Christ my life have given,
  Ever His alone to be;
Oh, what peace and blest assurance,
  That He has a plan for me!

Now I know that He is leading
  In His love so full and free;
I can rest in Him securely,
  For He has a plan for me.

As I walk along life's pathway,
  Though the way I cannot see
I shall follow in His footsteps,
  For He has a plan for me.

So I look to Him for guidance,
  Saviour, Lord and King is He;
I can trust Him — aye, forever,
  Since He has a plan for me!

Trusting Him in full assurance,
  This would be my only plea —
Reveal, Oh Lord, just step by step
  Thine own perfect plan for me!
                            ROSELLA THIESEN

———◆———

Please

Please God and you will please good men.

———◆———

Please God in all you do and be pleased with all God does.

———◆———

When you do what you please, do you do what pleases God?

———◆———

No man has a right to do as he pleases unless he pleases to do right.

———◆———

Pleasure

Not what we have, but what we enjoy constitutes our abundance.

———◆———

That man is richest whose pleasures are cheapest.   HENRY D. THOREAU

———◆———

Many a man thinks he is buying pleasure when he is really selling himself a slave to it.   BENJAMIN FRANKLIN

———◆———

Poise

A politician was speaking with his accustomed eloquence and poise. There were thousands of bugs flying around the bright light overhead. Some bugs zoomed around him like jets, but he remained calm and devoted to his speech. Every time he inhaled the people thought sure he would suck in a bug. Finally the inevitable happened — he did! "What will he do?" they questioned. When he got his breath, the politician said, "Served the bug right, he should have watched where he was going!"

189

When asked to define the word poise, the Dutchman said, "That's what girls go out with."

———•———

Poise is the art of raising the eyebrows instead of the roof.

———•———

Nonchalance is the ability to look like an owl when you have behaved like an ass.

Polite

Politeness is an inexpensive way of making friends.

———•———

Politeness is to do and say the kindest things in the kindest way.

———•———

The lady gave Tommy an orange. "What do you say to the lady, Tommy?" asked his mother.
"Peel it," said Tommy.

———•———

A small boy was told that when visitors came to the house it was his duty to pay them some attention.
Shortly afterward a Mrs. Daniel called, and the small boy shook hands with her politely and exclaimed in his best drawing-room manner:
"How do you do, Mrs. Daniel? I've just been reading about your husband in the den of lions."

———•———

Politics

A politician is a gent who works up his gums before election and gums up the works afterward. *Presbyterian Life*

———•———

We are not so much interested in where a politician "stands" as we are in which direction he's moving—if any.

———•———

Nothing is politically right which is morally wrong. LINCOLN

———•———

Crooked politicians get into office because honest men fail to do their duty.

Popular, Popularity

One of the easiest ways to become popular is to remember the nice things folks say about a person, and repeat them to him.

———•———

Possess, Possessions

If we don't have the things we want, let's want the things we have.

———•———

Don't let your possessions possess you. M. R. SIEMENS

———•———

Our children are the only earthly possessions we can take with us to glory.

———•———

The only difference between the man who has one million dollars and six children and the man who has one million dollars, is that the man with one million dollars wants more.

———•———

Poverty

Poverty in the way of duty is to be chosen rather than plenty in the way of sin.

———•———

Bein' poor is a problem, but bein' rich ain't the answer. C. GRANT

———•———

Power

The power to purpose in the heart is the spinal column of personality and the measure of manhood.

———•———

Horsepower was much safer when only horses had it.

———•———

If the heartbeats for a single day were concentrated into one huge throb of vital power, it might be sufficient to to throw a ton of iron 120 feet into the air. AUBREY J. CARPENTER

———•———

The power of God is given to enable us to do a spiritual thing in a spiritual way in an unspiritual world.
MALCOLM CRONK

Power cannot go from the rushing water to the high tension wire without going through the power house.

———◆———

Dynamite comes in small packages!

———◆———

Power

I ask not wealth, but power to take
And use the things I have aright;
Not years, but wisdom that shall make
My life a profit and delight.
PHOEBE CARY

———◆———

Praise

Try praising your wife, even if it does frighten her at first. BILLY SUNDAY

———◆———

Self-praise is half scandal.

———◆———

The hardest thing any man can do is to fall down on the ice when it's slippery, and get up and praise the Lord. JOSH BILLINGS

———◆———

If you would reap praise you must sow the seeds, gentle words and useful deeds. BENJAMIN FRANKLIN

———◆———

If you think that praise is due him, now's the time to slip it to him, for he cannot read his tombstone when he's dead. BERTON BRALEY

———◆———

The trouble with most of us is that we would rather be ruined by praise than saved with criticism.

———◆———

Prayer

Prayer is the key of the morning and the bolt of the night.

———◆———

It is good for us to keep some account of our prayers that we may not unsay them in our practice.

———◆———

A man may offer a prayer, beautiful in diction and perfect in the number of its petitions, but if it gives him gratification afterwards, that prayer cannot have been truly prayed. G. C. MORGAN

A coffee break is good; a prayer break is better; a praise break is best!

———◆———

You cannot stumble if you are on your knees.

———◆———

No nation has better citizens than the parents who teach their children how to pray.

———◆———

Prayer takes the very highest energy of which the human is capable. JOHN COLERIDGE

———◆———

What cannot be told to human ears can be poured into God's sympathetic ear.

———◆———

Fellowship with a holy God produces holiness among men.

———◆———

What the church needs today is not more machinery or better, nor new organizations or more and novel methods, but men whom the Holy Ghost can use — men of prayer, men mighty in prayer. The Holy Ghost does not flow through methods, but through men. He does not come on machinery, but on men. He does not anoint plans, but men — men of prayer. E. M. BOUNDS

———◆———

If stress and strife of the times causes us to become weak-kneed, perhaps we should let them collapse entirely and while in that position do a little serious praying.

———◆———

The doorway into the secret place of the Most High is always open to the hand of need, and at the knocking of that hand only.

———◆———

Prayer is not an easy way of getting what we want, but the only way of becoming what God wants us to be. STUDDERT KENNEDY

———◆———

The Christian on his knees sees more than the philosopher on tiptoe. AUGUSTUS TOPLADY

———◆———

A short prayer will reach the throne — if you don't live too far away.

191

The history of the church's progress is the history of prayer.

———♦———

If prayer does not drive sin out of your life, sin will drive prayer out.

———♦———

He stands best who kneels most.

———♦———

Prayer does not need proof; it needs practice.

———♦———

Prayer is to ask not what we wish of God, but what God wishes of us.

———♦———

Motto in a church: If you must whisper, whisper a prayer.

———♦———

The Bible doesn't say we should preach all the time, but it does say we should pray all the time.   JOHN R. RICE

———♦———

If the world is ever again to get on its feet, the church will have to get on its knees.

———♦———

Prayer does not fit us for the greater works; prayer is the greater work. We think of prayer as a common sense exercise of our higher powers in order to prepare us for God's work. In the teaching of Jesus Christ prayer is the working of the miracle of redemption in others by the power of God.

OSWALD CHAMBERS

———♦———

Prayer is the most important thing in my life. If I should neglect prayer for a single day, I should lose a great deal of the fire of faith.   MARTIN LUTHER

———♦———

Kneeling in prayer keeps you in good standing.

———♦———

Prayer is a serious thing. We may be taken at our words.   D. L. MOODY

———♦———

When it is hardest to pray, we ought to pray hardest.

———♦———

Prayer is releasing the energies of God. For prayer is asking God to do what we cannot do.   CHARLES TRUMBULL

———♦———

We organize instead of agonize.

The secret of prayer is prayer in secret.

———♦———

Nothing lies beyond the reach of prayer, except that which lies outside the will of God.

———♦———

It isn't the words we say on bended knee that count, but rather it's the way we think and live out our prayers.

———♦———

Prevailing prayer brings perpetual power.   *Sunday School Journal*

———♦———

Prayer is not overcrowding God's reluctance, but taking hold of God's willingness.

———♦———

The halting utterances of the consecrated pupil, earnest though inexperienced, are better than the mere fluency of long practice.

———♦———

Daily prayer is the gymnasium of the soul.

———♦———

Groanings which cannot be uttered are often prayers which cannot be refused.   C. H. SPURGEON

———♦———

No praying man or woman accomplishes so much with so little expenditure of time as when he or she is praying.   C. E. COWMAN

———♦———

Prayer is the first thing, the second thing, and the third thing necessary for a Christian worker. Pray, then, my dear brother, pray, pray and pray.

EDWARD PAYTON

———♦———

The godly man's prayers are his best biography, his most exact portrait. People who do a lot of kneeling don't do much lying.   *Moody Church News*

———♦———

If your knees knock, kneel on them.

———♦———

The only place we can hide from God's presence is in His presence.

———♦———

You can do more than pray *after* you have prayed, but you cannot do more than pray *until* you have prayed.

Prayer moves the arm that moves the world. G. D. WATSON

Why not change the pattern of your prayers now and then? Wake up some morning and ask, "Dear Lord, is there anything I can do for You today?"
Presbyterian Life

It has been reckoned that out of 667 prayers for specific things in the Bible there are 454 traceable answers. We spend too much time studying how to pray whereas we ought rather to pray. The Bible is predominantly a book of prayer.

Finney says prayer is not to change God but to change us.

Anchor yourself to the throne of God, then shorten the rope.

The only way to do much for God is to ask much of God.

Prayer is being intimate with God.

It is not the arithmetic of our prayers, how many they are; nor the rhetoric of our prayers, how eloquent they be; nor the geometry of our prayers, how long they may be; nor the music of our prayers, how sweet our voice may be; nor the logic of our prayers, how argumentative they may be; nor the method of our prayers, how orderly they may be; or even the theology of our prayers, how good the doctrine — which God cares for. Fervency of spirit is that which availeth much.
Moody Monthly

Two men praying the same prayers anywhere on earth will raise a commotion in heaven.
Blasts from the Ram's Horn

How deeply rooted must unbelief be in our hearts when we are surprised to find our prayers answered. HARE

Short prayers have the largest range and the surest aim.

The man who does all his praying on his knees does not pray enough.

Life gets scorched and lumpy when we forget to stir it up with prayer.

Satan trembles when he sees the weakest Christian on his knees.

All heaven listens when we send up a heartfelt prayer for an enemy's good.
Blasts from the Ram's Horn

I have so much to do that I must spend several hours in prayer before I am able to do it. JOHN WESLEY

Teachers, to be prepared you must be pre-prayered.

If you are too busy to pray, you are busier than you ought to be.

Hem in the day with prayer and it will be less likely to ravel out before night.

A child once prayed, "O Lord, make the bad people good, and the good people nice."

The Christian should have an appetite for prayer. He should want to pray. One does not have to force food upon a healthy child. Exercise, good circulation, health and labor demand food for sustenance. So it is with those who are spiritually healthy. They have an appetite for the Word of God, and for prayer.

Sin breaks fellowship with God. A little girl committed a certain offense and when her mother discovered it she began to question her daughter. Immediately the child lost her smile and a cloud darkened her face as she said, "Mother, I don't feel like talking." So it is with us when our fellowship with God is broken by sin in our lives. We do not feel like talking to Him. If you do not feel like praying, it is probably a good indication that you should start praying immediately. BILLY GRAHAM

193

PRAYER

When we pray for rain we must be willing to put up with some mud.

———◆———

Don't pray for tasks equal to your powers, but powers equal to your tasks.

———◆———

Abraham prayed and brought God down almost to his own terms.
Elijah prayed and called down fire from heaven.
Daniel prayed and was saved from the lions.
Paul prayed and the prison walls were shaken.
Luther prayed and the gates of Rome shook.
Knox prayed and Queen Mary trembled.
Wesley prayed and a great revival saved England.
Muller prayed and great orphanages were reared.
Roberts prayed and a Pentecost swept Wales. *Selected*

———◆———

A little girl was caught listening at the keyhole while her spinster aunt was saying her prayers. Her mother told her it was wrong to eavesdrop.

"But, Mommy," the child said, "Aunt Emma ended her prayer so funny."

"What did she say?" asked mother.

"Well, when she finished praying she said, 'World without men, ah me.'"

———◆———

The coed concluded her prayers with a modest appeal: "I'm not asking for myself, but please send my mother a son-in-law." *Glendale News Press*

———◆———

Here's the prayer of a child: "And, dear God, I hope You'll also take care of Yourself. If anything should happen to You, we'd be in an awful fix."

———◆———

One night a little two-and-one-half-year-old boy told his mother, "You can go now, Jesus can hear me without you here." But the mother listened at the door and heard her son say, "Jesus, will You help me to be a good boy? O.K. Amen." *Christian Parent*

Some folks are like the little boy who, when asked by his pastor if he prayed every day, replied, "No, not every day. Some days I don't want anything."

———◆———

One night little Susanne ended her prayers thus: "Good-by, dear Lord, we're moving to New York. It has been nice knowing You. Amen."

———◆———

Four-year-old Nancy's brother, Charles, had been tormenting her all afternoon by throwing stones. That night while praying, Nancy asked God to bless Charles and keep him from throwing stones. Then she remembered, after she had finished praying, that she had told God about this problem before so she added the following P.S.: "And by the way, dear God, I've mentioned this to You several times before."

———◆———

One day a mother noticed that her little girl was in her room a long, long time and she had said she was going in to pray to Jesus. Finally, when the little girl came out her mother asked her what she was doing in her room for such a long time when she had just gone in to pray.

"I was just telling Jesus that I love Him and He was telling me that He loves me. And we were just loving each other."

———◆———

When the searchers found a five-year-old boy who had been lost in the mountains for two days, they asked, "Were you afraid?"

"It was scary," the little boy answered, "but I prayed and God took good care of me."

———◆———

One day a Sunday school superintendent came to Sunday school with her arm in a cast because she had broken it. The children placed a marker in the Bible at the front of the room to mark the place where God promised to hear the prayers of His children. It was their custom to do this when

194

they had a special prayer request and today it was a request to heal the superintendent's arm.

Several weeks went by. The superintendent had forgotten that the children kept the marker in the Bible as a reminder of their request for her. She mentioned to a teacher that the doctor was going to remove the cast that week and she hoped the arm would be all right, and not need to be reset.

One little girl had heard the superintendent mention this and so she quickly spoke up: "Oh, your arm will be all right. I prayed for you and marked the Bible where God gives His promise. Your arm will be okay." And, of course, it was.

————◆————

During the afternoon a mother had to paddle her four-year-old daughter because she deliberately disobeyed her. That evening when the little girl prayed she said, "Dear Lord, please help me to understand my mother. Amen."

————◆————

Little Raymond returned home from Sunday school in a joyous mood. "Oh, Mother," he exclaimed as he entered the house, "the superintendent said something awfully nice about me in his prayer today."

"Isn't that wonderful!" said the mother. "What did he say?"

"He said, 'Oh, Lord, we thank Thee for food and Raymond,'" replied the lad.

————◆————

Roger and his mother were visiting an aunt during deer season. They knew there were a lot of hunters out but were surprised toward evening to hear shooting right in the barnyard. They rushed from the house just in time to see a wounded deer enter the orchard and start up the canyon. The hunters who had wounded the deer turned back for easier game. Knowing the deer to be badly wounded, Roger's mother took a rifle and followed its trail while Roger stayed with his aunt.

Time went on and it grew quite dark. Roger worried and finally went to his aunt and said: "It's getting blacker and blacker, Aunty, and Mother isn't back. Don't you think we'd better pray a little and set God on her trail?"

————◆————

One evening six-year-old Bobby asked his father for a pet.

"Sorry, Son," his father said, "not now. But if you pray real hard for two months, perhaps God will send you a baby brother."

Bobby prayed faithfully for a month, but it seemed futile to pray longer so he gave up.

How surprised he was, when a month later, a little baby boy arrived at their home, or so Bobby thought when he saw a squirming bundle beside his mother. His proud father drew back the cover and Bobby saw another baby. Twins!

"Aren't you glad you prayed for a baby brother?" asked his father.

"I sure am," said the boy. "But aren't you glad I stopped praying when I did?" *Together*

————◆————

President Eisenhower opened his second inaugural address with a plea for "the favor of almighty God" on the common labor of all Americans.

"And the hopes of our hearts fashion the deepest prayers of our people. May we pursue the right — without self-righteousness. May we know unity — without conformity. May we grow in strength — without pride of self. May we, in our dealings with all peoples of the earth, ever speak truth and serve justice."

————◆————

A British soldier one night was caught creeping stealthily back to his quarter from a near-by woods. He was immediately hauled before his commanding officer and charged with holding communications with the enemy. The man pleaded that he had gone into the woods to pray. That was his only defense.

"Have you been in the habit of

spending hours in private prayer?" growled the officer.

"Yes, sir."

"Then down on your knees and pray now!" he roared. "You never needed to so much."

Expecting immediate death, the soldier knelt and poured out his soul in prayer that for eloquence could have been inspired only by the power of the Holy Spirit.

"You may go," said the officer when he had finished. "I believe your story. If you hadn't drilled often, you couldn't have done so well at review."

Sunday School Promoter

———◆———

The Power of Prayer

Moses prayed, his prayer did save,
  A nation from death and from the grave.
Joshua prayed. The sun stood still
  His enemies fell in vale and hill.
Hannah prayed, God gave her a son;
  A nation back to the Lord he won.
Solomon prayed for wisdom.
  Then God made him the wisest of mortal men.
Elijah prayed with great desire,
  God gave him rain, and sent the fire.
Jonah prayed, God heard his wail;
  He quickly delivered him from the whale.
Three Hebrews prayed, through flames they trod;
  They had as a comrade the "Son of God."
Elisha prayed with strong emotion;
  He got the mantle and a "double portion."
Daniel prayed. The lion's claws
  Were held by the angel who locked their jaws.
Ten Lepers prayed, to the priests were sent;
  Glory to God! they were healed as they went.
Peter prayed, and Dorcas arose
  To life again, from death's repose.
The thief who prayed — for mercy cried,
  He went with Christ to Paradise.

The Church, she prayed, then got a shock;
  When Peter answered her prayer with a knock!
Abram stopped praying, cities fell,
  With all their sins, into hell!
The Disciples kept praying, the Spirit came,
  With "cloven tongue," and revival flame!
Conviction filled the hearts of men;
  Three thousand souls were "born again!"
When Christians pray, as they prayed of yore,
With living faith, for souls implore,
In one accord, united stand —
  Revival fires shall sweep the land!
And sinners shall converted be,
  And all the world God's glory see!

———◆———

My Gift

I cannot sway the multitudes
With words of grace sublime,
But I can pray for those who speak,
And God's anointing for them seek —
  This gift is mine!

I cannot go to lands afar
Engulfed in heathen night,
But I can give myself to prayer
For those who the glad tidings bear
  Of Christ, the light.

Yes, though I cannot preach or go,
Sin's strongholds I may sway
While on my knees before God's throne,
I intercede for all His own,
  For I can pray! AVIS B. CHRISTIANSEN

———◆———

Those Who Talk with God

How lovely are the faces
Of those who talk with God,
Lit with an inner sureness
Of the path their feet have trod.

Keen are the hands and feet—oh, yes!—
Of those who wait His will;
And clear as crystal mirrors
Are the hearts His love can fill.

AUTHOR UNKNOWN

Keep on Praying

Just keep on praying "Till light breaks
  through!"
The Lord will answer, will answer you,
God keeps His promise, His Word is
  true —
Just keep on praying "Till light breaks
  through!"

———♦———

The Importance of Prayer

Prayer is like . . .
  The porter — to watch the door of
  our lips.
  The guard — to keep the fort of our
  hearts.
  The hilt of the sword — to defend our
  hands.
  A *master workman* — who accomplishes things.
  A *barometer* — to show our spiritual
  condition.   Selected

———♦———

I met a poor soul in the depths of despair,
Who climbed to the heights in answer
  to prayer.

———♦———

A Sunday School Teacher's Prayer

  Several souls
  Will come to me today
  To hear of Thee.
  What I am,
  What I say,
  Will lead them to Thee,
  Or drive them away.
  Stand by, Lord, I pray.

———♦———

Prayer

Prayer is so simple;
It is like quietly opening a door
And slipping into the very presence of
  God,
There in the stillness
To listen to His voice;
Perhaps to petition,
Or only to listen;
It matters not.
Just to be there
In His presence
Is prayer.   Selected

Pray

When the great seething mass
  of others' need
    overwhelms me,
      I will pray.

When the great scalding blow
  of others' wrath
    falls round me,
      I will pray.

When the blind indifference
  of this world
    dismays me,
      I will pray.

When selfish greed and lack
  of faith hold sway,
    appall me,
      I will pray.

When the loved beauty of
  our Father's world
    enchants me,
      I will pray.

When His great loving kindness
  fills my soul,
    delights me,
      I will pray.

When God's mercy, His pardon
  and His grace
    challenge me,
      I will pray.

This His good gift to us
  His children here —
    that we may pray.
              MARY C. RIDER

———♦———

Prayer

If radio's slim fingers
Can pluck a melody
From night, and toss it over
A continent or sea —

If the petaled white notes
Of a violin
Are blown across a mountain
Or a city's din —

If songs, like crimson roses
Are culled from thin blue air,
Why should mortals wonder
If God hears prayer?
              EDITH ROMIG FULLER

PRAYER

The Christian's Prayer

Lord, make me free . . .
From fear of the future;
From anxiety of the morrow;
From bitterness toward anyone;
From cowardice in face of danger;
From failure before opportunity;
From laziness in face of work.

SOURCE UNKNOWN

———◆———

Bobbie's Prayer

Dear Father, there is this other boy
    tonight
Who's praying to a god that's made
    of wood:

He asks it to take care of him tonight
And love him — but it won't do any
    good.

He is so far I cannot make him hear.
I'd call to him and tell him if I could

That You'd take care of him, that You
    are near
And love him — but his god is made
    of wood.

I know he'd ask You if he only knew,
I know he'd love to know You if he
    could.

Dear God, take care of him and love
    him, too,
The other boy whose god is made of
    wood.

Selected

———◆———

Evening Prayer

Thank You, God, for this nice day,
Thank You for my work and play
For Your care the whole day through.
Thank You, God, for all You do. Amen.

———◆———

The Way

Have you ever watched a child
At the close of day —
Have you ever seen that child
Fold its hands and pray?

Not a thought of human pride,
Envy, doubt or care;
Not the love of earthly things
Can be reigning there.

Humble words and simple faith,
Trust in God, complete,
Eagerness to cast itself
At the Savior's feet.

So must you to find the way,
Mark the Savior's word;
As a humble, simple child,
Come unto the Lord.   RUDOLPH EVERS

———◆———

A Child's Prayer

Angel of God, my guardian dear,
To whom His love commits me here,
Ever this day be at my side
To light and guard, to rule and guide.
Amen.

———◆———

The Difference

I got up early one morning
And rushed right into the day;
I had so much to accomplish
That I didn't take time to pray.

Problems just tumbling about me,
And heavier came each task;
"Why doesn't God help me?" I won-
    dered.
He answered: "You didn't ask."

I wanted to see joy and beauty —
But the day toiled on, gray and bleak;
I wondered why God didn't show me,
He said: "But you didn't seek."

I tried to come into God's presence,
I used all my keys at the lock
God gently and lovingly chided:
"My child, you didn't knock."

I woke up early this morning
And paused before entering the day;
I had so much to accomplish
That I had to take time to pray.

Selected

———◆———

Heavenly Father, hear our prayer,
Keep us in Thy loving care.
Guard us through the livelong day
In our work and in our play.
Keep us pure and sweet and true
In everything we say and do.
Amen.

Now I lay me down to sleep;
I pray the Lord my soul to keep.
If I should die before I wake,
I pray the Lord my soul to take.

ISAAC WATTS, 1732

Morning Prayers

Father, we thank Thee for the night,
And for the pleasant morning light
For rest and food and loving care,
And all that makes the world so fair.

Help us to do the things we should,
To be to others kind and good,
In all we do in work and play
To grow more loving every day.
Amen.

Childlike Trust

"Now I lay me" — say it, darling;
"Lay me," lisped the tiny lips
Of my daughter, kneeling, bending,
O'er her folded finger tips.

"Down to sleep" — "to sleep," she mur-
mured,
And the curly head drooped low;
"I pray the Lord," I gently added,
"You can say it all, I know."

"Pray the Lord" — the words came
faintly,
Fainter still — "My soul to keep,"
Then the tired head fairly nodded,
And the child was fast asleep.

But the dewy eyes half opened
When I clasped her to my breast,
And the dear voice softly whispered,
"Mamma, God knows all the rest."

Oh, the trusting, sweet confiding
Of the child-heart! Would that I
Thus might trust my Heavenly Father,
He who hears my feeblest cry.
COL. THOS. H. AYERS

Table Graces

God is great and God is good;
Let us thank Him for our food.
By His hand we all are fed;
Thank You, God, for daily bread.
Amen.

Father in heaven, sustain our bodies
with this food, our hearts with true
friendship, and our souls with Thy
truth, For Jesus' sake. Amen.

Father, bless the food we take
And bless us all for Jesus' sake.
Amen.

Lord Jesus, be our holy Guest,
Our morning Joy, our evening Rest;
And with our daily bread impart
Thy love and peace to every heart.
Amen.

The Teacher's Prayer

Lord, who am I to teach the way
To little children, day by day —
So prone myself to go astray?

I teach them knowledge — but I know
How faint they flicker and how low —
The candles of my knowledge glow.

I teach them power to will and do —
But only now to learn anew
My own great weakness through and
through.

I teach them love for all mankind
And all God's creatures — but I find
My love comes lagging still behind.

Lord, if their guide I still must be,
O let the little children see
The teacher leaning hard on Thee.
EDWARD A. ESTAPER

The Secret

I met God in the morning
When the day was at its best,
And His presence came like sunrise,
Like a glory in my breast.
All day long the Presence lingered,
All day long He stayed with me
And we sailed in perfect calmness
O'er a very troubled sea.
Other ships were blown and battered
Other ships were sore distressed
But the winds that seemed to drive
them
Brought to us a peace and rest.
Then I thought of other mornings
With a keen remorse of mind

199

When I, too, had loosed the moorings
With the Presence left behind.
So I think I know the secret
Learned from many a troubled way
You must seek Him in the morning
If you want Him through the day.

AUTHOR UNKNOWN

The Kitchen Prayer

Lord of all pots and pans and things,
  since I've not time to be
A saint by doing lovely things or
  watching late with Thee
Or dreaming in the dawn light or
  storming Heaven's gates,
Make me a saint by getting meals
  and washing up the plates.
Although I must have Martha's hands,
  I have a Mary mind
And when I black the boots and
  shoes, Thy sandals, Lord, I find.
I think of how they trod the earth,
  what time I scrub the floor
Accept this meditation Lord, I haven't
  time for more.
Warm all the kitchen with Thy love,
  and light it with Thy peace
Forgive me all my worrying and
  make my grumbling cease.
Thou who dids't love to give men food,
  in room or by the sea
Accept this service that I do, I do it
  unto Thee.   AUTHOR UNKNOWN

Preach, Preacher, Preaching

The Preacher

If he's young, he lacks experience;
if his hair is gray he's too old.

If he has five or six children, he has
too many; if he has none, he isn't setting a good example.

If his wife sings in the choir, she's
being forward; if not, she's not interested in her husband's work.

If he speaks from notes, he has
canned sermons and is dry; if he is ex-
temporaneous, he's too deep.

If he spends too much time in his
study, he neglects his people; if he
visits he's a gadabout.

If he is attentive to the poor, he's

playing the grandstand; if to the
wealthy, he's trying to be an aristocrat.

If he suggests improvements, he's a
dictator; if he doesn't he's a figure-
head.

If he uses too many illustrations he
neglects the Bible; if not enough, he's
not clear.

If he condemns wrong, he is cranky;
if he doesn't he is a compromiser.

If he preaches an hour, he's windy;
if less, he's lazy.

If he preaches the truth, he's offen-
sive; if not, he's a hypocrite.

If he fails to please everyone, he's
hurting the church; if he does please
everyone, he has no convictions.

If he preaches tithing, he's a money
grabber; if he doesn't, he is failing to
develop his people.

If he receives a large salary he's mercenary; if a small salary it proves he's
not worth much.

If he preaches all the time, the people get tired of hearing one man; if
he invites guest preachers he's shirking
responsibility.

And some folks think the preacher
has an easy time.

AUTHOR UNKNOWN

Qualifications of a Pastor

The strength of an ox.
The tenacity of a building.
The daring of a lion.
The patience of a donkey.
The industry of a beaver.
The versatility of a chameleon.
The vision of an eagle.
The melodies of a nightingale.
The meekness of a lamb.
The hide of a rhinoceros.
The disposition of an angel.
The resignation of an incurable.
The loyalty of an apostle.
The faithfulness of a prophet.
The tenderness of a shepherd.
The fervency of an evangelist.
The devotion of a mother.

Christian Beacon

You can preach a better sermon with
your life than with your lips.

When I preach I regard neither doctors nor magistrates, of whom I have above forty in the congregation; I have all my eyes on the servant maids and on the children. And if the learned men are not well pleased with what they hear, well, the door is open.

MARTIN LUTHER

———◆———

As long as there are people in the world, so long must we preach the Gospel of Christ.   CHR. CHRISTIANSEN

———◆———

Preaching without emotion is not preaching, but beware of the cheap substitute.

———◆———

The preacher who does not evangelize will fossilize.

———◆———

The sexton had been laying the new carpet on the pulpit platform and had left a number of tacks scattered on the floor. "See here, James," said the parson, "what do you suppose would happen if I stepped on one of those tacks right in the middle of my sermon?"

"Well, sir," replied the sexton, "I reckon there'd be one point you wouldn't linger on!"

———◆———

A preacher who was in the habit of writing his sermons out carefully found himself at church one Sunday morning without his manuscript. "As I have forgotten my notes," he began his sermon, "I will have to rely on the Lord for guidance. Tonight I shall come better prepared."

———◆———

For an hour and a half the pastor droned on with his fervent sermon. Finally he asked: "What more can I say?"

There was a pause. Then from the rear pew: "You might say amen."

———◆———

A preacher was disturbed by the snoring of the grandpa at the front. He stopped preaching and asked the little boy to awaken him.

He promptly answered, "You wake him up, you put him to sleep."

A zealous preacher with a sense of humor posted this on his office door: "If you have troubles, come in and tell me about them. If not, by all means come in and tell me how you avoid them."   Presbyterian Life

———◆———

A preacher had succeeded in putting an elderly man asleep by his sermon. Preaching for a decision, in the midst of his sermon, he shouted, "Those who want to go to hell, *stand up.*" The old man heard the "Stand up" and did so.

He looked around, paused with a puzzled look on his face and said, "Preacher, I don't know what we're voting on, but it looks like you and I are the only ones for it."

———◆———

He who lives well is the best preacher.   CERVANTES

———◆———

A preacher's diet consists of cold shoulder and spiced tongue.

———◆———

The parson should tell folks how to get on, not where to get off.

C. GRANT

———◆———

"In time of trial," the preacher droned after seventy minutes of droning, "what brings us the greatest joy?"

Some sinner in the back row answered, "An acquittal!"   Presbyterian Life

———◆———

You can't tell how much a preacher is doing for the Lord by the size of his salary.

———◆———

Prejudice

When a prejudiced man thinks, he just rearranges his thoughts.

———◆———

People are usually down on what they are not up on.

———◆———

The tight skirts of prejudice shorten the steps of progress.

———◆———

We should never let our prejudices against certain people prejudice us against their ideas and their accomplishments.

There isn't a parallel of latitude but thinks it would have been the equator if it had had its rights.   MARK TWAIN

———♦———

A chip on the shoulder is the heaviest load you can carry.

———♦———

Prejudice has always been the greatest obstacle to progress.

———♦———

A prejudice is a vagrant opinion without visible means of support.   BIERCE

———♦———

Prepare, Prepared, Preparation

Before beginning, prepare carefully.
    CICERO

———♦———

Seventy-five per cent of the victory depends on preparation.
    DR. C. E. MATTHEWS

———♦———

The prepared man succeeds; the unprepared man fails.

———♦———

Press, Printing

The press is the foe of rhetoric, but the friend of reason.

———♦———

The Reformation was cradled in the printing press, and established by no other instrument.   AGNES STRICKLAND

———♦———

A drop of ink may make a million think.

———♦———

Four hundred years ago Martin Luther said, "We must throw the printer's inkpot at the devil."

———♦———

Pretender, Pretense

No Sense in Pretense

You tell what you are by the friends you seek,
By the manner in which you speak.
By the way you employ your leisure time,
By the use you make of dollar and dime.
You tell what you are by the things you wear,
By the spirit in which you burdens bear,
By the kind of thing at which you laugh,
By records you play on the phonograph.
You tell what you are by the way you walk,
By the things of which you delight to talk,
By the manner in which you bear defeat,
By so simple a thing as how you eat.
By the books you choose from the well-filled shelf;
In these ways and more, you tell on yourself.
So there's really no particle of sense
In any effort at pretense.
    AUTHOR UNKNOWN

———♦———

Children are quick to detect pretense and to shun the pretender. Only the genuine, the true man or woman, can hope to lead them long.   *Selected*

———♦———

Pride, Proud

Always hold your head up, but be careful to keep your nose at a friendly level.

———♦———

The remarkable thing about family pride is that so many people can be so proud of so little.

———♦———

Swallowing of pride seldom leads to indigestion.

———♦———

Don't let your pride get inflated — you may have to swallow it someday.

———♦———

The man who is not proud of his church seldom makes the church proud of him.   T. J. BACH

———♦———

The proud hate pride — in others.
    BENJAMIN FRANKLIN

———♦———

Problem, Problems

Problems are only opportunities in work clothes.   HENRY J. KAISER

Why can't life's problems hit us when we are 18 and know everything!

Glendale News Press

Show Us

Folks say we do a lot of things
We hadn't oughta had;
We never mean a bit of harm
Nor do them to be bad.

But when a chance just comes along
With fun a-peekin' through
We take it mostly just because
We've nothing else to do.

Kids are an awful problem
All the grownup people say
But honest all we really want
Is just a chance to play.

And all of us from country towns
And from the cities, too,
Will quit what you call mischief
If you show us what to do.

AUTHOR UNKNOWN

Procrastinate

You may delay, but time will not.

BENJAMIN FRANKLIN

Always put off until tomorrow the things you shouldn't do at all.

FRANCES RODMAN

Profane, Profanity

Someone has said that profanity is the effort of a feeble mind to express itself forcibly.

He knew not what to say, and so he swore.

LORD BYRON

Progress

It is a "little farther" that costs, but it is a "little farther" that counts.

You only go as far as you go on your knees.

Progress is the great law of life.

Progress has little to do with speed, but much with direction.

If you want to go higher, go deeper.

After Calvin Coolidge made known to the public that he "did not choose to run," he was besieged by newspaper reporters for a more elaborate statement. It seems that one was more persistent than the others.

"Exactly why don't you want to be president again?" he inquired.

"No chance for advancement," was the president's reply. WALTER J. BARTAZEK

Progress, like running a locomotive, requires cooperation.
The crew must be organized.
Machinery must be well-oiled.
It must be fired up.
There must be steam.
Someone must be at the throttle.

Promise, Promises

There is no more perishable freight than a bulging crate of promises.

A fair promise makes a fool merry.

He who promises runs in debt.

Tarry at the promise till God meets you there. He always returns by way of His promises.

While some stand on the promises, others just sit on the premises.

He who is most slow in making a promise is usually the most faithful in the performance of it. ROUSSEAU

Promises may get their friends, but non-performance will turn them into enemies. BENJAMIN FRANKLIN

Promote, Promotion

Promotion is achieved by motion.

If you want to go up, get down to work.

Two-thirds of promotion consists of motion.

Promptness

During a busy life I have often been asked, "How did you manage to do it all?" The answer is simple: Because I did everything promptly.

SIR RICHARD TANGYE

Prosperity

Sobriety is the door of prosperity.

Few of us can stand prosperity. Another man's, I mean.　　MARK TWAIN

Proverbs

A good anvil is not afraid of the hammer.

There is nothing new except what hath been forgotten.　　*English Proverb*

From saying to doing is a long stretch.　　*French*

Fuel is not sold in the forest, nor fish on the shore of a lake.　　*Chinese*

One dog barks at something, and a hundred bark at the sound.　　*Chinese*

He who wants to know himself should offend two or three of his neighbors.　　*Chinese*

Well begun is half done.

Little boats should keep the shore.

An old fox is not caught in a trap.

One flower does not make a garland.

An eagle does not feed on flies.

A bow too much bent is easily broken.

The statelier the tower the heavier the crash.

Glasses and lasses are brittle ware.

There is no compassion like the penny.

Man is caught by his tongue, and an ox by his horns.　　*Russian*

To perfect diligence nothing is difficult.　　*Chinese*

It is easy to cut thongs from other men's leather.　　*Dutch*

Fashion is more powerful than any tyrant.　　*Latin*

The great calabash tree has a seed as its mother.　　*African*

He is great whose failings can be numbered.　　*Hebrew*

A guest sees more in an hour than the host in a year.　　*Polish*

The heron's a saint when there are no fish in sight.　　*Bengalese*

Hunger changes beans into almonds.　　*Italian*

Everyone can keep house better than her mother until she trieth.　　*English*

It is not easy to straighten in the oak the crook that grew in the sapling.　　*Gaelic*

A man without religion is like a horse without a bridle.　　*Latin*

Many mickles make a muckle.

He that is warm thinks all so.

One swallow does not make a summer.

The handsome flower is not the sweetest.

Rashness is the parent of misfortune.

A cracked plate may last as long as a sound one.

Little brooks make great rivers.

204

A thousand probabilities do not make one truth.

———◆———

Rough stones grow smooth from hand to hand.

———◆———

In an orderly house all is soon ready.

———◆———

Running hares need no spurs.

———◆———

He that lies down with dogs rises with fleas.   *English*

———◆———

We can never see the sun rise by looking into the west.   *Japanese*

———◆———

For a good dinner and a gentle wife you can afford to wait.   *Danish*

———◆———

He who plants trees loves others besides himself.   *English*

———◆———

Provide, Provision

Winter finds out what summer has laid up.

———◆———

God gives every bird food, but he does not throw it into the nest.
                              J. G. HOLLAND

———◆———

Psychiatry, Psychology

Two psychologists met on the street one day. One said to the other, "You're fine today, how am I?"

———◆———

"Child psychology, as a rule," says a child psychologist, "always works better when it is applied like paint — with a brush."

———◆———

Psychiatrist: "Don't worry too much if your son likes to make mud pies, and even if he tries to eat them it is quite normal."
Mother: "Well I don't think so, and neither does his wife."

———◆———

Have you heard about the cannibal who went to a psychiatrist because he was fed up with people?

Do you know the difference between a neurotic, a psychotic and a psychiatrist?
A neurotic dreams about castles in the air.
A psychotic lives in castles in the air.
A psychiatrist collects the rent from those castles.

———◆———

"He's a psycho-ceramic."
"What's that?"
"A crackpot."

———◆———

Mother of small boy to child psychiatrist: Well, I don't know whether or not he feels insecure, but everyone else in the neighborhood certainly does.

———◆———

A psychiatrist is a guy who asks you a lot of expensive questions that your wife asks for nothing.

———◆———

A man went to a psychologist for help. "I have an inferiority complex," the man said.
"You don't have a complex," the psychologist said, "you are inferior."

———◆———

One young couple told their friends that they raised their first child according to "The Book" on child psychology. But they raised their second child on the covers of the book!

———◆———

Punctual, Punctuality

A teacher is late unless he's a half-hour early.

———◆———

Punctuality is the politeness of kings.

———◆———

Purity

Subdue your passion or it will subdue you.

———◆———

Purpose

The purposes of God are sometimes delayed, but never abandoned!

It is better to die for something than it is to live for nothing.
DR. BOB JONES, SR.

———◆———

A great purpose leads to great achievement.

———◆———

A teacher's purpose should be as great as the purpose of God.

———◆———

Poverty of purpose is worse than poverty of purse.

———◆———

A man without a purpose or goal is like a ship without a rudder, adrift on the foaming, trackless ocean.

———◆———

It is not the man with a motive but the man with a purpose who wins.

———◆———

The person with no purpose in life can never show progress.

The greatest thing in this world is not so much where we stand, as in what direction we are moving.
OLIVER W. HOLMES

———◆———

My Symphony

To live content with small means;
To seek elegance rather than luxury and refinement rather than fashion;
To be worthy, not respectable, and wealthy, not rich;
To listen to stars and birds, babes and sages with open heart;
To study hard;
To think quietly, act frankly, talk gently, await occasions, hurry never;
In a word, to let the spiritual, unbidden and unconscious, grow up through the common —
This is my symphony.
WILLIAM HENRY CHANNING

Q

Quality

Only a mediocre person is always at his best.
SOMERSET MAUGHAM

———◆———

God does not want us to do extraordinary things;
He wants us to do the ordinary things extraordinarily well.
BISHOP GORE

———◆———

Nothing comes out of a sack but what was put into it.

———◆———

All is not gold that glitters.

———◆———

Quarrel, Quarreling

Where one will not, two cannot quarrel.

———◆———

Quarrels would never last long if there were not faults on both sides.
LA ROCHEFOUCAULD

———◆———

A quarrelsome man has no good neighbors.
BENJAMIN FRANKLIN

Those who in quarrels interpose, must often wipe a bloody nose.
BENJAMIN FRANKLIN

———◆———

Questions, Quizzes

I can't understand why goods sent by ship are called cargo, while goods sent in a car are a shipment.

———◆———

We may not put a question mark where God puts a period.

———◆———

Who was a lady but was never a little girl? Eve.

———◆———

What man was never born? Adam.

———◆———

The Master's Question

Have ye looked for my sheep in the desert,
For those who have missed the way?
Have you been in the wild, waste places,

Where the lost and wandering stray?
Have ye trodden the lonely highway,
  The foul and the darksome street?
It may be ye'd see in the gloaming
  The print of My wounded feet.

Have ye folded home to your bosom
  The trembling, neglected lamb,
And taught to the little lost one
  The sound of the Shepherd's Name?
Have ye searched for the poor and
  needy
  With no clothing, no home, no
  bread?
The Son of Man was among them —
  He had nowhere to lay His head.

Have ye carried the living water
  To the parched and thirsty soul?
Have ye said to the sick and wounded,
  "Christ Jesus make thee whole"?
Have ye told My fainting children
  Of the strength of the Father's hand?
Have ye guided the tottering footsteps
  To the shore of the golden land?

Have ye stood by the sad and weary
  To soothe the pillow of death;
To comfort the sorrowful, stricken,
  And strengthen the feeble faith?
And have ye felt when the glory
  Has streamed through the open door,
And flitted across the shadows,
  That there I have been before?

Have ye wept with the broken-hearted
  In their agony of woe?
Ye might hear Me whispering beside
  you,
" 'Tis the pathway I often go!"
AUTHOR UNKNOWN

Quiet

Quietness

"Be still and know that I am God,"
That I who made and gave thee life
Will lead thy faltering steps aright;
That I who see each sparrow's fall
Will hear and heed thy earnest call.
  I am thy God.

"Be still and know that I am God,"
When aching burdens crush thy heart.
Then know I formed thee for thy part
And purpose in the plan I hold.
Thou art the clay that I would mold.
  Trust thou in God.

"Be still and know that I am God,"
Who made the atom's tiny span
And set it moving to my plan,
That I who guide the stars above
Will guide and keep thee in my love.
  Be thou still. AUTHOR UNKNOWN

———◆———

Beware of a silent dog and still
water.

———◆———

Quit

Don't Quit

When things get wrong, as they some-
  times will,
When the road you are trudging seems
  all up hill;
When the funds are low and the debts
  are high
And you want to smile, but you have
  to sigh;
When care is pressing you down a bit,
Rest if you must, but don't you quit.
Success is failure turned inside out;
The silver tint of the clouds of doubt.
And you can never tell how close you
  are
It may be near when it seems afar;
So stick to the fight when you're hard-
  est hit —
It's when things seem worst that you
  mustn't quit. AUTHOR UNKNOWN

———◆———

Too many people have finishing
fever.

———◆———

Someone worse than a quitter is
someone who finishes something he
should never have started.

———◆———

Trying times are no time to quit
trying.

R

Read, Readings

Time to Read the Bible

It takes 70 hours and 40 minutes to read the Bible at pulpit rate.

It takes 52 hours and 20 minutes to read the Old Testament.

It takes 18 hours and 20 minutes to read the New Testament.

In the Old Testament the Psalms take the longest to read: 4 hours and 28 minutes.

In the New Testament the Gospel of Luke takes 2 hours and 43 minutes to read.

———◆———

Reading is of no value unless we translate what we read into life itself.

———◆———

The number of people who can read is small, and the number of those who can read to any purpose, much smaller, and the number of those who are too tired after a hard day's work to read — enormous. But all except the blind and deaf can see and hear.
GEORGE BERNARD SHAW

———◆———

The man who does not read good books has no advantage over the man who can't read them.

———◆———

Reading is to the mind what exercise is to the body.   JOSEPH ADDISON

———◆———

To acquire the habit of reading is to construct for yourself a refuge from almost all the miseries of life.
SOMERSET MAUGHAM

———◆———

Show me a family of readers, and I will show you the people who move the world.   NAPOLEON

———◆———

Resolve to edge in a little reading every day. If you gain but 15 minutes a day, it will make itself felt at the end of a year.   HORACE MANN

Sales-minded executives should cultivate faster, more effective reading. Reading should not be regarded as an isolated skill. Many jobs presuppose the ability to read well. Sales executives have to read for a variety of purposes and should not have to read everything the same way. To be a flexible reader requires fast, effective reading habits. Reading, vocabulary, comprehension and rate can be improved through definite and systematic training. Effective reading habits may mean the difference between lacking self-confidence and having it. Improved reading will result in improved effectiveness in your job and you will be a greater asset to your company.   ELIZABETH A. SIMPSON

———◆———

Primary-age children enjoy reading. One day six-year-old Johnny, who had just started public school, volunteered to read the twenty-third Psalm for the Scripture lesson in primary church. Carefully he picked up the Bible, opened it and read the verses, letter-perfect.

The teacher, knowing Johnny had just started school, was so surprised that she slipped up behind him to observe his reading. Sure enough, he read the passage right, line for line, word for word — but the Bible was upside down!

———◆———

The love of reading enables a man to exchange the wearisome hours of life which come to everyone for hours of delight.   MONTESQUIEU

———◆———

Real, Reality

What you would seem to be, be really.   BENJAMIN FRANKLIN

———◆———

A rainbow is as real as a derrick.
RICHARD LE GALLIENNE

208

Water changes its color while passing through rocks and swift currents: for a moment it is churned into white foam. Reality often looks unreal when passing through tests and opposition.

———◆———

Reason, Reasonings

To everything there is a reason.

———◆———

A man without reason is out of season.

———◆———

It has been said that there are two reasons for everything we do — a good reason and the real reason. We can give a good reason to others. But to God we have to give the real reason.

———◆———

He who will not reason is a bigot; he who cannot is a fool; he who dares not is a slave. WALTER DRUMMOND

———◆———

Reason never shows itself so unreasonable as when it ceases to reason about things which are above reason.

———◆———

Hear reason or she'll make you feel her. BENJAMIN FRANKLIN

———◆———

"Are you in pain, my little man?" asked the kind old gentleman.
"No," answered the boy, "the pain's in me."

———◆———

Teacher: "Which is more important to us — the moon or the sun?"
Johnny: "The moon."
Teacher: "Why?"
Johnny: "The moon gives us light at night when we need it. The sun gives us light only in the daytime when we don't need it." Christian Herald

———◆———

The father played possum while his youngsters tried their best to rouse him from a Sunday afternoon nap to take them for a promised walk. Finally, his five-year-old daughter pried open one of his eyelids, peered carefully, then reported: "He's still in there." Reville

Recitation, Recite

A Methodist missionary to the Spanish mission in Florida was giving a program for the children and had given them pieces to learn. One day he received a note from a mother: "Dear Pastor — I am sorry Carlos will not be able to recite on Friday. The goat ate his speech." Together

———◆———

Albert was taking a part in a local concert. He was only seven years old, but recited so well that he was encored.
"Well, Albert, and how did you get on?" asked the proud father when he returned home.
"Why, I thought I did all right," replied the youngster, "but they made me do it again."

———◆———

Redemption

Redemption was not an afterthought with God.

———◆———

Refine, Refinement

The turning lathe that has the sharpest knives produces the finest work.

———◆———

Some people become so polished they cast reflections on everyone.

———◆———

Reform, Reformer

A reformer is one who insists upon his conscience being your guide. Town Journal

———◆———

Reform only yourself; for in doing that you do everything. MONTAIGNE

———◆———

A man who reforms himself has contributed his full share towards the reformation of his neighbor. NORMAN DOUGLAS

———◆———

Refuge

Can I find refuge
    in Jesus? — Question
I find refuge in Jesus. — Affirmative
Find refuge in Jesus. — Exhortation

Refuge in Jesus. — Consolation
In Jesus. — Exaltation
Jesus. — Satisfaction

——◆——

Regret

Why cry over spilt milk when it is already four-fifths water?

——◆——

Seven Things You Never Regret
Feeling reverence for your Maker.
Showing kindness to an aged person.
Destroying a letter written in anger.
Offering the apology that saves a friendship.
Stopping a scandal that could wreck a reputation.
Taking time to show loved ones consideration.
Accepting the judgment of God on any question.　　ANONYMOUS

——◆——

Religion, Religious

The religions of the world say "do and live." The religion of the Bible says, "live and do."　　DR. BOB JONES, SR.

——◆——

Religion is the best armor that a man can have, but it is the worst cloak.
　　　　　　　　JOHN BUNYAN

——◆——

It is natural to be religious; it is supernatural to be Christian.
　　　　　　　　W. M. CRAIG

——◆——

If men are so wicked with religion, what would they be without it?
　　　　　　BENJAMIN FRANKLIN

——◆——

It is a poor religion that is never strong except when the owner is sick.

——◆——

Sure religion costs — but irreligion's bill is bigger.

——◆——

The need of the hour is not more legislation. The need of the hour is more religion.　　ROGER BABSON

——◆——

"Are mosquitoes religious?"
"Yes. They first sing over you and then they prey on you."

Some people endure religion; others enjoy salvation.

——◆——

Some people never think of religion until they come in sight of a cemetery.

——◆——

A religion that never suffices to govern a man will never suffice to save him. That which does not distinguish him from a sinful world will never distinguish him from a perishing world.
　　　　　　　　JOHN HOWE

——◆——

People are not interested in religion but in reality.　　DR. HENRIETTA C. MEARS

——◆——

Religion

Get religion like a Methodist,
Experience it like a Baptist,
Be sure of it like a Disciple,
Stick to it like a Lutheran,
Pay for it like a Presbyterian,
Conciliate it like a Congregationalist,
Glorify it like a Jew,
Be proud of it like an Episcopalian,
Practice it like a Christian Scientist,
Propagate it like a Roman Catholic,
Work for it like a Salvation Army lassie,
And enjoy it like a colored man.
　　　　　DR. EDGAR DE WITT JONES

——◆——

Religion without morality is a tree without fruits; morality without religion is a tree without roots.
　　　　　　HAROLD W. RUOPP

——◆——

When asked why I was looking so healthy, I explained that I had taken up yogurt. My friend exclaimed, "It just shows that some of those funny foreign religions can really help a person!"

——◆——

Many have quarreled about religion that never practiced it.
　　　　　　BENJAMIN FRANKLIN

——◆——

The religion that makes a man look sick certainly won't cure the world.
　　　　　　PHILLIPS BROOKS

——◆——

The world does not need a definition of religion so much as it needs a demonstration.

Let your religion be not a goad but a goal.

———♦———

Still religion like still water freezes first.

———♦———

A religion that costs nothing does nothing.

———♦———

Remember, Recall

When We Were Kids

Some of us — but we'd hate to admit it — can remember when —
Nobody swatted the fly.
Nobody had appendicitis.
Nobody wore white shoes.
Cream was five cents a pint.
Cantaloupes were muskmelons.
Milk-shake was a favorite drink.
Advertisers were supposed to tell the truth.
You never heard of a gas wagon.
Doctors wanted to look at your tongue.
The hired girl received one-fifty a week.
And the hired man got ten dollars a month.
Farmers drove to town for their mail.
Nobody listened in on a telephone.
Nobody was bothered with static on the radio.
Nobody cared about the price of gasoline.
The butcher threw in a chunk of liver.
The clothing merchant threw in a pair of suspenders with a new suit.
Straw stacks were burned instead of baled.   ANONYMOUS

———♦———

Repent, Repentance

You cannot repent too soon, because you know not how soon it may be too late.

———♦———

Repentance is being so sorry for sin you quit sinning.

———♦———

Repentance is a change of heart, not an opinion.   *Eternity*

Reputation

Every dissipation of youth must be paid for with a draft on old age.
                DR. BOB JONES, SR.

———♦———

Honest confession is good for the soul but hard on the reputation.

———♦———

Do not be too concerned about what people think about you — chances are they seldom think about you at all.

———♦———

Reputation is to virtue what light is to a picture.

———♦———

Reputation is precious, but character is priceless.   *Youth's Companion*

———♦———

The only reputation that matters is your reputation in heaven.

———♦———

Glass, china and reputation are easily cracked and never well mended.
                BENJAMIN FRANKLIN

———♦———

Beware of him who regards not his reputation.   *Proverb*

———♦———

It takes a lifetime to build a good reputation: It may be lost in a moment.

———♦———

A good reputation always proves to be good business capital.

———♦———

Your ideal—what you wish you were.
Your reputation — what people say you are.
Your character — what you are.

———♦———

An ill wound but not an ill name may be healed.   BENJAMIN FRANKLIN

———♦———

The way to gain a good reputation is to endeavor to be what you desire to appear.   SOCRATES

———♦———

Research

It takes a lot to teach a little.

———♦———

You never get anything you don't dig for.

We do not need many researchers today; what we need are searchers.

LOUIS N. KATZ, M.D. in A.M.A. Journal

Resist

Every moment of resistance to temptation is a victory.

FABER

Better shun the bait than struggle in the snare.

DRYDEN

"I can resist everything," said the young lady, "except temptation."

Resolutions

The first things broken each new year are resolutions.

Good resolutions are like babies crying in church: They should be carried out immediately!

CHARLES M. SHELDON

He that resolves to mend hereafter resolves not to mend now!

Resources, Resourceful

It is seldom that we find out how great are our resources until we are thrown upon them.

BOVEE

A father was taking his blonde toddler on a tour of the zoo and they had stopped outside the lion's cage.

"Daddy," the little tyke asked, "if the lion gets out and eats you up, what bus do I take to get home?"

Responsible, Responsibilities

We measure ourselves by the responsibility we shoulder successfully.

Some people grow under responsibility; others swell.

Weary is the head that wears the crown.

Not your responsibility, but your response to God's ability is what counts.

Regal honors have regal cares.

A youth answered an advertisement for a responsible boy. "What makes you think you're responsible?" asked the employer.

"On every job I have ever had so far," the young man answered, "whenever anything went wrong, the boss has always said to me, 'You're responsible!' "

Responsibility is our response to God's ability.

In the great ocean family the whale and herring at one time were inseparable. One day, however, they had a serious quarrel and separated, vowing never to speak again. The entire ocean family was sad. Finally, one day, a mackerel was sent to investigate the situation and see what could be done. He talked at length with the whale who he thought should be big and remedy the situation. But the whale got tired of listening to the mackerel and asked, "Say, am I my brother's kipper?"

If I am decent merely because the neighbors require it, my decency is not really decent. But when I am honest, not because business demands it, but because I demand it . . . when I am generous, not because my friends insist upon it, but because my heart insists upon it . . . when I am decent, not because the neighbors require it, but because I require it . . . *then* I have found the secret of responsibility.

COTTON

Rest

Rest

Rest is not quitting
   The busy career;
Rest is the fitting
   Of self to its sphere.
'Tis loving and serving
   The highest and best!
'Tis onward, unswerving,
   And that is true rest.

J. S. DWIGHT

There's no rest for the wicked and the righteous don't need it.

———◆———

Resurrection

In resurrection stillness there is resurrection power.

———◆———

Our Lord has written the promise of the resurrection, not in books alone, but in every leaf in springtime.
MARTIN LUTHER

———◆———

Retribution, Revenge

In taking revenge a man is but equal to his enemy, but in passing it over he is his superior.
BACON

———◆———

'Tis more noble to forgive and more manly to despise, than to revenge an injury.
BENJAMIN FRANKLIN

———◆———

He who pelts every barking dog must pick up many stones.

———◆———

Do not look for wrong and evil;
You will find them if you do:
As you measure for your neighbor,
He will measure back to you.

———◆———

After a lengthy search through her purse, the lady who had just boarded a streetcar handed the conductor a twenty dollar bill.

"I'm sorry," she snapped, noting the conductor's disapproving glance, "but I don't have a nickel."

"Oh, don't worry lady," he reassured her. "You'll have three hundred and ninety-nine of them in a minute!"

———◆———

The only people you should try to get even with are those who have helped you in some way.
Hoard's Dairyman

———◆———

You can never get ahead of anyone as long as you are trying to get even with him.

———◆———

Don't lay for your enemies nor lie for your friends.

Reverence

Reverence for the things of God must be taught as well as caught. H. C. GARNER

———◆———

Reverence controls behavior, behavior does not control reverence.

———◆———

Revival

When Will We Have Revival?

When Christians wear out more carpets around the family altar than around the dressing table;

When Christians wear out more rubber tires calling on needy homes than they wear out on pleasure trips.

When Christians stop bickering over little things, and have fellowship in the spirit of divine love;

When "My people, which are called by my name, shall humble themselves and pray and seek my face and turn from their wicked ways; then will I hear from heaven, and will forgive their sins, and will heal their land" — then the revival will come.

When dad stays home from the club and lodge.

When mother stays away from the amusement places and parties.

When the car is left in the garage long enough to cool off;

When the radio and TV are turned off long enough for the entire family to tune in on God; then we shall have revival.

When preachers preach the Word of God, rather than essays on philosophy and psychology and the opinions of men.

When churches quit trying to hold together by means of entertainment and picnics.

When the folks all get back in one accord, rather than discord; then shall we have revival.

In genuine humility and submission, let us seek God's face. We must save our homes, our churches, our country.
BISHOP WM. F. ANDERSON

213

They tried to stamp out the fire of God in Jerusalem, but they scattered the embers all over the world.

HAROLD L. LUNDQUIST

———◆———

A revival spasm furnishes no permanent stimulation.

———◆———

Rich, Riches

A *Child of the King*

Poor? No, of course not! Why, how could I be,
When Christ, the King, is taking care of me?
Tired? Sometimes – yes, more than tired; but then,
I know a place where I can rest again!
Lonely? Ah, well I know the aching blight;
But now – I've Jesus with me day and night.
Burdens? I have them; oft they press me sore,
And then – I lean the harder, trust the more.
Worthy? Oh, no! The marvel of it is
That I should know such boundless love as His!
And so, I'm rich; with Christ I am "joint heir,"
Since He once stooped my poverty to share.

EDITH LILLIAN YOUNG

———◆———

It is not the fact that a man has riches which keeps him from the Kingdom of Heaven, but the fact that riches have him.

DAVID CAIRD

———◆———

The rich have plenty of relations.

———◆———

The rich are not always godly, but the godly are always rich.

———◆———

Riches exclude only one inconvenience, and that is poverty.

SAMUEL JOHNSON

———◆———

A man is rich in proportion to the number of things which he can afford to let alone.

THOREAU

Write it on your heart that every day is the best day in the year. He only is rich who owns the day, and no one owns the day who allows it to be invaded with worry, fret and anxiety. Finish every day and be done with it. You have done what you could.

RALPH WALDO EMERSON

———◆———

He who multiplies riches, multiplies cares.

BENJAMIN FRANKLIN

———◆———

Finances

When I think of the gold in the sunset,
And the silver of stars bright at night;
The platinum glow of the moonbeams,
And the pearls in a smile of delight,
I wonder if I am poor.

When I figure the emeralds in tree-tops,
And the turquoise of fresh bluebells,
The diamonds in sparkling dew,
And the wealth of a baby's yells,
I wonder if I am poor.

The gold and silver and platinum,
The sunsets rich and fine;
The diamonds and the emeralds
Are God's and God is mine.
Why, I'm rich!

VERNE ARENDS

———◆———

Ridiculous

The ridiculous man is one who never changes.

———◆———

Right, Righteous, Righteousness

No man has a right to all of his rights.

PHILLIPS BROOKS

———◆———

Our country, right or wrong. When right, to be kept right; when wrong, to be put right.

CARL SCHURZ

———◆———

I prefer to do right and get no thanks rather than to do wrong and get no punishment.

MARCUS CATO

———◆———

It is never right to do wrong!

God never alters the robe of righteousness to fit man, but the man to fit the robe.

Rut

The only difference between a rut and a grave is length.

S

Saints

Brother Mose said there were two kinds of people in his church: The saints and the ain'ts.

———♦———

Great saints are only great receivers.

———♦———

Salvation

Born once, die twice; born twice, die once.

———♦———

Salvation may come quietly, but we cannot remain quiet about it.

———♦———

Salvation of a child is like a multiplication table, capacity to win others.

———♦———

The recognition of sin is the beginning of salvation.   LUTHER

———♦———

If Christ is the way, why waste time traveling some other way?

———♦———

You asked me how I gave my heart
  to Christ,
I do not know;
There came a yearning for Him in my
  soul
So long ago;
I found earth's flowers would fade and
  die,
I wept for something that would
  satisfy
And then, and then, somehow I seemed
  to dare
To lift my broken heart to God in
  prayer.
  I do not know, I cannot tell you
  how;
I only know He is my Saviour now.
                ANONYMOUS

Which?

Just see how short this candle is,
This candle that I hold.
It represents a man who found
The Lord when he was old.
And though his light is shining now
And bright beyond a doubt
He hasn't much to give because
His light will soon be out.

This candle that I have will
Burn much longer than the other.
I love its glowing light, don't you?
It represents a mother.
She found the Lord in middle age
Her children were all grown.
If only she had known the Lord
When they were still at home.

This candle is a larger one
It represents a youth
Who gave his heart to God
And walks the path of right and truth.
His light can shine out long and bright
With many trophies won;
With more to give because
He found the Lord when he was young.

Which candle do you want to be?
The short one or the tall?
The voice of Jesus calls to you
Come now! Give Christ your all.
                AUTHOR UNKNOWN

———♦———

It has been said that chances are 5,000 to 1 against getting decisions for Christ between the ages of 18 and 25; 25,000 to 1 between 25 and 35; 80,000 to 1 between 35 and 45; 1,000,-000 to 1 between 45 and 85.

———♦———

There is but one ladder to heaven — the cross.

215

Better never to have been born at all, than never to have been born again.

———◆———

A little girl in the kindergarten department hurried home one day from Sunday school and weighed herself.

"Why did you weigh yourself again today when you just weighed yourself yesterday?" the mother asked.

"Because," the little girl replied, "I gave my heart to Jesus this morning and I wanted to see how much I weighed without it. And, Mommy, I weigh just the same."

———◆———

Suppose that Paul had been converted at seventy instead of twenty-five. There would have been no Paul in history. There was a Matthew Henry because he was converted at eleven and not at seventy; a Dr. Watts because he was converted at nine and not at sixty; a Jonathan Edwards because he was converted at eight and not at eighty; a Richard Baxter because he was converted at six and not at sixty.

How much more a soul is worth that has a lifetime of opportunity before it than the soul which has nothing! Lambs are of more worth than' sheep in the realm of souls as well as in the marketplace.   J. O. WILSON

———◆———

Too Little

Said a precious little laddie,
  To his father one bright day,
"May I give myself to Jesus,
  Let Him wash my sins away?"

"Oh, my son, but you're too little,
  Wait until you older grow,
Bigger folks, 'tis true, do need Him, but
  Little folks are safe, you know."

Said the father to his laddie
  As a storm was coming on,
"Are the sheep all safely sheltered,
  Safe within the fold, my son?"

"All the big ones are, my father,
  But the lambs, I let them go,
For I didn't think it mattered,
  Little ones are safe, you know."

Oh, my brother! Oh, my sister!
  Have you too made that mistake?
Little hearts that now are yielding
  May be hardened then — too late.

'Ere the evil days come nigh them,
  "Let the children come to Me,
And forbid them not," said Jesus,
  "For such shall My kingdom be."
    AUTHOR UNKNOWN

———◆———

I'm a Christian

I am a Christian, though I'm small;
  Jesus does not care at all
If we're three years old, or four;
  Or if we are fifty more.

If we come to Him and say,
  "Jesus, wash my sins away,"
And His Word we then believe,
  He will gladly us receive.
    AUTHOR UNKNOWN

———◆———

What Think Ye of Christ?

Youth: Too happy to think — time yet.

Manhood: Too busy to think — more gold.

Prime: Too anxious to think — worry.

Declining Years: Too aged to think — old hearts harder to get.

Dying Bed: Too ill to think — weak, suffering alone.

Death: Too late to think — the spirit has flown.

Eternity: Forever to think — God's mercy past. Into hell I am righteously cast, forever to weep my doom.
    AUTHOR UNKNOWN

———◆———

The A B C of Salvation

All have sinned, and come short of the glory of God. Romans 3:23

Behold the Lamb of God, which taketh away the sin of the world. John 1:29

Come now, and let us reason together, saith the Lord: though your sins be as scarlet, they shall be as white as snow; though they be red like crimson, they shall be as wool. Isaiah 1:18

"Dear Mother," said the little maid,
"Please whisper it to me —
Before I am a Christian
How old ought I to be?"

"How old ought you to be, dear child,
Before you can love me?"
"I always loved you, Mommy dear,
Since I was tiny, wee."

"I love you now, and always will,"
The little daughter said,
And on her mother's shoulder hid
Her golden curly head.

"How old, my girlie, must you be
Before you trust my care?"
"Oh, Mother dear, I do, I do,
I trust you everywhere."

"How old ought you to be my child,
To do the things I say?"
The little girl looked up and said,
"I can do that today."

"Then you can be a Christian, too,
Don't wait 'til you are grown.
Tell Jesus, now, you come to Him
To be His very own."

And so the little maid knelt down,
And said, "Lord, if I may,
I'd like to be a Christian now,"
He answered, "Yes; today."
                              AUTHOR UNKNOWN

Satisfaction

If you are satisfied with little in yourself, how can you demand much from others?

———◆———

When you have got a thing where you want it, it is a good thing to leave it where it is.   WINSTON CHURCHILL

———◆———

Scholarship

The riches of scholarship, the benignities of literature, defy fortune and outline calamity. They are beyond the reach of thief or moth or rust. As they cannot be inherited, so they cannot be alienated.   LOWELL

School

On the first day of school the little boy was telling his teacher about his dog.
Teacher: "What kind is it?"
Boy: "Oh, he's a mixed-up kind — sort of a cocker scandal!"

———◆———

The most difficult school is the school of hard knocks. One never graduates.

———◆———

Schools

There is a little school called home,
Where childhood's heart must learn
To meet aright the years to come,
Their hidden truth discern.

There is a larger school called books,
Where further facts are taught.
It is a tower that brightly looks
Across the world of thought.

There is a mighty school called life,
Where we must all make good
Courses conditioned in the strife
Of earlier studenthood.

The school of life will try the wit,
Nor are its courses free.
The less one waits to learn from it
The better it will be.
                              CLARENCE E. FLYNN

———◆———

School houses are the republican line of fortifications.   HORACE MANN

———◆———

School is not preparation for life, but school is life.   JOHN DEWEY

———◆———

After Tommy's first day at school, his mother asked him what happened during the day.
"Oh, nothin'," said Tommy. "A woman wanted to know how to spell 'cat,' and I told 'er."   *Florida School Journal*

———◆———

Scripture

It's not a matter of Scripture being hard to understand, but of our unwillingness to yield to it.   M. D. CHRISTENSEN

217

Different Rendering of Psalm 23:5
My cup runneth over. *Authorized Version*
My cup is teemin' fu'. *Broad Scotch*
My happiness cup fills to overflowing. *Chinese*
My cup He fills till it runs over. *Indian*
My drinking cup bubbles over. *Zulu*
Thou dost fill my cup to running over. *Tibetan*
Thou pourest out fullness to me. *German*
My cup runs over. Yes, happen what may, happiness and grace will accompany me. *French*   *Now*

———◆———

Sea

The Set of the Sail

I stood on the shore beside the sea;
The wind from the west blew fresh and free,
While past the rocks at the harbor's mouth
The ships went north and the ships went south.

And some sailed out on an unknown quest,
And some sailed into the harbor's rest;
Yet ever the wind blew out of the west.

I said to one who had sailed the sea
That this was a marvel unto me;
For how can the ships go safely forth,
Some to the south and some to the north,
Far out to sea on their golden quest,
Or into the harbor's calm and rest,
And ever the wind blow out of the west?

The sailor smiled as he answered me,
"Go where you will when you're on the sea,
Though head winds baffle and flaw a delay,
You can keep the course by night and day;
Drive with the breeze or against the gale;
It will not matter what winds prevail,
For all depends upon the set of the sail."

Voyager soul on the sea of life,
O'er waves of sorrow and sin and strife,
When fogs bewilder and foes betray,
Steer straight on your course from day to day;
Though unseen currents run deep and swift,
Where rocks are hidden and sandbars shift,
All helpless and aimless, you need not drift.

Oh, set your sail to the heavenly gale,
And then, no matter what winds prevail,
No reef shall wreck you, no calm delay,
No mist shall hinder, no storm shall stay;
Though far you wander and long you roam,
Through salt sea-spray and o'er white sea foam,
No wind that can blow but shall speed you home.   AUTHOR UNKNOWN

———◆———

Seasons

Autumn Time

With rustling rows of cornstalks,
Gay pumpkins heaped in mounds,
And hubbard squash in hummocks,
The countryside abounds.

In garb of gold and crimson,
The forest is arrayed,
The woodland wears a mantle
Of beauty on parade.

The summer sun retreating
Leaves tonic in the air,
And in the dawn there glistens
A frosty carpet fair.

It is a season teeming
With charm and festive cheer,
And life unfolds new treasures
When autumn days are here.   B. L. BRUCE

———◆———

Scarlet Ribbon

A country road is jubilant
When April runs its length
To find a fragile crocus cupped
Against a gray hill's strength;

And there is hushed tranquility
Upon the moonlit track,
Half-drifted-in, when snow lies deep
Where a country road runs back.

But when the frosted wayside vines
Hang crimson, and the curled
Bronze leaves drift underneath
Proud plumes the sumacs have un-
furled,
A country road goes up the hills
And down through autumn weather,
A gallant scarlet ribbon which
Ties farm and farm together.
RAMONA VERNON

Secrecy, Secret

When you part from your friend,
both should lock up their secrets and
exchange keys.

———•———

Don't have more secrets than you
can carry yourself.

———•———

The secret of life is not to do what
one likes, but to try to like what one
has to do. DINAH MULOCH CRAIK

———•———

Women can keep a secret as well as
men can, but it takes more of them to
do it.

———•———

Don't expect other people to keep
your secrets if you don't do it yourself!

———•———

If you would keep your secret from
an enemy, tell it not to a friend.
BENJAMIN FRANKLIN

———•———

It is wise not to seek a secret and
honest not to reveal it.
BENJAMIN FRANKLIN

———•———

Three can keep a secret if two of
them are dead. BENJAMIN FRANKLIN

———•———

Secretary

Dictated, But Not Read

"Now look here, I fired three girls
for revising my letters, see?" said the
boss to his new secretary.
"Yes, Sir."

"All right; now take a letter and take
it the way I tell you."

And the next morning Mr. C. J.
Squizz of the Squizz Soap Co., received
the following letter:

Mr. O., or A. J. or something, look
it up, Squizz, what a name, Soap
Company, Detroit, that's in Michigan, isn't it? Dear Mr. Squizz, hmmm.
The last shipment of soap you sent
us was of inferior quality and I want
you to understand — no, scratch that
out. I want you to understand —
hmmm — unless you can ship — furnish, ship, no, furnish us with your
regular soap you needn't ship us no
more, period, or whatever the grammar is.

Where was I? Paragraph. Your
soap wasn't what you said — I should
say it wasn't. Them bums tried to
put over a lot of hooey on us.
Whadda you want to paint your faces
up like Indians on the warpath?
We're sending back your last shipment tomorrow. Sure, we're gonna
send it back, I'd like to feed it to 'em
with a spoon and make 'em eat it,
the bums. Now read the letter over
—no, don't read it over, we've wasted
enough time on them crooks, fix it
up and sign my name. What do you
say we go out to lunch?

———•———

My typist has gone on hir holiday
My typist has gohn on a spree,
My typish hap gone oh hyr haliduy,
O gring bacq mu hypist to me.
Bling bac% oK Sring back
O bynk b4ck my tipishth to me, tu
mo,
Btung gicq ocsling Beck
Oh blynck ba'k mg tl/2pys? to mi.
No credit necessary

———•———

Security

At all times in history there have
been many who sought escape into
"security" from self-reliance.
HERBERT HOOVER

———•———

You cannot establish security on borrowed money. ABRAHAM LINCOLN

Self, Selfish, Selfishness

A man's Sunday-self and his week-self are like two halves of a round-trip ticket; not good if detached.

Link

———◆———

We can suffer from the paralysis of self-analysis. EUGENIA PRICE

———◆———

Self is the only prison that can bind the soul. HENRY VAN DYKE

———◆———

To have a respect for ourselves guides our morals; and to have a deference for others governs our manners.

LAURENCE STERNE

———◆———

Memo to Me:
"Others live here, too."

———◆———

Yourself

You know the model of your car,
You know just what its powers are,
You treat it with a deal of care,
Nor tax it more than it will bear,
But as to self — that's different!
Your mechanism may be bent,
Your carburetor gone to grass,
Your engine just a rusty mass,
Your wheels may wobble, and your cogs
Be handed over to the dogs.
And then you skip and skid and slide
Without a thought of things inside.
What fools indeed we mortals are
To lavish care upon a car,
With ne'er a bit of time to see
About our own machinery!

JOHN KENDRICK BANGS

———◆———

We have to make peace with our limitations. DR. HAROLD LINDSELL

———◆———

A man can stand a lot as long as he can stand himself. AXEL MUNTHE

———◆———

Self control is more often called for than self-expression. WILLIAM W. COMFORT

———◆———

The seed of strife is in selfish seeking for glory. T. C. HORTON

You Tell on Yourself

You tell on yourself by the friends you seek,
By the very manner in which you speak,
By the way you employ your leisure time,
By the use you make of dollar and dime.
You tell what you are by the things you wear
By the spirit in which you your burdens bear.
By the kind of things at which you laugh.
By the records you play on the phonograph.
You tell what you are by the way you walk,
By the things of which you delight to talk,
By the manner in which you bear defeat,
By so simple a thing as how you eat.
By the books you choose from the well-filled shelf;
By these ways and more, you tell on yourself;
So there's really no particle of sense
In an effort to keep up false pretense.

Selected

———◆———

Whenever you are too selfishly looking out for your own interest, you have only one person working for you — yourself. When you help a dozen other people with their problems, you have a dozen people working with you.

WILLIAM B. GIVEN, JR.

———◆———

The greatest difficulty with the world is not its inability to produce, but its unwillingness to share. ROY L. SMITH

———◆———

No one is fooled when you try to make him think that you have more than you have, know more than you know, are more than you are. This is one of the most pitiful gestures a young person can make. Avoid it. Be yourself. Someone is sure to like you for what you really are, and everyone will respect your lack of pretense.

S. S. Informer

Myself

I have to live with myself, and so,
I want to be fit for myself to know;
I want to be able as days go by
Always to look myself in the eye.

I don't want to stand with the setting
sun
And hate myself for the things I've
done.
I want to go out with my head erect;
I want to deserve all men's respect.

But here, in the struggle for fame and
wealth
I want to be able to like myself.
I don't want to look at myself and
know
That I'm a bluster, and bluff, and
empty show.

I can never hide myself from me
I see what others may never see;
I know what others may never know:
I can never fool myself and so
Whatever happens, I want to be
Self respecting, and conscience free.
Selected

———◆———

Make it thy business to know thyself,
which is the most difficult lesson in the
world. CERVANTES

———◆———

Master selfishness or it will master
you.

———◆———

He who lives to benefit himself confers on the world a benefit when he
dies. TERTULLIAN

———◆———

Far too frequently in this life we
are interested in only three persons:
Me, Myself and I.

———◆———

To some, "mine" is better than "ours."

———◆———

Mother: "Why Bobby, you ate all
that cake without thinking of your
little sister."
Bobby: "I was thinking of her all
the time. I was afraid she would come
before I finished it."

———◆———

It is dangerous to be self-satisfied.

Edith was a little country bounded
on the north, south, east and west by
Edith. *Reader's Digest*

———◆———

A Tea Party

I had a little tea party
This afternoon at three.
'Twas very small —
Three guests in all —
Just I, Myself and Me.

Myself ate all the sandwiches,
While I drank up the tea;
'Twas also I who ate the pie
And passed the cake to me.
AUTHOR UNKNOWN

———◆———

Sell, Selling

Tips on Selling

1. Look competent, well groomed,
   businesslike.
2. Create a pleasant buying atmosphere. Avoid pressure.
3. Be courteous, patient and helpful.
4. If you see that your customer is in
   a hurry, be quick. Indifference and
   slowness are irritating and explain
   many lost sales.
5. If you see that your customer is
   slow, wants to linger and look, adjust your speed to his. Be patient,
   be slow.
6. Do not make any criticism or comparison of any competitive merchandise to gain a sale.
7. Stress what is new, unusual or exclusive in the product.
8. Seem cooperative, sincere and convinced yourself.
9. Know the product you are selling.
   Selected

———◆———

The salesgirl at the perfume counter
leaned toward her young customer and
whispered: "If I may, let me give you
a word of advice — please don't use
this if you are bluffing."

———◆———

He who has a thing to sell
And goes and whispers in a well,
Is not so apt to get the dollars
As he who climbs a tree and hollers.

Don't Sell Me "Things"

Don't sell me clothes. Sell me neat appearance ... style ... attractiveness.

Don't sell me shoes. Sell me foot comfort and the pleasure of walking in the open air.

Don't sell me candy. Sell me happiness and the pleasure of taste.

Don't sell me furniture. Sell me a home that has comfort, cleanliness, contentment.

Don't sell me books. Sell me pleasant hours and the profits of knowledge.

Don't sell me toys. Sell me playthings to make my children happy.

Don't sell me tools. Sell me the pleasure and profit of making fine things.

Don't sell me refrigerators. Sell me the health and better flavor of fresh kept food.

Don't sell me tires. Sell me freedom from worry and low-cost-per-mile.

Don't sell me plows. Sell me green fields of waving wheat.

Don't sell me things. Sell me ideals ... feelings ... self-respect ... home life ... happiness.

Please don't sell me things!

Your Customer
Adventures in Salesmanship, Sears Roebuck & Co.

Sense

The average man has five senses: touch, taste, sight, smell and hearing. The successful man has two more: horse sense and common sense.

———◆———

The sermon is the house; the illustrations are the windows that let in the light. SPURGEON

———◆———

The most powerful part of a sermon is the man behind it. PHILLIPS BROOKS

———◆———

A good sermon consists in saying all that is necessary and nothing that is unnecessary. *Church Management*

Sermons

The Living Sermon

I'd rather see a sermon than hear one any day,
I'd rather one would walk with me than merely tell the way,
The eye's a better pupil and more willing than the ear;
Fine counsel is confusing, but example's always clear.
The best of all the preachers are the men who live their creeds.
For to see good put in action is what everybody needs.

I soon can learn to do it if you'll let me see it done,
I can watch your hands in action, but your tongue too fast may run;
The lectures you deliver may be very wise and true,
But I'd rather get my lessons by observing what you do.
I may not understand the high advice that you may give
But there's no misunderstanding how you act and how you live!
ANONYMOUS

———◆———

Sermonettes are just fine for Christian-ettes.

———◆———

You can preach a better sermon with your life than with your lips. OLIVER GOLDSMITH

———◆———

When Donald came out of church earlier than usual, his surprised friend Sandy asked in dismay, "What, Donald, is the sermon all done?"

"No," replied Donald. "It is all said, but it's not even started to be done." *Sunday School Journal*

———◆———

Ignoring a mouse can be difficult. A seminarian, pinch-hitting in a pulpit, tried for ten minutes to ignore the mouse that climbed his chancel flowers and cavorted while his congregation giggled. Finally he reacted with a logical fervor — rolled his sermon manuscript into a club and got rid of the intruder. Must have been some good solid material in that message! *Presbyterian Life*

The Alphabetical Test of a Message

It's Not The:	It's The:
Ability	Aim
Beauty	Book
Contention	Cross
Delivery	Decisions
Eloquence	Effect
Fragments	Fruit
Gloominess	Gladness
Hate	Harvest
Imagination	Instruction
Jesting	Justice
Knowledge	Kindness
Language	Love
Method	Message
Noise	New Birth
Offense	Object
Presentation	Power
Quantity	Quality
Reformation	Regeneration
Strength of Man	Spirit of God
Tradition	Truth
Understanding	Unction
Volume	Vision
Wisdom of Man	Word of God
eXcerpts	eXample
Yearns	Yieldedness
Zip	Zeal!

EDDIE WAGNER

A famous clergyman told his congregation, "Every blade of grass is a sermon."

A few days later a parishioner saw him mowing his lawn. "That's right, Reverend," the man said, "cut your sermons short."

———◆———

Serve, Service

What we can do for Christ is the test of service. What we can suffer for Him is the test of love.

———◆———

Service can put a new coat on a man. The grace of God alone can put a new man in the coat.

———◆———

The great violinist, Nicolò Paganini, willed his marvelous violin to the City of Genoa, on condition that it must never be played upon.

No service without separation from the world.

———◆———

Wood, while used and handled, wears but slightly. Discarded, it begins to decay. The lovely-toned violin has become worm-eaten and useless except as a relic. It is only a reminder that a life withdrawn from service to others becomes quite useless.   *Selected*

———◆———

Three things the Master asks of us,
And we who serve Him here below
And long to see His Kingdom come
May pray or give or go.
He needs them all — the open hand,
The willing feet, the praying heart,
To work together and to weave
A threefold cord that shall not part.
AUTHOR UNKNOWN

———◆———

I'll Go Where You Want Me to Go — Maybe

I'll go where you want me to go, dear Lord,
Real service is what I desire.
I'll sing a solo any time, dear Lord.
But don't ask me to sing in the choir.

I'll do what you want me to do, dear Lord,
I like to see things come to pass.
But don't ask me to teach boys and girls, O Lord.
I'd rather just stay in my class.

I'll do what you want me to do, dear Lord,
I yearn for thy kingdom to thrive.
I'll give you my nickels and dimes, dear Lord.
But please don't ask me to tithe.

I'll go where you want to me go, dear Lord.
I'll say what you want me to say.
I'm busy just now with myself, dear Lord
So I'll help you some other day.
Bible Crusader News

———◆———

The service that counts is the service that costs.

———◆———

Service is love in working clothes.

223

Service can never become slavery to one who loves. J. L. MASSEE

If we are devoted to the cause of humanity, we shall soon be crushed and brokenhearted, for we shall often meet more ingratitude from men than we would from a dog; but if our motive is love for God, no ingratitude can hinder us from serving our fellow men. OSWALD CHAMBERS

Only a burdened heart can lead to fruitful service. ALAN REDPATH

You do not do God a favor by serving Him. He honors you by allowing you to serve Him. VICTOR NYQUIST

To be of real service you must give something which cannot be bought or measured with money, and that is sincerity and integrity.

Service is the rent we pay for the space we occupy in this world.

You can measure what you would do for the Lord by what you do. T. C. HORTON

We are saved to serve, not to be served.

Share, Sharing

One child said to another, "If one of us would get off this tricycle, I could ride it much better." DR. HENRIETTA C. MEARS

Homily

Share your laughter every day;
Shun folks when you weep;
For joy was made to give away,
Sorrow made to keep. M. E. USCHOLD

Two children at a Sunday school picnic found a third who had no lunch. Remembering the lesson on the loaves and fishes in the Bible, Ronny said to his friend Timmy: "We are going to share our lunch with our new friend, aren't you, Timmy?"

The way to share much is to share a little each day. ELD

Don't share your troubles; people are already over-supplied.

Shine, Shining

There is no shining without burning.

Silence, Silent

Silence is the most satisfactory substitute for wisdom.

A man is wise until he opens his mouth.

Six young housewives living in the same apartment building in Canada fell into a dispute of such magnitude that it resulted in their being haled into court. When the case was called, they all made a concerted rush for the bench and, reaching it, all broke into bitter complaints at the same moment.

The judge sat momentarily stunned, as charges and countercharges filled the air. Suddenly he rapped for order. When quiet had been restored, the patient magistrate said gently, "Now, I'll hear the oldest first."

That closed the case.

It often shows a fine command of language to say nothing. ANONYMOUS

Luigi Tarisio was found dead one morning with scarce a comfort in his home, but with two hundred and forty-six fiddles, which he had been collecting all his life, crammed into an attic, the best in the bottom drawer of an old rickety bureau. In very devotion to the violin he had robbed the world of all that music all the time he treasured them; others before him had done the same, so that when the greatest Stradivarius was first played it had had one hundred and forty-seven speechless years. W. Y. FULLERTON

To sin by silence, when they should protest, makes cowards of men.
ABRAHAM LINCOLN

Simple, Simplicity

Simplicity is truth's most becoming garb. DR. BOB JONES, SR.

Simplicity, of all things, is the hardest to be copied. STEELE

Sin, Sinners

Sin in a Christian's life makes a coward of him.

There is no degree of sin in the sight of God.

God's children are made to smart when they yield to sin. But woe to the man who sins without pain; he feels no correction and sinneth again.

Sin is not hurtful
Because it is forbidden
But it is forbidden
Because it is hurtful.
BENJAMIN FRANKLIN

The sin that robs God of your soul will rob your soul of God.

There is more evil in a drop of sin than in a sea of affliction.

Sin can keep you from the Bible and the Bible can keep you from sin.

The wages of sin is death — thank God I quit before pay day.
REAMER LOOMIS

Sin, a moment of gratification; an eternity of remorse.

The best way to show that a stick is crooked is not to argue about it or to spend time denouncing it, but to lay a straight stick alongside it.
D. L. MOODY

Sin is the greatest of all detectives; be sure it will find you out.

The only people on the face of the earth for whom Christ can do anything are sinners.

Whether a man is an up-and-out or down-and-out sinner it is only when he recognizes that he is "out" that he is able to get "in."

The trouble with a little sin is that it won't stay little.

The biggest trouble with sin is the I in the middle of it. ELD

Christ hates sin but loves the sinner.

The easiest thing to confess is a neighbor's sin.

Sin is a clenched fist and its object is the face of God.

When sin pays, the corn is not enjoyed for long.

Sin has a medium of exchange that trades in sorrows, disillusionment and death.

A preacher recently announced there were 726 sins. He is now being beseiged by requests for the list by people who think they are missing something.

He that hath slight thoughts of sin never had great thoughts of God. OWEN

The Seven Modern Sins

Politics without principles.
Pleasures without conscience.
Wealth without work.
Knowledge without character.
Industry without morality.
Science without humanity.
Worship without sacrifice.
CANON FREDERIC DONALDSON

Sincere, Sincerity

Earnestness is the solemn realization of the soberness of your errand.

Earnestness is the salt of eloquence.
VICTOR HUGO

———◆———

Be sincere — you cannot sell anything you don't believe in.

———◆———

"Now we come to sincerity," declared the how-to-win friends expert. "Always be sincere, whether you mean it or not."

———◆———

Sing, Singing

They who wish to sing always find a song.

———◆———

You don't have to know how to sing, it's feeling as though you want to that makes the day successful.

———◆———

A former choir member was asked when he had stopped singing in the choir, and he gave an honest answer — "Since that Sunday I was absent, and everyone thought the organ had been tuned!"

———◆———

"What new thing did you learn in Sunday school today?" her mother asked Susan.

"For one thing," the little girl said, "we learned a song about carrots. It goes like this, 'He carrots for you, He carrots . . .'"

———◆———

When the teacher asked the children what song they wanted to sing one little boy said, "The Laundry Song."

"Tell us how it goes," the teacher said, not recognizing she had taught such a song.

"You know," the boy said. "Bringing in the sheets, bringing in the sheets; We shall come rejoicing, bringing in the sheets."

———◆———

A little girl kept singing seemingly strange words to the old familiar song, "Jesus died for all the children." Upon listening closely her mother heard these words: "Jesus diapered all the children."

The child came home happy from Sunday school and said, "Mommy, we learned the bear song today."

"Sing it to me, dear," said mother.

And so the child sang, "Jesus eyed the cross-eyed bear. . . ."

———◆———

Sleep, Sleepy, Sleepyhead

He that rises late must trot all day.
BENJAMIN FRANKLIN

———◆———

Early to bed, early to rise makes a man baggy under the eyes.

———◆———

Laugh and the world laughs with you, snore and you sleep alone.

———◆———

Some people count sheep and some people talk to the Shepherd!

———◆———

Oversleeping keeps a lot of dreams from coming true. CHARLEY GRANT

———◆———

"I tried counting sheep, as you advised me," a clothing manufacturer told his partner, "but I couldn't get to sleep. I counted thousands of sheep. Then, before I realized what I was doing I sheared them, combed the wool, spun it into cloth and made the cloth into suits. But I lost twenty dollars on each suit — and for the rest of the night I lay awake worrying."

———◆———

Kind Sleep

How good the pillow feels at night to him
Who kept a silent tongue when evil thought
Was on his lips! The heart fills to the brim
With satisfaction that his soul has bought.
How restless he may lie upon his bed
Who carried some choice gossip to a friend,
Which may have been much better left unsaid.
Quick spoken words are often hard to mend!

Kind sleep oft gently soothes the weary brow
Of him whose soul has found a battle won,
While wakefulness will very often plow
A deeper furrow, at some evil done.
The man who wears a bridle on his tongue
May surely keep the heart forever young. CHRISTINE GRANT CURLESS

Sorrow

Remorse is the echo of a lost virtue. BULWER-LYTTON

Only the soul that knows the mighty grief can know the mighty rapture. Sorrows come to stretch out spaces in the heart of joy. EDWIN MARKHAM

It sweetens every sorrow to know what can come of it.

The true way to mourn the dead is to take care of the living who belong to them. EDMUND BURKE

The young man who has not wept is a savage, and the old man who will not laugh is a fool. GEORGE SANTAYANA

God washes the eyes by tears until they can behold the invisible land where tears shall come no more.

Soul, Soul Winning

Christ's last act was winning a soul.
His last command was to win a soul.
His last prayer was forgiveness to a soul.

A man cannot touch his neighbor's heart with anything less than his own.

Personal Work

All can do it.
It can be done anywhere.
It can be done any time.
It reaches all classes.
It hits the mark.
It provides large results. R. A. TORREY

If we work upon marble,
It will perish;
If we work upon brass,
Time will efface it;
If we rear temples,
They will crumble into dust;
But, if we work upon immortal souls,
If we imbue them with principles,
With the just fear of God
And the love of fellow man,
We engrave on those tablets
Something which will brighten all eternity. DANIEL WEBSTER

We are not supposed to spend time making fishing tackle but to tackle fish.

He was an old man, tottering to the grave. After a class session in Ohio where he was visiting, he arose and said:

"I am an old man, but the greatest work I have ever done was to teach a Sunday school class. I arrived in an Ohio town a total stranger. The first Sunday morning I went to Sunday school and asked for a class but they didn't have one to give me.

"'If you want a class,' said the pastor, 'go out and get one.'

"I went and found four boys playing marbles in the street. I asked them to be my Sunday school class and they consented. I had the greatest time of my life with them. I stayed with them and they stayed with me. They write me every year on my birthday."

Who were they?

The old man went on to tell his story. "A few years have passed but here are three of those marble-playing boys:

"One is Charles Conway, a missionary to India. One became secretary to the President of the United States and one became President of the United States — Warren G. Harding."

That old man's name is lost. Who he was, the teacher of that Ohio class where the story was told, did not know, but the results of his teaching are unforgettable. *The Sunday School*

227

If we would win some we must be winsome.

———◆———

The seventy who went out did not hire a hall to preach Christ, they used their soles to go after souls.

———◆———

A Sunday School Teacher's Prayer

Several souls
Will come to me today
To hear of Thee —
What I am,
What I say,
Will lead them to Thee,
Or drive them away —
Stand by, Lord, I pray.

———◆———

If You Will

If God can make an ugly seed,
With a bit of earth and air,
And dew and rain, sunshine and shade —
A flower so wondrous fair;
What can He make of a soul like you,
With the Bible and faith and prayer,
And the Holy Spirit, if you do His will
And trust His love and care!

A. D. BURKETT

———◆———

A pastor was passing a large department store and followed a sudden impression to speak to the proprietor. He said, "I've talked carpets ˙ and beds but never my business with you. Will you give me a few minutes?"

Being led to the private office, the pastor took out his Testament and directed his attention to passage after passage, and urged him to become a Christian. Finally the tears began to roll down the man's cheeks.

"I'm seventy years old, I was born in this city and more than a hundred ministers and five hundred officers of the various churches have known me in a business way. You are the only man who has ever talked to me about my soul."

Service

———◆———

Speak, Speakers, Speeches

I was cut out to be a speaker all right, but I got sewed up all wrong.

Three essentials for a good speaker to remember:
1. Stand up.
2. Speak up.
3. Shut up.

———◆———

If the speaker cannot strike oil in the first twenty minutes there is no need to keep boring.

———◆———

Joe: "They really enjoyed my speech. After I finished they kept yelling, 'Fine! Fine!' "

Moe: "If you'd talked another ten minutes they'd have been yelling imprisonment!"

National Motorist

———◆———

On his return home from a meeting, the fond wife asked her husband, "How was your talk tonight?"

"Which one," he asked, "the one I was going to give, the one I did give, or the one I delivered so brilliantly to myself on the way home in the car?"

Watchman Examiner

———◆———

Charles Lamb was giving a talk at a mixed gathering and someone in the crowd hissed. A stunned silence followed. Finally Lamb calmly said, "There are only three things that hiss — a goose, a snake and a fool. Come forth and be identified."

———◆———

Toastmaster to guest speaker: "Shall we let the folks enjoy themselves a little longer, or do you think you'd better begin your speech now?"

———◆———

Toastmaster: "I cannot do justice to the speaker in the way of an introduction so I'll just let you listen to him and draw your own conclusions."

———◆———

Speaker's prayer: "Lord, fill my mouth with proper stuff, and nudge me when I've said enough."

———◆———

Speaker's lament: "I feel like an Egyptian mummy — pressed for time."

———◆———

Toastmaster: One who uses a few appropriated words.

ANONYMOUS

228

Chairman, introducing speaker: "There are two types of speakers — one needs no introduction; the other deserves none."

———◆———

Many good speakers have a head of steam and a fine train of thought but no terminal facilities.

———◆———

A man isn't a finished speaker until he sits down.

———◆———

Every speaker should remember to
Be good.
Be brief.
Be seated.

———◆———

A man walked out of a hall where a speaker was addressing a meeting. Someone in the corridor asked if the speaker had finished his speech. "Yes," was the reply, "but he hasn't stopped talking."

———◆———

A fashionable speech: long enough to cover the subject and short enough to be interesting.

———◆———

After the banquet speaker sat down from delivering a lengthy dissertation, profuse with unfamiliar words on the value of education, the toastmaster arose and commented, "Now we are all confused on a higher level."

———◆———

Commented one after-dinner speaker: "The trouble with us speakers is that after we eat the blood rushes from the head to the stomach and leaves us light-headed."

———◆———

A new minister was asked to speak at a civic banquet and was quite nervous about it. When he arose to speak he said, "Before I came there were two who knew what I was going to say, the Lord and I. Now only the Lord knows."

———◆———

Speech making, like a Texas longhorned steer, has a point here and there and a lot of bull in between.

It's all right to have a train of thought as long as you have a terminal in mind.

———◆———

If a thing goes without saying, let it go.

———◆———

A speaker ought to be the first person to know when he's through.

———◆———

A distraught speaker who had been left only a very few moments following lengthy preliminaries arose and said, "I have a very good address. It is at 123 Main Street. I am going there now, gentlemen. Good-by." And with that, he left.

———◆———

Someone has said that the writer of Psalm Ninety-one must have been speaking at a luncheon club when he wrote about "The Destruction that wasteth at noon day." Perhaps he referred to banquets when he spoke of "The Pestilence that walketh in darkness."

CHARLES F. BANNING in *Church Management*

———◆———

A long-winded speaker was continuing to deliver his dry and lengthy address. He was running long over time. The master of ceremonies tried to get him to stop, but couldn't attract his attention. Finally, in desperation, he picked up the gavel, aimed and fired, but missed the speaker and hit a man in the first row. The man slumped down, then groaned, "Hit me again, I can still hear him."

———◆———

In discussing dangerous weapons, one over-clubbed and over-banqueted gentleman said, "In my opinion, the most dangerous weapon is the jawbone of an ass."

———◆———

A colonel was speaking at a dinner given in his honor before embarking for Africa.

"I thank you," he concluded, "for your kind wishes regarding my welfare, and I want you to know that when I am far away, surrounded by ugly, grinning savages, I shall always think of you."

SPEAK

A speaker was telling his audience why he always used notes. A lady in the back remarked to a friend, "If he can't remember what he's saying, how does he expect us to?"

———◆———

A speaker was encouraging contributions to a worthy community fund. "All who will give $5.00 stand up," he said. But aside, to the orchestra leader he whispered, "Play the 'Star Spangled Banner.'"

———◆———

What grandpa used to say about getting water is true of speakers: "When you're through pumping, bud, let go the handle."

———◆———

Five crows were sitting on a pump handle. The farmer's wife opened the door and threw out some prunes.

One crow flew off the handle and ate some prunes. Soon he died. That left four crows. A second flew down and ate some prunes and soon he died. Three crows were left. After a time a third crow flew down and ate some prunes. Yes, he rolled over and died, too. That left only two crows. Finally a fourth crow was tempted by the prunes and he flew down and ate some. Of course he didn't live long. One crow remained. For a time he debated about the prunes and decided to try them. Well, it wasn't long until he was in crow heaven.

The moral of the story? Don't fly off the handle when you are full of prunes.

———◆———

An old man found his way to the speaker after the meeting and said, "It was a good talk, son, but you talked too long."

The man continued complimenting the speaker, then said, "And you talked too fast." He paused and added, "You didn't say anything either."

The speaker was at a loss for words but a friend tried to console him and said, "Don't worry, my friend, that poor old fellow isn't quite all there and he only repeats what he hears."

Some speakers talk so long they need a calendar instead of a clock to keep track of time.   ELD

———◆———

Better to be quiet and be thought a fool than to speak and remove all doubt.

———◆———

Most of us know how to say nothing; few of us know when.

———◆———

You earn the right to speak by listening.

———◆———

Learn to speak deliberately, so that the hearer will remember what he should never forget.

———◆———

The most important thing is not being prepared with a message, but for a message.   MILLIE STAMM

———◆———

"Mrs. Jones was outspoken at the knitting circle today, John."

"I can't believe it. Who outspoke her?"

———◆———

The Duke of Windsor tells about his first attempts at public speaking after he became the Prince of Wales:

"The more appearances I had to make, the more I came to respect the really first-class speech as one of the highest human accomplishments. No one I knew seemed to possess that rare and envied gift of speaking well in so high a degree as Mr. Winston Churchill, who was a sympathetic witness of some of my earliest attempts. 'If you have an important point to make,' he advised, 'don't try to be subtle and clever about it. Use the pile driver. Hit the point once, and then come back and hit it again, and then hit it the third time, a tremendous whack!'"

———◆———

If you think twice before you speak, you'll speak the better for it.

———◆———

I do not agree with a word you say, but I will defend to the death your right to say it.   VOLTAIRE

230

Love simple speech as much as you hate shallow thinking.

———◆———

Be careful to say nothing to embarrass new scholars or hurt the feelings of old ones.

———◆———

A young preacher was candidating in a rural area and was being entertained at the home of one of the faithful, godly women of the church. When Sunday evening supper was served the young preacher refused, saying: "I always speak better if I don't eat supper."

After the service was over, on the way home the anxious young man asked his hostess what she thought of his preaching.

"Young man," she said, "you might as well have 'et!"

———◆———

Don't say things. What you are stands over you the while, and thunders so that I cannot hear what you say to the contrary.   EMERSON

———◆———

Kind words don't wear out the tongue.   *Danish Proverb*

———◆———

Orville Wright, guest at a dinner, was reproached by a friend for not taking up the challenge of some that it was Professor Langley, and not the Wright brothers, who flew first.

"Your trouble," said the friend, "is that you're too taciturn. You don't assert yourself enough. You should press-agentize more. Talk man, talk!"

"My friend," replied Mr. Wright, "the best talker and the worst flier among the birds is the parrot!"

———◆———

Speech belongs half to the speaker, half to the listener.   MONTAIGNE

———◆———

Spirit, Spiritual

There are two world powers, the sword and the spirit, but the spirit has always vanquished the sword.
NAPOLEON

Let the Spirit in, in order that you may be emptied.   D. L. MOODY

———◆———

Empty yourself for the Spirit to come in.   A. J. GORDON

———◆———

In newspaper English, Galatians 5: 22, 23 would read something like this: "The fruit of the Spirit is an affectionate, lovable, disposition, a radiant spirit and a cheerful temper, a tranquil mind and a quiet manner, a forbearing patience, in provoking circumstances and with trying people, a sympathetic insight and tactful helpfulness, generous judgment and a big-souled charity, loyalty and reliableness under all circumstances, humility that forgets self in the joy of others, in all things self-mastered and self-controlled, which is the final mark of perfecting."
SAMUEL CHADWICK

———◆———

The Spirit of God can dwell with many people when the rest of us cannot.

———◆———

To solve one's spiritual problems one must remain spiritually solvent.

———◆———

Great men are they who see that spiritual force is stronger than any material force; that thoughts rule the world.   EMERSON

———◆———

God develops spiritual power in our lives through pressure of hard places.

———◆———

If nine-tenths of you were as weak physically as you are spiritually, you couldn't walk.   BILLY SUNDAY

———◆———

State, Statesmanship

True statesmanship is the art of changing a nation from what it is into what it ought to be.   W. R. ALGER

———◆———

Statesmanship and diplomacy have failed and the only remedy is Jesus Christ — it is either Christ or chaos.
DAVID LLOYD GEORGE

Statistics

Startling Statistics

Of every 100 church members in an average church:
5 cannot be found
20 never pray
25 never read the Bible
30 never attend worship service
40 never give to the church budget
50 never go to Sunday school
60 never go to church at night
65 are not in worship on a given Sunday
75 never give to missions
75 never do any church work
85 do not have family worship of any kind
90 never go to prayer services
95 do not tithe
95 never win another person to Christb

————◆————

The following notice appeared in a hotel room:

"This hotel is fully equipped with automatic sprinklers. Statistics show that loss of life has never occurred in a sprinklered building. In case of fire, you may get wet, but not burned."

After reading the notice a witty guest composed the following prayer to fit the circumstances:

Now I lay me down to sleep,
Statistics guard my slumber deep;
If I should die I'm not concerned,
I may get wet, but I won't get burned. *Church Management*

————◆————

Americans own:
71 per cent of the world's automobiles;
80 per cent of the hospital beds;
82 per cent of the bathtubs;
52 per cent of the high school enrollment;
48 per cent of the radio, telephone and telegraph facilities;
60 per cent of the life insurance policies;
34 per cent of the meat;
approximately 33⅓ per cent of the railroads.

You work, if an average worker:
4½ minutes to buy a pound of sugar, 9 minutes in England, 141½ in Russia;
32¼ minutes to buy a pound of butter, 33½ in England, 544 in Russia;
9½ minutes to buy a quart of milk, 29 in England, 59½ in Russia;
7 hours, 10 minutes to buy a pair of women's shoes, 15 hours in England, 98 in Russia.

You can earn $20 in real wages in:
8 hours in the United States, 19 hours in England, 81 in Russia.

You have:
140 doctors per 1,000,000 population, 114 in England, 103 in New Zealand, 75 in France, 4 in China.

You have:
6 per cent of the world's land and 7 per cent of the population, but you have created 45 per cent of the world's wealth. *The Weekly Messenger*

————◆————

Statistics can be used to support anything — especially statisticians.

————◆————

Stomach

A Boy's Remarks to His Stomach
(The Morning After)

What's the matter with you — ain't I always been your friend?
Ain't I been a pardner to you? All my pennies don't I spend
In getting nice things for you? Don't I give you lots of cake?
Say, stummick, what's the matter, that you had to go and ache?
Why, I loaded you with good things yesterday — I gave you more
Potatoes, squash and turkey than you'd ever had before.
I gave you nuts and candy, pumpkin pies and chocolate cake.
And last night when I got to bed you had to go and ache!

Say, what's the matter with you? Ain't
    you satisfied at all?
I gave you all you wanted; you was
    hard just like a ball;
And you couldn't hold another bit of
    puddin', yet last night
You ached most awful, stummick; that
    ain't treatin' me just right!
I've been a friend to you, I have; why
    ain't you a friend of mine?
They gave me castor oil last night be-
    cause you made me whine.
I'm awful sick this mornin' and I'm
    feelin' mighty blue,
Because you don't appreciate the things
    I do for you.   *Hubbard's Silent Salesman*

Story, Storytelling

Too many people want to tell a story
instead of having a story to tell.

A story with a hidden lesson is like
an operation under an anesthetic — the
work is being done while the patient
is unconscious of what is really happening.

Storytelling

See it —
    Feel it —
        Shorten it —
            Expand it —
                Master it —
                    Repeat it.

Strong, Strength

Be Strong

Be strong!
We are not here to play, to dream, to
    drift;
We have had work to do, and loads to
    lift;
Shun not the struggle — face it; 'tis
    God's gift.

Be strong!
Say not, "The days are evil. Who's to
    blame?"
And fold the hands and acquiesce —
    oh, shame!
Stand up, speak out, and bravely, in
    God's name.

Be strong!
It matters not how deep entrenched
    the wrong,
How hard the battle goes, the day how
    long;
Faint not — fight on! Tomorrow comes
    the song.   MALTBIE DAVENPORT BABCOCK

There are two ways of exerting one's
strength; one is pushing down, the
other is pulling up.   BOOKER T. WASHINGTON

Nothing makes one feel so strong as
a call for help.   GEORGE MACDONALD

Who is strong? He that can conquer
his bad habits.   BENJAMIN FRANKLIN

Study

The more we study the more we discover our ignorance.

Apply thyself wholly to the Scriptures and the Scriptures wholly to
thyself.

By studying diligently from eighteen to eighty a person can learn about
half as much as he thought he knew
at eighteen.

It is the glory of God to conceal a
thing but the honor of kings is to search
out a matter. Proverbs 25:2

Philosophy of college students: "Don't
let your studies interfere with your
education."

It is the studying that you do after
your school days that really counts.
Otherwise you know only that which
everyone else knows.   HENRY L. DOHERTY

Style

Style is a man's own; it is a part of
his nature.   BUFFON

Success, Successful

Success is a wonderful thing. You
meet such interesting relatives.

Teacher: "Be diligent and you will succeed. Remember my telling you of the great difficulty George Washington had to contend with?"

Little Jimmy: "Yes, ma'am, he couldn't tell a lie."

———◆———

The profit of life is life, not money.

CAMPBELL

———◆———

Make chariot wheels out of your difficulties and ride to success.

DR. BOB JONES, SR.

———◆———

What a wonderful world this would be if we all did as well today as we expect to do tomorrow.

———◆———

The secret of success for every man who is, or has ever been successful, lies in the fact that he has formed the habit of doing things that failures don't like to do.

———◆———

You cannot attain eminence by climbing on the fence.

———◆———

The man owns the world who remains its master.

——◆———

The fellow who wins success is the one who makes hay from the grass that grows under the other fellow's feet, and who doesn't restrict his efforts to the hours when the sun shines.

Reader's Digest

———◆———

Success lies not in achieving what you aim at but in aiming at what you ought to achieve.

———◆———

Ninety-nine per cent of success is built on former failure.

KETTERING of General Motors

———◆———

The door to the room of success swings on the hinges of opposition.

DR. BOB JONES, SR.

———◆———

Four things a man must learn to do
If he would make his record true:
To think without confusion, clearly,
To love his fellowmen sincerely;
To act from honest motives purely;
To trust in God and heaven securely.

HENRY VAN DYKE

The secret of success is constancy of purpose.

———◆———

To be able to carry money without spending it;
To be able to bear an injustice without retaliating;
To be able to do one's duty even when one is not watched;
To be able to keep at the job until it is finished;
To be able to accept criticism without letting it whip you;
This is success.

AUTHOR UNKNOWN

———◆———

Seven Steps to Success

1. Commencement by starting: "Ye must be born again." John 3:7
2. Confession of Christ by speaking: "Confess with thy mouth." Romans 10:9
3. Concentration by study: "Search the scriptures." John 5:39
4. Communion by seeking: "Pray without ceasing." I Thessalonians 5:17
5. Communication by serving: "Workers together with him." II Corinthians 6:1
6. Contribution by supplying: "Lay by him in store, as God hath prospered him." I Corinthians 16:2
7. Continuance by being satisfied: "Be thou faithful unto death." Revelation 2:10

———◆———

A man can't make a place for himself in the sun if he keeps taking refuge under the family tree.

———◆———

The successful man lengthens his stride when he discovers the signpost has deceived him; the failure looks for a place to sit down.

JOHN RUSKIN

———◆———

The man of the hour spent many days and nights getting there.

———◆———

Success is your birthright.

GREENVILLE KLEISER

———◆———

Most of us get what we deserve, but only the successful will admit it.

ANONYMOUS

We rise by the things we put under our feet.

———◆———

Every man owes it to himself to be a success. He also owes it to the collector of internal revenue.

Presbyterian Life

———◆———

One of the worst tragedies that can befall a man is to have ulcers and still not be a success.

———◆———

Behind every successful man there's a woman — constantly telling him he's not so hot.

———◆———

Behind every successful man can usually be found three people: his wife, and Mr. and Mrs. Jones.

National Motorist

———◆———

Success is not measured by the heights one attains, but by the obstacles one overcomes in their attainment.

BOOKER T. WASHINGTON

———◆———

Fortune smiles upon the person who can laugh at himself. BRENDAN FRANCIS

———◆———

Achieving success is more a matter of waking up than climbing up.

———◆———

God doesn't call us to be successful. He calls us to be faithful.

———◆———

For success, try aspiration, inspiration and perspiration.

———◆———

No rule of success will work if you don't.

———◆———

To get to the top, get to the bottom of things.

———◆———

Man can climb to the highest summits, but he cannot dwell there long.

GEORGE BERNARD SHAW

———◆———

Successful is the man who goes straight forward — with an aim on only what is right.

———◆———

Some men think they have made a success of life when all they have made is money.

Success consists of getting up just one more time than you fell down.

———◆———

You are not obligated to succeed. You are obligated only to do your best.

———◆———

Our aim should be service, not success.

———◆———

Success comes from mastering defeat.

———◆———

Success gives us certain assurance at first but in the end you are never really sure. FRANCOISE SAGAN

———◆———

How to succeed: Start at the bottom and wake up.

———◆———

The difference between success and failure is decided by little things, when you are least aware of it. MARTIN VANBEE

———◆———

Success is not the reverse of failure; it is the scorn of failure. Always dare to fail; never fail to dare.

STEPHEN S. WISE

———◆———

A Ladder of Success

100% I did
90% I will
80% I can
70% I think I can
60% I might
50% I think I might
40% What is it?
30% I wish I could
20% I don't know how
10% I can't
0% I won't

———◆———

A Moravian missionary named George Smith went to Africa. He had been there only a short time and had only one convert, a poor woman, when he was driven from the country. He died shortly after, on his knees, praying for Africa. He was considered a failure.

But a company of men stumbled onto the place where he had prayed and found a copy of the Scriptures he had left. Presently they met the one poor woman who was his convert.

A hundred years later his mission counted more than 13,000 living converts who had sprung from the ministry of George Smith. A. J. GORDON

In 1923 a group of the world's most successful financiers met at a Chicago hotel. Present were:

The president of the largest independent steel company.

The president of the largest utility company.

The greatest wheat speculator.

The president of the New York Stock Exchange.

A member of the President's cabinet.

The president of the Bank of International Settlements.

The head of the world's greatest monopoly.

Collectively, these tycoons controlled more wealth than there was in the United States Treasury, and for years newspapers and magazines had been printing their success stories and urging the youth of the nation to follow their examples. Twenty-five years later, let's see what happened to them.

The president of the largest independent steel company — Charles Schwab — lived on borrowed money the last five years of his life, and died penniless.

The greatest wheat speculator — Arthur Cutten — died abroad in poverty.

The president of the New York Stock Exchange — Richard Whitney — was recently released from Sing Sing.

The member of the President's Cabinet — Albert Fall — was pardoned from prison so he could die at home.

The president of the Bank of International Settlement — Leon Fraser — committed suicide.

The head of the world's greatest monopoly — Ivar Kreuger — committed suicide.

All of these men had learned how to make money, but not one of them had learned how to live.

United Evangelical Action

Suffer, Suffering

The school of suffering graduates rare scholars.

———◆———

God will not look you over for medals, degrees or diplomas, but for scars.

———◆———

Suffering is sin's index finger pointing out something wrong.

———◆———

To have suffered much is like knowing many languages: It gives the sufferer access to many more people.

———◆———

Most people are quite happy to suffer in silence, if they are sure everyone knows they're doing it.

———◆———

Summer

Summer: The season when children slam the doors they left open all winter.

———◆———

There's nothing wrong with summer that a little less heat, a little more lemonade, a little less humidity, and a little more swimming, a little less work, and a little more homemade ice cream wouldn't correct. *Presbyterian Life*

———◆———

Sunday

A world without a Sabbath would be like a summer without flowers.

HENRY WARD BEECHER

———◆———

The Sabbath is the golden clasp that binds together the volume of the week.

MACAULEY

———◆———

A man submerged in business all week had better come up for air on Sunday.

J. A. HOLMES

———◆———

Some people seem to think that Sunday is Funday.

———◆———

No Sabbath, no worship;
No worship, no religion;
No religion, no morals;
No morals, then — what?

CRAWFORD JOHNSON

The Lord's Day is the shadow of Christ on the hot highway of time.
R. E. SPIER

Recipe for a Useless Sunday

Stay in bed until ten;
Read Sunday papers until one;
Feed your face until three;
Lop around until nine;
Nothing doing; nothing done;
Good Night!
ANONYMOUS

Add It Up!

Every seventh day is a Sunday, therefore:

Every seven years one has lived a full year of Sundays.
A person 21 years old has had 3 years of Sundays for his spiritual improvement,
One of thirty-five has had five years,
One of seventy has had ten.

This is great addition if the Sundays are spent in church.

Sunday School (General)

Speak well of your Sunday school — you are a part of it.

You can have a Sunday school without a church, but you cannot have a church without a Sunday school.

The Sunday school that refuses to go is the goner.

The test of Sunday school courage comes when we are in the minority; the test of tolerance comes when we are in the majority.

Always keep in mind the fact that you run the school for the scholar and hence you must build on his interests and desires.

Someone asked John Wanamaker, "How do you get time to run a Sunday school with four thousand scholars in addition to the business of your stores and your work as Postmaster General?"

Instantly Mr. Wanamaker replied, "Why, the Sunday school is my business! All other things are just things. Forty-five years ago I decided that God's promise was sure, 'Seek ye first the Kingdom of God and His righteousness; and all these things shall be added unto you.'"
Sunday School Journal

Weak Sunday Schools

A non-missionary Sunday school.
A minister with no program.
A gossiping, fault-finding group.
Pessimistic officials.
A Sunday school run by some one person with a "rule or ruin" disposition.
A Sunday school in which everything is done by the same two or three people.
A Sunday school that pays little, talks a lot, and does nothing worth-while.
A Sunday school that gets in the rut and stays there, afraid to try anything new.
None of the members tithe.
Poor music and no leader.
The Sunday school always started late.
Nothing in a social way for the members.
Strangers are ignored, while friends visit together.
Members are content, have no craving for souls and are spiritually dead.
Dirt and dust everywhere; no paint, poor light, and not much fire.
ANONYMOUS

In solving Sunday school problems, teachers should not substitute prejudices for good judgment.

No Sunday school worker is ever used in a large way who cannot be trusted in a small emergency.

Would You?

Would you go to Sunday school if you had to sit on chairs so high that your feet dangled in mid-air?
Would you go to Sunday school if you had to be in a dingy basement?
Would you go to Sunday school if

the teacher read the lesson to you every Sunday?

Would you go to Sunday school if you didn't like and understand the songs?

Would you go to Sunday school if you thought the teacher considered her work a bore?

Would you go to Sunday school if you were told to keep still every time you talked?

No, you wouldn't. But this is just what the children in so many schools endure every week.

MARY ELIZABETH BREWBAKER

---◆---

Seven Reasons for Going to Sunday School

1. *The best book is studied* and taught, and I want to know it and follow it in my everyday life.

2. *The best day is utilized* and observed, and I wish to keep holy the holy day.

3. *The best people are assembled* and enlisted, and I desire the blessing of their fellowship and friendship.

4. *The best institution is awake* and at work for the Master, and I ought to invest myself where I will do my utmost for Christ and the Church.

5. *The best work is being done,* and I must not fail to do my part for the enlightenment, evangelization and upbuilding of my fellowmen.

6. *The best development is assured* and attained, and I yearn to grow mentally, morally and spiritually.

7. *The best equipment is supplied,* adopted and inspired, and I want to be thoroughly furnished unto all good works.

Exchange

---◆---

How to Kill, Embalm and Bury Your Sunday School

1. Don't go.
2. If you do go, be late.
3. If it is too wet, or too dry, or too hot, or too cold to go, publicize the fact.
4. When you go, be sure to find fault.

5. Refuse every invitation to help, then tell how forward and overbearing those are who do help.

6. Never encourage the other officers; criticize them and tell others how you would do the job.

7. Never take part in the service.

8. Point out all the mistakes you can to the workers and teachers and condemn them for making such mistakes.

9. Never put more than three cents in the offering. If you had no pennies with you last Sunday, don't give twice as much this Sunday.

10. Believe everything you hear about the Sunday school without any investigation.

11. Wear a sour face to show your disapproval of everything that's going on.

12. Stalk out of church as soon as Sunday school is over. Don't speak to anyone.

Our Sunday School Counsellor

---◆---

Purpose of the Sunday School Class

To bring in the unreached.

To win them for Christ and the Church.

To train for effective Christian service.

To support the program of the Church.

---◆---

The Sunday School Bees

Have you ever heard of the
Sunday school bees
Which buzz in your ears short
phrases like these?

O girls and boys, just hear what we hum:
On Sunday morning, to Sunday school come.

Be regular; every week in your place
Be cheerful, keeping a smile on your face;
Be punctual, every Sunday on time,
In your seat when the calling bell ceases to chime.
Be glad, lifting up your voices in song,
That the chorus of praise may be full and strong.

Be reverent, quietly bowing in prayer;
To those who are speaking, listen with
care.
Then everyone who your happy school
sees,
Will praise your swarm of Sunday
school bees.   MARY STARCK KERR

———————

Ten Beatitudes for Sunday School Leaders

BLESSED is the leader who has not
sought the high places, but
who has been drafted into
service because of his ability
and willingness to serve.

BLESSED is the leader who knows where
he is going, why he is going
and how to get there.

BLESSED is the leader who knows no
discouragement, who presents
no alibi.

BLESSED is the leader who knows how
to lead without being dicta-
torial; true leaders are humble.

BLESSED is the leader who seeks the
best for those he serves.

BLESSED is the leader who leads for the
good of the most concerned,
and not for the personal gratification of his own ideas.

BLESSED is the leader who develops
leaders while leading.

BLESSED is the leader who marches
with the group, interprets correctly the signs on the pathway that leads to success.

BLESSED is the leader who has his head
in the clouds but his feet on
the ground.

BLESSED is the leader who considers
leadership an opportunity for
service.   S. S. Memo

———————

"Say, Dad, did you go to Sunday
school when you were a boy?"

"Yes, Son, regularly."

"Well, then, I don't guess it will do
me any good either."   Together

Sunday School Training Pays

Max Jukes lived in the state of New
York. He did not believe in Christian
training. He married a girl of like
character. From this union they have
1,026 descendants. Three hundred of
them died prematurely. One hundred
were sent to the penitentiary for an
average of thirteen years each. One
hundred and ninety were public pros-
titutes. There were one hundred drunkards and the family cost the state
$1,200,000. They made no contribution
to society.

But . . .

Jonathan Edwards lived in the same
state. He believed in Christian training. He married a girl of like character. From this union they have 729
descendants. Out of this family have
come three hundred preachers, sixty-
five college professors, thirteen university presidents, sixty authors of good
books, three United States congress-
men and one vice-president of the
United States, and except for Aaron
Burr, a grandson of Edwards who married a questionable character, the family has not cost the state a single dollar. The difference in the two families:
Christian training in youth and heart
conversions.   A Good News folder

———————

Thirteen Sunday School Beatitudes

BLESSED is the Sunday School that is
striving for spirituality, evangelism and growth, in that order.

BLESSED is the Sunday school whose
teachers do not rely on word
pictures alone but who prepare visual aids.

BLESSED is the Sunday school which
has officers who are providing
the best possible equipment
and materials for its teachers.
Good lighting and ventilation,
clean classrooms and audi-
toriums, sand tables, visual

aid boards, blackboards, maps and charts are necessary provisions.

BLESSED is the Sunday school which operates in an evangelistic spirit.

BLESSED is the Sunday school whose teachers and officers pool their ideas through the means of the Workers' Conference.

BLESSED is the Sunday school whose workers are provided a Workers' Training class so that they may be better qualified to teach.

BLESSED is the Sunday school which has good records.

BLESSED is the Sunday school which has a definite visitation program.

BLESSED is the Sunday school whose superintendent plans and conducts interesting opening services.

BLESSED is the Sunday school whose teachers love to teach and are happy in their jobs.

BLESSED is the Sunday school whose workers are prompt and faithful to Sunday school and all services of the church.

BLESSED is the Sunday school whose workers set a living example of the principles they teach.

BLESSED is the Sunday school for verily it will grow and win souls for the kingdom of God.

AUTHOR UNKNOWN

———◆———

A pastor once said, "Do away with the Sunday schools for 15 years and the church will be cut half in its membership."

A. S. LONDON

———◆———

Judge Fawcett, of Brooklyn, New York, said that out of 2,700 boys brought before his court, not one of them was a Sunday school pupil.

A. S. LONDON

Sunday School (Departments)

The following interesting stories are recorded according to ages of children as they are grouped in Sunday school departments. Other stories, ascribed to these ages, are given throughout the book: see the index.

———◆———

Nursery: (Two and Three Years)

After a little two-year-old child returned from her first visit to the nursery department of the Sunday school, her mother asked her what she learned. Without hesitation the tot replied, "Jesus loves me."

———◆———

Dickie often went with his daddy over a toll bridge. "Why do you always shake hands with the man on the bridge?" the tot asked.

Daddy had to explain he was paying toll, not shaking hands.

The Christian Parent

———◆———

Three-year-old to younger child: Come, Freddie, sit on the floor. Your chair fits me better than it fits you.

———◆———

Kindergarten: (Four and Five Years)

The little girl was lying in bed, her teeth chattering and her feet sticking out beneath the covers.

"Gracious!" exclaimed her mother. "Put your feet under the covers."

"Uh-uh," protested the child. "I'm not putting those cold things in bed with me."

The Instructor

———◆———

For many weeks mother and daddy had cautioned little Al to "Please be still," during the church service — and their training was paying off, at least everyone thought so until one Sunday morning . . . at which time Al was thoroughly frustrated. The minister led the congregation in the singing of a hymn and the little boy turned to his parents and asked, "Why is everyone telling me to 'please be still'?" Quietly his mother comforted the lad by telling him the song they were singing was "Peace Be Still."

240

When the neighbor lady gave Tommy a piece of cake he politely said, "Thank you."

"Now I like to hear little boys say 'thank you,'" the kind neighbor said.

"If you want to hear me say it again," Tommy said, "you can put some ice cream on the cake."

———◆———

A little girl who went to Sunday school for the first time was telling her mother all about it. "Did you know," she asked mother, "that the teacher is baby Jesus' grandmother?"

"That's interesting," her mother replied. "And how do you know?"

"Because," the little girl said, "she talks about him all the time."

———◆———

Primary: (Six, Seven and Eight Years)

Little Diana had put through a very miserable day. Everything seemed to go wrong. Finally, her mother asked, "Diana, child, what in the world is wrong with you today?"

"Oh, Mummie," she sobbed wretchedly in her mother's arms, "I just can't seem to manage my aggravations."

Christian Home

———◆———

One day the teacher took her pupils on a trip to the Natural History Museum. Telling about it at home, little Jimmy said, "Our teacher took us to a dead circus today." *The Instructor*

———◆———

A first-grader, instructed to color the shirt blue on the sketch of a man, walked to the teacher's desk and asked for a white crayon.

"We're going to make the shirt blue, dear," said the teacher. "We don't need a white crayon."

"Maybe you won't," replied the youngster, "but he will. I wanna put white underwear on him first."

NEA Journal

———◆———

One version of why Adam and Eve were expelled from the Garden of Eden was contributed by a child as follows:

"One day Cain and Abel were talking to their father, Adam, and asked him just why it was they couldn't go back to the beautiful home God had given them. After thinking for a moment Adam said, 'Well boys, it's like this, one day your mother decided to eat us out of house and home.'"

———◆———

A Sunday school teacher had been telling a class of little boys about crowns of glory and heavenly rewards for good people.

"Now tell me," she said at the close of the lesson, "who will get the biggest crown?"

There was silence for a while then Johnnie replied, "Him wots got the biggest head." *Watchman Examiner*

———◆———

The teacher had carefully prepared a flannelgraph visual aid to use with the Bible story of Jesus ascending to heaven. She prepared the figure of Jesus so she could move it up and off the board. Of course the children were delighted with the story and listened breathlessly when the teacher told it.

When Terry got home he was so overwhelmed with the story that he insisted on his mother and dad sitting down and hearing him tell it. He got to the part where the disciples were with Jesus on the hill and he asked, "What do you think happened, then?"

"What?" asked the parents together.

"Well, then God used Scotch tape and string and took Jesus up to heaven!"

———◆———

A junior high school youth told his teacher not to be discouraged and quoted, "Blessed are they that go round in circles for they shall become big wheels."

———◆———

"I'm going to hurry and get married," the thirteen-year-old girl told her favorite teacher.

"Why are you going to do that?" her teacher asked.

"I want to have my children know you and learn from you, too," the girl told her teacher.

241

John came home from Sunday school one day and said:

"I'm afraid of my superintendent."

"Why, Johnny," said Mother, "why are you afraid of the superintendent? He seems like a nice Christian man to me, who loves Jesus."

"Maybe he loves Jesus but he said he would put us in a big furnace if we didn't come to Sunday school regular."

"Are you sure he said that?"

Johnny's mother was disturbed, so she paid a special visit to the superintendent who protested that he was innocent. Finally he said:

"I understand now . . . I did say once, 'Those who don't come regularly, we must finally drop from the register.'"

Christian Parent

———◆———

Junior: (Ages Nine, Ten, Eleven)

Last year, the first in our new school building, I was explaining the word EXIT over each door. One youngster said, "But all the doors say EXIT. Which one am I supposed to enter?"

The Instructor

———◆———

"What is the difference between results and consequences?" a teacher asked her class.

Little Billie answered: "Results are what you expect. Consequences are what you get."

———◆———

Youth: (Junior and Senior High)

When I was sixteen my father was an ignoramus; but when I was twenty-one I was amazed at how much progress the old man had made.

MARK TWAIN

———◆———

Superintendent

A superintendent is a person with *super*vision. How is your vision?

———◆———

The work of the Sunday school superintendent is comparable to an iceberg, that is, only a small percentage of it is visible above the surface. His public appearances represent only a fractional part of his work.

Christian Monitor

Mr. Superintendent

1. Wear a smile that won't rub off on a rainy day.
2. Common interest on week days may mean compound interest on Sunday.
3. The superintendent who never makes a mistake never makes progress.
4. Two things to observe with care: thyself and thy programs to prepare.
5. A book a month will keep the blues and blunders away.
6. A stitch in time may save nine boys and girls to the Sunday school; usually that stitch is a well-chosen teacher.
7. An efficient school is its own best advertisement.
8. No school has a right to sweep in new pupils until it does justice to the ones it already has.
9. Trained teachers mean bigger enrollment and better building.
10. Cease to learn, cease to lead.

Pittsburgh Conference Herald

———◆———

Some superintendents, like boats, toot loudest in the fog.

———◆———

Ten Commandments for Church School Superintendents

I. Thou shalt challenge thy teachers to grow continuously in personality, training and technique.

II. Thou shalt plan and hold regular Workers' Conferences for thy teachers; for verily, it is thy responsibility to keep them challenged, informed, inspired and interested.

III. Thou shalt select teachers wisely; for verily, they are the strength of the church school.

IV. Thou shalt not expect thy pastor to do thy work.

V. Thou shalt be a conscientious student of the Bible, a reader of religious books, a subscriber to thy church publications, and so "study to show thyself approved unto God, a workman that needeth not to be ashamed. . . ."

VI. Thou shalt see that accurate records are kept throughout the church school — for verily, the Lord's business demands utmost efficiency.

VII. Thou shalt encourage thy department superintendents and teachers to follow up absentees, and thy attendance will surely rise.

VIII. Thou shalt keep thy entire church informed of the work of the church school — its program, its plans and its needs.

IX. Thou shalt set an example of promptness for thy teachers on Sunday mornings.

X. Thou shalt challenge thy teachers to prepare their lessons well, to teach the Bible and its message, to continuously stress the meaning of stewardship, and to lead individuals to Christ and Christian maturity.

WILLIAM A. WARD *in The Church School*

———✦———

God never uses a superintendent in a large way who cannot be trusted in a personal emergency. *Sunday School Digest*

———✦———

A superintendent is only as busy as the things about which he busies himself.

———✦———

The main idea in Sunday school teaching is to drive home the point, not the audience.

———✦———

Blessed Is the Superintendent

WHO does not think he knows it all, but recognizes there are a few things yet to learn.

WHO does not work by the tick of the clock, but by the beat of the heart.

WHO does not make announcements twice in exactly the same way, but cultivates variety and surprise.

WHO does not surrender to a chance visitor the precious closing moments of the school.

WHO does not ride hobbies, but who seeks to develop the school symmetrically.

WHO does not resign when his toes are stepped on.

WHO never expects to be satisfied with attainment.

WHO does not blame others for going to sleep because he is not awake.
Selected

———✦———

Superlatives

Superlative Words

The greatest word is God.
The deepest word is soul.
The longest word is eternity.
The swiftest word is time.
The nearest word is now.
The darkest word is sin.
The meanest word is hypocrisy.
The broadest word is truth.
The strongest word is right.
The tenderest word is love.
The sweetest word is heaven.
The dearest word is Jesus.
Selected

———✦———

Christ

Absolutely necessary.
Exclusively sufficient.
Instantaneously accessible.
Perennially satisfying.
ANONYMOUS

———✦———

Suspicion

Most of our suspicions of others are aroused by what we know of ourselves.
ANONYMOUS

———✦———

Sympathy

Sympathy is what one woman gives another in exchange for all the details.

———✦———

The people who least live their creeds are not seldom the people who shout loudest about them. The paralysis which affects the arms does not, in these cases, interfere with the tongue. . . .

The homely illustration of the very tender sympathy which gushes inwards, and does nothing to clothe naked backs or fill empty stomachs, perhaps has a sting in it. . . . Sympathy, like every other emotion is meant to influence action. If it does not, what is the use of it? What is the good of getting up fire in the furnace, and making a mighty roaring of steam, if it all escapes at the waste-pipe, and drives no wheels? And what is the good of a "faith" which only rushes out at the escape-pipe of talk? It is "dead in itself." ALEXANDER MACLAREN

T

Tact

Tact is the knack of making a point without making an enemy. HOWARD W. NEWTON

Tact is the best oil to use to keep the church machinery running smoothly.

Tact is a remarkable human quality that allows you to know just how far to go too far.

Many people are so tactful that they never make contact with people.

Tact formula: Be brief, politely; be aggressive, smilingly; be emphatic, pleasantly; be positive, diplomatically; be right, graciously. ANONYMOUS

If you want to be popular, you must endure being taught many things that you already know.

Abraham Lincoln was once asked to give his definition of diplomacy. "Well," he mused, "I guess you might say that it's the knack of letting the other fellow have your way."

Talent

Too many people make cemeteries of their lives by burying their talents.

The real tragedy of life is not in being limited to one talent, but in the failure to use the one talent. EDGAR W. WORK

Talent is the capacity of doing anything that depends on application and industry; it is voluntary power, while genius is involuntary. HAZLETT

Nature has concealed at the bottom of our minds talents and abilities of which we are not aware. LA ROCHEFOUCAULD

Use what talents you have. The woods would be very silent if no birds sang there except those which sang the best. *Sunday School Journal*

If every man stuck to his talent, the cows would be well tended. J. F. DE FLORIAN

Talent that is used is multiplied.

Talk, Talking

Most of us know how to say nothing. Few of us know when.

Have more than thou showest; speak less than thou knowest. SHAKESPEARE

An ounce of illustration is worth a ton of talk.

What is in the well of your heart will show up in the bucket of your speech.

You are often sorry for saying a harsh word, but you never regret saying a kind one. BERT ESTABROOK

People who talk much say nothing.

Some people talk like the watch which ticks away the minutes but never strikes the hour.   SAMUEL JOHNSON

"What did you say?"
"Nothing."
"Of course. But how did you express it this time?"   *National Motorist*

We know a bird by its song and a man by his words.

Do more than talk, say something.

It takes a baby about two years to learn to talk, and some sixty or seventy years to learn to keep his mouth shut.

The only way to save face is to keep the lower end of it closed.

You may talk too much on the best of subjects.   BENJAMIN FRANKLIN

Don't ever prophesy — unless you know.   J. R. LOWELL

I have never been hurt by anything I didn't say.   CALVIN COOLIDGE

Great talkers should be cropped for they have no need of ears.
     BENJAMIN FRANKLIN

Some people have a line long enough to hang their clothes on.

It's when he doesn't keep his mouth shut that the fish gets caught.

Some people don't have much to say. The only trouble is you have to wait so long to find out.   *Town Journal*

The three main kinds of communication are: telephone, telegraph, tell a woman.

Polysyllables are not the signs of profanity. Often they are the cloak of poverty and bought at a jumble sale.

Never talk down to your audience; they are not there!

Great talkers, little doers.
     BENJAMIN FRANKLIN

As a man grows older and wiser, he talks less and says more.

A lot of people are like buttons — always popping off at the wrong time.

To talk and arrive nowhere is the same as climbing a tree to catch a fish.

The man who says nothing at the right time is a good talker.

The best rule for talking is the one carpenters use: measure twice, saw once.

There is nothing wrong with having nothing to say unless you say it aloud.

When in doubt about what to say, take a chance on getting by with the truth.

Some say very little . . . and yet talk all the time.

After all is said and done, more is said than done.

To be successful in conversing, try to be more interested than interesting.

Don't throw a stone into a well from which you have drunk.

It's often the blunt man who makes the most cutting remarks.

To know a man . . . listen carefully when he mentions his dislikes.

Two good tips: Always say less than you think, and remember that how you say it often means more than what you say.

As a rule anything that is either shouted or whispered isn't worth listening to. FREDERICK LANGBRIDGE

Discretion of speech is more than eloquence; and to speak agreeably to him with whom we deal is more than to speak in good words. BACON

The average man thinks about what he has said; the above average about what he is going to say.

Task

Rate the task above the prize. CONFUCIUS

Every man's task is his life preserver. *The Sunday School*

Taxation, Taxes

The income tax division of our government should be mighty glad the taxpayers have what it takes.

Whatever the government spends, its citizens must give up through taxation. EARL BUNTING

A taxpayer is one who has the government on his payroll.

Two things the country can always be sure of: taxes and children.

The person who remembers when the only kind of tax was carpet tacks is really an old-timer.

Teach, Teacher, Teaching

First I learned to love my teacher, then I learned to love my teacher's Bible, then I learned to love my teacher's Saviour. MARION LAWRENCE

He who teaches the Bible is never a scholar; he is always a student.

Many teachers who are not having great visions are dreaming troubled dreams.

A teacher should know more than he teaches, and if he knows more than he teaches, he will teach more than he knows.

Good teachers are not born so; they are made by conscientious labor.

All teachers are born; all teachers are *not* born made.

The teacher is the hinge on which the Sunday school swings.

The best teacher follows his own instruction.

It takes a lot of preparation to teach just a little.

Those who teach must be teachable.

The things which hurt, instruct. BENJAMIN FRANKLIN

If you want to succeed in the trade of teaching, you must be willing to learn the tricks of the trade.

A teacher teaches by —
what he says —
what he does —
what he is!

If you don't live it, don't teach it.

If you feel you have to teach, don't.

We can never teach more children than we can reach.

Take your decisions to class with you.

Much time is spent teaching young people how to make a living, yet few know how to make a life. DR. HENRIETTA C. MEARS

If you cannot control self, you cannot control your class.

Good teaching requires only one message but many dynamic techniques.

Children learn many things we have not planned to teach, such as coming in late, being absent, coming to class with lesson unprepared. You would be surprised, children learn from all that the Sunday school teacher *is* or *does!*

————♦————

To know how to suggest is the art of teaching.   HENRI F. AMIEL

————♦————

To effect an act, apply the fact.

————♦————

If one member of the teaching team fumbles the ball the whole team loses ground.

————♦————

If you listen while you teach you will learn a little.

————♦————

A poor teacher has to teach something; a good teacher has something to teach.

————♦————

Sunday school teachers must be:
    Saved —
    Sound —
    Separated —
    Stable in Character —
    Spirit-filled —
    Sanctified —
    Soul-burdened!

————♦————

Those teachers who try to memorize the Sunday school quarterlies are described thus: a Sunday school quarterly wired for sound.

————♦————

The teacher who is attempting to teach without inspiring the pupil with a desire to learn is hammering on cold iron.   HORACE MANN

————♦————

Measured by the best standards of pedagogy, Jesus was the greatest teacher in the world:
    He knew His subject;
    He knew His pupils;
    He lived what He taught.
        DR. BOB JONES, SR.

————♦————

Good tools do not make an excellent teacher but an excellent teacher makes good use of tools.

There are three powers in the mastery of teaching:
 1. The power of understanding.
 2. The power of sympathy.
 3. The power to communicate.
        Education Summary

————♦————

The object of teaching a child is to enable him to get along without his teacher.   ELBERT HUBBARD

————♦————

Many teachers are like rocking chairs — always in motion but getting no place.

————♦————

All teachers fall into some mould, but some are a little mouldier than others.

————♦————

You can lead a horse to water but you can't make him think.

————♦————

First student: "Why is teaching like a Model T Ford?"
Second student: "Why?"
First student: "A room full of nuts and a crank up front."

————♦————

A Sunday school teacher is a person whose job is to welcome a lot of live wires and see that they are well-grounded.

————♦————

Some teachers merely help the pupils to transfer information from the teacher's notebook to the pupil's notebook without going through the mind or heart of either.

————♦————

As all roads lead to Rome, all teaching should point to Christ.

————♦————

Teachers must be
    Producers
        Reproducers
            Reproducers of producers
                Reproducers of reproducers.
                    BILL GWINN

————♦————

Kindling of interest is the great function of the teacher. People sometimes say, "I should like to teach if only pupils cared to learn." But then, there would be little need of teaching.
        GEORGE HERBERT PALMER

TEACH

Good teachers cost more, but poor teachers cost most.
Delta Kappa Gamma Bulletin

———♦———

The question mark is the teacher's badge.
HERMAN H. HORNE

———♦———

The way you teach is important, and what you teach is more important, but how you live is most important.

———♦———

To teach something you don't know is like coming back from somewhere you haven't been.
VANCE HAVNER

———♦———

The teacher, under God, is the master key to every Sunday school problem.
Sunday School Journal

———♦———

A good teacher may overcome poor physical equipment, but the most modern schoolroom and the brightest pupils cannot function without a teacher. No mechanical device can replace the teacher. Thus far no substitute has been found for the impact of mind upon mind, personality upon personality. Teachers may overcome limitations in environment, but they themselves are absolutely essential.

———♦———

The teacher is like the candle, which lights others in consuming itself.
Italian Proverb

———♦———

The authority of those who teach is often an obstacle to those who wish to learn.
CICERO

———♦———

Learn of the skillful: He that teaches himself hath a fool for his master.
BENJAMIN FRANKLIN

———♦———

Would you write your name among the stars?
Then write it large upon
The hearts of children.
They will remember!
Have you visions of a nobler, happier world?
Tell the children!
They will build it for you.
CLARA TREE MAJOR

Experience may be the best teacher, but even the best teachers need pupils smart enough to learn.

———♦———

A Successful Teacher Needs
The education of a college president
The executive ability of a financier
The humility of a deacon
The adaptation of a chameleon
The hope of an optimist
The courage of a hero
The wisdom of a serpent
The gentleness of a dove
The patience of Job, and
The grace of God.
AUTHOR UNKNOWN

———♦———

What the Teacher Builds

Where teachers are building temples
With loving and infinite care,
Planning each arch with patience,
Laying each stone with prayer,
The temple the teacher is building
Will last while the ages roll:
For that beautiful unseen temple
Is a child's immortal soul.
Selected

———♦———

England's great and good Queen Victoria was being honored by a great celebration while visiting a city. On a corner of one street a large stand was built where a great company of children was assembled to sing for her.

That night after all the excitement was over, the mayor received a telegram. Perhaps he thought it was a compliment about the celebration.

But the message was a simple one straight from a motherly heart: "The Queen wants to know whether all the children got home safely."

Is not this the concern of our Heavenly King regarding the children in our classes?
ETHEL M. PATTERSON,
The Sunday School Times

———♦———

The Average Teacher

Surveys have been taken of a cross section of teachers without regard to size or kind of church. There are said to be 2,741,929 Sunday school teachers in the United States. The results of the survey picture the average teacher:

4 out of 5 teachers are women;

she is about 45 years of age;

she is the mother of two children;

her formal education is high school and one year of college;

she had no teaching experience except that gained in her own church's Sunday school;

she began teaching in her teens;

she spends less than one hour a week preparing her Sunday school lesson for teaching;

lesson preparation is usually done on Saturday night;

she relies entirely upon her Bible and quarterly;

she usually arrives at Sunday school late;

10 Sundays out of the year she is absent;

although many improvements have been made in materials and teaching methods, she makes little use of them;

in spite of the above evidence, the "average teacher" feels that her work as a teacher has been successful;

she attributes her success to her "thorough and regular" preparation. DR. GUY P. LEAVITT

Some Don'ts for Teachers

Don't take a class just to have something to do.

Don't expect to take the wiggles and giggles out of boys and girls with philosophical lectures.

Don't spend your time a-scoldin' and a-fussin' when you ought to be ringing the religious bell in the class.

Don't wait for absentees to die before you visit them.

Don't expect to do your winning of boys and girls on Sundays only.

Don't expect the pastor and the superintendent to carry all the Sunday school load.

Don't forget the place of God . . . prayer . . . souls . . . the church in your work. *Sunday School Digest*

Teachers May Be Classified in Three Divisions

1. Opportunity Makers—such teachers, if the way does not present itself, will make a way to serve and glorify God.

2. Opportunity Takers — These teachers may not go out of their way to find means of serving God and of glorifying Him, but if a way does present itself they will not turn it down.

3. Opportunity Breakers — chance after chance comes to promote the work of the Kingdom — to bear fruit for God—but the opportunity breakers disregard them. They kill their own opportunities.

Are you making and taking every opportunity you can to acknowledge God and to work for Him? *Sunday School Counsellor*

A Teacher Is Succeeding —

If his pupils are becoming his closest friends rather than Sunday morning acquaintances.

If he is able to instill into them high ideals for Christian living.

If the teacher and class mutually desire each other's companionship throughout the week.

If he can look his boys straight in the eye and know there is nothing hidden which would cause him to blush if his boys should know.

If he definitely knows he is giving God first place in his life.

If he sets aside a portion of each day for spiritual growth through communion with God (reading His Word and talking with Him).

If he takes advantage of every opportunity offered for improvement. (Teachers' training books, conventions, conferences and teachers' meetings.)

If he is unwilling for a single pupil to remain in his class unsaved.

If he becomes so dissatisfied when his entire class has been won to Christ that he is constrained to go forth and bring in others that he might teach and win them to a "saving knowledge of Jesus Christ." *Moody Church News*

The Unknown Teacher

I sing of the unknown teacher. Great generals win campaigns, but it is the unknown soldier who wins the war. It is the unknown teacher who delivers and guides the young. She lives in obscurity and contends with hardship. For her no trumpets blare, no chariots wait, no golden decorations are decreed. She keeps the watch along the borders of darkness and makes the attack on the trenches of ignorance and folly. She awakens sleeping spirits. She quickens the indolent, the unstable. She communicates her own joy in learning and shares with boys and girls the very best treasures of her mind. She lights many candles which, in later years will shine back to cheer her. This is her reward. HENRY VAN DYKE

The Consecrated Teacher

The glory of life is brightest
　When the glory of life is dim,
And she has most compelled me
　Who most has pointed to Him.
She has held me, stirred me, swayed me,
　I have hung on her every word,
'Till I fain would rise and follow
　Not her, not her, but her Lord.

The manager of a factory inquired whether a new man was progressing with his work. The foreman, who had not gotten along very well with the man in question exclaimed: "Progressing! I have taught him everything I know, and he is still a perfect idiot."

The Teacher's Prayer

Lord, who am I to teach the way
To little children, day by day —
So prone myself to go astray?

I teach them knowledge — but I know
How faint they flicker and how low
The candles of my knowledge glow.

I teach them power to will and do —
But only now to learn anew
My own great weakness through and
　through.

I teach them love for all mankind
And all God's creatures — but I find
My love comes lagging still behind.

Lord, if their guide I still must be,
O let the little children see
The teacher leaning hard on Thee.
　　　　　　　　　　EDWARD A. ESTAPHER

A seventh grader's quote from the Declaration of Independence: ". . . Every man should be divided equal." *NEA Journal*

Pupil's Valentine to His Teacher

The bees do the work
　And the bees get the honey,
But we do the work
　And you get the money.

A Teacher's Prayer

Lord, in another hour I stand
Before a wide-eyed, wond'ring band
Of little ones — and mine to teach —
My little school! What longings lie
Behind this moment now so nigh?
Now, ere from out my room I fare,
Hear Thou, O Lord, a teacher's prayer.

Great Teacher — God, oh, make Thou
　me
The teacher that I long to be —
Who sees beyond the smiles and tears
Of schoolroom life to coming years,
Who touches children now, that then
His impress may be seen on men,
Who labors not for fame, or fee,
Who teaches e'en as unto Thee.

Help me, O Lord, as comes each morn
And with it countless cares are born —
The little things that mean so much
To every childish heart I touch.
Help me to laugh, and tho' tired and
sad,
Help me to make my children glad,
Help me, O Lord, when things go
wrong,
To carry on with cheery song.

Keep Thou each day my lips, dear
Lord,
From sharp or harsh or hasty word,
Would patience yield to weary nerve,
Help me to remember Whom I serve.
I go to face this waiting band —
Oh, make me wise to understand
Each little heart within my care —
Grant Thou, O Lord, a teacher's prayer.

E. MARGARET CLARKSON

———◆———

One small boy in school always came in dirty clothing, and it was quite noticeable from his odor and appearance that he had little contact with water. The teacher sent home a note after a week or two which read: "Please give Johnny a bath so he will smell nice and clean."

Imagine the teacher's surprise when Johnny appeared as before, bearing a reply to the note which read, "It ain't your business to smell him, it's your business to learn him."

———◆———

A teacher is one who, in his youth, admired teachers. H. L. MENCKEN

———◆———

Those who can, do; those who can't, teach; and those who can't do anything at all, teach the teachers.

———◆———

The Teacher

A teacher
is a complex creature.
A saint
she ain't.
Nor could she be . . .
Nor should she be . . .
For she's human, just as
you and me,

But if she would charm her principal
she should be a gal
With these characteristics:
(Strictly conjecture — not statistics)
The Patience of a bird dog at point . . .
The Adaptability of a chameleon on
a crazy quilt . . .
A sense of Humor that enables her
to laugh even at herself . . .
The Self-control of a sphinx . . .
A Personality that glows like a candle
in a dark place . . .
The Objectivity of a research
chemist . . .
The Sincerity of a five-year-old telling
mother he loves her . . .
A professional Attitude rivaling that of
the surgeon . . .
The Promptness of a seventeen-year-old
calling on his first date . . .
The Wisdom of the prophets . . .
A Love of children that knows only
infinity as its bounds . . .
Superhuman? Impossible? I agree . . .
But should you find her
bind her
And send her to me!

HARRY A. HENDERSHOT, school principal

———◆———

A civics teacher reports on a ninth grader's written answer in a test. The student wrote of the "writ of hideous corpus." NEA Journal

———◆———

Soliloquy While Waiting for the Bell to Ring

To teach or not to teach: — that is the
question;
Whether 'tis nobler in the mind to
suffer
The slams and curses of outrageous
youth,
Or to take arms against the group of
brats,
And by opposing, end them.
To expel — to flunk — and more;
And by a flunk to say we end
The headaches and the thousand nervous shocks
That faculty is heir to — 'tis a position
Devoutly to be feared.
To expel — to flunk —

TEACH

To flunk. Perchance he may come back!
Ay, there's the rub.
For in that ensuing year what troubles may come
As to rob us of mind and reason
And make us old! There's the thing
That makes teaching of so long life;
For who could bear the scorns and jeers of youth,
The oppressor's wrong, the professor's contempt,
The pangs of disturbing conscience, the law's delay,
The impudence of office force and the sneers
That patient teachers of the unworthy take
When they themselves might quietus make
With a forty-five. Who would these burdens bear
To grunt and sweat under such a life,
But that the dread of an empty pay envelope,
A catastrophe in itself, puzzles the will
And makes us rather bear those ills we have
Than fly to those we know not of?
Thus teaching does make cowards of us all
And thus the lovely color of one's complexion
Is sicklied o'er with the pale cast of fear,
And faculty members of great frame and stature,
After teaching a month, their sunny smiles melt away
And they lose the name of humans.

PATRICIA MADDEN

———◆———

The names of Sunday school teachers are written on God's honor roll although few people in this world ever hear of teachers. Usually the pupils are the ones who are known and remembered as is D. L. Moody. Who was the Sunday school teacher who talked with him about Christ in the back room of his uncle's shoe store? It was Edward Kimball.

Advice to Sunday School Teachers

Don't argue.
Don't pull or use force.
Don't scathe or be mean.
Don't be too urgent with strangers.
Don't criticize their church.
Don't speak to the same person each church service.
Don't return to those who resent your coming.
Don't go to those with whom you may have had difficulty.
Don't embarrass a soul by keeping him standing while others are seated.
Don't put off until tomorrow that which you should do today.
Don't get discouraged because you do not see results.

JOHN HALL, *Sunday School Digest*

———◆———

A pastor was trying to persuade a woman to teach a class in the church school. She was well-qualified and had time for it. She declined, saying over and over, "I don't want to be tied down to things." Finally, the pastor had all of that he could take. He looked her in the eye and said, in a kindly voice, "You know we serve a Master who was willing to be *nailed* down to things. He was nailed to the Cross."

Christian Herald

———◆———

The Sunday school teacher was reviewing a lesson. "Who led the children of Israel out of Egypt?" There was no answer, so she pointed to a boy at the back of the room and repeated her question.

"It wasn't me," he said timidly. "We just moved here from Tulsa."

Together

———◆———

The Sunday school teacher had been telling her young class about the Christians who were thrown to the lions. Then she showed them a picture of the scene. One little boy looked so stricken that the teacher asked what was the matter. He pointed to the picture and wailed, "That poor lion didn't get any Christian!"

Together

A Teacher's Code

To come before my class each Sunday with a prepared lesson, prepared heart and a prepared attitude.

To make every effort to grow in grace and in the knowledge of the Lord Jesus Christ, and to lead my pupils to do the same.

To contact absentees promptly, personally and persistently.

To set an example in faithfulness, regular attendance, punctuality and stewardship.

To make my instruction personal and practical, adapting the lesson to the individual needs.

To make a conscientious effort to win every pupil to Christ and to help him live a Christian life.

To be loyal to my church and Sunday school.

To cooperate gladly with my pastor, superintendent, and other officers.

To investigate and appropriate every possible means of improving my teaching ministry.

To esteem Christ first, others second and self last.　　　C. V. EGEMEIER

———◆———

The Sunday school teacher told his eager-beaver class that "we are here to help others."

One bright lad asked, "Well, what are the others here for?"

Presbyterian Life

———◆———

The story is told of a woodsman in northern Minnesota who was tormented day and night by gnats and mosquitoes. When, with patience worn thin, he had almost reached the limit of endurance, he cried out in desperation, "Lord, deliver us from these pesky gnats and mosquitoes; we will take care of the bears, ourselves."

Sunday school teachers, likewise, often find that more grace is needed for the constant, annoying trifles than for the really big problems, but he who intelligently and masterfully overcomes the gnats and mosquitoes will be well prepared to face the big black bear when he stalks out of the woods.

Sunday School Journal

My Sunday School Teacher

A Sunday school teacher
I don't know his name,
A wonderful preacher
Who never found fame.
So faithful, so earnest
When I was a boy —
He stuck to his task
Though I tried to annoy.
He never was missing
In cold or in heat,
A smile his face lighted
The moment we'd meet.
He taught by example
As well as by word,
This splendid old teacher
Who honored his Lord,
He helped my young life
More than ever he knew
Later years I remembered
And tried to be true.
I suppose he has gone now
To join heaven's ranks
May it be my good fortune
Someday to say, thanks.

WILL H. HOUGHTON

———◆———

The Teacher's Psalm

The Lord is my helper, I shall not fear in guiding these pupils.

He leadeth me to the heart of the truth, and prepareth the minds of the pupils for the truth.

He giveth me a vision of the immortality of these lives.

He leadeth me to see the sacredness of teaching His Book.

Yea, though I become discouraged and despair at times, yet shall I lift my head, for His promises cannot fail me.

His Word will not return to Him void, and my faith undimmed shall burn through all the coming years.

Thou walketh before me that the seed planted shall grow.

Thou shalt stand by my side on Sunday, and speak through these lips so that these pupils feel the nearness of God.

Thou shalt cause each broken effort to gather sheaves through unnumbered years. My joy is full when I know that every effort in Thy name shall abide forever.

Surely Thy love and watchcare shall be with me every day of my life, and someday I shall live with those who turn many to righteousness for ever and ever. ROSALEE MILLS APPLEBY

———◆———

A Teacher's Prayer

My Lord, I do not ask to stand
As king or prince of high degree;
I only pray that hand in hand
A child and I may come to Thee.

To teach a tender voice to pray,
Two childish eyes Thy face to see,
Two feet to guide in Thy straight way —
This fervently I ask of Thee.

O grant Thy patience to impart
Thy holy law, Thy words of truth;
Give, Lord, Thy grace, that my whole heart
May overflow with love for youth.

As step by step we tread the way,
Trusting, and confident, and free —
A child and I, day by day,
Find sweet companionship with Thee.
The Sunday School World

———◆———

Parable of the Prodigal Teacher

A certain teacher had a Sunday school class; and one of his pupils said to this teacher, "Teacher, give us the portion of thyself and thy care and thy friendship and thy counsel which faileth us."

And he divided unto them his time in that he was present at Sunday school when it did not interfere with any of his own plans; he tried to visit each home, although somehow he never quite succeeded and he just never had time to attend the through-the-week activities of his class. Yet he continually told himself that he was doing everything for his class that could be expected of him.

And not many days after, the teacher gathered all his desires and plans and ambitions and took his journey into a far country, into a land of selfishness and complacency and good intentions and other things which do not help a Sunday school pupil and there he wasted his precious opportunity of being a chum to his own pupils.

And when he had spent the very best of his time and had gained material things but had failed to meet the needs in the lives of those he taught, there arose a mighty famine in his heart; and he began to be in want of the sense of satisfaction which comes to those in real service for their Lord whom they love wholeheartedly.

But he went and joined himself to one of the organizations of the community; and they elected him chairman of one committee after another and kept him busy doing many things. And he would fain have satisfied himself with the husks that other men did eat, but over and over again came the still small Voice saying, "I have called thee to teach and thou art neglecting thy class."

And when he came to himself, he said, "How many teachers of my acquaintance have pupils whom they understand and who understand them — pupils who look to their teachers for advice and counsel — who associate with their pupils and seem perfectly happy in their comradeship and I perish with a sense of guilt because one of my pupils has gone astray. I will arise and go to that one and will say unto him, 'Son, I have sinned against Heaven and against thee; I am no more worthy to be called thy teacher; make me as one of thy friends and let me help thee now in thy need.'"

And he arose and came to his wayward pupil, but while he was yet afar off, his pupil saw him and was moved with amazement. Instead of running and greeting his teacher, however, he drew back and was ill at ease.

And the teacher said unto the pupil, "Son, I have sinned against Heaven and against thee; I am no more worthy to be called thy teacher. Forgive me now and let me be thy friend and help thee in thy need."

But the pupil said, "Not so, I wish it were possible but it is too late now. There was a time when I needed you, when I wanted your friendship and I received counsel; but I got the wrong kind and now, alas, I am wrecked in soul and body and there is nothing you can do for me. It's too late, too late, too late!"

NELS M. ANDERSON in Christian Action

——————•——————

Traits of an Ideal Teacher

Tact
Earnestness
Adaptability
Character
Humility
Endurance
Reliability

——————•——————

Hints for Sunday School Teachers

I will teach you the good and the right way (I Samuel 12:23).

When the hour is come (Luke 22:14), do not fail to be
In your place; thus show a good example to your scholars.
Let some minutes, indeed, *before* school be occupied in
Loving, homely chats with them on their home life.

Take kindly notice of, as well as a keen interest in
Every scholar who enters the class. And, by all means,
Avoid favoritism among them. Be sure and see that each
Child is perfectly still as soon as the superintendent
Has rung the bell for the opening of the school.

You should also make sure that every scholar is possessed
Of a Bible and hymnbook and that these have their
Undivided attention while reading and singing are on.

The scholars, too, must be taught always to show the
Highest reverence during prayer time; and see that
Every eye is closed, and every tongue quite still.

Give the children to understand it is imperative that
Order must be maintained in the class, and
On no account give any the full number of marks unless
Deserving of them. "Be just before you're generous."

Always try to arrange the scholars in such a way that
None can escape your attention, the best position, and most
Desirable, being in the form of a circle or square.

The illustrations used (if any) should have point in them,
Helping to lodge the truth. As the feather to the arrow,
Even so, should the illustration be to the subject.

Regular attendance on the teacher's part is of as much
Importance as that of the scholars; and notice should be
Given to the superintendent always in the event of one's
Having to be absent on a Sunday, in order
That a suitable substitute may be provided.

Whatsoever ye do, do it as to the Lord (Col. 3:23).
And let each and every scholar in your class see that
Your one desire is their eternal soul's salvation. w. t. r.

——————•——————

"If" for Sunday School Teachers

If you can trust when all your pupils scorn you
And make a mockery of all you do;
If you can teach the truth, though few will hear you

255

And all who are concerned are blaming you;
If you can rest in God nor fret nor waver,
But quietly remain within His will;
Or, being snubbed, you do not curry favor;
When you are greatly wronged, keep silence still;

If you can stay calm when giggles interrupt you,
And boredom blunts the point you've toiled to make;
If you can pray when anger might disrupt you,
Meet jealousy and spite for Jesus' sake;
If, often criticized, you do not murmur,
Accept nor give sly flattery to win;
If you can fight for truth, then stand the firmer;
When tempted, do not yield to secret sin;

If you can pray and work for their conversion
And therefore set your heart on things above;
Uphold the cross in spite of their aversion
And to the most contentious child show love;
If you can hear the call to worldly pleasure,
And yet refuse because you want to be with Him;
Let Christ be joy to you beyond all measure,
Nor let your service be a slave to whim;

If you can smile when criticism's rudest, too,
And take the road of tact instead of might;
Yield humbly when your way seems right to you
To do the thing the elders think is right;
To saturate yourself in prayer that always
Your Lord can live His life through you each day;

Then He, not you, will teach that class on Sundays
And, which is more, He'll win them, too — His way.

FLORENCE H. PLUMSTEAD

———◆———

And There Were TEN TEACHERS

Then shall the average Sunday school be likened unto ten teachers which took their quarterlies on a Sunday morning and went forth to meet their Sunday school pupils. And five of them were wise, and five were foolish.

They that were foolish took only their quarterlies, and took no center of interest with them. But the wise took many types of interest centers with their quarterlies and Bibles.

While the worship service was conducted, they all sang and listened. And at 10:15 there was the announcement made, "It is time for classes, you are dismissed." Then all those teachers arose, and gathered their pupils together.

And the wise teachers preceded their pupils to the classroom and verily, the boys and girls were quiet before they entered the room. Each pupil went to his own seat which was cleverly marked and behold, Jimmy was not next to Johnny for much had been their fighting in past days.

And as the wise teachers had been studying the lesson for a week, they knew the story of Achan and his sin so they closed their quarterlies.

One wise teacher had for her center of interest some magazine pictures of animals who hide, and behold the boys and girls knew much information they could tell, too. Soon the wise teacher told of Achan hiding his sin.

Verily, another wise teacher brought a newspaper headline that mentioned the Middle East with her and the pupils looked at maps until they found where Achan abode.

And likewise, the third wise teacher made a white sugar cube turn black and many boys and girls said unto her, "Sin is awful."

And before the fourth wise teacher sat many pupils watching her take the chalk and draw exceedingly great things with circles and lines. They knew it was Jericho and the tents and Achan hiding his sin.

And unto her class the fifth wise teacher was showing feltograms of important little things and many were guessing — David's stones, the widow's mite, the boy's basket and then the important little thing in Achan's life.

Behold, the centers of interest were many for one story and all these children said, "We will come back and bring others with us."

And when classes were over the five foolish teachers arose and said unto the wise, "Give us of your ideas; for our attendance has gone down." And the wise answered saying, "It is so, the center of interest is easy to have. Let us sit down and talk with one another and share some different interest centers." And while they were discussing, the Sunday school superintendent and pastor came by and they agreed that there must be the center of interest.

Afterward, not many weeks hence, came the ten teachers saying, "Pastor, pastor, what will we do? Our rooms are small and our attendance is great."

But he answered and said, "Verily I say unto you, as our attendance increases, so will our rooms."

JOYCE DODGE

———◆———

A True Teacher

When the last diploma's granted
  And the race takes its degree,
And the worth-while things are graven
  In the Hall of History;
When the world's great benefactors
  Gather at the Master's call,
There will be one more deserving,
  One more worthy than them all.

When the deeds of men are measured
  And their services are weighed,
And the Master of all masters
  Hands to each his final grade,

Then the warrior, merchant, banker,
  Each shall take his separate place
'Round about a central figure,
  The most honored of our race.

Then the ones who fought for power
  And the ones who strove for pelf
Will discover that the greatest
  Was the one who offered self;
Then the teacher, true and faithful,
  Will be greeted from the Throne
By the greatest of all Teachers;
  "Ye shall reap as ye have sown!"

RILEY SCOTT

———◆———

A Teacher's Meditation

Behold, there was a teacher who had taught for many years.

And, as she sat down to prepare for the new church year she saw in her mind's eye the many experiences of the past.

And in her imagination each experience did appear as a stone, all cut and ready for use.

And that teacher did examine each stone.

Then carefully she placed stone beside stone and stone upon stone until she had builded close around herself a high wall of stone.

Then she said within herself, "This is good, I will stay here safe and secure within this enclosure;

For I have taught these many years; I need not worry any more.

I now know all of the procedures well, and as for the new ways of teaching, I do not approve of those

I will not journey further."

And behold there was a second teacher who also had taught for many years.

And, as she sat down to prepare for the new church year she saw in her mind's eye the many experiences of the past.

And in her imagination each experience did appear as a stone, all cut and ready for use.

And this teacher did examine each stone.

Then carefully she placed stone beside

stone and stone upon stone until she had builded before herself a steep but sturdy flight of stairs.

Then eagerly she climbed the stairs and gazed out across the vistas of the future.

Then she said within herself, "This is good, but I must not stay here. I must keep on building.

For lo, I have taught these many years, but there is still so much to learn.

New and challenging opportunities lie ahead.

I must yet journey farther."

And behold, there was a third teacher; and she was brand new in this field of teaching.

And, as she sat down to prepare for the new church year it was given to her the privilege to see the innermost thoughts of her two fellow workers.

And as she viewed the high forbidding wall, and as she saw the steep but sturdy stairs —

She wrestled within herself saying, "The decision lies before me; the choice is for me to make.

What kind of teacher will I become?"

ELIZABETH SUITER

Feed My Lambs

I meant to study all the week,
  And very carefully prepare;
I meant to kneel — yes, every day,
  And bear each pupil up in prayer.
But I was busy, and I found
  So many things that I must do,
Important things, that could not wait —
  The week was gone before I knew.
I meant to visit several homes,
  And mail some cards to absentees,
To let them know that they were missed,
  For such a word is sure to please
And often brings them quickly back;
  But somehow every day went by
And not a single card I sent.
  And now I ask, "Why didn't I?"
And so this morning when I rose
  I tried to study while I ate;

I briefly read my quarterly
  And hurried out, five minutes late.
I found them singing, and I dropped,
  Breathless, ashamed, into my seat —
For I intended to be there
  That I the earliest child might greet.
Time for the lesson, and a group
  Of eager voices beg their turn
To quote by heart the memory verse
  Which I, alas, forgot to learn!
And so I stumbled through the hour,
  And built with stubble, hay, and wood
Instead of gold and precious stones,
  And silver, as His servants should.
"Go feed my lambs," was His command;
  And shall I hope for them to live
On little morsels such as this,
  When mighty feasts are mine to give?
Forgive me, Lord, that I should treat
  Thy Word in such a shameful way,
And may I never stand again,
  Defeated, as I've done today.

BARBARA COMER RYBERG

The Schoolmaster's Prayer

My God, first of all, let me learn of Thee, and to teach them under my charge as Thou teachest all Thy creatures.

That is, let me lead them to be just because I am just, wise because I am wise, great because I am great.

And, if their keen eyes see that I do fall short in these qualities, let them also perceive that I recognize my shortcomings, that I pretend not to virtues I do not possess and that I honestly strive to improve.

My God, let me study Thy methods and imitate them.

As Thou dost bring all life to its possible perfection by growth, so let me duly value the element of time in my pupils and endeavor rather to guide them to maturity than to force them to perfection.

Teach me Thy noble disdain of force and Thy shrewd indirection; that I may always induce and never resort to the weakness of compulsion.

Let me be a gardener of souls and not a mere merchant of facts.

Imbue me with Thy patience that I may thoroughly learn the supreme art of teaching, which is to wait.

Let me see every pupil of mine as a candle of the Lord and know that my business is to light him.

May I stimulate curiosity and feed it. Show me how to handle fear and turn it into courage, to make the weak will strong, to cure indifference and transform it into ambition, to shame self-pity into self-confidence.

Give me the love of my pupils, for without love there is no teachableness.

Give me strength and that gentleness which is the garment of strength; and preserve me from weakness, and from petulance and tyranny, which are the signs of weakness.

Give me so mature a mind that I shall have a sense of values, that I may distinguish between essentials and non-essentials, and that I may not magnify little things.

Give me a wise blindness to the faults of exuberance and a wise evaluation of enthusiasm.

Make me sympathetic with youth, that I may not criticize as evil what is nothing but immaturity.

Teach me never to resort to the folly of reward and punishment, but to recognize that every human being wants to learn, wants to be strong and wants to be right; and show me how to uncover and how to develop these wants.

Let me never forget the profits of my calling, and that the greatest wealth one can gain in this world is the property right he clears in souls.

Invest me with the true dignity of my office, that I may always have a proper pride in knowing that mine is the highest of all callings, and that no man's business is nobler than his whose calling it is to guide and mold the unfolding mind.

Keep me humble that I may continue to learn while I teach.

May I strive not so much to be called master, as to be a master, not to show authority so much as to have authority.

And give me that joy in my work, the exaltation in my privilege and that satisfaction in my service that comes from the knowledge that, of all human occupations, that of teaching is most like the business of God Himself.

DR. FRANK CRANE

———◆———

Tears

Nothing dries sooner than a tear.

BENJAMIN FRANKLIN

———◆———

Water works: nothing but tears.

———◆———

Telephone

Did you hear about the preacher who called another preacher on the long distance telephone? It was a parson-to-parson call.

———◆———

Bad is he who breaks your slumber to mutter rudely, "Wrong number!" Worse is he who risks your wrath by phoning when you're in your bath. But worst of all is the pest who hisses in disguised voice, "Bet-you-can't-guess-who-this-is?"

———◆———

Television

Television has undoubtedly improved conversation. There's so much less of it.

———◆———

A poll was taken to find out how many people see television in taverns. The returns were staggering.

———◆———

A TV repairman was trying to locate the trouble in a friend's set. A six-year-old watching the operation said, "If you'd clean out all the old dead cowboys from the bottom of the set it might work again."

Corydon, Indiana, Democrat

259

Nowadays a husband and his wife have to have minds that run in the same channels . . . or else two television sets.

———◆———

The geography teacher asked Bobby a question about the English channel. "I don't know about that one," answered Bobby. "There's no such channel on our television set."

———◆———

First neighbor: "How do you like your new TV set?"
Second neighbor: "Fine, except for the jaberdizing."

———◆———

Temper, Temperamental

Every time you lose your temper you advertise yourself.

———◆———

A man's temper improves the more he doesn't use it.

———◆———

Temperament is temper that is too old to spank.   CHARLOTTE GREENWOOD

———◆———

Temperamental: Easy glum; easy glow.

———◆———

Temperamental: Ninety per cent temper, ten per cent mental.

———◆———

Temperance

We must plant the seed from which will grow the will to abstain!

———◆———

The drinking man commits suicide on the installment plan.

———◆———

We still want to meet the Christian who will tell us that Christ approved of drinking.

———◆———

Intemperance is one of the greatest — if not the greatest — of all evils known to mankind.   ABRAHAM LINCOLN

———◆———

Many a man has dug his grave with his teeth.

———◆———

Alcohol kills the living and preserves the dead.

Temptation

Of all essences, the devil likes acquiescence the best.

———◆———

Every temptation is an opportunity of our getting nearer to God.
                                    J. Q. ADAMS

———◆———

Find out what your temptations are, and you will find out largely what you are yourself.   HENRY WARD BEECHER

———◆———

Why comes temptation but for man to meet
And master and make crouch beneath his feet,
And so be pedestaled in triumph?
                                    BROWNING

———◆———

One young lady to another: "I can resist everything but temptation."

———◆———

To realize God's presence is the one sovereign remedy against temptation.
                                    FENELON

———◆———

Some temptations come to the industrious, but all temptations attack the idle.   SPURGEON

———◆———

It is one thing to be tempted, another thing to fall.   SHAKESPEARE

———◆———

To pray against temptations, and yet to rush into occasions, is to thrust your fingers into the fire, and then pray they might not be burnt.   SECKER

———◆———

Following the path of least resistance makes both rivers and men crooked.

———◆———

People cannot be judged by what others say about them, but they can be judged by what they say about others.

———◆———

No one can honestly or hopefully be delivered from temptation unless he has himself honestly and firmly determined to do the best he can to keep out of it.   RUSKIN

———◆———

Keeping away from the mire is better than washing it off.

TEMPTATION

Our greatest temptations come to us when we are off duty. How and where we spend our spare time will react upon our Christian experience.

———◆———

Temptation is the tempter looking through the keyhole into the room where you are living; sin is your drawing back the bolt and making it possible for him to enter.

J. WILBUR CHAPMAN

———◆———

Temptation rarely comes in working hours. It is in their leisure time that men are made or marred. W. T. TAYLOR

———◆———

Some people feel that the only way to handle temptation successfully is to yield to it.

———◆———

Teacher: "How do you resist temptation, Jerry?"

Jerry: "I always have a little talk with the devil. I just say, 'Get thee behind me, Satan, and don't you dare push.'"

———◆———

Bring up a Child

'Twas a dangerous cliff as they freely confessed
Though to walk near its crest was so pleasant
But over its terrible edge there had slipped
A Duke and full many a peasant.

So the people said something would have to be done
But their project did not at all tally
Some said, "Put a fence 'round the edge of the cliff."
Some, "An ambulance down in the valley."

But the cry for an ambulance carried the day,
For it spread to a neighboring city.
A fence may be useful or not it is true
But each heart became brim full of pity.

For those who slipped over the terrible cliff
And the dwellers in highway and alley

Gave pounds or gave pence, not to put up a fence
But an ambulance down in the valley.

"For the cliff is all right if you're careful," they said,
"And if folks ever slip and are dropping
It isn't the slipping that hurts them so much
As the shock down below when they're stopping."

So day after day, as the mishaps occurred
Quick forth would rescuers sally
To pick up the victims
Who fell from the cliff
With an ambulance down in the valley.

Better guard well the young than reclaim them when old,
For the voice of true wisdom is calling
To rescue the fallen is good, but 'tis best
To prevent other people from falling.

Better close up the source of temptation and crime
Than deliver from dungeon and galley
Better build a strong fence 'round the top of the cliff
Than an ambulance down in the valley!

AUTHOR UNKNOWN

———◆———

Three ten-year-old boys were discussing how they could obtain three toys by paying for just one.

"Go in and buy the airplane," one lad suggested to one of the others, "and be sure to get the sales slip. When you bring the package out, take out the toy and give the bag and sales slip to me. I'll go in the store, get a toy and put it in the bag. The clerk won't know the difference because I'll have the toy in the bag and will be able to show the sales slip for it. After I come out I'll give the bag and sales slip to Joe. See? We'll all have a plane — three for the price of one."

"I won't do it," Joe said, remembering the lesson his Sunday school teacher had taught the previous Sunday.

"Why, Joe?" the first lad asked.

"Because," said Joe simply but confidently, "I know Jesus wouldn't like for us to do this. It is wrong."

What happened? The boys did not get the toys.

———◆———

Test, Testing

Testing proves real worth.

———◆———

Thank, Thankful

Giving thanks is a course from which we never graduate.

———◆———

Thanksgiving is good, thanksliving is better.

———◆———

Be careful for nothing;
Be prayerful for everything;
Be thankful for anything.
                    D. L. MOODY

———◆———

Gratitude is a duty which ought to be paid, but which none have a right to expect.   ROUSSEAU

———◆———

Christian gratitude keeps life from sagging because there is something underneath life.

———◆———

Unfailing gratitude makes a human magnet out of a common personality.

———◆———

A grateful mind is a great mind.

———◆———

He who thanks but with the lips
Thanks but in part;
The full, the true Thanksgiving
Comes from the heart.

———◆———

When I find a great deal of gratitude in a poor man, I take it for granted there would be as much generosity if he were rich.   POPE

———◆———

The debts which gold can't pay
Would stand for aye,
If we should never have Thanksgiving
     Day.   FRED BECK

———◆———

Gratitude is not only the memory, but the homage of the heart — rendered to God for His goodness.   N. P. WILLIS

Say So

Does a neighbor help a little,
  As along the way you go —
Help to make your burden lighter?
  Then why not tell him so!

Does a handclasp seem to lift you
  From the depth of grief and woe,
When an old friend shares your sorrow?
  Then why not tell him so!

Does your Heavenly Father give you
  Many blessings here below?
Then on bended knee before Him
  Frankly, gladly, tell Him so!
                    GERALDINE SEARFOSS

———◆———

Gratitude is the memory of the heart.

———◆———

If you have nothing to be thankful for, make up your mind that there is something wrong with you.

———◆———

When the Sunday school teacher asked her class what they were thankful for, one little fellow replied, "My glasses."

He explained, "They keep the boys from fighting me and the girls from kissing me."   Together

———◆———

Father asked little Kathy if she didn't want to thank God for sending her such a fine new baby brother. Imagine his surprise when he heard this prayer: "Thank you, dear God, for Jimmy. I'm especially thankful that Jimmy wasn't twins like I heard the doctor say he might be."

———◆———

Think, Thinking, Thought, Thoughtful

There are two kinds of people:
  Those who stop to think and
  Those who stop thinking.

———◆———

It is the amount of thinking done with an ordinary amount of brains that gets an extraordinary amount accomplished, whether it be in religion or elsewhere.   Carillonic Peals

It is well to think well and it is divine to act well. HORACE MANN

———◆———

We think we are thinking when in reality we are only rearranging our thinking. C. T. JOHNSON

———◆———

No man has made any gain who only listens to the thing he already believes. The only man who is really thinking is the one who is waking up his mind. *K. V. P. Philosopher*

———◆———

An engineer on the Twentieth Century Limited was asked by an interviewer what he thought about as he sat in his cab rushing along at seventy miles an hour.

"I am thinking about a half mile ahead," was the engineer's reply.

Sunday school wrecks as well as train wrecks may be avoided by thinking ahead. When teachers and leaders keep their thoughts speeding far ahead, into the future, they clear the track for continued success. *Adapted*

———◆———

When everyone thinks alike, few are doing much thinking. *Nashua Cavalier*

———◆———

There's nothing either good or bad but thinking makes it so. SHAKESPEARE

———◆———

"I think" is the most overworked and exaggerated expression in the English language.

———◆———

As the gardener, by severe pruning, forces the sap of the tree into one or two vigorous limbs, so should you stop off your miscellaneous activity and concentrate your force on one or a few points. EMERSON

———◆———

The brain is as strong as its weakest think.

———◆———

What you think means more than anything else in your life: More than what you earn, more than where you live, more than your social position, and more than what anyone else may think about you. GEORGE MATTHEW ADAMS

Thinking, not growth, makes manhood. Accustom yourself, therefore, to thinking. Set yourself to understand whatever you see or read. To join thinking with reading is one of the first maxims, and one of the easiest operations. ISAAC TAYLOR

———◆———

Why can't somebody give us a list of things that everybody thinks and nobody says, and another list of things that everybody says and nobody thinks? OLIVER WENDELL HOLMES

———◆———

The Record Book

If all the things you ever said,
  Were written in a book:
And all your thoughts were on display,
  So all could take a look:
I guess there's not a living soul,
  Who wouldn't hang his head:
And feel ashamed before the Lord
  And wish that he were dead.

There is a record book I'm told
  With every deed and word;
It even keeps the records of
  Our thoughts that can't be heard;
The good, the bad and every sin
  For nothing has been missed:
It really makes me feel ashamed,
  To think what's on my list.

———◆———

We are what we think.

———◆———

Do more than think, *act.*

———◆———

And yet the pages of my past,
  Shall never condemn me;
For Jesus nailed them to His cross,
  One day at Calvary:
And now I stand in Him complete,
  Redeemed from sin and strife.
And with His blood He wrote my name
  Down in the book of life.
WALT HUNTLEY

———◆———

Broad-mindedness is the result of flattening high-mindedness out. GEORGE SANTAYANA

———◆———

Many a man fails because his train of thought is only a local.

THINK

The man who thinks he knows it all has merely stopped thinking.

————◆————

Watch Your Thoughts

Watch your thoughts,
Keep them STRONG;
High resolve
Thinks no wrong.
Watch your thoughts,
Keep them CLEAR;
Perfect love
Casts out fear.
Watch your thoughts,
Keep them RIGHT;
Faith and wisdom
Give you light.
Watch your thoughts,
Keep them TRUE;
Look to God
He'll govern you.

GRENVILLE KLEISER

————◆————

What a person thinks greatly determines what he becomes.

————◆————

One day a young man had an accident: He was struck with a thought.

————◆————

A great many people think they are thinking when they are merely rearranging their prejudices.   WILLIAM JONES

————◆————

It is easy to decide without thinking; it is easy to think and not decide; but it is hard to think fairly and decide courageously.   Youth's Companion

————◆————

To him whose elastic and vigorous thought keeps pace with the sun, the day is a perpetual morning.

HENRY D. THOREAU

————◆————

You can drive a child to reading but you can't make him think.

————◆————

You have powers that you never dreamed of. You can do things you never thought you could do. There are no limitations in what you can do except the limitations in your own mind as to what you cannot do. Don't think you cannot. Think you can.

DARWIN P. KINGSLEY

According to the American Medical Association, sitting up in bed increases your energy requirements ten per cent; standing nearly doubles it; chopping wood causes your needs to shoot up nearly eight times. Now here's a blow for you: Heavy thinking requires hardly any energy at all . . . something to think about!

————◆————

Think all you speak but speak not all you think.   PATRICK DELANEY

————◆————

Think! It may be a new experience.

————◆————

Thinking is not knowing.
Portuguese Proverb

————◆————

Most folks have presence of mind. The trouble is absence of thought.

HOWARD W. NEWTON

————◆————

If I can give a man a thought, I've helped him, but if I can make him think, I've done him a service.

ELBERT HUBBARD

————◆————

Forethought spares afterthought.

————◆————

Consideration for the rights of others is the strongest link in the chain of human friendship.

————◆————

Remember a Shut-In

Let's remember a shut-in on this day.
Remember one in some little way:
Send him a card, pay a visit or two;
It will cheer him when he's feeling blue.

Take him some books, or send him flowers,
It will ease the pain in the lonely hours.
A friendly smile, and a cheery hello
Means more to him than you'll ever know.

God will reward you someday I'm sure;
A visit from a friend can be the best known cure.
I know we all have a moment to spare
So please, visit a shut-in and show him you care.   HELEN SULEY

Associate reverently, and as much as you can, with your own loftiest thoughts.

THOREAU

Time

You have time to kill? How about working it to death?

———◆———

Everything comes to him who waits — except the precious time lost waiting.

PAUL STEINER

———◆———

Take Time

Take time to work — it is the price of success.

Take time to think — it is the source of power.

Take time to play — it is the secret of perpetual youth.

Take time to read — it is the foundation of wisdom.

Take time to worship — it is the highway to reverence.

Take time to be friendly—it is the road to happiness.

Take time to dream — it is hitching one's wagon to a star.

Take time to love and be loved — it is the privilege of the gods.

Take time to live — it is one secret of success.

Take time for friendship—it is a source of happiness.

Take time to laugh — it helps lift life's load.

Take time to worship — it is the highway of reverence.

Take time to pray — it helps to bring Christ near, and washes the dust of earth from our eyes.

Take time to be holy — for without holiness no man shall see the Lord.

Take time for God — it is life's only lasting investment.

Hawkinsville Dispatch News

———◆———

The Lord wants our precious time, not our spare time.

———◆———

Footprints in the sands of time were not made sitting down.

Americans have more time-saving devices and less time than any other people in the world.

———◆———

Waste of time is the most extravagant and costly of all expenses.

———◆———

Use time for the things that outlast time.

———◆———

He who kills time commits suicide.

FRED BECK

———◆———

You should take time before time takes you.

———◆———

Some people spend their time as recklessly as if it were just so much money.

A. C. LEE

Now

The time is now!
  It is not too soon,
For now it is late
  In the afternoon:
And our day is fading
  Without so seeming,
And into the sunset
  we go dreaming.
Awake, O nation —
  The Christ avow!
For God's salvation
  The time is now!

B. PHILIP MARTIN

———◆———

Time deals gently with those who take it gently.

ANATOLE FRANCE

———◆———

It takes less time to do a thing right than it does to explain why you did it wrong.

H. W. LONGFELLOW

———◆———

The Clock of Life

The clock of life is wound but once
And no man has the power
To tell just when the hand will stop —
At late or early hour.

Now is the only time you own!
Live, love, toil with will;
Place not faith in "tomorrow" for
The clock may then be still.

AUTHOR UNKNOWN

TIME

Time once lost is gone forever.

———◆———

One today is worth a dozen tomorrows.

———◆———

Time wasted is existence; used, life.
YOUNG

———◆———

Four things that never return:
  The spoken word,
  The sped arrow,
  The past life,
  The neglected opportunity.
ANONYMOUS

———◆———

Just a Minute

I have only just a minute
Just sixty seconds in it;
Forced upon me — can't refuse it,
Didn't seek it, didn't choose it.
I must suffer if I lose it,
Give account if I abuse it;
Just a tiny little minute
But eternity is in it.
AUTHOR UNKNOWN

———◆———

Time works wonders. So would most people if they worked twenty-four hours a day as time does.

———◆———

The man who makes the best use of his time has most to spare.

———◆———

If you have time, don't wait for time.
BENJAMIN FRANKLIN

———◆———

Perfect Timing

God's help is always sure
His methods seldom guessed;
Delay will make our pleasure pure,
Surprise will give it zest.
His wisdom is sublime,
His heart profoundly kind;
God never is before His time,
And never is behind.
ANONYMOUS

———◆———

Little drops of water
  Little grains of sand,
Make the mighty ocean
  And the pleasant land.
So the little moments,
  Humble though they be,
Make the mighty ages
  Of eternity.
AUTHOR UNKNOWN

One always has time enough if one will apply it.
GOETHE

———◆———

Time is an herb that cures all diseases.
BENJAMIN FRANKLIN

———◆———

A Minute

It's the time it takes to smile, or to give a warm "hello."
It's the time it takes to say, "Well done."
It's the time it takes to sympathize —
Or avoid calling someone what he "should be called."
It's the time it takes to cheer someone or make things better.
How much is a minute worth? It's priceless or worthless—depending on how you use it.
AUTHOR UNKNOWN

———◆———

Time is infinitely long and each day is a vessel into which a great deal may be poured, if one will actually fill it up.
GOETHE

———◆———

He who neglects the present moment throws away all he has.
SCHILLER

———◆———

Better than counting your years is to make your years count.

———◆———

This Age

This is the age
Of the half-read page,
And the quick hash
And the mad dash,
And the bright night
With the nerves tight,
The plane hop
And the brief stop,
The lamp tan
In a short span,
The big shot
And a good spot,
And the brain strain
And the heart pain,
And the cat naps
Till the spring snaps —
And the fun's done
And then comes taps.
VIRGINIA BRASIER

Since you are not sure of a minute throw not away an hour.

BENJAMIN FRANKLIN

———◆———

Secretary's definition of time: The stuff between paydays.

———◆———

One of the illusions of life is that the present hour is not the critical, decisive hour. Write it on your heart that every day is the best day of the year. He only is rich who owns the day, and no one owns the day who allows it to be invaded with worry, fret and anxiety. Finish every day, and be done with it. You have done what you could.

EMERSON

———◆———

Tithe, Tithing

Not only will a man rob God, but he will take an income tax deduction on it.

———◆———

God's Tenth

Nine parts for thee and one for me.
Nine for earth, and one for heaven;
The nine are thine, and one is mine,
But, oh, how slowly given!
In gospel land thy life is spanned,
With all Christ's blessings o'er thee,
While o'er the earth without new birth,
Lost millions sink before thee.
They sink to hell, while you could tell
The glorious gospel story;
Far from the gold which thou dost
hold,
My tithe could bring them glory.
Ten parts for thee and none for me;
All for earth, and none for heaven!
Far from my gold which thou dost
hold,
My tithe thou hast not given.
No souls for thee, no souls for me,
All for hell, and none for heaven!
For from my gold which thou dost
hold,
My tithe thou hast not given.

Selected

———◆———

Some pay their dues when due;
Some when overdue;
Some never do;
How do you do?

AUTHOR UNKNOWN

John D. Rockefeller is said to have once made the following statement concerning the habit of tithing: "I never would have been able to tithe the first million dollars I ever made if I had not tithed my first salary, which was $1.50 a week."

———◆———

Titles

It is not titles that reflect honor on men, but men on their titles.

MACHIAVELLI

———◆———

Toastmaster

Three reasons for the title, "Toastmaster":
Always popping up.
Always getting burned.
The wrong plug won't work!

———◆———

The master of ceremonies said, "You are very fortunate to have me here. There are many lousy speakers but in me you have a double feature: I'm good and lousy."

———◆———

Three hints on speech-making:
Be sincere,
Be brief,
Be seated.

———◆———

A speaker had informed the toastmaster that his address would be entitled "Shadrach, Meshach and Abednego." In preparing for the banquet, the toastmaster found he had trouble remembering the names and since he did not want to use notes, he was trying to find a way to help him remember these troublesome names. Finally a friend suggested that he write the three names on a slip of paper and pin it inside his coat. Then, when he was about to introduce the speaker he could enthusiastically gesture and open his coat and sneak a quick look at the names. And, that's just what he did — gestured and sneaked a quick look and said, "Our speaker's topic is Hart, Schaffner and Marx."

267

A machine has been invented that will unwrinkle raisins and blow up foods to as much as thirty times their true size. It must have been invented by the men who introduces public speakers.   ZULA B. GREEN *in Capper's Weekly*

———◆———

A toastmaster is one who introduces others with a few appropriated words.

———◆———

Three-B formula for toastmasters:
Be alert.
Be specific.
Be seated.

———◆———

Toastmaster to audience: "I neglected to tell you before our speaker's address that he was not feeling well; I hasten to do so now."

———◆———

Today

Today

Fill it with gladness
With courage, and love, and trust.
Treat it not lightly,
For it is a part of life
That, when spent, can never return.

———◆———

Today is the day in which to express your noblest qualities of mind and heart, to do at least one worthy thing which you have long postponed.   GRENVILLE KLEISER

———◆———

Today is the tomorrow we worried about yesterday.

———◆———

Begin Today

Dream not too much of what you'll do tomorrow,
How well you'll work another year;
Tomorrow's chance you do not need to borrow —
Today is here.

Boast not too much of mountains you will master
The while you linger in the vale below,
To dream is well, but plodding brings us faster
To where we go.

Talk not too much about some new endeavor
You mean to make a little later on.
Who idles now will idle on forever
Till life is gone.

Swear not some day to break some habit's fetter,
When this old year is dead and passed away;
If you have need of living, wiser, better
Begin today!   ANONYMOUS

———◆———

A Bit of Heaven

There's a "little bit of heaven" in each new passing day,
If you'll take the time to find it and not hurry on your way.
The smile of a loved one, when you are feeling blue,
Can banish all your cares away and make you start anew.

The handclasp of a true friend is worth far more than gold;
It is a priceless treasure that cannot be bought or sold.
There's a "little bit of heaven" when bright sunbeams entwine;
Also in a shaft of moonlight pouring silver on the vine.

In the laughter of a child you can hear the angels sing,
And a tiny, chubby hand in yours makes you richer than a king.
The crimson splash of sunset on a purple evening sky
Will paint your heart a memory that cannot, ever, die.

There's a "little bit of heaven" in the simple things of earth.
If you can only see them, your soul will find new birth.
Take time to look around you, beneath God's sky of blue —
And you'll find a "bit of heaven" right here on earth with you.
  LA VERNE P. LARSON

Tombstone

Even a tombstone will say good things about a fellow when he's down.

———◆———

The most upright thing about a dead criminal is his tombstone.

———◆———

The tombstone always sticks up for a man when he's down under.

———◆———

Tomorrow

Every tomorrow has two handles; we can take hold by the handle of anxiety or by the handle of faith.
HENRY WARD BEECHER

———◆———

Sometimes it helps a little, when the skies are overcast,
To remember that tomorrow, this day's troubles will be past;
And tomorrow always brings new strength, new courage too, some way,
For each dawn's a bright beginning, and each day's a brand new day.
AUTHOR UNKNOWN

———◆———

It was Anthony's first ride on a railroad. The train rounded a slight bend and plunged into a tunnel. There were gasps of surprise from the corner where Anthony was sitting. Suddenly the train rushed into broad daylight again, and a small voice was lifted in wonder. "It's tomorrow!" exclaimed the small boy.

———◆———

Yesterday is a cancelled check. Tomorrow is a promissory note. Today is ready cash. Use it wisely.

———◆———

Never put off 'til tomorrow what you can do today.

———◆———

A thing done right means less trouble tomorrow.

———◆———

I do not fear tomorrow, for I remember yesterday and I love today.
WILLIAM ALLEN WHITE

———◆———

Do it tomorrow—you've made enough mistakes today.

Tomorrow

He was going to be all that a mortal should be
Tomorrow.
No one should be kinder or braver than he
Tomorrow.
A friend who was troubled and weary he knew,
Who'd be glad of a lift and who needed it, too;
On him he would call and see what he could do
Tomorrow.

Each morning he stacked up the letters he'd write
Tomorrow
And thought of the folks he would fill with delight
Tomorrow.
It was too bad, indeed, he was busy today,
And hadn't a minute to stop on his way;
More time he would have to give to others, he'd say,
Tomorrow.

The greatest of workers this man would have been
Tomorrow
The world would have known him, had he ever seen
Tomorrow.
But the fact is he died and he faded from view,
And all that he left here when living was through
Was a mountain of things he intended to do
Tomorrow.
EDGAR A. GUEST

———◆———

Tongue

Let not your tongue cut your throat.

———◆———

Confine your tongue lest it confine you.

———◆———

If you keep your shoes tied tight your tongue won't wag.

———◆———

A still tongue makes a wise head.

A sharp tongue is the only edge tool that grows sharper with constant use.
WASHINGTON IRVING

———◆———

Kind Sleep

How good the pillow feels at night to him
Who kept a silent tongue when evil thought
Was on his lips! The heart fills to the brim
With satisfaction that his soul has bought.
How restless he may lie upon his bed
Who carried some choice gossip to a friend,
Which may have been much better left unsaid.
Quick spoken words are often hard to mend!
Kind sleep oft gently soothes the weary brow
Of him whose soul has found a battle won
While wakefulness will very often plow
A deeper furrow, at some evil done.
The man who wears a bridle on his tongue,
May surely keep the heart forever young.
CHRISTINE GRANT CURLESS

———◆———

The Tongue

"The boneless tongue so small and weak
Can crush and kill," declared the Greek;
"The tongue destroys a greater horde,"
The Turk asserts, "than does the sword."

The Persian proverb wisely saith,
"A lengthy tongue — an early death,"
Or sometimes takes this form instead,
"Don't let your tongue cut off your head."

"The tongue can speak a word, whose speed,"
Says the Chinese, "outstrips the steed,"
While Arab sages this impart:
"The tongue's great storehouse is the heart."

From Hebrew with the maxim sprung;
"Though feet may slip, ne'er let the tongue,"
The sacred writer crowns the whole;
"Who keeps his tongue, doth keep his soul."
Selected

———◆———

It takes a strong mind to hold an unruly tongue.

———◆———

The heart of the fool is in his mouth, but the mouth of the wise man is in his heart.
BENJAMIN FRANKLIN

———◆———

By examining the tongue of a patient physicians find out the diseases of the body, and philosophers the diseases of the mind.
JUSTIN

———◆———

Don't let your tongue cut off your head.
Persian Proverb

———◆———

A bit of love is the only bit that will bridle the tongue.
FRED BECK

———◆———

Usually the first screw that gets loose in a person's head is the one that controls the tongue.

———◆———

Nothing is so opened more by mistake than the mouth.

———◆———

The part of the body some people talk with is generally too big for the part they think with.

———◆———

Man's tongue is soft,
And bone doth lack;
Yet a stroke therewith
May break a man's back.
BENJAMIN FRANKLIN

———◆———

The most untameable thing in the world has its den just back of the teeth.

———◆———

Teach your child to hold his tongue, he'll learn fast enough to speak.
BENJAMIN FRANKLIN

———◆———

A slip of the foot you may soon recover, but a slip of the tongue you may never get over.
BENJAMIN FRANKLIN

The Tattler

I met an ardent tattler,
Of prominent renown;
Her form was tall and slender
Her coat was long and brown.
I knew her by her swagger,
When first I saw her walk;
And in my mind I settled it
That she was much to talk.

She had a polished manner,
About her person spread;
And though she was deceitful,
She seemed to be well bred.
She was so very friendly
With those who knew her not;
Unwittingly she trapped them
With gossip and with rot.

She seemed quite bent on mischief,
And labored hard and long
To cover up the works of right,
And drag out what was wrong;
Of tales and scandals on the folks,
She loved much to relate;
When love and peace were given out,
She always came in late.

She whispered on the preacher,
And talked about the folk;
Her fellow members in the church
She loved to slur and joke.
Her neighbors on the right of her
Were filthy, low and base;
And those upon the other side,
She said were in disgrace.

Train, Training

Small boy, in hospital, to visiting parents: "Do they train the trained nurses in cages like they train animals?"

It is noble to train a child in the way he should go. Still better is to walk that way yourself.

Acknowledging an introduction, a lecturer declared that he received his moral training at the knee of a devout mother and across the knee of a determined father. It takes both knees for successful rearing. *Link*

Transform, Transformed

The man who —
Knows that God is the central fact of life,
Feels the daily nearness of God,
Sees the constant evidence of God's love,
Offers himself in gratitude to God,
Is a transformed man!

If you want to set the world right, start with yourself.

If you would reform the world from its errors and vices, begin by enlisting the mothers. CHARLES SIMMONS

Travel

It isn't the travel that broadens one — it's all that rich foreign food.

Flying is against my religion. I'm a devout coward.

Many individuals are going too fast morally, too slow spiritually, too recklessly domestically for their eternal safety. MARK F. SMITH

If you want to travel fast, travel light — take off all your jealousies, prejudices, selfishness and fears. GLENN CLARK

In America there are two classes of travel — first class and with children. ROBERT BENCHLEY

A tourist is a fellow who travels many hundreds of miles in order to get a snapshot of himself standing by his automobile. *National Motorist*

Two vacationing old maids were back from the Holy Land, and their pastor asked them if they had visited Tyre and Sidon.

"Why, no," they answered, looking astonished. "Are they places? Always thought they were man and wife, like Sodom and Gomorrah."

271

God may not plan for us an easy journey but he plans a safe one.

———◆———

Treasures

Treasures in heaven are laid up only as treasures on earth are laid down.

———◆———

Trouble

When we think about people
Trouble grows;
When we think about God
Trouble goes.   AUTHOR UNKNOWN

———◆———

Troubles that you borrow soon become your own.

———◆———

Be careful how you sidestep trouble; you might miss duty.   C. A. LEE

———◆———

The most trouble is produced by those who don't produce anything else.

———◆———

The people we have the most trouble with is ourselves.

———◆———

Trouble may drive you to prayer, but prayer will drive away trouble.

———◆———

When we run from the Lord we run into trouble.

———◆———

They who have nothing to trouble them will be troubled at nothing.   BENJAMIN FRANKLIN

———◆———

Better never trouble trouble
Until trouble troubles you;
For you only make your trouble
Double-trouble when you do;
And the trouble, like a bubble,
That you're troubling about,
May be nothing but a cipher
With its rim rubbed out.   DAVID KEPPEL

———◆———

The shadow of a trouble is mostly blacker than the trouble itself.

———◆———

Borrowing trouble's as easy as pie, but the carrying charges run pretty high.

Troubles, like babies, grow larger by nursing.

———◆———

In the presence of trouble, some people grow wings; others buy crutches.   HAROLD W. RUOPP

———◆———

The best way to look at trouble is through the wrong end of a telescope.

———◆———

The brook would lose its song if you removed the rocks.   FRED BECK

———◆———

This world would be a better place in which to live if in these troubled times we turned to God and lived by His teachings.   J. EDGAR HOOVER

———◆———

Never attempt to bear more than one kind of trouble at once. Some people bear three kinds: all they had, all they have now, and all they expect to have.   EDWARD EVERETT HALE

———◆———

If you brood over your troubles, you will have a perfect hatch.   J. HOPKINS

———◆———

If you can laugh at your troubles, you will never run out of something to laugh at.   The Christian Parent

———◆———

Of all our troubles great or small, the greatest are those that don't happen at all.

———◆———

Whatever trouble Adam had,
No man in days of yore
Could say, when Adam cracked a joke,
I've heard that one before.   AUTHOR UNKNOWN

———◆———

Never go out to meet trouble. If you will just sit still, nine times out of ten someone will intercept it before it reaches you.   CALVIN COOLIDGE

———◆———

Trust

Trust

How often we trust each other,
And only doubt our Lord.
We take the word of mortals,
And yet distrust His word;

But, oh, what light and glory
Would shine o'er all our days,
If we always would remember
God means just what He says.

A. B. SIMPSON

———♦———

He that sells upon trust loses many friends, and always wants money.

BENJAMIN FRANKLIN

———♦———

If you worry you do not trust. If you trust you do not worry.

G. H. LUNN

———♦———

Let me no more my comfort draw
From my frail grasp of Thee;
In this alone rejoice with awe —
Thy mighty grasp of me.

Selected

———♦———

Trust before you try; repent before you die.

———♦———

Trust in yourself, and you are doomed to disappointment; trust in your friends, and they will die and leave you; trust in money, and you may have it taken from you; trust in reputation and some slanderous tongue may blast it; but trust in God, and you are never to be confounded in time or eternity.

D. L. MOODY

———♦———

Trust thyself and another shall not betray thee.

BENJAMIN FRANKLIN

———♦———

The passengers on the train were uneasy as they sped along through the dark, stormy night. The lightning was flashing, black clouds were rolling and the train was traveling fast. The fear and tension among the passengers was evident.

One little fellow, however, sitting all by himself, seemed utterly unaware of the storm or the speed of the train. He was amusing himself with a few toys.

One of the passengers spoke to him. "Sonny, I see you are alone on the train. Aren't you afraid to travel alone on such a stormy night?"

The lad looked up with a smile and answered, "No ma'am, I ain't afraid. My daddy's the engineer."

Brethren Quarterly

Fret not — He loves thee.   John 13:1
Faint not—He holds thee. Psalm 139:10
Fear not — He keeps thee. Psalm 121:5

———♦———

I have held many things in my hands, and I have lost them all; but whatever I have placed in God's hands, that I still possess.

MARTIN LUTHER

———♦———

He that on earthly things doth trust
Dependeth upon smoke and dust.

———♦———

The family was enjoying a camping trip and one evening after tucking four-year-old Bobby in bed, they were sitting about the campfire.

After a time Bobby called out saying, "I'm not afraid, Mommy. I'm not afraid, Daddy. God is watching over me."

"You're a big boy," his mother replied. "I know you are not afraid."

But soon again Bobby called out asking his mother to come into the tent.

"I just wanted to tell you why I'm not afraid," Bobby said. "You see all those bright stars up in the sky? They're the reason I'm not afraid. I know that they must be God's peepholes. He can look through them and watch over me."

———♦———

Truth

Truth is what God says about a thing.

———♦———

"Ye shall know the truth, and the truth shall make you free."

JOHN 8:32

———♦———

Who speaks the truth stabs falsehood to the heart.   JAMES RUSSELL LOWELL

———♦———

Know thou the truth thyself, if you the truth wouldst teach.

———♦———

Five Truths

All Sin.	Romans 3:23
All Loved.	John 3:16, Romans 5:8
All Raised.	John 5:28, 29
All Judged.	Romans 14:10
All Bow.	Philippians 2:10

Beware of a half-truth; you may get hold of the wrong half.

———◆———

There is no fit search after truth which does not, first of all, begin to live the truth it knows.

———◆———

The greatest homage we can pay to truth is to use it.   EMERSON

———◆———

Seven years of silent inquiry are needful for a man to learn the truth, but fourteen in order to learn how to make it known to his fellow men.

PLATO

———◆———

The sting of a reproach is the truth of it.   BENJAMIN FRANKLIN

———◆———

Naturalness and simple truth will always find their opportunity and pass current in any age. The freedom of speech of a man who acts without any self-interest attracts little suspicion.

MONTAIGNE

———◆———

Nothing is more harmful to a new truth than an old error.   GOETHE

———◆———

The best method of eradication of error is to publish and practice truth.

———◆———

Truth is like the sun — all that hides it is a passing cloud.

———◆———

Any time you find that truth stands in your way, you may be sure that you are headed in the wrong direction.

———◆———

If the world goes against truth, then Athanasius goes against the world.

ATHANASIUS

———◆———

The terrible thing about the quest for truth is that you find it.

ROMY DE GOURMONT

———◆———

The man who moves humbly in the direction of truth comes closer to it than the partisan who claims to have the truth assembled within the framework of some streamlined ideology.

OSCAR OSTLUND

———◆———

Old truths are always new to us, if they come with the smell of heaven upon them.   JOHN BUNYAN

Truth not translated into life is dead truth.

———◆———

The greatest and noblest pleasure which men can have in this world is to discover new truths; and the next is to shake off old prejudices.

FREDERICK THE GREAT

———◆———

Truth never fell dead in the streets. It has such affinity for the souls of men that seed, however broadcast, will catch somewhere and produce its fruit.

THEODORE PARKER

———◆———

Truth wears a different face to everybody, and it would be too tedious to wait till all the world were agreed. She is said to lie at the bottom of a well, for the very reason, perhaps, that whoever looks down in search of her sees his own image at the bottom, and is persuaded not only that he has seen the goddess, but that she is far better-looking than he had imagined.

JAMES RUSSELL LOWELL

———◆———

In quarreling the truth is always lost.

———◆———

Everyone wishes to have the truth on his side, but it is not everyone that wishes to be on the side of truth.

———◆———

Error is none the better for being common, nor truth the worse for having lain neglected.   JOHN LOCKE

———◆———

Error addresses the passions and prejudices; truth the conscience and understanding.

———◆———

Truth is the most robust and indestructible and formidable thing in the world.   WOODROW WILSON

———◆———

We must never throw away a bushel of truth because it happens to contain a few grains of chaff.   DEAN STANLEY

———◆———

Nothing ruins the truth like stretching it.

———◆———

Seek not greatness, but seek truth and you will find both.   HORACE MANN

Some people do not know what to do with truth when it is offered to them. CHARLES LAMB

Truth crushed to earth shall rise again;
The eternal years of God are hers;
But error, wounded, writhes with pain,
And dies among his worshippers. WILLIAM CULLEN BRYANT

Father: "I want an explanation and I want the truth."
Son: "Make up your mind, Dad, you can't have both."

There are three sides to every story: your side, my side, the truth.

Teacher: "Johnny, can you tell us what happens if you tell a lie?"
Johnny: "Sometimes I ride for half fare and sometimes I see a ball game for half price."

Try

In trying times, too many people stop trying.

U

Understand, Understanding

Many people are troubled about the Scriptures which are mysterious and hard to understand. I am most troubled about those which I can understand. MARK TWAIN

It is nothing to worry about if you are misunderstood. But you had better get all steamed up if you don't understand.

The man who understands one woman is qualified to understand well everything. JOHN BUTLER YEATS

Understanding others changes us.

It is better to understand a little than to misunderstand a lot. ANATOLE FRANCE

Unhappiness, Unhappy

Unhappiness invents no tools — discontent writes no song.

The discontented man finds no easy chair. BENJAMIN FRANKLIN

Is there anything men take more pains about than to make themselves unhappy? BENJAMIN FRANKLIN

How to Be Perfectly Miserable

1. Think about yourself.
2. Talk about yourself.
3. Use "I" as often as possible.
4. Mirror yourself continually in the opinion of others.
5. Listen greedily to what people say about you.
6. Expect to be appreciated.
7. Be suspicious.
8. Be jealous and envious.
9. Be sensitive to slights.
10. Never forgive a criticism.
11. Trust no one but yourself.
12. Insist on consideration and respect.
13. Demand agreement with your own views on everything.
14. Sulk if people are not grateful to you for favors shown them.
15. Never forget a service you may have rendered.
16. Be on the lookout for a good time for yourself.
17. Shirk your duties if you can.
18. Do as little as possible for others.
19. Love yourself supremely.
20. Be selfish.

This recipe is guaranteed to be infallible. *Gospel Herald*

275

The quickest way to make yourself miserable is to start wondering whether you're as happy as you could be.

————◆————

Unkind, Unkindness

Pray for a poor memory when people seem unkind.

————◆————

Unselfish, Unselfishness

Teaching children ethics and morals presents difficulties. Take the woman who had been lecturing her small son on the benefits of unselfishness. She concluded with: "We are in this world to help others."

After due consideration, he asked her: "Well then, what are the others here for?"

————◆————

Urgency, Urgent

Expedients are for the hour; principles for the ages. HENRY WARD BEECHER

Never lose your sense of urgency.
II Timothy 4:2, Phillips Translation

————◆————

Use, Useful, Usefulness

Everyone is of some use, even if nothing more than to serve as a horrible example.

————◆————

To be of use in the world is the only way to be happy.

————◆————

Egypt must be out of Moses as well as Moses out of Egypt before God can use him. WILLIAM POWELL

————◆————

Shamgar had an oxgoad,
David had a sling,
Samson had a jawbone,
Rahab had a string,
Mary had some ointment,
Aaron had a rod,
Dorcas had a needle,
All were used for God.
Harvester Mission

V

Vacations

Vacations for mothers are when boys go to summer camps.

————◆————

A vacation puts you in the pink but leaves you in the red.

————◆————

Vacations are simpler now. A man has a wife to tell him where to go, and a boss to tell him when. All he needs is someone to tell him how.

————◆————

Value

The price is what you pay, the value is what you receive.

————◆————

True values are proved under stress. It is the ability to withstand the shocks and strains and overload that proves character.

Values Compared

Longfellow could take a worthless sheet of paper, write a poem on it and make it worth $6,000—that's genius.

Rockefeller could sign his name to a piece of paper and make it worth a million — that is capital.

Uncle Sam can take silver, stamp an emblem on it, and make it worth a dollar — that's money.

A *mechanic* can take metal that is worth only $5.00 and make it worth $50.00 — that's skill.

An *artist* can take a 50 cent piece of canvas, paint a picture on it and make it worth $1,000 — that's art.

But . . . *God* can take a worthless sinful life, wash it in the blood of Christ, put His spirit in it, and make it blessing to humanity — that's salvation.
The Compass

Not long ago the worth of a man was reckoned at $1.50 — based on the value of the chemical content of his body. Now, with atomic power in view, all this is changed.

Some smart fellow has figured out that the atoms in the human body will produce 11,400,000 kilowatts of power per pound. If they could be harnessed, that is. At $570.00 for that amount of power, a man who weighs in at 150 pounds is worth $85,500. All too often these days the boss can't get enough energy out of a man to make him worth a day's wages. *Convoys News Roundup*

Victory

There are no victories without conflicts, no rainbow without a cloud and a storm.

———♦———

The hardest victory is the victory over self. ARISTOTLE

Vigilance

Eternal vigilance is the price of victory. THOMAS JEFFERSON

———♦———

Observe all men, thyself most. BENJAMIN FRANKLIN

Virtue

Virtue is as good as a thousand shields.

———♦———

You may be more happy than princes if you will be more virtuous. BENJAMIN FRANKLIN

———♦———

There was never yet any truly great man that was not at the same time truly virtuous. BENJAMIN FRANKLIN

———♦———

Few men have virtue to withstand the highest bidder. GEORGE WASHINGTON

———♦———

He is ill clothed that is bare of virtue. BENJAMIN FRANKLIN

———♦———

The whole of virtue consists in its practice. CICERO

Virtue and happiness are mother and daughter. BENJAMIN FRANKLIN

———♦———

Sell not virtue to purchase wealth nor liberty to purchase power. BENJAMIN FRANKLIN

———♦———

Vision

A superintendent is a person with *super* vision. How is your vision?

———♦———

The man who has vision and no task is a dreamer. The man who has a task and no vision is a drudge. The man who has a task and vision is a hero.

———♦———

If you don't build castles in the air you won't build anything on the ground.

———♦———

Men have sight; women insight. VICTOR HUGO

———♦———

A task without vision is drudgery. A vision without a task is a dream. A task with a vision is victory.

———♦———

"I keep seeing spots in front of my eyes . . . red spots, black spots, all kinds of spots."
"Have you seen an oculist?"
"No, just spots." *Glendale News Press*

———♦———

The sorriest man in town is the one who has caught up with his vision. PAUL ELLIOTT

———♦———

The little present must not be allowed wholly to elbow the great past out of view. ANDREW LANG

———♦———

It is always wise to look ahead, but difficult to look further than you can see. WINSTON CHURCHILL

———♦———

You must scale the mountains if you would view the plain. CHINESE PHILOSOPHER

———♦———

One day Michelangelo saw a block of marble which the owner said was of no value.
"It is valuable to me," said Michelangelo. "There is an angel imprisoned in it and I must set it free."

277

Visit, Visitation

The church needs a little more foot-shaking as well as some good hand-shaking. DR. HENRIETTA C. MEARS

———◆———

One visit is worth a basket full of letters.

———◆———

The best way to know the home of your pupils is to go there.

———◆———

The young minister said, in welcoming visitors, "We thank God for those who are not regularly with us today."

———◆———

There is no substitute for consecrated shoe leather. GEORGE A. BUTTERICK

———◆———

Rules for Visiting

1. Pray as you go.
2. Look your best, but don't over-dress.
3. Introduce yourself, your department, and your church at once.
4. Create a feeling of sincere interest.
5. Win confidence and approval of pupils as well as parents.
6. Stay long enough to accomplish the purpose of your call. But don't stay too long.
7. Be sure the advice you give is good. Take Christian literature with you that will meet their needs.
8. Don't discuss child's problems.
9. Remember you are visiting your pupil.
10. Don't let your first call be the last one.
11. Don't be irregular with your visits. INEZ SPENCE

———◆———

Visit

Christ needs you.
The church needs you.
Your pupils need you.
Your Sunday school department expects it.
Your ministers appreciate it.
You have promised to do it.
So, visit.

The non-church goer cannot be reached by the non-going church.

———◆———

Souls cost soles.

———◆———

Fish and visitors stink after three days. BENJAMIN FRANKLIN

———◆———

Visitation

V - italizes the work of the Sunday school.
I - ncreases the enrollment.
S - ecures home cooperation.
I - nspires regularity and punctuality in attendance.
T - ies the home closer to the church.
A - ids in the solving of problems.
T - ypifies the loving interest of the great Teacher.
I - nsures growth in grace on the part of the one who visits.
O - pens the doors of homes to the Lord Jesus Christ.
N - urtures friendliness and good will. *Baptist Outlook*

———◆———

V - erily, verily
I
S - ay unto thee,
I - f the Sunday school
T - eacher will visit
A - s he should,
T - he wonderful results
I - n his class will
O - vercome the absentee problem
N - ow facing him.

———◆———

To Visit or Not to Visit
(Paraphrase of Hebrews 12:1-17)

Therefore seeing we are compassed about with so great a crowd of unsaved people, let us lay aside all excuses and the hindrances which do so easily betray us, and let us walk with patience from door to door.

Looking unto Jesus, the author of personal evangelism, who for the joy of telling people of salvation, endured the problems, despising the reproach, and is now ready to go along with you.

For consider the salesman that endured such sales resistance against his products, lest ye be wearied and lose your courage.

Ye have not yet persisted unto blisters pushing doorbells.

And ye have forgotten the exhortation which speaketh unto you as Christians. Despise not thou the work of visitation evangelism, nor faint when thou art called upon to do some:

For whom the pastor respects, he calls, and keeps busy every member whom he receiveth.

If ye endure visitation, ye work then as good Christians; for what member is he who is not expected to do visitation.

But if ye be without any responsibility to personal visitation, whereof all needs must be, then are ye poor representatives of the Gospel of Christ and not good church members.

Furthermore, we have secular organizations which make similar demands of us and we respect them. Shall we not much rather be cooperative in this great crusade for souls, and live?

For they make unimportant demands reflecting their own interests, but this for our profit, that we might be participants in spreading the experience of heart holiness.

For no visitation at the moment will seem especially joyous, but rather strenuous: nevertheless, it yieldeth the glorious fruit of precious souls being brought into the Gospel of Jesus Christ.

Wherefore lift up the hands which hang down, and strengthen the feeble knees;

And make straight paths for your feet, lest those which are lazy fail to pound the pavement: rather, let them be revived.

Follow peace with all men and do personal evangelism, without which no church shall experience a real revival:

Looking diligently lest a man shirk responsibility, lest a flimsy excuse spring up to delay you, and thereby many be sidetracked;

Lest there be any fornicator, or profane person, as John Doe, who for a radio or television program, or as a visitor at your home, kept you from personal evangelism.

For you know that afterward, on Sunday, when he would have the church full, there were only a very few present, and he found no way of remedying his slothfulness at that time, though he prayed loudly and with tears in his eyes.

REV. DEWEY M. YALE, *Adapted in Sunday School Journal*

————◆————

V - ital

I - nterest

S - ends us

I - nto

T - he home.

————◆————

The A-B-C's of a Successful Visit

A - cquaint yourself with the family beforehand.

B - e prepared spiritually, mentally, physically.

C - all at the right time.

D - on't intrude if they are busy.

E - nter properly, introduce yourself.

F - ind a point of contact.

G - ive them a chance to talk.

H - ave things ready to talk about.

I - ntroduce them to the Saviour.

J - oin in with their interests.

K - eep from gossiping.

L - ead the conversation to spiritual things.

M - ake use of the Bible.

N - ever argue.

O - perate through the Holy Spirit.

P - ray as you visit.

Q - uiet their fears and misapprehensions.

R - adiate the love of Christ.

S - peak well of your church and pastor.

T - alk enthusiastically of your Sunday school.

U - nderstand and be patient with their needs.

V - ital personal witness to Christ is your best weapon.

W - atch the clock — don't stay too long.

X - pect unpleasant responses sometimes.

Y - ou may be Christ's only witness to them — press for decision.

Z - eal for God will always have a reward.

Wait, Waiting, Waits

He who waits obtains what he wishes.

———◆———

Waiting on God often brings us to our journey's end quicker than our feet.

———◆———

All things come to him who waits. But remember they come much more quickly to him who goes out to see what's the matter.   FRANK PIXLEY

———◆———

Don't wait for something to turn up, get a spade and dig for it.   T. JONES

———◆———

There is no time lost in waiting if you are waiting on the Lord.   *Eternity*

———◆———

Everything comes to him who hustles while he waits.   THOMAS A. EDISON

———◆———

A man would do nothing if he waited until he could do it so well that one could find no fault with what he has done.

———◆———

Walk

Don't let your talk exceed your walk.

———◆———

War

The war that will end war will not be fought with guns.

———◆———

Wars should be operated like street cars — pay as you enter. Then everyone would see what they're getting into, how much it will cost and where it will take them.

A battle is a terrible conjugation of the verb to kill: I kill, thou killest, he kills, we kill, they kill, all kill.
        CARLYLE

———◆———

Waste

Willful waste makes woeful want.

———◆———

Wealth

A good wife and health are a man's best wealth.

———◆———

The wealth of a man is the number of things he loves and blesses, which he is loved and blessed by.
        THOMAS CARLYLE

———◆———

It is not what you have in your pocket that makes you thankful but what you have in your heart.

———◆———

Wealth is of the heart, not of the hand.   MILTON

———◆———

Wealth: Any income that is at least one hundred dollars more a year than the income of one's wife's sister's husband.   H. L. MENCKEN

———◆———

Wealth is not his that has it, but his that enjoys it.   BENJAMIN FRANKLIN

———◆———

Riches are not an end of life, but an instrument of life.
        HENRY WARD BEECHER

———◆———

Jonathan Brown

I will tell you the story of Jonathan Brown
The wealthiest man in Vanastorbiltown.

He had lands, he had houses, and factories and stocks,
Good gilt-edged investments, as solid as rocks.
"Everything that I have," he so frequently said,
"Shall belong to the Lord just as soon as I'm dead."
So he made out his will, with particular care,
A few hundred here, and a few thousand there.

For the little home church in the village close by
He planned a new building with spire great and high,
And chimes to be heard for miles upon miles,
And deep crimson carpet all down its long aisles.
For his pastor, a new home, with rooms large and nice;
For the village library, a generous slice.
And then he remembered a college,
Where young folks were taught the essentials of knowledge.
The promising son of his very best friend
To prepare for the ministry he planned to send.
He'd pay for his board and his room and tuition,
Expecting the lad to fulfill a great mission.

His pastor, in old shoes, and shabbiest raiment,
Suggested the Lord might enjoy a down payment.
And said it weren't smart to do business that way.
"I'd end in the poorhouse for certain," he said,
"If I give up my money before I am dead."
He grumbled because the good preacher'd been rash,
And sat down again to figure his cash.

Now Satan stood by with a devilish grin,
Saw all that old Jonathan had to put in;

"Ahem," said the devil, concealing a smile,
"I'll see that this old fellow lives a long while."
So Satan chased off every menacing germ,
And sprayed with helseptic each threatening worm,
Until not a disease could get near Brother Brown,
And his excellent health was the talk of the town.
He survived epidemics of flu and of measles,
Of smallpox, diphtheria, Bavarian teasles;
He escaped the distress of acute 'pendicitis,
He couldn't so much as have old tonsillitis.
At sixty he still was quite hearty and hale,
At seventy he hadn't started to fail,
At eighty his step was still youthful and spry,
At ninety his nieces said, "Why don't he die?"

But the day after he was a hundred and two,
And Satan weren't looking, a germ wriggled through
And laid Brother Jonathan low in his grave,
And his relatives gathered in solemn conclave.
Lawyer Jones read the will in a voice deep and round,
But there wasn't a legatee that could be found.
The little home church he had loved in his youth
Had long since closed its doors and ceased spreading the truth.
His pastor had died poor a long time before
And the village library existed no more,
The college, they found when they wrote,
Was long ago sold on account of a note.
And the boy that he planned to send off to school

Had grown up in ignorance, almost a fool,
And had seven sons, each one worse than the rest,
And eleven grandchildren, the whole tribe a pest.
So his ungodly relatives each took a slice,
And his lawyers forgot and paid themselves twice,
And there wasn't a friend and there wasn't a mourner,
Not even the paper boy down at the corner.
And Satan still smiled, turned to tasks fresh and new,
Muttered, "Brother, let this be a lesson to you,"
Wagged his fingers and spat as the casket went down.
Thus ended the story of Jonathan Brown.   *Herald of Holiness, adapted*

Weather

During last summer's heat-wave, a church in the Midwest put this on its bulletin board: "You think it's hot here?"   *Reville*

Forecast for Mexico: chile today and hot tamale.

Wedding

A four-year-old lad went to a church wedding with his parents. He sat quietly, taking in every detail. Presently there was a hush as the organist began to play and the minister, bridegroom, and four attendants came from the side room to the altar. As they filed out, the boy whispered, "Mom, does she get to take her pick?"   *Together*

Weight

I always watch my waistline — I've got it out in front where I can keep my eye on it.

She's all right in her way, but she weighs too much.

A sure cure weight-reducing exercise is to push yourself away from the table three times a day.

The best reducing exercise is to move the head slowly from side to side when offered a second helping.

In a physiology class the teacher said, "Joey, can you give a familiar example of the human body as it adapts itself to changed conditions?"
"Yes, ma'am," answered Joey, "my aunt gained 50 pounds last year, and her skin never cracked."

Wicked

To swear is wicked because it is taking God's name in vain. To murmur is likewise wicked for it takes God's promises in vain.

There is no rest for the wicked and the righteous don't need it.

Wife

Of all home remedies, a good wife is the best.   ABE MARTIN

When a wife has a good husband it is easily seen in her face.   GOETHE

Mose: "Who introduced you to your wife?"
Jose: "We just happened to meet. I don't blame nobody."

May: "How did you meet your husband?"
June: "At a travel bureau. I was looking for a vacation and he was the last resort."

Will, God's Will

To know God's will is man's greatest treasure; to do His will is life's greatest privilege.

Every hour comes with some little fagot of God's will fastened upon its back.

Out of the will of God there is no such thing as success; in the will of God there cannot be any failure.

The Christian Chronicle

God will not change your will against your will.

God has given us a will with which to choose His will.

A will of your own is more likely to help you succeed than the will of a rich relative.

Indianapolis Times

Win, Winners, Winning

The cheerful loser is a sort of winner.

WILLIAM HOWARD TAFT

A winner never quits and a quitter never wins.

If we would win some, we must be winsome.

Wisdom

Wisdom is the ability to use knowledge so as to meet successfully the emergencies of life. Men may acquire knowledge, but wisdom is a gift direct from God.

DR. BOB JONES, SR.

There is this difference between happiness and wisdom: He that thinks himself the happiest man, really is so; but he that thinks himself the wisest is generally the greatest fool.

COLTON

Common sense, in an uncommon degree, is what the world calls wisdom.

COLERIDGE

The height of wisdom is to take things as they are, and look upon the rest with confidence.

MONTAIGNE

He is truly wise who gains wisdom from another's mistakes.

No one ever asks a wasp to sit down when it comes to see him.

Wisdom is the right use of knowledge.

SPURGEON

Wisdom is knowing what to do;
Skill is knowing how to do it;
Virtue is doing it.

DAVID STARR JORDAN

A wise man will not only bow at the manger but also at the cross.

To have a low opinion of our own merits, and to think highly of others, is an evidence of wisdom. All men are frail, but thou shouldst reckon none as frail as thyself.

THOMAS A' KEMPIS

The superior man measures his wisdom by watching people who have none.

A fool tells what he will do; a boaster what he has done; the wise man does it and says nothing.

There are four kinds of people:
Those who know not, and know not that they know not.
These are foolish.
Those who know not, and know they know not.
These are the simple, and should be instructed.
Those who know, and know not that they know.
These are asleep, wake them.
Those who know and know they know.
These are the wise, listen to them.

ARAB PHILOSOPHER

A wise man will make more opportunities than he finds.

BACON

He's a fool that cannot conceal his wisdom.

BENJAMIN FRANKLIN

He who learns the rules of wisdom without conforming to them in his life is like a man who labored in his fields, but did not sow.

SAADI

Culture

My music is the patter
Of happy little feet,
Exploring house and attic
And scampering down the street.

My art is crayon scribbling
On table, door and wall
In classic style and modern —
I treasure one and all.

My literature comprises
The books my children know
And old tales I remember
From childhood long ago.

The kind of culture I acquire
No colleges impart,
Yet wisdom only life can teach
I cherish in my heart.
KATHERINE KELLY WOODLEY

The doorstep to the temple of wisdom is a knowledge of your own ignorance. BENJAMIN FRANKLIN

Wit

Wit is the salt of conversation, not the food. WILLIAM HAZLITT

There's many witty men whose brains can't fill their bellies. BENJAMIN FRANKLIN

It is said that an Englishman gets three laughs from a joke: the first when it is told, the second when it is explained to him and the third when he catches on!

Half wits talk much but say little. BENJAMIN FRANKLIN

The person who lacks wit is not necessarily a half wit.

There are no fools so troublesome as those who have wit. BENJAMIN FRANKLIN

Witness, Witnessing

Instead of being question marks for Christ, we need to be exclamation points.

Too many teachers and preachers think that they are called to be lawyers for Christ instead of witnesses for Him. Just testify concerning the things you know about Him!

Some Christians are like arctic rivers — frozen at the mouth.

The true disciple is a witness to the fact that the Lord gives us His presence.

Be not simply a reflector of Christ; be a radiator. Christian Digest

Speak Out for Jesus

You talk about your business,
Your bonds and stocks and gold;
And in all worldly matters
You are so brave and bold.
But why are you so silent
About salvation's plan?
Why don't you speak for Jesus,
And speak out like a man?

You talk about the weather,
And the crops of corn and wheat;
You speak of friends and neighbors
That pass along the street;
You call yourself a Christian,
And like the gospel plan —
Then why not speak for Jesus,
And speak out like a man?

Are you ashamed of Jesus
And the story of the cross,
That you lower His pure banner
And let it suffer loss?
Have you forgot His suffering?
Did He die for you in vain?
If not, then live and speak for Jesus,
And speak out like a man.

I'd like to tell the story sweet
Of Jesus, wouldn't you?
To help some other folks to meet
Their Saviour, wouldn't you?
I'd like to travel all the way
To where I'd hear my Jesus say:
"You've helped my work along today."
I'd like that. Wouldn't you?
AUTHOR UNKNOWN

Every time you walk a mile to church and carry a Bible with you, you preach a sermon a mile long.   D. L. MOODY

———◆———

If God could speak through Balaam's ass, He could speak through you.

———◆———

We do not stand in the world bearing witness to Christ, but stand in Christ and bear witness to the world.   GORDON

———◆———

A little girl was playing with some lettered blocks one day. Her mother showed her how to spell the word, "good," and explained how important it was for little girls to be good and do good. After a while, as her mother was working in the kitchen, the little girl ran to her and said, "Come and see the two nice words I made out of the word good." When her mother looked she saw the words, "go" and "do."

———◆———

Woman, Women

A Woman in It

They talk about a woman's sphere
As though it had a limit;
There's not a task to mankind given,
There's not a blessing or a woe,
There's not a whispered "yes" or "no,"
There's not a life, there's not a birth
That has a feather's weight of worth
Without a woman in it.

———◆———

Women's faults are many,
Men have only two:
Everything they say,
And everything they do.

———◆———

There's only one way to handle a woman. The trouble is nobody knows what it is.   *Glendale News Press*

———◆———

There is in every true woman's heart a spark of heavenly fire, which lies dormant in the broad daylight of prosperity; but which kindles up, and beams and blazes in the dark hour of adversity.   WASHINGTON IRVING

Three women can keep a secret if two of them are dead.

———◆———

A sufficient measure of civilization is the influence of good women.   EMERSON

———◆———

A good woman inspires a man,
A brilliant woman interests him,
A beautiful woman fascinates him—
The sympathetic woman gets him.   HELEN ROWLAND

———◆———

To be happy in this life a woman needs the optimism of a child, the chic of a mannequin, the diplomacy of a prime minister, the nerves of a cold potato, the wisdom of Solomon and the complacency of a prize cat.

———◆———

A perfectly honest woman, a woman who never flatters, who never manages, who never conceals, who never uses her eyes, who never speculates on the effect which she produces — what a monster, I say, would such a female be!   THACKERAY

———◆———

When women live longer than men, it's often between birthdays.

———◆———

You can always tell a woman, but you cannot tell her much.

———◆———

Women have a wonderful instinct about things. They can discover everything except the obvious.   OSCAR WILDE

———◆———

When you find a great man playing a big part on life's stage you'll find in sight, or just around the corner, a great woman. Read history! A man alone is only half a man; it takes the two to make the whole.   ELBERT HUBBARD

———◆———

Nothing shall be impossible to the woman who knows how to cry in the right way, in front of the right man.   WINIFRED V. KNOCKER

———◆———

Woman was made from Adam's side that she might walk beside him, not from his foot that he should step on her.   DR. HAROLD LINDSELL

Being a woman is a terribly difficult trade, since it consists principally of dealing with men. JOSEPH CONRAD

———◆———

Intuition is suspicion in skirts.

———◆———

If you want to change a woman's mind, agree with her.

———◆———

Women have:
A smile for every joy,
A tear for every sorrow,
A consolation for every grief,
An excuse for every fault,
A prayer for every misfortune,
Encouragement for every hope. SAINT-FOIX

———◆———

Woman

She's an angel in truth, a demon in fiction,
A woman's the greatest in all contradiction;
She's afraid of a cockroach, she'll scream at a mouse,
But she'll tackle a husband as big as a house.

She'll take him for better, she'll take him for worse,
She'll split his head open and then be his nurse.
And when he is well and can get out of bed,
She'll pick up a teapot and throw at his head.

She's faithful, deceitful, keen-sighted and blind;
She's crafty, she's simple, she's cruel, she's kind.
She'll lift a man up, she'll cast a man down,
She'll take him apart and make him a clown.

You fancy she's this, but you'll find she is that,
For she'll play like a kitten and bite like a cat.
In the morning she will, at evening she won't,
And you're always expecting she does, but she don't! AUTHOR UNKNOWN

Generally when a man climbs to success, a woman is holding the ladder.

———◆———

Women's styles may change, but their designs remain the same. OSCAR WILDE

———◆———

God created women beautiful and foolish: beautiful so that men would love them, foolish so that they would love the men.

———◆———

Woman — A New Chemical Element

Symbol — woe
Atomic — 120 pounds, approximately.
Occurrence
1. Can be found wherever man exists.
2. Seldom in the free or natural state.
   Physical Properties
1. All sizes and colors.
2. Always appears in disguised conditions.
3. Boils at nothing and may freeze at any point.
4. Melts when properly heated.
5. Very bitter if not used correctly.
   Chemical Properties
1. Extremely active.
2. Great affinity for gold, silver, platinum, precious stones.
3. Able to absorb expensive food at any time.
4. Undissolved in liquids, but activity is greatly increased when saturated with spirit solution.
5. Sometimes yields to pressure.
6. Turns green when placed next to a better specimen.
7. Ages rapidly. The fresh variety has greater attraction.
8. Highly dangerous and explosive in inexperienced hands.

———◆———

Words

Kind words do not cost much. They never blister the tongue or lips. Though they do not cost much, they accomplish much. They make other people good-natured. They also produce their own image in other men's souls, and a beautiful image it is. PASCAL

Words

Words that are softly spoken,
Can build a world of charm.
Words of tender passion,
Can rescue a soul from harm.

Words of wondrous beauty,
Like silver imbedded in gold,
Can lift the brokenhearted
To heavenly joys untold.

Words of love and comfort,
Can calm a stormy sea.
Words of courage and wisdom,
Bring wonderful peace to me.

Words of hope like sunshine
Fill the heart and soul.
Wonderful words — how precious,
Are worth a future of gold.
CLAUDE COX

Colors fade, temples crumble, empires fall, but wise words endure.
THORNDIKE

Seest thou a man that is hasty in his words?
There is more hope of a fool than of him.
SOLOMON

One thing you can give and still keep is your word.

The knowledge of words is the gate of scholarship.
WILSON

Words break no bones; hearts though sometimes.
ROBERT BROWNING

Don't use a gallon of words to express a spoonful of thought.

There are two new words that have appeared in recent years that suggest the new tempo in business. The first of these is *pre-search* . . . it means preparing in advance, testing, planning, long before the time of need. The other word is *imagineering*, which is the wedding of imagination and engineering . . . and these two were meant for each other. It means hooking up vision and inspiration with technical knowledge. It pays to think ahead!
Selected

As we must account for every idle word, so we must for every idle silence.
BENJAMIN FRANKLIN

Words

Calm words in any stress
Of pride or ire,
Are like slow falling rain
Upon a fire.
LALIA MITCHELL THORNTON

Beware of the man who does not translate his words into deeds.
THEODORE ROOSEVELT

Words

A careless word may kindle strife.
A cruel word may wreck a life.
A brutal word may smite and kill.
A gracious word may smooth the way.
A joyous word may light the day.
A timely word may lessen stress.
A loving word may heal and bless.
WALTER

Words are like leaves, and where they most abound,
Much fruit of sense beneath is rarely found.
ALEXANDER POPE

Work

If a task is once begun
Never leave it till it's done.
Be the labor great or small,
Do it well or not at all.
ANONYMOUS

To work at the things you love, or for those you love, is to turn work into play and duty into privilege.
PARLETTE

When we are in the wrong place, the right place is empty.

Each morning sees some task begun,
Each evening sees its close;
Something attempted, something done,
Has earned a night's repose.
LONGFELLOW, The Village Blacksmith

The great thing with work is to be on top of it, not constantly chasing after it.
DOROTHY THOMPSON

287

WORK

Do your work and you shall reinforce yourself. EMERSON

———◆———

A willing heart lightens work.

———◆———

Work!
Thank God for the swing of it,
For the clamoring hammering ring of
it . . .
Oh, what is so fierce as the flame of it?
And what is so huge as the aim of it?
Thundering on through dearth and
doubt
Calling the plan of the Master out.
ANGELA MORGAN, *Work*

———◆———

There aren't any rules for success
that work unless you do. ANITA BELMONT

———◆———

An efficiency expert is smart enough
to tell you how to run your business
and too smart to start one of his own.
The Businessman's Book of Quotations

———◆———

Blessed are they that go 'round and
'round for they shall become big
wheels.

———◆———

It is easier to do a job right than
to explain why you did it.

———◆———

We are all good manufacturers —
either making good or making trouble.

———◆———

No one ever kicks a dead dog.

———◆———

Few things come to him who wishes;
all things come to him who works.

———◆———

I will go anywhere provided it is
forward. LIVINGSTON

———◆———

Men do less than they ought, unless
they do all that they can. CARLYLE

———◆———

The smartest person is not the one
who is quickest to see through a thing,
but it is the one who is quickest to see
a thing through. *Selected*

———◆———

Work as if you were to live 100
years, pray as if you were to die tomorrow. BENJAMIN FRANKLIN

Too frequently we have a Samaria
vision but only a Jerusalem zeal.

———◆———

Every man is as lazy as his circumstances permit him to be.

———◆———

Too many churches are full of willing workers: some are willing to work
and the rest are willing to let them
work.

———◆———

No one knows what he can do until
he tries.

———◆———

I'd like to compliment you on your
work — when will you start?

———◆———

Employer to new employee: "Young
man, we have a record for doing the
impossible in this place."
Young man: "Yes sir, I'll remember.
I'll be as impossible as I can."

———◆———

You can do anything you ought to
do. DR. BOB JONES, SR.

———◆———

It takes vision and courage to create
— it takes faith and courage to prove.
OWEN D. YOUNG

———◆———

Have plenty of time for work, none
to waste.

———◆———

It is no disgrace to fail. It is a disgrace to do less than your best to
keep from failing. DR. BOB JONES, SR.

———◆———

The world is blessed most by men
who do things, and not by those who
merely talk about them. JAMES OLIVER

———◆———

Anyone can do any amount of work
as long as it isn't the work he is supposed to be doing. ROBERT BENCHLEY

———◆———

Do More
Do more than exist, live.
Do more than touch, feel.
Do more than look, observe.
Do more than hear, listen.
Do more than listen, understand.
Do more than think, ponder.
Do more than talk, say something.
Baptist Bulletin

288

Make stepping stones out of your stumbling stones. DR. BOB JONES, SR.

———♦———

No work is too trifling to be well done.

———♦———

There is only one way to improve one's work — love it. PHILLIP BROOKS

———♦———

The following formula is credited to Carnegie as the way to manage any kind of business:
1. Organize — which means to have the right man in the right place.
2. Deputize — which is to give the man full authority to do the job you hired him for.
3. Supervise — which means to keep after the whole gang to see that they do what they are supposed to do. Advertisers' Digest

———♦———

A Christian worker should be like a good watch:
Open face,
Busy hands,
Pure gold,
Well regulated,
Full of good works. Matthew 5:16

———♦———

A servant works; a king speaks.

———♦———

It doesn't make any difference what brand of polish you use; you have to mix elbow grease with it to make it shine the shoes.

———♦———

When you know you are doing a job perfectly, look for ways to improve it, or someone else will. MARTIN VANBEE

———♦———

Work and study as though all depended upon you, but pray and trust as though all depended upon God.

———♦———

Some people are so busy learning the tricks of the trade that they don't learn the trade.

———♦———

People who take pains never to do any more than they get paid for, never get paid for any more than they do. ELBERT HUBBARD

When your work speaks for itself, don't interrupt it. HENRY J. KAISER

———♦———

Keep thy shop, and thy shop will keep thee. BENJAMIN FRANKLIN

———♦———

Only horses work, and they turn their backs on it. ANONYMOUS

———♦———

In the ordinary business of life, industry can do anything which genius can do, and very many things which it cannot. HENRY WARD BEECHER

———♦———

Most footprints on the sands of time were left by work shoes. Town Journal

———♦———

It is better to wear out than to rust out.

———♦———

"I have saved myself a great deal of trouble," a friend once told me, "by always following this precept: When you have anything to do, do it." SIR JOHN LUBBOCK

———♦———

I am not worried about the amount of work I have to do, it's the condition of the shovel that concerns me.

———♦———

Raise your hat to the past and take off your coat to the future.

———♦———

A worker who does only what he has to do, is a slave. One who willingly does more than is required of him, is truly a free man.

———♦———

No one can do his work well who does not think it of importance.

———♦———

The best jobs haven't been started. The best work hasn't been done. BERTON BRALEY

———♦———

Approach the easy as though it were difficult and the difficult as though it were easy; the first, lest overconfidence make you careless, and the second, lest faint-heartedness make you afraid.

———♦———

It isn't the number of hours a man puts in, it's what a man puts in the hours that really counts.

Don't drift along. Any dead fish can float downstream.

———♦———

A jockey always whispered this to his horse so he would win:
Roses are red, violets are blue,
Horses that lose are made into glue.

———♦———

A man who needed a job saw an ad in the paper for a position open at the zoo. He accepted the job and was to dress up as a monkey and perform in one of the cages. All went well for several days and then, as he was going from limb to limb he fell.
"Help, help," he cried.
"Shut up," said the lion in the next cage, "or we'll both lose our jobs."

———♦———

Don't always fret about your work
And rewards that are small and few,
Remember that the mighty oak
Was once a nut like you.

———♦———

Nothing is really work unless you would rather be doing something else.
SIR JAMES BARRIE

———♦———

There are four kinds of church workers:
Jaw-bone,
Wish-bone,
Back-bone,
Knee-bone.

———♦———

Work for Christ

1. The *field* is large. Matthew 13:38
2. The *need* is great. John 4:35
3. The *time* is now. Galatians 1:10
4. The *call* is urgent. Matthew 20:6
5. The *work* is varied. I Corinthians 12:12
6. The *partner* is almighty. II Corinthians 6:1
7. The *means* are provided. Luke 19:15

———♦———

I do not work my soul to save —
That my Lord hath done;
But I will work like any slave
For love of God's dear Son.

———♦———

Do not let work divorce itself from imagination.

The things nearest are best . . .
breath in your nostrils,
light in your eyes,
flowers at your feet,
duties at your hand,
the path of right just before you.
Then do not grasp at the stars, but do life's plain, common work as it comes, certain that daily duties and daily bread are the sweetest things of life.
ROBERT LOUIS STEVENSON

———♦———

Workers with Him

Little is much when God is in it;
Man's busiest day's not worth God's minute,
Much is little everywhere,
If God the labor does not share;
So work with God and nothing's lost,
Who works with Him does best and most:
Work on! Work on!
A. A. REES

———♦———

The church needs to be a place full of wide-awake workers and not a dormitory of sleepyheads.

———♦———

John Wesley traveled two hundred and fifty thousand miles on horseback, averaging twenty miles a day for forty years; preached forty thousand sermons; produced four hundred books; knew ten languages. At eighty-three he was annoyed that he could not write more than fifteen hours a day without hurting his eyes, and at eighty-six he was ashamed he could not preach more than twice a day. He complained in his diary that there was an increasing tendency to lie in bed until 5:30 in the morning.
The Arkansas Baptist

———♦———

Work wrought out in activities which bless others produces joy in the heart of the one who does it.

———♦———

Now I get me up to work,
I pray the Lord I may not shirk.
If I should die before tonight,
I pray the Lord my work's all right.
ANONYMOUS

A thing done right means less trouble tomorrow.

———◆———

The man who watches the clock never becomes the "Man of the Hour."

———◆———

Work is the best narcotic.

MAURICE MOLNAR

———◆———

What the country needs is dirtier fingernails and cleaner minds.

WILL ROGERS

———◆———

A new employee had been caught coming in late for work three times and the fourth morning the foreman decided to read the riot act.

"Look here," he snapped, "don't you know what time we start work around here?"

"No, sir," said the man, "they're always working when I get here."

———◆———

Your Field of Labor

If you cannot on the ocean
    Sail among the swiftest fleet,
Rocking on the highest billows,
    Laughing at the storms you meet,
You can stand among the sailors
    Anchored yet within the bay;
You can lend a hand to help them,
    As they launch their boats away.

If you are too weak to journey
    Up the mountain steep and high,
You can stand within the valley
    While the multitudes go by;
You can chant in happy measure
    As they slowly pass along,
Though they may forget the singer,
    They will not forget the song.

Do not, then, stand idly waiting
    For some greater work to do;
Fortune is a lazy goddess,
    She will never come to you;
Go, and toil in any vineyard,
    Do not fear to do or dare;
If you want a field of labor,
    You can find it anywhere.

ELLEN H. COTES

World

We can only change the world by changing men.

CHARLES WELLS

———◆———

We cannot have a better world without first having better men.

Newsweek

———◆———

A ship is safe in the ocean as long as the ocean is not in the ship, and a Christian is safe in the world so long as the world is not in the Christian.

———◆———

The earth is a swinging cemetery of the dead.

———◆———

This World

This world is not so bad a world
    As some would like to make it;
Though whether good or whether bad,
    Depends on how we take it.
For if we scold and fret all day
    From dewy morn till even,
This world will ne'er afford to man
    A foretaste here of heaven.

This world in truth's as good a world
    As e'er was known to any
Who have not seen another world,
    And these are very many;
And if the men, and women, too,
    Have plenty of employment,
Those surely must be hard to please
    Who cannot find enjoyment.

This world is quite a clever world
    In rain or pleasant weather,
If people would but learn to live
    In harmony together;
Nor seek to burst the kindly bond
    By love and peace cemented,
And learn the best of lessons, yet
    To always be contented.

AUTHOR UNKNOWN

———◆———

He who would have no trouble in this world must not be born in it.

Italian Proverb

———◆———

The world is a globe that revolves on its taxes.

———◆———

When you deplore the condition of the world, ask yourself, "Am I part of the problem or part of the solution?"

MURRAY D. LINCOLN

291

Worry

Worry is interest paid on trouble before it is due.   DEAN INGE

———◆———

Worrying takes up just as much time as work, but work pays better dividends.

———◆———

Our worst misfortunes never happen, and most miseries lie in anticipation.

———◆———

Worry, like a rocking chair, will give you something to do, but it won't get you anywhere.

———◆———

Those who live in a worry invite death in a hurry.   ANONYMOUS

———◆———

The eagle that soars in the upper air does not worry itself as to how it is to cross rivers.   Selected

———◆———

There are two days we should not worry over — yesterday and tomorrow.

———◆———

There is a great difference between worry and concern.
A worried person sees a problem, and the concerned person solves a problem.   J. HAROLD STEPHENS

———◆———

Worry can cast a big shadow behind a small thing.

———◆———

In days of stress and strife, it is well to remember that worry is no one's friend, but everyone's enemy.
There are 773,692 words in the Bible but one will search in vain for a single occurrence of the word "worry" among them!
"Worry" is not in God's vocabulary and should not be in ours.

———◆———

Worry kills more people than work because more people worry than work.

———◆———

I never met a healthy person who worried much about his health, or a really good person who worried much about his soul.

JOHN BURTON S. HALDANE

Said the robin to the sparrow,
  I should really like to know
Why these anxious human beings
  Rush about and worry so.

Said the sparrow to the robin,
  I think that it must be
They have no Heavenly Father
  Such as cares for you and me.

———◆———
                          The Prairie Pastor

Nobody's Friend

I'm old man Worry, and I'm nobody's
  friend,
Though I'm called in many a home.
When trouble comes, for me they will
  send,
And it matters not where they roam.

For me they will lay awake many a
  night,
And I pay them in shattered nerves.
But they hold me and cuddle me
  tight —
I'm an old man whom many a one
  serves.

The rich and the poor invite me in,
And I go wherever they ask.
But they should know I hurt like sin,
And unfit them for any task.

I rob them of friends, as well as health,
And things that are held most dear.
And it matters not if they have wealth,
They are not happy when I am near.

But there are two smart ones where I
  can't abide —
They are Faith and Hope, I declare!
Wherever they go I stay outside —
No room to crowd in there.   H. J. ANDREWS

———◆———

Worry affects the circulation, the heart, the glands, the whole nervous system, and profoundly affects the health. I have never known a man who died from overwork, but many who died from doubt.   DR. CHARLES MAYO

———◆———

Worship

Satan doesn't care what we worship, as long as we don't worship God.
                          D. L. MOODY

The man who bows the lowest in the presence of God stands the straightest in the presence of sin.

———◆———

Worship is fellowship with God.

———◆———

Gold has more worshipers than God.

———◆———

Worship is written upon the heart of man by the hand of God.

———◆———

Worship is the first step to wisdom.

———◆———

You can worship God in the woods . . . but you don't!
You can worship God on the lakes . . . but you don't!
You can worship God in your auto . . . but you don't!
You can worship God in a different church each Sunday . . . but you don't!
You can worship God by sending the children to Sunday school . . . but you don't!
The best place to worship God on Sunday is at your church!

———◆———

Ten Commandments for Worshipers

I. Thou shalt not come to service late
   Nor for the amen refuse to wait.
II. When speaks the organ's sweet refrain
   Thy noisy tongue thou shalt restrain.
III. But when the hymns are sounded out
   Thou shalt lift up thy voice and shout.
IV. And when the anthem thou shalt hear
   Thy sticky throat thou shalt not clear.
V. The endmost seat thou shalt leave free
   For more must share the pew with thee.
VI. The offering plate thou shalt not fear
   But give thine uttermost with cheer.
VII. Thou shalt the minister give heed
   Nor blame him when thou art disagreed.
VIII. Unto thy neighbor thou shalt bend
   And if a stranger, make a friend.
IX. Thou shalt in every way be kind,
   Compassionate, and of tender mind.
X. And so, by all thy spirit's grace,
   Thou shalt show God within this place. ANONYMOUS

———◆———

Write, Writing

Writing requires an application of a coat of glue to the seat of the chair.

———◆———

Scholars' pens carry farther and give a louder report than thunder. SIR THOMAS BROWNE

———◆———

Say it with flowers,
Say it with mink,
But never, oh, never
Say it with ink.

———◆———

Though authors use the same words, some do seem to string 'em together better.

———◆———

An author is never successful until he has learned to make his words smaller than his ideas. R. W. EMERSON

———◆———

He that composes himself is wiser than he that composes books. BENJAMIN FRANKLIN

———◆———

Dedication in a scientific book: "To my wife, without whose absence this book could not have been written."

———◆———

Editor: "You wish a position as a proofreader?"
Applicant: "Yes, sir."
Editor: "Do you understand the requirements of that responsible position?"
Applicant: "Perfectly. Whenever you make any mistakes in the magazine, just blame 'em on me, and I'll never say a word."

WRITE

Asked to paraphrase the sentence, "He had a literary bent," a city scholar gave this version:
"He was very round shouldered through excessive writing."

———◆———

The learned fool writes his nonsense in better language than the unlearned, but still 'tis nonsense.

———◆———

The teacher had asked the pupils to write a short composition on the subject, "Water."
One boy wrote: "Water is a white wet liquid which turns black when you wash in it."

———◆———

A student-made distinction: "The difference between prose and poetry is that prose is written all the way across the page, and poetry is written only half way across." LAURA GLOVER

———◆———

If you would not be forgotten, as soon as you are dead and rotten, either write things worth reading or do things worth the writing. BENJAMIN FRANKLIN

———◆———

Do right and fear no man; don't write and fear no woman.

———◆———

Reading makes a full man; conversation a ready man, writing an exact man.

———◆———

"The nose," wrote little Susie in her school paper, "is that part of the body which shines, snubs, snoops and sneezes." *Presbyterian Life*

———◆———

Newspaper editor to hopeful young writer: "Do you write for pay or do you write free verse?"

———◆———

Four men died on the same day. One was a struggling author; he left his family only $5. The second was a bookseller; he left $50. The third was a publisher; he left $500. The fourth was a dealer in waste paper. He left $50,000!

To Our Contributors

If you have a thing to say,
    Cut it down!
Something you must write today,
    Cut it down!
Let your words be short and few,
Aim to make them clear and true,
Monosyllables will do,
    Cut it down!

If you're writing to the press,
    Cut it down!
Make it half or even less,
    Cut it down!
Editors like pithy prose,
Lengthy letters are their foes,
Take a hint from "one who knows,"
    Cut it down!

Have to make a speech tonight?
    Cut it down!
Wish to have it take all right?
    Cut it down!
Do not be a talking bore,
Better far to listen more,
Don't monopolize the floor,
    Cut it down! GRENVILLE KLEISER

———◆———

Typographical Error

The typographical error
    Is a slippery thing and sly
You can hunt till you are dizzy,
    But it somehow will get by.
Till the forms are off the presses,
    It is strange how still it keeps
It shrinks down into a corner
    And it never stirs or peeps,
That typographical error,
    Too small for human eyes!

Till the ink is on the paper
    When it grows to mountain size,
The boss he stares with horror,
    Then he grabs his hair and groans.
The copy reader drops his head
    Upon his hands and moans —
The remainder of the issues
    May be clean as clean can be,
But that typographical error
    Is the only thing you see.
AUTHOR UNKNOWN

294

The Poet's Truest Friend

The kindest friend the poet has,
(Though poets least suspect it)
Is the editor who'll scan his verse,
Then mercifully reject it.

Like battercakes, on griddle hot,
Ambitious poems sizzle,
But, were they baked on slower fire,
They'd not be such a fizzle!

When the editor returns my verse
I think him very hateful,
Yet, when I read that poem through,
I'm really, deeply grateful.

'Twould never do to let it go,
Just as I firstly wrote it;
For, till I've made it over new,
No one would ever quote it.

'Tis best, you see, when writing verse,
To polish and to shine it.
Or else, some brilliant editor,
Will instantly decline it!
News and Courier

The Editor's Request

If you have a tale to tell,
Boil it down!
Write it out and write it well,
Being careful how you spell;
Send the kernel, keep the shell;
Boil it down! Boil it down!

If you want the world to know,
Boil it down!
If you have good cause to crow
If you'd tell how churches grow,
Whence you came or where you go,
Boil it down! Boil it down!

Then, when all the job is done,
Boil it down!
If you want to share our fun,
Know just how a paper's run,
Day by day from sun to sun,
Boil it down! Boil it down!

When there's not a word to spare,
Boil it down!
Heave a sigh and lift a prayer,
Stamp your foot and tear your hair,
Then begin again with care —
Boil it down! Boil it down!

When all done, you send it in,
We'll boil it down.
Where you end, there we begin;
This is our besetting sin;
With a scowl or with a grin,
We'll boil it down; boil it down.
The Presbyterian Advance

Boil It Down

If you've got a thought that's happy,
Boil it down;
Make it short and crisp and snappy,
Boil it down;
When your brain its coin has minted
Down the page your pen has sprinted—
Boil it down.

Take out every useless letter,
Boil it down;
Fewer syllables the better;
Boil it down;
Make it plain, express it
So we'll know, not merely guess it;
Then, my friend, ere you address it,
Boil it down.

Boil out all the useless trimmings,
Boil it down;
Skim it well, then skim the skimmings,
Boil it down;
When you're sure 'twould be a sin to
Cut another sentence into,
Send it on and we'll begin to
Boil it down.   JOE LINCOLN

I would I were beside the sea,
Or sailing in a boat,
With all the things I've got to write —
wrote.

I would I were away from town
As far as I could get,
With all the bills, I've got to meet —
met.

I would I were out on a farm,
A-basking in the sun,
With all the things I've got to do —
done.   AUTHOR UNKNOWN

It is hard to meet a deadline for a
man who likes to change things and
says, "That's fine, just what I want,
let's make these few changes, but finish
it today."

Wrong

Nothing is politically right which is morally wrong. DANIEL O'CONNELL

If you think the world is all wrong, remember that it contains people like you. GANDHI

Fear to do ill and you need fear nothing else. BENJAMIN FRANKLIN

To avoid doing wrong is not necessarily doing good.

A man should never be ashamed to own he has been in the wrong, which is but saying that he is wiser today than he was yesterday. ALEXANDER POPE

If you are willing to admit you are all wrong when you are all wrong, you are all right!

To always be "consistent" is to be frequently wrong.

If a thing is not *all* right it is *all* wrong. ELD

You may sometimes be much in the wrong, in owning your being in the right. BENJAMIN FRANKLIN

And now among the fading embers,
These in the main are my regrets;
When I am right, no one remembers;
When I am wrong, no one forgets.

Yesterday

The weak days are yesterday and tomorrow. Watch your step!

Yield

Some people say "Let God go" instead of "Let go and let God."

Youth

Youth to father: "Dad, could you go to a private P.T.A. meeting tonight with me and the principal?"

Teenagers are too old to be children and too young to be adults. They subsist on hot dogs, noise, potato chips, giggles, food, telephone talk, emotional outbursts, and ice cream sodas. Their normal habitats are the schoolroom, the hot rod, the drive-in theater, and the swimming pool. They are not readily domesticated, but can be trained to do astonishing tricks if rewarded frequently with increased praise and/or an increased allowance. Their principal

enemies are parents, but teachers also frequently prey upon them. Some authorities – who do not have to live intimately with them – rank them as our nation's most valuable wild life. *Presbyterian Life*

An adolescent is an it turning into a he or a she.

Growing up is the period spent in learning that bad manners are tolerated only in grownups. *Changing Times*

Adolescence is that period when children feel their parents should be told the facts of life.

Adolescence is that period of life when a boy refuses to believe that someday he will be as dumb as his father.

Seminary student's definition of "epistle": The wife of an apostle.

Until a boy is sixteen he's a boy scout, after that he's a girl scout.

Ninety per cent of most youth problems is adult.   DR. LOUIS H. EVANS

"If" for Youth

If you can live as youth today are living
And keep your feet at such a dizzy
  pace;
If you can greet life's subtleties with
  candor
And turn toward all its care a smiling
  face;
If you can feel the pulse of youthful
  vigor
Beat in your veins and yourself subdue;
If you can see untruth knee-deep about
  you
And still to God and self and home be
  true;
If you can cross the brimming flood of
  folly,
And not dip from the stream to quench
  your thirst;
If you can note life's changing scales
  of values;
And still in your own life keep first
  things first;
If you can feel the urge of disobedi-
  ence,
Yet yield yourself to conscience rigid
  rule;
If you can leave untouched the fruit
  forbidden,
And daily learn in virtue's humble
  sehool;
If you can play the game of life with
  honor,
And losing, be inspired to strive the
  more;
If you can teach men how to live life
  better,
The world will beat a pathway to your
  door.   Alberta Temperance Review

Youth prefers to learn the hard way,
and some people never seem to grow
old.

A youth is a person who is going to
carry on what you have started. He is
going to sit right where you are sitting,
and, when you are gone, attend to
those things which you think are im-

portant. You may adopt all the policies
you please, but how they will be carried out depends on him.

He will assume control of your cities,
states and nations. He is going to move
and take over your churches, schools,
universities and corporations.

All your books are going to be
judged, praised or condemned by him.
The fate of humanity is in his hands.

So it might be well to pay him some
attention!   War Cry

Love them, work them, feed them —
and you'll have them.
    DR. HENRIETTA C. MEARS

At four they know all the questions;
at fourteen they know all the answers.

If the world seems to beat a path to
your door, you probably have a pretty
teen-age daughter.

Youth is that time of life when boys
have the open-mouth disease.
    DR. HENRIETTA C. MEARS

The trouble with the younger generation is that so many of us don't
belong to it any more.   Kansas Teacher

The flower of youth never appears
more beautiful than when it bends
toward the sun of righteousness.
    MATTHEW HENRY

Teen-Age Commandments

  I. Stop and think before you drink.
 II. Don't let your parents down,
     they brought you up.
III. Be humble enough to obey. You
     will be giving orders yourself
     someday.
 IV. At the first moment turn away
     from unclean thinking.
  V. Don't show off when driving. If
     you want to race, go to Indian-
     apolis.
 VI. Choose a date who would make
     a good mate.
VII. Go to church faithfully. The
     Creator gives us a week. Give
     Him back at least an hour.

VIII. Choose your companions carefully. You are what they are.
IX. Avoid following the crowd. Be an engine, not a caboose.
X. Recall the original Ten Commandments. BY A TEENAGER

Denunciation of the young is a necessary part of the hygiene of older people and greatly assists in the circulation of their blood. *Scholastic Teacher*

Z

Zeal
Zeal without tolerance is fanaticism.
JOHN KELMAN

SUBJECT INDEX

SUBJECT INDEX

SUBJECT INDEX

SPEAKERS
SOURCEBOOK
II

PLEASE SHARE ANOTHER SOURCEBOOK . . .

which I have enjoyed preparing for you to use when you need an illustration, aphorism, ancedote, poem, quotation or attention-getter.

This book began several years ago when I came across two notebooks containing materials which I had wanted to use but could not find while preparing the *Speaker's Sourcebook* manuscript. I began adding to these cherished scrapbooks and often had occasion to share their content with others. A high school neighbor boy needed illustrations for an essay, a collegian requested quotations to support a report, a minister wanted some sentence-sermons for the church bulletin, a toastmaster needed stories, a school teacher asked for maxims, a service club friend wanted attention-getters for a meeting, a Sunday school teacher needed a paraphrase, a writer asked for anecdotes about children. . . . And, because others, many others, found the collection helpful, this new Sourcebook was prepared.

Since this book originated from scrapbooks compiled for personal use, it contains materials selected primarily for their practical helpfulness and not necessarily for their literary quality. Many selections are from great books, others from outstanding incidents and persons in history, some from personal experiences and the experiences of friends. Still others are from the delightful world of children. And a number are from sources and authors unknown to me although every possible effort was made to acknowledge the publications and/or author. Regrettably numerous selections bear the credit line, "Author Unknown," "Source Unknown," "Anonymous," etc.

The more than 5000 selections in this book are arranged under more than 600 alphabetized subjects. This broad classification and the carefully detailed index are dependable guides in finding practical helpfulness and personal enjoyment as you share the pages of my second sourcebook.

ELEANOR DOAN

Glendale, California

ACKNOWLEDGMENTS

Grateful acknowledgment is made to the following who have granted permission to include copyrighted selections in this book:

ABINGDON PRESS for the quotation on p. 187 from Costen J. Harrell, *Walking With God*. Copyright renewal 1956. Reprinted by permission.

Herm Albright for the quotation on p. 252 which appeared in *Family Weekly*.

ALLIANCE WITNESS for poems and quotations by A. B. Simpson.

AMERICAN SUNDAY-SCHOOL UNION for two stories on pp. 230 and 335 from *Sunday School World*.

ASSOCIATION PRESS for the poem on p. 241, "Take Time to Live" by Thomas Curtis Clark; for the paragraph headings on p. 152 from Harry Emerson Fosdick, *The Meaning of Faith*, Chapter I.

Frances Benson for the anecdote on p. 123 from *Family Weekly*.

GEOFFREY BLES LTD., London, England, for four quotations from C. S. Lewis, *Mere Christianity*.

William M. Bower for two poems on pp. 44 and 166 by Helen Frazee-Bower, "The Book" and "The Land of the Free" which appeared in *The King's Business*.

THE BRETHREN PRESS for the poem on p. 115, "Seed" by Myra Brooks Welch, from her book *The Touch of the Master's Hand*, copyright © 1957.

CHRISTIAN HERALD for the quotations on pp. 291 and 305 by J. C. Penney, and other anecdotes.

CHRISTIAN LIFE PUBLICATIONS for the selections from *Christian Life* Magazine, copyright by Christian Life Publications, Inc., Gunderson Drive and Schmale Road, Wheaton, Illinois 60187.

CHURCH MANAGEMENT for the poem on p. 95, "Birth of a Committee" by Leslie Conrad, Jr.; the poem on p. 260 "First Missionaries" by Donna Dickey Guyer; the paragraphs on p. 380 by Dr. William H. Leach. Copyright Church Management, Inc., reprinted by permission.

DAVID C. COOK PUBLISHING COMPANY for the item on p. 43 from *The Leader*; the story on p. 267 from *The Christian Mother*.

THE CURTIS PUBLISHING COMPANY for quotations from the *Saturday Evening Post*, one each from Franklin P. Jones (Copyright October 11, 1952 by The Curtis Publishing Company); Raymond Duncan (Copyright February 25, 1956 by The Curtis Publishing Company); G. Norman Collie (Copyright November 22, 1958 by The Curtis Publishing Company); Chon Day (Copyright February 13, 1960 by The Curtis Publishing Company).

DECISION Magazine for quotations by Billy Graham, Roy W. Gustafson, Sherwood E. Wirt, and the Christmas greeting from the *Decision* staff, "A Square, Honest Look" by Sherwood E. Wirt on pp. 84-85.

DEFENDER Magazine for "A Christmas Compliment" on p. 85, and the poem "Preachers Can Talk" on p. 297.

T. S. DENISON & COMPANY, INC. for the poem on p. 319, "School Days" by Nick Kenny, from *Poems to Inspire* by Nick Kenny, published by T. S. Denison & Co., Inc., Minneapolis, Minn.

DOUBLEDAY & COMPANY, INC. for two quotations from Billy Graham, *The Secret of Happiness*.

LIFE Magazine for the quotation on p. 144 by Billy Graham from the article "Billy Graham Makes Plea for an End to Intolerance," October 1, 1956.

LOG OF THE GOOD SHIP GRACE for poems, illustrations, anecdotes, etc. by various authors; for poems, sayings, illustrations by Nat Olson.

LOIZEAUX BROTHERS, INC. for four lines by Frances R. Havergal on p. 244 from the poem "Seldom Can a Heart . . ." from the November 25th meditation in *Opened Treasures* by Frances Ridley Havergal, published by Loizeaux Brothers, and reprinted by permission.

LUTHERAN STANDARD for the poem on p. 189, "Grandma" by Ann Johnson. Copyright Augsburg Publishing House, *The Lutheran Standard*, February 16, 1963.

THE MACMILLAN COMPANY for the selection on pp. 196-197 from J. B. Phillips, *Your God Is Too Small*, first published in the United States by The Macmillan Company, 1953; for four quotations on pp. 39, 97, 102, 104 from C. S. Lewis, *Mere Christianity*, copyright 1952 by The Macmillan Company, New York.

Virgil Markham for poems by Edwin Markham: two stanzas on p. 59 entitled "Why Build?" and four lines on p. 323.

METHODIST PUBLISHING HOUSE for selections from *Together* Magazine, copyright 1959, 1960, 1961 by Lovick Pierce Publisher; copyright 1963 by The Methodist Publishing House, Nashville, Tennessee.

Phyllis C. Michael for the poems "On Graduating," p. 134, and "A Girl Is A Girl," pp. 172-173, copyright 1963 by Phyllis C. Michael in *Poems for Mothers*, Zondervan Publishing House.

Wanda Milner for her poem on p. 75, "Fingers," which appeared in December 1963 *Decision* Magazine.

MOODY MONTHLY for the selection on p. 254 by Anne Nunemaker, reprinted by permission.

MOODY PRESS for seven poems by Martha Snell Nicholson: p. 40, "My Advocate," copyright 1938; p. 262, "The Voice of One Who Wept," copyright 1943; p. 362, "Treasures," copyright 1946; p. 325, "Remembered Sin," copyright 1952 in *Her Best For the Master;* p. 200, "From a Loved One in Heaven," and p. 366, "Trusting," copyright 1945 in *In Heaven's Garden;* p. 131, "Easter," copyright 1950 in *Her Heart Held High*.

NATIONAL CONFERENCE OF CHRISTIANS AND JEWS, INC. for the poem on p. 67 by Jo Tenjford, "Some Children Are."

NATIONAL EDUCATION ASSOCIATION JOURNAL for stories and quotations and the poem on p. 345 by Beth Blue. Copyright *NEA Journal*.

Tom and Marie Olson for poems and illustrations from *Now*.

Theo Oxenham for three poems by John Oxenham: p. 108, "Credo" from *Bees in Amber;* p. 153, "Lord, Give Me Faith," and p. 110, "The Cross of Calvary," copyright by Theo Oxenham.

PENTECOSTAL EVANGEL for the anecdotes on pp. 164, 194.

RAND MCNALLY & COMPANY for the poems of Ella Wheeler Wilcox, copyright by the W. B. Conkey Company.

Lucy Lolli Rankin for the poem "One Weigh" which appeared in *Family Weekly*.

READER'S DIGEST for five anecdotes by the following: Mrs. Roy Carter, p. 130; Mrs. Frank Watson, p. 189; Louise Paw, pp. 249-250; Ethel M. Anderson, p. 281; Lula M. Olds, p. 329.

REFORMED CHURCH IN AMERICA for the item by William R. Buitendorp, "You Are Not Cheap," from the *Church Herald*.

HENRY REGNERY COMPANY for Edgar A. Guest's poems: p. 42, "Believe in Yourself"; p. 101, "The Signal Lights"; p. 231, "It's the Laymen"; p. 326, four lines from "He Did It"; copyright Henry Regnery Company, Reilly & Lee Company, Chicago.

FLEMING H. REVELL CO. for the quotation on p. 151 from Vance Havner, *Peace in the Valley*.

May Richstone for her poem "Might Have Been" on p. 307.

THE RODEHEAVER COMPANY for the two poems on pp. 267 and 334 by Strickland Gillilan from *Gillilan, Finnigan and Company* published by The Rodeheaver Co.: "Stewardship," and four lines from "The Reading Mother."

THE SALVATION ARMY for materials from *The War Cry.*

Margaret E. Sangster for her poem on p. 86, "The Christmas List."

CHARLES SCRIBNER'S SONS for the following by Henry van Dyke: pp. 26-27, "America For Me" from *The Poems of Henry van Dyke,* copyright 1911, Charles Scribner's Sons, renewal copyright 1939, Tertius van Dyke; pp. 79-80, "The Psalm of the Good Teacher" from *Songs Out of Doors,* copyright 1922 by Charles Scribner's Sons, renewal copyright 1950 by Tertius van Dyke; pp. 45-46, an excerpt from *Companionable Books,* copyright 1922 by Charles Scribner's Sons, renewal copyright 1950 by Tertius van Dyke; p. 355, six lines entitled "Time Is" from "Katrina's Sun Dial" from *Music and Other Poems,* 1904; and four lines from "Three Best Things" p. 229, stanza 4 of "The Gospel of Labor" from *The Toiling of Felix.*

SCRIPTURE PRESS PUBLICATIONS for the poem on p. 73, "My Choice" by Bill McChesney, copyright 1965, Scripture Press Publications, Inc., Wheaton, Illinois, reprinted by permission from *Power for Living;* p. 60, the poem "Too Busy?" and other anecdotes and sayings from *The Christian Parent.*

THE SOCIETY FOR PROMOTING CHRISTIAN KNOWLEDGE, London. England, for the poem by Amy Carmichael on p. 371.

STANDARD PUBLISHING for the quotation on p. 340 from James DeForest Murch, *Christian Education and the Local Church,* copyright 1943; revised edition copyright 1958.

THE SUNDAY SCHOOL BOARD OF THE SOUTHERN BAPTIST CONVENTION for the six selections on pp. 66, 144, 168, 189, 295 from *Home Life,* copyright by the Sunday School Board of the Southern Baptist Convention, Nashville, Tenn., and used by permission.

THE SUNDAY SCHOOL TIMES for the poem on pp. 174, 192-193 and 315 by Barbara C. Ryberg, and other stories and paragraphs. Copyright by The Sunday School Times.

THE SUNSHINE PRESS for "Marking Time" by Luther Markin, p. 53; "Business Trends," p. 59; "Life's Melody by Ruth Smeltzer, p. 236; the poem by Paul P. Wentz, p. 248; selection by Doris LaGasse, p. 321; and other materials, reprinted from *Sunshine Magazine.*

THIS DAY for the poem on p. 221, "Instruction" by Beth Applegate. Copyright 1957 by *This Day* Magazine.

THE UNITED PRESBYTERIAN CHURCH IN THE UNITED STATES OF AMERICA for Mary Seth's article on p. 243; the poem "First Bible" on pp. 48-49, from the *United Presbyterian.*

WORLD VISION for excerpts from Paul Rees's editorial, "Heal as You Travel," copyright *World Vision* Magazine.

ZONDERVAN PUBLISHING HOUSE for excerpts from Martin P. Simon, *Points for Parents;* the excerpt on p. 230 from *Religious Digest;* the quotation on p. 233 by C. B. Eavey; the poem on p. 350 by Clifford Lewis from *212 Victory Poems;* quotations by Richard C. Halverson from *Perspective.*

Diligent effort has been made to locate the original source of all copyrighted materials in this book and to secure permission for their inclusion. If such acknowledgments have been inadvertently omitted, the compiler and publisher would appreciate receiving full information so that proper credit may be given in future editions.

A

Abide

Abiding And Confiding

I have learned the wondrous secret
  Of abiding in the Lord;
I have found the strength and sweet-
    ness
  Of confiding in His word.
I have tasted life's pure fountain;
  I am drinking of His blood;
I have lost myself in Jesus,
  I am sinking into God.

I am crucified with Jesus,
  And He lives and dwells with me;
I have ceased from all my struggling;
  'Tis no longer I but He.
All my will is yielded to Him,
  And His Spirit reigns within,
And His precious blood each moment
  Keeps me cleansed and free from sin.

For my words I take His wisdom,
  For my works, His Spirit's power;
For my ways, His ceaseless Presence
  Guards and guides me every hour.
Of my heart, He is the portion,
  Of my joy, the boundless spring;
Saviour, Sanctifier, Healer,
  Glorious Lord and Coming King!

A. B. SIMPSON

———o———

The Blessed Secret
(Philippians 4:11)

I have learned the blessed secret
  Of the soul that's satisfied,
Since the Saviour dwells within me
  And in Him I now *abide*.
I have learned the joy of trusting
  In the sureness of His Word,
Knowing that each promise spoken
  Will be honored by my Lord.

In the silence I have heard Him:
  (O, the music of His voice!)
*"Peace I give thee, be not troubled,
  Let thy heart and soul rejoice."*
Yes, I've found my Lord sufficient,
  For He meets my ev'ry need,
Satisfies my soul's deep longings,
  Guards and guides each thought and
    deed.

Peace that passeth understanding
  Is His gift of grace so free.
And the power of His presence
  Is His promise unto me.
Blessed peace, divine contentment
  From the heart of God above!
All the shadows turn to sunshine,
  Walking with the Lord of love.

AUTHOR UNKNOWN

Ability

Ability means responsibility.

———o———

There is great ability in knowing how to conceal one's ability.

FRANÇOIS, DUC DE LA ROCHEFOUCAULD,
Maxim 245

———o———

Every one excels in something in which another fails.

PUBLILIUS SYRUS, Maxim 17

———o———

They can because they think they can.

VIRGIL, Aeneid

———o———

There is something that is much more scarce, something rarer than ability. It is the ability to recognize ability.

ROBERT HALF

———o———

Ability is a poor man's wealth.

M. WREN

———o———

Most of us live too near the surface of our abilities, dreading to call upon our deeper resources. It is as if a strong man were to do his work with only one finger.

JOHN CHARLES WYNN

———o———

We are sometimes born into wealth, but not ability. Ability must be acquired by an earnest effort; it is not inherited.

PAUL P. PARKER

———o———

As we advance in life, we learn the limits of our abilities.

JAMES ANTHONY FROUDE

Heal As You Travel

Dr. Paul Rees talks about life for the Christian as a "healing journey." "The Samaritan concerned himself with just one thing: saving the life of a mortal brother. Compassion . . . oil and wine . . . his own beast . . . two pence — he gave it all."

The healing journey, Dr. Rees explains, is made according to ability and not according to expediency.

Expediency says: "I must look after my own safety."

Ability says: "At all cost I must rescue this dying man."

Expediency asks: "How little can I get by with?"

Ability asks: "How much can I do?"

Expediency mumbles: "I must save up for a rainy day."

Ability cries: "I must give now, for this may be my last day."

Yes, for the Samaritan life was a healing journey. He took the wounded of the way and made them whole.

The Great Physician is looking for more "Samaritans" who will walk the way of the wounded with Him.

PAUL REES *in* World Vision Magazine

———o———

A man seldom knows what he can do until he tries to undo what he did.

Leader, Bridgeport, Ill.

———o———

Most men underestimate their ability but overestimate their performance.

———o———

You can do anything you ought to do.

Voice for Health

———o———

Ability is of little value without dependability.

———o———

It is not enough to know how to load the Gospel gun; you have to be able to shoot it.

AN UNKNOWN CHRISTIAN

Absence, Absentminded

Distance sometimes endears friendship, and absence sweeteneth it.

JAMES HOWELL, *Familiar Letters*

Our hours in love have wings; in absence crutches.

COLLEY CIBBER, *Xerxes*

———o———

Four-year-old Danny and his family went camping for their vacation. Since they weren't near a church, the family had Sunday school together at their campsite. During prayer time Danny prayed, "Dear God, please help my Sunday school teacher to be able to get along without me this morning!"

MRS. IRIS ELDRIDGE, *Teach*

———o———

A Pastor Explains His Absence

Dear Members:

I feel that a word of explanation is due concerning my absence from the pulpit last Sunday morning. I had not anticipated it causing such an uproar among the members, but I feel that when you hear of the circumstances you'll understand.

I had fully intended to be present as usual, but Saturday afternoon a whole carload of my wife's folks from Arkansas pulled into the driveway. We hadn't seen them in almost a year and since they had their children with them, we packed a hurried picnic supper and headed for the lake. It was after dark when we got back and aside from the fact that I hadn't been able to finish my sermon preparation; my wife's relatives had decided that they would spend the night with us and leave right after lunch Sunday to drive on to the mountains.

I tried to phone the chairman of our deacons, but as most of you know he is out of town a great deal and I was unable to contact him. However, I did leave a message with his wife and she promised to let him know as soon as he got home. Naturally, I felt that this was all that was necessary and that everything would work out fine.

I stayed home Sunday morning visiting with the folks, and it wasn't until Sunday afternoon, when the committee from the deacons came to visit me, that I found out that you hadn't been able to line up a supply preacher. I had just taken for granted that the chairman's wife would tell her husband when he came in Saturday night and that he would work something out. And besides this, how was I to know that this was the Sunday our organist had planned to be out of town, and that our choir director would be called away to announce a Sunday baseball game.

I regret that you had to dismiss the services. It just never occurred to me that the more than 500 people present had come expecting to hear me preach. And, I was deeply sorry to hear from the deacons' committee that there were four people present who had come to make a profession of faith but had to leave disappointed. I'll try not to let this happen again, but I can't promise anything, at least until vacation is over.

So, as my favorite barber tells me when I get my hair cut, "I'll see you next Sunday, unless company drops in."

Almost sincerely,
Your Pastor

P.S. — Absurd? Unthinkable? Yes, but the same Person who expects the pastor to be present is depending just as much on every Sunday school teacher and officer to be present too — Jesus Christ. He's the one whom we fail.

Original Source Unknown, printed in *Biblical Recorder*

———o———

If absence really made the heart grow fonder, a lot of people would miss church more than any place in the world.

———o———

I am not absentminded. It is the presence of mind that makes me unaware of everything else.

GILBERT KEITH CHESTERTON

Accidents, Accidental

Some people get to the top just by being stuck in the back of the elevator.

———o———

Accidents will occur in the best regulated families.

CHARLES DICKENS, *David Copperfield*

At first laying down, as a fact fundamental,
That nothing with God can be accidental.

HENRY W. LONGFELLOW

———o———

A man became sleepy. He rammed his motorcycle into a parked trailer truck, and he was killed. Two trailer trucks stopped at the scene. Two motorcycles smashed into the rear truck, killing both the motorcyclists. Another truck, unable to stop in time, hit the wreckage and hurled two bodies over an embankment. A fourth motorcyle plunged into that truck. Rider and another critically injured. Six automobiles piled up in opposite lane. Traffic stalled for hours. All because of one man!

Newspaper item

Accomplish, Achieve

I found Rome brick, I left it marble.

AUGUSTUS CAESAR

———o———

Almost never killed a fly.
German Saying

———o———

Take the obvious, add a cupful of brains, a generous pinch of imagination, a bucketful of courage and daring, stir well and bring it to a boil.

BERNARD BARUCH

———o———

If you would go to the top, first go to the bottom.

THOMAS A. EDISON

———o———

It is impossible for a man who attempts many things to do them all well.
Xenophon

———o———

Others have done so much with so little, while we have done so little with so much.

BOB PIERCE

———o———

All men are born equal, but what they are equal to later on is what counts.

I "can't" is a quitter;
I "don't know" is too lazy;
I "wish I could" is a wisher;
I "might" is waking up;
I "will try" is on his feet;
I "can" is on his way;
I "will" is at work;
I "did" is now boss.

AUTHOR UNKNOWN

———o———

The shortest way to do anything is to do only one thing at a time.

MARTIN LUTHER

———o———

Nothing is impossible to the man who doesn't have to do it himself.

———o———

It isn't what you wish to do, it's what you will do for God that transforms your life.

HENRIETTA C. MEARS

———o———

I long to accomplish a great and noble task, but it is my chief duty to accomplish tasks as though they were great and noble. The world is moved along, not only by the mighty shoves of its heroes, but also by the aggregate of the tiny pushes of each honest worker.

HELEN KELLER

———o———

The fellow who's on his toes doesn't usually have any trouble keeping other people from stepping on them.

———o———

People forget how fast you did a job . . . but they remember how well you did it.

HOWARD W. NEWTON

———o———

Not by self-seeking, but by self-sacrifice, not by dodging difficulties, but by overcoming them; not by giving supreme attention to outer things, but to inner worth — do men achieve.

CLIFF COLE

———o———

We have achieved plenty but lost quality.

The life of achievement is a life of hard work.

Councillor

———o———

It isn't how much you know, but what you get done that the world rewards and remembers.

DONALD LAIRD

Account, Accountable

God's Plan

If we don't like the sermon we can
    turn the dial
And tune in another station;
If we don't like the church we can
    stay away
For this is a broad creation.

But stop and think as you go your way:
    We'll each have to answer to God
    some day;
There'll be no dial that we can turn,
    There'll be no way of escape;
We'll face our God, and to Him
    A full confession make.

AUTHOR UNKNOWN

———o———

God Keeps Account

Of every self-denial true,
Of every thing we say or do,
Of every good intention, too,
    God keeps account.

Of each cup of cold water given,
Of each encouragement toward heaven,
To one, despairing, tempest driven,
    God keeps account.

Of every prayer to heaven we send,
Of every helping hand we lend,
Of every brother's wrong we mend,
    God keeps account.

May every word and deed and thought
Be prompted by the love of God,
And prove that I have only sought
    A good account.

O. F. HINZ

———o———

Bankrupt

One midnight, deep in starlight still,
I dreamed that I received this bill:
"(. . . . . in account with Life):

Five thousand breathless dawns all
new;
Five thousand flowers fresh in dew;
Five thousand sunsets wrapped in gold;
One million snow-flakes served ice-
cold;
Five quiet friends; one baby's love;
One white-mad sea with clouds above;
One hundred music-haunted dreams
Of moon-drenched roads and hurrying
streams;
Of prophesying winds, and trees;
Of silent stars and browsing bees;
One still night in a fragrant wood;
One heart that loved and understood."
I wondered when I waked at day,
How — how in God's name — I could
pay!

CORTLAND W. SAYRES,
Golden Book of Faith

Accuse

The breath of accusation kills an innocent name,
And leaves for lame acquittal the poor
life,
Which is a mask without it.

PERCY BYSSHE SHELLEY, *The Cenci*

———o———

When you point your finger accus-
ingly at someone else, you've three
fingers pointing at yourself.

Acts, Actions, Active
(See also Do, Doing)

Everywhere in life, the true question
is not what we gain, but what we do.

THOMAS CARLYLE

———o———

It is not necessary for all men to be
great in action. The greatest and sub-
limest power is often simple patience.

HORACE BUSHNELL

———o———

I have never heard anything about
the resolutions of the apostles, but a
great deal about their acts.

HORACE MANN

———o———

Actions, not words, are the true characteristic mark of the attachment of
friends.

GEORGE WASHINGTON

Distinction between virtuous and
vicious actions has been engraven by
the Lord in the heart of every man.

JOHN CALVIN

———o———

Do unto others as though you were
the others.

———o———

The need of the hour is not so much
to discuss the genuineness of the Bread,
as to break it and pass it out to the
hungry multitude.

———o———

Have you ever noticed that there
are two kinds of people who always
seem to be in bad luck; those who did
it but never thought, and those who
thought but never did it?

———o———

It is better to wear out than to rust
out.

BISHOP RICHARD CUMBERLAND

———o———

If I rest, I rust.

MARTIN LUTHER

———o———

The great end of life is not knowledge but action.

THOMAS H. HUXLEY,
Technical Education

———o———

Every man feels instinctively that all
the beautiful sentiments in the world
weigh less than a single lovely action.

JAMES RUSSELL LOWELL

———o———

It is not always your actions that
count, but your reactions.

———o———

It is possible to be so active in the
service of Christ as to forget to love
him.

PETER TAYLER FORSYTH

———o———

To be active for God is one thing
. . . but to be *effective* in that work is
quite another thing.

———o———

The story is told of a supersalesman
who sold an incredibly efficient filing

system to a certain business concern. A few months later he dropped by the office of the company to check up on its operation.

"How is the system working?" he inquired eagerly.

"Beyond our wildest dreams," the manager replied.

"And how's business?" the salesman asked.

The manager smiled, "We had to give up our business in order to run the filing system!"

———o———

You can't plow a field by turning it over in your mind.

———o———

When You Do An Act

You can never tell when you do an act
Just what the result will be;
But with every deed you are sowing a
    seed,
Though its harvest you may not see.

Each kindly act is an acorn dropped
In God's productive soil;
Though you may not know, yet the
    tree shall grow
And shelter the brows that toil.
AUTHOR UNKNOWN

Adapt

One learns to itch where one can scratch.
ERNEST BRAMAH

———o———

You might as well fall flat on your face as to lean over too far backward.

———o———

He who does not stretch himself according to the coverlet, finds his feet uncovered.
JOHANN WOLFGANG VON GOETHE

———o———

The wise man does no wrong in changing his habits with the times.
DIONYSIUS CATO

———o———

You must cut your coat according to your cloth.
Old Proverb

Admire

In reality, we do not admire a man so much for his success as we do for the qualities he has that makes success possible.

———o———

We always love those who admire us, and we do not always love those whom we admire.
FRANÇOIS, DUC DE LA ROCHEFOUCAULD,
Maxim 294

———o———

The greatest admiration gives rise, not to words, but to silence.
MUSONIUS

———o———

Admiration is our polite recognition of another man's resemblance to ourselves.
AMBROSE BIERCE

Adolescence
(See also Age)

Adolescence is a time of rapid changes. Between the ages of 12 and 17, for example, a parent ages as much as 20 years.
Changing Times, The Kiplinger Magazine

———o———

Adolescence is that period when a boy refuses to believe that some day he will be as ignorant as his parents.

———o———

Adolescent: One who is well informed about anything he doesn't have to study.

———o———

The world is full of people suffering from delayed or ingrown adolescence.
STORM JAMESON

Adopted

Ode To An Adopted Child

Not flesh of my flesh,
Nor bone of my bone;
But still, miraculously, my own!

Never forget, for a single minute:
You didn't grow under my heart
But in it!
FLEUR CONKLING HEYLINGER

Advantage

Shed no tears over your lack of early advantages. No really great man ever had any advantages that he himself did not create.

ELBERT HUBBARD

———o———

Next to knowing when to seize an opportunity, the most important thing in life is to know when to forego an advantage.

BENJAMIN DISRAELI

Adversary, Adversities

When the adversary strikes, watch God's answer. It may seem long in coming, but let us always remember that God will have the last word.

———o———

Adversities act as if they were the victors, but inwardly they are the vanquished.

RUSSELL H. VOIGHT

———o———

Adversity brings out talents which in prosperous circumstances would have lain dormant.

———o———

Be modest in good fortune, prudent in misfortune.

PERIANDER

———o———

Prosperity is a great teacher; adversity is a greater.

WILLIAM HAZLITT

———o———

Gold is tried by fire, brave men by affliction.

SENECA

———o———

Prosperity proves the fortunate, adversity the great.

PLINY THE YOUNGER

———o———

He who has not tasted bitter does not know what sweet is.

From the German

———o———

Storms make oaks take deeper root.

Kites rise highest against the wind — not with it.

SIR WINSTON CHURCHILL

———o———

It is in the furnace of affliction that our Savior watches for Christlikeness to be brought out in us. He is pictured as a purifier and refiner of silver, and we are told that he counts the process complete only when he can see his likeness in the molten metal.

NORMAN B. HARRISON

———o———

My business as a preacher is to afflict the comfortable and comfort the afflicted.

RALPH W. SOCKMAN

Advertising

The Sunday school teacher had carefully prepared his lesson. He was lecturing the youngsters on keeping their minds as clean as their bodies. Then, to emphasize his point, he held up a bar of soap.

"Oh, oh," murmured one lad. "Here comes the commercial."

Presbyterian Life

———o———

Advertising is the mouthpiece of business.

JAMES R. ADAMS

———o———

When business is good, it pays to advertise;
When business is bad you've got to advertise.

———o———

The first time six-year-old Lisa attended Sunday School she brought home a Sunday School paper.

"What is that?" her mother asked, reaching for the paper.

"Oh," said Lisa, "It's a give-away sheet full of ads about heaven!"

Advice

A woman's advice is not worth much, but he who doesn't heed it is a fool.

PEDRO CALDERON DE LA BARCA

———o———

A famous pediatrician was asked by

a mother what the best time was to put her children to bed.

"While you still have the strength," was the answer.

———o———

We wonder why it is that well-meant advice and constructive criticism, like a hat someone else has put on your head, never feels just right.

———o———

There is no situation in human life or experience for which advice from God cannot be found in the Bible — whether it be personal, social, national or international.

G. CAMPBELL MORGAN

———o———

We give advice by the bucket, but take it by the grain.

WILLIAM R. ALGER

———o———

Be quiet enough to hear it,
 The plan of God.
Be brave enough to speak it,
 The message of God.
Be honest enough to live it,
 The life of God.

———o———

One little hint may be worth a ton of advice.

———o———

Many receive advice, few profit by it.

PUBLILIUS SYRUS, *Maxim 149*

———o———

To stimulate her young pupils, a first-grade teacher arranged to take her class on an "educational tour" of a farmyard. But one small boy saw right through her scheme. "Don't look, don't look!" he warned his buddy. "If we look we'll have to tell about it tomorrow."

AL RHOADES, Newburgh, N.Y.,
Newburgh-Beacon News

———o———

Advice is like castor oil, easy enough to give but dreadful uneasy to take.

"JOSH BILLINGS"
(HENRY WHEELER SHAW)

———o———

When Billy Sunday was converted and joined the church, a Christian man put his arm on the young man's shoulder and said, "William, there are three simple rules I can give to you, and if you will hold to them you will never write 'backslider' after your name.

"Take fifteen minutes each day to listen to God talking to you; take fifteen minutes each day to talk to God; take fifteen minutes each day to talk to others about God."

The young convert was deeply impressed and determined to make these rules of his life. From that day onward throughout his life he made it a rule to spend the first moments of his day alone with God and God's Word. Before he read a letter, looked at a paper or even read a telegram, he went first to the Bible, that the first impression of the day might be what he got directly from God.

———o———

Advice is what you take for a cold.

THOMAS J. O'BRIEN

———o———

To a young man learning to perform on the flying trapeze a veteran circus performer once said, "Throw your heart over the bars and your body will follow."

———o———

To find fault is easy; to do better may be difficult.

———o———

Doctor: "The thing for you to do is to stop thinking about yourself; try burying yourself in your work."
Patient: "Mercy, and me a concrete mixer!"

———o———

Walk softly, speak tenderly, pray fervently, do not run up stairs, do not run down God's people.

T. J. BACH

Advocate

My Advocate

I sinned. And straightway, posthaste, Satan flew
Before the presence of the most High God,

And made a railing accusation there.
He said, "This soul, this thing of clay
    and sod,
Has sinned. 'Tis true that he has named
    Thy Name,
But I demand his death, for Thou hast
    said,
'The soul that sinneth, it shall die.'
    Shall not
Thy sentence be fulfilled? Is justice
    dead?
Send now this wretched sinner to his
    doom.
What other thing can righteous ruler
    do?"
And thus he did accuse me day and
    night,
And every word he spoke, oh God, was
    true!

Then quickly One rose up from God's
    right hand
Before whose glory angels veiled their
    eyes,
He spoke, "Each jot and tittle of the law
Must be fulfilled; the guilty sinner dies!
But wait — suppose his guilt were all
    transferred to Me, and that I paid his
    penalty!
Behold My hands, My side, My feet!
    One day
I was made sin for him, and died that
    he
Might be presented faultless, at thy
    throne!"
And Satan fled away. Full well he knew
That he could not prevail against such
    love,
For every word my dear Lord spoke
    was true!

                MARTHA SNELL NICHOLSON

Age

If you want to be a dear old lady at
seventy you have to begin early, say
about seventeen.

                MAUDE ROYDEN

———o———

To avoid old age keep taking on new
thoughts and throwing off old habits.

———o———

Middle age is the time of life when
your idea of getting ahead is to stay
even.

The most dangerous age for women is
poundage.

———o———

When a man has a birthday he takes
the day off, but when a woman has a
birthday, she takes a year off.

———o———

Going On

Growing old, but not retiring
    For the battle still is on;
Going on without relenting,
    Till the final victory's won.
Ever on, nor think of resting,
    For the battle rages still,
And my Saviour still is with me
    And I seek to do His will.

Years roll by, the body weakens;
    But the spirit still is young;
Breath of God — it never ages,
    Is eternal, ever strong.
Rather, year by year it strengthens,
    Gaining o'er the things of sense.
By Thy Spirit, lead my spirit,
    Saviour, till Thou call me hence.
Things of earth decrease in value,
    Brighter shines the light above;
Less the power of human hatred,
    Sweeter far the Saviour's love.
Let me tell it to the needy,
    Far and wide Thy worth proclaim;
That my closing years may praise Thee
    Glorify Thy blessed name.

Let me labor in Thy harvest
    More than ever in the past,
Reaping in what Thou hast planted,
    Till I dwell with Thee at last;
That before Thy throne eternal
    I may have some fruit to bring,
Not my work — the fruit of Calvary,
    All are Thine, my Lord and King.

                AUTHOR UNKNOWN

———o———

To keep young, associate much with
young people. To get old in a hurry,
try keeping up with them.

———o———

You are as young as your faith,
As old as your doubt,
As young as your self-confidence,
As old as your fear,

As young as your hope,
As old as your despair.
                                                    CINDY

———o———

The Ages Of Man

Baby	Working
Bottle	Saving
Rocking crib	Bride and groom
Walking	Children
Talking	Cottage
Tidy bib	Money boom
Pencil	Christmas
Paper	Easter
Grammar school	Mountain lakes
Reading	Meetings
Writing	Hobbies
Golden Rule	Leaves and rakes
Growing	Prestige
Learning	Wall Street
In a daze	Pain in head
Rockin'	Doctors
Rollin'	Ulcers
Hi Fi craze	Rest in bed
College	False teeth
Buddies	Fatty
Actions rude	Lots of dough
Liquor	Fifty
Army	Sixty
Language crude	Had to go

GEORGE LOUKIDES in *Suburbia Today*

———o———

Some folks go to seed long before
spring planting time.

———o———

No man is really old until his mother
stops worrying about him.
                                        WILLIAM RYAN

———o———

Why is it that a person your own age
always looks older than you do?

———o———

When a woman filling out an application blank came to the square marked
"Age," she didn't hesitate. She simply
wrote: "Atomic."

Adolescence is when you think you'll
live forever. Middle age is when you
wonder how you've lasted so long.

———o———

To be seventy years young is sometimes far more cheerful and hopeful
than to be forty years old.
                            OLIVER WENDELL HOLMES

———o———

Middle age is when you start for
home about the same time you used to
start for somewhere else.
                            Review, Conrad, Iowa

———o———

For Friends Of The Aged

BLESSED are they who understand
My faltering step and palsied hand.
BLESSED are they who know that my
    ears today
Must strain to catch the things they
    say.
BLESSED are they who seem to know
That my eyes are dim and my wits
    are slow.
BLESSED are they who looked away
When coffee was spilled at table to-
    day.
BLESSED are they who never say:
    "You've told that story twice today."
BLESSED are they who know the ways
To bring back memories of yester-
    days.
BLESSED are they who make it known
That I'm loved, respected and not
    alone.
BLESSED are they who know I'm at a
    loss
To find the strength to carry the
    Cross.
BLESSED are they who ease the days
Of my journey home in loving ways.
                        ESTHER M. WALKER,
                        The Glass "Chatterbox"

———o———

Middle age is the time when you can
do everything you could in your youth,
but not until tomorrow.
                                    CHICK WELCH

———o———

Look them over and you will find that
people don't stop playing because they

get old, but they get old because they stop playing.

———o———

You're an old-timer if you can remember when a housewife's meals were carefully thought out instead of thawed out.

ANNA HERBERT

———o———

Age makes you take twice as long to rest and half as long to get tired.

———o———

Old age and the wear of time teach many things.

———o———

A Prayer For Older Folk

Lord, Thou knowest that I am growing older.
Keep me from becoming talkative and possessed with the idea that I must express myself on every subject.
Release me from the craving to straighten out everyone's affairs.
Keep my mind free from the recital of endless details. Give me wings to get to the point.
Seal my lips when I am inclined to tell of my aches and pains. They are increasing with the years and my love to speak of them grows sweeter as time goes by.
Teach me the glorious lesson that occasionally I may be wrong.
Make me thoughtful but not nosey; helpful but not bossy.
With my vast store of wisdom and experience it does seem a pity not to use it all, but Thou, knowest, Lord, that I want a few friends left at the end. Amen!

AUTHOR UNKNOWN

———o———

Life Begins At Forty?

I completed my preparations,
   But, alas, I found with chagrin,
I had worked so hard getting ready
   That I was too tired to begin.

———o———

At age twenty we don't care what the world thinks of us; at age fifty we find out it wasn't thinking of us at all.

When a man ceases to grow, no matter what the years, then and there he begins to be old.

———o———

Talking about growing old, a man isn't old until everything seems wrong. It may happen at seventy or twenty.

CLIFF COLE

———o———

Isn't it silly to fuss about getting old? When we stop growing older, we're dead.

———o———

About the only thing that comes to us without effort is old age.

———o———

Several elderly church members were being asked to what they attributed their longevity. "And why do you think God has permitted you to reach the age of 92?" one wealthy old lady was asked.
   Without hesitation she responded: "To test the patience of my relatives."

MARY LYNN SHELTON, *Reader's Digest*

———o———

We do not count a man's years, until he has nothing else to count.

RALPH WALDO EMERSON

———o———

Adult to small boy: "How old is your father?"
   Small boy: "He's in the middle ages."

———o———

Middle age is the time when a man is always thinking that in a week or two he will feel as good as ever.

DONALD ROBERT PERRY MARQUIS

———o———

Age, A Quality Of Mind

Age is a quality of mind;
If you have left your dreams behind,
If hope is cold,
If you no longer look ahead,
If your ambition's fires are dead,
Then you are old.

But if from life you take the best,
And if in life you keep the zest,
If love you hold,
No matter how the years go by,
No matter how the birthdays fly,
You are not old.

AUTHOR UNKNOWN

Agree

The quickest way to take the starch out of a man who is always blaming himself is to agree with him.

"JOSH BILLINGS" (HENRY WHEELER SHAW)

———o———

Be pretty if you can;
Be witty if you must;
But be agreeable if it kills you.

———o———

The Home With The Two Bears

It was observed by friends that old Brother and Sister Brown were getting on more agreeably together than they had formerly done. Asked for an explanation, Brother Brown replied: "Well, about a year ago we decided to keep two bears in the house all the time. One of these bears is 'bear ye one another's burdens,' and the other is 'Forbear one another in love.' And since we took these two bears in we have found the going easier."

———o———

When you say that you agree to a thing in principle you mean that you have not the slightest intention of carrying it out.

OTTO VON BISMARCK

———o———

When everyone agrees, there is very little thinking.

———o———

Fools bite one another, but wise men agree.

———o———

When two men in business always agree, one of them is unnecessary.

WILLIAM WRIGLEY, JR.

———o———

You can't expect people to see eye to eye with you if you look down on them.

Aim

Slight not what's near through aiming at what's far.

EURIPIDES, Rhesus

Next in importance to having good aim is to recognize when to pull the trigger.

ELMER G. LETERMAN

———o———

Everything worth-while has a high wall around it; but by looking to God He will give you the key to open the gate and go through.

———o———

An aim in life is the only fortune worth finding.

ROBERT LOUIS STEVENSON

———o———

The Christian's aim should be less at goods and more at goodness.

———o———

When man understands that the aim of life is not material profit but life itself, he ceases to fix his attention exclusively on the external world. He considers more attentively his own existence and the existence of those around him. He realizes that he depends on others and that others depend on him.

ALEXIS CARREL

Alcohol

The liquor dealers advertise
In many magazines,
We see their "ads" on street cars, too,
And on the movie screens.
Pictures of happy, laughing girls
And wholesome, healthy lads;
But where's their finished product?
It's never in their ads.

———o———

Balanced judgment will certify that intoxicating liquor leaves an unbalanced budget, unbalanced men and women, an unbalanced home and an unbalanced social order.

CLIFF COLE

———o———

Our Silly Ways

We license a saloon to teach vice and then tax people for schools to teach virtue!
We license a man to make drunken pau-

pers and then tax sober men to take care of them!

We license a man to sell that which will make a man drunk, and then punish the man for being drunk!

SOURCE UNKNOWN

———o———

A physician once said of alcoholic beverages:

It gives you a red nose,
a black eye,
a white liver,
a dark brown breath,
a blue outlook.

But who wants that color scheme in life?

———o———

Abstinence is as easy to me as temperance would be difficult.

SAMUEL JOHNSON

———o———

Some of the domestic evils of drunkenness are houses without windows, gardens without fences, fields without tillage, barns without roofs, children without clothing, principles, morals or manners.

BENJAMIN FRANKLIN

———o———

The steady drinker soon becomes the unsteady drinker.

———o———

Liquor talks mighty loud when it gets loose from the bottle.

———o———

The man who drinks a little, drinks too much.

Alone

Never Alone

"I will never leave thee, nor forsake thee" (Hebrews 13:5).

I'm never alone in the morning
  As I rise at the break of day,
For Jesus who watched through the darkness
  Says, "Lo, I am with you alway."

I'm never alone at my table,
  Though loved ones no longer I see;
For dearer than all who have vanished,
  Is Jesus who breaks bread with me.

I'm never alone through the daylight,
  Though nothing but trials I see;
Though the furnace be seven times heated,
  The "form of the fourth" walks with me.

I'm never alone at the twilight
  When darkness around me doth creep;
And spectres press hard round my pillow,
  He watches and cares while I sleep.

I'm walking and talking with Jesus,
  Each day as I journey along;
I'm never alone, Hallelujah!
  The joy of the Lord is my song.

AUTHOR UNKNOWN

———o———

I was never less alone than when by myself.

EDWARD GIBBON

———o———

Who lives unto himself, he lives to none.

FRANCIS QUARLES

———o———

There's a path that leads through a woodland — a path that I love to trod,
To get away from this wild world's rush and be alone with God.

From a Very Old Scrapbook

Alphabet

Bible Alphabet

A—Ask and it shall be given you.
B—Be still, and know that I am God.
C—Commit thy works unto the Lord.
D—Do good, O Lord, unto those that do good.
E—Enter into his gates with thanksgiving.
F—For by grace are ye saved through faith.
G—Give, and it shall be given unto you.

H—Honor and majesty are before him.
I — In his hands are the deep places of the earth.
J—Judge not, that ye be not judged.
K—Keep thy heart with all diligence.
L—Let all the people praise thee, O God.
M—My help cometh from the Lord.
N—Nevertheless, I tell ye the truth.
O—O worship the Lord in the beauty of holiness.
P—Praise ye the Lord.
Q—Quench not the Spirit.
R—Rest in the Lord, and wait patiently for him.
S—Sing unto the Lord a new song.
T—Take my yoke upon you.
U—Unto thee lift I up mine eyes.
V—Vanity, vanity, all is vanity.
W—Where there is no vision, the people perish.
X—(X-ray).
Y—Ye are my witnesses, saith the Lord.
Z—Zion heard and was glad.

VERNA B. WADDELL

Ambition

Your ambition, not your worded prayer, is your real creed.

ELLA WHEELER WILCOX

———o———

Ambition can move mountains — providing the tools are there to do the job.

———o———

Some people are like blisters, they do not show up until the work is done.

———o———

Many a man with an ambition to find fame and fortune failed because he didn't find himself first.

———o———

A little boy came home from Sunday School and said to his grandmother "We have been singing 'Jesus wants me for a sunbeam.'"
"How lovely," replied Grandmother.
Looking rather put out, the little chap said: "But Granny, I want to be an engine driver."

Life Story

The evolution of a man's ambitions:
To be a circus clown.
To be like dad.
To be a fireman.
To do something noble.
To get wealthy.
To make ends meet.
To get the old-age pension.

Sunshine Magazine

———o———

The tallest trees are most in the power of the winds, and ambitious men of the blasts of fortune.

WILLIAM PENN

———o———

A man will remain a rag-picker as long as he has only the vision of a rag-picker.

O. S. MARDEN

———o———

Every man is capable of being something better than he is.

ROY L. SMITH

———o———

The desire of power in excess caused the angels to fall; the desire of knowledge in excess caused man to fall; but in charity there is no excess, neither can angel or man come in danger by it.

FRANCIS BACON, *Essay: Of Goodness*

———o———

Well it is known that ambition can creep as well as soar.

EDMUND BURKE

———o———

Let proud Ambition pause
And sicken at the vanity that prompts
His little deeds.

DAVID MALLETT, *The Excursion, Cante ii*

———o———

There is a loftier ambition than merely to stand high in the world. It is to stoop down and lift mankind a little higher.

HENRY VAN DYKE

America

"America For Me"

'Tis fine to see the Old World, and travel up and down

Among the famous places and cities of
renown,
To admire the crumbly castles and
statues of the Kings, —
But now I think I've had enough of
antiquated things.

So it's home again, and home again,
America for me!
My heart is turning home again, and
there I long to be,
In the land of youth and freedom be-
yond the ocean bars,
Where the air is full of sunlight and the
flag is full of stars.

Oh, London is a man's town, there's
power in the air;
And Paris is a woman's town, with
flowers in her hair;
And it's sweet to dream in Venice, and
it's great to study Rome;
But when it comes to living there is no
place like home.

I like the German fir-woods, in green
battalions drilled;
I like the gardens of Versailles with
flashing fountains filled;
But, oh, to take your hand, my dear,
and ramble for a day
In the friendly western woodland where
Nature has her way!

I know that Europe's wonderful, yet
something seems to lack:
The Past is too much with her, and
people looking back.
But the glory of the Present is to make
the Future free, —
We love our land for what she is and
what she is to be.

Oh, it's home again, and home again,
America for me!
I want a ship that's westward bound
to plough the rolling sea,
To the blessed Land of Room Enough
beyond the ocean bars,
Where the air is full of sunlight and the
flag is full of stars.

HENRY VAN DYKE

———o———

It's a great country, but you can't live
in it for nothing.

WILL ROGERS

The World In Miniature

Imagine that we could compress the
world's population of more than three
and a quarter billion into one town of
1,000 persons in the exact proportions in
which the world population is actually
divided. In such a town of 1,000 there
would be only 60 Americans! And these
60 Americans would receive half the income of the entire town. Only about
330 of the remaining 940 townsfolk
would be classed as Christians. At least
80 townspeople would be practicing
Communists and 370 others under Communist domination.

The 60 Americans would have an
average life expectancy of 70 years;
the other 940 less than 40 years. The
60 Americans would have 15 times as
many possessions per person as all of
their neighbors. The Americans would
produce 16 percent of the town's food
supply and, although they'd eat 72 percent above the maximum food requirements, they would either eat most of
what they grew, or store it for their
own further use, at enormous cost.
(With most of the 940 non-Americans
hungry, the food supply disparity might
understandably lead to some ill-feel-
ing.)

There would be 53 telephones in this
one-town world . . . Americans would
have 28 of them. The Americans would
enjoy a disproportionate share of electric power, coal, fuel, steel, and general
equipment.

The lowest income group among the
Americans would be better off by far
than the average of the other towns-
men. The 60 Americans and about 200
others representing Western Europe
and a few classes in South America,
South Africa, Australia, and Japan
would be relatively well off, by comparison.

Half of the inhabitants of our one-
town world would be ignorant of Jesus
Christ, but more than half would have
heard, and would continue to hear of
Karl Marx, Lenin, Stalin, and Khrush-
chev.

Out of his average income of $3,000
per year, the gift of each American per-

son for all purposes other than private and personal gifts would average less than $60 per year. This might raise a question as to how seriously he regards the Christian faith or the meaning of Christmas with its emphasis on peace and good will among men.

HENRY SMITH LEIPER

———o———

Of This I Am Proud

That I am an American
  And have the right to vote as
  And for whom I please

That I have the right to choose
  My friends
  And live where I please

That I have the right to worship
  At the church and religion of my
    choice
  When and where I please

That I have the right
  And may always live worthy of
  And do honor to this country
  Of which I am proud

STERLING SNYDER

———o———

Let independence be our boast,
Ever mindful what it cost;
Ever grateful for the prize,
Let its altar reach the skies!

JOSEPH HOPKINSON, Hail, Columbia

———o———

I shall know but one country. The ends I aim at shall be my country's, my God's and Truth's. I was born an American; I will live an American; I shall die an American.

DANIEL WEBSTER

———o———

Give me your tired, your poor,
Your huddled masses yearning to
  breathe free,
The wretched refuse of your teeming
  shore,
Send these, the homeless, tempest-
  tossed to me:
I lift my lamp beside the golden door.

EMMA LAZARUS —
Inscription on the Statue of Liberty

Ancestors

Little Tommy: "What kind of things are ancestors?"

Papa: "Well, I'm one and so is Grandpa."

Little Tommy: "Then why is it people go around bragging about them?"

———o———

It is indeed a desirable thing to be well descended, but the glory belongs to our ancestors.

PLUTARCH

———o———

They that on glorious ancestors enlarge,
Produce their debt, instead of their discharge.

EDWARD YOUNG, Love of Fame

———o———

He who serves well his country has no need of ancestors.

VOLTAIRE

———o———

People will not look forward to posterity who never looked backward to their ancestors.

EDMUND BURKE

———o———

If there be no nobility of descent, all the more indispensable is it that there should be nobility of ascent — a character in them that bear rule so fine and high and pure that as men come within the circle of its influence they involuntarily pay homage to that which is the one pre-eminent distinction, the royalty of virtue.

HENRY CODMAN POTTER

———o———

The kind of ancestors we have had is not as important as the kind of descendants our ancestors have.

———o———

A man who has ancestors is like a representative of the past.

EDWARD GEORGE BULWER-LYTTON

———o———

Many a family tree needs trimming.

FRANK MCKINNEY HUBBARD

Angels

Five-year-old Betty had been told that the noise of a thunderstorm was only the angels making their beds. One morning, after a storm in which there had been considerable thunder and lightning, the little girl said:

"You know, Mommy, I didn't mind the noise when the angels made their beds last night, but I certainly didn't like it when they couldn't make up their minds whether to turn the lights off or not."

———o———

It's easy to be an angel when nobody ruffles your feathers.

Anger, Angry

It is he who is in the wrong who first gets angry.
                                        WILLIAM PENN

———o———

Anger improves nothing except the arch of a cat's back.
                                        COLEMAN COX

———o———

Consider how few things are worthy of anger, and thou wilt wonder that any fool should be wroth.
                                        ROBERT DODSLEY

———o———

Getting mad will never get you anything else!

———o———

When tempted to anger, read —

   The Humility Verse — Job 18:4
   The Punishment Verse — Matthew 5:22
   Cruel Wrath — Proverbs 27:4
   A Soft Answer — Proverbs 15:1

———o———

He who can suppress a moment's anger may prevent a day of sorrow.
                                        TRYON EDWARDS

———o———

When angry, count ten before you speak; if very angry, count a hundred.
                                        THOMAS JEFFERSON

———o———

Form the habit of closing your mouth firmly when angry.

———o———

If you are patient in one moment of anger, you will escape a hundred days of sorrow.
                                        Chinese Proverb

———o———

Be strong enough to control your anger instead of letting it control you.

———o———

Be not angry that you cannot make others as you wish them to be, since you cannot make yourself as you wish to be.
                                        THOMAS À KEMPIS

———o———

Whatever is begun in anger ends in shame.

———o———

He that strives not to stem his anger's tide,
Does a wild horse without a bridle ride.
                                        COLLEY CIBBER, *Love's Last Shift*

Animals

I have found . . . that those who love
   a deer, a dog, a bird and flowers . . .
are usually thoughtful of the larger
   needs that may be ours . . .
. . . Who for God's creatures small will
   plan . . . will seldom wrong his fellow man.
                                        AUTHOR UNKNOWN

———o———

You can't buy loyalty, they say.
I bought it though, the other day.
You can't buy friendship tried and true.
Well, just the same, I bought that, too.

I made my bid, and on the spot
Bought love and faith and a whole job lot
Of happiness; so all in all
The total price was pretty small.

I bought a simple, trusting heart
That gave devotion from the start.
If you think these things are not for sale,
Buy a brown-eyed pup with a wagging tail!
                                        AUTHOR UNKNOWN

———o———

Animals are such agreeable friends — they ask no questions, they pass no criticisms.
                                        GEORGE ELIOT (MARY ANN EVANS)

When the donkey saw the Zebra
He began to switch his tail;
"Well, I never," was the comment,
"Saw a mule that's been in jail."

Southwest Collegian

———o———

School Essay On The Cow

The cow is an animal. At the back it has a tail. On it hangs a brush. With this it sends the flies away so that they do not fall into the milk. The head is for the purpose of growing horns and so the mouth can be somewhere. The horns are to butt with, and the mouth is to moo with. Under the cow hangs the milk. It is arranged for milking. When people milk, the milk comes. How the cow does it, I don't know. The cow has a fine sense of smell. One can smell it far away; this is the reason for fresh air in the country. The cow does not eat much, but eats it twice, so that it gets enough. When it is hungry, it moos, but when it says nothing, it is because it is all full up with grass.

SIR ERNEST GOWERS, *Plain Words*
Observer

———o———

The first-grade children in a Raleigh, N.C., school were having a wonderful time playing with a stray cat. After a while one little lad asked the teacher if it was a boy cat or a girl cat. Not wishing to get into that particular subject, she said that she didn't believe she could tell. "I know how we can find out," said the boy.

"All right," said the teacher, resigning herself to the inevitable. "How can we find out?"

"We can vote," said the child.

SAM RAGAN, Raleigh, N.C.,
News and Observer

———o———

The Tale Of A Dog

There was a dachshund, once, so long
He hadn't any notion
How long it took to notify
His tail of his emotion;
And so it happened, while his eyes
Were filled with woe and sadness,
His little tail went wagging on
Because of previous gladness.

AUTHOR UNKNOWN

Why a dog has so many friends: his tail wags instead of his tongue.

———o———

During World War II a mother and her little girl were sent from a city to the country home of parents. One day the little girl came in and said, "Mummy, I saw four little pigs blowing up the mother pig!"

———o———

There was a young man from a city
Who saw what he thought was a kitty.
He gave it a pat, said nice little cat —
And they buried his clothes out of pity.

———o———

It's nice for children to have pets until the pets start having children.

The Wildrooter

———o———

Dachshund

A dog-and-a-half long
And a half-a-dog high;
All the family can pet him
While he's passing by.

VIRGIE EVANS ROGERS

Announcement

A Clean Announcement

DUZ you just DREFT along with the TIDE of unconcern? VEL now is the time to CHEER up. If you want real JOY the TREND is for ALL the family to BREEZE right into our Sunday School. Hear our SOS. Don't let us have to DIAL you this week to have you WHISK yourself to Sunday School next Sunday. Come on and let's ALL pull together like a 20 MULE TEAM.

Temple Evangelist

———o———

A young wife, wishing to announce the birth of her first child to a friend in a distant city, sent this telegram: "Isaiah 9:6."

Her friend, not familiar with the Scriptures, said to her husband:

"Margaret evidently has a boy who weighs nine pounds and six ounces, but why on earth did they name him Isaiah?"

Answer

Gracious Care

God answered prayer!
Not in the way I sought:
Not in the way that I had thought He
    ought!
But in His own good way and I could
    see
He answered in the fashion best for me.
And I was glad that I had such a share
In His parental love and gracious care,
    That thus He answered prayer.

God answered prayer!
But not in my brief hour:
I looked to see the fruit ere yet the
    flower
Had shed its gales of sweetness o'er my
    path!
But I have learned that slowest blos-
    soms yield
The choicest fruit; and so I leave them
    there
Upon the boughs, assured that they
    will bear
In time my answered prayer!

God answered prayer!
So sweetly that I stand
Amid the blessing of His wondrous
    Hand,
And marvel at the miracle I see,
The fashion that His love has wrought
    for me.
Pray on for the impossible and dare,
Upon thy banner this brave motto bear,
    "My Father answers prayer."

The Good Shepherd

———o———

Usually reluctant to participate in
class discussions, Alfred was wildly
waving his hand in response to the
question, "What causes tides?" I was
happy to call on him.

"Dead people!" he said with some
smugness. "It says so right in the geography book: 'Tides are caused by
heavenly bodies.'"

MARTHA VOGEN in *Grade Teacher*

———o———

The trouble with some people who
always "have all the answers" is that
so few of them are the right ones.

A child can ask a thousand questions
that the wisest man cannot answer.

JACOB ABBOTT

———o———

God's Answer

One day I prayed that God would lay
a soul upon my heart;
And in my prayer I promised Him that
I would do my part.
I'd call on strangers, write some cards,
and use the telephone;
Then trust Him — in His wisdom — to
lead me to that one.

Just then my doorbell rang so hard it
shook me from my prayer.
Before me stood a ten-year-old, his
head and feet were bare.
His small, dark face was far from clean,
his speech was bold and rough.
His brother said, "He's awful mean";
his manner said, "I'm tough."

But as I stood there at the door, the
Saviour whispered low,
"Here is that soul I charge to you. Oh,
do not let him go!"
That's why I baked these cookies; I've
put them out to cool
For my small friend — no longer tough
— he's in our Sunday school.

AUTHOR UNKNOWN

———o———

It is a good answer which knows
when to stop.

Italian Proverb

———o———

There cannot be a precise answer to
a vague question.

WENDELL JOHNSON

———o———

It is not every question that deserves
an answer.

PUBLILIUS SYRUS, *Maxim 581*

———o———

If you desire a wise answer, you must
ask a reasonable question.

JOHANN WOLFGANG VON GOETHE

———o———

A Sunday school teacher was telling
a Junior boy the story of Zacchaeus.
When he came to the part where Jesus
looked up into the tree and saw Zac-

chaeus, he asked, "What did Jesus say to the little man?" Without hesitation the lad answered, "Don't climb trees!"

MOLLIE MCCALL

Anticipation

As watchmen look for the morning, so do we look for Thee, O Christ. Come with the dawning of the day, and make Thyself known to us in the breaking of the bread; for Thou art our God for ever and ever.

Clare College Rite

———o———

Not many sounds in life, and I include all urban and all rural sounds, exceed in interest a knock at the door.

CHARLES LAMB, *Essays of Elia.*
Valentine's Day

———o———

Many count their chickens before they are hatched.

MIGUEL DE CERVANTES, *Don Quixote*

———o———

Let's fear no storm, before we feel a shower.

MICHAEL DRAYTON, *The Baron's Wars*

———o———

The misfortunes hardest to bear are those which never came.

JAMES RUSSELL LOWELL

———o———

Nothing is so good as it seems beforehand.

GEORGE ELIOT (MARY ANN EVANS),
Silas Marner

Anxiety

What does your anxiety do? It does not empty tomorrow, brother, of its sorrow; but ah! it empties today of its strength. It does not make you escape the evil; it makes you unfit to cope with it if it comes.

IAN MCLAREN

———o———

There is such a thing as taking ourselves and the world too seriously, or at any rate too anxiously. Half of the secular unrest and dismal, profane sadness of modern society comes from the vain idea that every man is bound to be a critic of life, and to let no day pass without finding some fault with the general order of things, or projecting some plan for its general improvement. And the other half comes from the greedy notion that a man's life does consist, after all, in the abundance of things that he possesseth, and that it is somehow or other more respectable and pious to be always at work trying to make a larger living, than it is to lie on your back in the green pastures and beside the still waters, and thank God that you are alive.

HENRY VAN DYKE

———o———

Oh, how great peace and quietness would he possess who should cut off all vain anxiety and place all his confidence in God.

THOMAS À KEMPIS

———o———

Nothing in the affairs of men is worthy of great anxiety.

PLATO

———o———

Anxiety reveals a lack of faith.

———o———

Anxiety is the poison of human life; the parent of many sins and of more miseries.

HUGH BLAIR

———o———

You cannot carry easily and well today's duties if you pile anxiety concerning the morrow on top of them.

Apology

A preacher's small son had to apologize for forgetting his aunt's birthday. He wrote, "I am sorry I forgot your birthday. I have no excuse, and it would serve me right if you forgot mine, which is next Friday."

———o———

From a son, now twice the age of which he speaks, came to his parents this one-line note: "If I was ever sixteen, pardon me!"

Apologies only account for that which they do not alter.

BENJAMIN DISRAELI

Appearance

You can't judge a horse by the harness.

Old Proverb

———o———

All is not false which seems at first a lie.

ROBERT SOUTHEY

———o———

Appearances to the mind are of four kinds. Things either are what they appear to be; or they neither are, nor appear to be; or they are, and do not appear to be; or they are not, and yet appear to be. Rightly to aim in all these cases is the wise man's task.

EPICTETUS

———o———

Half the work that is done in this world is to make things appear what they are not.

ELIAS ROST BEADLE

———o———

Appearances do not make the man, but it will pay any man to make the best appearance possible.

ROY L. SMITH

———o———

The dress does not make the monk.

FRANÇOIS RABELAIS

Application
(See also Action)

If a girl sits and reads the recipes in the cook-book, and does nothing more about it, she will never get a dinner ready. Reading the Bible can be done in the same easy way — with the same lack of results.

The Brethren Evangelist

———o———

Few men are lacking in capacity, but they fail because they are lacking in application.

CALVIN COOLIDGE

———o———

When a minister in a new parish preached the same sermon three Sundays in a row there was quite a bit of fuss and talk.

At last, one of the deacons called the young minister aside and said, "Pastor, you have used the sermon three times in a row. When are you going to preach a new one?"

The young pastor answered, "I will preach a new sermon when the people of my church start practicing the message of this one."

The Log of the Good Ship Grace

———o———

Application is the price to be paid for mental acquisition. To have the harvest we must sow the seed.

———o———

Application in youth enriches old age.

CHARLES SIMMONS

Appreciation
Appreciation

Let me be very patient with the old
And gladly listen to their tales thrice-
 told;
My hurrying feet I would more gently
 stay,
And fit my steps to theirs, along the
 way.

Perhaps the fertile future holds for me
Bright days the lonely old shall never
 see;
And so I fain would share their joy,
 their pain,
Because they shall not pass this way
 again.

Then let me not forget to give my smile,
And let me not forget that all the while
The old are giving too, of wisdom rare,
Rich gifts to me, though I be unaware.

RUBY M. SLOAN
in *South Carolina Methodist Advocate*

———o———

The only place you can be sure to find appreciation is in the dictionary.

———o———

Don't be stingy with words of appreciation when they are justly due.

He who seeks only for applause from without has all his happiness in another's keeping.

OLIVER GOLDSMITH

———o———

Applause is the spur of noble minds, the end and aim of weak ones.

CHARLES CALEB COLTON

———o———

Prayer For Appreciation

Oh teach me, Lord, to treasure much
The simple things of life — the touch
Of wind and snow, of rain and sun;
And when the hours of work are done,
The quietness of rest, the fair
And healing sustenance of prayer.
And, Lord of living, help me keep
A shining, singing gladness deep
Within for blessings yet to be
Through all eternity.

AUTHOR UNKNOWN

Architects

All are architects of fate,
Working in these walls of Time;
Some with massive deeds and great,
Some with ornaments of rhyme.

HENRY WADSWORTH LONGFELLOW

———o———

Every man is the architect of his own fortune.

SALLUST

———o———

Every man's fortune is moulded by his character.

CORNELIUS NEPOS

———o———

If you seek a monument, look about you.

Inscription on Sir Christopher Wren's Tomb, in St. Paul's Cathedral, London

———o———

We must not only be architects of our fate; we must also be builders.

———o———

Let us not say, Every man is the architect of his own fortune; but let us say, Every man is the architect of his own character.

GEORGE DANA BOARDMAN

Argue, Argument

A man who has only an argument is no match for a Christian who has an experience.

———o———

No matter what side of an argument you get on, you will always find some people with you that you wish were on the other side.

JASCHA HEIFETZ

———o———

Many a person can recall ruefully having gone out of his way to get an argument, only to lose it.

Glendale News-Press, Glendale, Calif.

———o———

The best way I know of to win an argument is to start by being in the right.

LORD HAILSHAM

———o———

One way to avoid arguments is to be a good listener.

———o———

Note found in a Wauwatosa, Wisconsin, household written by a nine-year-old girl after an argument: "Good-bye family. You all hate me. I love you all very much. God bless you.
"P.S. In case of fire, I'm in the attic."

———o———

The only people who listen to both sides of an argument are the neighbors.

———o———

When all is said and done makes a a dandy time to quit arguing.

Changing Times, The Kiplinger Magazine

———o———

You can't prove anything in an argument, except that you're just as bull-headed as the other fellow.

———o———

I never make the mistake of arguing with people for whose opinions I have no respect.

EDWARD GIBBON

———o———

Don't win the argument and lose the sale.

ROY L. SMITH

Argument is the worst sort of conversation.

JONATHAN SWIFT

———o———

In a heated argument we are apt to lose sight of the truth.

PUBLILIUS SYRUS

———o———

There is no good in arguing with the inevitable. The only argument available with an east wind is to put on your overcoat.

JAMES RUSSELL LOWELL

———o———

A long dispute means that both parties are wrong.

VOLTAIRE

———o———

Behind every argument is someone's ignorance.

LOUIS DEMBITZ BRANDEIS

Aspiration

What we truly and earnestly aspire to be, that in a sense we are.

———o———

The one who aspires highly is the one who achieves highly.

———o———

What shall I do to be forever known, And make the age to come my own?

ABRAHAM COWLEY

———o———

Our aspirations are our possibilities,

ROBERT BROWNING

———o———

There is not a heart but has its moments of longing, yearning for something better, nobler, holier than it knows now.

HENRY WARD BEECHER

Assets

If you count all your assets, you always show a profit.

ROBERT QUILLEN

———o———

Enthusiasm is the greatest asset in the world. It beats money and power and influence.

HENRY CHESTER

Good will is the one and only asset that competition cannot undersell or destroy.

MARSHALL FIELD

———o———

The greatest asset of a man, a business or a nation is faith.

THOMAS J. WATSON

Assurance

This I Know

I do not know the depths of love
  It took to die on Calvary;
I do not know the shame and grief
  He suffered there to set me free.
Nor can I tell how bitter was
  His cup in dark Gethsemane,
The pain He bore — heartbroken, poor;
  But this I know: He died for me!

I know not why that for my sins
  His precious blood so freely flows,
Nor fathom why the Lord of All
  Did not such cruel death oppose.
I cannot understand the power
  Which triumphed over death and
    foes.
They sealed His tomb 'midst dark'ning
    gloom;
  But this I know: for me He rose!

I do not know why oftentimes
  The skies are dark and overcast;
Nor why, in grave temptations, all
  My problems seem so hard, so vast.
I cannot tell what things may come —
  Sore heartaches, all my hopes to blast
The shades of night obscure the light;
  But this I know: He'll hold me fast.

GRACE V. WATKINS

———o———

Rock And Roll

I'm on the roll up there
and on the rock down here.

———o———

Robert Louis Stevenson tells the story of a ship at sea in time of storm. The passengers were in great distress. After a while one of them, against orders, went up on deck and made his way to the pilot.

The seaman was at his post of duty at the wheel and when he saw the man was greatly frightened he gave him a reassuring smile. Then the passanger turned and went back to the other passengers and said, "I have seen the pilot and he smiled, 'All is well.'"

When our small boat of life is storm-tossed and our hearts are fearful, we may push through the storm to our Pilot who is standing at the wheel, and when we see His face we shall know that all is well.

Atheist

I can see how it might be possible for a man to look down upon the earth and be an atheist, but I cannot conceive how a man could look up into the heavens and say there is no God.

ABRAHAM LINCOLN

He who does not believe that God is above all is either a fool or has no experience of life.

CAECILIUS STATIUS, *Fragments No. 15*

It takes no brains to be an atheist.

DWIGHT DAVID EISENHOWER

An atheist has a reason, but no hope for his reason. A hypocrite has a hope, but no reason for his hope. A Christian has a reason for his hope and hope for his reason.

The United Brethren Magazine

An atheist is a man without any invisible means of support.

JOHN BUCHAN, LORD TWEEDSMUIR

An atheist cannot find God for the same reason a thief cannot find a policeman.

The atheist's most embarrassing moment is when he feels profoundly thankful for something but can't think of anybody to thank for it.

MARY ANN VINCENT

An atheist spent a few days with Fenelon, a saintly Christian. He was moved to say: "If I stay here much longer, I shall become a Christian in spite of myself." Fenelon had used no word of controversy or of pleading. It was only the quiet, convincing argument of a holy life — a consistent walk and conversation.

"There is no God," the wicked saith,
    "And truly it's a blessing,
For what He might have done with us
    It's better only guessing."

Some others also, to themselves
    Who scarce so much as doubt it,
Think there is none, when they are well
    And do not think about it.

And almost every one when age,
    Disease, or sorrows strike him,
Inclines to think there is a God,
    Or something very like Him.

ARTHUR HUGH CLOUGH, *Dipsychus*

The science to which I pinned my faith is bankrupt. . . . Its counsels which should have established the millennium led directly to the suicide of Europe. I believed them once. . . . In their name I helped to destroy the faith of millions of worshippers in the temples of a thousand creeds. And now they look at me and witness the great tragedy of an atheist who has lost *his* faith.

GEORGE BERNARD SHAW,
Too True To Be Good

Attention

If a pupil is not giving attention, he's absent.

The easiest way for a man to get his wife's attention is by looking comfortable.

Attention is the stuff that memory is made of, and memory is accumulated genius.

JAMES RUSSELL LOWELL

When you can do the common things of life in an uncommon way you will command the attention of the world.

GEORGE WASHINGTON CARVER

What makes men great is their ability to decide what is important, and then focus their attention on it.

Attitude

The posture of Christianity toward the religions of the world is not one of condemnation. It is rather one of illumination and the offering of the Good News.

GARY W. DEMAREST

——o——

One's attitude toward life is determined largely by one's altitude.

——o——

The best attitude to have toward one's daily work is a keep-at-it-tude.

——o——

One ship drives east and another west,
  With the self-same winds that blow;
'Tis the set of the sails and not the gales
  That determines where they go.
Like the winds of the sea are the ways
  of fate,
  As we voyage along through life;
'Tis the set of a soul that decides the
  goal —
And not the calm or the strife.

REBECCA R. WILLIAMS

Authority

The best time for a man to assert his authority and let his wife know who's boss is the first time he gets up the courage.

——o——

Greatness does not depend on the size of your command, but on the way you exercise it.

MARSHALL FERDINAND FOCH

——o——

Nothing pleases a little man more than an opportunity to crack a big whip.

——o——

The one in authority has responsibility.

——o——

Nothing so soon overthrows a weak character as a bit of authority.

Authors

Choose an author as you choose a friend.

WENTWORTH DILLON, EARL OF ROSCOMMON,
Essay on Translated Verse

——o——

A small number of men and women think for the million; through them the million speak and act.

JEAN-JACQUES ROUSSEAU

——o——

I think the author who speaks about his own books is almost as bad as a mother who talks about her own children.

BENJAMIN DISRAELI

——o——

The greatest part of a writer's time is spent in reading, in order to write; a man will turn over half a library to make one book.

SAMUEL JOHNSON

——o——

A man may write at any time if he will set himself doggedly to it.

SAMUEL JOHNSON

Automation

Automation is man's effort to make work so easy that woman can do it all.

In a Nutshell

——o——

We are turning out machines that act like men, and men that act like machines.

ERICH FROMM

——o——

A tool is but the extension of a man's hand and a machine is but a complex tool; and he that invents a machine augments the power of man and the well-being of mankind.

HENRY WARD BEECHER

Automobile

Nothing keeps the family together as much as owning just one car.

——o——

"This car is the opportunity of a lifetime," remarked the enterprising salesman.

"Yes," replied the prospective buyer, "I can hear it knocking."

———o———

The trouble is that the car of tomorrow is being driven on the highway of yesterday by the driver of today.

———o———

Car sickness: The feeling you get each month when the payment's due.

———o———

Safety slogan: Look out for school children — especially if they are driving cars.

———o———

The worst kind of car trouble is when the engine won't start and the payments won't stop.

Autumn

God painted all the autumn leaves
And put to sleep the flowers,
And told the birds to find a place
To spend their winter hours.

CHARLES BOWMAN

———o———

Coming Of Autumn

Autumn came this morning
Scarlet slippers on her feet,
Her eyes were blue as asters,
Her breath was honey sweet.

Like a brook's soft whispering
She crooned a lullaby,
And all the flowers nodded
As she passed by.

She walked along the roadside,
And where her footsteps fell
Swamp maple and young sassafras
Felt her magic spell.

Low dogwood and the sweet-gum,
Pin oak and tulip, too,
Stood clad in gold and scarlet
When she passed through.

She ran across the marshes
Free as the sea-blown air,
And turned to gold the sedges
To warn the heron there.

They heeded not her warning,
But stood with me to stare
At all the wealth of beauty
Around us, everywhere.

M. K. S.

———o———

It takes two kinds of people to make the world — poets to write about the glories of autumn and the rest of us to rake them.

MARJORIE JOHNSON in NEA Journal

———o———

Autumn is when an unwatched boy, raking, leaves.

———o———

November

November is an outdoor month
Of crisp and sparkling weather,
A time for playing outdoor games,
For doing chores together.
November is a harvest month
Of richly laden tables,
A time for roaring winter fires
And barnyard turkey fables.
November is a solemn month,
A time reserved for prayer
Of thankfulness for blessings past
And for God's loving care.

CHRISTINE GRAHAME

Average

The average man never gets mad, because he never thinks the things being said about the average man mean him.

Press, London, Ohio

———o———

It is so much easier to live down to the average than to rise above it.

B

Baby

What Is A Baby?

What is a baby?
A baby is a lot of things:
A baby is a soft little hand, curling warmly around your finger. . . .
A baby is a lively little pair of legs, kicking happily in the air after a bath. . . .
A baby is a puckered and trembling lower lip, trying hard, — oh so hard — to tell you something. . . .
A baby is a cry in the night, calling you swiftly out of sleep and to its crib. . . .
A baby is an eloquent pair of eyes — one time dancing with glee and sparkle as they watch a bouncing toy, another time staring at you with sober and steady reflection, until you wonder what goes on within that little head. . . .
And above all a baby is a priceless gift from God. Those little hands must learn to move in His service . . . those little feet must grow up to walk in His ways . . . those little eyes must learn to focus on His Word.

EWA Family Counselor

———o———

As a young mother was bathing her baby, a neighbor's little girl was holding a doll minus an arm.
"How long have you had your baby?" asked the little visitor.
"Three months," replied the mother.
And the little girl said: "But you've kept her nice."

Bachelor

She: "And how is your bachelor friend?"
He: "When I saw him last he was mending very slowly."
She: "Indeed. I didn't know he'd been ill."
He: "He hasn't been. He was darning his socks."

A bachelor is a person who has to fix only one breakfast.

———o———

A bachelor is a fellow who can take a nap on top of a bedspread.

Spectator, Somerset, Mass.

———o———

A bachelor should learn to sew on his own buttons and darn his socks — he may marry some day.

Bargain

It's a bad bargain where nobody gains.

English Proverb

———o———

It is extraordinary to what an expense of time and money people will go in order to get something for nothing.

ROBERT LYND

———o———

Two small children were engaged in selling pink lemonade, side by side. Tom's glasses were the same size as Mike's but his lemonade was marked "2 glasses for 5c" while Mike's were marked "5c each." Of course Tom was doing a bigger business.
Feeling sorry for Mike, a neighbor stopped to buy a glass of lemonade from him. "Your lemonade looks just the same as Tom's and your glasses are the same size," he said. "How is it that your price is higher than Tom's?"
"Well, you see," Mike explained, "the cat fell into Tom's bucket just before our sale began so he's having a bargain sale!"

Beauty

Beautiful young people are accidents of nature, but beautiful old people are works of art.

———o———

Beauty is the mark God sets on virtue.

RALPH WALDO EMERSON

Everything has its beauty, but not everyone sees it.

CONFUCIUS

There is no beautifier of complexion, or form, or behavior, like the wish to scatter joy and not pain around us.

RALPH WALDO EMERSON, *Conduct of Life*

"What do you think of mul as a beautifier?"
"It hasn't done much for pigs."

A man should hear a little music, read a little poetry, and see a fine picture every day of his life, in order that worldly cares may not obliterate the sense of the beautiful which God has implanted in the human soul.

JOHANN WOLFGANG VON GOETHE

Beauty without grace is a hook without a bait.

NINON DE LENCLOS

Beauty is but a flower,
Which wrinkles will devour.

THOMAS NASH

A beautiful mother, a more beautiful daughter.

HORACE

That is the best part of beauty, which a picture cannot express.

FRANCIS BACON, *Of Beauty*

Begin, Beginning

Be active
Be vital
Be responsible
Begin

A good start makes for a good ending only if you don't start something you can't finish.

A mosquito doesn't wait for an opening, he makes one.

Life is full of endings, but every ending is a new beginning.

You will never reach second base if you keep one foot on first base.

VERNON LAW

The beginning is the most important part of the work.

PLATO, *The Republic*

Tender twigs are bent with ease,
Aged trees do break with bending.

ROBERT SOUTHWELL, *Loss in Delay*

Behavior

Behavior is a mirror in which everyone shows his true image.

JOHANN WOLFGANG VON GOETHE

To really know a man, observe his behavior with a woman, a flat tire and a child.

Always behave like a duck. Remain calm and unruffled on the surface, but keep paddling like fury underneath.

If one fights for good behavior, God makes one a present of the good feelings.

JULIANA H. EWING

The Art Of Getting Along

Sooner or later, a man, if he is wise, discovers that life is a mixture of good days and bad, victory and defeat, give and take.

He learns that it doesn't pay to let things get his goat; that he must let some things go over his head like water off a duck's back.

He learns that carrying a chip on his shoulder is the quickest way to get into a fight.

He learns that buck-passing acts as a boomerang.

He learns that carrying tales and gossip about others is the surest way to become unpopular.

He learns that giving others a mental lift by showing appreciation and praise is the best way to lift his own spirits.

He learns that the world will not end when he fails or makes an error; that there is always another day and another chance.

He learns that all men have burnt toast for breakfast now and then, and that he shouldn't let their grumbling get him down.

He learns that people are not any more difficult to get along with in one place than another, and that "Getting along" depends about 98% on his own behavior.

"As much as lieth in you, live peaceably with all men." Romans 12:18.

WILFRED A. PETERSON

———o———

The sum of behavior is to retain a man's own dignity, without intruding upon the liberty of others.

FRANCIS BACON

———o———

The Sunday school teacher had finished her talk on behavior.

"Now, Billy," she questioned, "tell me what we must do before we can expect forgiveness of sin."

There was a moment's thought, then Billy replied, "We gotta sin."

———o———

Perfection consists not in doing extraordinary things, but in doing ordinary things extraordinarily well.

ANGÉLIQUE ARNAULD

———o———

Your moral behavior is governed by your inner grace.

Believe

If you believe in God, in the principles on which our nation was founded, in a personal code of ethics, then exemplify them for us.

Spoken by a Youth

———o———

Teacher to parent about child: Don't believe everything he tells you about me and I won't believe everything he tells me about you.

———o———

I did not use to believe the story of Daniel in the lions' den until I had to take some of these awful marches [through the leopard forests of Nigeria]. Then I knew it was true, and that it was written for my comfort.

MARY SLESSOR

I Believe God

I believe God —
Though angry breakers
Cast their spray
Upon the shore,
I know that through the storm
He'll keep me safe
Forevermore.

I believe God —
Though neither sun
Nor stars appear
For many days,
I trust Him in the darkest,
Wildest hours.
He knows my ways.

I believe God —
Though this frail ship
Be swept along
By tempest force,
I am assured at last
Of Harbor Home.
He charts my course.

PAUL T. HOLLIDAY

———o———

Why is it that some people so often will more readily believe a lie than the truth?

———o———

Believe God's Word

It is strange we trust each other
And only doubt our Lord.
We take the word of mortals
And yet distrust His Word.
But oh, what light and glory
Would shine o'er all our days,
If we always would remember
God means just what He says.

A. B. SIMPSON

———o———

The world says, "show me and I'll

believe." Christ says, "Believe Me and I'll show you."

———o———

To those who believe no explanation is necessary; to those who do not believe no explanation will satisfy.

FRANZ WERFEL

———o———

One who does not believe in God does not believe in self.

ROGER BABSON

———o———

Philanthropic unbelievers and unphilanthropic believers are equally monstrosities.

———o———

A London missionary, who had before him three hundred ragged children, placed a coin under a book on the table and said, "Whosoever believeth, let him come and take it." He waited; they were all "whosoevers," but only one was "whosoever believeth;" a little ragged chap who came up, lifted the Bible, and took the coin, saying, "Thank you, Sir."

"What is your name?" asked the missionary.

"Cecil Smithers."

"I did not say Cecil Smithers could have the coin.

"No, Sir," said the half-frightened boy, "but you did say 'whosoever,' and that means me."

The missionary's "whosoever" meant anyone, and the boy believed it; and God's "whosoever" means anyone. Have you believed this?

"Whosoever believeth in Him (that is, in Christ, Who died and rose again) shall receive the remission (the pardon) of sins."

The Little Lutheran

———o———

One person with a belief is equal to a force of ninety-nine who have only interests.

JOHN STUART MILL

———o———

People will believe anything if you whisper it.

Believe In Yourself

Believe in yourself! Believe you were made
To do any task without calling for aid.
Believe, without growing too scornfully proud,
That you, as the greatest and least are endowed.
A mind to do thinking, two hands and two eyes
Are all the equipment God gives to the wise.

Believe in yourself! You're divinely designed
And perfectly made for the work of mankind.
This truth you must cling to through danger and pain;
The heights man has reached you can also attain.
Believe to the very last hour, for it's true,
That whatever you will you've been gifted to do.

The wisdom of ages is yours if you'll read
But you've got to believe in yourself to succeed.

EDGAR A. GUEST

———o———

Upon the wreckage of thy yesterday
Design thy structure of tomorrow, lay
Strong corner-stones of purpose, and prepare
Great blocks of wisdom cut from past despair.
Shape mighty pillars of resolve, to set
Deep in the tear-wet mortar of regret.
Believe in God — in thine own self believe,
All thou hast hoped for thou shalt yet achieve.

ELLA WHEELER WILCOX

———o———

If I believed [the Gospel], I would crawl across England on broken glass on my hands and knees to tell men it was true!

CHARLES PEACE, *On The Scaffold*

———o———

A belief that does not express itself in action soon ceases to be even a belief.

I believe in God as I believe in my friends, because I feel the breath of his affection, feel his invisible and intangible hand drawing me, leading me, grasping me.

MIGUEL DE UNAMUNO, *Prosa Diversa*

———o———

He does not believe that does not live according to his belief.

THOMAS FULLER

Best

God's Best

God has His best things for the few
  That dare to stand the test;
God has His second choice for those
  Who will not have His best.

It is not always open ill
  That risks the Promised Rest;
The better, often, is the foe
  That keeps us from the best.

Some seek the highest choice,
  But, when by trials pressed
They shrink, they yield, they shun the
    cross
And so they lose the best.

Give me, O Lord, Thy highest choice;
  Let others take the rest.
Their good things have no charm for
    me,
  I want Thy very best.

I want, in this short life of mine,
  As much as can be pressed
Of service true for God and man:
  Make me to be Thy best.

A. B. SIMPSON

———o———

Do the very best you can today and tomorrow you can do better.

MARTIN VANBEE

———o———

God does not seek better methods, or better means, but He seeks for better men.

———o———

It is a sin to take the good when the best can be had.

———o———

The search for the best is a constant challenge to high adventure.

When we do the best that we can, we never know what miracle is wrought in our life, or in the life of another.

HELEN KELLER

Betray

Thomas Cranmer, Archbishop of Canterbury in the sixteenth century, was cast into prison because of his faith. His imprisoners thrust a written document into his hands and said: "Sign that!" When Cranmer read it, he exclaimed: "Nay, 'tis a downright denial of my Christ! I will not sign." "Sign it or die," they threatened, and they badgered and tortured him until in a weak moment he took the pen and wrote his name. When he finished, the horror of his betrayal leapt upon his soul, and he stared at his right hand that had signed his name. For days and nights he was tormented with remorse. Jesus had said: "If thy hand offend thee, cut it off," and he gladly would have taken a knife and severed his traitor hand. When, in spite of his recantation, they led him out to die, he walked to the martyr pyre and thrust his right arm first into the flames. "This unworthy hand," he said, "this which hath sinned, having signed the writing, must be the first to suffer," and he held it there until it was blackened and consumed. Then he plunged into the fire himself.

The Leader

Bible

The Bible! There It Stands!

Where childhood needs a standard
  Or youth a beacon light,
Where sorrow sighs for comfort
  Or weakness longs for might,
Bring forth the Holy Bible,
  The Bible! There it stands!
Resolving all life's problems
  And meeting its demands.

Though sophistry conceal it,
  The Bible! There it stands!
Though Pharisees profane it,
  Its influence expands;

It fills the world with fragrance
Whose sweetness never cloys,
It lifts our eyes to heaven,
It heightens human joys.

Despised and torn in pieces,
By infidels decried —
The thunderbolts of hatred
The haughty cynic's pride —
All these have railed against it
In this and other lands,
Yet dynasties have fallen,
And still the Bible stands!

To paradise a highway,
The Bible! There it stands!
Its promises unfailing,
Nor grievous its commands;
It points man to the Saviour,
The lover of his soul;
Salvation is its watchword,
Eternity its goal!

JAMES M. GRAY

God's Book does not yield up its secrets to those who will not be taught of the Spirit.

JAMES I. PACKER

The Bible is a great and powerful tree. Each word is a mighty branch. Each of these branches have I well shaken. And the shaking of them has never disappointed me.

MARTIN LUTHER

Sampling the Word of God only occasionally will never give you a real taste for it.

Give me a Bible and a candle and shut me up in a dungeon and I will tell you what the world is doing.

CECIL DICHARD

Apply yourself to the whole text, and apply the whole text to yourself.

J. A. BENGEL

A Navy chaplain had just completed a lengthy tour of sea duty and was happily headed for home when he was ordered back to sea. Disturbed, he wired the office of the chief of chaplains: "How long, O Lord? Isaiah 6:11."

His chief's reply came fast: "It would be for a time, two times, and half a time. — Daniel 12:7."

SHIRLEY LINDE in *Together*

Men do not reject the Bible because it contradicts itself but because it contradicts them.

The Book

The books men write are but a fragrance blown
From transient blossoms crushed by human hands;
But high above them, splendid and alone,
Staunch as a tree, there is a Book that stands
Unmoved by storms, unchallenged by decay:
The winds of criticism would profane
Its sacred pages, but the Truth, the Way,
The Life are in it — and they beat in vain.

Oh, traveler from this to yonder world,
Pause in the shade of God's magnificent,
Eternal World — that tree whose roots are curled
About our human need. When strength is spent,
Stretch out beneath some great, far-reaching limb
Of promise and find rest and peace in HIM.

HELEN FRAZEE-BOWER

It is of the greatest importance then that we should feed our minds with facts; with reliable information; with the results of human experience; and above all with the teachings of the Word of God. It is matter for the utmost admiration to notice how full the Bible is of biography and history: so that there is hardly a single crisis in our lives that may not be matched from those wondrous pages. There is no book like the Bible for casting a light on the dark landings of human life.

F. B. MEYER

The Holy Scriptures are full of divine gifts and virtues . . . In a word, the Holy Scripture is the Highest and Best of Books, abounding in comfort under all afflictions and trials. It teaches us to see, to feel, to grasp and to comprehend faith, hope and charity. . . . And when evil oppresses us, it teaches how these virtues throw light upon the darkness and how, after this poor, miserable existence of ours on earth, there is another and an eternal life.

MARTIN LUTHER

Secret Study

Pre-eminent, supreme among the helps to secret prayer I place, of course, the secret study of the holy written Word of God.

Read it on your knees, at least on the knees of your spirit. Read it to reassure, to feed, to regulate, to kindle, to give to your secret prayer at once body and soul.

Read it that you may hold faster your certainty of being heard.

Read it that you may know with blessed definiteness whom you have believed, and what you have in Him, and how He is able to keep your deposit safe.

Read it in the attitude of mind in which the apostles read it, in which the Lord read it. Read it, not seldom, to turn it at once into prayer.

H. C. G. MOULE

Does It Matter What I Say?

What if I say —
"The Bible is God's Holy Word,
Complete, inspired, without a flaw" —
But let its pages stay
Unread from day to day,
And fail to learn therefrom God's law;
What if I go not there to seek
The truth of which I glibly speak,
For guidance on this earthly way —
Does it matter what I say?

What if I say —
"That Jesus Christ is Lord divine — "
Yet fellow-pilgrims can behold
Naught of the Master's love in me,
No grace of kindly sympathy?

If I am of the Shepherd's fold,
Then shall I know the Shepherd's voice
And gladly make His way my choice.
We are saved by faith, yet faith is one
With life, like daylight and the sun.
Unless they flower in our deeds,
Dead, empty husks are all the creeds.
To call Christ Lord, but strive not to obey —
Belies the homage that with words I pay.

MAUD FRAZER JACKSON

Heed the exhortation of one who, with all the passion of his heart, urges you to lay hold on the Bible until the Bible lays hold on you.

WILL H. HOUGHTON

Other books were given for our information; the Bible was given for our transformation.

God's Word

Where is comfort for your sorrow,
    Wounded heart that peace would know?
Where is help to aid and strengthen,
    Weary pilgrim here below?
Where is wisdom that will guide you,
    Puzzled youth with questioning plea?
Where is cleansing for transgression,
    Sinner longing to be free?
All is answered, all provided
    In God's Word to you and me.

DELLA ADAMS LEITNER

The Bible

Born in the East and clothed in Oriental form and imagery, the Bible walks the ways of all the world with familiar feet and enters land after land to find its own everywhere. It comes to the palace to tell the monarch that he is a servant of the Most High, and into the cottage to assure the peasant that he can be a son of God. Children listen to its stories with wonder and delight, and wise men ponder them as parables of life.

It has a word of peace for the time of peril, a word of comfort for the time of calamity, a word of light for the hour of darkness. Its oracles are repeated in the assembly of the people, and its counsels whispered in the ear of the lonely. The wicked and the proud tremble at its warnings, but to the wounded and penitent it has a mother's voice.

No man is poor or desolate who has this treasure for his own. When the landscape darkens and the trembling pilgrim comes to the valley named of the shadow, he is not afraid to enter; he takes the rod and staff of Scripture in his hand, he says to his friend and comrade, "Goodbye, we shall meet again"; and comforted by that support, he goes toward the lonely pass as one who walks through darkness into light.

HENRY VAN DYKE

———o———

A preacher entered a Sunday school class while the lesson was in progress and asked this question, "Who broke down the walls of Jericho?" A boy answered, "Not me, sir." The preacher turned to the teacher and asked, "Is this the usual behavior in this class?" The teacher answered, "This boy is honest and I believe him. I really don't think he did it."

Leaving the room, the preacher sought out an elder and explained what had happened. The elder said, "I have known both the teacher and the boy for years, and neither of them would do such a thing."

By this time the preacher was heartsick and reported it to the Department of Christian Education. They said, "We see no point in being disturbed. Let's pay the bill for the damage to the walls and charge it to upkeep."

Modern Maturity

It is illegal to read the Bible in the public schools of Illinois, but a law requires the STATE to provide a Bible for every convict! Don't worry, young people, if you can't read the Bible in school, you'll be able to when you get to prison!

Baptist Beacon

———o———

I have spent seventy years of my life studying that Book to satisfy my heart; it is the Word of God. I bank my life on the statement that I believe this Book to be the solid rock of Holy Scripture.

WILLIAM EWART GLADSTONE

———o———

A scholarly Chinese was employed to translate the New Testament into the Chinese language. After a while, he exclaimed, "What a marvelous Book this is!"

"Why do you think so?" asked the missionary.

"Because it tells me so exactly about myself. It knows all that is in me. The One who made this Book must be the One who made me!"

As we read God's Word, it searches our innermost being. It reveals to us the sinfulness of the human heart — "deceitful above all things, and desperately wicked." It prescribes the sure remedy for our spiritual sickness: "The blood of Jesus Christ his Son cleanseth us from all sin." (I John 1:7).

———o———

Comments By Great Men
About The Bible

Abraham Lincoln — I am profitably engaged in reading the Bible. Take all of this Book upon reason that you can and the balance by faith, and you will live and die a better man.

George Washington — Above all, the pure and benign light of Revelation has had a meliorating influence on mankind, and increased the blessings of society.

Thomas Jefferson — I always have said, and always will say, that the studious perusal of the sacred Volume will make better citizens, better fathers, and better husbands.

John Quincy Adams — The first and almost the only Book deserving of universal attention is the Bible. I speak as a man of the world . . . and I say to you, "Search the Scriptures."

Zachary Taylor — It was for the love of the truths of this great and good Book that our fathers abandoned their native shore for the wilderness.

Daniel Webster — The Bible is a book of faith, and a book of doctrine, and a book of morals, and a book of religion, of special revelation from God; but it is also a book which teaches man his own individual responsibility, his own dignity, and his equality with his fellow-man.

William H. Seward, Secretary of State in Lincoln's cabinet — I know not how long a republican form of government can flourish among a great people who have not the Bible.

Herbert Hoover — There is no other book so various as the Bible, nor one so full of concentrated wisdom. Whether it be of law, business, morals or that vision which leads the imagination in the creation of constructive enterprises for the happiness of mankind, he who seeks for guidance . . . may look inside its covers and find illumination.

William Ewart Gladstone — I have known ninety-five great men of the world in my time and of these eighty-seven were followers of the Bible.

———o———

Where To Look In The BIBLE

When God seems far away, read Psalm 139.

When sorrowful, read John 14; Psalm 46.

When men fail you, read Psalm 27.

When you have sinned, read Psalm 51; I John 1.

When you worry, read Matthew 6:19-34; Psalm 43.

When in sickness, read Psalm 41.

When in danger, read Psalm 91.

When you have the blues, read Psalm 34.

When you are discouraged, read Isaiah 40.

When you are lonely or fearful, read Psalm 23.

When you forget your blessings, read Psalm 103.

When you want courage, read Joshua 1:1-9.

When the world seems bigger than God, read Psalm 90.

When you want rest and peace, read Matthew 11:25-30.

When you want assurance, read Romans 8.

When looking for joy, read Colossians 3.

When you leave home to travel, read Psalm 121.

When you grow bitter or critical, read I Corinthians 13.

When you think of investments, read Mark 10:17-31.

Some rules of conduct? Read Romans 12.

Why not follow Psalm 119:11?

———o———

Search The Scriptures

When Jesus walked the shore of Galilee,
Not all Capernaum turned out to see;
When He worked miracles within that town,
Some even turned their casement shutters down!

And Nazareth? He did no wonders there!
To thrust Him from its cliff they'd even dare;
But there were some who followed Him, and learned
His way of life, and truth — of hearts which burned.

A wistful feeling lies with men today,
Who wish that they could meet Him on their way
Down country lanes, or on some city street,
Or resting by a rock in desert heat.

And He is there — if one has faith to see;
And He abides in men like you and me —

His living temples — passing to and
fro
Along the very way He bid them go.
In Nazareth, men spurned God's holy
writ,
And people still are few who study it;
Your footsteps — do they press the
world's Broadway?
Then read, lest when you meet, it's
Judgment Day.

MILDRED ALLEN JEFFERY

Bobby Richardson, Yankee baseball
star, says this about the Bible: "Put a
man in a baseball suit, give him a
glove and a hat — but all that doesn't
make him a star. Nor will all the practice in the world get some people into
the major leagues. Something more is
needed.

"It's also true if you put a man in
church and give him a hymn book or
a Bible, it doesn't make him a Christian. Not singing all the hymns in the
world will do that — or even reading
the Bible from cover to cover.

"That's why something more is needed when you read the Bible. We call
it the Spirit. Read the Bible and let
its message live in you, for 'not the
readers of the law are just before God,
but the doers shall be justified.'"

"I have never in my whole life met
a man who really knew the Bible, and
rejected it. The difficulty has always
been an *unwillingness* to give it an
honest trial. Our Lord Himself says,
'Ye will not come unto me, that you
may have life.'"

HOWARD A. KELLY

A man who loves his wife will love
her letters and her photographs because they speak to him of her. So if
we love the Lord Jesus we shall love
the Bible because it speaks to us of
him.

JOHN R. W. STOTT

If you accept the Bible with reservations, the devil has a reservation for
you.

RALPH BREWER

The English Bible is the first of our
national treasures.

GEORGE V, KING OF ENGLAND

The Bible is a revelation of God's
thoughts for the happiness of His children.

If a man's Bible is coming apart, it
is an indication that he himself is fairly
well put together.

JAMES E. JENNINGS

I consider an intimate knowledge of
the Bible an indispensable qualification
of a well-educated man.

ROBERT ANDREWS MILLIKAN

The Bible is criticized most by those
who read it the least.

The Bible contains the vitamins of
soul health.

PALMER

A Christian woman wrote upon the
fly-page of her Bible the following
words: "Lay any burden upon me, only sustain me; send me anywhere,
only go with me; sever any tie but that
which binds me to thy service and to
thy heart."

If our children have the background
of a godly, happy home and this un-
shakeable faith that the Bible is indeed
the Word of God, they will have a
foundation that the forces of hell cannot shake.

MRS. BILLY GRAHAM

The Bible is broad as life, having,
indeed, the same Author.

SCHMAUK

The Bible and Children

First Bible

A little boy's first Bible
Is the greatest thrill he's known;
There's a sweet, unique excitement
In a Bible all his own!

And yet my heart is smitten
As this touching sight I see —
Has his reverence for that Bible
Depended much on me?
As I see him with his Bible,
I bow my head and pray —
May he always love that Bible
The way he does today.
Then I hear a voice within me
Speak in solemn words and true;
How he cherishes that Bible
Will depend a lot on you!
I love my Bible better
Since I've seen the beaming joy
This wonderful possession
Has afforded to my boy.
May I seek to give mine daily
A devotion he can see,
For the love he bears his Bible
Will depend a lot on me.

AUTHOR UNKNOWN

———o———

"Mother, I found an old dusty thing
High on the shelf — just look!"
"Why, that's a Bible, Tommy dear;
Be careful — that's God's book!"
"God's book!" the child exclaimed;
"Then, mother, before we lose it,
We'd better send it back to God,
For, you know, we never use it."

Christian Life

———o———

Dusty Bibles

When the pastor called he found little Mary crying, and inquired as to the cause of her tears.

"Mamma got my apron all dirty," she sobbed.

"And how did that happen?" he asked.

"When she saw you coming she used it to wipe the dust off the Bible."

———o———

The preacher was visiting the home, and asked if he might read a chapter from the Bible. The man of the house said to his little son, "Bobby, go and get the Bible — you know, the big Book we read so much."

In a little while Bobby came in carrying the mail-order catalog!

Big

God is looking for men who are big enough to be small enough to be used of Him in a big way.

Christian Digest

———o———

Only a truly big person can graciously accept a favor he doesn't deserve and may never be able to repay.

———o———

What a superb thing it would be if we were all big enough in mind to see no slights, accept no insults, cherish no jealousies and admit into our heart no hatred!

ELBERT HUBBARD

Birth (New)

We really begin to live only when we are born twice.

———o———

Second Birth

I never loved the pleasant earth
So much as since my second birth!
The shy forget-me-not's soft blue
Seems bits of Heaven shining
through!
The golden buttercup's bright face
Proclaims the glory of *His* face.
The red of maples in the fall,
His precious Blood that washes all.
My sin forever far away,
As white as hawthorn buds in May —
The saints' new shining linen dress —
The robe of His own righteousness.
I touch the pansy's purple face —
His kingly majesty I trace.
Green pasture breathes refreshment,
rest,
And sweet communion on His breast;
While bird song from the orchard trees
Suggests celestial harmonies.
I see in river, hill and glen
New charms since I've been born
again!

LOIS REYNOLDS CARPENTER

Blessings

Whatever seeming calamity happens to you, if you thank God and praise him for it you turn it into a blessing.

WILLIAM LAW

———o———

God gives our blessings, but we have to take them.

———o———

Reflect upon your present blessings, of which every man has many; not on your past misfortunes, of which all men have some.

CHARLES DICKENS

———o———

Our Business

We are not store-rooms, but channels;
We are not cisterns, but springs;
Passing our benefits onward,
Fitting our blessings with wings;

Letting the water flow outward
To spread o'er the desert forlorn.
Sharing our bread with our brothers,
Our comfort with those who mourn.

AUTHOR UNKNOWN

———o———

Countless Blessings

For the quiet of the forest
And the grandeur of the hills,
For the glory of the sunsets
And the music of the rills,
For the flowers that bloom so sweetly
Along the woodland ways —
For these, and countless blessings,
Dear Lord, we render praise!

A. M. S. ROSSITER

———o———

The blessings we evoke for another descend upon ourselves.

EDMUND GIBSON

———o———

No Christian can be an "avenue" of blessing if he's not willing to cross the "street" to church.

NAT OLSON

———o———

With Blessings Everywhere

(Ezekiel 16:49)

Not only, Lord, in time of trial
Would I hold fast to Thee,
Not only when false friends revile,
Seek help on bended knee;
But also when victorious,

When pain has found release,
When all my way is glorious,
When I am filled with peace
Would I rejoice in Thee, my Friend,
For all the good that Thou dost send.
Not only then, when troubles breed
Would I seek Thee in prayer,
But also in the greater need
With blessings everywhere.
For in Thy holy Word, we know
Men seek Thee to be fed,
And then forget the thanks they owe
When they are filled with bread.
Thou callest this iniquity;
From it, O God, deliver me.

MILDRED ALLEN JEFFERY

Blind

My Personal Testimony

I cannot see that of which others tell:
The beauties of this earth on which we dwell;
The jeweled perfection of the starry sky;
Great sights that please and tantalize the eye.

But there are precious jewels which are not seen:
Things everlasting, wholesome, pure, and clean.
Such gems are found within God's Holy Book,
Wherein a man, though blind, may freely look.

And I have looked within that Book, and found
A source of perfect peace, a footing sound.
I've found, portrayed therein, a gracious Friend,
Whose tender loving care will never end.

So now I see His hand upon my life,
Directing all my way, through peace or strife;
And though my way is dark, I'm not alone;
With Christ I am content, while walking home.

ALVY E. FORD

Boast

Boasters by nature are from truth aloof.

GEOFFREY CHAUCER

———o———

There's less chance of your friends not letting you down if you don't build yourself up so high.

———o———

You can't push yourself ahead by patting yourself on the back.

———o———

The saying is true, "The empty vessel makes the greatest sound."

WILLIAM SHAKESPEARE, *King Henry V*

———o———

We rise in glory, as we sink in pride;
Where boasting ends, there dignity begins.

EDWARD YOUNG

———o———

Boasting is the refuge of those more able to talk than to do.

———o———

Deeds done and work accomplished need not be bolstered by words.

———o———

For every person who brags about being bright, there are a dozen ready to polish him off.

———o———

The trouble with singing your own praises is that you seldom get the right pitch.

ARNOLD GLASGOW

———o———

The trouble with blowing one's own horn is that it seldom leaves any wind for climbing.

———o———

Some folks would rather blow their own horn than listen to a military band.

Whenever you boast too much, you pray too little.
Whenever you pray too little, you act too soon.

Body

If there are a thousand miles of blood vessels in my body, if there are 1,500,000 sweat glands on its surface, if my lungs are composed of 700,000,-000 cells, if my heart-beats for a single day were "concentrated into one huge throb of vital power, it would be sufficient to throw a ton of iron 120 feet into the air" then, since it has already beat 3,000,000,000 times since I was born, and has lifted what would equal the weight of 600,000 tons, if my nervous system is controlled by a brain that has 3,000,000,000,000 nerve cells of which 9,200,000,000 are in the cortex or covering of the brain alone, and if in my veins there are 3,000,000 white corpuscles and 180,000,000,000,000 red ones — then it is *some job* for (it just to evolve) . . . I grant! It sounds to me more like the work of God!

The Psalmist wrote: "*I will praise Thee: for I am fearfully and wonderfully made.*" (Psalm 139:14).

W. B. RILEY

———o———

Our body is a wonderful engine of marvelous energy. Overfed, underfed, over-burdened, neglected, abused, weakened, shamefully talked about, yet it goes on generating from year to year the most divine thing in the universe — Life.

DR. CROFT

———o———

Definition Of Anatomy
(by a very small boy)

"Your head is kind of round and hard, and your brains are in it. Your hair is on it. Your face is the front of your head where you eat and make faces. Your neck is what keeps your head out of your collar. It is hard to keep clean . . . Your stummick is something that if you don't eat enough it hurts, and spinach don't help none. Your spine is a long bone in your back that keeps you from folding up. Your back is always behind you no matter how quick you turn around. Your arms you have to have to pitch with and so you can reach the butter. Your fingers stick out of your hand so you can throw a curve and add up rithmetic. Your legs is what if you have not got two of you can't get to first base. Your feet are what you run on; your toes are what always get stubbed. And that's all there is to you except what's inside and I never saw it."

———o———

God gave us two ears and one mouth to use in that proportion.

Bold

What you can do, or dream you can — begin it. Boldness has genius, power, and magic in it.

JOHANN WOLFGANG VON GOETHE

———o———

A minister without boldness is like a smooth file, a knife without an edge, a sentinel that is afraid to let off his gun. Men will be bold in sin, and ministers must be bold to reprove.

WILLIAM GURNALL

———o———

Be bold in what you stand for, but careful what you fall for.

———o———

Boldness is unembarrassed freedom of speech.

———o———

We make way for the man who boldly pushes past us.

———o———

He who never ventures will never cross the sea.

Books

A house without books is like a room without windows.

HORACE MANN

———o———

There is no reason to make either books or education easy, any more than

tennis or football is easy. . . . Books require a certain amount of hard work and practice and, like sports, they can be both a challenge and a delight.

GILBERT W. CHAPMAN

———o———

Books are the quietest and most constant of friends; they are the most accessible and wisest of counsellors, and the most patient of teachers.

CHARLES WILLIAM ELIOT

———o———

A book is a book only when it is in the hands of a reader. The rest of the time it is an artifact.

WILLIAM SLOANE

———o———

Get books and read and study them carefully.

ABRAHAM LINCOLN

———o———

When we are collecting books, we are collecting happiness.

VINCENT STARRETT

———o———

The books that help you most are those that make you think the most.

THEODORE PARKER

———o———

Even in life the best friendships are based not so much on propinquity and contact as on the touching of minds and spirits, and this is almost completely obtainable in a book.

MARY WRIGHT PLUMMER

———o———

Read not to contradict and confute; nor to believe and take for granted; nor to find talk and discourse; but to weigh and consider. Some books are to be tasted, others to be swallowed, and some few to be chewed and digested: that is, some books are to be read only in parts, others to be read, but not curiously; and some few to be read wholly, and with diligence and attention.

FRANCIS BACON, *Of Studies*

———o———

There are three schoolmasters for everybody that will employ them — the senses, intelligent companions, and books.

HENRY WARD BEECHER

———o———

Someone has said that the three most important books are the Bible, the Cook Book, and the Check Book.

———o———

A book is a success when people who haven't read it pretend they have.

———o———

The true University of these days is a Collection of Books.

THOMAS CARLYLE, *Heroes and Hero Worship*

———o———

But words are things, and a small drop of ink,
Falling like dew upon a thought, produces
That which makes thousands, perhaps millions, think.

LORD BYRON, *Don Juan*

———o———

It is a man's duty to have books. A library is not a luxury, but one of the necessaries of life.

HENRY WARD BEECHER

———o———

One man browsing in a bookstore is worth 100 men gathering in the market place.

———o———

Books are lighthouses erected in the great sea of time.

EDWIN PERCY WHIPPLE

———o———

A taste for books is the pleasure and glory of my life. I would not exchange it for the riches of the Indies.

EDWARD GIBBON

———o———

Except a living man there is nothing more wonderful than a book! A message to us from the dead — from human souls whom we never saw, who lived perhaps thousands of miles away; and yet these, on those little sheets of paper, speak to us, teach us, comfort us, open their hearts to us as brothers.

CHARLES KINGSLEY

A home without books and ideas can be almost as bad for a child as a broken home, an alcoholic home, or a criminal home, because it leaves a vacuum into which rush corrupting values.

MAX LERNER

———o———

The voice of books can be heard for years!

Sunshine Magazine

———o———

Marking Time

A book is more than printer's ink.
It is a friend who helps me think;
In a short time I can obtain
What took him many years to gain.

LUTHER MARKIN in *Sunshine Magazine*

———o———

Books are sepulchres of thought.

HENRY WADSWORTH LONGFELLOW

———o———

Books, the children of the brain.

JONATHAN SWIFT, *Tale of a Tub*

———o———

Wear the old coat and buy the new book.

AUSTIN PHELPS

———o———

Dreams, books are each a world;
And books, we know,
Are a substantial world,
Both pure and good;
Round these, with tendril strong
As flesh and blood,
Our pastime and our happiness
Will grow.

WILLIAM WORDSWORTH, *Personal Talk*

———o———

Since the invention of printing about 18,000,000 different titles of books have been published, and about one-third of these have appeared since 1960.

Bore, Boredom

Bore: a person who talks when you wish him to listen.

AMBROSE BIERCE

Some people can stay longer in an hour than others can in a week.

———o———

The secret of being a bore is to tell everything.

VOLTAIRE

———o———

We may forgive those who bore us, we cannot forgive those whom we bore.

FRANÇOIS, DUC DE LA ROCHEFOUCAULD

———o———

A man of learning is never bored.

JEAN PAUL RICHTER

———o———

Work is the best escape from boredom.

ELEANOR L. DOAN

———o———

America is said to have the highest per capita boredom of any spot on earth. We know because we have the greatest variety and number of artificial amusements of any country. People have become so empty that they can't even entertain themselves. They have to pay other people to amuse them, to make them happy and comfortable for a few minutes, to try to lose that awful, frightening, hollow feeling of being lost and alone.

BILLY GRAHAM

Borrow

Don't worry if you borrow, only if you lend.

Russian Proverb

———o———

The borrower runs in his own debt.

RALPH WALDO EMERSON

———o———

Neither a borrower nor a lender be;
For a loan oft loses both itself and friend,
And borrowing dulls the edge of husbandry.

WILLIAM SHAKESPEARE, *Hamlet*

Boys

Definition Of A Junior Boy

After a male baby has grown out of long clothes and triangles, and has acquired pants, freckles, and so much dirt that relatives don't dare to kiss it between meals, it becomes a boy. A boy is nature's answer to that false belief that there is no such thing as perpetual motion. A boy can swim like a fish, run like a deer, climb like a squirrel, balk like a mule, bellow like a bull, eat like a pig, or act like a fool. He is called a tornado because he comes in at the most unexpected times, hits most unexpected places, and leaves everything a wreck behind him. He is a piece of skin stretched over an appetite. A noise with smudges. He is a growing animal of superlative promise to be fed, watered, and kept warm; a joy forever, a periodic nuisance, the problem of our times, the hope of a nation.

Every boy born is evidence that God is not discouraged with man. Were it not for boys, newspapers would go unread and a thousand TV shows would go bankrupt. Boys are useful in running errands. A boy can easily do the family errands with the help of five or six adults. The zest with which a boy does an errand is equaled only by the speed of a turtle on a hot day in July.

The boy is a natural spectator. He watches parades, fires, ballgames, automobiles, boats, and airplanes with equal fervor, but will not watch the clock. The man who invents a clock that will stand on its head and sing a song when it strikes will win the undying gratitude of millions of families whose boys are forever coming to lunch about suppertime. Boys faithfully imitate their dads in spite of all efforts to teach them good manners. A boy, if not washed too often and if kept in a cool, quiet place after each accident, will survive broken bones, hornets, swimming holes, fights, and nine helpings of pie.

AUTHOR UNKNOWN

———o———

A boy becomes a man when he wears out the seat of his pants instead of the soles of his shoes.

———o———

Small boys are washable, though most of them shrink from it.

Times, Fort Mill, S.C.

Diamonds In The Rough

A diamond in the rough
Is a diamond sure enough,
For, before it ever sparkled,
It was made of diamond stuff.
Of course someone must find it
Or it never will be found.
And then, someone must grind it
Or it never will be ground.

But when it's found, and when it's
    ground
And when it's burnished bright,
That diamond's everlastingly
Flashing out its radiant light.
O! Christian, please, who'er you be,
Don't say you've done enough,
That worst boy in the class may be
A Diamond in the Rough.

AUTHOR UNKNOWN

A Little Boy In Church

He ruffles through his hymn book,
He fumbles with his tie,
He laces up his oxfords,
He overworks a sigh;
He goes through all his pockets,
Engrossed in deep research;
There's no one quite so busy
As a little boy in church.

THELMA IRELAND

A boy is a bank where you can deposit your most precious treasures — the hard won wisdom, the dreams of a better world. A boy can guard and protect these, and perhaps invest them wisely and with a profit — a profit larger than you ever dreamed. A boy will inherit your world. All the work will be judged by him. Tomorrow he will take your seat in Congress, own your company, run your town. The future is his and through him the future is yours. Perhaps he deserves a little more attention now.

SOURCE UNKNOWN

For Any Mother Of A Small Boy

Was it for this I rendered sterile
Bottles, blankets, and apparel,
Scrubbed and boiled and disinfected,
Let no one touch unless inspected,
That now, quite innocent of soap,
My erstwhile pride, my one-time hope,
In spite of all the books assert
Should thrive on good old-fashioned
    dirt?

ELIZABETH-ELLEN LONG

Seven Year Old

STEM the force behind a tide!
Have you tried?

Direct the hurricane's wild path,
Appease its wrath;

Reduce the forest's red-tongued flames
With words and names;

Then you have curbed with order's
    rules
Beyond the power of sages, fools,

What's in a boy!

Electric, alien, proud creation!
But you'll have silenced the ovation
Nature raised to Joy!

IDA ELAINE JAMES
in *The Christian Parent*

A little girl was once asked to write an essay on boys. She wrote: Boys are noisy, pesty, and dirty. They hate soap and never wash themselves. They have bugs and worms in their pockets. I don't want to play with them. But girls are nice. They are quiet and play together in a ladylike way. My daddy must have been a little girl when he was a little boy because he is so nice.

Church School Teacher

Among the papers of the late Dr. Harper of the University of Chicago was found a memorandum which read like this:
"If I were a boy again, I would strive to find out from good books how good men lived.
"If I were a boy again I would more and more cultivate the company of those whose graces of person and mind would help me on in my work. I would always seek good company.
"If I were a boy again, I would study the life and character of our

Savior persistently, that I might become more and more like Him.

"If I were a boy again, I would study the Bible even more than I did. The Bible is a necessity to every boy."

War Cry

Brain

You must nourish the brain as well as the body. The man who despises music as a luxury and non-essential is doing the Nation an injury.

THOMAS ALVA EDISON

———o———

I use not only all the brains I have, but all I can borrow.

WOODROW WILSON

———o———

As we sit and watch the train go by, along with a hundred other autoists, it occurs to us that the human brain is somewhat like a freight car, guaranteed to have a certain capacity, but too often running empty.

———o———

The Brain

The top-floor apartment in the Human Block, known as the Cranium, and kept by the Sarah Sisters — Sarah Brum and Sarah Belum, assisted by Medulla Oblongata. All three are nervous, but are always confined to their cells. The Brain is done in gray and white and furnished with light and heat, hot or cold water, (if desired), with regular connections to the outside world by way of the Spinal Circuit. Usually occupied by the Intellect Bros. — Thoughts and Ideas — as an Intelligence Office.

———o———

The brain is as strong as its weakest think.

———o———

Our brains, like our bodies, don't come with a set of directions attached.

KEYES

———o———

A brain is known by its fruit.

H. G. WELLS

Brave, Bravery

Bravery is the capacity to perform properly even when scared half to death.

OMAR BRADLEY

———o———

The brave man seeks not honor of man but does always the best he can.

———o———

The brave man is not one who feels no fear, but one who conquers his fear and boldly does his duty.

Brevity

A short saying often carries much wisdom.

SOPHOCLES

———o———

'Tis better to be brief, than tedious.

WILLIAM SHAKESPEARE

———o———

Brevity is the best recommendation of speech, whether in a senator or an orator.

MARCUS TULLIUS CICERO

———o———

Whatever you teach, be brief, that your readers' minds may readily comprehend and faithfully retain your words. Everything superfluous slips from the full heart.

HORACE

———o———

Have something to say; say it, and stop when you've done.

TRYON EDWARDS

———o———

Brevity is very good when we are, or are not, understood.

SAMUEL BUTLER

———o———

Brevity is not a virtue; it is a result. In a word, if you would be brief, first be long. To make a telephone conversation short, think it over and anticipate as far as possible what needs to be said. To make . . . an annual report pointed, let it first be written in fullness, or at least outlined in some . . . detail. Only then will it be possible to make it brief.

CHARLES W. FERGUSON in *THINK*

Bride

Dear Bride

Love in your heart . . . a ring on your
    finger;
Flowers in your hand . . . a groom to
    share life with;
The prospect of a future family of your
    own.
What more could a woman ask for?
You stand there, hands slightly trem-
    bling
Yet with confidence in your heart —
Confident that yours will be the "per-
    fect marriage."
And it can be just that!
O, there will be those well-meaning
    friends
Who will tell you otherwise.
But don't you listen to them in their
    unhappiness.
If you will keep the love you feel to-
    day;
If you will guard the confidence you
    sense today,
Yours can be "a bit of heaven on earth."
Go walking daily with your lover
Through the pages of God's Word, es-
    pecially I Corinthians 13
For there you will find the secret of
    "abiding love" that never fails!

NAT OLSON
in *The Log of the Good Ship Grace*

———o———

Two Brides

A faithful bride, in garments spotless,
    fair,
    Is waiting, watching, for her coming
    lord.
She knows that he will quickly meet
    her there
    Because she has the promise of his
    word.

The Bride of Christ, in garments spot-
    less, fair,
    Is waiting, watching, for her coming
    Lord.
She knows that she will meet Him in
    the air
    Because she has the promise of His
    Word.

EMMA BELLE YOURDON in *Today*

A wise bride is one who loses her
temper — permanently.

HAL CHADWICK

Build

Building For The Future

The angels from their thrones on high
    Look down on us with wondering
    eye,
That where we are but passing guests
    We build such strong and solid nests;
And where we hope to dwell for aye
    We scarce take heed a stone to lay.

The Sunday School Times

———o———

Why Build?

We are all blind until we see
That in the human plan
Nothing is worth the making, if
It does not make the man.

Why build those cities glorious
If man unbuilded goes?
In vain, we build the work, unless
The builder also grows.

EDWIN MARKHAM, *Man-Making*

———o———

The loftier the building the deeper
must the foundation be laid.

THOMAS À KEMPIS

No matter what your lot, build something on it.

———o———

You cannot erect a sound super-
structure on a foundation of thinking
based upon error.

———o———

I watched them tearing a building
    down,
A gang of men in a busy town.
With a ho-heave-ho and a lusty yell,
They swung a beam, and the sidewall
    fell.
I asked the foreman: "Are these men
    skilled?
"And the men you'd hire if you had to
    build?"
He gave a laugh and said: "No, in-
    deed
"Just common labor is all I need.

"With them I can wreck in a day or
two,
"What builders have taken years to do."
So I thought to myself as I went my
way,
Which of these roles have I tried to
play?
Am I a builder who works with care,
Measuring life by the rule and square?
Am I shaping my deeds to a well made
plan,
Patiently doing the best I can?
Or am I a wrecker, who walks the
town,
Content with the labor of tearing
down?

AUTHOR UNKNOWN

Burden

The greatest burden we have to carry
in life is self. The most difficult thing
we have to manage is self.

HANNAH WHITALL SMITH

———o———

Pray not for lighter burdens but for
stronger backs.

THEODORE ROOSEVELT

———o———

None knows the weight of another's
burthen.

GEORGE HERBERT, *Jacula Prudentum*

———o———

Burdens become light when cheerfully borne.

OVID

———o———

A biologist tells how he watched an
ant carrying a piece of straw which
seemed almost too heavy for it to drag.
The ant came to a crack in the ground
which was too big for it to cross. It
stood still for a time, as though perplexed by the situation, then put the
straw across the crack and walked over
on the straw.

If only we were as wise as that ant!
We speak much about the burdens
we must bear. But have we ever
thought of converting our burdens into
bridges, of having our burdens bear *us*
up instead of us bearing *them* up?

The Log of the Good Ship Grace

Not the load but the overload kills.

Spanish Proverb

———o———

The story is told of a poor man who
plodded along toward home in an Irish
town carrying a huge bag of potatoes.
A horse and wagon carrying a stranger
came along, and the stranger stopped
the wagon and invited the man on foot
to climb inside. This the poor man
did, but when he sat down in the
wagon he held the bag of potatoes in
his arms. And when it was suggested
that he should set it down, he said very
warmly: "Sure, I don't like to trouble
you too much. You're giving me a ride.
I'll carry the potatoes!"

Sometimes we think we are doing
the Lord a favor when we carry the
burden. But the work is His, and the
burden is His, and He asks us only to
be faithful.

ISAAC PAGE

———o———

Our Burden Bearer

The little sharp vexations
And the briars that catch and fret,
Why not take all to the Helper
Who has never failed us yet?

Tell Him about the heartache,
And tell Him the longings, too;
Tell Him the baffled purpose
When we scarce know what to do.

Then, leaving all our weakness
With One divinely strong,
Forget that we bore the burden,
And carry away the song.

PHILLIPS BROOKS

———o———

Everyone thinks his own burden
heavy.

French Proverb

Business

A Busy Business Man's Prayer

Take my wife and let her be
Consecrated, Lord, to Thee.
Take her moments and her days;
Leave me mine for my own ways.

Take my weekly offering
That so grudgingly I bring

Yet report as 10 per cent
So that more will be exempt.

Take my voice and let me pray
Sundays — maybe twice that day;
Otherwise, O Lord, my mother
Handles prayers for me and others.

Take my children, show them how
Respect is due me here and now;
Make them do just what I say,
Not to follow in my way.

Finally, Lord, at end of life
Make me faithful as my wife,
That together we may be
Ever, only, all for Thee!

FRANCES R. LONGINO

Sign in store window: "This is a non-profit organization — please help us change."

Business Trends

"My business is looking up," said the astronomer.
"Mine is all write," declared the author.
"Mine is growing," boasted the farmer.
"Mine is picking up," chuckled the cheerful rag picker.
"Mine is just sew, sew," ventured the tailor.
"Mine is looking better," smiled the optician.
"Mine is pretty light," snapped the electric light man.

Sunshine Magazine

To be a success in business: Be daring, be first, be different.

MARCHANT

Business makes a man, as well as tries him.

No business is a success which must ruin men to make money.

ROY L. SMITH

Success or failure in business is caused more by mental attitude even than by mental capacities.

WALTER DILL SCOTT

The men who made fortunes in business always precede, never follow, the crowd.

Some people regard private enterprise as a predatory tiger to be shot. Others look on it as a cow they can milk. Not enough people see it as a healthy horse pulling a sturdy wagon.

SIR WINSTON CHURCHILL

Busy

Too Busy

"I sometimes think we are in danger of being too busy to be really useful," said an old lady, thoughtfully. "We hear so much about making every minute count, that there is no place left for small wayside kindnesses. We visit the sick neighbor, and relieve the poor neighbor, but for the common, everyday neighbor, who has not fallen by the way, we haven't a minute to spare. But everybody who needs a cup of cold water isn't calling the fact out to the world. There are a great many little pauses by the way which are no waste time."

SELECTED

If You Were Busy

If you were busy being kind,
Before you knew it you would find
You'd soon forget to think 'twas true
That someone was unkind to you.

If you were busy being glad,
And cheering people who are sad,
Although your heart might ache a bit,
You'd soon forget to notice it.

If you were busy being good,
And doing just the best you could,
You'd not have time to blame some man
Who's doing just the best he can.

If you were busy being true
To what you know you ought to do,
You'd be so busy you'd forget
The blunders of the folks you've met.

If you were busy being right,
You'd find yourself too busy, quite,
To criticize your neighbor long
Because he's busy being wrong.

REBECCA FORESMAN

Too Busy?

You are too busy this morning
In the maelstrom of family care,
The husband must rush to the office,
So there isn't a moment for prayer?

The children are sent to the school-
room,
And the grind of the day then begins
With no Word from God to remember,
Nor the echo of strengthening hymns?

What wonder the burdens seem heavy
And the hours seem irksomely long!
What wonder that rash words are spo-
ken
And life seems discordant and wrong!

Oh, pause for a little each morning
And again at the close of the day,
To talk to the Master, who loves you.
Remember, He taught us to pray!
AUTHOR UNKNOWN

———o———

If you're too busy to read God's Word,
If you're too busy to pray,
If you're too busy to hear His voice,
You're too busy today.

———o———

I Was Too Busy

The Lord Christ wanted a tongue one
day
To speak a message of cheer
To a heart that was weary and worn
and sad,
And weighed with a mighty fear.
He asked me for mine, but 'twas busy
quite
With my own affairs from morn till
night.

The Lord Christ wanted a hand one
day
To do a loving deed;
He wanted two feet, on an errand for
Him
To run with gladsome speed.
But I had need of my own that day;
To his gentle beseeching I answered,
"Nay!"

So all that day I used my tongue,
My hands, and my feet as I chose;
I said some hasty, bitter words
That hurt one heart, God knows.
I busied my hands with worthless play,
And my wilful feet went a crooked way.

And the dear Lord Christ, was His
work undone
For lack of a willing heart?
Only through men does He speak to
men?
Dumb must He be apart?
I do not know, but I wish today
I had let the Lord Christ have His way.
Christian Endeavor World

C

Call

The Call of Calls

I am the everlasting Christ.
I stand and call from the heights,
   in the places of the paths,
      at the coming in at the doors,
And my voice is to the sons of men.

Hear, for I will speak of excellent
      things,
   and my mouth shall say truth:
The life which I am
   is better than rubies
      and fine gold
         and choice silver;
Earth has nothing to compare with it.

Counsel is mine, and sound wisdom;
I am understanding, I am strength.
I lead in the wheelruts of righteousness,
In the paths of justice;
For it is by me that rulers declare
   what is just.
The kind of honor and substance that
      I give
   is the kind that endures.

To seek me early is to find me,
   for I love those who love me,
And my delight is with the sons of
      men,
   to endow them
      with the treasures of their hearts.

It has always been this way;
I was with the Father from the be-
    ginning;
Before the hills were did I set forth
    to teach men to hate the evil way,
    to live in me and for me
        and to rejoice in the dowry of
        earth.

Hear instruction, then, and be wise:
Watch for me, wait for me, listen for
    me;
Discern the riffling of the water,
    the waving of the treetops,
        the moving of the Spirit,
Lest you fall in love with death
    and lose out on eternity.

The man who finds me finds life,
    the only real life there is,
        in the favor of the Lord.
            Adapted from Proverbs 8:2-35

————o————

There is a terrible fact that if I
hadn't heard the call of Christ, I might
have been a physician in Harley Street
being driven about in my Rolls-Royce.
                    SIR WILFRED GRENFELL,
                a missionary to Labrador

Camp

Summer camps are places where little boys and girls go for mother's vacation.

————o————

Counselor to new boy at camp: "We
want you to be happy, so enjoy yourself here. If there's something you want
we haven't got, I'll show you how to
get along without it."

————o————

Thank You, God

Thank you, God, for all these things —
    For the moon, the stars and the sun;
Thank you for the beautiful sky
    When the day has just begun.

Thank you, God, for mountains high,
    Thank you for the trees;
Thank you for all creatures that live;
    For the mighty, crashing seas.

Thank you for my friends so dear,
    Thank you for my family;

Thank you for the whole wide world,
    And especially, God, for me.

Thank you for Jesus Christ
    And all that He has done,
That we may go to heaven
    And live with Thee as one.

*This poem was written by a ten-year-old
girl at Forest Home Christian Conference
Center, Calif.*

Can't

The man who says, "It can't be done,"
is liable to be interrupted by someone
doing it.

————o————

It can't be done, it never has been
done; therefore I will do it.

————o————

When someone says something can't
be done, it only means *he* can't do it.

————o————

"I can't do it" never yet accomplished anything; "I will try" has performed wonders.

                    GEORGE P. BURNHAM

Care

If a care is too small to be turned
into a prayer, it is too small to be made
into a burden.

————o————

Careful For Nothing

Casting all your care upon Him; for He careth
for you. (I Peter 5:7)

Cease your thinking, troubled Chris-
    tian;
    What avail your anxious cares;
God is ever thinking for you,
    Jesus every burden bears.
Casting all your care upon Him,
    Sink into His blessed will;
While He folds you to His bosom,
    Sweetly whispering, "Peace be still."

Jesus knows the way He leads me,
    I have but to hold His hand;
Nothing from His thought is hidden,
    Why need I to understand?

Let me, like the loved disciple,
  Hide my head upon His breast;
Till upon His faithful bosom,
  All my cares are hushed to rest.
                              A. B. SIMPSON

———o———

Millions dying there have never heard.
Millions living here have never cared.

———o———

Out In The Fields

The little cares that fretted me,
  I lost them yesterday
Among the fields above the sea,
  Among the winds at play;
Among the lowing of the herds,
  The rustling of the trees,
Among the singing of the birds,
  The humming of the bees.

The foolish fears of what may happen,
  I cast them all away
Among the clover-scented grass,
  Among the new-mown hay;
Among the hushing of the corn
  Where drowsy poppies nod,
Where ill thoughts die and good are
    born,
  Out in the fields with God.
                              ANONYMOUS

———o———

"It Matters To Him About You"

Casting all your care upon Him; for He careth
for you. (I Peter 5:7)

Be not troubled with thought of the
    morrow —
Of duties you surely must do —
On the Lord cast thy burden of sor-
    row —
"It matters to Him about you!"

Be not weary in fighting with Satan —
But, buckle His armour so true —
He will make all your troubles to
    straighten —
"It matters to Him about you!"

Be patient, until His appearing —
'Tis dawn, almost, now, on your
    view —
The mists of this dark age are clear-
    ing —
"He is planning in love about you!"
                              AUTHOR UNKNOWN

Challenge

These Slogans are Timely

Have voice . . . . will invite
Have phone . . . . will call
Have pen . . . . . will write
Have interest . . . will come
Have car . . . . . will bring
Have concern . . . will pray
Have ability . . . . will use
Have conviction . . will share
Have hope . . . . will rejoice
Have money . . . . will tithe

———o———

Before Napoleon Bonaparte invaded
Russia, he told the Russian ambassador
that he would destroy that empire. The
ambassador's reply was, "Man proposes,
but God disposes." "Tell your master,"
thundered the arrogant and self-con-
fident Corsican, "that I am he that
proposes, and I am he that disposes."
It was a challenge to the living God
to show who was the ruler of this
world, and God accepted the challenge.
He moved not from His august throne.
But He sent one of His most humble
messengers, the crystal snowflake, from
Heaven to punish the audacious boaster. Napoleon flung his army into Mos-
cow, but in his retreat he left on the
frozen plains the bulk of his vast army,
and the official returns of the Russian
authorities reported 213,516 French
corpses and 95,816 dead horses.
                              A. T. PIERSON

———o———

Never challenge another to do
wrong, lest he sin at thy bidding.

———o———

Flaming Torch

That flaming torch — it fell,
It fell among the trees,
Cut down by cruel hands.
It fell, and falling cast
Long shadows on the ground,
Shadows of men in chains,
Shadows of prison walls.

It fell, and yet it burns —
Not smoldering, not flickering,
But sending up long fingers
To the sky,

Fingers that point,
Fingers that plead,
Fingers that beckon me
To quit this life of deadly ease
And lift that torch on high.

O God,
And shall my heart
Be cold —
When men go out to die
For Thee?

E.L.S., *Source Unknown*

Chance

Chance is a nickname for Providence.
SEBASTIEN R. N. CHAMFORT,
Maxims and Thoughts

———o———

The successful man is one who had the chance and took it.
ROGER BABSON

———o———

Every day gives you another chance.

———o———

Chances rule men and not men chances.
HERODOTUS

Change

When one life is changed, the world is changed.
THOMAS L. JOHNS

———o———

Blessed is the man who has discovered that there is nothing permanent in life but change.
A. P. GOUTHEY

———o———

A wise man changes his mind, a fool never.
Spanish Proverb

———o———

Changing one thing for the better does more good than proving a dozen things are wrong.

———o———

Lincoln used to tell the story of a man who heated a piece of iron in the forge, not knowing just what he was going to make out of it. At first he thought he would make a horseshoe; then he changed his mind and thought he would make something else out of it. After he had hammered on this design for a little while, he changed his mind and started on something else. By this time, he had so hammered the iron that it was not good for much of anything; and, holding it up with his tongs, and looking at it in dusgust, the blacksmith thrust it hissing into a tub of water. "Well, at least I can make a fizzle out of it!" he exclaimed.
CLARENCE E. MACARTNEY

———o———

The past cannot be altered; the future can.

Character

You can't carve rotten wood.
Chinese Proverb

———o———

Character is a victory, not a gift.
Try Square

———o———

A wise observer of human nature once said that a sure test of a person's character was for him to list honestly what things are luxuries to him and what are necessities. Try it. The result will show what kind of a person you are. Under the heading "necessities," some people will put down such items as an expensive car, a house in a "nice" neighborhood, fashionable clothes, membership in exclusive clubs. These will soon crowd out things needed for the life of the soul. Other people will put down as necessities integrity and independence of spirit, no matter what they cost in social approval. They will put down the religious quality and influence of the home, and the sharing of one's goods in the work of the Kingdom of God. What are the "necessities" of life to you?

———o———

You cannot dream yourself into a character; you must hammer and forge yourself into one.
JAMES ANTHONY FROUDE

———o———

The grand aim of man's creation is the development of a grand character — and grand character is, by its very nature, the product of probationary discipline.
AUSTIN PHELPS

Reputation is what you have on arrival. Character is what you have on departure.

———o———

A river becomes crooked by following the line of least resistance! So does a man!

———o———

Character is like the foundation to a house . . . it is below the surface.

———o———

Youth and beauty fade; character endures forever.

———o———

A noble character is the sum of many ordinary days well used.

———o———

Persons with any weight of character carry, like planets, their atmosphere along with them in their orbits.

THOMAS HARDY

———o———

Character is Destiny.

HERACLITUS

———o———

Character cannot be made except by a steady, long continued process.

PHILLIPS BROOKS

———o———

The measure of a man's real character is what he would do if he knew he would never be found out.

THOMAS BABINGTON MACAULAY

———o———

How a man plays the game, shows something of his character. How he loses, shows all of it.

———o———

Character is a by-product; it is produced in the great manufacture of daily duty.

WOODROW WILSON

———o———

Reputation is what men think we are; character is what God knows we are.

LEVIER

———o———

If I take care of my character, my reputation will take care of itself.

DWIGHT L. MOODY

In times like these it is our task to build into America's children what psychologists call 'internalized systems.' This capacity for self-discipline is called character: the building of character is a life-long process; it is built at the mother's knee — and sometimes over the mother's knee.

REV. FRED GREVE
in The Log of the Good Ship Grace

———o———

Every man has three characters: that which he exhibits, that which he has, and that which he thinks he has.

A. KARR

———o———

A man shows what he is by what he does with what he has.

———o———

Character is not a gift but an achievement.

H. A. PARK

Charity

It is not charity to any man to give him what he needs. Offer him an opportunity to earn what he needs and you are his benefactor.

———o———

People who have no charity for the faults of others are generally stoneblind to their own!

———o———

What Is Charity?

It's silence when your words would hurt;
It's patience when your neighbor's curt;
It's deafness when the scandal flows;
It's thoughtfulness for another's woes;
It's promptness when stern duty calls;
It's courage when misfortune falls.

World Christian Digest

———o———

Real charity doesn't care if it's tax-deductible or not.

DAN BENNETT

———o———

Charity is a virtue of the heart, and not of the hands.

JOSEPH ADDISON, *The Guardian*

Feel for others — in your pocket.
CHARLES HADDON SPURGEON

Charm

"Charm" — which means the power to effect work without employing brute force — is indispensable to women.

Charm is a woman's strength just as strength is a man's charm.
HAVELOCK ELLIS

———o———

Prescription For Charm

For *lips* — truth, kind, words, and a smile.

For *eyes* — friendliness and sympathetic understanding.

For *ears* — courteous attention and wholesome listening.

For *hands* — honest work and thoughtful deeds.

For *figure* — helpful and right living.

For *voice* — prayer, praise, and the lilt of joy.

For *heart* — love for God, for life, and for others.
AUTHOR UNKNOWN

Cheerful

A cheerful heart makes its own blue sky.

———o———

Brightening up the life of someone else will put a fresh shine on your own.

———o———

Give a cheerful, kind and courteous answer to the meanest grouch (if there is such a person) and you are mighty sure to have a kind answer in return.

———o———

Well, you're richer tonight than you were this morning, if a little child has smiled at you, or a stray dog has licked your hand, or if you have managed to be cheerful even though harassed and troubled.

———o———

Cheerfulness keeps up a kind of daylight in the mind, and fills it with a steady and perpetual serenity.
JOSEPH ADDISON, *The Spectator*

Cheerfulness means a contented spirit; a pure heart, a kind and loving disposition; it means humility and charity, a generous appreciation of others, and a modest opinion of self.
WILLIAM MAKEPEACE THACKERAY

———o———

Cheerful people, the doctors say, resist disease better than the glum ones. In other words, the surly bird catches the germ.

———o———

Merely to share another's burden is noble. To do it cheerfully is sublime.

———o———

Cheerfulness and content are great beautifiers, and are famous preservers of youthful looks.
CHARLES DICKENS

Children

Let Me Guide A Little Child!

Dear Lord, I do not ask
That Thou should'st give me some high work of Thine,
Some noble calling, or some wondrous task.
Give me a little hand to hold in mine;
Give me a little child to point the way
Over the strange, sweet path that leads to Thee;
Give me a little voice to teach to pray;
Give me two shining eyes Thy face to see.
The only crown I ask, dear Lord to wear
Is this: that I may teach a little child.
I do not ask that I may ever stand
Among the wise, the worthy, or the great;
I only ask that softly, hand in hand,
A child and I may enter at the gate.
AUTHOR UNKNOWN

———o———

The most important in child training is love.
REX

———o———

We are apt to forget that children watch examples better than they listen to preaching.
ROY L. SMITH

Children are what we make them.
French Proverb

———o———

The Heart Of A Child

The heart of a child is a tremulous
thing;
Lovely and frail as a butterfly's wing.

Kissed by the beam of a summer sun,
Or crushed by the word of a careless
one.

A look or a smile will cause it to sing,
For the heart of a child is a tremulous
thing.
                         MILLICENT M. SLABY

———o———

Be careful of your life lest a child
stumble over you.

———o———

Children are contagious to character
and conduct.

———o———

I love little children, and it is not a
slight thing when they, who are fresh
from God, love us.
                         CHARLES DICKENS

———o———

A torn jacket is soon mended, but
hard words bruise the heart of a child.
                 HENRY WADSWORTH LONGFELLOW

———o———

Mothers who raise
A child by the book,
Can, if sufficiently vexed,
Hasten results
By applying the book
As well as the text.
                         Evangelical Beacon

———o———

The thing most apt to drive a parent
wild,
Is a child behaving like a child.

———o———

Children: Today's investment, tomorrow's dividend.

———o———

The Child's Appeal

I am the Child.
All the world waits for my coming.
All the earth watches with interest to
see what
I shall become.
Civilization hangs in the balance,
For what I am, the world of tomorrow
will be.

I am the Child.
I have come into your world, about
which
I know nothing.
Why I came I know not;
How I came I know not.
I am curious; I am interested.

I am the Child.
You hold in your hand my destiny.
You determine, largely, whether I shall
succeed or fail.
Give me, I pray you, those things that
make
for happiness.
Train me, I beg you, that I may be a
blessing
to the world.
                         MAMIE GENE COLE

———o———

Trail Of Woe

There's a well-trodden path from nursery to sink
From eternal nocturnally fetching his
drink.
                 PAT CUNNINGHAM in *Home Life*

———o———

Personalized Music

In spite of all the toys I buy
Equipped with "built-in" tunes
My child prefers to improvise
With my best *pans* and *spoons!*
                         CATHERINE CLARK

———o———

Four

It's such a sweet and helpful age;
Too bad it's just a passing stage.
                 ALICE CHANDLER DUCH in *Home Life*

———o———

There's no faith like that of children.
They know that God is quiet and calm
and wonderful — big and interested in
them, and kind. Their requests of God
usually are reasonable and honest,

modest. They seldom ask for more than they deserve. They know of no reason why the world, in fact, shouldn't be mostly good.

Leader, Stuttgart, Ark.

———o———

Children are God's apostles sent forth, day by day, to preach of love, and hope and peace.

JAMES RUSSELL LOWELL

———o———

Those that allow and countenance their children in any evil way and do not use their authority to restrain and punish them, do in effect honor them more than God being more tender of their reputation than of His glory, and more desirous to humor them than to honor Him.

MATTHEW HENRY

———o———

Children begin by loving their parents; as they grow older they judge them; sometimes they forgive them.

OSCAR WILDE, *The Picture of Dorian Gray*

———o———

Some Children Are . . .

Some children are brown
  like newly baked bread,
some children are yellow
  and some are red,
some children are white
  and some almost blue.
Their colors are different —
  the children like you!

Some children eat porridge
  and some eat figs,
some children like ice-cream
  and some roasted pigs!
Some eat raw fishes
  and some Irish stew —
Their likings are different —
  the children like you!

Some children say "yes"
  and some say "oui"
some say "ja"
  and some say "si,"
some children say "peep,"
  and some say "booh —"
Their words may be different
  the children like you!

Some children wear sweaters
  and some rebozos,
some children wear furs
  and some kimonos,
some children go naked
  and wear only their queue.
Their clothes may be different —
  the children like you!

Some children have houses
  of stone in the streets,
some live in igloos,
  and some live on fleets.
Some live in old strawhuts
  and some in new —
Their homes may be different —
  the children like you!

Oh, if they could dance
  and if they could play
altogether together
  a wonderful day!
Some could come sailing
  and some could just hike!
So much would be different —
  the children alike!

JO TENJFORD

———o———

Children now love luxury, have bad manners, contempt for authority, show disrespect for their elders, and love chatter in place of exercise. Children are now tyrants, not the servants of their households. They no longer rise when elders enter the room. They contradict their parents, chatter before company, gobble up their dainties at table, cross their legs and tyrannize over their teachers.

SOCRATES

———o———

First talk to God about your children — Then talk to your children about God.

———o———

Rearing children is like drafting a blueprint; you have to know where to draw the line.

———o———

Our earnest suggestion to the person who feels that she has been hurrying through life a bit too fast and has, in the process, grown a bit indifferent to life: Take the hand of a three-year-old

and walk with him two or three blocks.
The child can do to a person what any
amount of philosophizing cannot.

News-Herald, Morning Sun, Iowa

———o———

Father our children keep!
  We know not what is coming on the
    earth;
Beneath the shadow of Thy heavenly
    wing
  O keep them, keep them, Thou who
    gav'st them birth.

Father, draw nearer us!
  Draw firmer round us Thy protecting
    arm;
Oh, clasp our children closer to Thy
    side,
  Uninjured in the day of earth's alarm.

Oh, keep them undefiled!
  Unspotted from a tempting world of
    sin;
That, clothed in white, through the
    bright city gates,
  They may, with us, in triumph enter
    in.

HORATIUS BONAR

———o———

The Child Was Shy

The child was shy.
One moist hand
Clung tightly to her mother.
Quite close she stood,
Her head pressed hard
Against her dress.
But between two fingers
A troubled eye
Peered into a strange, new world,
The Nursery Room.
For a long time she stood —
Afraid.

And then she saw
A small, familiar thing —
A crooked house
Built out of blocks.
Slowly she made her way
Across the room,
Forgetful of its strangeness.
And as her hand
Caught up a block,
She smiled back at her mother.
"You can go," she said,
"I think I'll build a house."

AUTHOR UNKNOWN

The Faith Of A Child

As I tucked my little boy into bed and
    waited
for the prayers he always said,
He closed his eyes, and with his hands
    held
tight, said "Jesus, I'm tired, so I'll
just say good night."
And the smile on his face showed a
    faith so
grand that I knew in my heart God
would understand.

As I left him all snuggled with peace
    and content,
I thought to myself if I was this con-
    fident,
And this child-like faith was at my
    command,
so I'd put my hand in the nail-scarred
    hand
And leave it there all nestled tight so
    God
would guide me day and night.
I'd have no fear of the future then for
    my
broken dreams I know He'd mend,
And if life at times seemed hard to
    take I'd
know my God had made no mistake.
I'd just hold tighter to His arm and
    He would
quiet the raging storm.

Some folk would say such a faith is
    "blind"
and think they had it well defined.
But I've never seen any brighter eyes
    than
those of a child who completely
    relies
On the mighty grace of God above and
    there
abides within His love.

VELMA WOODS
in *Log of the Good Ship Grace*

———o———

Children's Beatitudes

Blessed is the child who has someone who believes in him, to whom he
can carry his problems unafraid.

Blessed is the child who is allowed
to pursue his curiosity into every worthwhile field of information.

Blessed is the child who has someone who understands that childhood's griefs are real and call for understanding and sympathy.

Blessed is the child who has about him those who realize his need of Christ as Saviour and will lead him patiently and prayerfully to the place of acceptance.

Blessed is the child whose love of the true, the beautiful, and the good has been nourished through the years.

Blessed is the child whose imagination has been turned into channels of creative effort.

Blessed is the child whose efforts to achieve have found encouragement and kindly commendation.

Blessed is the child who has learned freedom from selfishness through responsibility and cooperation with others.

AUTHOR UNKNOWN

——o——

Sayings And Stories Of Children

PRESCHOOL AGES

Three-year-old Nancy was going down the stairs, holding a cup and saucer.

"Be careful you don't fall down the steps, dear!" her mother called out to her.

"Oh, that's all right, Mother. I won't fall," Nancy replied blithely. "I'm holding real tight to the cup."

ALICE CHRISTIE in *The Instructor*

——o——

Three children were debating whether they dared take candy mints to church to eat during the service.

"Mother wouldn't let us," Terry warned.

"Then put them in my pocket," the smallest volunteered. "She thinks I'm too little to know better."

REX CAMPBELL in *Together*

——o——

My small daughter had spent some time with her grandmother and broke something for which she had been reprimanded.

A few days later, she was listening

to a discussion a friend and I were having about weapons, and afterward my daughter asked me what the word meant. I answered that it usually referred to an object that did damage.

She thought about this for a moment, then asked in a little voice, "Mother, am I a weapon?"

MRS. W. H. DE MOURE in *Coronet*

——o——

Little Mary was visiting her grandmother in the country. Walking in the garden, Mary chanced to see a peacock, a bird that she had never seen before.

After gazing in silent admiration, she ran into the house and cried out: "Oh, Granny, come and see! One of your chickens is in bloom!"

Christian Herald

——o——

When my baby brother was three or four years old, he had to be watched quite closely as he liked to play with kitchen knives.

One day, however, he did manage to sneak a sharp, pointed paring knife out of the house. He carried it carefully across the fields to where my uncle worked at quite a distance from home. Handing it to him he said, "Please put this in your pocket so the kids don't get it."

MRS. R. J. G. in *The Christian Parent*

——o——

Grandmother brought home some lovely color books and crayons to her little four-year-old granddaughter, Vickie. She did not want the little girl to mark the book carelessly, so she patiently tried to show her how to color within the confines of the book. Vickie did her best, but Grandmother wanted her to do better. Vickie tried, but finally to her Grandmother's numerous suggestions replied, "Grandma, this is the first time you have ever hounded me!"

——o——

The father took his young son (five years old) to a nursery school to be enrolled, and the teacher brought out a long form and started asking questions.

"Does the boy have any older brothers?" she asked.

"No."

"Any younger brothers?"

"No."

"Younger sisters?" "No."

"Older sisters?" "No."

Young Johnny, who had been looking more and more unhappy during this dialogue, finally burst out wistfully, "But I've got friends."

———o———

A pre-schooler with considerable TV-watching experience wasn't stumped for a remedy when her mother lost her voice in a recent siege of laryngitis. "You got no sound, Mama," diagnosed the tot. "Maybe you need a new tube."

Christian Herald

———o———

Johnny was very grown-up for his four-and-one-half years. One day I was inspecting our gardens after returning from a vacation and this little fellow from next door joined me. "Look at those nice gourds, Johnny," I said. Johnny disagreed, "They're not gourds, they're squash." "No, Johnny," said I, "those are gourds." "Well," said the little gardener, "they're gourds in your yard, but they're squash in my yard.!"

ELEANOR L. DOAN

———o———

KINDERGARTEN AGES

The beginners' Sunday school teacher used gold stars at the top of pupils' papers to reward excellent work.

One boy who received a large zero on his took the paper home and explained to his mother: "Teacher ran out of stars, so she gave me a moon!"

FLORENCE NAGLE in *Together*

———o———

Tommy and his little brother Jack had taken their sled out to have some fun while the snow lasted. After a little while mother looked out of the window to see how they were getting on. "I hope you are letting Jack have his share, Tommy," she said. "Oh, yes, Mother," was the reply. "I have it down hill and he has it up."

A little girl at Christmas had ten cents given her — ten bright, new pennies. "This," she said, laying aside one, "is for Jesus."

"But," said her mother, "you have already given one to Jesus."

"Yes," said the child, "but that belonged to Him; this is a present."

Selected

———o———

Young Susan, an avid television fan, was told to come to the dinner table to say grace. Bowing her head, but with her mind still on the program, she said in a clear small voice: "Thank Thee, God, for the food we are about to receive and speed it up so I can get back to Woody Woodpecker."

Watchman Examiner

———o———

The family was preparing to go to the mission field, and each person had to receive several shots. Finally little Janie asked her mother, "Mommie, do you have to get a shot to go to heaven?"

MRS. EARL CARTER in *Teach*

———o———

PRIMARY AGES

One of my seven-year-old twins came to me one day and said, "Daddy, when we sin we get smaller, don't we?" "No," I replied. "Why do you say that?" "Well," she exclaimed, "the Bible says, 'All have sinned and come short!'"

R. J., Norwalk, Calif.

———o———

"It's Sunday, Bobby. Don't play in the street. Go out and play in the back yard," his mother instructed.

"But, Mother, it's Sunday there, too," Bobby replied.

———o———

"Mommy, Mommy," called Richard half crying.

"What is it, dear?" Mother asked.

"I was just trying to whistle like Daddy," explained Richard, "and my teeth stepped on my tongue."

———o———

The Sunday school teacher asked the class to act out the Bible story they had just heard of Joseph's brothers selling him to an Egyptian merchant. This delighted the children, particularly one little boy who took the part of the merchant. Carefully he began to count out the money. "One . . . two . . . three . . . four . . . five . . . six . . . seven . . . Oh, this is so much work," the lad complained. "I'll just write out a check!"

MRS. BILL SMITH, Chattanooga, Tenn.

———o———

It was Promotion Sunday in our church. Wondering how much my primary class understood about this concept, I asked, "Who can tell me what special day this is?"

Without hesitation one bright-eyed youngster said, "I know! It's COMMOTION SUNDAY!"

MRS. F. W. ROSEBURG in *Teach*

———o———

A third-grader's definition:

"A contraction is made by putting two words together to make one word. You leave out some of the letters, but you put in a catastrophe."

BETTY KOWALLIK in *NEA Journal*

———o———

When classes were dismissed for the day at Goodman Point School, a first-grader walked up to teacher, Mrs. Marie Story, tugged on her skirt, and said: "Mrs. Story, could you please tell me what I learned in school today? My daddy always wants to know."

Cortez, Colo. (AP)

———o———

Our seven-year-old daughter looks forward each evening to reading time when we all gather in the living room while Daddy reads. It was following family devotions after studying a series on the Gospel of John, that she asked Christ to be her Saviour.

While discussing the Bible story about Pilate's attempt to release Jesus, our 3½-year-old daughter said, "But they wanted the bunnies instead." Our first thought was that she had not been listening as we read the story, but her further comment that "they wanted

the rabbits" revealed her interpretation of the name Barabbas.

MRS. JOHN R. COLOMBO
in *The Christian Parent*

———o———

A small boy in church with his mother heard the preacher talk on *What Is a Christian?* Every time he asked the question, the minister banged his fist on the pulpit.

"Mama, do you know?" the boy whispered to his mother.

"Yes, dear, now be quiet," she replied.

Finally, when the minister demanded once more, "What is a Christian?" and banged especially hard, the boy yelled, "Mama, tell 'im!"

GLENDA GOSS in *Together*

———o———

Immediately after opening exercises, Robin waved an urgent hand for attention. I called on her, and she asked, "What is a widget?"

In response to my obvious mystification, she explained: "You know, in the pledge we say, 'I pledge allegiance for widget stands . . .'"

BONNIE K. PEZZOPANE in *Grade Teacher*

———o———

JUNIOR AGES

Doctors had conferred with the parents of a ten-year-old boy suffering with an incurable disease. They agreed to explain the true situation to him. After this was done, the boy faced the doctors and asked, "How shall we break the news to my parents?"

———o———

The solar system was the subject and the teacher had permitted each pupil in her fourth grade to select his own topic about which to study and report to the rest of the class. Jim took "Pluto," Henry "Mars," but Walter selected "Earth," and his reason seemed most logical. Explained Walter, "It's the only planet I have visited."

———o———

Sunday School Teacher: "In what order do the Gospels come?"

Student: "One after the other."

A San Jose teacher suggested that her sixth graders stage a United Nations session. One of the first youngsters to volunteer to represent a nation was a boy who wanted to be Russia. When the session got underway, the "Russian" delegate promptly got up and walked out of the room.

FRANK FREEMAN
in San Jose, Calif., *Mercury*

———o———

The Sunday school teacher was telling the class about the Christian's armor. After speaking of the breastplate of righteousness and a shield of faith, she said, "And Paul also says we should carry a weapon, which he says is the Word of God. Do you remember what he called the Word of God?"

There was no answer so she added, "It's something very sharp, something that cuts."

Then one little fellow answered vigorously, "I know. I know. It's the axe of the Apostles!"

Baptist & Reflector

———o———

"If you had been living when Noah was building the ark, what would you have said about him if you had watched him?" the first grade Sunday School teacher asked her class. "Martha, do you want to tell us?"

"I would have said, 'Noah is a silly, foolish man!'" the little girl replied.

"Now," said the teacher, "pretend that I am Noah and tell me what you would say to me."

"No," objected Martha. "I don't know what I would say to you."

"But you just said it," the teacher reminded her.

"Yes, I know," Martha replied. "But I didn't say it to his face!"

———o———

Recently, our young son was listening to a broadcast of the Milwaukee Braves ball game which opened with the singing of the national anthem.

During the singing, he stood up very solemnly and, as the anthem came to a close, he sang, "And the homers of the Braves."

MRS. M. OTTERBEIN in *Coronet*

Asked if she could spell banana, a little girl said, "I know how to spell banana but I never know when to stop."

QUOTED BY CHARLES POORE
in *New York Times*

Choice

It's not a question of good or bad — but a choice of good or best.

———o———

The rich young ruler, in his famous interview with Christ,
Asked the *right* question,
Asked the *right* Person,
Received the *right* answer,
But made the *wrong* choice.

BILLY GRAHAM

———o———

It is not in life's chances but in its choices that happiness comes to the heart of the individual.

———o———

This Thing I Choose

Some folk enjoy talking about trouble,
    and insults, and burdens, and pain;
They talk about losses and crosses,
    but seldom of sunshine and gain.
Their troubles they list without number,
    but blessings, if ever, are told;
No wonder they bog down in spirit,
    and grow sad before they grow old.

Sure I could join them in sadness,
    for sorrow has oft come to me;
I could tell all my blights and my blunders,
    and heartache that folks cannot see.
But would this make our world any brighter?
    Wouldn't I lend to its sorrow and care?
Why then scatter gloom in this dark world,
    When God has sunbeams to spare?

No, I won't join the ranks of complainers,
    for God's been too good to me;
I refuse to find fault with His leadings;
I refuse to weep on bitterly.

I want to be grateful and humble,
and ever His sweet praises sing;
I want to enjoy every moment the
victory
that Christ came to bring!

NAT OLSON
in *The Log of the Good Ship Grace*

———o———

Three choices every young person needs to make right: master, mission, and mate.

———o———

Evangelist Billy Graham told an interesting story about a man who had trouble with his eyes. In fact, he was rapidly becoming blind.

The doctor advised that he have an operation. So this was done. The man's eyesight became normal, but his memory seemed affected. So the doctor operated once more. The man's memory improved, but his eyesight failed. Finally the perplexed doctor asked his patient, "What do you choose — your memory or your eyesight?"

After a moment of deep thought, the man replied, "I choose my eyesight because I would rather spend my life looking ahead than remembering the things that are past."

———o———

Make worthy choices but avoid taking foolish chances.

———o———

Where there is no choice, we do well to make no difficulty.

GEORGE MACDONALD

———o———

If you are willing to choose the seeming darkness of faith instead of the illumination of reason, wonderful light will break out upon you from the Word of God.

ADONIRAM J. GORDON

———o———

My Choice

Written during his training days by Bill McChesney, who became a missionary martyr in the Congo, November 25, 1964

I want my breakfast served at "eight,"
With ham and eggs upon the plate;
A well-broiled steak I'll eat at "one,"
And dine again when day is done.

I want an ultra modern home,
And in each room a telephone;
Soft carpets, too, upon the floors,
And pretty drapes to grace the doors.

A cozy place of lovely things,
Like easy chairs with innersprings,
And then I'll get a small TV —
Of course, "I'm careful what I see."

I want my wardrobe, too, to be
Of neatest, finest quality,
With latest style in suit and vest.
Why shouldn't Christians have the best?

But then the Master I can hear,
In no uncertain voice, so clear,
"I bid you come and follow Me,
The lowly Man of Galilee.

"Birds of the air have made their nest,
And foxes in their holes find rest;
But I can offer you no bed;
No place have I to lay My head."

In shame I hung my head and cried.
How could I spurn the Crucified?
Could I forget the way He went,
The sleepless nights in prayer He spent?

For forty days without a bite,
Alone He fasted day and night;
Despised, rejected — on He went,
And did not stop till veil He rent.

A Man of sorrows and of grief,
No earthly friend to bring relief —
"Smitten of God," the prophet said —
Mocked, beaten, bruised, His blood ran red.

If He be God and died for me,
No sacrifice too great can be
For me, a mortal man, to make;
I'll do it all for Jesus' sake.

Yes, I will tread the path He trod,
No other way will please my God;
So, henceforth, this my choice shall be,
My choice for all eternity.

BILL MCCHESNEY, *Power For Living*

Christ

Christ is not valued at all — unless He is valued above all.
ST. AUGUSTINE

All that I had, He took; all that He has, He has given me in Jesus Christ!
SUBODH SAHU, "Evangelism and The Church" in *Commission, Conflict, Commitment*

Christ with me sleeping,
Christ with me waking,
Christ with me watching
Every day and night
Each day and night.

God with me protecting,
The Lord with me directing,
The Spirit with me strengthening
Forever and forevermore,
Ever and evermore. Amen.
Translated from the Gaelic

What the sunshine is to the flower, the Lord Jesus Christ is to my soul.
ALFRED, LORD TENNYSON

Christ never says He is a high delicacy, a rare luxury, a feast which the rich alone can afford. He says that He is Bread, He is Water, He is Light, He is the Door, He is the Shepherd. These words, so simple, stretch their meaning around the whole circle of human life.
Selected

The world doesn't want Christ, but it needs Him.
DR. EARLE STEVENS

John 14:6

I am the Way, the Truth, and the Life. Without the Way, there is no going, Without the Truth there is no knowing, Without the Life there is no living.

My Saviour

There is no time too busy for His leisure,
There is no task too hard for Him to share.

There is no soul too lowly for His notice,
There is no need to trifling for His care.
There is no place too humble for His presence,
There is no pain His bosom cannot feel.
There is no sorrow that He cannot comfort,
There is no sickness that He cannot heal.
From *The Banner* — Bethany Presbyterian Church, Fort Lauderdale, Florida

Our Wonderful Lord

Whatever Christ touched was transformed by His love
The manger, the cross and the tomb.
The Light of the World turned sin's night into day,
And death has been shorn of its gloom.

The multitudes fed of the bread from His hand;
The lame leaped for joy at His word;
The blind saw His beauty, and shouted His praise;
The leper was healed by the Lord.

One wonderful day His great love touched my heart,
And then by His mercy and grace
The darkness all fled as His love-light shone in,
Transformed by His tender embrace.

Then let us speak forth the glad tidings anew,
And words of salvation proclaim;
For still He is mighty to save and to keep
Through faith in His marvelous Name.
ALBERT SIMPSON REITZ

Excellency Of Christ

He is a path, if any be misled;
He is a robe, if any naked be;
If any chance to hunger, he is bread;
If any be a bondman, he is free;
If any be but weak, how strong is he!
To dead men life is he, to sick men, health;

To blind men, sight, and to the needy, wealth;
A pleasure without loss, a treasure without stealth.

GILES FLETCHER

————o————

Christ has outlived the empire which crucified Him nineteen centuries ago. He will outlast the dictators who defy Him now.

RALPH W. SOCKMAN

————o————

If Jesus Christ is a man —
And only a man — I say,
That of all mankind I will cleave to Him,
And to Him will I cleave alway.

If Jesus Christ is God —
And the only God — I swear,
I will follow Him through heaven and hell,
The earth, the sea and the air!

RICHARD WATSON GILDER,
The Song of a Heathen

————o————

Jesus Christ is a FRIEND of sinners; but a COMPANION only of the godly.

————o————

We know what God is like because we know the character of Jesus Christ.

GEORGE HODGES

————o————

Jesus was not a man of remarkable spiritual powers with big and ambitious ideas. He was a man under orders. His unique vocation was to establish the Kingdom of God.

W. R. FORRESTER

————o————

There is a reward for the obedient disciple, there are power and authority for the faithful disciple, there is glory of achievement for the zealous disciple; but there is the whisper of his love, the joy of his presence, and the shining of his face, for those who love Jesus for himself alone.

SUSAN B. STRACHAN

Christ's Birth
(See also Christmas)

Fingers

Newborn petal-pink fingers destined to
Tangle Mary's hair.

Clasp a magi's thumb,
Handle saw and plane,
Explore the Law and the Prophets,

Beckon to fishermen,
Cleanse and heal,
Wash a sinner's feet,
Dangle from a gibbet,
Break bread at Emmaus!

WANDA MILNER

————o————

Sadhu Sundar Singh used to illustrate the incarnation mystery in this way. A simple countryman was being shown a red glass bottle full of milk. They asked him what was in the bottle. "Wine? Brandy? Whiskey?" he replied, questioningly. He could not believe it was filled with milk till he saw the milk poured out from it. The redness of the bottle hid the color of the milk.

So, he said, it was and is with our Lord's humanity. Man saw Him tired, hungry, suffering, weeping, and thought He was only man. "He was made in the likeness of men," yet He ever is "God over all, blessed for ever."

————o————

The whole question of the virgin birth of Jesus need not afflict the average man. If Jesus is unique, unlike any other person, it is not illogical to believe that his birth was unique.

WILLIAM LYON PHELPS

————o————

If Christ Had Not Been Born. . .

Suppose that Christ had not been born
That far away Judean morn.
Suppose that God, Whose mighty hand
Created worlds, had never planned
A way for man to be redeemed.
Suppose the wise men only dreamed
That guiding star whose light still glows
Down through the centuries. Suppose
Christ never walked here in men's sight,
Our blessed Way, and Truth, and Light.

Suppose He counted all the cost,
And never cared that we were lost,
And never died for you and me,
Nor shed His blood on Calvary

Upon a shameful cross. Suppose
That having died, He never rose,
And there was none with power to save
Our souls from death beyond the grave!
Oh, far away Judean morn —
Suppose that Christ had not been born!

But praise His name, the Christ was
born
That far away Judean morn —
Beloved of our Father God, Whose
mighty hand
Created worlds; and while they stand,
Redemption's door is open still
Through Him proclaimed on Judah's
hill!
The guiding star leads to Him now
And we may in the presence bow
Of Him who walked here in men's
sight
Our blessed Way, and Truth, and
Light.

He never stopped to count the cost,
Oh, how He loved His sheep — the
lost!
Christ gave His life for you and me
And shed His blood on Calvary,
Upon a shameful cross. But none
Could overcome God's only Son! —
Assurance of His power to save
Our souls from death beyond the grave.
O far away Judean morn —
We praise Him in the manger born!

MARTHA SNELL and MARY R. KEFFER

———o———

Lamb Of God

We think it strange the Son of God
Should in a manger lie;
His room, a stable floored with sod,
And animals close by.

We think it strange; we sigh and
mourn.
A stable seems so odd.
But where else should a lamb be born?
Behold the Lamb of God!

BESS A. OLSON

Christ's Death

As A Lamb

As a Lamb to the slaughter my Saviour
was led,
With the thorns in His heart, and the
thorns on His head.

By His stripes I am healed, by His
death I now live,
And He died that my sins He might
fully forgive.

In the Garden of Sorrows He suffered
for me,
In the cold judgment hall He was sentenced for me,
In the midst of the mob He was nailed
to the tree
And in love He was willing to die there,
for me.

In this wonderful Saviour no fault
could be found,
But through envy they led Him to
Calvary's mound
"O forgive them" He cried, ere in an-
guish He died,
And He loved to the end, my dear
Lord crucified.

Oh, how can I repay Thee, my Saviour
divine.
All I am and I have shall forever be
Thine.
I will give Thee my life, I will give
Thee my love,
And forever I'll praise Thee in man-
sions above.

ALBERT SIMPSON REITZ

———o———

The biggest fact about Joseph's tomb
is that it wasn't a tomb at all, it was
a room for a transient. Jesus just
stopped there a night or two on his
way back to glory.

HERBERT BOOTH SMITH

Christ's Return

The King Is Coming . . .

The skies are growing darker,
With the passing of the years,
And life becomes more restless,
And on every hand are fears:
Men know not what is coming,
Yet feel something lies ahead,
Which fills them with foreboding
And a solemn sense of dread.

But Christians we are waiting
For the breaking of the day:
We are certain Christ is coming —
He may now be on the way.

Deeper still will grow earth's dark-
ness —
Still more awesome grow its night,
But for Christ our eyes are looking,
Quick may come the Rapture bright.
Doorstep Evangel

---o---

Looking

There are two ways of looking at the
Lord's coming: a looking *for* it and a
looking *at* it. It is possible to look at it
with keen intellect and profound interest, and yet have it mean nothing to
us personally. It is also possible to
know but little of the theology of the
subject, and yet have a deep and holy
longing for our Lord to appear. May
this theme be not only our study but
also our personal hope; for "unto them
that look for him shall he appear a
second time without sin unto salvation."
A. B. SIMPSON

---o---

What Would He Say?

If He should come today
And find my hands so full
Of future plans, however fair,
In which my Saviour had no share,
What would He say?

If He should come today
And find I had not told
One soul about my heavenly Friend
Whose blessings all my way attend,
What would He say?

If He should come today,
Would I be glad, quite glad?
Remembering He had died for all,
And none through me had heard His
call,
What would He say?
AUTHOR UNKNOWN

---o---

Are You Ready?

The Scriptures give constant testimony to the fact that our Lord Jesus
Christ will come again. If you take
your Bible and read through from the
beginning you will be amazed at the
reiterated truth of the Second Advent.
If we were to take out of the Bible

every reference to the second coming
of the Lord we would have a terribly
mutilated Book! This is no "pet theory"
accepted by a few "cranks"; it is a
major doctrine of the Word of God. It
has been said by scholars that the
second coming of Christ is mentioned
no less than 1,200 times in the Old
Testament and 300 times in the New
Testament. If we read our Bible and
believe our Bible we cannot do other
than be certain that our Saviour is coming again. The fact of His return is
clearly and emphatically stated, in
prediction, type, parable and promise.
REV. FRANCIS W. DIXON

---o---

He Is Coming Again

I stood one day on a busy street
And watched the restless throng.
And heard the tramp of countless feet,
As they hurriedly marched along.
All bent on pleasure; no thought of
care,
The rich, the poor all were there;
Making the most of the time at hand,
But starving their souls in a bounte-
ous land.
And I thought of the Master, as He
wept to see
The thoughtless crowd at Galilee.
I thought of the awful price He paid
When all of our sins on Him were
laid.
How He bore the cross — endured the
pain:
We know He's coming back again.
What a wondrous morning that will be
When all of His glory we shall see.
We'll reign with Him a thousand years;
No more heartaches, no more tears,
No more sorrow, grief or pain
When Jesus comes to earth again.
W. A. BARNES

---o---

A Wonderful Day

Glorious day when we stand in His
presence,
All of our heartaches and sorrows are
past,
No more burdens too heavy to carry —
We shall see Jesus at last!

Wonderful day when we shall be like
  Him,
    Features were marred by sin here
    below,
Now they are radiant, beautiful, glori-
  ous!
    Cleansed by His blood, made whiter
    than snow.

Marvelous day, all suffering ended,
    Glorious bodies now, like to His own;
We will be kings and priests in God's
  kingdom,
    With glory and honor around the
    white throne.

Radiant day — the day of His crowning —
    The thought of this day is immea-
    surably sweet;
Then we will stand transformed in His
  likeness,
    Casting our trophies and crowns at
    His feet.

Victorious day — the day of the Rapture,
    The Lamb who was slain is now be-
    come King!
The Bride of the Lamb in garments all
  glorious
    Is singing sweet songs the Bride only
    can sing.

Triumphant day — great day of His
  power!
    All the kingdoms of earth will crum-
    ble and fall;
The saints of all ages in garments of
  splendor
    Are crowning Him King to rule over
    all!
                                    A. H. DIXON

Christian

As burning candles give light until
they be consumed, so likewise godly
Christians must be occupied in doing
good so long as they shall live.
                                    CAWDRAY

——o——

A *Christian's Relationships*:

Get right with God;
Get together with other Christians;
Get going for others.
                          SAMUEL M. SHOEMAKER

It doesn't take much of a man to be
a Christian . . . it takes all of him.
                          DAWSON TROTMAN

——o——

If every Christian in your church
were the kind of Christian that you
are, what kind of a church would your
church be?

——o——

A visitor asked an old bedridden
woman who said she was trying to be
a Christian: "Are you trying to be Mrs.
Whyte?"
"No, I am Mrs. Whyte."
"How long have you been Mrs.
Whyte?"
"Ever since this ring was put on my
finger."
"That is how it is with me. I do not
try to be a Christian. I have been one
ever since I put out my empty hand
and received Christ as my Saviour."
                          The Prairie Overcomer

——o——

What is a Christian put into the
world for, except to do the impossible
in the strength of the Lord?
                          GENERAL S. C. ARMSTRONG

——o——

It has been said that a Christian is
one who believes what Christ believes,
hates what Christ hates, and loves what
Christ loves.

——o——

Christians are like the first half of a
round trip ticket — not good if detached.
                          ROBERT E. SPEER

——o——

Some Christians are like porcupines.
They have many fine points but it's
hard to get next to them.
                          VANCE HAVNER

——o——

Many Christians are like the man
who bought a book on reducing exercises and lies down to read it.

——o——

A Christian should be a striking likeness of Jesus Christ. You have read
lives of Christ, beautifully written; but
the best life of Christ is His living

biography, written out in the words and action of His people.

CHARLES HADDON SPURGEON

---o---

Three Pictures

A believer may see three pictures of himself in God's Word — what he was, what he is, and what he shall be. As to his former condition, he reads in Ephesians 2:12: "That at that time ye were without Christ, being aliens from the commonwealth of Israel, and strangers from the covenants of promise, having no hope, and without God in the world." As to his present position, he reads in I John 3:2: "Beloved, now are we the sons of God." As to his future glory, he reads in the same verse: "It doth not yet appear what we shall be: but we know that . . . we shall be like Him."

F. J. HORSEFIELD

---o---

The true Christian is marked by his selflessness.

RODGER GOODMAN

---o---

Only a great Christian can be a great Biblical scholar.

KENNETH SCOTT LATOURETTE

---o---

A Christian is someone to whom God entrusts all his fellow men.

DWIGHT L. MOODY

---o---

If a man cannot be a Christian in the place where he is, he cannot be a Christian anywhere.

HENRY WARD BEECHER

---o---

This cold world needs warm-hearted Christians.

---o---

Some Christians crawl into a spiritual bomb shelter and sing, "Safe am I."

---o---

When a Christian is in the wrong place, his right place is empty.

T. J. BACH

A true and faithful Christian does not make holy living a mere incidental thing. It is his great concern. As the business of the soldier is to fight, so the business of the Christian is to be like Christ.

JONATHAN EDWARDS

---o---

These Christians love each other even before they are acquainted!

CELUS, Roman anti-Christian philosopher, 3rd Century A.D.

---o---

Christians and camels receive their burdens kneeling.

AMBROSE BIERCE

---o---

Christians are in the world to do the things that unbelievers say cannot be done!

---o---

One can be a Confucianist without knowing Confucius. One can be a Mohammedan without knowing Mohammed. One can be a Buddhist without knowing Buddha. But one cannot be a Christian without knowing Christ.

CARL ARMERDING

---o---

Without Christ I was like a fish out of water. With Christ I am in the ocean of love.

SADHU SUNDAR SINGH

Christian Education

The Psalm Of The Good Teacher

The Lord is my teacher,
I shall not lose the way.
He leadeth me in the lowly path of learning,
He prepareth a lesson for me every day;
He bringeth me to the clear fountains of instruction,
Little by little he showeth me the beauty of truth.

The world is a great book that he hath written,
He turneth the leaves for me slowly;
They are all inscribed with images and letters,

He poureth light on the pictures and
the words.

He taketh me by the hand to the hill-
top of vision,
And my soul is glad when I perceive
his meaning;
In the valley also he walketh beside me,
In the dark places he whispereth to my
heart.

Even though my lesson be hard it is not
hopeless,
For the Lord is patient with his slow
scholar;
He will wait awhile for my weakness,
And help me to read the truth through
tears.

HENRY VAN DYKE

───o───

Pod Of Christian Peas

The goal and aim of every Sunday
School board can be summed up in
this group of Christian P's.
CHRISTIAN Planning.
CHRISTIAN Praying.
CHRISTIAN Playing.
CHRISTIAN Purpose.

In *P.A.S.S.*

───o───

To help the individual develop into
an ever better Christian in all of life's
relationships is an aim of Christian education.

Christian Living

Do not strive to make yourself holy
by working, but by believing, by living
out of yourselves, entirely on the
strength of Christ; the believer's life is
a life hid with Christ in God.

───o───

The Weaver

My life is but a weaving
    Between my Lord and me,
I cannot choose the colors
    He worketh steadily.

Ofttimes He weaveth sorrow,
    And I in foolish pride
Forget He sees the upper
    And I, the underside.

Not till the loom is silent
    And the shuttles cease to fly
Shall God unroll the canvas
    And explain the reason why.

The dark threads are as needful
    In the Weaver's skillful hand
As the threads of gold and silver
    In the pattern He has planned.

AUTHOR UNKNOWN

───o───

The Christian life is like an airplane;
when you stop, you drop.

───o───

The argument for the risen Christ is
the living Christian.

WINIFRED KIRKLAND

───o───

Christian love is a road sign to the
lost.

HAROLD G. SARLES

───o───

The Way of the Cross is not a free-
way: the toll is heavy.

RALPH BREWER

───o───

Christian ABC's

Act instead of Argue
Build instead of Brag
Climb instead of Criticize
Dig instead of Deprecate
Encourage instead of Envy
Fight instead of Faint
Give instead of Grumble
Help instead of Harm
Invite instead of Ignore
Join instead of Jeer
Kneel instead of Kick
Love instead of Lampoon
Move instead of Mould
Nurture instead of Neglect
Obey instead of Obstruct
Pray instead of Pout
Quicken instead of Quit
Rescue instead of Ridicule
Shout instead of Shrink
Try instead of Tremble
Undergird instead of Undermine
Vindicate instead of Vilify
Witness instead of Wilt

Exterminate instead of Excuse
Yield instead of Yell
Zip instead of Zigzag.

ALVY E. FORD

———o———

One advantage of traveling the straight and narrow is that no one is trying to pass you.

Clarion-Ledger, Jackson, Mississippi

———o———

The straight and narrow way seems to have no detours nor places to park, and the folk who travel it are supposed to keep going right on to its end.

———o———

I grew up in the generation of the giants — John R. Mott and his disciples — among whom it was taken for granted that if you were going to live the Christian life at all, you would give at least one hour daily, before the first meal of the day, to seeking God through his Word and to listening to his voice.

BISHOP STEPHEN NEILL

———o———

If you do not feel as close to God as you once did, make no mistake about which one of you has moved.

———o———

In religion, as in every other profession, practicing is the great thing. Lawyers practice law, doctors practice medicine, and ministers must practice what they preach. So, too, Christians must practice their religion.

JACOBUS

———o———

Serving Christ is not overwork but overflow.

CURTIS B. AKENSON

———o———

Keep your lamp burning, and let God place it where He will.

———o———

An old story always worth a chuckle is the story of the little girl who stood before her mother one day, the picture of guilt and dejection.

"Mother," she began, "you know the priceless vase that has been handed down in our family from one generation to another? Well, this generation just dropped it!"

But the story ceases to be funny when one realizes that in many families the Christian religion is suffering the fate of that priceless vase.

As a Christian, you owe it to yourself and God to be an evangelist for Christ. Invite people to come to church. Be a witness. Express your faith. Evangelism is the calling of your faith.

Evangelism Committee

———o———

God doesn't need lawyers, He needs witnesses.

J. STEWART HOLDEN

———o———

A Christian worker is a physician of souls.

———o———

The Mind Of Christ In Me

May the mind of Christ our Saviour,
  Live in me from day to day,
By His love and power controlling
  All I do and say.

May the Word of God dwell richly
  In my heart from hour to hour,
So that all may see I triumph
  Only through His power.

May the peace of God my Father
  Rule my life in everything,
That I may be calm to comfort
  Sick and sorrowing.

May the love of Jesus fill me,
  As the waters fill the sea,
Him exalting, self abasing,
  This is victory.

May I run the race before me,
  Strong and brave to face the foe,
Looking only unto Jesus
  As I onward go.

May His beauty rest upon me
  As I seek the lost to win,
And may they forget the channel,
  Seeing only Him.

KATE B. WILKINSON

Christianity

According to Wilberforce, the great English preacher, Christianity can be condensed into four words — admit, submit, commit, transmit.

———o———

Christianity has not been tried and found wanting; it has been found difficult and *not* tried.

GILBERT KEITH CHESTERTON

———o———

Christianity is not a human speculation about God, it is a divine revelation to man.

———o———

Christianity demands the homage of the intellect, that the truth be believed; it also requires the homage of the heart, that truth be felt; and of the life, that truth be obeyed.

CLIFF COLE

———o———

Christianity is like the seafaring life — a smooth sea never made a good sailor.

———o———

The primary declaration of Christianity is not "This do!" but "This happened!"

EVELYN UNDERHILL

———o———

What reality is there in your Christianity if you look at men struggling in darkness and you are content to congratulate yourselves that you are in the light?

FREDERICK WILLIAM ROBERTSON

———o———

The greatest proof of Christianity for others, is not how far a man can logically analyze his reasons for believing, but how far in practice he will stake his life on his belief.

T. S. ELIOT

———o———

Is your Christianity ancient history or current events?

SAMUEL M. SHOEMAKER

———o———

Christianity begins where conventionality leaves off; it turns the other cheek, goes the second mile, does more than the expected, and learns what it is to sacrifice.

———o———

The world is equally shocked at hearing Christianity criticized and seeing it practiced.

D. ELTON TRUEBLOOD

———o———

There are no crown-wearers in heaven who were not cross-bearers here below.

CHARLES HADDON SPURGEON

———o———

When Christianity assumes an aggressive attitude, the first result is a great exhibition of Satanic power.

GEORGE BOWEN,
American missionary to India

———o———

A Christianity which does not prove its worth in practice degenerates into dry scholasticism and idle talk.

ABRAHAM KUYPER

———o———

Columbus discovered America. Yes, but what did he find out about its rivers, lakes, and plains? Just so with one who "discovers" Christianity. Wait till you explore!

———o———

Christianity is either relevant all the time or useless anytime. It is not just a phase of life; it is life itself.

RICHARD C. HALVERSON

———o———

He who shall introduce into public affairs the principles of primitive Christianity will change the face of the world.

BENJAMIN FRANKLIN

———o———

My understanding of Christianity is God in search of lost men, not men in search of a lost God.

RONALD R. HATCH
in a letter to *Time Magazine*

———o———

It is not Christianity that is failing, but Christians who fail to do their task.

JAMES BOLARIN

Some people use Christianity like a bus; they ride on it only when it is going their way.

———o———

Too many of us have been inoculated with small doses of Christianity — which keep us from catching the real thing.

LESLIE D. WEATHERHEAD

———o———

The world does not doubt Christianity as much as it does Christians.

Christmas

Christmas Meditation

I wonder — if Christ were here today
In person, as we are, face to face —
Could I place in His hand this offering,
And say, "It is all I have to bring
To spread the work of redeeming grace"?
Watching our gifts of thankfulness,
Could I make this offering honestly,
With His loving eyes fixed full on me,
And feel it was something He could bless?
I wonder! *For Christ is here* today
And no heart motive is hid from Him.
Can it be that He finds me hesitate
To sacrifice for a cause so great?
It was worth a Cross to Him!

Selected

———o———

A little boy in a Christmas program had but one sentence to say, "Behold, I bring you good tidings." After the rehearsal he asked his mother what tidings meant, and she told him it meant "news." When the program was put on, he was stage-struck and forgot his line. Finally the idea came back to him and he cried out, "Hey, I got news for you!"

———o———

God's Gift

He did not use a silvery box,
Or paper green and red;
God laid His Christmas gift to men
Within a manger bed.

No silken cord was used to bind
The gift sent from above.

'Twas wrapped in swaddling clothes and bound
In cords of tender love.

There was no evergreen to which
His precious gift was tied:
Upon a bare tree on a hill
His gift was hung . . . and died.

'Twas taken down from off the tree
And laid beneath the sod,
But death itself could not destroy
The precious gift of God.

With mighty hand He lifted it
From out the stony grave;
Forevermore to every man
A living gift He gave.

RUTH PRENTICE
in *The Log of the Good Ship Grace*

———o———

Christmas in the Heart

It's Christmastime throughout the land
And trees are white with silver snow,
Come, let us take each other's hand
And wander back to long ago.
The wind is cold, the air is clean,
The church bells chime for all to hear.
What loveliness stands in between
Our hearts and God, this time of year!

What happy faces do we see,
Their cares forgotten every one,
This is the way it ought to be
From dawn until the set of sun.
These blessed days of joy and peace,
Bedecked with wonder, set apart,
Through all our years will never cease,
If we keep Christmas . . . in our heart!

GRACE E. EASLEY

———o———

To see his star is good, but to see his face is better.

DWIGHT L. MOODY

———o———

Return of Christmas

The happy Christmas comes once more,
The heavenly Guest is at the door;
The blessed words the shepherds thrill,
The joyous tidings: Peace, good-will!

To David's city let us fly,
Where angels sing beneath the sky;
Through plain and village pressing near,

And news from God which shepherds
hear.

Oh, let us go with quiet mind,
The gentle Babe with shepherds find,
To gaze on Him who gladdens them,
The loveliest Flower of Jesse's stem!

The lowly Saviour meekly lies,
Laid off the splendour of the skies;
No crown bedecks His forehead fair;
No pearl or gem or silk is there.

No human glory, might, and gold,
The lovely infant's form enfold;
The manger and the swaddlings poor
Are His whom angels' songs adore.

Oh, wake our hearts, in gladness sing!
And keep our Christmas with our King,
Till living song, from loving souls,
Like sound of mighty waters rolls.

O Holy Child! Thy manger streams,
Till earth and heaven glow with its
beams,
Till midnight noon's broad light has
won,
And Jacob's Star outshines the sun.

Thou, patriarchs' joy, Thou, prophets'
song,
Thou, heavenly Day-spring, looked for
long,
Thou, Son of man, Incarnate Word,
Great David's Son, great David's Lord!

Come, Jesus, glorious, heavenly Guest,
Keep Thine own Christmas in our
breast!
Then David's harp strings, hushed so
long,
Shall swell our jubilee of song.
CHARLES P. KRAUTH
(Translated from the Danish)

———o———

This old Christmas greeting from a
letter written between 1387-1455 by
Giovanni da Fiesole (Fra Angelico):

I salute you. I am your friend, and
my love for you goes deep. There is
nothing I can give you which you have
not already; but there is much, very
much, which though I cannot give it,
you can take. No heaven can come to
us unless our hearts find rest in today.
Take heaven. No peace lies in the
future which is not hidden in this
precious little instant. Take peace.
The gloom of the world is but a shadow. Behind it, yet within our reach, is
joy. There is radiance and courage in
the darkness could we but see it; and
to see, we have only to look. Life is so
generous a giver, but we, 'judging its
gifts by their coverings, cast them away
as ugly or heavy or hard. Remove the
covering, and you will find beneath it a
living splendor, woven of love, and
wisdom, and power. Welcome it, greet
it, and you touch the angel's hand that
brings it.

Everything we call a trial, a sorrow,
a duty, believe me, that angel's hand
is there, the gift is there, and the wonder of an overshadowing Presence. Our
joys, too, be not content with them as
joys. They, too, conceal diviner gifts.
Life is so full of meaning and purpose,
so full of beauty beneath its covering,
that you will find earth but cloaks your
heaven. Courage, then, to claim it, that
is all! But courage you have, and the
knowledge that we are pilgrims wend-
ing through unknown country our way
home.

And so, at this Christmas time, I
greet you, not quite as the world sends
greeting, but with profound esteem
now and forever.

The day breaks and the shadows
flee away.

———o———

A little child . . .
A shining star,
A stable rude . . .
The door ajar.
Yet in that place . . .
So crude, forlorn,
The Hope of all . . .
The world was born.
AUTHOR UNKNOWN

———o———

A Square, Honest Look

The people were being heavily taxed,
and faced every prospect of a sharp
increase to cover expanding military
expenses.

The threat of world domination by
a cruel, ungodly, power-intoxicated

band of men was ever just below the threshold of consciousness.

Moral deterioration had corrupted the upper levels of society and was moving rapidly into the broad base of the populace.

Peace propaganda was heard everywhere in the midst of preparations for war.

The latest rulers were covering the landscape with their statues and images, invoking a subtle form of state-worship.

Intense nationalistic feeling was clashing openly with new and sinister forms of imperialism.

Conformity was the spirit of the age.

Government handouts were being used with increasing lavishness to keep the population from rising up and throwing out the leaders.

Interest rates were spiraling upward in the midst of an inflated economy.

External religious observance was considered a political asset.

An abnormal emphasis was being placed upon sports and athletic competitions.

Social life centered around the banquet and the pool.

Racial tension was at the breaking point.

In such a time and amid such a people, a child was born to a migrant couple who had just signed up for a fresh round of taxation, and who were soon to become political exiles.

The child was called, among other things, the Prince of Peace.

When he had grown up and had entered upon his ministry, he said, "Peace I leave with you, my peace I give unto you . . . Let not your heart be troubled, neither let it be afraid."

SHERWOOD E. WIRT in *Decision Magazine*

———o———

Too often the Christmas bells with the merriest jingle are on the cash register.

———o———

"When Christmas is over," said a merchant to a minister, "it's over, and it's our job to rid this store completely of Christmas in a day."

"Well," said the minister, "I've a bigger job — to keep Christmas in the hearts of my people for a lifetime."

———o———

A little slum lad, whose parents were dead, was left in charge of a drunken woman, who beat and half-starved him.

The greatest delight in his life was to gaze at the beautiful Christmas toys in the shop windows. He knew, however, that these toys were not for him, for there was ever the glass between.

One day the little fellow was run over and taken to a hospital. About a week having passed, to his surprise he saw other children playing with toys they had received for Christmas.

Soon he himself sat up in bed when, wonder of wonders, on the bed were a number of toys for him.

Hardly able to believe his eyes, he stretched out his hand, and said, "There's no glass between!"

It is only sin that can come between us and Jesus, God's loving gift to the world. But sin can be removed through Christ's atoning blood, so that nothing may be between.

Defender

———o———

Lost Christmas

Why wait till Christmas time again is
  here?
Why spend those precious hours in
  hectic ways
Doing the things that you could do all
  year
And let the noise of whirl of festival
  days
Drown out the angels' song? Why not
  take time
To lift the eyes to candles in the sky;
To walk some silent night, while carols
  chime
And hear the hush of wings brush
  softly by?
Take time to meditate: to catch the
  spell
Of childish trust, that simple faith you
  knew
When love was everywhere, and all
  was well . . .
The gift you lost may now come back
  to you.

Seek not for Christmas in the busy mart
But cradled somewhere in a trusting heart.

RACHEL VAN CREME

———o———

Christmas-Time

I am the spirit of Christmas-time, when all should gladness be.
I am the light that you see shining upon each Christmas tree.
I am the thought that brings each gift from ones we hold so dear.
I am the good that permeates the world with Christmas cheer.
I am the joy that brightens homes and guides our thoughts above.
All heaven and earth rejoice in me, for I am known as Love.

LEBARON SHARP

———o———

The miracle of Christmas — that a baby can be so decisive.

———o———

There is love at Christmas because Christmas was born of love. Let us, each one, keep alive this spirit of love and glorify God.

JOSEPHA EMMS

———o———

The Christmas List

Give a gift of laughter,
Give a gift of song,
Give a gift of sympathy
To last a whole life long.
Give a cheerful message,
Give a helping hand,
Tell your sorry neighbor
That you understand!
Give a newsy letter
To a far-off friend;
Give a garden flower
With the book you lend.
Wash the supper dishes,
Help to dust the room;
Give a smile to leaven
Someone's hour of gloom!
Give a gift of sharing,
Give a gift of hope;
Light faith's gleaming candle
For the ones who grope
Slowly through the shadows.

Sweeten dreary days
For the lost and lonely.
Give yourself, ALWAYS!

MARGARET E. SANGSTER

———o———

Carol and Tommy were helping put up Christmas decorations. The conversation went like this:

"I like Christmas time — especially Christmas Day," said Tommy thoughtfully. "There's so much to think about. I wish I had been born on Christmas Day, like Jesus was."

Carol's answer was emphatic: "Jesus wasn't born on Christmas Day! He was born on a regular day. But it became Christmas because he was born that day. Before then it wasn't Christmas at all. Now it's Christmas everywhere! Don't you see? He makes it Christmas!"

"But it isn't Christmas everywhere," Tommy disagreed. "Some places don't have Christmas. Can you imagine a place without Christmas?"

"It can be Christmas even if places don't have it," Carol reasoned. "People can have Christmas. When Jesus lives in your heart he makes it Christmas!"

———o———

After Christmas

She needed pots and a new floor broom
And window shades for the children's room;
Her sheets were down to a threadbare three
And her table cloths were a sight to see.
She wanted scarfs and a towel rack
And a good, plain, useful dressing sack,
Some kitchen spoons and a box for bread,
A pair of scissors and sewing thread.
She hoped some practical friend would stop
And figure out that she'd like a mop,
Or a bathroom rug or a lacquered tray
Or a few plain plates for every day.
She hoped and hoped and she wished a lot,
But these, of course, were the things she got:
A cut glass vase and a bonbonniere,

A china thing for receiving hair,
Some oyster forks, a manicure set,
A chafing dish and a cellaret.
A boudoir cap and a drawn-work mat,
And a sterling this and a sterling that;
A gilt-edge book on a lofty theme,
And fancy bags till she longed to scream;
Some curious tongs and a powder puff,
And a bunch of other useless stuff.
And though she inwardly raged, she wrote
To all her friends the self-same note.
And said to all of her generous host —
"Just how did you guess what I needed most?"

ELLA BENTLEY ARTHUR

Church
(Attendance, Membership, etc.)

The holiest moment of the church service is the moment when God's people — strengthened by preaching and sacrament — go out of the church door into the world to be the Church. We don't go to church; we are the Church.

CANON ERNEST SOUTHCOTT

———o———

The church which neglects the children will have children who neglect the church.

———o———

What shall it profit a church if it go round the world to make converts and lose its own sons and daughters?

———o———

A church is a hospital for sinners, not a museum for saints.

ABIGAIL VAN BUREN, McNaught Syndicate

———o———

A Little Poem

The members sleep a little late,
They go to Church a little late,
Then they'll chew their gum a little,
Joke a little, doodle a little.
Brethren in class argue a little,
Commune a little, give a little,
After dismissal they gossip a little,
Go home and forget what little they heard,
And act like they cared but little,
For the greatest, holiest and most Precious institution on earth —
The Church of the Lord Jesus Christ.
I may have exaggerated a little,
But very little, and I think in some cases have omitted a little.
Brethren, will you think on this a little?

SOURCE UNKNOWN

———o———

The Church's preoccupation must be Christ. Jesus did not say, "I will build *your* Church; or *you* will build my Church." He said, "*I* will build my Church."

ARTHUR F. FOGARTIE in *Presbyterian Journal*

———o———

Three ministers who served churches near railroad tracks were exchanging troubles.
"Our first Sunday morning hymn is always interrupted by the C & O when it rumbles past the window," the first complained.
"That's nothing," replied the second minister. "Right in the middle of our prayer the L & N drowns me out."
"Brothers," lamented the third, "I wish all I had was your troubles. Everytime the deacons in my church take up collections, I look down the aisle and there comes the Nickel Plate!"

BERNICE SNELL in *Together*

———o———

Two things ruin a church: loose living and tight giving.

NAT OLSON

———o———

The church's business is not to catch the spirit of the age but to correct it.

———o———

When our daughter was four, she went to church for the first time with her grandma. On her return her father asked her what the minister's sermon was about.
"I don't know, Daddy. He didn't say."

MRS. RANDALL NEAL in *Together*

The purpose of going to church is not to show that we are better than others but to bring out the best in ourselves.

The Thief

"Yes, sir, I'm saved and going to heaven," a man told the minister.

Surprised, the minister replied, "Why that's fine. Have you ever united with a church?"

"No. The dying thief didn't and he went to heaven."

"Have you ever partaken of the Lord's Supper?"

"No. The dying thief didn't and Christ accepted him."

"Have you ever given to missions?"

"No. But the dying thief didn't either."

"Well, my friend," the minister replied, "the difference I see between you and the dying thief — is that you are a *living* one!"

C. H. KILMER

When I see the same fellows ushering year after year in a church I wonder if folks don't think it's short on man power. Perhaps they don't know that one of nature's good masterpieces is a good usher.

The church is not a gallery for the exhibition of eminent Christians, but a school for the education of imperfect ones, a nursery for the care of weak ones, a hospital for the healing of those who need special care.

HENRY WARD BEECHER

When you take opportunity to criticize the church and tell how you stay away from its services because of imperfect members, did you ever think how lonely you'd be in a perfect church?

Two reasons why churches do not do something:

1. They've never tried it before.
2. They've tried it and "it won't work."

It Isn't The Church, It's You!

If you want to have the kind of a Church
Like the kind of the Church you like,
You needn't slip your clothes in a grip
And start on a long, long hike.
You'll only find what you left behind,
For there's nothing really new.
It's a knock at yourself when you knock
  at your Church;
It isn't the Church — it's you!

When everything seems to be going
  wrong,
And trouble seems everywhere brewing;
When prayer meeting, young people's
  meeting, and all,
Seem simmering slowly stewing,
Just take a look at yourself and say,
"What's the use of being blue?"
Are you doing your "bit" to make things
  "hit"?
It isn't the Church — it's you!

It's really strange sometimes, don't you
  know,
That things go as well as they do,
When we think of the little — the very
  small mite —
We add to the work of the few.
We sit, and stand round, and complain
  of what's done,
And do very little but fuss!
Are we bearing our share of the burdens to bear?
It isn't the Church — it's us!

AUTHOR UNKNOWN

Skyscraper Church

As noon approaches every day,
Chimes from the church across the way
Rise over the city's busy din
And climb to where the clouds begin.
Here in my office in the sky,
Old hymns plead their way in and vie
With my insistent clicking keys
That type their brisk monotonies.
"Dear Sirs: We have received your bill,
And when the merchandise is stored,"
*"Faith of our fathers living still,
In spite of dungeon, fire and sword."*
"We are indeed surprised to know
That you will never guarantee,"

"Oh, love that will not let me go,
I rest my weary soul in thee."
They make a very strange duet,
The typewriter and the chimes, and yet
I wonder why it should seem odd
To mix up offices and God!
AUTHOR UNKNOWN

————o————

The church must either send or end.

————o————

On Church bulletin board:
"You aren't too bad to come in.
You aren't too good to stay out."

————o————

Many people find the church cold because they insist on sitting in "Z" row. Get up front where it's warm!

————o————

One of the things that is wrong with the church is that it dwells too much on what's wrong with it, and overlooks its own greatness and destiny.

————o————

This Is My Church

This is my church. It is composed of people like me. We make it what it is. I want it to be a church that is a light on the path of pilgrims, leading them to Goodness, Truth and Beauty. It will be, if I am. It will be friendly, if I am. Its pews will be filled, if I help to fill them. It will do a great work, if I work. It will bring other people into its worship and fellowship, if I bring them. It will be a church of loyalty and love, of fearlessness and faith; if I who make it what it is, am filled with these. Therefore, I dedicate myself to the task of being what I want my church to be.
Brooklyn Central Church Bulletin

————o————

I Found All This

A room of quiet, a temple of peace,
The home of faith where doubting cease,
A house of comfort where hope is given,
A source of strength to make earth heaven,
A shrine of worship, a place to pray —
I found all this in my church today.
AUTHOR UNKNOWN

————o————

One thing that may still be said about "a struggling church." As long as it is struggling, it isn't dead.

————o————

The best way to heat a church is to have the stove in the pulpit.

————o————

Churches do take many offerings and collections, and so there are many of us who figure that religion is a costly thing; but irreligion costs many times as much. Think it over.

————o————

It's very strange that heat on Sunday
Seems so much hotter than on Monday,
And weekday pains, that we ignore,
On Sundays seem to hurt much more,
Till we decide to stay in bed
When we should go to church instead.

————o————

In church recently a boy ran a toy engine up and down the seat, much to the annoyance of an elderly gent seated in the pew behind.
At long last the man protested: "Shh! Shh!" he said.
The small boy beamed. "Oh," he exclaimed, "do you play trains, too?"
CHARLES KENNEDY

————o————

The church that is married to the spirit of the age will find itself a widow in the next generation.
JOSEPH SIZOO

————o————

The best days of the church have always been its singing days.
THEODORE LEDYARD CUYLER

————o————

Prayerless pews make powerless pulpits.

————o————

Satan does not do his most subtle work in the saloon, but in the sanctuary.
RALPH H. STOLL

CHURCH 90

Now I set me down to sleep
The prayer is long; the subject's deep.
If he should stop before I wake
Please give me a pinch, for goodness' sake.

———o———

The church is so subnormal that if it ever got back to the New Testament normal it would seem to people to be abnormal.

VANCE HAVNER

———o———

My Church

I want my church to be a place
Where I can meet God face to face
And meditate upon His grace.

I want each worship hour so sweet
That I can think each time we meet
A Presence comes and takes His seat.

I want her doors to stand so wide
No hungry soul who waits outside
Will think that he has been denied.

I want my church to be much more
Than stone and mortar, pew and door
Or carpet laid upon a floor.

But, oh, I know that it can be
No more than that is found in me,
So teach me, Lord, to show forth Thee.

JESSIE MERLE FRANKLIN

———o———

Churches

Churches!
Thank God for the sight of them,
The beauty, the dreams and the right of them,
In country and city, on mountain and moor,
Churches with welcome at the door.

Churches that silently testify,
With spires and crosses reared to the sky.
That makes us think every time we look,
Of God and right and the Holy Book.

Churches!
Thank God for the heart of them,
The people who live as a part of them,
Praying and learning the things to do,

Giving and labouring, proving them true,
Mastering lethargy, selfishness, fear,
Dreaming of Heaven, building it here.

Churches!
Thank God for the scope of them,
For the aims and the deeds and the hope of them.

CHAUNCEY R. PIETY

———o———

Urgently in need of sleeping cars, a Canadian railroad inserted the following advertisement in one of the trade journals:
"300 Sleepers Wanted. At Once."
A short time later they received a letter from a minister of a church in Iowa offering his entire congregation.

MELVIN E. LUKENBACH in *Coronet*

———o———

The old problem of getting congregations to occupy the front pews has been solved by the Trenton, Michigan, Community Presbyterian Church. The first three rows — and only the first three rows — are temptingly equipped with foam-rubber cushions.

———o———

A church exists for the double purpose of gathering in and sending out.

———o———

The reason that rain or shine keeps you away from the church is the reason why the church is necessary.

———o———

Are You Going?

It was
Sunday morning
At the breakfast
Table,
And my host asked
Mrs. Host —
Meaning his wife —
If she was
Going to church.

And I thought
That was funny —
If that's the
Right word.

Strange is better
Maybe —
Or tragic —
Or unfortunate.

I couldn't see why
It should be a
Matter for debate;
Because she was
In good health,
And they were
Members of the
Church.

AUTHOR UNKNOWN

———o———

When you think of yourself and your relation to your church it might be a good motto to "be square all week and be 'round on Sunday."

CLIFF COLE

———o———

Across The Pastor's Desk

Sometime ago, a newspaper carried a story about Mrs. Lila Craig, 81, who had not missed in her church attendance in 1,040 Sundays — a perfect record for twenty years. With tongue in cheek, the writer asked, "What's wrong with Mrs. Craig?"

1. Doesn't Mrs. Craig ever have company on Sunday?

2. Doesn't she ever go anywhere on Saturday night, so that she gets up tired on Sunday morning?

3. Doesn't she ever have headaches, colds, nervous spells, tired feelings, poor breakfasts, sudden trips out of the city, business trips, Sunday picnics, family reunions?

4. Doesn't she ever sleep late on Sunday morning?

5. Doesn't she have any friends who invite her to go on a weekend trip?

6. Doesn't she ever read the Sunday paper?

7. Doesn't it ever rain or snow in her town on Sunday?

8. Doesn't she ever become angry at the minister or her teacher?

9. Doesn't she ever get her feelings hurt by someone at church?

10. Doesn't she have a radio or TV set so that she can stay home and hear some good services?

Church attendance is a privilege which each of us has as a Christian. It is a witness to what we believe. It is fortification for our lives. It is the opportunity to meet God in the beauty of His sanctuary.

See you in church!

Chimes of Hope

———o———

You Arx Important!

Whxn you arx txmptxd to takx a Sunday off, and you think that thx absxncx of onx pxrson won't makx too much diffxrxncx at church, you placx your ministxr in thx samx position as a fxllow trying to typx with onx kxy missing. Hx can makx substitutions just as wx havx donx, but thx rxsult is nxvxr thx samx as whxn hx's with all thx mxmbxrs of thx congrxgation!

———o———

A pastor in Daytona Beach, Florida had a good idea. In a recent bulletin he ran a check list; across the top were the words, "I cannot attend church services because: . . ." And then . . . "Please check." Following were some reasons that a person could check: "Too busy. Must go to the movies. Pleasure trip. Company. Have to go fishing. Disinterestedness. Radio and TV programs. Need to rest." And then there was this instruction across the bottom: "Please tear off and mail to God."

ROBERT E. GOODRICH, JR.

———o———

Moribus Sabbaticus

Sunday sickness, or *moribus sabbaticus,* is a sickness peculiar to church members, and it recurs every seventh day. There will be no suggestion of the disease until Sunday morning, and without the least difficulty it can develop very quickly.

The symptoms vary, but the disease never interferes with the appetite. It never lasts more than twenty-four hours, and often much less. It is never necessary to call a physician, yet the disease is very contagious. No symptoms are felt on Saturday night, but the attack develops suddenly on Sunday morning. The patient awakens as usual, feeling well, and eats a hearty breakfast. About nine o'clock the first attack comes on and lasts usually until noon. And in the afternoon, the patient is much improved and is able to ride and read the Sunday papers.

The aftermath is that on Monday morning the patient who is subject to Sunday sickness, is out bright and early, meeting friends at the drugstore corner and attending to business with the usual interest and briskness.

This strange disease has proved very much of an epidemic. In nearly every home there will be one or more cases every Sunday.

Christian Life

————o————

The minister was inquiring of one of his flock why he had not attended church recently. "Well, you see, sir," said the man, "I've been troubled with a bunion on my foot."

"Strange," said the minister, "that a bunion should impede the pilgrim's progress."

Watchman Examiner

————o————

The new preacher looked coldly at Deacon Smith and said he had heard that the deacon went to a ball game instead of to church last Sunday. "That's a lie!" the shocked deacon cried, "And I've got the fish to prove it."

————o————

What kind of church
   Would my church be,
If everyone in it
   Were just like me?

————o————

An Ordinary Member

Just an ordinary member of the church,
   I heard him say.
But you'd always find him present,
   even on a rainy day.
He had a hearty handclasp for the
   stranger in the aisle,
And a friend who was in trouble found
   sunshine in his smile.
When the sermon helped him, he told
   the preacher so

And when he needed comfort, he let
   the pastor know.
He always paid up promptly, and tried
   to do his share
In all the ordinary tasks for which some
   have no care.
His talents were not many but his love
   for God was true;
His prayers were not in public, but he
   prayed for me and you.
An ordinary member? I think that I
   would say
He was extraordinary in a humble sort
   of way.

LILLIAN M. WEEKS

in *First Methodist Messenger*, Pasadena, Calif.

————o————

A statistician has figured that 5% of all church members do not exist; 10% of them cannot be found; 25% never go to church; 50% never contribute a cent to the Lord's work; 75% never attend a midweek prayer service; 90% do not have family worship in their homes, and more than 95% have never tried to win a soul to Christ!

Easygoing religions make the going easy for the devil.

Circumstances

Man is not the creature of circumstances. Circumstances are the creatures of men.

BENJAMIN DISRAELI, *Vivian Grey*

————o————

People are always blaming their circumstances for what they are. I don't believe in circumstances. The people who get on in the world are the people who get up and look for the circumstances they want, and, if they can't find them, make them.

GEORGE BERNARD SHAW,
Mrs. Warren's Profession

————o————

There are no circumstances, no matter how unfortunate, that clever people do not extract some advantage from; and none, no matter how fortunate, that the unwise cannot turn to their own disadvantage.

FRANÇOIS, DUC DE LA ROCHEFOUCAULD

It is our relation to circumstances that determine their influence over us. The same wind that carries one vessel into port may blow another off shore.

———o———

Circumstances are like featherbeds. So long as you're on top of your circumstances, you're fine. But if you allow those circumstances to get on top of you, they'll suffocate you with the pressure of discouragement and hopelessness.

———o———

It is not the circumstances of our lives that give them character, but our relationships to God under any circumstances.

———o———

The ideal man bears the accidents of life with dignity and grace, making the best of the circumstances.

ARISTOTLE

———o———

Superiority to circumstances is one of the most prominent characteristics of great men.

HORACE MANN

———o———

Circumstances may prevent you from building a fortune, but they have no power to prevent you from building character.

Civilization

Perhaps the supreme product of civilization is people who can endure it.

FRANKLIN P. JONES

———o———

Let us not condemn civilization. It has brought us marvels . . . Civilization is good to have; it is dangerous to be lost in.

RABBI ABRAHAM HESCHEL

———o———

It would have helped a lot if the pioneers had located cities closer to airports.

Advertiser, Salisbury, Maryland

Civilization is just a slow process of being kind.

CHARLES L. LUCAS

———o———

When a civilization reaches the phase of worshipping comfort, it is unfailingly conquered by one of tougher ambitions.

WILLIAM S. SCHLAMM

Clean

Church Cleaning

We cleaned our little church today —
Wiped all the dust and dirt away.
We straightened papers, washed the floors;
Wiped off the light and painted doors.

We brushed the dirt stains from the books
And whisked the cobwebs from the nooks.
We polished windows so we'd see
The newly greening shrub and tree.

The menfolks, too, raked up the yard —
They laughed and said it wasn't hard,
And, oh, it felt so very good
To have the place look as it should.

We said, "How wonderful 'twould be
"If we cleaned out what we can't see —
"Such things as grudges, hates, and lies,
"And musty thoughts much worse than flies."

Selected, from *Christian Witness*

———o———

Clean living makes the undertaker wait longer for his money.

———o———

Just as Jesus found it necessary to sweep the money-changers from the Temple porch, so we ourselves need a lot of housecleaning.

DALE EVANS

———o———

Lord, that my words may be as clean
As any sunshine-whitened stone
Within a meadow, vernal-fair;
My thoughts as clean as mountain air
Along a sky-reflecting lake
Where morning-joyful birds awake;

My heart as clean as when beside
An ocean with a shining tide
I stood with Thee and saw the Grace
Upon Thy holy, selfless face.

GRACE V. WATKINS

———o———

Between the dark and the daylight,
When the night is beginning to lower,
Little paws, black from day's occupations,
Make what is known as the "Children's Scour!"

———o———

Cleanliness is, indeed, next to godliness.

JOHN WESLEY

Clothing

Tommy: "Is it true that pigskins make the best shoes?"
Johnny: "I don't know, but banana skins make the best slippers."

———o———

Keeping your clothes well pressed will keep you from looking hard pressed.

COLEMAN COX

———o———

You are never fully dressed until you wear a smile.

———o———

The fashion wears out more apparel than the man.

WILLIAM SHAKESPEARE,
Much Ado About Nothing

———o———

My Sunday Cloak

My Sunday cloak's a lovely thing,
Its pattern woven by a King.
It wraps me close in special grace,
Which knows no strangeness anyplace.
"I'm all you need," it seems to say,
"Why don't you wear me everyday?"

But it doesn't match my Monday shoes.

My feet have many things to do,
Important things that I pursue.

The gods entice; I must adore,
To win their blessing just once more.
Just one more time to know their touch,
Just one more time — that's not too much.

(My Sunday cloak's a lovely thing,
Its pattern woven by a King.)

But it doesn't match my Tuesday mask.

This face pretends it cannot see;
It honors none — not even me.
It makes believe no choices burn,
And so evades its soul's concern.
It's wearing thin? Oh, yes, I know.
But still I cling — I need it so.

(My Sunday cloak's a lovely thing,
Its pattern woven by a King.)

But it doesn't match my Wednesday gloves.

But gloves somehow don't hide my hands
Outstretched to kill with their demands.
They point with hate and faith deny
The love which came — and stayed to die.
But wash them clean from nail to wrist?
I can't; I can't unclench my fist.

(My Sunday cloak's a lovely thing,
Its pattern woven by a King.)

But it doesn't match my Thursday beads.

And stone by stone my necklace glows
To feed the lusts on which it grows.
God's offered plans ignored, denied;
I have my own. They must be tried.
But if they fail, then hear my plea:
"Why me, Oh God? Why Me? Why Me?"

(My Sunday cloak's a lovely thing,
Its pattern woven by a King.)

But it doesn't match my Friday purse.

And to this purse I have to hold,
For this is where I store my gold.
Here the thefts and lies unfurled;
These my treasure — this my world.
For this is how I pay my way!
And give it up? I can't today.

(My Sunday cloak's a lovely thing,
Its pattern woven by a King.)

But it doesn't match my Saturday mood.

This mood screams back in grim despair,
"It isn't right! It isn't fair!
"Why always theirs and never mine?
"Is this God's plan? A plan divine?"

But still He comes to help me pray.
— To hold my cloak — To lead the way.

My Sunday cloak's a lovely thing,
Its pattern woven by a King.
It wraps me close in special grace,
Which knows no strangeness anyplace.
"I'm all you need," it seems to say,
"Why don't you wear me everyday?"

BLANCHE SMITH

Comfort

Oh, the comfort, the inexpressible comfort, of feeling safe with a person having neither to weigh thoughts nor measure words, but pouring them all right out, just as they are, chaff and grain together, certain that a faithful hand will take and sift them, keeping what is worth keeping, and with the breath of kindness blow the rest away.

DINAH MARIA MULOCH CRAIK

———o———

God often comforts us, not by changing the circumstances of our lives, but by changing our attitude towards them.

S. H. B. MASTERMAN

———o———

The Psalm Of Comfort

The Lord is my Counselor, I shall not feel insecure.
He leads me into quiet moments of meditation;
I hear Him bid me be still.
He restores my soul.
He leads me in paths of service that I may glorify His name.
Even though the darkness of selfishness, greed and hate would destroy me, I am not afraid.
The promise of His word keeps me firm.
In the presence of my sin and failure He proves His love.
His forgiveness washes away all guilt, my joy knows no bounds.

Surely as I serve Him with love and humility
He shall abide with me and I shall know His peace.

MARGARETTE A. WOOD

———o———

Consolation

When I sink down in gloom or fear,
Hope blighted or delayed,
Thy whisper, Lord, my heart shall cheer,
" 'Tis I, be not afraid!"

Or, startled at some sudden blow,
If fretful thoughts I feel,
"Fear not, it is but I!" shall flow,
As balm my wound to heal.

JOHN H. NEWMAN

Committee

If you want to get a job done, give it to an individual; if you want to have it studied, give it to a committee.

———o———

Committee work is like an easy chair — easy to get into but hard to get out of.

———o———

Birth Of Committees

We sat in committee all morning,
   discussing the "cons and the pros,"
At noon we adjourned by creating
   . . . more committees to re-dig our rows.

LESLIE CONRAD, JR.
in Church Management

———o———

It's a mighty good thing that the Ten Commandments were handed down direct instead of being obliged to pass through the hands of a few committees.

CLIFF COLE

———o———

A committee of one gets things done.

JOE RYAN, Ben Roth Syndicate

———o———

A committee consists of those who are unwilling to do the unnecessary.

If machines get too powerful we can organize them into committees, and that will do them in.

————o————

Standing committees should sit down often because they tire easily and others especially!

Common Sense

I read, I study, I examine, I listen, I reflect, and out of all this I try to form an idea into which I put as much common sense as I can.

LAFAYETTE

————o————

The only way to play it cool is to wait until you're through being hot under the collar.

————o————

Common sense is instinct. Enough of it is genius.

GEORGE BERNARD SHAW

————o————

O God, give the world common sense, beginning with me.

————o————

Common sense in an uncommon degree is what the world calls wisdom.

SAMUEL TAYLOR COLERIDGE

————o————

A handful of common sense is worth a bushel of learning.

Spanish Proverb

————o————

The finest education is useless without common sense.

E. F. GIRARD

————o————

Lord, if I dig a pit for others
Let me fall into it;
But if I dig it for myself,
Give me sense enough to walk around it.

SHERWOOD E. WIRT

————o————

Those who keep their feet on the ground aren't likely to lose standing.

Good sense is a thing all need, few have, and none think they want.

BENJAMIN FRANKLIN

Communication

Communication is depositing a part of yourself in another person.

————o————

Strides in communication now permit us to talk with people around the globe, but cannot bridge the ever-widening gaps within our own families.

GLORIA FRANCE

Communion

Communion

In memory of the Saviour's love,
  We keep the sacred feast,
Where every humble, contrite heart
  Is made a welcome guest.
By faith we take the Bread of Life
  With which our souls are fed,
The Cup in token of His blood
  That was for sinners shed.
In faith and memory thus we sing
  The wonders of His love,
And thus anticipate by faith
  The heavenly feast above.

The Evangel

————o————

If the individual can commune with God, then he must matter to God; and if he matters to God, he must share God's eternity.

JOHN BAILLIE

————o————

Silent Communion

O teach me, Lord, that I may teach
The precious things Thou dost impart:
And wing my words that they may reach
The hidden depths of many a heart.
Amen.

FRANCES RIDLEY HAVERGAL

————o————

The measure of the worth of our public activity for God is the private communion we have with Him.

OSWALD CHAMBERS

Oh, to reach up to the heights that He
   planned,
Though they be rough.
Finding His smile and the touch of His
   hand
Always enough.

Communism

To Fight Communism . . .

Alert yourself – learn the true nature
   and tactics of communism.
Make civic programs for social improvement your business.
Exercise your right to vote; elect representatives of integrity.
Respect human dignity – communism
   and individual rights cannot coexist.
Inform yourself . . . know your country
   – its history, traditions and heritage.
Combat public apathy toward communism – indifference can be fatal
   when national survival is at stake.
Attack bigotry and prejudice wherever
   they appear; justice for all is the
   bulwark of democracy.

J. EDGAR HOOVER

———o———

A communist is like a crocodile.
When it opens its mouth you cannot
tell whether it is trying to smile or
preparing to eat you up.

SIR WINSTON CHURCHILL

———o———

Communism possesses a language
which every people can understand.
Its elements are hunger, envy, and
death.

HEINRICH HEINE

———o———

In a communist country they name
a street after you one day and chase
you down it the next.

The Irish Digest

———o———

What is a communist? One who has
yearnings for equal division of unequal
earnings. Idler or bungler, he is willing to fork out his penny and pocket
your shilling.

EBENEZER ELLIOTT

It is clear that we can never cope
with Communism simply by fearing it
and hating it. We must recapture our
own national sense of purpose, our devotion to a great cause, and a vital
faith.

BILLY GRAHAM

———o———

Every human ideology comes to an
end sometime and Communism, too,
will be a thing of the past, maybe much
sooner than anyone presently thinks.
There already are traces of crumbling
and falling down.

BISHOP OTTO DIBELIUS

Compensation

Most people don't care how much
they pay for something, as long as it's
not all at once.

———o———

Those who reason that "the world
owes me a living" are likely to discover
that the pay days are somewhat irregular.

———o———

My Wages

I bargained with Life for a penny and
   Life would pay no more,
However I begged at evening, as I
   counted my scanty score.
For Life is just an employer, he gives
   you what you ask;
But once you have set the wages, you
   must perform the task.
I worked for a menial's hire, only to
   learn, dismayed,
That any wage I had asked of Life,
   Life would have gladly paid.

AUTHOR UNKNOWN

Competition

A group of clergymen were discussing whether or not they ought to invite
Dwight L. Moody to their city. The
success of the famed evangelist was
brought to the attention of the men.
One unimpressed minister commented, "Does Mr. Moody have a monopoly
on the Holy Ghost?"

Another man quietly replied, "No, but the Holy Ghost seems to have a monopoly on Mr. Moody."
Sunday

———o———

Don't be afraid of opposition. Remember a kite rises against, not with, the wind.
HAMILTON W. MABIE

———o———

Competition comes in place of monopoly; and intelligence and industry ask only for fair play and an open field.
DANIEL WEBSTER

Complain

A noted preacher had a special black book labeled "Complaints of Members Against One Another." When one of his congregation told him about the faults of another, he would say, "Here is my complaint book. I will write down what you say, and you can sign it. Then when I have time I will take up the matter officially concerning this brother." The sight of the open book and the ready pen had its effect. "Oh, no, I couldn't sign anything like that!" they would say. In 40 years this preacher never got anyone to write a line in it.
Voice of Truth

———o———

A repining life is a lingering death.
BENJAMIN WHICHOUTE

———o———

A Christian lady was complaining to a friend about the hardness of life and the circumstances that buffeted her and in anger said: "Oh, I would to God that I had never been made!" "My dear child," replied the friend, "you are not yet made; you are only being made, and you are quarreling with God's processes."

———o———

Constant complaint is the poorest sort of play for all the comforts we enjoy.
BENJAMIN FRANKLIN

Everyone sympathizes with the chronic grouch when he has to be by himself!

———o———

It is easier to complain than it is to get out and hustle.

Compliment

Everybody knows how to express a complaint, but few can utter a graceful compliment.

———o———

Success in dealing with other people is like making rhubarb pie — use all the sugar you can, and then double it.
Banking

———o———

J. A. Persson of Sweden, missionary to Africa, was going home on furlough, and the Christians at his station were having a farewell dinner. An African native paid the missionary the highest compliment he could think of: "Mr. Persson may have a white skin, but his heart is as black as any of us."
Presbyterian Survey

———o———

Everybody likes a praise-giver. Nobody likes a praise-grabber.

———o———

A man's body is so sensitive that when you pat him on the back, his head swells.

———o———

Praise loudly, blame softly.

Compromise

A compromise is the art of dividing a cake in such a way that everyone believes that he has got the biggest piece.
LUDWIG ERHARD, German Minister of Economics in *The Observer*, London

———o———

Compromise is always wrong when it means a sacrifice principle.

———o———

Many things are worse than defeat and compromise with evil is one of them.

Remember the uncertain soldier in our Civil War who, figuring to play it safe, dressed himself in a blue coat and gray pants and tip-toed out into the field of battle. He got shot from both directions.

Paul Harvey News

———o———

The concessions of the weak are the concessions of fear.

EDMUND BURKE

Computer

The only thing a computer can do when a request is made is to call on its memory bank, which is intake. Eventually it may suffer from hardening of the categories.

———o———

Computers will not really have replaced people until and if somebody figures out a way to discipline them for their mistakes.

Conceit

Conceit is what makes a little squirt think that he is a fountain of knowledge.

———o———

A conceited man is like a man up in a balloon: everybody looks small to him and he looks small to everybody.

———o———

I always like to hear a man talk about himself, because then I never hear anything but good.

WILL ROGERS

———o———

Conceit is a closer companion of ignorance than of learning.

———o———

Conceit may puff a man up, but never prop him up.

JOHN RUSKIN

———o———

If you want to know how important you are in the world, stick your finger in a pan of water and see the hole that is left.

The head never begins to swell until the mind stops growing.

———o———

Conceit is a form of disease that makes everybody sick except the one who has it.

———o———

Conceit causes more conversation than wit.

———o———

The arrogant and self-centered fellow is to be pitied: he has no true friends; for in prosperity he knows nobody, and in adversity nobody knows him.

———o———

He that falls in love with himself will have no rivals.

BENJAMIN FRANKLIN

Concern

Could I climb to the highest place in Athens, I would lift up my voice and proclaim: Fellow citizens, why do ye turn and scrape every stone to gather wealth, and take so little care of your children, to whom one day you must relinquish it all?

SOCRATES

———o———

Walter, who was not quite five, knew much about the Lord Jesus and had accepted him as Saviour. The forgiveness of his sin made him happy.

He surprised us with the question, "Did the Lord Jesus know how many people there were in the world and how many more there would be when He died for them?"

Is the fact that One died for all the sins of all people still able to move us? Does that once-and-for-all offering of Jesus still have anything to say in this day and age?

HEDWIG GUT, Berlin, Germany
in *The Gospel Call*

———o———

When To Be Alarmed

If you find yourself . . .
coveting any pleasure
more than your prayer times,

enjoying any book
more than your Bible,
reading the newspapers for relaxation
more than the Bible or some spiritual book,
reverencing any house
more than the House of God,
satisfied with any table
more than the Lord's Table,
loving any person
more than our Lord Jesus Christ,
seeking the fellowship of men
more than that of the Holy Spirit,
or delighted with any prospect
more than that of the return of Jesus,
. . . then take alarm.

AUTHOR UNKNOWN

Confidence

Confidence is the feeling you have before you know better.

———o———

Why should there not be a patient confidence in the ultimate justice of the people? Is there any better or equal hope in the world?

ABRAHAM LINCOLN

———o———

A little girl was taking a long journey, and in the course of the day her train crossed a number of rivers. The water seen in advance always awakened doubts and fears in the child. She did not understand how it could safely be crossed. As they drew near the river, however, a bridge appeared and furnished the way over. Several times the same thing happened, and finally the child leaned back with a long breath of relief and confidence: "Somebody has put bridges for us all the way." So God does likewise for His children all through life.

Selected

———o———

The best way to acquire self-confidence is to do exactly what you are afraid to do.

———o———

Our confidence in Christ does not make us lazy, negligent or careless, but on the contrary it awakens us, urges us on, and makes us active in living righteous lives and doing good. There is no self-confidence to compare with this.

ULRICH ZWINGLI

———o———

A well-adjusted person is one who makes the same mistake twice without getting nervous!

JANE HEARD in *The Progressive Farmer*

———o———

Confidence is a thing not to be produced by compulsion. Men cannot be forced into trust.

DANIEL WEBSTER

———o———

Confidence is that feeling by which the mind embarks on great and honorable courses with a sure hope and trust in itself.

MARCUS TULLIUS CICERO

———o———

Skill and confidence are an unconquered enemy.

Confusion

Why do those who "run in circles" never realize that they always end up right where they started?

———o———

Give a man some facts and he will draw his own confusions.

———o———

When you are confused it's when you don't know enough about a thing to be worried.

WILL ROGERS

Conquer

A conqueror is one who wins by fighting; a "more than conqueror" is one who wins without fighting.

———o———

Me

Today I had a battle,
The fight was hard and long;
My opponent was so stubborn,
And I knew him to be wrong.

We didn't need a referee,
Because, when we were through,
The decision was unquestioned,
Nor did we start anew.
I never did like fighting,
And yet I fail to see
How I could help but cheer a bit
When I had conquered ME.
HAZEL V. WOLFE
in *The Log of the Good Ship Grace*

———o———

They conquer who believe they can.
JOHN DRYDEN

———o———

Make me a captive, Lord,
And then I shall be free.
Force me to render up my sword,
And I shall conqueror be.
GEORGE MATHESON

———o———

If thou wouldst conquer thy weakness thou must not gratify it.
WILLIAM PENN

———o———

I count him braver who overcomes his desires than him who conquers his enemies; for the hardest victory is the victory over self.
ARISTOTLE

———o———

Who has a harder fight than he who is striving to overcome himself?
THOMAS À KEMPIS

———o———

Conquest pursues where courage leads the way.
SIR SAMUEL GARTH, *The Dispensary*

———o———

Don't try to overcome the inevitable — just don't let the inevitable overcome you.

Conscience

Conscience and reputation are closely related — a man who has a good conscience seldom gets a bad reputation.

———o———

A good conscience is a continual Christmas.
BENJAMIN FRANKLIN, *Poor Richard*

A twinge of conscience is a glimpse of God.
PETER USTINOV

———o———

Conscience is that small voice that makes us feel small when we do something small.
EVA JO STEPHEN

———o———

Guilty consciences always make people cowards.
PILPAY

———o———

Man's conscience is the oracle of God.
LORD BYRON, *The Island*

———o———

The Signal Lights

"It was well you stopped when the red
    light flashed,"
She said, as we drove along,
"For an officer stood at the corner
    there,
In charge of the traffic throng."
And I smiled and said to my daughter
    fair,
As we waited on the spot,
"I always stop when the red light
    shows,
Be an officer there or not."
Then she sat in thought as we drove
    along
And suddenly this she said,
"There ought to be lights for us all
    through life —
The amber and green and red.
What help 'twould be if a red light
    flashed
Where danger and shame were near,
And we all might wait till the green
    light came
To show that the road was clear."
"My dear," said I, "we have tried to
    light
Life's road for your feet to fare,
And pray you'll stop when the red
    light glows,
Though none of us may be there.
We have tried to teach you the signs
    of wrong
And the way to a life serene,
So stop when your conscience post
    shows red —
And go when it flashes green."
EDGAR A. GUEST

Conscience gets a lot of credit that should really belong to cold feet.

———o———

Conscience warns us as a friend before it punishes us as a judge.

STANISLAS I (King of Poland)

———o———

"Conscience," said an Indian, "is a three-cornered thing in my heart that stands still when I am good, but when I am bad, it turns around and the corners hurt a lot. If I keep on doing wrong, the corners wear off and it does not hurt any more."

Construction Digest

———o———

Conscience is thoroughly well bred, and soon leaves off talking to those who do not wish to hear it.

SAMUEL BUTLER

———o———

The most painful wound in the world is a stab of conscience.

JOHN ELLIS LARGE

———o———

Asked to describe her conscience, one young girl said: "It's a gray ghost inside you with a friendly face but it stops smiling when your nerves begin to write a note to it when you want to do something bad and when the ghost sees this bad note he gets very angry and yells 'Stop!' "

The Secret World of Kids

———o———

Conscience is a weak, inner voice that sometimes doesn't speak your language.

———o———

Conscience is the chamber of justice.

———o———

Conscience is never dilatory in her warnings.

Consecration

A life totally consecrated to God sees all of its tasks as God-appointed.

———o———

I go out to preach with two proposi-tions in mind. First, every person ought to give his life to Christ. Second, whether or not anyone else gives Him his life, I will give Him mine.

JONATHAN EDWARDS

———o———

Consecration

Lord, my greatest is so little,
  And my most is yet so small,
When I measure it with Jesus
  There is nothing left at all,
And I hesitate to answer
  When I hear Thee call.

Can the Lord, who owns the cattle
  On a thousand fertile hills,
He who speaks in voice commanding
  And the angry water stills —
Can the Lord, who died for sinners
  On the cross of Calvary,
Use me even in my weakness?
  Yes, for He demands of me
Perfect strength, and then He gives it
  In His all-sufficiency.
Take my greatest, Lord — 'tis noth-
    ing —
  And my strongest, though 'tis less.
Thou canst use the little, Father,
  And the humble offering bless;
And I'll serve Thee, Lord, forever
  And Thy blessed name confess.

AUTHOR UNKNOWN

———o———

"Kept By The Power Of God"
(I Peter 1:5)

My Life Kept for Jesus. Colossians 3:3, 4
My Time Kept for Jesus. Psalm 31:15
My Hands Kept for Jesus. Psalm 24: 3, 4
My Feet Kept for Jesus. I Samuel 2:9
My Voice Kept for Jesus. Psalm 40:3
My Lips Kept for Jesus. Psalm 51:15
My Intellect Kept for Jesus. Isaiah 26: 3
My Will Kept for Jesus. Hebrews 13: 20, 21
My Heart Kept for Jesus. Luke 24:32
My Love Kept for Jesus. I John 4:19, 21

REV. J. BECHTEL (*Based on a hymn by* FRANCES RIDLEY HAVERGAL, 1874, "Take My Life and Let it Be.")

To be crucified means, first, the man on the cross is facing only one direction; second, he is not going back; and third, he has no further plans of his own.

A. W. TOZER

———o———

Consecration is not giving to God, but taking hands off what belongs to God.

———o———

You cannot give to the world any more than you give to God.

———o———

Our business is to do the will of God. He will take care of the business.

Consequence

Our deeds still travel with us from afar, And what we have been makes us what we are.

GEORGE ELIOT (MARY ANN EVANS)

———o———

No action, whether foul or fair, Is ever done, but it leaves somewhere A record, written by fingers ghostly, As a blessing or a curse.

HENRY WADSWORTH LONGFELLOW, *The Golden Legend*

Consistent

A foolish consistency is the hobgoblin of little minds.

RALPH WALDO EMERSON

———o———

We need to learn to set our course by the stars and not by the lights of every passing ship.

OMAR BRADLEY

———o———

Those who honestly mean to be true contradict themselves more rarely than those who try to be consistent.

OLIVER WENDELL HOLMES

———o———

Always endeavor to be really what you would wish to appear.

GRANVILLE SHARP

———o———

The true man professes only what he practices.

Content, Contentment

It is right to be content with what we have, never with what we are.

SIR JAMES MACKINTOSH

———o———

As Noah's dove found no footing but in the ark, so a Christian finds no contentment but in Christ.

MASON

———o———

O what a happy soul am I; although
    I cannot see,
I am resolved that in this world
Contented I will be;
How many blessings I enjoy
That other people don't!
To weep and sigh because I'm blind,
I cannot, and I won't!

FANNY JANE CROSBY

———o———

Suppose all the joys, the cares, and the opportunities afforded you in life could be gathered into a bag which you could carry on your shoulders. And suppose each person in the world brought his burden to one common heap, there to be given the privilege of depositing his bag and selecting any other bag of his choice. Do you know what would happen? Invariably, each one would be content once again to pick up the bag he had deposited on the heap and go his way.

Based on PLUTARCH, *Consolation to Apollonius*

———o———

Contentment comes when we remember that what God chooses is far better than what we choose.

———o———

Sweet are the thoughts that savour of content;
The quiet mind is richer than a crown.
    . . .
A mind content both crown and kingdom is.

ROBERT GREENE, *Farewell to Folly*

———o———

Content's a kingdom.

THOMAS HEYWOOD

He that wants money, means, and content is without three good friends.
WILLIAM SHAKESPEARE, *As You Like It*

———o———

Contentment is natural wealth.
SOCRATES

Control

When it comes to the control of our lives, we are either "body" men or "spirit" men.
ERIC LINDHOLM

———o———

Controls

You cannot control the length of your life, but you can control its width and depth.

You cannot control the contour of your countenance, but you can control its expression.

You cannot control the other fellow's opportunities, but you can grasp your own.

You cannot control the weather, but you can control the moral atmosphere which surrounds you.

You cannot control the distance that your head shall be above the ground, but you can control the height of the contents of your head.

You cannot control the other fellow's faults, but you can see to it that you yourself do not develop or harbor provoking propensities.

Why worry about things you cannot control? Why not get busy controlling the things that depend on you.
Highway of Happiness

Conversation

Conversation is the laboratory and workshop of the student.
RALPH WALDO EMERSON

———o———

Good talk is like good scenery – continuous, yet constantly varying, and full of the charm of novelty and surprise.
RANDOLPH S. BOURNE

———o———

The reason why so few people are agreeable in conversation, is, that each is thinking more of what he is intending to say, than of what others are saying; and we never listen when we are planning to speak.
FRANÇOIS, DUC DE LA ROCHEFOUCAULD

———o———

It may be difficult to practice, but it seems to us that one of the main rules of conversation is never to speak when you ought to be listening. Also it's a fine builder of personal appreciation.

———o———

For a really fetching conversation, three persons are required: two to talk and one to be the topic.
Dixie County Advocate,
Cross City, Florida

———o———

It's surprising how many conversations develop into a monologue.

———o———

A clever young lady was asked to attend a public function. She was assigned a place between a noted bishop and an equally famous rabbi. It was her chance to break into high company and she meant to use it.

"I feel as if I were a leaf between the Old and New Testaments," she said brilliantly, during a lull in the conversation.

"That page, Madam," replied the rabbi, "is usually a blank."

———o———

It's all right to hold a conversation, but you should let go of it now and then.

———o———

The value of the average conversation could be enormously improved by the constant use of four simple words: "I do not know."
ANDRÉ MAUROIS

———o———

A single conversation across the table with a wise man is worth a month's study of books.
Chinese Proverb

———o———

Conversation is an art in which a man has all mankind for competitors.
RALPH WALDO EMERSON

The best guide to conversation is to ask questions.

———o———

Silence is one of the great arts of conversation.

MARCUS TULLIUS CICERO

Conversion

Conversion is not a repairing of the old building; but it takes all down and erects a new structure. It is not the sewing on a patch of holiness; but with the true convert, holiness is woven into all his powers, principles and practice.

JOSEPH ALLEINE,
An Alarm to the Unconverted

———o———

If good books did good, the world would have been converted long ago.

———o———

A man may be convicted yet never converted, but no man is converted unless he has first been convicted.

D. THURLOW YAXLEY

Conviction

If you don't stand for something, you'll fall for anything.

———o———

He who floats with the current, who does not guide himself according to higher principles, who has no ideal, no convictions — such a man is a mere article of the world's furniture — a thing moved, instead of a living and moving being — an echo, not a voice. The man who has no inner life is the slave of his surroundings, as the barometer is the obedient servant of the air at rest and the weathercock the humble servant of the air in motion.

———o———

I can only say that I have acted upon my best convictions, without selfishness or malice, and that by the help of God I shall continue to do so.

ABRAHAM LINCOLN

Real convictions disturb. They also attract.

———o———

In one of the great crises of Martin Luther's life, when he was standing firmly and alone for a conviction that he refused to surrender, he was confronted furiously by a powerful opponent. Did he realize, asked that opponent, what he was doing and what power he was defying? Did he expect any force worth mentioning to take up arms and come to his help? "No," said Luther quietly, "I do not expect that."
"Then where will you be?" thundered the dignitary who had come to challenge him. "Where will you be?"
And to that Luther answered in words that seem to go to the very heart of things, "I shall be where I have always been — in the hands of Almighty God."

———o———

The men who succeed best in public life are those who take the risk of standing by their own convictions.

JAMES A. GARFIELD

Cooperate

Horse Sense

A horse can't pull while kicking
This fact we merely mention,
And he can't kick while pulling,
Which is our chief contention.

Let's imitate the good horse
And lead a life that's fitting;
Just pull an honest load, and
Then there'll be no time for kicking.

———o———

Begin this morning by saying to thyself, I shall meet with the busybody, the ungrateful, arrogant, deceitful, envious, unsocial. All these things happen to them by reason of their ignorance of what is good and evil. But I who have seen the nature of the good, that it is beautiful, and of the bad and that it is ugly, and the nature of him who does wrong, that it is akin to me, not only of the same blood but that it participates in the same intelligence and the same portion of the divinity, I can neither be injured by any of them, nor can I be angry with my kinsman nor hate him. For we are made for cooperation, like feet, like hands. To act against one another, then, is contrary to nature, and it is acting against one another to be vexed and to turn away. The best way of avenging thyself is not to become like the wrong-doer. Men exist for the sake of one another. Teach them, then, or bear with them.

MARCUS AURELIUS

———o———

Getting along in this world depends a lot on getting along well with others.

———o———

A man said to his body, "Today I will go with you three times to eat, but you will come with me three times to pray."

AUTHOR UNKNOWN

———o———

A little boy asked his father for assistance in repairing his broken wagon. When the job was done, the boy looked up and said, "Daddy, when I try to do things by myself, they go wrong. But when you and I work together, they turn out just fine."

———o———

Light is the task when many share the toil.

HOMER

———o———

Cooperation is spelled with two letters — WE.

G. M. VERITY

Cost

It will cost me to be loyal to Christ — but it will also pay.

———o———

What Then?

You've counted the cost of high living, my friend,
The heat, light, water and food.

You've counted the rent, car insurance and gas, all of them,
But have you counted the cost if your soul should be lost? What then?

You've counted the days till your pay check comes,
You've counted the dollars withheld and why,
You've counted the dollars that you can bring home,
And how much those dollars will buy.
But have you counted the cost if your soul should be lost? What then?

You've counted the distance you travel to work,
And the distance you come back again.
You've counted the bills you cannot shirk,
How you can pay them, and when.
But have you counted the cost if your soul should be lost? What then?

You've counted the cost of a new home perhaps,
And the beauties that make home so bright,
Of the children playing around your door —
All of which is proper and right —
But have you thought, my brother, that sometime you'll die, and when?
Have you counted the cost if your soul should be lost? What then?

EDNA UBER
in *The Log of the Good Ship Grace*

Country

To live in the country one must have the soul of a poet, the mind of a philosopher, the simple tastes of a hermit — and a good station wagon.

———o———

The country for a wounded heart.

English Proverb

Courage

The Difference

Sure, it takes a lot of courage
  To put things in God's hands . . .
To give ourselves completely,
  Our lives, our hopes, our plans;

To follow where He leads us
    And make His will our own . . .
But all it takes is foolishness
    To go the way alone!
                        BETSEY KLINE

————o————

Courage is, on all hands, considered as an essential of high character.
                JAMES ANTHONY FROUDE

————o————

Remember you are your own doctor when it comes to curing cold feet.

————o————

Courage is fear that has said its prayers.

————o————

Courage is no more necessary on the battlefield than in the hourly choice between right and wrong!

————o————

Courage consists not in hazarding without fear, but being resolutely minded in a just cause.
                        PLUTARCH

————o————

Courage is a great thing. One may lose his money which is much, he may lose a friend and that is worse, but if he loses his courage he almost loses all.

————o————

If the glory of God is to break out in your service, you must be ready to go out into the night.
                M. BASILEA SCHLINK

————o————

Courage is the virtue that makes other virtues possible.
                SIR WINSTON CHURCHILL

————o————

Oftimes the test of courage becomes rather to live than to die.
            VITTORIO ALFIERI, Oreste

————o————

Two small boys entered a dentist's office and one addressed the dentist as follows: "Say, Doc, will you pull a tooth right this minute? Don't want any gas or nothin'. Just give her one yank."

"Surely," replied the dentist. "My lit-tle man, that's what I call being brave and courageous. Now just show me the tooth you want pulled."

"Come, Wilfred, show Doc your tooth."

Courtesy

Courtesy, after all, is only kindliness, politeness and civility.

————o————

Courtesy is the eye which overlooks your friend's broken gateway — but sees the rose which blossoms in his garden.
                        LYMAN ABBOTT

————o————

Courtesy, good cheer, friendliness — the ability to serve without ostentation, the willingness to give freely of that spirit of welcome that warms the heart — this makes friends.

————o————

Once upon a time a man gave up his seat on a bus to a woman. She fainted. On recovering, she thanked him. Then he fainted.

————o————

How sweet and gracious, even in common speech,
    Is that fine sense which men call Courtesy!
Wholesome as air and genial as the light,
    Welcome in every clime as breath of flowers,
It transmutes aliens into trusting friends,
    And gives its owner passport round the globe.
            JAMES THOMAS FIELDS, Courtesy

————o————

We must be as courteous to a man as we are to a picture, which we are willing to give the advantage of a good light.
                RALPH WALDO EMERSON,
                Conduct of Life, Behaviour

————o————

Courtesy comes from the heart. It is the unmistakable sign of good breeding.

Courtesy is made up of petty sacrifices.

———o———

That false courtesy, that smirking smile which comes from the lips only — is like a cheap gold plating, the baser metal soon shows through.

———o———

Some people should be sentenced to solitary refinement.

———o———

Courtesy is a science of the highest importance which ought to be on the curriculum of every Christian.

———o———

The small courtesies sweeten life; the greater ennoble it.
CHRISTIAN NESTELL BOVEE

Coward

There comes a time when silence is not golden — just plain yellow!

———o———

Necessity makes even the coward brave.
Old Proverb

———o———

Coward: one who in a perilous emergency thinks with his legs.
AMBROSE BIERCE

———o———

To sin by silence when they should protest makes cowards out of men.
ABRAHAM LINCOLN

Create, Creation

God creates out of nothing. Wonderful, you say. Yes, to be sure, but He does what is still more wonderful: He makes saints out of sinners.
SÖREN KIERKEGAARD

———o———

God never mends. He creates anew.
DWIGHT L. MOODY

———o———

Posterity will some day laugh at the foolishness of modern materialistic philosophy. The more I study nature, the more I am amazed at the Creator.
LOUIS PASTEUR

The probability of life originating from accident is comparable to the probability of the unabridged dictionary resulting from an explosion in a printing shop.
EDWIN CONKLIN

———o———

A little Ohio lad attending church school for the first time was asked by his teacher, "Who made you?"
"Made me?"
"Yes, who made you?"
"Why, God made me 'bout so long," holding his hands a few inches apart, "but I growed all the rest."
ORIGINAL SOURCE UNKNOWN

———o———

Nothing was made in vain, but the fly came near it.
MARK TWAIN

———o———

God created the world out of nothing. As long as you are not yet nothing, God cannot make something out of you.
MARTIN LUTHER

Credit

Many people would have skinny wallets if they removed the credit cards.

———o———

No man's credit is as good as his money.
EDGAR WATSON HOWE

———o———

You can accomplish almost anything if you don't care who gets the credit for it.

Creeds

I envy those men and women who know how to keep their creeds intact and unchanged throughout the entire journey of life. Their path is peace and their hope is sure.
SIR ARTHUR KEITH

———o———

Credo

Not what, but WHOM, I do believe,
That, in my darkest hour of need,
Hath comfort that no mortal creed

To mortal man may give;
Not what, but WHOM!
    For Christ is more than all the
      creeds,
    And His full life of gentle deeds
    Shall all the creeds outlive.
Not what I do believe, but WHOM!
    WHO walks beside me in the gloom?
    WHO shares the burden wearisome?
    WHO all the dim way doth illume,
    And bids me look beyond the tomb
    The larger life to live?
Not what I do believe,
But WHOM!
Not what,
But WHOM!

                JOHN OXENHAM

———o———

Here is my creed:
I believe in one God, creator of the
    Universe.
    That He governs it by His provi-
    dence.
    That He ought to be worshipped.
    That the most acceptable service we
    can render Him is doing good to
    His other children.
    That the soul of man is immortal,
    and will be treated with justice in
    another life respecting its conduct
    in this life.

                BENJAMIN FRANKLIN

———o———

The creed of today becomes the
deed of tomorrow.

                E. STANLEY JONES

Crime

Permit a child to always get what
he wants when he wants it — and you
have a criminal in the making.

                J. EDGAR HOOVER

———o———

The crime of the Christian church is
that we have withheld the Gospel from
the masses of people.

                A. B. SIMPSON

———o———

Seven National Crimes

Seven so-called "national crimes,"
which are in reality unwholesome
mental attitudes are as follows:

1. I don't think.
2. I don't know.
3. I don't care.
4. I am too busy.
5. I leave well enough alone.
6. I have no time to read and find
    out.
7. I am not interested.

                The Record

———o———

Whoever profits by the crime is
guilty of it.

                French Proverb

———o———

He who spares the guilty threatens
the innocent.

                Legal Maxim

———o———

Every unpunished murder takes
away something from the security of
every man's life.

                DANIEL WEBSTER

———o———

Murder may pass unpunished for a
    time,
But tardy justice will o'ertake the
    crime.

                JOHN DRYDEN

Criticize

The world has so many critics because it is so much easier to criticize
than to appreciate.

    LUC DE CLAPIERS VAUVENARGUES

———o———

He who throws mud loses ground.

            Presbyterian News

———o———

He who shrinks from criticism cannot safely be showered with praise.

———o———

You have to be little to belittle.

———o———

Nothing is easier than fault-finding;
no talent, no self-denial, no brains, no
character is required to set up in the
grumbling business.

———o———

At the close of a meeting a cynic
approached Mr. Moody and said:

"Mr. Moody, during your address this evening I counted eighteen mistakes in your English."

Looking at his critic, Mr. Moody answered:

"Young man, I am using for the glory of God all the grammar that I know. Are you doing the same?"

————o————

Let me give so much time to the improvement of myself that I shall have no time to criticize others.

DEAN CRESHAM

————o————

It is easy to shoot a skylark, but it is not so easy to produce its song.

LIONEL B. FLETCHER

————o————

He has a right to criticize who has a heart to help.

ABRAHAM LINCOLN

————o————

Don't fear criticism. Ford forgot to put a reverse gear in his first automobile.

————o————

Some folks escape criticism by doing nothing.

RALPH BREWER

————o————

. . . how much easier it is to be critical than to be correct.

BENJAMIN DISRAELI

————o————

Most of the time, people criticize in order to forget their own weaknesses.

RALPH BREWER

————o————

Everything you reprove in another, you must carefully avoid in yourself.

MARCUS TULLIUS CICERO

————o————

Criticism, like charity, should begin at home.

————o————

A critic is a person who is unable to do a thing the way he thinks it ought to be done.

————o————

I looked upon my brother with the microscope of criticism, and said, "How coarse my brother is!" I looked at him with the telescope of scorn, and said, "How small my brother is!" I looked into the mirror of truth, and I said, "How like me my brother is!"

Cross

We all have crosses to bear, but let us not forget that it depends on the spirit in which we bear the cross as to whether it becomes an agony or a glory.

CLIFF COLE

————o————

The Cross Of Calvary

The Cross of Calvary
Was verily the key
By which our Brother Christ
Unlocked the door
Of immortality
To you and me;
And, passing through Himself before,
He set it wide
Forevermore,
That we, by His grace justified
And by His great love fortified,
Might enter in all fearlessly,
And dwell forever by His side.

JOHN OXENHAM

————o————

The cross is rough, and it is deadly, but it is effective. It does not keep its victim hanging there forever. There comes a moment when its work is finished. . . . After that is resurrection glory and power, and the pain is forgotten for joy that the veil is taken away and we have entered in actual experience the Presence of the living God.

A. W. TOZER, The Pursuit of God

————o————

The Cross is a symbol of God's heartbreak over a world that is gone astray.

SAM JONES

————o————

Jesus hath many lovers of His kingdom but few bearers of the cross. . . . All are disposed to rejoice with Him, but few to suffer for His sake.

THOMAS À KEMPIS, The Imitation of Christ

Crowds

It was the great Methodist evangelist, John Wesley, who told his young preachers: "Don't worry about how to get crowds. Just get on fire and the people will come to see you burn."

————o————

The more the merrier.

JOHN HEYWOOD,
Proverbs (a collection, 1546)

————o————

The reason the way of the transgressor is hard is that it is so crowded.

FRANK MCKINNEY HUBBARD

Culture

By culture many people mean stuffing modern houses full of antique furniture.

PABLO PICASSO

————o————

Culture is not Christianity but Christianity is culture. Christian culture is the apex of all culture.

HUGH C. BENNER

————o————

Culture . . . is a study of perfection.

MATTHEW ARNOLD, *Culture and Anarchy*

————o————

Culture is the fruit of acquainting ourselves with the best that has been known and said in the world.

MATTHEW ARNOLD

————o————

The soul of culture is the culture of the soul.

ALICE REID

————o————

A man should be just cultured enough to be able to look with suspicion upon culture.

SAMUEL BUTLER

Culture is the habit of being pleased with the best and knowing why.

HENRY VAN DYKE

Curiosity

Curiosity is, in great and generous minds, the first passion and the last.

SAMUEL JOHNSON

————o————

Ask me no questions, and I'll tell you no fibs.

OLIVER GOLDSMITH,
She Stoops to Conquer

————o————

The public have an insatiable curiosity to know everything — except what is worth knowing.

OSCAR WILDE

————o————

The farmer was milking a cow who was eating some hay when a child visitor asked, "If you feed your cow milk, will it give some hay?"

Cynic

A cynic is but a sentimentalist on guard.

————o————

It takes a clever man to turn cynic, and a wise man to be clever enough not to.

FANNIE HURST

————o————

A cynic is a man who, when he smells flowers, looks around for a coffin.

H. L. MENCKEN

————o————

What is a cynic? A man who knows the price of everything, and the value of nothing.

OSCAR WILDE, *Lady Windermere's Fan*

D

Daughter

A pretty good way to arrange additional closet space is to marry off a daughter.

Leader, Earlville, Illinois

———o———

Daughter am I in my mother's house;
But mistress in my own.

RUDYARD KIPLING, *Our Lady of the Snows*

———o———

Oh, my son's my son till he gets him a wife,
But my daughter's my daughter all her life.

DINAH MARIA MULOCK CRAIK,
Young and Old

———o———

Raise your daughter to know the Lord and she will have a built-in chaperon.

Day

Days are like suitcases: all nearly the same size, but some people can pack a lot more into them.

———o———

One Day At A Time

One day at a time, with its failures and fears,
With its hurts and mistakes, with its weakness and tears,
With its portion of pain and its burden of care;
One day at a time we must meet and must bear.

One day at a time to be patient and strong,
To be calm under trial and sweet under wrong,
Then its toiling shall pass, and its sorrow shall cease;
It shall darken and die, and the night shall bring peace.

One day at a time – but the day is so long,
And the heart is not brave and the soul is not strong.
O Thou pitiful Christ, be Thou near all the way;
Give courage and patience and strength for the day.

Swift cometh His answer, so clear and so sweet;
"Yea, I will be with thee, thy troubles to meet;
I will not forget thee, nor fail thee, nor grieve;
I will not forsake thee; I never will leave."

Not yesterday's load we are called on to bear,
Nor the morrow's uncertain and shadowy care;
Why should we look forward or back with dismay?
Our needs, as our mercies, are but for the day.

One day at a time, and the day is His day;
He hath numbered its hours, though they haste or delay.
His grace is sufficient; we walk not alone;
As the day, so the strength that He giveth His own.

ANNIE JOHNSON FLINT

———o———

Think that day lost whose descending sun
Views from thy hand no noble action done.

JACOB BOBART

———o———

Count the day lost in which you have not tried to do something for others.

HAROLD C. HOWARD

———o———

Morning

Open the window! Let in the sun!
Let in the morning! Day has begun!
Here at the height of it,
Warm to the sight of it,

Move in the light of it,
Wakening one!
Come from your dreaming in darkness
   and shade
Into a radiance never to fade!
Here at the start of it,
Close to the heart of it,
Know yourself part of it —
All He has made!

                              IRENE STANLEY

Death

I think of death as a glad awakening from this troubled sleep which we call life; as an emancipation from a world which, beautiful though it be, is still a land of captivity.

                              LYMAN ABBOTT

Death has nothing terrible which life has not made so. A faithful Christian life in this world is the best preparation for the next.

                              TRYON EDWARDS

Death to an enemy does not determine who was in the right!

He that lives to live forever, never fears dying.

                              WILLIAM PENN

The fear of death is cancelled by faith in Christ.

Warning!

If you are not prepared to die:

Do *not* ride in or get in the way of automobiles, as they are the cause of 20 percent of all accidents.

Do *not* stay at home, as 17 percent of all accidents happen inside the home. If you must be at home, stay outside; only 8.5 percent of all accidents occur around the outside of the house.

Do *not* walk on the street if you can avoid it, as 14 percent of all accidents occur to pedestrians.

Do *not* travel by air, rail, or water, because 6 percent of all accidents are the result of traveling.

Do *not* indulge in sports or recreation under any circumstances, for 20 percent of all accidents result from this.

Do *not* do anything or go anywhere, for a multitude of miscellaneous accidents may waylay you.

BUT . . . you can "believe on the Lord Jesus Christ, and thou shalt be saved" (Acts 16:31). Then you *will* be prepared to die anytime, anywhere.

                    T. M. OLSON in *The Shantyman*

When the small-town minister turned out on Sunday morning, he saw in the church driveway a dead mule, victim of a Saturday night driver. The preacher hastened to the phone and called the mayor.

"Why tell me?" asked his Honor. "I thought you preachers buried the dead."

"We do," said the preacher, "but first we always like to notify next of kin."

                              LUELLA DAHLSTROM

One of the world's great tragedies is that so many people die for nothing.

A man's conception of *death* will determine his philosophy of *life*.

The Christian Hope

BLESSED ARE THE DEAD WHICH DIE IN THE LORD.

"With Christ — which is far better" (Philippians 1:23).

Fallen asleep in Jesus!
How precious is that word!
Enjoying now for evermore
The presence of the Lord.
This is not death! 'tis only sleep;
The Lord doth now thy loved one
   keep.

The earthen vessel's broken,
The Treasure now has flown,
The Lord hath taken back again
What is by right His own.
But when He takes what most we store
It is that He may give thee more.

Thou wouldst have gladly kept her
A little longer here,
To soothe, and nurse, and cherish,
And make her wants thy care.
But He, who doeth what is best,
Hath called her to Himself to rest.

As members of one body
In sympathy we weep —
And yet rejoice — because we know
In Jesus she doth sleep.
For all her pain and suffering's o'er;
And joy her portion evermore.

'Tis not "Goodbye," beloved,
'Tis only just "Farewell."
A little while — a "moment,"
We too with Christ shall dwell:
And so we dry the falling tear,
Because we know the Lord is near.

O, may the God of Comfort
His richest grace impart!
Himself fill up the aching void,
Bind up thy broken heart;
And give thee now to look above,
And rest in His unchanging love.

AUTHOR UNKNOWN

———o———

Low-sunk life imagines itself weary
of life; but it is death, not life, it is
weary of.

GEORGE MACDONALD

———o———

Dying is the last thing I ever intend
to do.

———o———

I dreamed Death came the other night,
And Heaven's gate swung wide,
With kindly grace an Angel came,
And ushered me inside.
And there to my astonishment,
Stood folks I'd known on Earth.
Some I'd judged and called "unfit,"
And some of "little worth."
Indignant words rose to my lips,
But never were set free,
For every face showed stunned sur-
prise,
Not one expected me!

AUTHOR UNKNOWN

———o———

'Tis not the dying for a faith that's so

hard . . . 'tis the living up to it that's
difficult.

WILLIAM MAKEPEACE THACKERAY,
Henry Esmond

———o———

A few hours before entering the
"Homeland" Dwight L. Moody caught
a glimpse of the glory awaiting him.
Awakening from a sleep, he said,
"Earth recedes, Heaven opens before
me. If this is death, it is sweet! There
is no valley here. God is calling me,
and I must go!" His son, who was
standing by his bedside, said, "No, no,
father, you are dreaming."
"No!" said Mr. Moody, "I am not
dreaming: I have been within the
gates: I have seen the children's faces."
A short time elapsed and then, following what seemed to the family to
be the death struggle, he spoke again:
"This is my triumph; this is my coro-
nation day! It is glorious!"

———o———

One can survive everything nowadays except death.

OSCAR WILDE

———o———

Dear God

(Poem found on the body of an unknown
American soldier)

"Dear God, I've never spoken to you,
But now I desperately want to know
you, too.
You see, God, they told me you didn't
exist,
And, like a fool, I believed all this.
Last night from a shell-hole I saw your
sky;
I figured right then they'd told me a
lie.
Had I taken time to see things you
had made
I'd have known they weren't calling a
spade a spade.
I wonder, God, if you'd take my hand;
Somehow I feel that you will under-
stand.
Strange I had to come to this hellish
place
Before I had time to see your face.
Well, I guess there isn't much more to
say,

But I'm sure glad, Lord, you opened
   the way.
I guess zero hour will soon be here.
But I'm not afraid since I know you
   are near.
The signal! Well, God, I guess I'll
   have to go.
I love you, Lord — this I want you to
   know.
Look now, this will be a horrible fight!
Who knows, I may come to your house
   tonight.
Though I wasn't friends with you be-
   fore,
I wonder, Christ, if You'd wait at Your
   door?
Look, I'm crying — me shedding tears.
How I wish I'd known You these many
   years!
Well, I have to go now, God. Good-
   bye.
Strange, since I met You I'm not
   scared to die."
        The Log of the Good Ship Grace

John Wesley when dying said:
"Brethren, farewell. The greatest thing
is that God still lives."

Last words of Francis Willard: "How
beautiful to be with God!"

Deceive

It is easier to deceive yourself than
to deceive anyone else.

Oh, what a tangled web we weave,
When first we practise to deceive!
        SIR WALTER SCOTT, *Marmion*

However much we may deceive others and ourselves, we never deceive
God.

Fool me once, shame on you;
Fool me twice, shame on me.
        Chinese Proverb

When we put up a bluff we are
sure to tumble over it.

A story is told of old Thomas K.
Beecher, who could not bear deceit in
any form. Finding that a clock in his
church was habitually too fast or too
slow he hung a placard on the wall
above it, reading in large letters:
"DON'T BLAME MY HANDS — THE TROU-
BLE LIES DEEPER." That is where the
trouble lies with us when our hands
do wrong, or our feet, or our lips, or
even our thoughts." The trouble lies
so deep that only God's miracle power
can deal with it. Sin indeed goes deep,
but Christ goes deeper.
        The Elim Evangel

Decision
(See also Choice)

Whenever you face a decision you
have three chances: Do what you
please; do what others do; or do what
is right.
        A. BANNINGISM

Seed
Seed that is planted in the mind
   Bears fruitage after its own kind;
The choice of which shall die or grow
   Rests with the one who wields the
      hoe.
        MYRA BROOKS WELCH

When we let somebody else decide
what our reaction shall be, we are no
longer free persons, whether we decide
to agree or disagree.
        SYDNEY J. HARRIS

A layman visited a great city church
during a business trip. After the service, he congratulated the minister on
his service and sermon. "But," said
the manufacturer, "if you were my
salesman, I'd discharge you. You got
my attention by your appearance, voice
and manner; your prayer, reading and
logical discourse aroused my interest;
you warmed my heart with a desire
for what you preached; and then —
and then you stopped without asking
me to do something about it. In business the important thing is to get them
to sign on the dotted line."
        JAMES DUFF

When an old Indian Chief first heard of the Savior, he said, "The Jesus road is good, but I've followed the old Indian road all my life, and I will follow it to the end."

A year later he was on the border of death. Seeking a pathway through the darkness, he said to the missionary, "Can I turn to Jesus now? My road stops here. It has no path through the valley."

———o———

I saw a tiny little boy in a candy store. He wandered from case to case with the utmost gravity, studying each assortment with deep seriousness.

His mother, tired of waiting, called to him, "Hurry up, son, spend your money. We must be going."

To this he replied, "But Mama, I've only one penny to spend, and I've got to spend it carefully."

———o———

Once to every man and nation comes the moment to decide,
In the strife of Truth with Falsehood, for the good or evil side.
JAMES RUSSELL LOWELL, *The Present Crisis*

Dedication

God wants your heart every hour in the day, and every day in the week, and every week in the year.
ULDINE UTLEY

———o———

A Mother's Dedication

Dear Lord, I bring to Thee my son
Whose tender years have scarce begun;
In this wee frame I know full well
A living soul has come to dwell
Who needs Thee now at childhood's gate
Ere he shall grow to man's estate.
I covenant through hours apart
To pray for him with fervent heart,
To teach Thy Word with winsome voice
By day and night until his choice
Be but Thy blood for sin's deep stain,
And my small son is born again;
Then onward shall I pray the more

And teach Thy precepts o'er and o'er
That he may grow, each boyhood hour
By Thine indwelling risen power.
Lord, some small boys with none to care
Will never hear a mother's prayer;
Prepare my son with love aflame
To reach them with Thy saving name;
And make him, Lord, a polished tool,
A learner in Thy highest school.
A mother's part seems, oh, so frail!
But Thy strong arm can never fail;
To teach, to pray, to stand are mine;
The miracles must all be Thine.
Expectantly, I yield to Thee
The little boy Thou gavest me.
LOUISE B. EAVEY

———o———

If I had 300 men who feared nothing but God, hated nothing but sin, and were determined to know nothing among men but Jesus Christ, and Him crucified, I would set the world on fire.
JOHN WESLEY

———o———

Many of us would love to have sin taken away. Who loves to have a hasty temper? Who loves to have a proud disposition? Who loves to have a worldly heart? No one. You ask Christ to take it away, and He does not do it. Why does He not do it? It is because you wanted Him to take away the ugly fruits while the poisonous roots remained in you. You did not ask that henceforth you might give up self entirely to the power of His Spirit. Do you suppose that a painter would want to work out a beautiful picture on a canvas which did not belong to him? No. Yet people want Jesus Christ to take away this temper or that other sin while as yet they have not yielded themselves utterly to His command.
ANDREW MURRAY

———o———

The Instrument

As ocean waves that sing upon the sand,
Or as a bow held in a master's hand
That sweeps that taut and waiting strings, —
So shall my spirit, tuned to heavenly things,

Give forth, as they, its tenderest melodies
When God's own hand sweeps o'er the silent keys.
My life an instrument through which is poured
Ecstatically, the music of the Lord!

BERNIECE AYERS HALL

———o———

O that I could dedicate my all to God! This is all the return I can make Him.

DAVID BRAINERD

———o———

No candle on the altar of a church will ever substitute for a flame in the heart of the preacher in the pulpit.

ROY L. SMITH

Deeds

Give me the ready hand rather than the ready tongue.

GIUSEPPE GARIBALDI

———o———

The smallest *deed* is better than the greatest *intention*.

———o———

Little deeds of kindness, little words of love,
Help to make earth happy, like the heaven above.
Little deeds of mercy sown by careful hands,
Grow to bless the nations far in heathen lands.

JULIA A. FLETCHER CARNEY, *Little Things*

———o———

Our deeds are like stones cast into the pool of time; though they themselves may disappear, their ripples extend to eternity.

Our Daily Bread

———o———

Small deeds done are better than great deeds planned.

PETER MARSHALL

———o———

If our faith were greater, our deeds would be larger.

If any little word of ours has made one heart the lighter,
If any little deeds of ours has made one life the brighter;
Lord, take that little word or deed, or any bit of singing,
And drop it in some lonely vale, and set the echoes ringing.

AUTHOR UNKNOWN

———o———

Deeds are the X-rays which enable others to discern our inner life. What we are within is revealed through what we are without.

———o———

I count this thing to be grandly true,
That a noble deed is a step toward God,
Lifting the soul from the common sod
To a purer air and a broader view.

JOSIAH GILBERT HOLLAND, *Gradatim*

Defeat

When we start talking of defeat, too often the devil has the victory already.

JESS KAUFFMAN

———o———

Some defeats are only installments to victory.

JACOB A. RIIS

———o———

There are some defeats more triumphant than victories.

MICHEL EYQUEM DE MONTAIGNE, *Of Cannibals*

———o———

Man learns little from victory, but much more from defeat.

Japanese Proverb

———o———

Helen Keller became deaf, dumb, and blind shortly after birth . . . her entire life has served as evidence that no one ever is defeated until defeat has been accepted as a reality.

———o———

Robert E. Lee was one of American's greatest men. He was a great general, but his real greatness was shown in defeat. He accepted it without fear, hate, or rancor.

WILLIAM ROSS

———o———

Defeat never comes to any man until he admits it.

———o———

No defeat is final unless you choose to make it so.

Definitions

Alarm Clock: A mechanism used to scare the daylights into you.

———o———

During an oral test the teacher asked one of the students to give a sentence using the word *ambushed.* Answer: "Well, I sat through two TV horror pictures last night and today I sure ambushed!"

———o———

Antique: A piece of furniture that is paid for.

———o———

Auction Sale: Where you get something for nodding.

———o———

Bachelor: A man who believes in life, liberty, and the happiness of pursuit.

———o———

Blarney is simply baloney coated with an Irish smile!

———o———

Modern *Bridegroom*: A fellow who expects some finance firm to carry practically everything over the threshold except the bride.

———o———

Broadmindedness is highmindedness flattened out by experience.

Clipper, Lexington, Nebraska

———o———

Bureaucracy is a giant mechanism operated by pygmies.

HONORÉ DE BALZAC

Career Girl: A girl who'd rather bring home the bacon than fry it.

———o———

Collection: A church function in which many take no more than a passing interest.

HOWIE LASSETER

———o———

Desperation: A man in want of bread is ready for anything.

French Proverb

———o———

Discussion: A method of confronting others in their errors.

AMBROSE BIERCE

———o———

Do-gooder: A person trying to live beyond his spiritual income.

H. A WILLIAMS

———o———

Equator: Menagerie lion running around the earth and ending in Africa with all the wild animals.

———o———

Faith: Reason grown courageous. What Christ asks is that we shall try it out.

WILFRED GRENFELL

———o———

Friend: One who knows everything about us, and yet knows nothing except that which is good.

FRANK JOHNSON

———o———

Generation: The period between the time when a town tears down an historic landmark and the time when it has a fund-raising drive to build an authentic reproduction of it.

———o———

Gentleman: A man who can disagree without being disagreeable.

———o———

Good Breeding: That quality that enables a person to wait in well-mannered silence while the loud mouth gets the service.

———o———

Honeymoon: The period between "I do" and "You'd better."

Kleptomaniac: A rich thief.
AMBROSE BIERCE

———o———

Lyric: Something written to be sung by a liar.

———o———

Manuscript: Something submitted in haste and returned at leisure.
OLIVER HERFORD

———o———

Mealtime: When youngsters sit down to continue eating.
The Office Economist

———o———

Minister: One who will burst inside unless a message from God gets said.
FRANK JOHNSON

———o———

Mockery: Mockery is the child of ignorance; we jest at what we know nothing of.
HONDRÉ DE BALZAC

———o———

Neurotic: A person in a clash by himself.

———o———

Four-year-old's definition of *nursery school*: A place where they try to teach children who hit, not to hit; and children who don't hit, to hit back.
M. S. N. in *Parents' Magazine*

———o———

Optimist: A fellow who never reads the headlines on today's newspapers.

———o———

Pedestrian: A husband who didn't think the family needed two cars.

———o———

Poise: The ability to continue talking about something else while the other fellow picks up the check.

———o———

Positive: Being mistaken at the top of one's voice.
AMBROSE BIERCE

Radical: A fellow who can out-talk you on any subject.

———o———

A wife's definition of *retirement*: Twice as much husband on half as much income.

———o———

Self-Made Man: One who absolves God of a great responsibility.
FRANK JOHNSON

———o———

Seminary: A place where they bury the dead.

———o———

Sermon: Something that takes a lifetime of experience and twenty hours to prepare, but must be spoken in twenty minutes.
FRANK JOHNSON

———o———

Social Grace: The ability to yawn and not open your mouth.

———o———

Spring: God thinking in gold, laughing in blue, and speaking in green.
FRANK JOHNSON

———o———

One old brother said, "*Status quo* is Latin for the mess we're in."

———o———

Thinking: The talking of the soul with itself.

Delinquent

Rules for Raising Delinquent Children

1. Begin with infancy to give the child everything he wants. In this he will grow up to believe the world owes him a living!

2. When he picks up bad words, laugh at him. This will make him think he's cute. It will also encourage him to pick up "cuter" phrases!

3. Never give him any spiritual training. Wait until he is 21 and then let him decide himself!

4. Avoid use of the word "wrong." It might develop a guilt complex!

5. Pick up everything he leaves lying around — books, shoes, clothes. Do

everything for him so that he will be experienced in throwing all responsibility on others!

6. Let him read any printed matter he can get his hands on. Be careful that the silverware and drinking glasses are sterilized, but let his mind feed on garbage!

7. Quarrel frequently in the presence of your children. In this way they will not be too shocked when the home is broken up later!

8. Give the child all the spending money he wants. Never let him earn his own. Why should he have things as tough as you did!

9. Satisfy his every craving for food, drink and comfort. See that every sensual desire is gratified. Denial may lead him to harmful frustration!

10. Take his part against neighbors, teachers and policemen. They are all prejudiced against your child!

11. When he gets into real trouble, apologize for yourself saying, "I never could do anything for him."

12. Prepare for a life of grief. You will be likely to have it!

Houston, Texas, Police Department

Democracy

Democracy is a method of getting ahead without leaving any of us behind.

T. V. SMITH

———o———

A democracy, — that is a government of all the people, by all the people, for all the people; of course, a government of the principles of eternal justice, the unchanging law of God; for shortness sake I will call it the idea of Freedom.

THEODORE PARKER, *The American Idea*

———o———

While democracy must have its organization and controls, its vital breath is individual liberty.

CHARLES EVANS HUGHES

———o———

The strength of democracy is judged by the quality of its services rendered by its citizens.

PLATO

Desire

An inquirer once asked a student what three things he most wanted, and he said, "Give me books, health and quiet." He asked a miser and he cried, "Money, money, money." He asked a pauper, and he said faintly, "Bread, bread, bread." The drunkard called loudly for strong drink. He turned to the multitude around him, and he heard in a confused cry, "Wealth, fame, pleasure!" Then he asked a poor man who had long been an earnest Christian. He replied that all his wants and wishes were met in Christ. He spoke seriously and explained: "I greatly desire three things: first, that I may be found IN Christ (Philippians 3:9); secondly, that I may be LIKE Christ (Philippians 3:10-11); and thirdly, that I may be WITH Christ (Philippians 1:23).

DWIGHT L. MOODY

———o———

Any unmortified desire which a man allows will effectually drive and keep Christ out of the heart.

CHARLES WESLEY

———o———

Some of us don't know what we want, but feel sure we don't have it.

———o———

Lord, grant that I may always desire more than I can accomplish.

MICHELANGELO

———o———

It is not our changing circumstances, but our unregulated desires that rob us of peace.

ALEXANDER MACLAREN

———o———

There is not one whom we employ who does not, like ourselves, desire recognition, praise, gentleness, forbearance, patience.

HENRY WARD BEECHER

———o———

A young fellow was looking at his pastor's new car.

"My, it's beautiful," he said excitedly. "I'm so glad you could get it."

"Well," his pastor replied, "I'm glad you like it. But, to tell you the truth, I didn't buy it. On my salary, I just couldn't afford it. My brother Bob bought it and gave it to me free of charge."

The pastor expected the usual reaction, the whiney, "My, I wish I had a brother like that."

But instead, the young boy looked up at the pastor thoughtfully and said, "My, I wish I *could be* a brother like that!"

———o———

The man who really wants to do something finds a way; the other kind finds an excuse.

———o———

If you want to be miserable, think about yourself. If you want to be perplexed, think about others. If you want to be filled with joy, meditate on the Lord Jesus Christ.

———o———

The stomach is the only part of man which can be fully satisfied. The yearning of man's brain for new knowledge and experience and for more pleasant and comfortable surroundings never can be completely met. It is an appetite which cannot be appeased.

THOMAS A. EDISON,
quoted in *This Week Magazine*

Destiny

One's destiny is determined, not by what he possesses, but by what possesses him.

———o———

Where one goes hereafter depends largely upon what he goes after here!

———o———

Destiny waits in the hand of God, not in the hands of statesmen.

T. S. ELIOT

———o———

Details will decide destiny.

———o———

The tissue of Life to be
We weave with colors all our own,
And in the field of destiny,
We reap as we have sown.

JOHN GREENLEAF WHITTIER, *Raphael*

Determination

If you have spunk enough, you can make quite a successful career of doing what others should but would rather not.

Times-Leader, West Point, Mississippi

———o———

Let us not be content to wait and see what will happen, but give us the determination to make the right thing happen.

PETER MARSHALL

———o———

A determined soul will do more with a rusty monkey-wrench than a loafer will accomplish with all the tools in a machine shop.

RUPERT HUGHES

———o———

When man is determined to have his own way, he will refuse to examine any evidence that may prove him wrong.

———o———

When life kicks you, let it kick you forward.

E. STANLEY JONES

———o———

A man without determination is but an untempered sword.

Chinese Proverb

———o———

To him that is determined it remains only to act.

Italian Proverb

———o———

What people say you cannot do, you try and find that you can.

HENRY DAVID THOREAU

Devil, Satan

Although the devil be the father of lies, he seems, like other great inventors, to have lost much of his reputation by the continual improvements that have been made upon him.

JONATHAN SWIFT

There are five or six devils working against you and me, affecting our usefulness, our happiness, and our health. They are worry, hate, hurry, fear, disappointment and pride.

———o———

The devil is the top hidden persuader — the master of subliminal motivation.

JESS C. MOODY

———o———

Asked one time how he overcame the Devil, Martin Luther replied: "Well, when he comes knocking upon the door of my heart, and asks, 'Who lives here?' the dear Lord Jesus goes to the door and says, 'Martin Luther used to live here but he has moved out. Now I live here.' The Devil, seeing the nail-prints in His hands, and the pierced side, takes flight immediately."

———o———

The one concern of the devil is to keep Christians from praying.

SAMUEL CHADWICK

———o———

The devil is worthy of some honor; he minds his business and is wide awake in this sleepy, drowsy age.

———o———

The devil is diligent at his plough.

BISHOP HUGH LATIMER,
Sermon on Ploughers

———o———

The cry of theologians that "God is dead" proves very much that the Devil is alive!

The Gospel Call

———o———

Undertake some worthwhile labor that the devil may always find you occupied.

———o———

If the devil catches a man idle, he will set him to work.

———o———

Billy Sunday used to say, "Yes, I know Satan — I've done business with him."

Some people don't seem to realize that whenever they turn their back on God, they face the devil.

Selected

———o———

Satan has many wiles. His favorite is "Wait awhile."

Devotion, Devotional Life

Rules For Daily Life

Begin the day with God,
　Kneel down to Him in prayer;
Lift up thy heart to His abode;
　And seek His love to share.

Open the Book of God
　And read a portion there,
That it may hallow all thy thoughts
　And sweeten all thy care.

Go through the day with God,
　Whate'er thy work may be;
Where e'er thou art — at home, abroad
　He is still near to thee.

Conclude the day with God:
　Thy sins to Him confess,
Trust in His cleansing blood,
　And plead His righteousness.

Lie down at night with God
　Who gives His servants sleep;
And when thou treadest the vale of
　death,
　He will thee guard and keep.

AUTHOR UNKNOWN

———o———

One Day To Live

Had I but this one day to live,
One day to love, one day to give,
One day to work and watch and raise
My voice to God in joyful praise,
One day to succour those in need,
Pour healing balm on hearts that bleed,
Or wipe the tears from sorrow's face,
And hearten those in sad disgrace —
I'd spend, O God, much time with
　THEE
That Thou might'st plan my day for
me.
Most earnestly I'd seek to know
The way that Thou would'st have me
go,

For Thou alone canst see the heart —
Thou knowest man's most inward
parts.
A.M.M.

———o———

A moment in the morning, take your
    Bible in hand,
And catch a gleam of glory from the
    peaceful promised land;
It will linger still before you, when
    you seek the busy mart,
And like flowers of hope will blossom
    into beauty in your heart;
The precious words like jewels, will
    glisten all the day
With a rare effulgent glory that will
    brighten all the way.

———o———

Thou hast made us O Lord for Thyself and our heart shall find no rest
till it rest in Thee.
SAINT AUGUSTINE, Confessions

———o———

Hurried "devotions" become nothing
but religious "commotions."

Diet

One thing you can always be sure of
— there are more people going on diets
tomorrow than are going on diets today.

———o———

Eat all you can cart
Today without sorrow;
You always can start
Your diet tomorrow.

———o———

To find out what a poor loser you
are, just start dieting.

———o———

Diets are for persons who are thick
and tired of it.
Tit-Bits

———o———

A young mother thought it was time
to break her little boy of thumb-suck-
ing, and she decided to do it by psychology. "Now, tell me, Johnny, does
your thumb taste good?"
"No," the boy admitted.
"Is it good to chew on?"

The boy shook his head.
"Then what is good about sucking
your thumb?"
"Well," the boy said after some
thought, "it's non-fattening."
FRANCES BENSON in Family Weekly

———o———

Who ends the day with wholesome
food, begins the next in a happy mood.
Ancient Saying

———o———

Some persons diet on any kind of
food they can get.

Difference

Honest differences of views and
honest debate are not disunity. They
are the vital process of policy-making
among free men.
HERBERT HOOVER

———o———

There's only a slight difference between keeping your chin up and sticking your neck out, but it's worth knowing.
Grit

———o———

Each of us lives a life that never has
been, or ever will be, exactly like that
of any other human being.
KEYES

———o———

When men come face to face, their
differences often vanish.

Difficulties

There Are Difficulties
And There Are "Difficulties"

A Marine who hadn't got mail for
weeks was finally handed a letter
while lying in a foxhole on Saipan
with bullets whizzing overhead. It was
a bill for $3.52, and the note read, "If
this bill is not paid in five days, you
will find yourself in serious trouble."

———o———

One of the grandest things to live
for is to make life less difficult for
other people.
CLIFF COLE

Write it over all your difficulties, pen it across all your disappointments, inscribe it on all your fears, post it over all your troubles — GOD IS ABLE.

————o————

Settle one difficulty and you keep a hundred others away.

Chinese Proverb

————o————

Difficulties are opportunities.

Proverb

————o————

Many men owe the grandeur of their lives to their tremendous difficulties.

CHARLES HADDON SPURGEON

————o————

Difficulties increase the nearer we approach our goal.

JOHANN WOLFGANG VON GOETHE

————o————

Some men make difficulties; some difficulties make men.

————o————

It takes the storm to prove the real shelter.

————o————

Out of difficulties grow miracles.

JEAN DE LA BRUYÈRE

————o————

When you are face to face with a difficulty, you are up against a discovery.

————o————

A hard fall means a high bounce — if you're made of the right material.

Diligence

It is better for a pot to boil over than never to boil at all.

————o————

Too many people itch for what they want but won't scratch for it.

Few things are impossible to diligence.

SAMUEL JOHNSON

————o————

Patience and diligence, like faith, remove mountains.

WILLIAM PENN

————o————

Diligence is the mother of good fortune.

MIGUEL DE CERVANTES, *Don Quixote*

————o————

Diligent working makes an expert workman.

Danish Proverb

Diplomacy

Diplomacy is the art of saying, "nice doggy" until you have time to pick up a rock.

————o————

Diplomacy is the art of letting someone else have your way.

————o————

Men, like bullets, go farthest when they are smoothest.

JEAN PAUL RICHTER

Direction

Society has erected the gallows at the end of the lane instead of guide posts and direction boards at the beginning.

EDWARD GEORGE BULWER-LYTTON

————o————

The greater thing in this world is not so much where we stand, as in what direction we are going.

OLIVER WENDELL HOLMES

————o————

Whenever things seem to go dead wrong, it wouldn't be a bad idea to stop and see if you're not facing in the wrong direction.

————o————

God judges a man not by the point he has reached, but by the way he is facing; not by distance, but by direction.

Too often we run across some fellow who seems to think he is ahead of the times, when infact the times are not going in his direction at all.

———o———

When God does the directing our life is useful and full of promise, whatever it is doing and discipline has its perfecting work.

H. E. COBB

———o———

If you don't know where you are going, then you are lost before you start.

Disagree

A church furnishings committee was meeting in the basement because there were no lights in the church auditorium. One committee member made a motion that the church purchase chandeliers. An older man on the committee objected for three reasons. "First," he said, "no one can play it. Second, we can't afford it, and third, we need lights!"

———o———

Some hair-splitters don't stop with hairs, they go right on through the head.

JOE BLINCO

———o———

It is regrettable that, among the Rights of Man, the right of contradicting oneself has been forgotten.

CHARLES BAUDELAIRE

Discipline

Discipline of Sunday school pupils is making disciples of them.

———o———

Command discipline, do not demand it.

———o———

Raising Billie

Papa said, "Now Billie, don't!"
  But Billie said, "I will," and did;
And Papa went to get the rod,
  But Mama said, "Don't beat the kid."

So Papa laid aside the rod
  While Billie smiled at "poor old Dad,"
And Mama stroked "dear Billie's" head
  And called him her poor little lad.

The years have passed and Bill is gone —
  Buried in a sinner's grave —
While Mom and Dad still linger on,
  So sad they let him misbehave.

The lesson's clear for all to see:
  If you would raise a son for God,
Father and Mother must agree
  When Billie needs it, use the rod!

R. H. BURROWS

———o———

Sometimes you can straighten out a youngster by bending him over.

Herald, Troy, Alabama

———o———

A lot of child welfare can be done with razor strap.

WILLIAM WARD AYER

———o———

Nothing impresses the young go-to-schooler
Like a teacher who uses the Golden Ruler.

SUSAN LLOYD in *Coronet*

———o———

Discipline effects destiny.

———o———

If a child annoys you, quiet him by brushing his hair. If this doesn't work, use the other side of the brush on the other end of the child.

Shawano, Wisconsin County Journal

———o———

About the only thing that gets an old-fashioned licking around most homes nowadays is a postage stamp.

———o———

The quickest way to be convinced that spanking is unnecessary is to become a grandparent.

———o———

Parents who are afraid to put their foot down usually have children who step on their toes.

What is discipline? As any small boy knows, it's something unpleasant Daddy had when he was little.

———o———

If parents don't mind that their kids don't mind, the kids don't.

———o———

Master easy, servant slack.

Chinese Proverb

———o———

There was more pathos than humor in what a disgruntled five-year-old boy said to his preacher father when the latter tried to take over the discipline in one of his rare visits home at meal time. "Aw, Dad," said the boy, "why don't you go to a meeting?"

Southern California Presbyterian

———o———

More board meetings in the woodshed would mean fewer cases in the juvenile courts.

———o———

On juvenile delinquency we would say with the poet, "Oh, for the smack of a vanished hand on the place where the spank ought to be."

———o———

A young businessman returned home tired from a hard day at the office to find his two children rushing madly about the house. He gave them both a scolding and sent them to bed as soon as possible. The next morning he found this note pinned to his bedroom door:
"Be good to your children and they will be good to you. Yours truly, God."

Discontent

Discontent is the price we pay for not being thankful for what we have.

———o———

Discontent may become either spur or spite.

DAGOBERT D. RUNES

———o———

Pliny informs us that Zeuxis once painted such a realistic picture of a boy holding a dish full of grapes that the birds were deceived and flew to the grapes to peck at them. Zeuxis, notwithstanding, was dissatisfied with the picture. "For," said he, "had I painted the boy as well as he ought to have been painted, the birds would have been afraid to touch them." Thus does the Christian dwell more on his shortcomings than on his attainments.

F. F. TRENCH

Discouragement

Let discouragement harden your determination, never your heart.

———o———

Discouragement is a handle that fits many tools.

———o———

Perhaps nothing more effectually cripples achievement than does discouragement.

Discover

When I want to discover something, I begin by reading up everything that has been done along the line in the past. I see what has been accomplished at great labor and expense in the past. I gather the data of many thousands of experiments as a starting point, and then I make several thousand more.

THOMAS A. EDISON

———o———

All human discoveries seem to be made only for the purpose of confirming more and more strongly the truths contained in the Holy Scriptures.

SIR JOHN HERSCHEL

———o———

When we find Christ, we find *everything;* when Christ finds us, He finds *nothing.*

———o———

The greatest discovery I made in life was that God was probably right when I thought Him to be wrong.

REUBEN A. TORREY

Disposition

It isn't your position but your disposition that makes you happy or unhappy.

——o——

The most destructive acid in the world is found in a sour disposition.

——o——

Your emotions shape your disposition. You can give way to hate, resentment, worry, fear, jealousy, and grumbling; or you may let love, faith, hope, goodwill, and kindness predominate.

——o——

Most people are just like cats in that if you rub them the right way, they will purr, but if you rub them the wrong way, they will bite and scratch.
WILLIAM ROSS

——o——

The wearer of smiles and the bearer of a kindly disposition needs no introduction, but is welcome anywhere.
O. S. MARDEN

Do, Doing
(See also Acts, etc.)

One never knows what he can do until he tries.

——o——

The world is blessed mostly by men who do things, not by those who merely talk about doing.

——o——

There never was a person who did anything worth doing who did not receive more than he gave.
HENRY WARD BEECHER

——o——

The more we do, the more we can do.
WILLIAM HAZLITT

——o——

No one ever climbed a hill by looking at it.

——o——

As I grow older, I pay less attention to what men say. I just watch what they do.
ANDREW CARNEGIE

——o——

Even though you are on the right track, you will be run over if you sit still.

——o——

Whatever is worth doing at all is worth doing well.
LORD CHESTERFIELD

——o——

Content yourself with doing, leave the talking to others.
BALTASAR GRACIÀN

——o——

Our chief want in life is somebody who shall make us do what we can.
RALPH WALDO EMERSON, Conduct of Life,
Considerations by the Way

——o——

The great pleasure in life is doing what people say you cannot do.
WALTER BAGEHOT

——o——

The shortest answer is doing.
GEORGE HERBERT

Doctor

A man took his wife to the doctor, who put a thermometer in her mouth and told her to keep her mouth shut for three minutes. When departing, the husband called the doctor aside and said, "What will you take for that thing, Doc?"

——o——

The best doctors in the world are Doctor Diet, Doctor Quiet, and Doctor Merryman.
JONATHAN SWIFT, *Polite Conversation*

——o——

No man is a good physician who has never been sick.
Arabian Proverb

——o——

I dressed his wounds, but God healed him.
AMBROISE PARÉ (father of modern surgery)

Inside information is what a doctor gets.

Doors

Doors

Doors are opened many ways,
By a key, or beam of light,
By gentle touch, or sudden jar,
Or by the wind at night.

Doors are opened many ways
Which we may understand;
But most important are the doors
God opens with His hand.

MILDRED ALLEN JEFFERY

——o——

All doors open to the man with a smile.

Doubt

There lives more faith in honest doubt,
Believe me, than in half the creeds.

ALFRED, LORD TENNYSON, In Memoriam

——o——

Philosophy goes no further than probabilities, and in every assertion keeps a doubt in reserve.

JAMES ANTHONY FROUDE

——o——

Skepticism is slow suicide.

RALPH WALDO EMERSON

——o——

If we begin with certainties, we shall end in doubt; but if we begin with doubts, and are patient in them, we shall end in certainties.

FRANCIS BACON

Dream

The Dreamer

They said: "He is only a dreamer of dreams,"
And passed him by with a smile;
But, out of his dreams he fashioned a song
That made life more worth while.

And who shall say he was less a part
Of the universal plan,
If, instead of building a mighty bridge,
He molded the life of a man?

ANNA M. PRIESTLY

——o——

Dreams are but interludes which fancy makes.

WILLIAM SHAKESPEARE

——o——

We cannot dream ourselves into what we could be.

——o——

Dreams are of great worth if they are carried into practice.

——o——

Dreaming has its values, but never should it become a substitute for work that needs to be done.

Drive, Driver

When motorists ignored "No parking" signs put on the private lot of a minister of one church, he put up a placard reading "Thou Shalt Not Park." It worked.

——o——

He who weaves his car in and out of traffic may be crocheting a shroud.

——o——

Instead of devoting so much time to developing more horsepower for their cars, maybe the auto manufacturers should try to find a way to put more horse sense into drivers.

——o——

Garage attendant to woman driver of badly battered car: "Sorry, lady, we just wash cars — we don't iron them."

CAVALLI in True

——o——

Traffic sign near school: Use your eyes and save the pupils.

Exchange

——o——

Man, teaching wife to drive: "Go on green, stop on red, take it easy when I turn white."

Sign on a cemetery along a well-traveled street: "Drive carefully. We can wait."

————o————

Always try to drive so that your license will expire before you do.

————o————

If more drivers would give some ground, there would be fewer of them in it.

————o————

Second-grader boasting about mother's progress in learning to drive: "She's getting real good at paralyze parking."
This Week Magazine

————o————

It's better to have one foot on the brake than six feet under the ground.

————o————

A traffic-choked bridge in London is called "the car-strangled spanner."
Evening Standard, London

————o————

Prayer For Motorists

O ever-present Lord, I pray,
Be with me at the wheel today.
Fill every corner of my mind,
So roaming thoughts no lodging find.
And take control of my two eyes,
That I may be alert and wise,
And take my feet, and take my hands,
That they react to quick demands.
Give me thy guidance, Friend Divine,
For other folks as well as mine.
Then, when we come to journey's end,
My prayer to heaven will ascend
In utter thankfulness to Thee,
Who kept the wheel all day with me.
REV. F. OSWALD BARNETT (Australia)

Duty

Life's Common Duties

Dream not of noble service elsewhere wrought,
The simple duty that awaits thy hand

Is God's voice uttering a divine command;
Life's common duties build what saints have thought.

In wonder-workings, or some bush aflame,
Men look for God and fancy Him concealed;
But in earth's common things He stands revealed,
While grass and flowers and stars spell out His name.
MINOT J. SAVAGE,
In Common Things

————o————

Do the Duty which lies nearest thee; which thou knowest to be a Duty! Thy second Duty will already have become clearer.
THOMAS CARLYLE, *Sartor Resartus*

————o————

The reward of one duty is the power to fulfil another.
GEORGE ELIOT (MARY ANN EVANS)

————o————

Your first duty is to do your duty first.

————o————

You should never wish to do less than your duty.
ROBERT E. LEE

————o————

The best way to get rid of your duties is to discharge them.

————o————

Duty and today are ours; results and the future belong to God.

————o————

When in Rome, do as the Romans ought to do.

————o————

A duty dodged is like a debt unpaid; it is only deferred, and we must come back and settle the account at last.
JOSEPH FORT NEWTON

E

Early

The early morning hours have gold in their mouth.

Dutch Proverb

————o————

Starting an hour earlier in the morning may make you an achiever instead of an almost.

DONALD LAIRD

————o————

Our five-year-old Jeanie took to rising at 5:30 each morning and puttering around just long enough to wake the rest of us before climbing back into bed. Her reason was always the same — she had to see if there was a surprise. Finally we told her firmly that she must stop and that there wouldn't be any surprises until Christmas, which was months away.

"I wasn't talking about living-room surprises," she said through her tears. "I was talking about like yesterday morning it was raining, and this morning real summer's here, and tomorrow morning I'll probably find some pink in the rosebuds."

Jeanie still gets up each morning at 5:30.

MRS. ROY F. CARTER in *Reader's Digest*

————o————

One school morning as I tried for the second or third time to awaken my six-year-old son, he half-opened his eyes, looked at me in disgust, and remarked, "Whoever invented morning sure made it too early."

MRS. JACQUELINE AHLSTRAND in *Teach*

————o————

He that would thrive must rise at five;
He that has thriven may lie till seven.

Ease, Easy

What is easy is seldom excellent.

SAMUEL JOHNSON

————o————

A life of ease is a difficult pursuit.

WILLIAM COWPER

It is easier to go down a hill than up, but the view is best from the top.

ARNOLD BENNETT

Easter

Easter Dawning

There's a whisper in the garden in the
morning very early,
And the flowers nod serenely in the
silver of the moon;
And the warbling of the songbirds in
the olives gnarled and hoary
Tell the story — tell the story
That our Lord is rising soon.

There's a stirring in the branches in
the morning in the moonlight,
Glad musicians fill the whole earth
with a burst of wondrous song;
And the sun's rays gild with splendor
and unearthly light His prison,
And the sky cries: "He is risen!"
While hosannas sweep along.

Sing, my heart, for He is risen, Christ
is risen, Christ is risen!
Let the mountains shout for gladness,
let the hills break forth and sing.
Let the seas make known His message,
let the stars tell out the story,
Let the world proclaim His glory.
He is Lord and He is King!

LOUIS MERTINS

————o————

The message of Easter cannot be written in the past tense. It is a message for today and the days to come. It is God's message which must re-echo through your lives.

FRANK D. GETTY

————o————

Easter Prayer

Lord, make my heart a garden,
As real a place of prayer
As was night-hushed Gethsemane
When Jesus suffered there.

Make it a place of flowers,
Whose fragrant cups distill
The dews of living water
Ensweetened in Thy will.

Plant there the trees of kindness,
  Where all who look above
May find the shadows softened
  By sunshine of Thy love.

Fill it with Easter gladness
  As fresh and new as spring.
Keep it the clean, pure dwelling
  Of Christ, the risen King.
                    ESTHER BALDWIN YORK

————o————

If Easter Be Not True

If Easter be not true,
Then faith must mount on broken
  wing;
Then hope no more immortal spring;
Then love must lose her mighty urge;
Life prove a phantom, death a dirge —
  If Easter be not true.

If Easter be not true —
But it is true, and Christ is risen!
And mortal spirit from its prison
Of sin and death with Him may rise!
Worthwhile the struggle, sure the
  prize,
Since Easter, aye, is true!
                    HENRY H. BARSTOW

————o————

Let us place more emphasis on the
Easter heart than on the Easter hat.

————o————

Easter

What whispers to the bulb, " 'Tis
  spring"?
Behold this shriveled, wrinkled thing —
It stirs and grows, bursts into bloom;
Its fragrance perfumes all the room.

Who tells the silent prisoner,
The little worm in tight cocoon,
"Wake up and work, and burst your
  bonds;
"You will be winged and flying soon"?

Who tells the acorn in the ground
To keep on reaching toward the sky?
How could it dream that it would be
A spreading oak tree, wide and high?

Who speaks within my sickroom, where
I live, a prisoner of pain,

And tells me, though this body die,
This very flesh shall live again?

Because He rose, I too shall rise,
Shall rise and walk and dance and
  sing;
And there shall be no grief, no pain,
Nor any tears, remembering!
                MARTHA SNELL NICHOLSON

————o————

Easter is an awakening
Of every living thing.
A time when soul and spirits rise,
As heaven receives its King.
                    OLIVE DUNKELBERGER

Eat

"Now," said the mother, "you just
eat your spinach. It will put color in
your cheeks."
"Yes," the little boy said, "but who
wants green cheeks?"

————o————

It's not the minutes you spend at
the table that make you fat, it's the
seconds.

————o————

"Most accidents happen in the kitchen," said a husband reading from
his newspaper. "And we men," he
added grimly, "have to eat them."

————o————

Let Christ stay throughout the meal.
Don't dismiss Him with the blessing.

————o————

Poor Mary

Mary had a little lamb,
A lobster and some prunes;
A glass of rum, a piece of pie
And then some macaroons.
It made the cafe waiters grin
To see her order so,
And when they carried Mary out
Her face was white as snow.
                    Uncle Mat's Magazine

Dad kept passing the pie to the others, finally his little son remarked, "They're all the same size, Dad, it's no use."

Selected

———o———

Part of the secret of success in life is to eat what you like and let the food fight it out inside.

———o———

The discovery of a new dish does more for the happiness of a man than the discovery of a star.

ANTHELME BRILLAT-SAVARIN

———o———

Tell me what you eat, and I will tell you what you are.

ANTHELME BRILLAT-SAVARIN,
Physiology of Gout

———o———

A dinner lubricates business.

WILLIAM SCOTT, LORD STOWELL,
quoted in Boswell's *Life of Dr. Johnson*

———o———

After a good dinner one can forgive anybody, even one's own relatives.

OSCAR WILDE

———o———

Eating little and speaking little can never do harm.

Economy

Economy: A way of spending money without getting any fun out of it.

———o———

Economy is half the battle of life; it is not so hard to earn money as to spend it well.

CHARLES HADDON SPURGEON

———o———

I favor the policy of economy, not because I wish to save money, but because I wish to save people.

CALVIN COOLIDGE

———o———

Economy, the poor man's mint.

MARTIN FARQUHAR TUPPER

———o———

There can be no economy where there is no efficiency.

BENJAMIN DISRAELI

Without economy none can be rich, and with it few will be poor.

SAMUEL JOHNSON

———o———

Whatever you have, spend less.

SAMUEL JOHNSON

———o———

Economy, industry, honesty and kindness form a quartet of virtue that will never be improved upon.

JAMES OLIVER

———o———

Limit your wants to your wealth.

———o———

Even a penny is too much to pay for something which is not needed.

———o———

Just about the time you think you can make ends meet, someone moves the ends!

Education

When a young man was applying for a job the manager said, "I'll give you a job. Sweep out the store."
Amazed, the young applicant said, "But I'm a college graduate."
The manager quietly replied, "Well, that's all right, I'll show you how."

———o———

Not all educated men are college graduates, nor are all college graduates educated men. An educated man is one who is useful to humanity, his profession or trade, and to himself.

Financial Management

———o———

It is a common fault never to be satisfied with our fortune, nor dissatisfied with our understanding.

FRANÇOIS, DUC DE LA ROCHEFOUCAULD

———o———

It is sometimes difficult to talk to a university man because he is so educated.

———o———

Education is what you have left over when you subtract what you've forgotten from what you learned.

The best education in the world is that got by struggling to get a living.

WENDELL PHILLIPS

———o———

In an honor system no one learns. The professors have the honor and the kids have the system.

———o———

Some kind of education is always going on. Education is not optional with the church.

HERMAN J. SWEET

———o———

It is not education that costs. It is ignorance that is expensive.

HEROLD C. HUNT

———o———

As often as not, adult education is left up to teen-agers.

FREDERIC G. HOULE

———o———

A pastor from a Latin American country was visiting various churches in the United States to observe operational procedures. While attending a meeting of the budget committee he observed in one report that the church had spent $800. for kitchen supplies and $100. for Teacher Training supplies.

Following the meeting the host pastor asked if there was anything in particular that had impressed him.

Without hesitation the visitor replied, "You spend more eating than you do feeding!"

———o———

When Woodrow Wilson was president of Princeton University, an anxious mother was questioning him closely about what Princeton could do for her son. Wilson replied: "Madam, we guarantee satisfaction or you will get your son back."

———o———

The entire object of true education is to make people not merely do the right things, but enjoy them — not merely industrious, but to love industry — not merely learned, but to love knowledge — not merely pure, but love purity — not merely just, but to hunger and thirst after justice.

JOHN RUSKIN

———o———

The great end of education is to discipline rather than to furnish the mind; to train it to the use of its own powers, rather than fill it with the accumulation of others.

TRYON EDWARDS

———o———

The object of education is to prepare the young to educate themselves throughout their lives.

ROBERT MAYNARD HUTCHENS

———o———

Those who have not distinguished themselves at school need not on that account be discouraged. The greatest minds do not necessarily ripen the quickest.

JOHN LUBBOCK

———o———

An educated man is one who has finally discovered that there are some questions to which nobody has the answers.

Boston Globe

———o———

Education without God is like a ship without a compass.

———o———

The primary purpose of education is not to teach you to earn your bread, but to make every mouthful sweeter.

JAMES ANGELL

———o———

Girl graduate: "Four years of college — and whom has it got me?"

———o———

Said one speaker, in referring to a long string of honorary degrees, "They're like the curl in the tail of a pig — following the main part of the animal, highly ornamental, but in no way improving the quality of the ham."

———o———

The real function of education, as we all well know, is not so much to teach us how to make a living as how to live while we are earning a living.

Too many of us have the cart before the horse.

———o———

Professor: "What three words are used most among college students?"
Freshman: "I don't know."
Professor: "Correct!"

Voiceways

———o———

We can only stimulate a person to education — we cannot stuff it into him.

———o———

Being educated means to prefer the best not only to the worst but to the second-best.

WILLIAM LYON PHELPS

———o———

Education would be much more effective if its purpose was to ensure that by the time they leave school every boy and girl should know how much they do *not* know, and be imbued with a lifelong desire to know it.

SIR WILLIAM HALEY

———o———

I thoroughly believe in a university education; but I believe a knowledge of the Bible without a college course is more valuable than a college course without the Bible.

WILLIAM LYON PHELPS

———o———

For adult education nothing beats children.

Banking

———o———

A man is not educated who does not know the basic truths of the Bible.

———o———

Education is something you get when your father sends you to college. But it isn't complete until you send your son there.

Washington Journal,
quoted in *Chicago Tribune*

———o———

Any man is educated who knows where to get knowledge when he needs it, and how to organize that knowledge into definite plans of action.

NAPOLEON HILL

Education is the ability to listen to almost anything without losing your temper.

ROBERT FROST

———o———

On one occasion Aristotle was asked how much educated men were superior to those uneducated: "As much," said he, "as the living are to the dead."

DIOGENES LAERTIUS, *Aristotle*

———o———

No one is ever finished with an education and the mark of an educated man is the constant struggle for more and more knowledge.

W. BERAN WOLFE

———o———

Men, while teaching, learn.

SENECA

———o———

The world is full of educated derelicts.

CALVIN COOLIDGE

———o———

On Graduating

Well, this is the last
  Of your high school days
Dear grownup lad
  With the winning ways.
I do not know
  What the future holds;
But day by day
  As time unfolds
May you find the hope
  The joy, the love
That comes from serving
  Your God above.
May you find the strength
  And the courage, too,
To do each task
  He plans for you;
Your work is not finished —
  It's just begun;
The world needs a "doer,"
  May you be the one.

PHYLLIS C. MICHAEL

———o———

Martin Luther gave the best reason for further education when he wrote: "The prosperity of a country depends, not on the abundance of its revenues, nor on the strength of its fortifications, nor on the beauty of its public buildings, but it consists in the number of its men of enlightenment and character."

Efficient

Efficiency expert: A man who waits to make up a foursome before going through a revolving door.
Irish Digest

——o——

Efficiency produces more with less effort.
ADMIRAL HUSBAND EDWARD KIMMEL

——o——

The efficient man is the man who thinks for himself and is capable of thinking hard and long.
CHARLES WILLIAM ELIOT

——o——

Efficiency is the ability to do a job well, plus the desire to do it better.
PAUL H. GILBERT

Effort

To achieve success, not by heritage but by individual effort, is the greatest joy of life.
J. P MORGAN

——o——

There is no ceiling on effort!
HARVEY FRUEHAUF

——o——

Prize fruit remains at the top of the tree because it is safer there from lazy pickers.

——o——

The best angle to use in approaching a problem is probably the try angle.

——o——

The Man Who Is Doing His Best

No matter how little he's getting,
    No matter how little he's got,
If he wears a grin, and is trying to win,
    He is doing a mighty lot!
No matter how humble his job is
    If he's striving to reach the crest,
The world has a prize for the fellow
    who tries —

The man who is doing his best!
Today he may be at the bottom
    Of the ladder to wealth or fame;
On the lowest rung, where he's bravely clung,
    In spite of the knocks — dead game!
And slowly he's gaining a foothold,
    His eyes on the uppermost roun';
It's a hard old climb, but he knows in time
    He will "land" — and be looking down!
The fellow who never surrenders,
    And is taking things as they come;
Who never says "quit," and exhibits grit,
    When the whole world is looking glum;
The fellow who stays to the finish,
    That nothing can hinder or stop,
And who works like sin, is the man who'll win —
    And some day he'll land on top!
AUTHOR UNKNOWN

——o——

Adam Clarke, a well-known theologian and commentator, was an early riser.
A young preacher wanted the eminent minister to tell him how he managed it. "Do you pray about it?" he asked.
"No," was the reply. "I just get up."
The Standard

——o——

The persistent exercise of a little extra effort is one of the most powerful forces contributing to success.
Grit

——o——

When my five-year-old son came to the table with his hands very dirty, I told him he must go wash and not come back until they were clean.
After a good deal of time had passed, I called, "Billy, how are your hands — are they clean yet?"
"Not clean," he replied. "But I got them to match!"
CAROLINE BECKER in *Grit*

——o——

Two frogs fell into a can of milk,
    Or so I've heard it told;

The sides of the can were shiny and
   steep,
The milk was deep and cold.

"Oh, what's the use?" croaked Number
   One,
"'Tis fate; no help's around.
"Goodbye, my friend! Goodbye, sad
   world!"
And weeping still, he drowned.

But Number Two, of sterner stuff,
   Dog-paddled in surprise,
The while he wiped his milky face
And dried his milky eyes.

"I'll swim awhile, at least," he said —
   Or so I've heard he said.
"It really wouldn't help the world
   "If one more frog were dead."

An hour or two he kicked and swam,
   Not once he stopped to mutter,
But kicked and kicked and swam and
   kicked —
Then hopped out, via butter!
           T. C. HAMLET in *The Target*

———o———

There's no need to put your best
foot forward if you drag the other one.

———o———

The men who try to do something
and fail are better than those who try
to do nothing and succeed.

———o———

If effort is organized, accomplishment follows.

Egotist, Egotism

Egotism is the opiate that the devil
administers to dull the pains of medi-
ocrity.

———o———

An egotist is a conceited dolt who
thinks he knows as much as you do.
           HAL CRANE

———o———

An egotist is not a man who thinks
too much of himself; he is a man who
thinks too little of other people.
           JOSEPH FORT NEWTON

To be pleased with oneself is the
surest way of offending everybody
else.
           EDWARD GEORGE BULWER-LYTTON

———o———

Egotist: One who likes mirrors, but
can't understand what others see in
them.
           HAROLD COFFIN in *Coronet*

———o———

Egotism: An internally generated
anesthetic which enables a conceited
person to live painlessly with himself.

———o———

Egotist: A person of low taste, more
interested in himself than in me.
           AMBROSE BIERCE

———o———

Through A Mirror

I have a little ego that is very fond of
   me,
Though what can be the use of him
   I often cannot see.
He follows close beside me wherever
   I may go;
Whenever I'd be good, he always tells
   me, "No!"
He is my sensitive feelings that are
   always getting hurt;
He is my self-conceit that needs rub-
   bing in the dirt;
He's all the little cranky ways to which
   I am so wont.
Lord, help me to get rid of him, this
   pesky little runt!
           IRENE T. COLE in *Clear Horizons*

Eloquence

He from whose lips divine persuasion flows.
           HOMER, *Iliad*

———o———

He is an eloquent man who can treat
humble subjects with delicacy, lofty
things impressively, and moderate
things temperately.
           MARCUS TULLIUS CICERO

———o———

When Demosthenes was asked what
was the first part of oratory, he an-

swered, "Action"; and which was the second, he replied, "Action"; and which was the third, he still answered, "Action."

PLUTARCH, *Lives of the Ten Orators*

———o———

Nothing is more eloquent than ready money.

French Proverb

———o———

Eloquence is the power to translate a truth into language perfectly intelligible to the person to whom you speak.

Employment

Never be unemployed and never be triflingly employed.

JOHN WESLEY

———o———

For he lives twice who can at once employ
The present well, and ev'n the past enjoy.

ALEXANDER POPE, *Imitation of Martial*

———o———

When men are employed, they are best contented.

BENJAMIN FRANKLIN, *Autobiography*

———o———

Employment gives health, sobriety, and morals.

DANIEL WEBSTER

———o———

Notice of employer on bulletin board to employees: "Bread is the staff of life, but that is no reason for the life of our staff to be one continual loaf!"

———o———

To All Employees

Due to increased competition and a keen desire to remain in business, we find it necessary to institute a new policy. Effective immediately, we are asking that somewhere between starting time and quitting time, and without infringing too much on the time usually devoted to lunch period, coffee breaks, rest periods, story telling, ticket selling, golfing, vacation planning, and the rehashing of yesterday's TV programs, that each employee endeavor to find some time that can be set aside and known as the "work break."

To some this may seem a radical innovation, but we honestly believe the idea has great possibilities. It can conceivably be an aid to steady employment and it might also be a means of insuring regular pay checks. While the adoption of the "work break" plan is not compulsory, it is hoped that each employee will find enough time to give the plan a fair trial. It is also hoped that those employees not in favor of adopting the "work break" idea will have fully completed their vacation plans.

Weaver Publishing Company

Encouragement

Encouragement is oxygen to the soul.

GEORGE M. ADAMS

———o———

Saying amen to a preacher is like saying siccum to a dog.

———o———

Correction does much, but encouragement does more. . . . Encouragement after censure is as the sun after a shower.

JOHANN WOLFGANG VON GOETHE

———o———

Secretary to downhearted boss whose desk is piled high with papers: "Allowing for holiday excitement, office parties, postseason letdown and normal absenteeism, we should have December's work cleaned up by January 25th."

HERBRAM in *The Christian Science Monitor*

———o———

A helping word to one in trouble is often like a switch on a railroad track — but one inch between a wreck and smooth rolling prosperity.

HENRY WARD BEECHER

Enemies

An enemy is a danger, but the danger is not what he can do to you. It is what he makes you do. If he fills you with envy, malice, hatred and all uncharitableness, he has done you real harm. But you can prevent that. Pray for him. If you say you cannot trust him, then watch and pray. But you cannot hate a man you pray for.

E. S. WATERHOUSE

———o———

Our foes are feeble in comparison with our Source of Strength.

SANFORD D. RICKER

———o———

He makes no friend who never made a foe.

ALFRED, LORD TENNYSON,
Lancelot and Elaine

———o———

The man who has no enemies has no following.

DON PLATT

———o———

What is a man's chief enemy? Each man is his own.

ANACHARSIS

———o———

Wise men learn much from enemies.

ARISTOPHANES, *Birds*

———o———

It is possible to learn from an enemy things we cannot learn from a friend.

———o———

If you tend to your work, and let your enemy alone, someone will come along some day, and do him up for you.

EDGAR WATSON HOWE

———o———

If you must have enemies — be careful in choosing them.

Energy

To be energetic, act energetic.

CLEMENT STONE

———o———

The world belongs to the energetic.

RALPH WALDO EMERSON

———o———

When men are young, they want experience and when they have gained experience, they want energy.

BENJAMIN DISRAELI

Enjoyment

You were made for enjoyment, and the world was filled with things you will enjoy.

JOHN RUSKIN

———o———

Some people are making such thorough preparation for rainy days that they aren't enjoying today's sunshine.

WILLIAM FEATHER

———o———

Enjoy the little you have while the fool is hunting for more.

Spanish Proverb

———o———

He who is convinced that there remains naught for him to do but to enjoy himself is little more than an erect animal.

RABBI J. LEONARD LEVY

Enthusiasm

Fires cannot be made with dead embers, nor can enthusiasm be stirred by spiritless men.

BALDWIN

———o———

Every man is enthusiastic at times. One man has enthusiasm for thirty minutes, another for thirty days, but it is the man who has it for thirty years who makes a success in life.

EDWARD B. BUTLER

———o———

We need fire without wild fire.

———o———

Every production of genius must be the production of enthusiasm.

BENJAMIN DISRAELI

———o———

The man who is capable of generating enthusiasm can't be whipped.

EDWARD GEORGE BULWER-LYTTON

———o———

A man can succeed at almost anything for which he has unlimited enthusiasm.

CHARLES SCHWAB

None are so old as those who have outlived their enthusiasm.

HENRY DAVID THOREAU

————o————

Merit begets confidence, confidence begets enthusiasm, enthusiasm conquers the world.

WALTER COTTINGHAM

————o————

The world belongs to the enthusiast who keeps cool.

WILLIAM MCFEE,
Casuals of the Sea. Book I

————o————

Enthusiasm is the genius of sincerity, and truth accomplishes no victories without it.

EDWARD GEORGE BULWER-LYTTON

————o————

Be a live wire, then people won't step on you.

Environment

We should seek the atmosphere and the surroundings which call forth the best that is in us.

COUNCILLOR

————o————

There's many a life of sweet content Whose virtue is environment.

WALTER LEARNED

Envy

Too many Christians envy the sinners their pleasure and the saints their joy, because they don't have either one.

MARTIN LUTHER

————o————

Expect not praise without envy until you are dead.

CHARLES CALEB COLTON

————o————

Envy is but the smoke of low estate, Ascending still against the fortunate.

LORD BROOKE

————o————

One cannot be envious and happy at the same time.

HENRY GREBER

Envy is littleness of soul.

WILLIAM HAZLITT

————o————

Envy is an open door to bitterness.

————o————

The envious person is a miserable person.

Epitaph

If tombstones told the truth, everybody would wish to be buried at sea.

JOHN W. RAPER

————o————

The Tired Woman's Epitaph

Here lies a poor woman, who always was tired;
She lived in a house where help was not hired.
Her last words on earth were: "Dear Friends, I am going
"Where washing ain't done, nor sweeping, nor sewing;
"But everything there is exact to my wishes;
"For where they don't eat there's no washing of dishes.
"I'll be where loud anthems will always be ringing,
"But, having no voice, I'll be clear of the singing.
"Don't mourn for me now; don't mourn for me never —
"I'm going to do nothing for ever and ever."

AUTHOR UNKNOWN

————o————

Friend, in your epitaph I'm grieved So very much is said;
One-half will never be believed, The other never read.

————o————

Epitaph of Robert Byrkes:
That I spent, that I had;
That I gave, that I have;
That I left, that I lost.

A.D. 1579

————o————

Epitaph Of Faith

A godly old man asked that on his tombstone be carved the legend "The

Inn of a Traveler on His Way to the New Jerusalem."

He looked on this life as a journey toward the heavenly city where real life would begin. Having set his course toward the full enjoyment of the presence of God, the grave became merely a stopping place on the way.

KATHERINE BEVIS

———o———

Epitaph: A belated advertisement for a line of goods that has permanently been discontinued.

IRVIN SHEWSBURY COBB

———o———

A man once lived the kind of life that inspired his friends to place this epitaph at his grave:
Unawed by opinion,
Unseduced by flattery,
Undismayed by disaster,
He confronted life with courage,
And death with Christian hope.

Errors

Things could be worse. Suppose our errors were tabulated and published every day like those of a ball player.

———o———

Some people throw away a bushel of Truth because it contains a grain of Error; while others swallow a bushel of Error because it contains a grain of Truth.

———o———

Navy Chaplain Lt. Daniel Litt was at 11th Naval District headquarters when a phone call came for another chaplain.

The secretary replied: "We only have one chaplain here just now, and he is Litt."

After what seemed to be an embarrassed silence, the caller hung up.

———o———

A typographical error in a church bulletin was not far off. A roster of the church staff included the name of the "Dustodian."

Minneapolis Tribune

She ended the program with a prelude and fudge by Bach.

Daily Record, Wooster, Ohio

———o———

The least error should humble, but we should never permit even the greatest to discourage us.

WILLIAM JAMES POTTER

———o———

Without error there can be no such thing as truth.

Chinese Saying

———o———

Errors, like straws, upon the surface flow;
He who would search for pearls must dive below.

JOHN DRYDEN, *All For Love*

———o———

Ignorance is a blank sheet on which we may write; but error is a scribbled one on which we must first erase.

CHARLES CALEB COLTON

———o———

Typographical Error

The typographical error is a slippery thing and sly
You can hunt till you are dizzy, but it somehow will get by.
Till the forms are off the presses, it is strange how still it keeps
It shrinks down into a corner and it never stirs or peeps,
That typographical error, too small for human eyes!
Till the ink is on the paper when it grows to mountain size
The boss he stares with horror, then he grabs his hair and groans.
The copy reader drops his head upon his hands and moans —
The remainder of the issues may be clean as clean can be,
But that typographical error is the only thing you see.

AUTHOR UNKNOWN

———o———

The following collection of students' boners are on file in St. Michael's school in Hoban Heights, Pennsylvania:

A *blizzard* is the inside of a fowl.

A *goblet* is a male turkey.

A *spinster* is a bachelor's wife.

A *virgin forest* is a forest in which the hand of man has never set foot.

They only raise *alpaca* grain in Kansas, and they have to irritate it to make it grow.

An *adjective* is a word hanging down from a noun.

The *Prodigal Son* went out a dude and came back a bum.

———o———

It is error only, and not truth, that shrinks from inquiry.

THOMAS PAINE

Eternity

In this world life becomes a new and thrilling thing; in the world to come eternal life with God becomes a certainty.

WILLIAM BARCLAY

———o———

Life with Christ is an endless hope; without Him it is a hopeless end.

———o———

We must live *for* Christ here, if we would live *with* Him hereafter.

———o———

With God Forever

The stars shine over the earth,
  The stars shine over the sea;
The stars look up to the mighty God,
  The stars look down on me.
The stars have lived for a million years
  A million years and a day,
But God and I shall love and live
  When the stars have passed away.

AUTHOR UNKNOWN

———o———

Eternity gives nothing back of what one leaves out of his minutes.

———o———

One life — a little gleam of time between two eternities.

PETRARCH

Church announcement board outside Christ Episcopal Church, New Brighton, Pennsylvania: "Christian funeral directors provide many valuable services . . . but they can't 'phone ahead for reservations — you must apply in person for Eternal Life."

Ethics

Evangelical faith without Christian ethics is a travesty on the gospel.

V. RAYMOND EDMAN

———o———

Ethics is the science of human duty.

DAVID SWING

———o———

A man without ethics is a wild beast loosed upon this world.

MANLY HALL

———o———

Ethics and equity and the principles of justice do not change with the calendar.

DAVID LAWRENCE

Etiquette

Ten Commandments For Church Etiquette

I. Thou shalt not come to service late, nor for the Amen refuse to wait.

II. Thy noisy tongue thou shalt restrain when speaks the organ its refrain.

III. And when the hymns are sounded out, thou shalt join in, not look about.

IV. The endmost seat thou shalt leave free, for more to share the pew with thee.

V. Forget thou not the off'ring plate, nor let the usher stand and wait.

VI. Thou shalt not make the pew a place to vainly decorate thy face.

VII. Thou shalt give heed to worship well, and not in thine own business dwell.

VIII. Thou shalt the Sabbath not misuse, nor come to church to take thy snooze.

IX. 'Tis well in church thy friend to meet, but let thy ardor be discreet.

X. Be friendly at the church's door, so shall the stranger love God more.

ARTHUR JAMES LAUGHLIN, JR.

———o———

Etiquette: How you behave every day of your life. Acquiring good manners and skill in the art of gracious living comes in a three-way package: reading, observation, and practice.

Evangelism

Let us go . . .

Because He commands us to go
Because He has made us ambassadors
Because we love Him
Because we do care for the lost

into the highways and hedges

Where a baby is born every two seconds
Where an immigrant crosses our border every two minutes
Where life's highway leads to school, shop, office, store, farm . . .
Where people are groping for reality

and compel them to come in

That the seeker may find the truth
That the weary may find rest.
That the troubled may find peace
That the sinner may find eternal life
That the Christian may find a blessing in service.

A. C. MCKENSIE

———o———

Of all the subjects that have to be discussed and prayed about, there is none which in my judgment is more fascinating and more important than the conversion of children.

F. B. MEYER

———o———

The Redemption Of Youth

Nineteen out of every twenty who ever get saved do so before they reach the age of twenty-five.

After twenty-five, only one in 10,000.

After thirty-five, only one in 50,000.
After forty-five, only one in 200,000.
After fifty-five, only one in 300,000.
After sixty-five, only one in 500,000.
After seventy-five only one in 700,-000.

Dr. Wilbur Chapman tested a meeting where 4,500 were present. The result was:

400 were saved before ten years of age.

600 were saved between twelve and fourteen.

600 were saved between fourteen and sixteen.

1,000 were saved between sixteen and twenty.

Twenty-five were saved after thirty years of age.

1,875 were unsaved.

———o———

Admit God's Word to be His message for you.

Submit to the authority of the book.

Commit Scriptures to memory.

Transmit the message to someone else.

———o———

If you should live to preach the gospel forty years, and be the instrument to saving only one soul, it will be worth all your labors.

———o———

Fireworks evangelism is like a rocket. It goes up in fire and falls like a dead stick.

———o———

Evangelism stands for a certain interpretation of Christianity emphasizing the objective atonement of Christ, the necessity of a new birth, or conversion, and salvation through faith.

W. W. SWEET

———o———

Told of thousands of souls going to Christless graves in foreign lands, men and women are stirred, but they are not stirred by the man dying in the next block into whose home no pastor has ever entered with the Gospel message. Somehow souls far away seem more valuable in the sight of God than souls nearby, or in the next town. There is a confusion of values among us, not derived from the Scriptures.

CHESTER E. TULGA

---o---

Things Not To Do

Don't argue and don't lecture!

Never talk boastfully or sound too familiar.

Don't point your finger in the person's face.

Don't interrupt while someone is speaking; there is danger of offending him and prejudicing him against you and against Christ through you.

Don't run down the person's church.

Don't beg or coax.

Avoid long stories or illustrations.

Don't be in a hurry.

Don't pick green fruit. (Try for an early decision, but don't force one . . . it might be the wrong decision.)

AUTHOR UNKNOWN

---o---

You can hardly have evangelism unless you have Christian scholarship; and the more Christian scholarship you have, so much the more evangelism.

J. GRESHAM MACHEN

---o---

In evangelism we seek the lost; in revival the lost are running to the Lord.

EDWIN ORR

Evil

We could add a fourth monkey to the Chinese where one hears no evil, one sees no evil and one speaks no evil. Our fourth monkey would "think no evil." Seems to us that it is the most important.

---o---

If a man's face is turned toward evil, and he is following his face, you'll find it hard to believe he's on the road to Heaven no matter what he says about it.

Out Or In?

All the water in the world
However hard it tried
Could never sink a ship
Unless it got inside.
All the evil in the world,
The wickedness and sin
Can never sink your soul's fair craft
Unless you let it in.

AUTHOR UNKNOWN

---o---

Evil does not disappear merely by being ignored.

---o---

Evil to him who evil thinks. (*Honi soit qui mal y pense.*)

EDWARD III, King of England
— Motto of the Order of the Garter

---o---

For himself doth a man work evil in working evils for another.

HESIOD

---o---

The truest definition of evil is that which represents it as something contrary to nature. Evil is evil because it is unnatural.

FREDERICK WILLIAM ROBERTSON

Exaggerate

An exaggeration is a truth that has lost its temper.

KAHLIL GIBRAN

---o---

You can tell a parrot from a human being because the parrot is content to repeat just what it hears without trying to make a good story out of it.

---o---

The fellow who is always slapping you on the back does this to help you swallow all he tells you!

---o---

When inclined to exaggerate, talk only to yourself.

---o---

We exaggerate misfortune and happiness alike. We are never so wretched or so happy as we say we are.

HONORÉ DE BALZAC

Examination

Examinations are formidable even to the best prepared, for the greatest fool may ask more than the wisest man can answer.

CHARLES CALEB COLTON

———o———

A teacher, annoyed with his clock-watching students, covered the clock with a cardboard which said: "Time will pass. Will you?"

Sunshine Magazine

———o———

In an examination, a high school student defined the humerus as "that part of the body which is commonly called the funny bone."

———o———

In answer to the question, "How can one attain a good posture?" one boy wrote on his class examination paper: "Keep the cows off of it, and let it grow awhile."

Example

(see also Influence)

When he was a small boy his teacher made him stay after school and write fifty times on the board, "I must not talk in class."

Now he was a big boy and a judge and into his court came his former teacher, charged with speeding.

The sentence? She must pay a fine of ten dollars and write one hundred times, "I must not exceed the speed limit."

———o———

A Primary-age child prayed in the worship service, "Dear God, please make me as much like my Jesus as my Sunday School teacher."

———o———

Example is always more efficacious than precept.

SAMUEL JOHNSON, *Rasselas*

———o———

Right example bolsters effectively the fruit of the lips.

Since truth and constancy are vain,
Since neither love, nor sense of pain,
Nor force of reason, can persuade,
Then let example be obey'd.

GEORGE GRANVILLE

———o———

I do not give you to posterity as a pattern to imitate but as an example to deter.

JUNIUS

———o———

Example is the school of mankind, and they will learn at no other.

EDMUND BURKE

Turning the Fable

When telling your children a story
And you use yourself as a sample,
Perhaps you should do it as warning
And not as a shining example!

LAVONNE MATHISON in *Home Life*

———o———

It's what you are when you pray that influences me.

———o———

Example is not the main thing in influencing others. It is the only thing!

ALBERT SCHWEITZER

———o———

Good example has twice the value of good advice.

———o———

A great man once said: "In early life I had nearly been betrayed into the principles of atheism, but there was one argument in favor of Christianity that I could not refute, and that was the consistent character and example of my own father."

———o———

Shortly after the close of the Civil War, a Negro entered a fashionable church in Richmond, Virginia, one Sunday morning while communion was being served. He walked down the aisle and knelt at the altar. A rustle of shock and anger swept through the congregation. Sensing the situation, a distinguished layman immediately stood up, stepped forward to the altar and knelt beside his colored brother. Captured by his spirit, the congregation followed this magnanimous example. The layman who set the example: Robert E. Lee.

BILLY GRAHAM in *Life*

———o———

Fathers who want their children to end up right must walk upright themselves.

NAT OLSON

———o———

The world wants to see demonstrators of the faith rather than defenders of the faith.

———o———

Nothing is so infectious as example.

CHARLES KINGSLEY

———o———

Not so long ago one of my two boys spoke these sobering words to me. He said, "When the two of us were young, there were times when you and mom would obviously set out to tell me how to live the good life. We could always recognize those moments and we would close our ears and our minds. Your most influential moments were your most inadvertent ones. We were apt to imitate what you really were — not what you said you were or even what you may have believed you were."

JOSEPH N. WELCH in *The Pioneer*

Excellence

Whoever I am or whatever I am doing, some kind of excellence is within my reach.

JOHN W. GARDNER

———o———

There is no excellence uncoupled with difficulties.

OVID

———o———

Excellent things are rare.

PLATO

———o———

Excellence is never granted to man but as the reward of labor.

SIR JOSHUA REYNOLDS

Of course it will only be a matter of time till you reach the top if you can contrive each day to outclass the fellow you were yesterday.

Excess

In the cross of Christ excess in men is met by excess in God; excess of evil is mastered by excess of love.

LOUIS BOURDALOUE

———o———

Excess in anything is a defect.

MONVEL

———o———

Excess kills more than the sword.

———o———

Nothing in excess.

TERENCE

Exclusive

A small Christian sect of an exclusive temperament was holding a convention. Outside the auditorium where they met there was displayed the motto, "Jesus Only."
A strong wind blew away the first three letters and left the sign, "us Only."

HARRY A. IRONSIDE

Excuse

Parents have always found excuses for their children when they failed to make it to school. Some of them have been honest, and some of them have stretched the truth a bit. One of the most widely used, and sometimes abused, excuses has been the breakdown of transportation. To show how this excuse has changed through the years, Frederich J. Moffitt in *Nation's Schools* gives this "History of Transportation."

1860 — Dear Teacher: Please excuse Mary for absence from school yesterday because it was her brother's turn to wear the shoes.

1900 — Dear Professor: John missed school today because the horse succumbed to an attack of glanders on Murder Hill.

1910 — Dear Principal: Jane was absent yesterday because her father broke his arm cranking the Ford.

1950 — Dear Superintendent: Willie overslept, and the school bus wouldn't wait for him.

1960 — Dear Announcer: K a r e n missed her lesson yesterday because the TV tube blew out.

Quote

———o———

We've heard a few times, "No, I didn't get to church but was there in spirit." As a preacher, I've found that it's not easy to preach to disembodied spirits; bodies are really indispensable.

———o———

He that is good at making excuses is seldom good at anything else.

BENJAMIN FRANKLIN

———o———

Church member X: "We really shouldn't be out here fishing on prayer meeting night."

Church member Z: "Oh, well I couldn't be at church tonight anyway. I've got a sick child at home."

Today

———o———

There aren't nearly enough crutches in the world for all the lame excuses.

———o———

"I'm sorry to be late, Mom," said ten-year-old Jimmy as he rushed home from school. "We were making a science display, and I had to stay to finish the universe."

———o———

He who excuses himself accuses himself.

GABRIEL MEURIER

Executive

An executive is a person who is working on the solution of a problem or else is a part of the problem.

———o———

Executive: A man who can make a decision and stick to it — no matter how wrong he is.

An executive is a man who can take as long as he wants to make a snap decision.

———o———

It isn't difficult to determine which executives are big wheels and which are merely spokesmen.

———o———

How to stay in the groove without making it a rut is the problem of every executive.

———o———

A good executive is one who wears the worried look — upon his assistant's face.

MAX SCHUSTER

———o———

The able executive is the man who can train assistants more capable than himself.

ANDREW CARNEGIE

———o———

The ability to influence people is a foremost requirement for every executive.

WILLIAM L. BATT

Exercise

The best exercise for the heart is to reach down and pull other people up.

———o———

Scientists tell us that exercise kills germs. Trouble is in trying to talk them into taking it.

———o———

The only exercise some people get is jumping to conclusions, running down their friends, sidestepping responsibility, and pushing their luck.

Expect

The small-town boy who had gone to fame and fortune decided to visit his birthplace after a twenty-year absence so he could gloat a little over his boyhood friends and surviving relatives.

Half expecting an official greeting and a turnout of the town band, he arrived at high noon to find empty streets, the same sleepy central square, and the old railroad station broiling in the sun.

Getting out of his train, his suitcase in his hand, he wandered over to the white-haired baggage handler and stood waiting for a sign of recognition and welcome.

The old man shuffled forward, squinted in the sun, and smiled. "Hello, Jimmie," he said. "Going away?"

———o———

Life is much like Christmas — you are more likely to get what you expect than what you want.

———o———

It is always first class when we do not expect anything better.

T. J. BACH

———o———

When you expect something for nothing, you deserve to be disappointed. No one is entitled to more than he gives.

THEODORE LANG

Experience

When a youngster sets out to gain experience, he should be cautioned that some experience is a definite loss.

———o———

Experience is what enables you to recognize a mistake when you make it again.

EARL WILSON

———o———

Even if you drop out of the school of experience, it has a wonderful home study program which keeps you constantly in touch.

———o———

I am a part of all that I have met;
Yet all experience is an arch wherethrough
Gleams that untraveled world whose margin fades
For ever and for ever when I move.

ALFRED, LORD TENNYSON, *Ulysses*

How Fresh Is Your Experience?

A story is told of an old man who had a wonderful experience twenty-five years ago, so wonderful that he wrote it all down and called it his "Blessed Experience." When people visited him he often would bring it out and read it through to them.

One night when a friend called in he said to his wife, "My dear, just run upstairs and bring down my 'Blessed Experience' from the drawer in the bedroom."

She went upstairs to get it and, on returning, she said, "I am sorry, but the mice have been in the drawer, and have eaten up your 'Blessed Experience'!"

And a good thing, too! If you had a blessing twenty-five years ago, and have not had one since, you had better forget it and get an up-to-date experience.

A. LINDSAY GLEGG in *Gospel Herald*

———o———

On a credit application the applicant signed his name "Bill Smith, BBBFF."

"You have an unusual degree," commented the credit manager. "Where did you get your education?"

"Experience," replied Bill Smith. "Three bankruptcies and two fires!"

———o———

Experience can be costly. But the right kind can be more than a refund in full.

———o———

One reason experience is such a good teacher is that she doesn't allow dropouts.

Changing Times, The Kiplinger Magazine

———o———

We need an experience of Christ in which we think everything about the Christ and not about the experience.

PETER TAYLOR FORSYTH

———o———

Learning teacheth more in one year than experience in twenty.

ROGER ASCHAM, *The Schoolmaster*

He gains wisdom in a happy way, who gains it by another's experience.
                                                                        PLAUTUS

———o———

Sad experience leaves no room for doubt.
                                                        ALEXANDER POPE

———o———

Experience is by industry achieved And perfected by the swift course of time.
                                                        WILLIAM SHAKESPEARE,
                                                        Two Gentlemen of Verona

———o———

Experience is what keeps a man who makes the same mistake twice from admitting it the third time around.
                                                TERRY MCCORMICK in *Quote*

Expert

An expert is a fellow that can hit a bull's eye without shooting the bull.

———o———

An expert is like the bottom part of a double boiler: builds up a lot of steam but doesn't know what's cooking.

———o———

An expert is a person who can take something you already know and make it sound confusing.

———o———

An expert is a man away from home with a set of slides.

———o———

Every skilled person is to be believed with reference to his own art.
                                                        Legal Maxim

Explanation

When the grass looks greener on the other side of the fence, it may be that they take better care of it over there.
                                                CECIL SELIG in *Quote*

———o———

One cool morning I was trying to convince my three-year-old son to put on his bathrobe. When I told him he was shivering, he replied: "I am not. I'm just bouncing my teeth."
                                                        MRS. HARRY WESTON
                                                        in *The Chicago Tribune*

———o———

The boy explained to his teacher why he hadn't yet returned his report card to her. "You gave me three A's, and the card still is on the rounds of the relatives."
                                        Times Leader, West Point, Mississippi

———o———

Jay, age three, put his cousin's roller skates on and tried to skate. But he said, "My one foot doesn't wait for the other one."
                                                        Christian Living

———o———

A four-year-old was overheard by his mother as he talked to his new puppy. "You mustn't chew me," he was saying. "Bones are for chewing. People are for lapping."

———o———

"And what did my little angel do while mother was shopping?" a mother asked her pride and joy.

"I played postman, Mommy," replied the youngster. "I put a letter in every mail box on the street. They were real letters, too. I found a big bundle of them in your drawer tied up in a pink ribbon."
                                                        V. D. PALAT

Extra

And Then Some . . .

A retired business executive was once asked the secret of his success. He replied that it could be summed up in three words: "and then some."

"I discovered at an early age," he said, "that most of the differences between average people and top people could be explained in three words. The top people did what was expected of them — and then some.

"They were thoughtful of others, they were considerate and kind — and then some.

"They were good friends to their friends — and then some.

"They could be counted on in an emergency — and then some.

"And so it is when we put our trust in God's goodness. He returns our love — and then some."

AUTHOR UNKNOWN

F

Face (Expression)

Take care that the face which looks out from your mirror in the morning is a pleasant one. You may not see it again all day, but others will.

———o———

A long face shortens your list of friends.

———o———

A gesture of a hand, a look upon a face, the silent message sensed in a chance glimpse of another's eyes often speak more eloquently than the finest prose or poetry, the most stirring music, or all the words in the dictionary.

———o———

Some persons think they have to look like a hedgehog to be pious.

BILLY SUNDAY

———o———

One small boy to another, shopping for Halloween masks: "Take your time. Don't fall for the first ugly face ya see!"

HANK KETCHAM, Hall Syndicate

———o———

It Will Show

You don't have to tell how you live every day,
You need not reveal if you work or play;
For a trusty barometer's always in place —
However you live it will show in your face.

The truth or deceit you would hide in your heart,
They will not stay inside when once given a start;
Sinews and blood are like thin veils of lace —

What you wear in your heart you must wear on your face.

If you've battled and won in the great game of life,
If you've striven and conquered through sorrow and strife,
If you've played the game fair but reached only first base,
It shows in your face.

AUTHOR UNKNOWN

———o———

God gave you your face; you make your own countenance.

———o———

A beautiful face is a silent commendation.

FRANCIS BACON

———o———

He had a face like a benediction.

MIGUEL DE CERVANTES, Don Quixote

———o———

A sanctimonious face is no proof of a Spirit-filled heart.

Facts

Jumping at conclusions is not half as good exercise as digging for facts.

———o———

Too many people decide what they want to believe, then go looking around for half-facts to prove they are right.

War Cry

———o———

Every story has three sides — yours, mine and the facts.

———o———

Mark Twain, in his reporting days, was instructed by an editor never to state anything as a fact that he could not verify from personal knowledge. Sent out to cover an important social event soon afterward he turned in the following:

A woman giving the name of Mrs. James Jones, who is reported to be one of the society leaders of the city, is said to have given what purported to be a party yesterday to a number of alleged ladies. The hostess claims to be the wife of a reputed attorney."

———o———

Small boy to friend: "Well, I know all the facts of life, but I don't know if they're true."

CHON DAY in *The Saturday Evening Post*

———o———

God formed us.
    Sin deformed us.
        One Christ can transform us.

———o———

Facts do not cease to exist because they are ignored.

———o———

Facts are stubborn things.

ALAIN RENÉ LE SAGE, *Gil Blas*

———o———

Nothing is so fallacious as facts, except figures.

GEORGE CANNING, quoted by SIDNEY SMITH

Failure

Don't worry when you stumble. Remember, a worm is about the only thing that can't fall down.

———o———

Every unfriendly individual is a failure, so let's all be a success.

———o———

It is better to fail in doing right than to succeed in doing wrong.

———o———

It ain't no disgrace for a man to fall, but to lay there and grunt is.

"JOSH BILLINGS" (HENRY WHEELER SHAW)

———o———

Man takes account of our failures but God of our striving.

The fellow who keeps looking back will soon find himself going that way.

———o———

Straight from the Mighty Bow this truth is driven:
They fail, and they alone, who have not striven.

CLARENCE URMY

———o———

In the lexicon of youth, which fate reserves
For a bright manhood, there is no such word
As "fail."

EDWARD GEORGE BULWER-LYTTON

———o———

More men fail through ignorance of their strength than fail through knowledge of their weakness.

———o———

Not failure, but low aim, is crime.

JAMES RUSSELL LOWELL,
For an Autograph

———o———

A lot of people spend six days sowing wild oats, then go to church on Sunday and pray for a crop failure.

FRED ALLEN

———o———

No man's success should be built on another man's failure.

———o———

Someone asks why so many church members fail. Here's one answer in a parable: When a boy was asked why he fell out of bed, he replied, "I guess it's because I stayed too close to the getting-in place."

Faith

Prayer is the faith that asks; thanksgiving is the faith that takes.

———o———

All I have seen teaches me to trust the Creator for all I have not seen.

RALPH WALDO EMERSON

Faith makes all things possible, and love makes them easy.

———o———

I believe the promises of God enough to venture an eternity on them.

ISAAC WATTS

———o———

Faith marches at the head of the army of progress. It is found beside the most refined life, the freest government, the profoundest philosophy, the noblest poetry, the purest humanity.

THEODORE T. MUNGER

———o———

Skepticism has never founded empires, established principles, or changed the world's heart. The great doers in history have always been men of faith.

EDWIN HUBBELL CHAPIN

———o———

Faith never stands around with its hands in its pockets.

———o———

Faith is more like a verb than a noun . . . Faith *accepts* the Word of God, *affirms* confidence in that Word and *acts* upon it. You never really get going until you act upon what you accept and affirm. Then you are "faithing" your way along.

VANCE HAVNER, *Peace In The Valley*

———o———

Faith gets the most; humility keeps the most; but love works the most.

DWIGHT L. MOODY

———o———

In actual life every great enterprise begins with and takes its first forward step in faith.

AUGUST WILHELM VON SCHLEGEL

———o———

Dwight L. Moody described three kinds of faith in Jesus Christ: struggling faith, which is like a man in deep water; clinging faith, which is like a man hanging to the side of a boat; and resting faith, which finds a man safely within the boat, and able moreover to reach out with a hand to help someone else.

Our faith is tried in order that His faithfulness may be experienced.

———o———

The faith that does not act, is it truly faith?

JEAN BAPTISTE RACINE

———o———

Dr. A. J. Gordon, while traveling on a train, engaged in a spirited conversation with a fellow passenger on the subject of faith. "I differ with you," said the man, "in that any person is admitted to heaven because of a little bit of theological scrip called 'faith.' I believe that when God receives one into heaven He makes a searching inquiry as to his character rather than inspection of his faith."

Presently the conductor came along and examined the tickets. When he had passed, Dr. Gordon said: "Did you ever notice how a conductor always looks at the ticket but takes no pains to inspect the passenger? A railway ticket, if genuine, certifies that the person presenting it has complied with the company's conditions and is entitled to transportation. So faith alone, my friend, entitles one to that saving grace which produces a character well-pleasing to God."

———o———

Faith

Oh for a faith that will be strong
  When angry foes beset,
A faith that will stand fast until
  The victory is met.

Though dark and long the battle rage,
  I pray for faith sincere,
A faith that will stand out, unmoved,
  A strength in time of fear.

A courage born of trust alone,
  I know will see me through;
So Lord, I pray, Thou mayest now,
  My feeble faith renew.

JOHN CALDWELL CRAIG

———o———

Faith makes the uplook good, the outlook bright, the inlook favorable, and the future glorious.

V. RAYMOND EDMAN

Faith

Faith came singing into my room
And other guests took flight;
Fear and anxiety, grief and gloom
Sped out into the night.
I wondered that such peace could be.
But Faith said gently, "Don't you see,
"They really cannot live with me."

AUTHOR UNKNOWN

———o———

Faith is dead to doubt, dumb to discouragement, blind to impossibilities, and knows nothing but success in God.

———o———

Faith is not believing that God can. It is knowing that He *will.*

———o———

While faith makes all things possible, it is love that makes all things easy.

EVAN H. HOPKINS,
in *The Wesleyan Methodist*

———o———

Faith is the eye by which we look to Jesus. A dim-sighted eye is still an eye; a weeping eye is still an eye.

Faith is the hand with which we lay hold of Jesus. A trembling hand is still a hand. And he is a believer whose heart within him trembles when he touches the hem of the Saviour's garment, that he may be healed.

Faith is the tongue by which we taste how good the Lord is. A feverish tongue is nevertheless a tongue. And then we may believe, when we are without the smallest portion of comfort; for our faith is founded, not upon feelings but upon the promises of God.

Faith is the foot by which we go to Jesus. A lame foot is still a foot. He who comes slowly nevertheless comes.

GEORGE MUELLER

———o———

Lord,
in spite of having been with you,
like Peter, James and John,
I find I still can't cope with so much
that seems wrong and frightening in
the world.

Give me the kind of faith that knows
that even if I can't cope
you can.

S. P. G., London

———o———

I prayed for faith and thought it would strike me like lightning. But faith did not come. One day I read, "Now faith comes by hearing, and hearing by the Word of God." I had closed my Bible and prayed for faith. I now began to study my Bible and faith has been growing ever since.

DWIGHT L. MOODY

———o———

It is strange we trust each other
And only doubt our Lord.
We take the word of mortals
And yet distrust His Word.
But oh, what light and glory
Would shine o'er all our days,
If we always would remember
God means just what He says.

A. B. SIMPSON

———o———

Faith is only worthy of the name when it erupts into action.

CATHERINE MARSHALL

———o———

When faith in God goes, man, the thinker, loses his greatest thought.
When faith in God goes, man, the worker, loses his greatest motive.
When faith in God goes, man, the sinner, loses his greatest help.
When faith in God goes, man, the sufferer, loses his securest refuge.
When faith in God goes, man, the lover, loses his fairest vision.
When faith in God goes, man, the mortal, loses his only hope.

HARRY EMERSON FOSDICK,
The Meaning of Faith

———o———

Faith: you can do very little with it, but you can do nothing without it.

SAMUEL BUTLER THE YOUNGER

———o———

I had faith
That God could,
I had hope
That God would;

Then my love
Pleased God
That He should.
FRANCES RHOADS LA CHANCE

---o---

Now that we have seen something of the greatness of faith, let us not forget that Christ is greater than faith in Him. As Maurice says, we spend half our time in thinking of faith, hope and love, instead of believing, hoping and loving.
JAMES HASTINGS

---o---

Lord, Give Me Faith

Lord, give me faith! — to live from day to day,
With tranquil heart to do my simple part,
And, with my hand in Thine, just go Thy way.

Lord, give me faith! — to trust, if not to know;
With quiet mind in all things Thee to find,
And, child-like, go where Thou wouldst have me go.

Lord, give me faith! — to leave it all to Thee,
The future is Thy gift, I would not lift
The veil Thy love has hung 'twixt it and me.
JOHN OXENHAM

---o---

Keystone

At first I only gave God thanks
If I felt well that day,
And everything was tranquil
And going just my way;
But when I learned to thank our Lord
When not one thing went right —
I found His hand was leading me,
His presence my delight,
His keystone *faith*, not sight.
MILDRED ALLEN JEFFERY

---o---

Faith is something like walking over a bridge you know will hold you up.
RAYMOND LINDQUIST

---o---

Faith lets Christ do for us and with us what we could never do alone.

Faithful

I cannot do great things for Him,
Who did so much for me,
But I should like to show my love,
Dear Jesus, unto Thee;
Faithful in very little things,
O Saviour, may I be.

---o---

His Choice Or Ours?

I would like to do something great, but God may appoint something little, and grace in doing that cheerfully may be greater in His sight. Elisha was ploughing, not dreaming, when Elijah brought God's message. Peter and Andrew were fishing, and James and John were mending their nets. "He that is faithful in that which is least is faithful also in much" (Luke 16:10). If we are glorifying God in that which He appoints today, we may be fitted for something more tomorrow. But we are not to live tomorrow today.
Selected

---o---

Fret not because thy place is small.
Thy service need not be,
For thou canst make it all there is
Of joy and ministry.

The dewdrop, as the boundless sea,
In God's great plan has part;
And this is all He asks of thee;
Be faithful where thou art.
Selected

---o---

It is not success that God rewards but faithfulness in doing His will.
Selected

Fame

Fame is a vapor, popularity an accident, riches take wings. Only one thing endures, and that is character.
HORACE GREELEY

---o---

I had rather men should ask why no statue has been erected in my honor, than why one has.
MARCUS PORCIUS CATO,
quoted in PLUTARCH's *Political Precepts*

Fame is no plant that grows on mortal soil.

JOHN MILTON, Lycidas

———o———

Seldom comes glory till a man be dead.

ROBERT HERRICK

———o———

Fame is the thirst of youth.

LORD BYRON, *Childe Harold's Pilgrimage*

Family

Someone has said, "The solution of the American family problems is contained in one word — CHRIST."

———o———

"A family man," says Roby Goff, who is one, "is a fellow who has replaced the currency in his wallet with snapshots."

Presbyterian Life

———o———

A family altar would alter many a family.

———o———

What Is Required

There are six essentials of good family life needed by all children.

First — love, affection and security, preferably with their own parents in their own home.

Second — full-time adult supervision and the teaching of self-control.

Third — parents with whom the child learns he can love on the basis of mutual trust.

Fourth — a close sense of family unity, where the members of the family eat together, take vacations together, go to church together.

Fifth — parents who take an interest in the education of their children.

Sixth — parents who set an example of living in accordance with the principles of their religious faith.

JUDGE GEORGE EDWARDS

———o———

Linda, aged nine, went with a neighbor playmate to a revival meeting one night. In telling her experience to the family she said, "The preacher asked everyone who had family *commotions* at their house to raise their hand, so I did."

Christian Home Builder

———o———

It is easy to govern a kingdom, but difficult to rule one's family.

———o———

You Can Always Tell Where a Family Lives

You can always tell where a family lives
By the gay effect that the hallway gives.
There are hooks arranged in a nice, straight row,
And the coats grow shorter and shorter, so
At the very first glance you can surmise
That the people vary in shape and size.
Hats that have streamers mean little girls,
With perky haircuts or ribboned curls.

A wagon and ball and bat reveal
That a boy lives there; and a slim, high heel
Or an overshoe is a certain clew
That a grown-up sister's an inmate, too.
A doll that flopped with a broken neck,
A toy train bunched ˉ in a pleasant wreck . . .
The rooms may be still as a sleeping mouse,
But you know there's a family in the house!

HELEN WELSHIMER

———o———

How To Hold A Family Worship

1. Choose a regular time to hold family worship each day — either in the morning or evening.
2. The father will be the leader.
3. Family worship should be a happy gathering, but remember that it must be reverent, too.
4. Let the Bible be the center of family worship. The Bible reading should be clear, careful, and brief.
5. Follow a definite course of Bible reading, either going through one book at a time — e.g. one of the

Gospels — or choosing passages which contain great verses or prayers, or tell of important events and prophecies. Where there are children, it is good to use the Psalms.

6. With young children it is sometimes better to tell a Bible story instead of reading it, or to read from a Bible picture book, which will help to hold their interest.

7. Children should be allowed to ask questions if they wish. They can also recite memory verses.

8. Prayers should be short, and the children encouraged to take part.

9. Invite friends to share in your family worship when they are visiting your home.

10. Remember that the saying of grace before meals is part of family worship too!

SOURCE UNKNOWN

Father

Father's Day

Father's Day, as some might assume, was not conceived in the egotism of a man, but was originated by a woman.

To Mrs. John Bruce Dodd belongs the honor.

The day actually came into being about forty-three years ago on a very small scale, when a woman, Mrs. John Dodd, in Spokane, Washington, remembered her father as she sat in church on Mother's Day.

Mrs. Dodd was one girl among six children, the other five were boys. She could recall the day when her mother died.

As little children, they did not understand the finality of death and that night one of the little boys rushed out of the door and started for the cemetery where they had put his mother. Her father ran after him and caught up the little fellow in his arms and brought him back and put his arm about all of them.

"From that moment he became both father and mother to us," she said.

Mrs. Dodd remembered how her father through the years tried to throw about those six children the best influence, how he taught them to live by the Golden Rule, and gave them a faith to live by. He brought the preacher into their home again and again.

Mrs. Dodd went to the ministerial association in Spokane with the idea of honoring her father.

Selected

———o———

Tommy, doing his homework: "Daddy, why is our language called the mother tongue?"

Dad: "Because fathers hardly ever get a chance to use it."

———o———

Nurse: "Congratulations! You are the father of triplets."

Building Contractor: "Whew! I've exceeded my estimate again!"

———o———

Many a son has lost his way among strangers because his father was too busy to get acquainted with him.

WILLIAM L. BROWNELL

———o———

God And Father

My little boy came to me one day,
Placed his tiny hand in mine and said:
"Daddy, what is God like?"
And I said, "God is like love and sunshine,
And all the good things you know."
He smiled into my eyes and said:
"Then, Daddy, God must be just like you!"
I remember how Jesus said
That God is like a father;
And I had to bow my head in shame
That I, a father, was so unlike God!

GEORGE A. TURNER
in *The Log of the Good Ship Grace*

———o———

A little girl was showing her playmate her new home. "This is daddy's den," she explained as they entered one room. "Does your daddy have a den?"

"No," was the answer, "my pop just growls all over the house."

———o———

Small boy's definition of Father's Day: "It's just like Mother's Day, only you don't spend as much on the present."

Toronto Star

———o———

Reflections Of A Father

Say, fellows, I want to tell you I'd be
happy as a clam
If I was just the Daddie that my laddie
thinks I am.
He thinks I'm a wonder and believes
his dear old Dad
Could never think of mixing with mean
things that are bad,
And sometimes I just sit and think how
nice it would be,
If I was just the Daddie that my laddie
thinks he is.

CHELEY

———o———

One father is more than a hundred
schoolmasters.

GEORGE HERBERT, *Jacula Prudentum*

———o———

Definition of an exceptional father:
One who lets the children play with
their Christmas toys more than he does.

———o———

Many a boy at sixteen can't believe
that some day he will be as dumb as
his dad!

———o———

A Father's Ten Commandments

By My Example

I. I shall teach my child respect
for his fellow man.
II. I shall teach him good sportsmanship in work and play.
III. I shall instill in him an appreciation of religion and the family,
the backbone of society.
IV. I shall strive for companionship
and mutual understanding.
V. I shall impart to him a desire
to love and honor his country
and obey its laws.
VI. I shall encourage him to apply
himself to difficult tasks.
VII. I shall teach him the importance
of participation in community
affairs and local government.
VIII. I shall teach him self-reliance
and help him develop an independent spirit.
IX. I shall help him develop a sense
of responsibility in planning for
the future.
X. I shall, above all, prepare him
for the duties and responsibilities of citizenship in a free
society.

Glendale News Press,
Glendale, Calif.

———o———

A Father's Day Prayer

Mender of toys, leader of boys,
Changer of fuses, kisser of bruises,
Bless him, dear Lord.
Mover of couches, soother of ouches
Pounder of nails, teller of tales,
Reward him, O Lord.
Hanger of screens, counselor of teens,
Fixer of bikes, chastiser of tykes,
Help him, O Lord.
Raker of leaves, cleaner of eaves,
Dryer of dishes, fulfiller of wishes . . .
Bless him, O Lord.

JO ANN HEIDBREDER in *The Sign*

———o———

Giddap, Dad

The men who ride in rodeos
Need to be tough, of course —
But they should have a two-year-old
And spend time as a horse!

LAVONNE MATHISON

———o———

Fatherhood

I could have lost him, but pride and
joy
Curbed sharp impatience with my boy.

I shared his joy at triumph's fame
Restored his faith when failure came.

Sometimes with wisdom, often with
hope,
I answered as his mind would grope

In eager questioning. And I would
pray
For guidance for myself, to lead his
way.

I salved his woes, calmed fears and
cries

And saw the father worship in his eyes.

Tired feet trod with his strong ones
To greater heights, to bright new suns!
ROY Z. KEMP

———o———

We think our fathers fools, so wise we
grow;
Our wiser sons, no doubt, will think us
so.
ALEXANDER POPE, *Essay on Criticism*

———o———

A Father's Prayer

Build me a son, O God, who will be
strong enough to know when he is
weak and brave enough to face himself when he is afraid; one who will be
proud and unbending in honest defeat, but humble and gentle in victory.
Build me a son whose wishes will not
replace his actions — a son who will
know Thee, and that to know himself
is the foundation stone of knowledge.
Send him, I pray, not in the path of
ease and comfort but the stress and
spur of difficulties and challenge; here
let him learn to stand up in the storm;
here let him learn compassion for those
who fail.

Build me a son whose heart will be
clear, whose goal will be high; a son
who will master himself before he seeks
to master others; one who will learn to
laugh, yet never forget how to weep;
one who will reach into the future,
yet never forget the past, and after all
these things are his, this I pray, enough
sense of humor that he may always be
serious yet never take himself too seriously. Give him humility so that he
may always remember the simplicity
of true greatness, the open mind of
true wisdom, the meekness of true
strength; then I, his father, will dare
to whisper, "I have not lived in vain."
Quoted by the late
GENERAL DOUGLAS MACARTHUR

Faults

From Day To Day

We all have faults to conquer
You do and I do, too.
We make mistakes quite often
In something that we do.

Not one of us is perfect.
We can only progress,
From day to day attempting
To make our faults grow less.

Then may we aid each other,
Not harshly criticize.
How sweet is understanding
From those who sympathize.

The helping hand, the kindly heart
Are needed everywhere
So let us reach out daily
And show someone we care
LOUISE DARCY

———o———

We can often do more for other men
by correcting our own faults than by
trying to correct theirs.

———o———

We ought to avoid in ourselves the
faults that we blame in others.
MENANDER

———o———

To acknowledge our faults when we
are blamed is modesty; to discover
them to one's friends, in ingenuousness,
is confidence; but to proclaim them to
the world, if one does not take care, is
pride.
CONFUCIUS

———o———

Nothing is easier than faultfinding;
no talent, no self-denial, no brains, no
character are required to set up in the
grumbling business.
The Herald

———o———

What you dislike in another, take
care to correct in yourself.
THOMAS SPAT

———o———

It is a satisfaction for some to exhibit another's faults even if they must
wait six months for a chance.

———o———

But, friend, to me
He is all fault who hath no fault at all.
ALFRED, LORD TENNYSON
Idylls of the King, Lancelot and Elaine

———o———

He has no faults, except that he is
· faultless.
PLINY THE YOUNGER

A fault confessed is half redressed.

———o———

To increase your happiness, forget your neighbor's faults.

———o———

I dare no more fret than I dare curse and swear. Nothing is more sure to destroy the joy and peace of a home. Nothing is more sure to finally divide and even separate a home than this habit of fretfulness, grumbling and fault-finding.

JOHN WESLEY

Fear

Near acquaintance doth diminish reverent fear.

SIR PHILIP SIDNEY

———o———

There is much in the world to make us afraid. There is much more in our faith to make us unafraid.

FREDERICK W. CROPP

———o———

The people to fear are not those who disagree with you but those who disagree with you and are too cowardly to let you know.

NAPOLEON BONAPARTE

———o———

He has not learned the lesson of life who does not every day surmount a fear.

RALPH WALDO EMERSON

———o———

Afraid? Of What?

Afraid? Of what?
To feel the spirit's glad release?
To pass from pain to perfect peace?
The strife and strain of life to cease?
Afraid — of that?

Afraid? Of what?
Afraid to see the Savior's face?
To hear His welcome, and to trace
The glory gleam from wounds of grace?
Afraid — of that?

E. H. HAMILTON

No power is strong enough to be lasting if it labors under the weight of fear.

MARCUS TULLIUS CICERO

———o———

We can easily forgive a child who is afraid of the dark; the real tragedy of life is when men are afraid of the light.

PLATO

———o———

Six-year-old Tommy was far from anxious to enter the first grade when school started in a few weeks. Finally he told his parents the reason for his fears. "I don't want to go to first grade because my teeth will begin to fall out like Johnny's did when he started to school!"

———o———

He who fears the Lord can expect help when his case is at the worst.

———o———

No one loves him whom he fears.

ARISTOTLE, Rhetoric

———o———

Our fears do make us traitors.

WILLIAM SHAKESPEARE, Macbeth

———o———

To be free from all fear, we must have but one fear — the fear of God.

———o———

What we are afraid to do before men we may well be afraid to think before God.

———o———

The function of fear is to warn us of danger, not to make us afraid to face it.

Fellowship

A habit of devout fellowship with God is the spring of all our life, and the strength of it. Such prayer, meditation and converse with God restores and renews the temper of our minds; so that by this contact with the world unseen we receive continual accesses of strength.

HENRY E. MANNING

Fellowship is heaven, and lack of fellowship is hell: fellowship is life, and lack of fellowship is death: and the deeds that ye do on earth, it is for fellowship's sake that ye do them.

WILLIAM MORRIS

———o———

I remember what an African said to a missionary. They had been praying together [in Africa], after the blessing. One was an African Christian, the other a missionary from England. The missionary saw what had happened in the life of this African, that he was changed, and that he came to the missionary and opened his heart — to the amazement of the Englishman. But after a number of times of having a little prayer time in the missionary's house . . ., the missionary turned to the African and said, "Look here. You haven't got as much fellowship with me as you have with your dear African brother [naming a friend]. What's wrong?" The African replied, "Look, we are here like two boxes. Imagine two boxes trying to have fellowship — one having the lock on, and the other wide open. Tell me if that is practical. Can these two boxes have fellowship as long as one is locked?"

Of the two men, one was open.

FESTO KIVENGERE,
in Commission, Conflict, Commitment

———o———

Tell God all that is in your heart, as one unloads one's heart to a dear friend. People who have no secrets from each other never want subjects of conversation; they do not weigh their words, because there is nothing to be kept back. Neither do they seek for something to say; they talk out of the abundance of their hearts, just what they think. Blessed are they who attain to such familiar, unreserved intercourse with God.

FRANÇOIS DE SALIGNAC DE LA MOTHE
FENELON (1651-1715)

Fight

If you aren't wounded then you haven't fought.

The tree that never had to fight
For sun and sky and air and light,
That stood out in the open plain
And always got its share of rain,
Never became a forest king,
But lived and died a scrubby thing.
Where thickest stands the forest growth
We find the patriarchs of both;
And they hold converse with the stars
Whose broken branches show the scars
Of many winds and much of strife.
This is the common law of life.

———o———

One day my youngster brought home a note from his teacher, saying he had been fighting in the schoolyard. "Johnny and I weren't fighting when the teacher came along," my son insisted. "We were just trying to separate each other."

MRS. LILY JACOBSEN in Coronet

———o———

It is easier to fight for one's principles than to live up to them.

ALFRED ADLER

———o———

It is often asked whether the Christian is not to fight in the conflict with personal sin. The answer is that of course he must fight, but it is necessary to remember that it is the "good fight of faith" (I Timothy 6:12), and it is particularly important to realize that the fight is not to obtain, but to maintain. It is a struggle not for a position, but from a position. As has been well said, the Christian is not like a man in the valley struggling to reach the top of the hill, but like a man on the top of the hill fighting to maintain his position there against enemies who are trying to drag him down.

GRIFFITH W. THOMAS

Fire

The same fire that melts the wax hardens the steel.

———o———

Men ablaze are invincible. Hell trembles when men kindle with the flame and fervor of the Holy Spirit. The stronghold of Satan is proof against everything but fire.

SAMUEL CHADWICK

————o————

The supreme need of the Church is the same in the twentieth century as in the first: it is men on fire for Christ.

JAMES S. STEWART

————o————

I will blaze the trail, though my grave may only become a stepping-stone that younger men may follow.

C. T. STUDD

————o————

You cannot kindle a fire in another until it is burning within yourself.

Fish, Fishing

Never fish in troubled waters.

————o————

Seeking diversion by fishing in the streams of Scotland, a literary man went from the city with patent pole and a complete outfit of the most expensive kind. After hours of effort without even a bit, he came across a country boy with only a switch for a pole and a bent pin for a hook — but he had a long string of fish.

"Why is it that I can't catch any?" the man inquired.

"Because you don't keep yourself out of sight," the boy replied.

This is the secret of fishing for men as well as trout. Hold up the Cross of Christ. Send the people away talking about Him, instead of praising you.

————o————

A fishing rod is an instrument with a worm at one end and a fool at the other.

————o————

You will find angling to be like the virtue of humility, which has a calmness of spirit and a world of other blessings attending upon it.

IZAAK WALTON, *The Compleat Angler*

Flag

Flag Day

"I pledge allegiance to my flag" and
  all for which it stands,
  The cradle-home of Freedom, and
    hearts of many lands,
And may I never dim its stars with
  touch of greedy hands!

"One nation indivisible," one banner,
  and one soul,
  For whom through years of blood
    and toil our fathers paid the toll,
And may I come to understand the
  vision of the whole!

"With liberty and justice," for each his
  fighting-chance
  To prove his worth, and win his
    dream in battled circumstance,
And may I never bar the way, nor
  break another's chance!

"I pledge allegiance to my flag," north,
  south, east and west,
  I know not what the years shall bring
    to put me to the test,
But may I guard it with my life, and
  serve it with my best!

MARTHA HASKELL CLARK

————o————

"A song for our banner?" The watchword recall
Which gave the Republic her station;
"United we stand, divided we fall!"
It made and preserves us a nation!

GEORGE POPE MORRIS,
The Flag of Our Union

————o————

The American Flag

When Freedom from her mountain
  height
  Unfurled her standard to the air,
She tore the azure robe of night,
  And set the stars of glory there.
She mingled with its gorgeous dyes
The milky baldric of the skies,
And striped its pure, celestial white,
With streakings of the morning light.

Flag of the free heart's hope and home!
  By angel hands to valor given;
Thy stars have lit the welkin dome,

And all thy hues were born in heaven.

Forever float that standard sheet!
Where breathes the foe but falls before us,
With Freedom's soil beneath our feet,
And Freedom's banner streaming o'er us?

JOSEPH RODMAN DRAKE

Flattery

Flattery is to be used like perfume — smell and enjoy it, but don't swallow it.

———o———

Flattery is soft soap
and soap is 90% lye.

Christian Leader

———o———

Flattery is often a gift-wrapped insult.

———o———

Flattery is the art of telling another person exactly what he thinks of himself.·

———o———

Flatterers look like friends, as wolves like dogs.

GEORGE CHAPMAN

———o———

Flattery corrupts both the receiver and the giver; and adulation is not of more service to the people than to kings.

EDMUND BURKE

———o———

He that loves to be flattered is worthy of the flattery.

WILLIAM SHAKESPEARE

———o———

'Tis an old maxim in the schools,
That flattery's the food of fools;
Yet now and then your men of wit
Will condescend to take a bit.

JONATHAN SWIFT, *Cadenus and Vanessa*

Follow

Followers

They followed Him by thousands when He took some fish and bread
And a banquet in the desert by His miracle was spread.

They sang aloud, "Hosanna!" and they shouted, "Praise His name!"
When in an hour of glory to Jerusalem He came.
They followed when He told them of a kingdom and a throne,
But when He went to Calvary, He went there all alone.

It seems that many people still would follow Him today
If He only went to places where everything was gay.
For the kingdom that they're seeking isn't one the world scorns,
And the crown of which they're singing isn't one that's made of thorns.
Oh, they'll follow for the fishes over land and over sea,
And they'll join the church at Zion, but not at Calvary.

It's so easy, friends, to follow when the nets are full of fish,
When the loaves are spread before you and you're eating all you wish,
When no lands, nor lots, nor houses and no friendships are at stake,
When there's no mob to mock you and you have no cross to take.
But you'll need some faith to follow down through Gethsemane,
And you'll need some love to follow up to Calvary!

AUTHOR UNKNOWN

———o———

If you haven't learned to follow, you can't lead.

HENRIETTA C. MEARS

———o———

A telegram was received by a famous girls' school in which the father of the applicant, on observing the question, "Outline the leadership capabilities of your daughter," responded by saying, "My daughter has no leadership capacities. However, she is an intelligent follower."
    The president of the college telephoned the father directly and admitted his daughter to the college without qualification, stating that, of the thousands of applicants to the college, this was the first girl who was not a natural-born leader.

GENE L. SCHWILCK in *Indiana Teacher*

When I follow someone I at least want to know where he's going.

CLARA FRANCES SMITH

———o———

Others follow in your footsteps quicker than they follow your advice.

———o———

Anyone can praise Christ, but it takes a man of courage to follow Him.

———o———

The grandchildren of Mr. and Mrs. W. W. Evans, owners of a ranch near Panhandle, Texas, were thrilled by the gift of seventeen sheep — which they played with and fed until one day the sheep wandered off the ranch. Another rancher, finding the strays and thinking they belonged to his son, put them in with his son's 200 sheep. When he realized he had taken the Evans children's sheep, he was quite sorry and willing to give them back. But how could they tell which of the sheep belonged to which owner?

Then Billy, one of the children, had an idea. Taking a bucket of oats, he went out to the flock, and gave his usual feed call. Immediately sixteen of the sheep hurried to him — and the seventeenth followed as soon as he came near enough to hear!

This brings home Christ's description of Himself as the Good Shepherd calling to His sheep: "And the sheep follow Him: for they know His voice" (John 10:4).

Fool, Foolish

A foolish man uses wisdom to explain his foolishness; a wise man uses foolishness to explain his wisdom.

———o———

Much more painful than acting like a fool is suddenly to realize that you were not acting!

———o———

You can always tell a fool, but the chances are he won't know what you're talking about.

Many a man who is counted a fool by financiers has laid up an enviable fortune in Heaven.

———o———

He who asks a question is a fool for five minutes; he who does not ask a question remains a fool forever.

Chinese Proverb

If there were a law against being foolish, we'd all be in jail.

———o———

Being considered a fool for Christ's sake is not a license to act like one.

C. J. FOSTER

———o———

If things go awry, must we then turn the world over into the hands of the fools?

———o———

The only way to keep from seeing a fool is to remain in your bedroom and break the mirror.

———o———

Dr. P. S. Hensen was engaged to speak for a Chautauqua on the subject of "Fools." He was introduced by Bishop John H. Vincent with the remark, "Ladies and Gentlemen, we are about to have a lecture on 'Fools' by one of the most distinguished . . ." The bishop paused as if finished, then resumed: ". . . men of Chicago." Dr. Hensen, unperturbed began his speech: "I am not so great a fool as Bishop Vincent . . ." The audience gasped during his pause, and then he concluded: ". . . would have you think."

———o———

Wise men learn more from fools than fools from wise men; for wise men avoid the faults of fools, but fools will not imitate the good examples of wise men.

MARCUS PORCIUS CATO,
quoted in PLUTARCH's *Lives*

Forbearance

If I Knew You And You Knew Me

If I knew you and you knew me,
'Tis seldom we would disagree;

But never having yet clasped hand,
Both often fail to understand
That each intends to do what's right
And treat each other "honor bright,"
How little to complain there'd be
If I knew you and you knew me.

Whene'er I ship you my mistake
Or in your bill some error make,
From irritation you'd be free
If I knew you and you knew me.
Or when the checks don't come on
    time
And customers send nary a line,
I'd wait without anxiety
If I knew you and you knew me.

Or when some goods you "fire back,"
Or make a "kick" on this or that,
I'd take it in good part, you see,
If I knew you and you knew me.
With customers a million strong,
Occasionally things go wrong —
Sometimes my fault, sometimes theirs —
Forbearance would decrease all cares.
Kind friend, how pleasant things would
    be
If I knew you and you knew me!
Herbalist Almanac, 1938

————o————

Cultivate forbearance till your heart
yields a fine crop of it. Pray for a short
memory as to all unkindnesses.
CHARLES HADDON SPURGEON

Foreign

After hearing his teacher talk about
a missionary family which the church
supported serving in a foreign field, the
three-year-old prayed as follows during
the prayer time: "Dear God, help the
Butler family in the corn field."

————o————

A Foreigner

Within the walls of hate and shunning
I am placed.
I am a foreigner.
Outside the walls of love and friend-
    ship
I am placed.
I am a foreigner.
Because I am dark,
Because I speak with an unharmoniz-
    ing tone,

Because I am a foreigner
I am placed
Within the walls of ridicule,
Outside the walls of understanding.
MARYBETH ANDERSON

Forget

Forget yourself for others, and others
will never forget you.

————o————

When a man forgets himself, he usually does something that everyone else
remembers.

————o————

The Year That Has Gone

Let us forget the things that vexed and
    tried us.
The worrying things that caused our
    soul to fret,
The hopes that cherished long, where
    still denied us,
Let us forget.

Let us forget the little slights that
    pained us,
The greater wrongs that rankle some-
    times yet,
The pride with which some lofty one
    disdained us,
Let us forget.

But blessings manifold past all deserv-
    ing,
Kind words and helpful deeds, a count-
    less throng,
The fault o'ercome, the rectitude un-
    swerving —
Let us remember long.

The sacrifice of love, the generous giv-
    ing,
Where friends were few, the hand-
    clasp warm and strong,
The fragrance of each life of holy liv-
    ing,
Let us remember long.

So pondering well the lesson it has
    taught us,
We tenderly may bid the year "Good-
    bye,"
Holding in memory all the good that
    it has brought us,
Letting the evil die.
AUTHOR UNKNOWN

Your brother's sins write in the sand
Where waters may erase them
But carve his virtues in your heart
And let not time efface them!
JAMES GALLAGHER

———o———

The Forward Look

Lord, make me deaf, and dumb and
  blind
To all, "those things which are behind."
Dead to the voice that memory brings,
Accusing me of many things.
Dumb to the things my tongue could
  speak,
Reminding me when I was weak.
Blind to the things I still might see,
When they come back to trouble me.
Let me press on to Thy high calling,
In Christ, who keepeth me from falling.
Forgetting all that lies behind —
Lord, make me deaf, and dumb and
  blind.
Like Paul, I then shall win the race,
I would have lost but for Thy grace!
Forgetting all that I have done —
'Twas Thee, dear Lord, not I that won!
GEORGE T. KENYON
in Herald of His Coming

Forgive

He who has mastered the grace of
forgiveness is far more triumphant than
he who has managed to see that no
wrong to him is gone unavenged.
LLOYD D. MATTSON

———o———

How can we gain a forgiving heart?
Only by going to the Cross and there
seeing how much our Lord has forgiven us and at what a cost. Then we
shall see that the utmost we are called
upon to forgive, compared with what
we have been forgiven, is a very little
thing.

———o———

Forgiveness of sins does not qualify
a person to live; it only qualifies him
to die.
LLOYD AHLEM

———o———

Dinny Malone, a retired sea captain
of unusual integrity, was reading his
Bible when the minister came to call.
The 80-year-old seaman greeted the
minister with the news that he had
been trying to get God to forgive him
for six years — "and He won't!"
  The minister looked at him keenly.
"Have you repented?" Dinny nodded
solemnly. "Have you trusted God?"
"Yes," answered Dinny. "Then you
must have found Him!"
  Dinny shook his head. "I never feel
it in my heart — the forgiveness."
  The minister took the Bible from
Dinny's hand and together they went
over the invitations of Christ and such
verses as I John 1:9: "If we confess our
sins, he is faithful and just to forgive us
our sins, and to cleanse us from all
unrighteousness."
  "Dinny," said the minister, "when
you give your word, do you keep it?"
"Sure I do!" roared Dinny. "Doesn't
a gentleman always?" The minister
leaned toward him. "Dinny, don't you
think God is a gentleman?"
  A light that never was on land or sea
shone on Dinny's face. "What a fool
I've been! I see it now. He does forgive me, and now I feel it!"
The Pentecostal Evangel

———o———

Forgiveness does not leave the
hatchet handle sticking out of the
ground.

———o———

The offender never pardons.
GEORGE HERBERT, Jacula Prudentum

———o———

Being all fashioned of the self-same
  dust,
Let us be merciful as well as just.
HENRY WADSWORTH LONGFELLOW

———o———

When you are forgiven, someone
must pay, and the one who forgives is
the one who suffers.
EDWIN ORR

———o———

Yesterday

A typical day, crowded full of things —
Household chores and a phone that
  rings

The children rushing in at three —
Shouting with laughter and full of glee.

She tried to be helpful — saying, "Here I'll pour"
And milk is spilled on the freshly waxed floor.
"Shame on you — now see what you've done."
(Was that my voice?) "You naughty one!"

"I'm sorry, Mommy" — "Sorry, won't do —
You go to your room 'til I call you."
The hours slip by — supper is past,
The children are bathed and in bed at last.

When out of the darkness a question from Sue,
"When you're naughty, Mommy, who punishes you?"
The house is quiet — my day is through
And so I turn, Dear God, to You —

To You who gives me each new day.
Another chance to go Thy way.
Another chance — all sins forgiven,
A gift of love from God in Heaven.

And suddenly the teardrops start,
For I have failed to do my part,
To teach my children the kind of love,
Given to us from God above.

I, whose sins are so much more
Than a glass of milk spilled on the floor,
Forget how much I count on Thee accepting
"I'm sorry" each day from me.

Forgive me, Father — Forgive me, Sue —
And help me remember my whole life through
"When you're naughty, Mommy — who punishes you?"

MARIAN PALMER

Fortune

When Fortune is on our side, popular favor bears her company.
PUBLILIUS SYRUS, *Maxim 275*

Not only is fortune herself blind, but she generally blinds those on whom she bestows her favors.
MARCUS TULLIUS CICERO

———o———

Fortune makes him a fool, whom she makes her darling.
FRANCIS BACON

———o———

Fortune is like glass — the brighter the glitter, the more easily broken.
PUBLILIUS SYRUS, *Maxim 280*

Free, Freedom

Once upon a time there was a kite who wanted to be free. He was quite thrilled the day his master took him out, and he rose high above the earth. But suddenly he found he could go no farther. His master had quit letting out the string.
"Why does he hold me back like this?" he fretted. "You think I am high in the sky now, but if my master would only let me loose and give me freedom, I'd show you how high I could go."
One day while the kite was fretting thus, the string broke. The kite wavered for a minute, was blown from side to side, then suddenly turned topsy-turvy, and came floating down, down, down, unable to right itself. Finally it was swept by the strong wind up against a telegraph wire and there it hung, all tattered and torn. Its freedom was its ruin.
The Evangelical Christian

———o———

Let us give thanks that we live in a free country where a man can say what he thinks if he isn't afraid of his wife, his neighbors, or his boss, and if he's sure it won't hurt his business.
Changing Times, The Kiplinger Magazine

———o———

False freedom leaves a man free to do what he likes; true freedom, to do what he ought.

———o———

Moody tells of a man who said he would like to come to Jesus, but he was chained and could not break away. A

Christian said to him, "But, man, why don't you come, chain and all?" He said, "I never thought of that. And I will." He did and Christ broke every fetter.

———o———

One who knows by the assurance of the witnessing Spirit that he is born of God, knows he must be free.

BISHOP WARREN CANDLER

———o———

Christianity promises to make men free; it never promises to make them independent.

WILLIAM R. INGE

———o———

You have freedom *of* choice but not freedom *from* choice.

WENDELL JONES

———o———

. . . freedom of religion; freedom of the press; freedom of person under the protection of the *habeas corpus*. . . . these principles form the bright constellation which has gone before us, and guided our steps through an age of revolution and reformation.

THOMAS JEFFERSON,
First Inaugural Address

———o———

No one can be free who does not work for the freedom of others.

———o———

Sunsets For Sale

Suppose that people had to pay
To see a sunset's crimson play
And the magic stars of the Milky Way.
Suppose it was fifty cents a night
To watch the pale moon's silvery light,
Or watch a gull in graceful flight.

Suppose God charged us for the rain,
Or put a price on a song-bird's strain
Of music — the dawn-mist on the plain.
How much would autumn landscapes cost,
Or a window etched with winter's frost,
And the rainbow's glory so quickly lost?

How much, I wonder, would it be worth
To smell the good, brown, fragrant earth

In spring? The miracle of birth —
How much do you think would people pay
For a baby's laugh at the close of day?
Suppose God charged us for them, I say!

Suppose we paid to look at the hills,
For the rippling mountain rills,
Or the mating song of whippoorwills,
Or curving breakers of the sea,
For grace and beauty and majesty?
And all these things He gives us free!

Ah! what poor return for these
We yield at night on bended knees,
Without thanksgiving we mumble pleas;
Ignoring the moonlight across the floor,
The voice of a friend at the open door,
We beg the Master for more and more!

AUTHOR UNKNOWN

———o———

Without a free press there can be no free society.

FELIX FRANKFURTER

———o———

Land Of The Free

Freedom to worship God.
Our pilgrim fathers came
Bearing aloft this torch,
A high and holy flame.

Freedom to worship God.
With this they lit the world;
Beneath this burning brand
A bright new flag unfurled.

Freedom to worship God.
And now, on speeding wheels,
Their children crowd the earth.
Today, who bows, who kneels?

Freedom to worship God.
This was their battle cry.
And now that we are free —
Have we forgotten why?

HELEN FRAZEE-BOWER

———o———

Three Needs

I know three things must always be,
To keep a nation strong and free;
One, a hearthstone, bright and clear

With busy, happy loved ones near.
One is a ready heart and hand
To love and serve, and keep the land.
One is a worn and beaten way
To where the people go to pray.
So long as these are kept alive,
Nation and people will survive.
God keep them always, everywhere —
The hearth, the flag, the place of prayer.

BERTHA CLARKE HUGHES

———o———

Here is J. Edgar Hoover's answer to the question, "Where do you believe freedom has its beginnings?"

In religion. Christ championed the sanctity of the individual. There is respect for human dignity only where Christ and the Bible are a way of life. The philosophy of Christ has meant freedom from despair and tyranny throughout history.

Friend

The older we grow the more we are disquieted over the lack of attention people show to their friends. An old Scandinavian adage puts it this way: "Go often to the house of thy friend, for weeds choke up an unused path."

———o———

A friend of mine dropped by, dear God, for just a friendly chat . . .
We sipped a cup of coffee and we talked of this and that . . .
Our visit was not planned at all, but as he passed my way . . .
My friend just stopped to say "hello" and pass the time of day . . .

You know how much I'm grateful, God, for kind and thoughtful friends . . .
It's folks like these that bring my life its richest dividends . . .
Because they bring a friendly word, they share a smile or two . . .
And skies that had a tinge of gray become a brighter blue.

GEORGE BILBY WALKER

———o———

It is my joy in life to find
At every turning of the road

The strong arms of a comrade kind
To help me onward with my load.
And since I have no gold to give
And love alone can make amends,
My only prayer is, "While I live,
God, make me worthy of my friends!"

AUTHOR UNKNOWN

———o———

A real friend is one who will continue to talk to you over the back fence even though he knows he's missing his favorite television program.

———o———

The ornaments of a house are the friends who visit it.

———o———

Old Friends

Make new friends, but keep the old;
Those are silver, these are gold.
New-made friendships, like new wine,
Age will mellow and refine.

Friendships that have stood the test —
Time and change — are surely best;
Brow may wrinkle, hair grow gray,
Friendship never knows decay.

For 'mid old friends, tried and true,
Once more we our youth renew.
But old friends, alas! may die,
New friends must their place supply.

Cherish friendship in your breast —
New is good, but old is best;
Make new friends, but keep the old;
Those are silver, these are gold.

JOSEPH PARRY

———o———

He who would have friends must show himself friendly. Love begets love. Kindness secures kindness. Whatsoever we sow we shall reap.

———o———

Treat your friend as if he might become an enemy.

PUBLILIUS SYRUS, *Maxim 402*

———o———

Some take their gold in minted mold
And some in harps hereafter;
But give me mine in friendship fine;
Keep the change in laughter.

I awake this morning with devout thanksgiving for my friends, the old and the new.

RALPH WALDO EMERSON

———o———

The way to keep a circle of friends is to keep on the square with them.

———o———

We can never replace a friend. When a man is fortunate enough to have several, he finds they are all different. No one has a double in friendship.

JOHANN VON SCHILLER

———o———

A friend is someone you can count on to count on you.

———o———

A friend whom it has taken years to win should not be displeasing to you in a moment. A stone is many years becoming a ruby — take care that you do not destroy its luster in an instant.

———o———

True friendship is loyalty to a friend in trouble.

RALPH BREWER

———o———

Prosperity makes friends and adversity tries them.

PUBLILIUS SYRUS, Maxim 872

———o———

To God, thy country, and thy friend be true.

HENRY VAUGHAN,
Rules and Lessons, No. 8

———o———

Chance makes our parents, but choice makes our friends.

JACQUES DELILLE

———o———

I lay it down as a fact that, if all men knew what others say of them, there would not be four friends in the world.

BLAISE PASCAL, Pensées

———o———

Unless you bear with the faults of a friend you betray your own.

PUBLILIUS SYRUS

Growing Friendship

Friendship is like a garden of flowers, fine and rare,
It cannot reach perfection except through loving care;
Then, new and lovely blossoms with each new day appear . . .
For Friendship like a garden, grows in beauty year by year.

AUTHOR UNKNOWN

———o———

Friendship is a chain of God
Shaped in God's all perfect mold.
Each link a smile, a laugh, a tear,
A grip of the hand, a word of cheer.
Steadfast as the ages roll,
Binding closer soul to soul.
No matter how far or heavy the load,
Sweet is the journey on friendship's road.

AUTHOR UNKNOWN

Fruitful

Fruitful Christian witness grows from roots of faithful obedience to Christ.

———o———

The fruits of the Spirit are nothing but the virtues of Christ.

FRIEDRICH ERNST SCHLEIERMACHER

———o———

He that plants thorns must never expect to gather roses.

PILPAY

Frustration

A good definition of frustration: Missing your turn in a revolving door.

———o———

Frustration

Traveling with a four-year-old
Explains the word "frustration" . . .
You have to stop . . . he has to go
At every service station.

ALBERTA KNOCH in Home Life

———o———

He overcomes the frustration of the times whose plans and purposes belong to God.

Fun

Mix a little folly with your wisdom;
a little nonsense is pleasant now and
then.

                          HORACE, *Odes*

———o———

There ain't much fun in medicine,
but there's a good deal of medicine
in fun.

———o———

When a thing is funny, search it for
a hidden truth.

                  GEORGE BERNARD SHAW

———o———

A little folly is desirable in him that
will not be guilty of stupidity.

    MICHEL EYQUEM DE MONTAIGNE, *Of Vanity*

———o———

A little nonsense now and then
Is relished by the wisest men.

                          ANONYMOUS

———o———

Your funny-bone is where you laugh
in your sleeve.

———o———

Everything is funny as long as it is
happening to somebody else.

        WILL ROGERS, *The Illiterate Digest*

Funeral

A new minister, who was called to
pastor a church in a small town in
Oklahoma, the first few days visited the
homes of the members, urging them to
attend his first service that coming Sunday.

But when Sunday came, only a handful of people showed up.

The next day, in desperation, the
young minister placed a notice in the
local newspaper stating that, because
such-and-such a church was dead, it
was his duty, as a minister, to give it a
decent Christian burial.

"The funeral will be held the following Sunday afternoon at the Church"
the advertisement said.

Morbidly curious, the entire community turned out for this unusual funeral.

In front of the pulpit, they saw a
casket, smothered with flowers. The
pastor read the obituary and delivered
the eulogy.

He then invited his congregation to
step forward and pay their respect to
the dearly beloved who had departed.

The long line filed by. Each "mourner" peeped into the coffin, and turned
away with a guilty, sheepish look.

In the coffin, tilted at the correct
angle, was a large mirror.

Each person saw himself — as the
reason for the death of the old church.

Future

The Uncertain Future

We know not what the future holds
In times like these today;
The castles that we start to build
May crumble and decay,
With all earth's vast uncertainty —
Some poverty, some wealth,
For some the best that heart could
  wish;
For others failing health.

Hold on to God's unchanging hand
No matter where you go;
Relinquish not your trust in Him
Though weakened by the foe.
May God's eternal leadership
Our stronghold ever be.
Oh, strengthen, Lord, our faith and
  hope
For what we cannot see!

                      AUTHOR UNKNOWN

———o———

The future is always a fairy land to
the young.

———o———

To The Future

The past has its store of joys we re-
  member,
The future is ours undefiled . . .
Let us carry our weight with courage
  of men,
But proceed with the trust of a child.

                  KATHLEEN PARTRIDGE

———o———

I do not know what the future holds,
but I do know who holds the future.
Because of the character and the invincible purpose of God, there can be

no doubt of the ultimate triumph of righteousness.

GEORGE W. TRUETT

I know of no way of judging the future but by the past.

PATRICK HENRY, *Speech*, March 23, 1775

G

Gain

A great point is gained when we have learned not to struggle against the circumstances God has appointed for us.

H. L. SIDNEY LEAR

———o———

I gave up all for Christ, and what have I found? I have found everything in Christ.

JOHN CALVIN

———o———

He who seeks for gain must be at some expense.

PLAUTUS

Gambling

Gambling is the child of avarice, the brother of iniquity, and the father of mischief.

GEORGE WASHINGTON

———o———

Gambling is the one sure way of getting nothing for something.

———o———

He who gambles picks his own pockets.

———o———

There are two times in a man's life when he should not speculate: when he can't afford it, and when he can.

———o———

The gambling known as business looks with austere disfavor upon the business known as gambling.

AMBROSE BIERCE

Games

Little Diane was lying on her back on the floor singing a happy song. The next time her mother looked, she was lying on her stomach, shrilling a different tune.

"Playing a game, dear?" Mother asked.

"Yes," Diane replied. "I'm pretending I'm a phonograph record, and I've just turned myself over."

The Instructor

———o———

Dare to err and to dream; a higher meaning often lies in childish play.

JOHANN CHRISTOPH FRIEDRICH VON SCHILLER

———o———

In play there are two pleasures for
  your choosing —
The one is winning, and the other losing.

LORD BYRON

Garden

God almighty first planted a garden; and, indeed, it is the purest of human pleasures. It is the greatest refreshment to the spirits of man; without which buildings and palaces are but gross handiworks. . . .

FRANCIS BACON, *Of Gardens*

———o———

My Garden

A Garden is a lovesome thing, God
  wot!
Rose plot,
Fringed pool,
Ferned grot —
The veriest school
Of Peace; and yet the fool
Contends that God is not —
Not God! in Gardens! when the eve is
  cool?
Nay, but I have a sign:
'Tis very sure God walks in mine.

THOMAS EDWARD BROWN

Practically everybody grows five things in the garden: peas, radishes, beans, tomatoes, and tired.

———o———

Gardening tip: To tell real plants from weeds, pull them out. If they come up again, they're weeds.

———o———

In order to live off a garden, you practically have to live in it.

FRANK MCKINNEY HUBBARD

———o———

Oh, Adam was a gardener, and God who made him sees
That half a proper gardener's work is done upon his knees.

RUDYARD KIPLING,
The Glory of the Garden

———o———

What a man needs in gardening is a cast-iron back, with a hinge in it.

Generous

A farmer had just finished telling his friend how much he loved the Lord and how much he loved to give. His friend asked him, "John, if you had twenty horses, would you give God two of them?"

"Why, of course," replied the farmer; "however, I have no horses."

"But if you had ten cows, would you give God one of them?"

"Certainly," was his prompt answer, "but I have no cows."

"Well, John, if you had ten pigs, would you give one of them to God?"

"Hold on there," cried John. "That isn't fair! You know I've got ten pigs!"

IVY MOODY

———o———

Men are very generous with that which costs them nothing.

———o———

Generosity during life is a very different thing from generosity in the hour of death; one proceeds from genuine liberality and benevolence, the other from pride or fear.

HORACE MANN

Genius

One of the strongest characteristics of genius is the power of lighting its own fire.

JOHN WATSON FOSTER

———o———

A genius is usually a crackpot until he hits the jackpot.

———o———

Genius is one per cent inspiration and ninety-nine per cent perspiration.

THOMAS A. EDISON

———o———

Genius, that power which dazzles mortal eyes,
Is oft but perseverance in disguise.

HENRY WILLARD AUSTIN,
Perseverance Conquers All

———o———

Talent is that which is in a man's power; genius is that in whose power a man is.

JAMES RUSSELL LOWELL
Rousseau and the Sentimentalists

———o———

Patience is a necessary ingredient of genius.

BENJAMIN DISRAELI, *The Young Duke*

———o———

Genius is mainly an affair of energy.

MATTHEW ARNOLD

———o———

It is the privilege of genius that to it life never grows commonplace as to the rest of us.

JAMES RUSSELL LOWELL

———o———

If people knew how hard I have to work to gain my mastery it wouldn't seem wonderful at all.

MICHELANGELO

Gentle, Gentlemen

Give me a gentle heart, that I may do
Naught but the gentle thing my whole life through.
Give me a heart as kind as heart can be,

That I may give before 'tis asked of me.

PERCY THOMAS

———o———

Nothing is so strong as gentleness; nothing so gentle as real strength.

ST. FRANCIS DE SALES

———o———

The gentleness of Christ is the comeliest ornament that a Christian can wear.

WILLIAM D. ARNOT

———o———

Be gentle in old age; peevishness is worse in second childhood than in first.

GEORGE D. PRENTICE

———o———

A gentleman is a man who can disagree without being disagreeable.

———o———

A man can never be a true gentleman in manner until he is a true gentleman at heart.

CHARLES DICKENS

———o———

A man may learn from his Bible to be a more thorough gentleman than if he had been brought up in all the drawing-rooms in London.

CHARLES KINGSLEY

Gifts

Instead of a gem, or even a flower, cast the gift of a lovely thought into the heart of a friend.

GEORGE MACDONALD

———o———

Rings and jewels are not gifts, but apologies for gifts. The only gift is a portion of thyself.

RALPH WALDO EMERSON, *Essays: Gifts*

———o———

The finest gift a man can give to his age and time is the gift of a constructive and creative life.

———o———

By the gates of the treasury still He sits,
And watches the gifts we bring —
And He measures the gold that we give to Him
By the gold to which we cling.
How much to revive a starving world?
How much for our pampered plates?
How much to extend the King's frontiers?
How much for our own estates?

F. C. WELLMAN

———o———

The most valuable gift of a man or woman to this world is not money, nor books, but a noble life.

———o———

It is the will, and not the gift that makes the giver.

GOTTHOLD EPHRAIM LESSING

———o———

Don't let the abundance of God's gifts make you forget the Giver in your satisfaction over the gifts.

Girls

The man is, as a first creation, genuine;
The woman is the clearer, softer, and diviner,
For he was from the inorganic dirt unfolded,
But she came forth from clay which life before has molded.

JOHN DRYDEN

———o———

A Girl Is A Girl

A girl is a girl so frilly and sweet
You'd just like to hug her the moment you meet.

She's little pink ruffles and nylon and lace;
She's an innocent look on a little pink face;

She's dozens of dollies of ev'ry known size —
This cute little angel with stars in her eyes;

She's little toy dishes and parties and teas —
A princess at heart, you can say what you please;

She's all kinds of ribbons and buttons
and bows,
A pleasure to have as any one knows.

She's little play houses and red rocking
chairs
Soft pink eyed bunnies and brown
teddy bears;

She's the pictures she colored and
wants you to see,
This wee little pixie who climbs on
your knee;

She's roses and sunshine, yes, she's all
that —
Wearing pink gloves and a little pink
hat;

In Mother's lace curtain this miniature bride
Is really quite charming it can't be denied.

She's an artist, a teacher, a nurse all in
white,
Yet the mother of four from morning
till night;

She's perfume and powder and all
pretty things
Like bracelets and beads and play
diamond rings;

She's ice cream and candy and pink
birthday cake
She's also the cookies she helped Mother bake;

She's the one perfect nuisance to each
little boy
But she's Daddy's own sweetheart, his
pride and his joy;

She can pout, she can stomp, she can
tease, she can cry,
But still she's his pet, the very apple of
his eye.

She's kittens and everything cuddly
and nice —
Ah, sure 'n she's a bit of God's own
paradise.

PHYLLIS C. MICHAEL,
Poems for Mothers

Give

If you want to give something very
small to the Lord, give yourself.

All that we have comes from God,
and we give it out of His hand.
I Chronicles 29:14b, Dutch Paraphrase

——o——

Give all He asks;
Take all He gives.
S. D. GORDON

——o——

Getters generally don't get happi-
ness; givers get it. You simply give to
others a bit of yourself:
A thoughtful act,
A helpful idea,
A word of appreciation,
A lift over a rough spot,
A sense of understanding,
A timely suggestion.
You take something out of your
mind, garnished in kindness out of your
heart, and put it into the other fellow's
mind and heart.
CHARLES H. BURR

——o——

All that we can hold in our dead
hands is what we have given away.
Sanskrit Proverb

——o——

If you want to be rich, give; if you
want to be poor, grasp; if you want
abundance, scatter; if you want to be
needy, hoard!

——o——

God has given us two hands — one
to receive with and the other to give
with. We are not cisterns made for
hoarding; we are channels made for
sharing. If we fail to fulfill this divine
duty and privilege we have missed
the meaning of Christianity.
BILLY GRAHAM

——o——

What I kept I lost.
What I spent I had.
What I gave I have.
Persian Proverb

——o——

True Giving

We lose what on ourselves we spend:
We have as treasure without end,
Whatever, Lord, to Thee we lend
Who givest all.

Whatever, Lord, we lend to Thee,
Repaid a thousand-fold will be;
And gladly will we give to Thee,
Who givest all.
CHRISTOPHER WORDSWORTH,
Giving to God

———o———

For Our Sakes

He did not even own a bed,
He had no place to lay His head;
A cattle stall, His crib at birth;
He had no bank account on earth.
He laid the wealth of Heaven down
For earthly rags, and thorny crown.
He passed the praise of angels by,
And came where men cried
"Crucify!"
He left a throne for you and me
And bore our sins upon a tree.
So strong His claim, so clear His call,
How dare I give Him less than all?
BARBARA C. RYBERG

———o———

Let Your Dollars Testify

An anxious father, fearful that his
son had lost all interest in the church,
asked the minister to speak with the
boy.

At the first opportunity the minister
said to the boy, "I should think you
would want to keep your interest in
the church if for no other reason than
that your father is so interested."

"You don't know my father," the boy
replied, adding, "By the way, how
much does Dad give to the church
each year?"

The minister thought for a moment
and said, "I'm not so sure what he
gives, but I know he is one of our
most generous members. I should say
he gives five dollars a Sunday."

The boy figured a bit. "That makes
$260 a year. But it costs him $600
a year to belong to the country club,
and he gave $5,000 to help elect his
friend the mayor. You say I ought to
attend church because Dad is so interested. I don't think he is as interested as you think. Go ask him to
give $500 a year to the church and
then come and talk with me."
ARTHUR V. BOAND

No man is known by what he receives, but by what he gives.

———o———

He gives double who gives unasked.

———o———

The preacher wrote to some parishioners asking financial aid for the
church. One man turned him down
with a curt note: "So far as I can see,
this Christian business is one continuous give, give, give." The pastor meditated on that, then wrote the man
again. "Thank you for the best definition of the Christian life I have ever
heard."

———o———

God requires our persons before He
asks our purses.

———o———

Who gives to me teaches me to
give.
Dutch Saying

———o———

The world will never be won to
Christ with what people can conveni-
ently spare.
BERNARD EDINGER

———o———

A godly woman unexpectedly received a legacy of $5,000. True to her
practice maintained in poverty, she at
once put $500 into her tenth box and
it was used in Christ's work. She never
mentioned the disposal of the tenth,
but after her death there was found
entered in her diary the day she received the legacy: "Quick, quick, before my heart gets hard."

———o———

Let Me Be A Giver

God, let me be a giver, and not one
Who only takes and takes unceas-
ingly;
God, let me give so that not just my
own,
But others' lives as well, may richer
be.

Let me give out whatever I may hold
Of what material things life
May be heaping.

Let me give raiment, shelter, food or
   gold,
  If these are, through Thy bounty,
   In my keeping.

But greater than such fleeting treas-
   ures,
  May I give my faith and hope and
   Cheerfulness,
Belief and dreams and joy and laughter
Gay some lonely soul to bless.

MARY DAVIES

I have held many things in my hands
and lost them all; but whatever I have
placed in God's hands, that I still possess.

MARTIN LUTHER

Giving

It is strange, but very true — giving
   just enriches you.
If you give a kindly deed, if you plant
   a friendship seed,
If you share a laugh or song, if your
   giving rights a wrong,
Then joy you feel and share makes
   more goodness everywhere.
It is strange, but very true — *giving*
   just enriches *you!*

How Much Ought I To Give?

Give as you would if an angel
Awaited your gift at the door;
Give as you would if tomorrow
Found you where giving was o'er.
Give as you would to the Master
If you met His loving look;
Give as you would of your substance
If His hand your offering took.

AUTHOR UNKNOWN

Spender

The fountains flash across his lawn,
His yard is full of flowers.
His house has thirty rooms or more
With half a dozen showers.
He slumbers in a massive bed,
Some king once owned it, it seems.
The table where he eats is long
And silver brightly gleams.
He drives a gleaming mammoth car

That has the latest shape.
He sits before a mighty desk
And reads a ticker tape.
He goes to church when Sunday comes,
He sits up very straight,
And with a pious look he drops
A dollar in the plate!

LON WOODRUM

Let Me Give

I do not know how long I'll live,
  But while I live, Lord, let me give,
Some comfort to someone in need,
  By smile or nod, kind word or deed.
And let me do whate'er I can
  To ease things for my fellow man.
I want naught but to do my part
  To lift a tired or weary heart,
To change folks' frowns to smiles again.
  Then I will not have lived in vain.
And I'll not care how long I'll live
  If I can give — and give — and give.

AUTHOR UNKNOWN

Most people apportion their giving
according to their earnings. If the process were reversed and the Giver of
All were to apportion our earnings according to our giving, some of us would
be very poor indeed.

The Christian

Three Kinds Of Giving

There are three kinds of giving:
Grudge giving, duty giving, and thanks
giving. Grudge giving says, "I hate to";
duty giving says, "I ought to"; thanks
giving says, "I want to."

The first comes from constraint, the
second from a sense of obligation and
the third from a full heart. Nothing
much is conveyed in grudge giving,
since the gift without the giver is
bare. Something more happens in duty
giving, but there is no song in it.
Thanks giving is an open gate into
the rewards.

ROBERT N. RODENMAYER

Little Ships

I sent my little ships to sea,
But none returned to comfort me;

Then Jesus came, and I'm content
Because He told me where they went:

"The tracts went where you cannot go;
Supplies sent folk you do not know;
The little ships you sent to sea,
All that you gave — returned to Me."

And I am glad that this is so,
For giving is a debt I owe
To Him who gave His life for me
Upon the cross of Calvary.

MILDRED ALLEN JEFFERY

———o———

Giving And Receiving

Is thy cruse of comfort wasting?
  Rise and share it with another,
And through all the years of famine
  It shall save thee and thy brother,
Love divine will fill thy warehouse,
  Or thy handful still renew;
Scanty fare for one will often
  Make a royal feast for two.

For the heart grows rich in giving;
  All its wealth is living grain;
Seeds which mildew in the garner,
  Scattered, fill with gold the plain.
Is thy burden hard and heavy?
  Do thy steps drag wearily?
Help to bear thy brother's burden;
  God will bear both it and thee.

Numb and weary on the mountain,
  Wouldst thou sleep amidst the snow?
Chafe that frozen form beside thee,
  And together both shall glow.
Art thou stricken in life's battle?
  Many wounded round thee moan;
Lavish in their wounds thy balsams,
  And that balm shall heal thine own.

Is thy heart a well left empty?
  None but God its void can fill;
Nothing but a ceaseless fountain,
  Can its ceaseless longing still.
Is thy heart a living power?
  Self-entwined its strength sinks low;
It can only live in loving,
  And by serving love will grow.

AUTHOR UNKNOWN

———o———

Seven Ways Of Giving

1. The Careless Way — To give something to every cause that is pre-sented without inquiry into its merits.
2. The Impulsive Way — To give from impulse, as much and as often as love and pity and sensibility prompt.
3. The Lazy Way — To make a special offer to earn money for benevolent objects by fairs, festivals, etc.
4. The Self-Denying Way — To save the cost of luxuries and apply them for purposes of religion and charity. This may lead to asceticism and self-complacence.
5. The Systematic Way — To lay aside as an offering to God a definite portion of our gains: one-tenth, one-fifth, one-third or one-half. This is adaptable if this method were generally practiced.
6. The Equal Way — To give to God and the needy just as much as we spend on ourselves, balancing our personal expenditures by our gifts.
7. The Heroic Way — To limit our own expenditures to a certain sum, and give away all the rest of our income. This was John Wesley's way.

A. T. PIERSON

———o———

If truth takes possession of a man's heart, it will direct his hand to his pocketbook.

———o———

Numbers 7 is the longest chapter in the Bible, containing nearly 2,000 words — all about giving.

———o———

When the heart is converted the purse will be inverted.

———o———

"What! Giving again?"
  I asked in dismay,
"And must I keep giving
  And giving alway?"
"Oh no," cried the Angel,
  Piercing me through.
"Just give 'til the Father
  Stops giving to you."

AUTHOR UNKNOWN

Glory

How swiftly passes the glory of the world!

THOMAS À KEMPIS,
The Imitation of Christ

———o———

Glory is like a circle in the water,
Which never ceaseth to enlarge itself
Till by broad spreading it disperse to nought.

WILLIAM SHAKESPEARE,
King Henry VI, Part I

Goals

Promise yourself:

To be so strong that nothing can disturb your peace of mind;
To talk health, happiness and prosperity;
To make your friends feel that there is something in them;
To look on the sunny side of everything;
To think only of the best;
To be just as enthusiastic about the success of others as you are about your own;
To forget the mistakes of the past and profit by them;
To wear a cheerful countenance and give a smile to everyone you meet;
To be too large for worry, too noble for anger, too strong for fear, and too happy to permit the presence of trouble.

CHRISTIAN D. LARSON

———o———

The ripest peach is highest on the tree.

JAMES WHITCOMB RILEY,
The Ripest Peach

———o———

If called to be a missionary, don't stoop to be a king.

CHARLES HADDON SPURGEON

———o———

The man that I want to be is so much better than the man that I am that I am desperately afraid that the man I am can never be the man I want to be. How is it with you?

Before you can score you must first have a goal.

Greek Proverb

———o———

Obstacles are those frightful things you see when you take your eyes off the goal.

HANNAH MORE

———o———

Not everything that is desirable is attainable, and not everything that is worthwhile knowing is knowable.

JOHANN WOLFGANG VON GOETHE

———o———

People with goals find a meaning in life.

God

The living God is my Partner.

GEORGE MUELLER

———o———

My great concern is not whether God is on our side; my great concern is to be on God's side.

ABRAHAM LINCOLN

———o———

Any step away from the true, living God is a step in the direction of strife.

BILLY GRAHAM

———o———

Evidence

The fool has said in his heart,
"There is no God,"
But the fool has not the mind to know.
Cycles of coppery suns and silvered moons
Declare the wonderment of God,
And all the things of earth
Silently proclaim His handiwork.
He spoke, and there was light;
He breathed, and man became a living soul.
Aeons of time declare the everlastingness of Him.
The fragrance of a flower,
And the mystery of a throbbing heart
Witness to His creative power.
The wise have not the minds to understand,
Yet, they must say in all humility,
"There is a God!"

HELEN MILLER LEHMAN

If

If man could fling a trillion stars
Beyond the sun and moon and Mars,
Far out in vast sidereal space,
And keep them spinning in their place;

If man could make a tiny flower
And make it grow by his own power;
If he the ocean could command
And measure it within his hand;

If man could make a living soul
That should endure while ages roll;
Would I be then by man so awed
That I'd acclaim him e'en as God?

Ah, no! for had he all this might,
He could not guide his life aright;
He could not cleanse his own lost soul,
Nor make a sin-sick sinner whole.

Though man-made spheres may come
    and go,
There's only one true God, I know,
Who holds the worlds within His hand,
And on that Rock secure I'll stand.
                        MARGARET K. FRASER

————o————

A man should be ashamed to run
his own life the minute he finds out
there is a God.
                        PAUL RADER

————o————

A little boy being asked, "How many
Gods are there?" replied "One!" "How
do you know that?" "Because," said
the boy, "there is only room for one,
for He fills heaven and earth."

————o————

God always fills in all hearts all the
room which is left Him there.
                        FREDERICK W. FABER

————o————

God be in my head,
    And in my understanding;
God be in my eyes,
    And in my looking;
God be in my mouth,
    And in my speaking;
God be in my heart,
    And in my thinking;
God be at my end,
    And at my departing.
            Old Sarum Primer, 1558

When I think of God, my heart is so
full of joy that the notes leap and
dance as they leave my pen; and since
God has given me a cheerful heart, I
serve Him with a cheerful spirit.
                        FRANZ JOSEPH HAYDN

————o————

Thou Art God

Thou art the triumph of the race well
    run,
The spring of virtue, rock of purity,
The Giver of all blessings through Thy
    Son,
And spark of hope set fire at Calvary.
In Thee alone I find abiding peace;
Thou art my fruitful valley, rich and
    deep.
Thy Grace and tender mercy shall not
    cease,
For time is Thine to fashion and to
    keep.

And yet I sorrow that these make-
    shift thoughts
Are as toy boats upon a mighty sea,
Or sparrows that would follow eagle
    wings:
Frail evidence of insufficiency.
O might my thunder peal Thy Name
    abroad!
Instead I choke and whisper, "Thou
    art God!"
                        ESTHER BELLE HEINS

————o————

God In A Box

God in a box? Unlikely thought —
And yet men do declare
It came to pass (Sing, angels, sing!),
And in a manger bare.

God in a box? Say rather, tent —
Not metal, wood or stone,
But like our own: See the Lord
    Christ
Wrapped 'round with flesh and bone.

God in a box? A coffin bleak,
So dark, and cold, and grim?
Yes, even here God stooped to seek
Men who would bury him.

See, then! This box, though doubly
    bound

With sin and death's strong cord,
Still could not hold his majesty —
Behold! The risen Lord!

RUTH HEARD

———o———

I fear God, yet am not afraid of
Him.

SIR THOMAS BROWNE

God's Goodness

God's Extras

God could have made the sun to rise
Without such splendor in the skies;
He could have made the sun to set
Without a glory greater yet.

He could have made the corn to grow
Without that sunny, golden glow;
The fruits without those colors bright,
So pleasant to the taste and sight.

And caused the apple trees to bloom
Without the scent that doth perfume
Those dainty blossoms, pink and white,
That fill our hearts with sheer de-
light.

He could have made the ocean roll
Without such music for the soul —
The mighty anthem, loud and strong —
And birds without their clear, sweet
song.

The charm of kittens' dainty grace,
The dimples in a baby's face —
All these are "extras" from His hand,
Whose love we cannot understand.

The God Who fashioned flowers and
trees,
Delights to give us things that please,
And all His handiwork so fair
His glory and His love declare.

Yes, He Who made the earth and skies
Gave "extras" for our ears and eyes,
And while my heart with rapture sings,
I thank Him for the "extra things."

MARGARET K. FRASER

———o———

God's ways are not like human ways,
He wears such strange disguises;
He tries us by His long delays
And then our faith surprises.

While we in unbelief deplore
And wonder at His staying,
He stands already at the door
And interrupts our praying.

J. E. RANKIN

———o———

He Giveth More

He giveth more grace when the burdens grow greater,
He sendeth more strength when the
labors increase;
To added affliction He addeth His
mercy,
To multiplied trials, His multiplied
peace.

When we have exhausted our store of
endurance,
When our strength has failed ere the
day is half done,
When we reach the end of our hoarded
resources,
Our Father's full giving is only begun.

His love has no limit, His grace has no
measure,
His power no boundary known unto
men;
For out of His infinite riches in Jesus
He giveth and giveth and giveth again.

ANNIE JOHNSON FLINT

———o———

God gives our blessings but we have
to take them.

God's Love and Care

No foe can cast me down,
No fear can make me flee,
No sorrow fill my life with ill;
Thy love surroundeth me.

Warm as the glowing sun,
So shines Thy love on me;
It wraps me round with kindly care,
It draws me unto Thee.

OSCAR CLUTE

———o———

I know not where His islands lift
Their fronded palms in air;
I only know I cannot drift
Beyond His love and care.

JOHN GREENLEAF WHITTIER,
The Eternal Goodness

The God of Love

And can he who smiles on all
Hear the wren with sorrows small,
Hear the small bird's grief and care,
Hear the woes that infants bear,

And not sit beside that nest,
Pouring pity in their breast;
And not sit that cradle near,
Weeping tear on infant's tear;

And not sit both night and day
Wiping all our tears away?
Oh, no! never can it be!

Never, never can it be!
He doth give his joy to all;
He becomes an infant small;
He becomes a man of woe.
He doth feel the sorrow too.

Think not thou canst sigh a sigh,
And thy Maker is not by;
Think not thou canst weep a tear,
And thy Maker is not near.

WILLIAM BLAKE,
On Another's Sorrow

———o———

How often we look upon God as
our last and feeblest resource! We go
to Him because we have no where
else to go. And then we learn that the
storms of life have driven us, not upon
the rocks, but into the desired havens.

GEORGE MACDONALD

———o———

If God did not hold us back every
moment, we should be devils incarnate.

DAVID BRAINERD

———o———

You can rest the weight of all your
anxieties upon God, for you are always
in His care.

Paraphrase of *I Peter 5:7*

God's Power and Greatness

God tempers the wind . . . to the
shorn lamb.

LAURENCE STERNE, *A Sentimental Journey*

———o———

God regulates the cold to the shorn
lamb.

HENRI ESTIENNE, *Prémices*

God is as great in minuteness as He
is in magnitude.

———o———

When Martin Luther's friends wrote
despairingly of the negotiations at the
Diet of Worms, Luther replied from
Coburg that he had been looking up at
the night sky, spangled and studded
with stars, and had found no pillars
to hold them up. And yet they did
not fall. God needs no props for His
stars and planets. He hangs them on
nothing. So, in the working of God's
providence, the unseen is prop enough
for the seen.

AUGUSTUS HOPKINS STRONG

———o———

And I smiled to think God's greatness
flowed around our incompleteness, —
Round our restlessness His rest.

ELIZABETH BARRETT BROWNING,
Rhyme of the Duchess May

———o———

As the marsh-hen secretly builds on the
watery sod,
Behold I will build me a nest on the
greatness of God:
I will fly in the greatness of God as the
marsh-hen flies
In the freedom that fills all the space
'twixt the marsh and the skies:
By so many roots as the marsh-grass
sends in the sod
I will heartily lay me a-hold on the
greatness of God.

SIDNEY LANIER, *The Marshes of Glynn*

God's Presence

My Presence Shall Go With Thee

Life's dark shadows turn to sunshine
When the Light of Life appears;
And the rainbow of His promise
Brightly beams above my fears.

He who guides the countless planets
Through the endless realms of space,
Walks beside me, guards and guides
me
By His never-failing grace.

He whom angels serve and worship
In the Glory Land above,

Deigns to be my blest companion,
In the greatness of His love.

Why then should I grieve my Savior
By my needless fret and care?
He will never, never leave me,
All my burdens He will share.

Heartaches? He knows all about them;
His own heart was pierced for me.
"Man of Sorrows" once they called Him,
He who died to make me free.

Yes, His presence will go with me,
For He always keeps His word,
And my soul shall rest serenely
In the love of Christ, my Lord.

ALBERT SIMPSON REITZ

God Is Here

(The following words are to be found engraved on the floor of the church where John Wesley preached his first sermon.)

Enter this door
As if the floor
Within were gold
And every wall
Of jewels, all
Of wealth untold;
As if a choir
In robes of fire
Were singing here
Nor shout, nor rush
But hush —
For God is here.

AUTHOR UNKNOWN

We are always punched in on God's timecard.

RICHARD RIIS

Tomorrow

God is in every tomorrow,
  Therefore I live for today,
Certain of finding at sunrise
Guidance and strength for the way;
Power for each moment of weakness,
  Hope for each moment of pain,
Comfort for every sorrow,
  Sunshine and joy after rain.

God is in every tomorrow,
  Planning for you and me;

E'en in the dark will I follow —
Trust where my eyes cannot see;
Stilled by His promise of blessing,
Soothed by the touch of His hand,
  Confident in His protection,
Knowing my life path is planned.

God is in every tomorrow,
  Life with its changes may come;
He is behind and before me;
  While in the distance shines Home!
Home — where no thought of tomorrow
  Ever can shadow my brow;
Home — in the presence of Jesus
  Through all eternity — now.

Exchange

God is the silent partner in all great enterprises.

ABRAHAM LINCOLN

God's Strength and Help

It is at the point where we are just about to faint, that God gives us strength to go on.

Only when you attempt the impossible do you test the resources of God.

Cheered by the presence of God, I will do each moment, without anxiety, according to the strength which He shall give me, the work that His providence assigns me.

FRANCOIS DE SALIGNAC DE LA MOTHE FÉNELON

Never does he who clings to God despair, because he is never without resources.

JACQUES BÉNIGNE BOSSUET

God's Ways

God's ways are behind the scenes, but He moves all the scenes which He is behind.

JOHN NELSON DARBY

Never make a plan without seeking God's guidance; never achieve a success without giving God the praise.

Though the mills of God grind slowly,
Yet they grind exceeding small;
Though with patience He stands wait-
ing,
With exactness grinds He all.
                HENRY WADSWORTH LONGFELLOW
(Translation of *Retribution* by F. VON LOGAN)

———o———

God writes with a pen that never
blots, speaks with a tongue that never
slips, acts with a hand that never fails.

———o———

Going God's Way

I arise today, equipped and fortified
to meet life's problems, with —
    God's strength to pilot me.
    God's wisdom to guide me.
    God's eye to look before me.
    God's ear to hear me.
    God's Word to speak for me.
    God's hand to guard me.
    God's way of life before me.
    God's shield to protect me.
    God's host to save me.
                                    Selected

God's Will

God's Will

It is God's will that I should cast
    My care on Him each day (I Peter
    5).
He also asks me not to cast
    My confidence away (Hebrews 10).
But, oh, how stupidly I act
    When taken unaware;
I cast away my confidence
    And carry all my care.
                                    T. BAIRD

———o———

Missionary Betty Elliot, whose husband was murdered by the fierce Auca
Indians of Ecuador, tells why she went
back to the Aucas. "I didn't return
because I thought it would be safe, or
even to carry on my husband's work.
The only reason is my belief that going back is the next step in a series of
steps that God wills."

———o———

William E. Gladstone, talking about
the questions of the day, said, "There
is but one question, and that is the will
of God. That settles all other questions."

———o———

If the will of God is our will, and
if He always has His way, then we
always have our way also.
                    HANNAH WHITALL SMITH

———o———

Those Things Beyond My Control

There are some things in life, O God,
    Beyond my own control.
And when they come,
    I pray that they will never warp my
    soul.

Sometimes my well-laid plans don't
    work,
    And everything goes wrong.
And then it is that
    I'm in need of courage to be strong.

In times that I have spent my strength
    In trying to resist,
The things that I could never change,
    It seems I've always missed.
A living opportunity to help myself
    adjust
To changeless situations, God,
And walk with You in trust.
                    GEORGE BILBY WALKER

———o———

O Thou who hast taught us that we
are most truly free when we lose our
wills in Thine, help us to gain that
liberty by continual surrender unto
Thee, that we may walk in the way
which Thou hast prepared for us, and
in doing Thy will may find our life,
through Jesus Christ our Lord.
                    Gelasian Sacramentary

———o———

Try to make an instantaneous act of
conformity to God's will, at everything
which vexes you.
                    EDWARD B. PUSEY

———o———

Through His will, loved and done,
lies the path to His love.
                    ANDREW MURRAY

———o———

A man should be encouraged to do
what the Maker of him has intended

by the making of him, according as the gifts have been bestowed on him for that purpose. His happiness, and that of others around him, [depends upon] such a relation to the Maker's will.

THOMAS CARLYLE

——o——

Grace To Do Without

My heart rejoices in God's will,
    'Tis ever best — I do not doubt;
He may not give me what I ask,
    But gives me grace to do without!

I blindly ask for what I crave,
    With haughty heart and will so stout;
He oft denies me what I seek,
    But gives me grace to do without!

He makes me love the way He leads,
    And every fear is put to rout;
When with my fondest wish denied,
    He gives me grace to do without!

O blessed, hallowed will of God,
    To it I bow with heart devout;
I will abide in all God's will,
    His way is best, I do not doubt;
He may not give me what I ask,
    But gives me grace to do without!
Selected

——o——

"Everything goes against me," said a man to Luther. "None of my wishes come true. My hopes go wrong. My plans never work out."

"My dear friend, that is your own fault," said Luther.

"My own fault?"

"Yes," said Luther. "Why do you pray every day, '*Thy* will be done'? You ought to pray, *My* will be done. But if you pray that God's will should be done and not yours, you should be satisfied if God does as you pray."
Lutheran Witness

——o——

When I was crossing the Irish Channel one dark, starless night, I stood on the deck by the captain and asked him, "How do you know Holyhead Harbor on so dark a night as this?"

He said, "You see those three lights? Those three must line up behind each other as one, and when we see them so united we know the exact position of the harbor's mouth."

When we want to know God's will there are three things which always concur: the inward impulse, the Word of God, and the trend of circumstances! God in the heart, impelling you forward; God in His book corroborating whatever He says in the heart; and God in circumstances, which are always indicative of His will. Never start until these three things agree.
F. B. MEYER

——o——

God's Will

I wanted to go, He said stay.
I wanted to do, He said pray;
I wanted to work, He said wait,
I wanted to live for His sake!
"Love Me, child," He softly said,
"Oh, yes, Lord," I bowed my head;
"I want your way, I am your son,
Not my will, but Thine be done!"
GRACE OPPERMAN

——o——

The hardness of God is kinder than the softness of men, and His compulsion is our liberation.
C. S. LEWIS, *Surprised by Joy*

——o——

Jesus taught, first, that a man's business is to do the will of God; second, that God takes upon Himself the care of that man; third, therefore, that a man must never be afraid of anything, and so, fourth, be left free to love God with all his heart, and his neighbor as himself.
GEORGE MACDONALD

——o——

A knowledge of the will of God is relative to one's desire to do the will of God. God does not reveal His will to those who are not gladly committed to it. A commission from God is relative to our commitment to God. Commitment is prerequisite to commission. There is no substitute for the bent knee, the surrendered heart, the open Bible, the listening ear and the voice of the Spirit in discovering the will of God.
DON W. HILLIS
in *The Missionary Broadcaster*

Sooner or later you will find that it is harder to shun the will of God than it is to yield yourself to it.

———o———

Passive to His holy will
Trust I in my Master still,
Even though He slay me.
JOHN GREENLEAF WHITTIER,
Barclay of Ury

God's Work

God's work done in God's way will never lack God's supplies.
J. HUDSON TAYLOR

———o———

God works slowly but surely; we spoil His work when we get in a hurry and interfere.

———o———

God requires on our part, nothing that we are unable, with His help, to do.

Godliness

Keep company with the more cheerful sort of the godly; there is no mirth like the mirth of believers.
RICHARD BAXTER

———o———

Unless there is within us that which is above us, we shall soon yield to that which is about us.
PETER TAYLOR FORSYTHE

———o———

Godliness is the knowledge of God in the mind; the grace of God in the soul; the love of God in the heart; the obedience to God in the life.
JAMES DRUMMOND BURNS

Good, Goodness

There is a very simple test by which we can tell good people from bad: if a smile improves a man's face, he is a good man; if a smile disfigures his face, he is a bad man.
WILLIAM LYON PHELPS

———o———

Be not only good; be good for something.
HENRIETTA C. MEARS

Goodness and love mold the form into their own image, and cause the joy and beauty of love to shine forth from every part of the face. When this form of love is seen, it appears ineffably beautiful, and effects with delight the inmost life of the soul.
EMANUEL SWEDENBORG

———o———

The truly good do good for no other reason than doing good.
ROY DALE

———o———

There are two kinds of people: good and bad. The classifying is done by the good.

———o———

Four-year-old Jimmie was saying his prayers one evening. His mother was shocked to hear him say:
"O God, make me a good boy — not real good, but just good enough to keep from getting spanked."
Gospel Banner

———o———

Good, the more
Communicated, more abundant grows.
JOHN MILTON, *Paradise Lost, Book IV*

———o———

If you can see good in everybody, almost everyone will see some good in you.
HENRY F. HENRICHS

———o———

It is not enough to do good; one must do it the right way.
JOHN VISCOUNT MORLEY, *On Compromise*

———o———

People seldom get dizzy from doing good turns.

———o———

"Who's telling the truth?" asked nine-year-old Bill.
"Why?" asked Father.
"Because," the boy explained, "my Sunday School teacher said that if I was good I would go to heaven and you said that if I was good I would go to the circus."

———o———

A Christian should always remember that the value of his good works is not based on their number and excellence, but on the love of God which prompts him to do these things.

SAN JUAN DE LA CRUZ

Gospel

The Gospel is a declaration, not a debate.

JAMES S. STEWART

——o——

We do not need to defend the Gospel, we need only to proclaim it.

——o——

The world has many religions; it has but one Gospel.

GEORGE OWEN

——o——

The Gospel is not a challenge, it is an offer.

JOE BLINCO

——o——

The Gospel is not simply for the sanctuary but for the open road.

RICHARD C. HALVERSON

——o——

The Gospel is not something we go to church to hear; it is something we go from church to tell.

VANCE HAVNER

——o——

The Gospel is God's News — not Man's Views.

JAMES L. FOWLE

——o——

Hear the good news — then tell it!

——o——

A thief broke into a Buffalo, New York, church and got away with some valuable equipment and several dollars from a collection box. The next day the church's outdoor bulletin board carried the words, "If the person who burglarized this church will contact the pastor, he will receive important news."

Interested, reporters called on the pastor. "What's the good news?" they wanted to know.

Replied the pastor, "If we confess our sins, He is faithful and just to forgive us our sins, and to cleanse us from all unrighteousness."

A man may want liberty, and yet be happy; a man may want food, and yet be content; a man may want clothing, and yet be comfortable; but he that wants the Gospel, wants everything that can do him good in this life and the next. Nothing worse can be imagined than to be without hope and without God in this world.

Traveller's Guide

Gossip

Tale-bearers are as bad as the tale-makers.

RICHARD BRINSLEY SHERIDAN,
School for Scandal

——o——

Gossip always travels faster over grapevines that are slightly sour.

——o——

A gossip turns an earful into a mouthful.

——o——

A gossip is a person who will never tell a lie when the truth will do more damage.

——o——

If we had buttons or zippers on our lips, we'd do less gossiping, and hold on to our respect for others.

——o——

Gossip

The longer I live, the more I feel the importance of adhering to the following rules, which I have laid down for myself in relation to such matters:

1. To hear as little as possible what is to the prejudice of others.
2. To believe nothing of the kind until I am absolutely forced to.
3. Always to moderate, so far as I can, the unkindness which is expressed toward others.
4. Always to believe that, if the other side were heard, very different accounts would be given of the matter.

An Old Scotch Writer

——o——

A five-year-old "preacher" lined his friends up on the curb and gravely announced, "This morning we will preach the gossip."

Teach

———o———

Had you ever thought that while we despise the gossiper it is almost as bad to listen eagerly, like most of us do, to his tales? Should we refuse to listen to gossip, it is likely that none would ever be spread.

———o———

Never believe anything bad about anybody unless you feel that it is absolutely necessary — and that God is listening while you tell it.

HENRY VAN DYKE

———o———

Someone has said that a gossip is one who talks too much about others. A bore is one who talks too much about himself. A wise man is one who talks little but says much.

———o———

Thy friend has a friend, and thy friend's friend has a friend, so be discreet.

The Talmud

———o———

Great minds discuss ideas, average minds discuss events, small minds discuss people.

———o———

Gossip is what no one claims to like — but everybody enjoys.

JOSEPH CONRAD

———o———

There is nothing that can't be made worse by telling.

TERENCE

Govern

Men must be governed by God or they will be ruled by tyrants.

WILLIAM PENN

———o———

A man must first govern himself, before he is fit to govern a family; and his family before he is fit to bear the government of the Commonwealth.

SIR WALTER RALEIGH

No man is good enough to govern another man without the other's consent.

ABRAHAM LINCOLN

———o———

Realms are households which the great must guide.

JOHN DRYDEN

———o———

They that govern the most make the least noise.

JOHN SELDEN, *Table Talk; Power*

———o———

It is impossible to govern the world without God.

GEORGE WASHINGTON

———o———

God rules in the realms to which he is admitted.

MARY WELCH

———o———

Never expect to govern others until you have learned to govern yourself.

———o———

The rule that governs my life is this: Anything that dims my vision of Christ, or takes away my taste for Bible study, or cramps my prayer life, or makes Christian work difficult, is wrong for me, and I must, as a Christian, turn away from it. This simple rule may help you find a safe road for your feet along life's road.

J. WILBUR CHAPMAN

Government

History has demonstrated that nations thrive and grow strong as they develop individual citizens. Law and order without loss of individual freedom can be maintained only as the personal ethics of individual citizens call for and support the laws of the state. Good government can exist and persist only as it is rooted in self-government by the millions of individual citizens.

DR. ALFRED HAAKE

———o———

A grade school teacher reports this answer was turned in on a question about government: "The main political parties are the GOP, AFL, CIO, and PTA."

Glendale News Press, Glendale, Calif.

———o———

If we did not believe in the spiritual character of man, we would be foolish indeed to be supporting the concept of free government in the world.

DWIGHT DAVID EISENHOWER

———o———

Whenever the pillars of Christianity shall be overthrown, our present republican forms of government, and all the blessings which flow from them, must fall with them.

JEDIDIAH MORSE

———o———

Government is a trust, and the officers of the government are trustees; and both the trust and the trustees are created for the benefit of the people.

HENRY CLAY, *Speech,* March, 1829

———o———

The lessons of paternalism ought to be unlearned and the better lesson taught that while the people should patriotically support their Government, its functions do not include the support of the people.

GROVER CLEVELAND, *Inaugural Address,* March 4, 1893

———o———

The Bible is for the government of the people, by the people, and of the people.

WYCLIFFE AND HEREFORD (Preface to their translation of the Bible — 1384)

———o———

The people's government, made for the people, made by the people, and answerable to the people.

DANIEL WEBSTER, *Speech,* January 26, 1830

———o———

. . . our aim in founding the Commonwealth was not to make any one class specially happy, but to secure the greatest possible happiness for the community as a whole.

PLATO, *The Republic*

There is no qualification for government but virtue and wisdom.

EDMUND BURKE

Grace

An ounce of quiet-working grace does what tons of effort can never accomplish.

———o———

There is a saving grace for sinners and a serving grace for Christians.

———o———

I was going to say that faith turns on the faucet of Grace, but I'll put it the other way: unbelief turns the faucet off.

WILLIAM R. NEWELL

———o———

The Father never fails to cheer our hearts with sweet surprises of His Grace. He hides them through all our fleeting years, and every day we are finding them: friends old and new, the joys of home, new aspirations, new tasks, new fields of labor, new knowledge. new understandings of the heart of Christ, new experiences with Him. Often they fall into our laps when we are least expecting them.

This is God's antidote for weariness and dullness. We greet each day with expectancy. We grow old gracefully, eagerly waiting to know what is that grandest gift of all — eternal life.

COSTEN J. HARRELL, *Walking With God*

———o———

'Twas grace that taught my heart to fear,
And grace my fears relieved;
How precious did that grace appear
The hour I first believed.

JOHN NEWTON, *Amazing Grace*

———o———

God's Grace is the only Grace,
And all Grace is the Grace of God.

COVENTRY PATMORE

———o———

It takes less grace to criticize than to cooperate.

J. B. CHAPMAN

Sin had no sooner come into the world than God came in Grace seeking the sinner, and so from the first question, "Adam where art thou?" on to the incarnation, God has been speaking to man.

HARRY A. IRONSIDE

——o——

Grace freely justifies me and sets me free from slavery to sin.

ST. BERNARD OF CLAIRVAUX

——o——

If we do less under grace than we do under law, it is a disgrace.

——o——

The word 'Grace' is unquestionably the most significant single word in the Bible.

ILION T. JONES

——o——

God's providence will never place you where His grace cannot keep you.

——o——

One who is saved by grace should live graciously.

——o——

Grace humbles man without degrading him and exalts him without deflating him.

——o——

Grace is everything for nothing to one who deserves nothing but judgment and destruction.

——o——

The dross of my cross gathered a scum of fears in the fire, doubtings, impatience, unbelief, challenging of Providence as sleeping and not regarding my sorrow. But my Goldsmith, Christ, was pleased to take off the scum and burn it in the fire. And blessed be my Refiner, He has made the metal better, and has furnished new supply of Grace, to cause me hold out weight; and I hope that He has not lost one grain-weight by burning His servant.

SAMUEL RUTHERFORD

Grammar

Christian Grammar

A well-known Bishop of the Church of England gave a class he was teaching a lesson in what he called "Christian Grammar."

"We have all learned to say in school:
'First person — I;
Second person — Thou;
Third person — He.'

"But that is wrong in Christian grammar, so wrong that to put it right, one has to turn it upside down. The Christian's grammar is:
'First person — He;
Second person — Thou;
Third person — I.'

"And 'he' means God, the first person in the first place. Then 'thou' means one's fellow-man; and 'I' myself comes last."

——o——

My son had been having trouble with his grammar studies in school. For several weeks we worked at night on the three degrees of adjectives and adverbs. After patiently emphasizing that the comparative degree was stronger and that the superlative was strongest, I dictated a list of words to compare, which included the adjective "high."

On his tablet I was amazed to find: "Positive degree — Hi. Comparative degree — Hello. Superlative degree — How do you do?"

ERNEST BLEVINS in *Your Life*

——o——

Grammar In A Nutshell

Three little words you often see
Are Articles — A, An, and The.

A Noun's the name of anything,
As School, or Garden, Hoop or Swing.

Adjectives tell the kind of Noun,
As Great, Small, Pretty, White or Brown.

Instead of Nouns the Pronouns stand —
Her head, His face, Your arm, My hand.

Verbs tell of something being done —
To Read, Count, Laugh, Sing, Jump or
Run.

How things are done the Adverbs tell,
As Slowly, Quickly, Ill, or Well.

Conjunctions join the words together,
As men And women, wind Or weather.

The Preposition stands before
A Noun, as In or Through a door.

The Interjection shows surprise
As Oh! how pretty! Ah! how wise!

The Whole are called Nine Parts of
Speech,
Which reading, writing, speaking teach.
AUTHOR UNKNOWN

———o———

Teacher: "Name three relative pronouns."
Student: "Aunt, uncle, brother."

———o———

Teacher: "What gender is the word
hurricane?"
Boy student: "Neuter gender, singular number."
Girl student: "No it isn't! Don't you
remember Mrs. Roseberry said last
week, 'Who ever heard of a *him*acane.
It's always a *her*-a-cane!'"
RUTH ROSEBERRY

———o———

One day in an English class a boy
was asked, "What parts of speech are
'my' and 'mine'?"
Quickly he replied, "Aggressive pronouns."
RUTH ROSEBERRY

———o———

One of our elementary school teachers gave her small charges a lecture on
the merits of brevity and then asked
them to write a sentence or two describing something exciting. One of
them promptly submitted the following: "Help! Help!"
PATRICIA LAITIN in *Coronet*

Grandparents

Grandma

My grandma likes to play with God,
They have a kind of game.

She plants the garden full of seeds,
He sends the sun and rain.

She likes to sit and talk with God
And knows He is right there.
She prays about the whole wide world,
Then leaves us in His care.
ANN JOHNSON, age 8 in
The Lutheran Standard

———o———

One of the most influential hand-
clasps is that of a grandchild around
the finger of a grandparent.
Gazette, High Bridge, New Jersey

———o———

Any grandmother can tell you what's
new in people. And she has pictures
to go with her wonderful story.
Herald, Azusa, California

———o———

My sister, the harassed mother of
five, was asked by a friend, "Well, Nell,
what do you want your next one to
be?"
"A grandchild!" she replied.
MRS. FRANK WATSON in *Reader's Digest*

———o———

Grandbabies are better than babies.
You can tote them around the church,
collecting compliments, whereas it
would be unseemly if you were merely
the father.
OREN ARNOLD in *Home Life*

Gratitude

Thou hast giv'n so much to me;
Give one thing more — a grateful heart.
. . . .
Not thankful when it pleases me
As if Thy blessings had spare days,
But such a heart, whose pulse may be
Thy praise.
GEORGE HERBERT, *Gratefulness*

———o———

Gratitude is a fruit of great cultivation; you do not find it among gross
people.
SAMUEL JOHNSON, *Tour to the Hebrides*

———o———

Gratitude takes three forms: a feeling in the heart, an expression in
words, and a giving in return.

We Thank Thee

A little sunshine, a little rain,
A little loss and a little gain,
Courage to walk the unknown road,
Strength to carry the tiring load,
Blossoming flowers and beauteous trees,
Singing birds – for all of these
  We thank Thee, God.

For memories of voices sweet,
Of beauty fresh and eager feet
That will not run again our way,
For all the joys of yesterday,
For vision to undo the bars
Of doubting night and see the stars,
  We thank Thee, God.

ADELAIDE R. KEMP

———o———

Gratitude is the sign of noble souls.

AESOP, *Androcles*

Great

The greatest truths are the simplest; and so are the greatest men.

AUGUSTUS WILLIAM HARE

———o———

The price of greatness is responsibility.

SIR WINSTON CHURCHILL

———o———

Those people who are always improving never become great. Greatness is an eminence, the ascent to which is steep and lofty, and which a man must seize on at once by natural boldness and vigor, and not by patient, wary steps.

WILLIAM HAZLITT

———o———

He is great who inspires others to think for themselves.

ELBERT HUBBARD

———o———

If a man is not great when it doesn't matter . . . he will not be when it does!

RICHARD C. HALVERSON

———o———

The all-important factor in national greatness is national character.

THEODORE ROOSEVELT

Popularity comes from pleasing people, but greatness comes from pleasing God.

———o———

No man is greater than his prayer life.

LEONARD RAVENHILL

———o———

They're only truly great who are truly good.

GEORGE CHAPMAN, *Revenge for Honour*

———o———

The smallest things become great when God requires them of us; they are small only in themselves; they are always great when they are done for God, and when they serve to unite us with Him eternally.

FRANCOIS DE SALIGNAC DE LA MOTHE FÉNELON

———o———

Great men never feel great.
Small men never feel small.

Chinese Saying

———o———

It is not required of every man and woman to be or do something great. Most of us must content ourselves with taking small parts in the chorus, as far as possible without discord.

HENRY VAN DYKE

———o———

Great Things

Great things are only done by men
Who, having failed, will try again:
Who risk their all to venture out,
And having ventured, never doubt:
Whose confidence in self is strong,
And dare defy the doubting throng.

AUTHOR UNKNOWN

———o———

A really great man is known by three signs: generosity in the design, humanity in the execution, and moderation in success.

OTTO VON BISMARCK

———o———

Great men never complain about the lack of time. Alexander the Great and John Wesley accomplished everything they did in 24-hour days.

FRED SMITH

Signs of True Greatness

The ability to apologize; to forgive and forget;
To avoid arguments; to avoid being self-conscious;
To take snubs and reproof well; to have mastery over the flesh;
To stoop to help others.

———o———

The great man is he who does not lose his child's heart.

———o———

The world's greatness is measured by authority and lordliness, but divine greatness is a meek and gentle influence.

———o———

The world's great men have not commonly been great scholars, nor the great scholars great men.

OLIVER WENDELL HOLMES,
The Autocrat of the Breakfast Table

———o———

Man is not great until he beholds his own littleness.

Grief

Some of your griefs you have cured,
And the sharpest you still have survived;
But what torments of pain you endured
From evils which never arrived!

RALPH WALDO EMERSON,
Borrowing (from the French)

———o———

Ah, surely nothing dies but something mourns.

LORD BYRON, *Don Juan*

———o———

Those who have known grief seldom seem sad.

BENJAMIN DISRAELI

———o———

The flood of grief decreaseth when it can swell no longer.

FRANCIS BACON

There is not a grief which time does not lessen and soften.

MARCUS TULLIUS CICERO

———o———

Nothing speaks our grief so well as to speak nothing.

RICHARD CRASHAW

Grow

God never puts any man in a place too small to grow in.

———o———

Every youth who is ambitious to grow to the full stature of noble manhood must make up his mind at the start that he has got to be bigger than the things that are trying to down him. If he doesn't, he will go down with them.

———o———

When a child was asked why a tree in his yard was crooked, he replied, "I 'sposed somebody must have stepped on it when it was a little fellow."

———o———

There could be no growth if there were not something planted . . . Until the new man is born, or begotten, the soul abideth in death, and therefore cannot grow.

HORACE BUSHNELL

———o———

If you are alive, you will grow; death begins where growth ends.

———o———

Most of us get so scared, so civilized, that we invent a disguise for ourselves, and we walk around looking serious and acting self-important, and we call it Grown Up.

ALLAN SHERMAN

———o———

We always grow in the direction in which we express ourselves.

———o———

An acorn is not an oak tree when it is sprouted. It must go through long summers and fierce winters; it has to endure all that frost and snow and side-striking winds can bring before it is a full grown oak. These are rough teachers; but rugged schoolmasters make rugged pupils. So a man when he is created; he is only begun. His manhood must come with years.

HENRY WARD BEECHER

———o———

Unless you try to do something beyond what you have already mastered, you will never grow.

———o———

Everybody wants to be somebody; nobody wants to grow.

JOHANN WOLFGANG VON GOETHE

Grudge

The high-minded man does not bear grudges, for it is not the mark of a great soul to remember injuries, but to forget them.

ARISTOTLE

———o———

Very often the chip on a person's shoulder is just bark.

———o———

No matter how much you nurse a grudge, it won't get better.

———o———

The heaviest piece of wood in the world is the chip a man carries on his shoulder.

———o———

The most inflammable wood is the chip on a Christian's shoulder.

———o———

Grudges are too heavy a load to bear.

———o———

To nurse a grudge is to keep alive a thing that will destroy you.

———o———

The surest way to knock the chip off a fellow's shoulder is by patting him on the back.

Guide, Guidance

When a door slams behind you, look for the one God is opening.

———o———

Divine Guidance

Forth into the darkness passing
  Nothing can I hear or see,
Save the Hand outstretched to guide me,
  And the Voice that calls to me.
"I will bring the blind by pathways
  That they know not, nor have known;
'Tis a way untried, untrodden,
  But they shall not walk alone."

Lead the way then, where Thou pleasest,
  Only keep me close to Thee,
Craving not to see the distance,
  Well content that Thou dost see.
Have I not my all committed
  To Thy keeping long ago?
Knowing Him Whom I have trusted,
  More I do not need to know!

AUTHOR UNKNOWN

———o———

I helped a little child to see
That God had made a willow tree,
And God became more real to me.
I tried to lead a child through play
To grow more Christlike every day,
And I myself became that way.
I joined a little child in prayer,
And as we bowed in worship there,
I felt anew God's loving care.
Thank You, dear Lord;
How grandly true:
By guiding children, we find You!

———o———

Step By Step

He does not lead me year by year
  Nor even day by day.
But step by step my path unfolds;
  My Lord directs my way.

Tomorrow's plans I do not know,
  I only know this minute:
But He will say, "This is the way,
  By faith now walk ye in it."

And I am glad that it is so;
 Today's enough to bear,
And when tomorrow comes, His grace
 Shall far exceed its care.

What need to worry then or fret;
 The God who gave His Son
Holds all the moments in His hand,
 And gives them one by one.
BARBARA C. RYBERG

———o———

If God has made your program, He
will carry it out.

———o———

A sound head, an honest heart, and
a humble spirit are the three best
guides through time and eternity.

———o———

Men give advice; God gives guidance.
LEONARD RAVENHILL

———o———

My Pilot

I care not if the tempest rage,
 Or if the billows roar,
I care not if the surges roll
 And break upon the shore;
I have a Pilot in my ship
 Whom wind and wave obey,
And when He whispers, "Peace, be
 still!"
The storm must die away.

I care not if the sky be black
 And wild the lightning flash,
I care not if the fierce winds blow,
 And loud the thunders crash;
I have a Pilot in my ship
 Who made the mighty sea,
Who made the thunder and the storm,
 And He abides with me.

I care not if the waves wash high,
 And treacherous waters roll,
O'er hidden bar, and jagged rock,
 Or over perilous shoal;
I have a Pilot in my ship
 Who knows the trackless sea,
And He will guide me safely Home
 To His Eternity!
E. MARGARET CLARKSON

Guilt, Guilty

Loud shouting about the sins in another person's life is often due to the
fact that those same sins are in the life
of the shouter
DAVID HAMMAR

———o———

The burden of guilt is a heavy burden.

———o———

Suspicion always haunts the guilty
 mind;
The thief doth fear each bush an officer.
WILLIAM SHAKESPEARE, King Henry VI,
Part III

Habits

Nothing so needs reforming as other
people's habits.
MARK TWAIN, Pudd'nhead Wilson

———o———

Talk about the slave habit! The true
galley slave is the man who, because
he is not the slave of habit, is always
mislaying things and hunting for them.
ROBERT LYND

———o———

Habits are at first cobwebs, then
cables.
Old Proverb

The chains of habit are generally too
small to be felt till they are too strong
to be broken.
SAMUEL JOHNSON

———o———

Habit is a cable. We weave a thread
of it every day until it becomes so
strong we cannot break it.
HORACE MANN

———o———

We first make our habits, and then
our habits make us.

———o———

Habit, if not resisted, soon becomes
necessity.
ST. AUGUSTINE

A bad habit is at first a caller, then a guest, and at last a master.

———o———

Guess Who I Am?

It is mighty hard to shake me,
In my brawny arms I take thee;
I can either make or break thee,
  I am Habit!
Through each day I slowly mold thee;
Soon my tightening chains enfold thee;
Then it is with ease I hold thee;
  This is Habit!
Choose me well when you are starting,
Seldom is there easy parting;
I'm a devil or a darling!
  I am habit!

ROBERT E. SLY, in *Junior Class Paper*

———o———

Our bad habits make us prisoners, and our false pride is the jailor that keeps us there.

———o———

Habits are either bobs or sinkers, cork or lead. They hold you up or hold you down.

———o———

I never knew a man to overcome a bad habit gradually.

JOHN R. MOTT

Hands

His Hands

The hands of Christ
  Seem very frail
For they were broken
  By a nail.

But only they
  Reach heaven at last
Whom these frail, broken
  Hands hold fast.

JOHN RICHARD MORELAND

———o———

My Mother's Hands

My mother's hands! So capable!
  I love them — every wrinkle there.
Though toil has made them rough and
    worn
These hands to me are wondrous fair.

AUTHOR UNKNOWN

Hands

Hands given to God, surrendered
    hands,
  Muscle and bone, and nerve and rich
    red blood,
Hands made for service and for selfless
    toil;
  I yield them gladly to the Lord I
    love,
For His high tasks as His wise love
    demands;
  But should I tire of work and minis-
    try,
If to life's challenge I disloyal am,
  And stretch not forth my hands in
    helpful deed,
Then, Jesus, in Thy mercy let me see
  Thy hands that toiled and served in
    Galilee,
Thy nail-pierced hands upon the sa-
    cred Tree,
  Lord, show me then the hands that
    bled for me;
So stab my soul that I may follow Thee,
  That life and hands re-dedicated be.

KENRED SMITH

———o———

Blessed are the horny hands of toil.

JAMES RUSSELL LOWELL,
A Glance Behind the Curtain

———o———

Helen Keller, the famous blind personality, says: "The hands of those I meet are dumbly eloquent to me. The touch of some hands is an impertinence. I have met people so empty of joy that when I clasped their frosty fingertips it seemed as if I were shaking hands with a north east storm. Others there are whose hands have sunbeams in them, so that their grasp warms my heart. It may be only the clinging touch of a child's hand, but there is as much potential sunshine in it for me as there is in a living glance for others (who can see)."

Happiness, Happy

The Way To Happiness

I met a man the other day
Whose sunny manner seemed to say
That he had found the happy way.
I asked the secret of his smile;

He gave a thoughtful look the while
And answered somewhat in this style:
"Six things have I that spell content,
Six things that mean a life well-spent,
That make for real accomplishment.
A peaceful mind,
A grateful heart,
A love for all that's true,
A helping hand,
Real tolerance,
And lots of things to do."
I took my way with courage new,
With kindlier feelings, broader view,
Trying to think his answer through.
That man had found the secret key
Of how to live and what to be,
And passed it on to you and me.
Then let us try his simple plan
Of faith in God and love for man,
And imitate him if we can.

S. W. GRAFFIN

———o———

On Finding Happiness

Once there was a little puppy chasing its tail. It kept chasing its tail all day long, day after day. The puppy never seemed to tire of chasing its tail.

But one day a large dog stopped near where the puppy was chasing its tail, and the puppy stopped long enough to have a short conversation with the large dog.

The large dog said to the puppy, "Why are you always chasing your tail?"

"Well," answered the puppy, "when I was a very young puppy I learned that happiness was in my tail. So long as it was up and wagging, I was happy. When it dropped, or fell between my legs, I was not so happy. So I've just decided to always chase my tail, since that is my source of happiness. But the trouble is that I never really catch it!"

The older and more mature dog said to the puppy, "When I was a puppy like you that's exactly the way I thought too. But one day I forgot to chase my tail. And, lo and behold, when I looked around, happiness was following me where I went."

C. EDWIN HOUK

———o———

God cannot give us happiness and peace apart from Himself, because it is not there. There is no such thing.

C. S. LEWIS,
Mere Christianity, What Christians Believe

———o———

Much happiness is overlooked because it doesn't cost anything.

OGDON

———o———

Recipe For A Happy Day

1 cup of friendly words
2 cups of understanding
4 heaping tablespoons of time
A pinch of warm personality
A dash of humor
Mix well and serve in generous portions.

———o———

A Recipe For Happiness

I mixed a little loving with my giving,
  And found it made my life much
    more complete;
I mixed some understanding with my
  living,
  And found it made the bitter waters
    sweet.

I took some oil of gladness in the morning
  And mixed it with the work I had to
    do,
Then suddenly I found my heart was
  warming,
  And I felt at peace with every one I
    knew.

I took some sympathy for those in
  trouble
  And mixed it very gently with a
    smile;
Then I felt the joy within begin to
  bubble,
  And I knew I'd found a mixture
    quite worthwhile.

I took a lot of love and godly pleasure
  And mixed it all together with the
    rest;
I then poured in more faith than I
  could measure,
  And it made a life of joy and happiness.

HOWARD ALEXANDER

Happiness is that certain something you acquire while you're too busy to be miserable.

————o————

The Happy Heart

The happy heart is that which is content with little things,
The heart that loves the simple life, the heart from which there springs
A sense of joy with each fresh day; a prayer of gratitude
For the morning miracle of health and strength renewed.

The heart that builds about itself a shell of quietness,
A heart that keeps its faith amidst disaster and distress;
A heart serene, unmoved by envy, doubt, defeat or fear,
Filled with hope unfailing, rich in charity and fear.

No greater gift could be bestowed than this: the happy heart.
The world becomes a better place when once we've learned the art
Of putting golden edges round the clouds that blow along,
Of turning sorrows into smiles and discord into song.

PATIENCE STRONG

————o————

The secret of happiness is not in doing what one likes, but in liking what one has to do.

GEORGE V, King of England

————o————

There is no personal charm so great as the charm of a cheerful and happy temperament.

HENRY VAN DYKE

————o————

Happiness in one respect is like potato salad: when shared with others, it's a picnic.

RALPH SCOTT

————o————

Nine-tenths of our unhappiness is selfishness, and is an insult cast in the face of God.

G. H. MORRISON

The greatest happiness of life is the conviction that we are loved, loved for ourselves, or rather loved in spite of ourselves.

VICTOR HUGO

————o————

The happiness which brings enduring worth to life is not the superficial happiness that is dependent on circumstances. It is the happiness and contentment that fills the soul even in the midst of the most distressing of circumstances and the most bitter environment.

BILLY GRAHAM

————o————

Now, if happiness were only as contagious as the common cold.

————o————

Whoever wishes to be happier than he is no longer is happy.

BEN THOMAS

————o————

It isn't your position that makes you happy or unhappy; it's your disposition.

————o————

In the happiness of others, I find my own happiness.

PIERRE CORNEILLE

————o————

There is no duty we underrate so much as the duty of being happy.

ROBERT LOUIS STEVENSON,
Virginibus Puerisque,
An Apology for Idlers

————o————

Making an issue of little things is one of the surest ways to spoil happiness.

————o————

Man's happiness consists in present peace, even in the midst of the greatest trials, and in more than hope of a glorious future.

CHARLES G. GORDON

————o————

Most People Think:

Happy are the pushers:
        For they get on in the world.
Happy are the hard-boiled:
        For they never let life hurt them.

Happy are they who complain:
   For they get their own way in
      the end.
Happy are the blasé:
   For they never worry over their
      sins.
Happy are the slave-drivers:
   For they get results.
Happy are the knowledgeable men of
      the world:
   For they know their way
      around.
Happy are the trouble-makers:
   For people have to take notice
      of them.

Jesus Christ Said:

Happy are those who realize their
      spiritual poverty:
   They have already entered the
      kingdom of reality.
Happy are they who bear their share
      of the world's pain:
   In the long run they will know
      more happiness than those
      who avoid it.
Happy are those who accept life and
      their own limitations:
   They will find more in life than
      anybody.
Happy are those who long to be truly
      "good":
   They will fully realize their
      ambition.
Happy are those who are ready to
      make allowances and to for-
      give:
   They will know the love of
      God.
Happy are those who are real in their
      thoughts and feelings:
   In the end they will see the
      ultimate Reality, God.
Happy are those who help others to
      live together:
   They will be known to be do-
      ing God's work.
                              J. B. PHILLIPS,
                     Your God Is Too Small

———o———

Seek not happiness; bestow it, and
it will come to you.

Happiness is nothing more than good
health and a bad memory.
                           ALBERT SCHWEITZER

———o———

The happier the time, the quicker it
passes.
                           PLINY THE YOUNGER

———o———

Be merry if you are wise.
                                    MARTIAL

———o———

A light heart lives long.
                       WILLIAM SHAKESPEARE

———o———

Happiness is not a station you arrive
at; but a manner of traveling.
                      MARGARET LEE RUNBECK

———o———

Possibly the greatest source of human happiness is in personal achievement.
                            HERBERT HOOVER

———o———

You traverse the world in search of
happiness, which is within the reach
of every man. A contented mind confers it on all.
                                    HORACE

———o———

The way to bliss lies not on beds of
   down,
And he that has no cross deserves no
   crown.
                       FRANCIS QUARLES, *Esther*

Hate

Hate is a prolonged form of suicide.
JOHANN CHRISTOPH FRIEDRICH VON SCHILLER

———o———

Unless love embrace the world, hate
will crush it.

———o———

Hate and mistrust are the children
of blindness.
                           WILLIAM WATSON

———o———

We are more inclined to hate one
another for points on which we differ
than to love one another for points on
which we agree.

One of the fine arts — to hate sin without hating sinners.

———o———

I shall allow no man to belittle my soul by making me hate him.
BOOKER T. WASHINGTON

———o———

Hatred is by far the longest pleasure, Men love in haste, but they detest at leisure.
LORD BYRON

———o———

Contempt is a kind of gangrene, which, if it seizes one part of a character, corrupts all the rest.
SAMUEL JOHNSON

———o———

Who love too much, hate in the like extreme.
HOMER

Head

To handle yourself, use your head; to handle others, use your heart.
The English Digest

———o———

A man is like a tack, he can go only as far as his head will take him.

———o———

I think there is only one quality worse than hardness of heart and that is softness of head.
THEODORE ROOSEVELT

———o———

One good head is better than a hundred strong hands.

———o———

Nobody can steal what's in your head or in your heart.
HAL STEBBINS

Health

Health Note: One way to keep your "ticker" ticking is not to continually wind it too tight.

———o———

He who has health, has hope; and he who has hope, has everything.
Arabian Proverb

Health is a trust from God.

———o———

To be the picture of health, keep in a good frame of mind.

———o———

Our good health always seems much more valuable after we lose it.

———o———

Health is a gift, but you have to work to keep it.
HUBBARD

———o———

He spent his health to get his wealth, and then with might and main
He turned around and spent his wealth to regain his health again.

———o———

Life is not mere living, but the enjoyment of health.
MARTIAL

———o———

Late to bed, early to rise, Makes dark circles under your eyes.

———o———

I cannot take care of my soul. God can keep that. But my body is for me to take care of.
GEORGE MUELLER

Hear

He hears but half who hears one side only.
AESCHYLUS

———o———

What you hear never sounds half so important as what you overhear.

———o———

Nature has given to men one tongue, but two ears, that we may hear from others twice as much as we speak.
EPICTETUS

———o———

The hearing ear is always found close to the speaking tongue.
RALPH WALDO EMERSON

———o———

Hear twice before you speak once.

Heart

God will accept a broken heart, but He must have all the pieces.

———o———

The best exercise for the heart is to bend down several times a day to help someone else.

———o———

The human heart generates enough energy in twelve hours to lift sixty-five tons one foot off the ground!

———o———

Whatever is seen, touched, heard, tasted, or smelled is likely to produce reactions in the heart!

———o———

"This is where your heart is," said the teacher, pointing to her chest.

"Mine is where I sit down," a little boy called from the back of the class.

"Whatever gave you that idea?" the startled teacher asked.

"Well," the youngster replied, "every time I do something good, my grandmother pats me there and says, 'Bless your little heart.'"

EDWARD JAMES BERRY

———o———

As God Sees

Man sees the kingly features,
　The confidence and charm,
The large, impressive stature,
　The strength of will and arm;
But God looks through the semblance
　And reads the hidden part,
And chooses for His servants
　The truly great at heart.
Man hears the spacious promise,
　The boast of statesmanship,
And worships him whose praises
　Are heard on every lip;
But God's ears are attentive
　To hear the thought instead,
And catch the secret meaning
　Of everything that's said.
God's ways with men are baffling,
　And oft to our surprise
He passes by the famous,
　The mighty and the wise.

He searches out a shepherd,
　A tollman in the mart,
And fishers by the seaside —
　The truly great at heart.

RALPH T. NORDLUND

———o———

It is not flesh and blood but the heart which makes us fathers and sons.

JOHANN CHRISTOPH FRIEDRICH VON SCHILLER

———o———

Whatever is to reach the heart must come from above.

LUDWIG VON BEETHOVEN

———o———

A Quiet Heart

O Lord, give me a quiet heart—
　So oft my heart is filled with fear;
I need the peace Thou canst impart;
　I need to feel that Thou art near.

Help me to walk by faith each day.
　Though shadows hide the path from
　　view;
Give me a quiet heart, I pray
　To trust Thee as Thou bid'st me do.

I cannot see the journey's end,
　I know not what lies just ahead;
But, oh I have a Heav'nly Friend
　Who knows the path my feet must
　　tread.

So now, my heart, be still and trust,
　Although thou canst not see the way:
For He who formed thee from the dust
　Wilt lead thee on from day to day.

A quiet heart — a quiet heart,
　From which are banished doubts
　　and fears;
O Lord, give me a quiet heart
　That trusts Thee for the coming
　　years.

W. M. NIENHUIS

———o———

The average heart is made to pump 2,000,000,000 times without failure, or more than ten times the performance expected from a cylinder in the engine of the highest-priced car.

———o———

In days of great need the world around there are too many folks worrying about hardening of the arteries who ought to be treated for hardening of the heart.

———o———

No man can tell whether he is rich or poor by turning to his ledger. It is the heart that makes a man rich. He is rich according to what he is, not according to what he has.

HENRY WARD BEECHER

———o———

If there is righteousness in the heart, there will be beauty in character, there will be harmony in the home. If there is harmony in the home, there will be order in the nation. Where there is order in the nation, there will be peace in the world.

Chinese Proverb

Heaven

Weep Not For Me

Would you like to know where I am?
I am at home in my Father's house, in the mansions prepared for me there.
I am where I would be —
No longer on the stormy sea, but in the safe and quiet harbor.
My working time is done and I am resting;
My sowing time is done and I am reaping;
My joy is as the joy of harvest.

Would you know how it is with me?
I am made perfect in holiness.
Grace is swallowed up in glory.
The top-stone of the building is brought forth.

Would you know what I am doing?
I see God.
I see Him as He is, not as through a glass darkly, but face to face,
And the sight is transforming, it makes me like Him.
I am in the sweet enjoyment of my blessed Redeemer.
I am here singing hallelujahs incessantly to Him who sits upon the throne,
And rest not day or night from praising Him.

Would you know what company I keep?
Blessed company —
Better than the best on earth.
Here are holy angels and the spirits of just men made perfect.
I am set down with Abraham, Isaac and Jacob in the Kingdom of God,
With the blessed Paul and Peter,
James and John and all the saints.
And here I meet with many of my old acquaintances with whom I worked,
And with whom I prayed who came hither before me.
And lastly . . .

Would you know how long this is to continue?
It is a garland that never withers,
The crown of glory that fades not away.
After millions and millions of ages it will be as fresh as it is now,
And therefore, weep not for me.

Ascribed to MATTHEW HENRY

———o———

From A Loved One In Heaven

I would not have you grieve for me today
Nor weep beside my vacant chair.
Could you but know my daily portion here
You would not, could not, wish me there.

I know now why He said, "Ear hath not heard."
I have no words, no alphabet.
Or even if I had I DARE not tell
Because you could not bear it yet.

So, only this — I am the same, though changed,
Like Him! A joy more rich and strong
Than I had dreamed that any heart could hold,
And all my life is one glad song.

Sometimes when you are talking to our Lord
He turns and speaks to me . . . Dear heart,
In that rare moment you and I are just
The distance of a word apart!

And so my loved ones, do not grieve
  for me
Around the family board today;
Instead, rejoice, for we are one in Him,
And so I am not far away.

MARTHA SNELL NICHOLSON

———o———

Billy was gazing at his one-day-old brother, who lay squealing and yelling in his cradle.

"Has he come from Heaven?" inquired Billy.

"Yes, dear."

"No wonder they put him out."

———o———

A devout Scotchman, being asked if he ever expected to go to Heaven, gave this reply: "Why, mon, I live there!" All the way to Heaven is Heaven begun to the Christian who walks near enough to God to hear the secrets He has to impart. There is such a thing as having an inner Heaven in the heart. "The Kingdom of God is within you."

B. F. HALLECK

———o———

Heaven is a prepared place for a prepared people, and they that enter shall find that they are neither unknown or unexpected.

BISHOP RYAL

———o———

A would-be soapbox orator who had reached the argumentative stage sat down next to a clergyman on a bus. Wishing to get into an argument, he turned and said, "I'm not going to heaven because there is no heaven."

His words, however, got no response.

"I said I'm not going to heaven because there is no heaven," he said again, almost shouting as he came to the end of his sentence.

"Well, then," replied the clergyman calmly, "go to hell, but be quiet about it."

———o———

Teacher: "How many of you children want to go to heaven?"

The children all raised their hands except Johnny.

Teacher: "But, Johnny, don't you want to go to heaven?"

Johnny: "I can't, teacher, 'cause mother told me to come home right after school."

———o———

A little girl taking an evening walk with her father looked up at the stars and exclaimed, "Oh, Daddy, if the wrong side of heaven is so beautiful what must the right side be!"

———o———

Think —

Of stepping on shore and finding it
  Heaven;
Of taking hold of a hand and finding
  it God's hand;
Of breathing a new air and finding it
  celestial air;
Of feeling invigorated and finding it
  immortality;
Of passing from storm and tempest to
  an unbroken calm;
Of waking up, and finding it Home!"

ANONYMOUS

———o———

In order to be heaven-bound, we must be heaven-born.

———o———

He who is on the road to heaven will not be content to go there alone.

———o———

Sequence

After the sea, the harbor;
  After the storm, the calm;
After the road, the arbor;
  After the bleeding, balm;
After the gladness, weeping;
  After the bloom, the clod;
After the labor, sleeping;
  After the sleeping — God!

EDGAR DANIEL KRAMER

———o———

One tear, one sigh, one fear, one loss, one thought of trouble cannot find lodging there.

———o———

Jesus came to earth from heaven that we might go to heaven from earth.

We can't enter heaven before heaven enters us!

———o———

There is a land of pure delight
Where saints immortal reign;
Infinite day excludes the night,
And pleasures banish pain.

ISAAC WATTS, *Hymn 66*

———o———

When I can read my title clear
To mansions in the skies,
I'll bid farewell to every fear,
And wipe my weeping eyes.

ISAAC WATTS, *Hymn 65*

———o———

Trying to impress on my son that he should take good care of a souvenir from Jerusalem, I said, "This is from the Holy Land, and it is so far away we'll never be able to go there."

Next day when showing his gift to a neighbor girl, he announced, "This is from heaven, and that's one place our family will never go."

MRS. B. J. WILZ in *Together*

———o———

The man who expects to go to heaven should take the trouble to learn what route will get him there!

———o———

If you read history you will find that the Christians who did most for the present world were just those who thought most of the next. The Apostles themselves who set on foot the conversion of the Roman Empire, . . . the English Evangelicals who abolished the Slave Trade, all left their mark on Earth, precisely because their minds were occupied with Heaven. It is since Christians have largely ceased to think of the other world that they have become so ineffective in this. Aim at Heaven and you will get earth "thrown in"; aim at earth and you will get neither.

C. S. LEWIS,
Mere Christianity, Christian Behaviour

———o———

A discussion of heaven with the boys and girls in children's church brought to light a hitherto unexplored advantage when four-year-old Becky said,

"We won't have to take naps when we get there!"

IRENE ROYCE in *Teach*

———o———

The blue of heaven is larger than the clouds.

ELIZABETH BARRETT BROWNING

———o———

If God hath made this world so fair
Where sin and death abound,
How beautiful beyond compare
Will paradise be found.

JAMES MONTGOMERY

Hell

Time flies, death urges, knells call, heaven invites, hell threatens.

EDWARD YOUNG

———o———

As sure as night follows day and winter follows summer, so shall wrath follow sin.

———o———

The wisest of men are those who spend most pains in keeping out of hell rather than to exercise themselves with disputes about it.

Help

When God puts a burden upon you He puts His own arm under you.

———o———

Boy Overboard

A surgeon on an ocean-going vessel told how a boy fell overboard, and the crew rescued him. They brought him on board, worked his hands and feet, and tried to revive him, but in vain. When the surgeon arrived on the scene the crew members said, "It's no use; he's dead."

The surgeon replied, "I think you have done all you could," and he was about to turn away, when a sudden impulse told him he ought to examine the boy and make sure there was nothing he could do to revive him.

When he went to where the lad was and looked down into his face, he discovered it was his own son!

The surgeon immediately got busy.

He pulled off his coat, bent over the boy, breathed into his mouth, blew into his nostrils. He turned him over and over. He prayed. For four hours he worked, and at last he saw signs of life in his boy.

"Oh, I will never see another boy drown," said the surgeon, "without taking off my coat and doing all I can to save him — just as if I knew he were my own boy!"

When we see a boy or girl in spiritual danger, are we as sympathetic and as concerned as if it were our own child? Do we really do all we can to help the situation?

The Log of the Good Ship Grace

———o———

The woman who helps her neighbor does herself a good turn.

BRENDAN FRANCIS

———o———

No one is useless in this world who lightens the burden of it to any one else.

CHARLES DICKENS

———o———

Not enough people realize that the helping hand they always are looking for is at the end of their own wrist.

NICK KOZMENIUK

———o———

The truest help we can render to an afflicted man is not to take his burden from him, but to call out his best strength, that he may be able to bear the burden.

PHILLIPS BROOKS

———o———

No man can sincerely try to help another without helping himself.

J. B. WEBSTER

———o———

The hands that tend the sick tend Christ.

ARTHUR F. WINNINGTON INGRAM

———o———

It would be much nicer if everyone tempted to point a finger would instead hold out a hand.

———o———

It is not so much our friends' help that helps us as the confidence in their help.

EPICURUS

———o———

To look up and not down,
To look forward and not back,
To look out and not in, and
To lend a hand.

EDWARD EVERETT HALE,
Ten Times One Is Ten

———o———

Nothing lightens one's burdens so quickly as helping others carry theirs.

———o———

You can't help someone else uphill without getting closer to the top yourself.

———o———

One lightning bug to another: "Give me a push; my battery's dead."

———o———

The Lord helps those who help others.

———o———

When my third-graders come to an unfamiliar word in oral reading, they usually stop and wait until I pronounce it for them.

One day I was reading a story when one child began whispering. Hoping that silence would remind her of her good manners, I stopped reading but did not look up. Whereupon a boy said sympathetically, "If you'll spell the word for me, Miss Carroll, maybe I can tell you what it is."

DOROTHY M. CARROLL in *NEA Journal*

Heredity

Heredity is when a teen-age boy winds up with his mother's big brown eyes and his father's long yellow convertible.

———o———

Heredity: Something you believe in when your child's report card is all A's.

DR. L. BINDER in *Coronet*

———o———

Every man believes in heredity until his son begins making a fool of himself.

Heredity is what makes the mother and father of teen-agers wonder a little about each other.

———o———

When one has nothing else to blame, he falls back on his heredity.

———o———

It is of no consequence of what parents a man is born, so he be a man of merit.

HORACE

Heroes

God is preparing His heroes and when the opportunity comes, he can fit them into their places in a moment and the world will wonder where they came from.

A. B. SIMPSON

———o———

Heroes are as necessary to a child's growth as vitamins.

———o———

Whosoever excels in what we prize,
Appears a hero in our eyes.

JONATHAN SWIFT

———o———

Unbounded courage and compassion joined proclaim him good and great, and make the hero and the man complete.

JOSEPH ADDISON

———o———

Heroes are made every little while, but only one in a million conduct themselves afterwards so that it makes us proud that we honored them at the time.

WILL ROGERS

———o———

As employment interviewer for a large aircraft company, I meet and talk with many kinds of people. I thought nothing could surprise me, but the other day a recently discharged sailor set me back on my heels.

Well-dressed in civvies, he wore on his lapel the Purple Heart, as well as his honorable discharge button. However, it was another large gold star-shaped medal, suspended from a ladder of ten bars, which really took my eye.

My curiosity grew. I was sure he had won the medal through some unprecedented act of valor. The details of his employment being completed, I did something I don't ordinarily do. I asked him how it happened.

"Oh," he replied proudly, yet with the modesty befitting a hero, "I got that *before* I went into the Navy. I won it for going to Sunday School for ten years without missing a Sunday."

ALFRED SEALE in *Coronet*

History

There is properly no history, only biography.

RALPH WALDO EMERSON

———o———

History keeps right on repeating itself, while statesmen act as though they expected it to do something different.

———o———

Some of the biggest improvements in history are made by writers of history.

Record-Herald, Butler, Indiana

———o———

The supreme purpose of history is a better world.

HERBERT HOOVER

———o———

What are all histories but God manifesting himself, shaking down and trampling under foot whatever he hath not planted.

OLIVER CROMWELL

———o———

[History] hath triumphed over time, which besides it nothing but eternity hath triumphed over.

SIR WALTER RALEIGH, *Historie of the World*

———o———

History is only a confused heap of facts.

LORD CHESTERFIELD

He is happiest of whom the world says least, good or bad.

THOMAS JEFFERSON

———o———

There is a saying among men, that a noble deed ought not to be buried in the silent grave.

PINDAR

Holy

A holy God could require of man nothing less than holiness.

———o———

Holiness

1. Not inability to sin, but ability not to sin.
2. Not freedom from temptation, but power to overcome temptation.
3. Not infallible judgment, but earnest and honest endeavor to follow the higher wisdom.
4. Not deliverance from infirmities of the flesh, but triumph over all bodily affliction.
5. Not exemption from conflict, but victory through conflict.
6. Not freedom from liability and falling, but gracious ability to prevent falling.
7. Not the end of progress, but deliverance from standing still.

What real Christians would not desire the beauty and blessedness of such a life?

G. CAMPBELL MORGAN

———o———

More holiness give me,
More striving within;
More patience in suffering,
More sorrow for sin;
More faith in my Savior,
More sense of His care;
More joy in His service,
More purpose in prayer.

P. P. BLISS

———o———

I am certain of nothing but the holiness of the heart's affections and the truth of imagination.

JOHN KEATS,
Letter to Benjamin Bailey

Holiness is righteousness expressed.

Holy Spirit

Without the Holy Spirit, the preacher is as helpless before a sinner needing a Saviour, as Samson before Delilah.

ARTHUR F. FOGARTIE in *Presbyterian Journal*

———o———

If the Church is to rise to its fullest stature in God, if it is to enjoy the abundant life, if it is to meet all foes in the spirit of triumph, it must rely, not upon its numbers or skills, but upon the power of the Holy Spirit.

AUTHUR J. MOORE

———o———

I am in Christ
    Christ is in me,
My body his temple,
    Sin's captive set free;
My heart His altar,
    Divine love the flame,
Cleansing for service
    In His matchless Name;
My life and His life
    Co-mingled shall be,
With God's very Spirit
    Enthroned in me.

FRANCES RHOADS LA CHANCE

———o———

I have learned to place myself before God every day as a vessel to be filled with His Holy Spirit. He has filled me with the blessed assurance that He, as the everlasting God, has guaranteed His own work in me.

ANDREW MURRAY

———o———

A man praying at a conference in England for the outpouring of the Holy Spirit, said: "O Lord, we can't hold much, but we can overflow lots."

S. D. GORDON

———o———

Every time we say, "I believe in the Holy Spirit," we mean that we believe that there is a living God able and willing to enter human personality and change it.

J. B. PHILLIPS

All that has been done by God the Father and by God the Son must be ineffectual to us, unless the Spirit shall reveal those things to our souls.

CHARLES HADDON SPURGEON

———o———

To build temples is easier than to be temples of the Holy Spirit.

———o———

One taught by the Spirit knows the will of God.

Home

Most of our homes are having this painful contemplation: A child is born in the home and for twenty years makes so much noise we think we can hardly stand it, and then he departs leaving the home so silent that we think we'll go mad.

———o———

Children may learn at home those things which enable them to live rich, happy, useful lives or they may become unhappy, maladjusted people, suspicious of the motives of others and unwilling to cooperate with anyone. Most children fall somewhere between these two extremes.

ALICE SOWERS

———o———

Home is the chief school of human virtues.

———o———

A house is built by human hands, but a home is built by human hearts.

———o———

The Christian Home

How God must love a friendly home
Which has a warming smile
To welcome everyone who comes
To bide a little while!

How God must love a happy home
Where song and laughter show
Hearts full of joyous certainty
That life means ways to grow!

How God must love a loyal home
Serenely sound and sure!
When troubles come to those within,
They still can feel secure.

How God must love a Christian Home
Where faith and love attest
That every moment, every hour,
He is the honored Guest!

GAIL BROOKS BURKET

———o———

Friday Night

The house is full of the gayest noise,
It's Friday night, and our two big boys
Are home from college, and the place
    seems glad;
The spaniel's crazy, the cat's gone mad;
The old stairs creak, and the windows
    rattle,
We gird our loins for banter and battle,
For clash of wits and laughter and
    song,
For the week-end's short, and they'll
    soon be gone.
The old house rumbles, and the shingles crack,
As it chuckles for joy, when the boys
    come back!

MARGERY COFFMAN in Gospel Herald

———o———

Men make a camp; a swarm of bees a
    comb;
Birds make a nest; a woman makes a
    home.

ARTHUR GUITERMAN

———o———

Nothing makes your home look so attractive as pricing the new ones.

FRANKLIN P. JONES

———o———

Tied Down

I am tied down . . .
By clothes lines
On which I hang
Small blue and yellow rompers.
By strings . . .
Just commonplace white threads
With which I sew on buttons,
Mend wee pockets,
Patch faded threadbare little suits.
Ropes tie me down,
Red jumping ropes
And those that pull
Small animals about.
Young, bleeding grimy thumbs there
are

To kiss and bind with lengths
Of clean white gauze.
And baby arms about my neck . . .
Oh, yes . . . I am tied down . . . thank
    God!

AUTHOR UNKNOWN

Motto For A Home

Lord, enter Thou my home with me,
Until I enter Thine with Thee.

A house is built of logs and stone,
    Of tiles and posts and piers;
A home is built of loving deeds
    That stand a thousand years.

VICTOR HUGO

God bless this home and those who
    love it;
Fair be the skies which bend above it.
May never anger's thoughtless word
Within these sheltering walls be heard.
May all who rest beside this fire
And then depart, glad thoughts in-
    spire;
And make them feel who close the
    door,
Friendship has graced their home once
    more.

God bless this house and those who
    keep it;
In the sweet oils of gladness steep it.
Endow these walls with lasting wealth,
The light of love, the glow of health,
The palm of peace, the charm of mirth,
Good friends to sit around the hearth;
And with each nightfall perfect rest —
Here let them live their happiest.

AUTHOR UNKNOWN

A visitor in a large Eastern city was
being taken around by a friend.
Among other features of interest he
was shown the beautiful homes of the
fine residential area. "Your homes are
palatial," the visitor remarked. "Yes,"
replied his host, "it is not so difficult
for us to build palatial mansions, but
it is extremely difficult to build princely men to live in them."

Light

If you want to find the pot of gold
at the end of the rainbow, start digging at home.

A house is not home unless it contains food and fire for the mind as
well as for the body.

Homes are the building blocks of
civilization.

ARNOLD J. TOYNBEE

Blest be that spot, where cheerful
    guests retire
To pause from toil, and trim their
    evening fire;
Blest that abode, where want and pain
    repair,
And every stranger finds a ready chair;
Blest be those feasts with simple
    plenty crowned,
Where all the ruddy family around
Laugh at the jests or pranks that never
    fail,
Or sigh with pity at some mournful
    tale,
Or press the bashful stranger to his
    food,
And learn the luxury of doing good.

OLIVER GOLDSMITH, *The Traveller*

Honesty

A commentary on the times is that
the noun "honesty" now is preceded
by the adjective "old-fashioned."

Modern Times

Make yourself an honest man, and
then you may be sure there is one
rascal less in the world.

THOMAS CARLYLE

I hope I shall always possess firmness and virtue enough to maintain
what I consider the most enviable of
all titles, the character of an honest
man.

GEORGE WASHINGTON

Honesty is the first chapter of the
book of wisdom.

THOMAS JEFFERSON

An honest man's the noblest work of God.

ALEXANDER POPE,
Essay on Man, Epistle IV

———o———

How happy is he born and taught,
That serveth not another's will;
Whose armour is his honest thought
And simple truth his utmost skill!

SIR HENRY WOTTON

———o———

The badge of honesty is simplicity.

———o———

To be honest with others, one must be thoroughly honest with himself.

Honor

No one was ever honored for what he received; honor is the reward for what he gave.

———o———

He who wishes to retain his honor, let him be humble and seek no honors; for in trying to receive honors and recognition, he reveals that he lacks something.

———o———

God has given us something to do in this world. Do we appreciate the honor?

———o———

Honor lies in honest toil.

GROVER CLEVELAND

Hope

Next to the gospel of love, the gospel of hope is perhaps the most blessed story in life. It makes us optimists for tomorrow, and we look for bright skies, good health, congenial work, true friends and a happy future.

AUTHOR UNKNOWN

———o———

Other men see only a hopeless end, but the Christian rejoices in an endless hope.

GILBERT M. BEENKEN

———o———

While there is life there is hope.

MARCUS TULLIUS CICERO

As froth on the face of the deep,
As foam on the crest of the sea,
As dreams at the waking of sleep,
As a gourd of a day and a night
As harvest that no man shall reap,
As vintage that never shall be
Is hope if it cling not aright,
O my God, unto Thee.

CHRISTINA GEORGINA ROSSETTI

———o———

Hope, alone, accomplishes nothing. Thought, effort, determination — these are among the other ingredients of accomplishment. But without hope, there is naught to nourish these other elements in our souls, minds and sinews.

———o———

Whatever happens don't lose your hold on the two main ropes of life: Hope and Faith. If you do, God pity you because then you are adrift without sail or anchor.

WILLIAM L. BROWNELL

———o———

Everything that is done in the world is done by hope.

MARTIN LUTHER

———o———

There is no medicine like hope, no incentive so great, and no tonic so powerful as expectation of something better tomorrow.

O. S. MARDEN

———o———

The time I live in is a time of turmoil, my hope is in God.

FREDERICK THE GREAT, King of Prussia

———o———

Be still, sad heart, and cease repining;
Behind the clouds the sun is shining;
Thy fate is the common fate of all,
Into each life some rain must fall,
Some days must be dark and dreary.

HENRY WADSWORTH LONGFELLOW,
The Rainy Day

———o———

Hope ever urges on, and tells us tomorrow will be better.

TIBULLUS

———o———

Hope, like the gleaming taper's light,
Adorns and cheers our way;

And still, as darker grows the night,
Emits a brighter ray.
OLIVER GOLDSMITH, *The Captivity*

Hospitality

The ultimate in hospitality is to be able to make your guest feel at home when you wish he were.

———o———

Alike he thwarts the hospitable end
Who drives the free or stays the hasty
    friend;
True friendship's laws are by this rule
    expressed,
Welcome the coming, speed the part-
    ing guest.
HOMER

———o———

Come in the evening, or come in the
    morning,
Come when you're looked for, or come
    without warning,
Kisses and welcome you'll find here
    before you,
And the oftener you come here the
    more I'll adore you.
THOMAS O. DAVIS, *The Welcome*

Housework

Housework is something you do that nobody notices unless you don't do it.

———o———

A Minneapolis housewife went in-to her kitchen early one morning on April Fool's Day and found a "Good Morning!" sign hung from the center light fixture. The door of a cabinet had been removed for fixing. At that point she found a sign "Closed For Repair." In the refrigerator crisper was another message "Lettuce Pray." In the freezer was another: "Help! I'm freezing!" In the egg compartment she found "I'll bet you didn't eggspect me in here." In the sink was "What depths some people won't sink to!" The dustpan had a note: "Remember, man, that thou art dust." A bar of soap was decorated with "Once again, Ivory returned." In the kitchenware drawer was "Hey! I've discovered sil-ver!" On the glassware shelf she found:

"Big Tyrone presents: 'The Glass Me-nagerie.'" Inside a rubber glove was "Why, we would just glove to have you." These were thought up and planted by her sons, ages 12 and 19.
BOB MURPHY

———o———

Christ moves among the pots and pans.
ST. THERESA

Human

Human beings divide the human race horizontally: upper class, middle class, lower class. But Christ divides it vertically: to the right and to the left; and it's Christ's division which will stand.

———o———

He who helps a child helps hu-manity with an immediateness which no other help given to human creatures in any other stage of their life can pos-sibly give again.
PHILLIPS BROOKS

———o———

Human beings generally respond to loving concern. There is more power in a thimbleful of tears than in a barrel of logic.
C. FRANKLIN ALLEE

———o———

Honor humanity, if for no other rea-son than that Jesus died and shed His blood for all.

———o———

Human action can be modified to some extent, but human nature can-not be changed.
ABRAHAM LINCOLN

Humility

The late Queen Mary visited a hos-pital ward one day and paused for a moment at the bed of a little girl. She asked the child where she lived and the child said in Battersea, a poor district in London.
"Where do you live?" the girl asked, unaware of the rank of her visitor.
"Oh, just behind Gorringe's depart-ment store," Queen Mary replied.
New York Herald Tribune

Whom God would greatly exalt He first humbles.

———o———

A city boy visiting on a farm for the first time saw a field of ripening wheat. He noticed that some of the yellowing stems stood up tall and straight while others gracefully bent their heads. "Those stalks that stand up so tall and straight must be the best," he remarked to the farm boy who was his companion. "They look as if they were proud of what they were doing."

The country boy laughed. "That's because you don't know much about wheat," he explained. He plucked a head of each and rubbing them in his hands showed that the tall, straight stalks held very little grain, while the bending heads were filled with the promise of a rich harvest. One of the surest evidences of greatness is a humble spirit.

———o———

Do you want to enter what people call "the higher life"? Then go a step lower down.

ANDREW MURRAY

———o———

The Lord fishes on the bottom, and if you want to get his bait and hook, brother, you've got to get right down on the bottom.

SAM JONES

———o———

I believe the first test of a truly great man is his humility.

JOHN RUSKIN

———o———

A humble person can neither be put down nor exalted; he can neither be humiliated nor honored: he remains the same person under all circumstances.

———o———

He that is down need fear no fall,
    He that is low no pride;
He that is humble ever shall
    Have God to be his guide.

JOHN BUNYAN,
Pilgrim's Progress, Part II

———o———

Humility is the acceptance of the place appointed by God, whether it be in the front or in the rear.

God will deny no blessing to a thoroughly humbled spirit.

CHARLES HADDON SPURGEON

———o———

The man who humbly bows before God, is sure to walk upright before men.

———o———

Humbleness is always grace; always dignity.

JAMES RUSSELL LOWELL

———o———

Sense shines with a double luster when it is set in humility. An able and yet humble man is a jewel worth a kingdom.

WILLIAM PENN

———o———

Humility is the solid foundation of all the virtues.

CONFUCIUS

———o———

He who blushes at the discovery of his own hidden virtues is a true gentleman.

———o———

Few people have a lower opinion of themselves than they deserve.

———o———

Humility is a virtue all preach, none practice, and yet everybody is content to hear.

JOHN SELDEN

———o———

The flower of sweetest smell is shy and lowly.

WILLIAM WORDSWORTH

———o———

In becoming a little child, and remaining a little child, there is all the difference between a simpleton and a saint.

Humor

A sense of humor . . . is not so much the ability to appreciate humorous stories as it is . . . the capacity to recognize the absurdity of the positions one gets into from time to time together with skill in retreating from them with dignity.

DANA L. FARNSWORTH in Think

Humor is emotional chaos remembered in tranquillity.

JAMES THURBER

———o———

A pun is the lowest form of humor — when you don't think of it first.

LEVANT

———o———

Lost!

I lost my sense of humor. Oh, wherever did it go?
Didn't know I'd lost it 'til it was needed so.
It wasn't in the kitchen; I couldn't find it there.
It wasn't in the parlor or in the room of prayer.

I couldn't laugh with children. Their pranks had vexed me sore.
I couldn't see the humorous side; I found life such a bore.
I took myself too seriously. My errors left me smarting.
I found the faults of those about excuse for my departing.

I wanted more perfection in everyone, and me,
Expected right to be the way I wanted it to be.
Then I heard God's chiding whisper, and suddenly I knew
I'd lost my sense of humor. Whatever could I do?

I looked and searched most everywhere
To find this needed treasure,
And there is was, obscured from sight,
By SELF grown out of measure.

DORIS REICHERT

———o———

A sense of humor is the lubricant of life's machinery.

———o———

Man is the only creature endowed with the gift of laughter; is he not also the only one that deserves to be laughed at?

FULKE GREVILLE

———o———

Cheer up and smile; it's gravity that holds things down.

Humor is the harmony of the heart.

DOUGLAS JERROLD

———o———

Good humor is a tonic for the mind and body.
It is the best antidote for anxiety and depression.
It is a business asset.
It attracts and keeps friends.
It lightens human burdens.
It is the direct route to serenity and contentment.

GRENVILLE KLEISER

———o———

More to be pitied than the unlearned person who cannot appreciate intellectual conversation is the learned person who cannot enjoy nonsense.

———o———

A humorist is a man who feels bad but who feels good about it.

———o———

There are very few good judges of humor, and they don't agree.

"JOSH BILLINGS" (HENRY WHEELER SHAW)

———o———

Humor makes the educated mind a safer mind.

WALTER LIPPMANN

———o———

A man, fond of practical jokes, late one night sent his friend a telegram out of a clear sky, collect which read: "I am perfectly well."
A week later the joker received a heavy parcel, collect, on which he had to pay considerable charges. On opening it, he found a big block of concrete on which was pasted this message:
"This is the weight your telegram lifted from my mind."

———o———

Mirth cannot move a soul in agony.

WILLIAM SHAKESPEARE

Hurry

Someone has said that modern life can be spelled in three words, "Hurry, worry, bury." One thinks of a senator who was asked, as he rushed breathlessly along, "What do you think of the world crisis?"

He replied, "Don't bother me; I'm in a hurry to make a radio speech. A crisis like this is no time to think!"

The Bible has as much to say about resting as about working. Our Lord would have us come apart and rest awhile, for if we don't we shall come apart!

VANCE HAVNER

———o———

I will not hurry through this day.
Lord, I will listen by the way
To humming bees and singing birds,
To murmuring trees and friendly words;
And for the moments in between
Seek glimpses of thy great unseen.

I will not hurry through this day,
I will take time to think and pray;
I will look up into the sky
Where fleecy clouds and swallows fly;
And somewhere in the day, maybe
I will catch whispers, Lord, from Thee.

ROBERT SPAULDING CUSHMAN

———o———

No man who is in a hurry is quite civilized.

WILL DURANT

———o———

Though I am always in haste, I am never in a hurry.

JOHN WESLEY

———o———

Christ was never in a hurry. There was no rushing forward, no anticipating, no fretting over what might be. Each day's duties were done as every day brought them, and the rest was left with God.

MARY SLESSOR

———o———

To go slowly and to live a long time are two brothers.

Dutch Proverb

———o———

Make haste slowly.

AUGUSTUS CAESAR

———o———

Ease and speed in doing a thing do not give the work lasting solidity or exactness of beauty.

PLUTARCH

Hurt

They say the world is round, and yet,
   it must be square;
So many little hurts we get from corners here and there.
We flatter those we scarcely know, we
   please the fleeting guest,
And deal full many a thoughtless blow to those we love the best.

WALTER LOG

———o———

Sometimes we are helped by being hurt. A skilled physician about to perform a delicate operation upon the ear said reassuringly, "I may hurt you, but I will not injure you." How often the Great Physician speaks to us the same message if we would only listen! Richer life, more abundant health for every child of His — that is His only purpose. Why defeat that purpose?

The Sunday School Times

Husband

Often, you can make him a good husband by making him a good wife.

Times, Holbrook, Massachusetts

———o———

Husband: A bachelor who became a yes-man.

———o———

The average husband is one who lays down the law to his wife and then accepts all the amendments.

———o———

A husband is a man who lost his liberty in the pursuit of happiness.

———o———

Good husband: One who feels in his pockets every time he passes a mailbox.

———o———

Husband: A curious creature who buys his football tickets in June and his wife's Christmas present on December 24.

Hypocrisy

Hypocrisy Versus Life

Ye call Me Master and obey Me not;
Ye call Me Light and see Me not;
Ye call Me Way and walk not;

Ye call Me Life and desire Me not;
Ye call Me Wise and follow Me not;
Ye call Me Fair and love Me not;
Ye call Me Rich and ask Me not;
Ye call Me Eternal and seek Me not;
Ye call Me Gracious and trust Me not;
Ye call Me Mighty and honor Me not;
Ye call Me Just and fear Me not;
If I condemn you blame Me not!

———o———

Hypocrisy is the homage that vice pays to virtue.

FRANCOIS DUC DE LA ROCHEFOUCAULD

———o———

Our Father

There is one thing more pitiable, almost worse, than even cold, black, miserable atheism:

To kneel down and say, "Our Father," and then to get up and live an orphaned life.

To stand and say, "I believe in God the Father Almighty," and then to go fretting and fearing.

Saying with a thousand tongues, "I believe in the love of God!" — but it stoppeth short at the stars.

To say, "I believe in the providence of God!" — but it is limited to the saints in Scripture.

To say, "I believe that the Lord reigneth" — only with reference to some far-off time with which we have nothing to do.

That is more insulting to our Heavenly Father, more harmful to the world, more cheating to ourselves, than to have no God at all.

MARK GUY PEARSE

———o———

For neither man nor angel can discern
Hypocrisy, the only evil that walks
Invisible, except to God alone.

JOHN MILTON, *Paradise Lost, Book III*

———o———

The man who says he is kept away from religion by hypocrites is not influenced by them in any other area of life.

Business is full of them, but if he sees a chance at making money he does not stop for that.

Society is crowded with them, and yet he never thinks of becoming a hermit.

Married life is full of them, but that doesn't make him remain a bachelor.

Hell is full of them, and yet he doesn't do a thing to keep himself from going there.

He wants to have you think that he is trying to avoid the society of hypocrites, and yet he takes not a single step toward Heaven, the one place where no hypocrites go!

Today

Idea, Ideas

A mind, once stretched by a great idea, can never return to its original dimensions.

OLIVER WENDELL HOLMES

———o———

Man is always ready to die for an idea, provided that idea is not quite clear to him.

———o———

I like people who have ideas and talk about them. Deliver me from the sphinxes of the world. A simple "yes" or "no" leaves me feeling flat and depressed. One of the nicest things in life is communicating with fellow creatures. There's just no substitute for good talk. There are three levels of conversation: the lowest is about other people, the second concerns events, and the highest is about ideas.

Journal, Louisville, Mississippi

———o———

Good ideas are subjected to solitary confinement when they get into an empty head.

GENTRY SERENADER

The university is not engaged in making ideas safe for students; it is engaged in making students safe for ideas.

KERR

———o———

We always think a man's ideas are good if they coincide with ours.

———o———

The man with an idea has ever changed the face of the world.

———o———

Nothing is as powerful as an idea whose time has come.

VICTOR HUGO

———o———

Ideas control the world.

JAMES A. GARFIELD

———o———

Man is a dispenser of words and a generator of ideas.

ERNEST REEVES

Ideals

Some people are more concerned about "deals" than ideals.

———o———

To live with a high ideal is a successful life. It is not what one does, but what one tries to do, that makes the soul strong and fit for a noble career.

E. P. TENNEY

———o———

He who dedicates his life to a great ideal, himself becomes great.

GILL R. WILSON

———o———

Ideals are like tuning forks: sound them often to bring your life up to standard pitch.

S. D. GORDON

———o———

Our ideals are our better selves.

AMOS BRONSON ALCOTT

———o———

Ideals are worthless unless we act on them.

———o———

The ideal man is the man who knows how to get what he ought to want.

EDWARD SHEFFIELD BRIGHTMAN

Idle

To be idle and to be poor have always been reproaches, and therefore every man endeavors with his utmost care to hide his poverty from others, and his idleness from himself.

SAMUEL JOHNSON

———o———

Too much idleness, I have observed, fills up a man's time much more completely, and leaves him less his own master, than any sort of employment whatsoever.

EDMUND BURKE

———o———

Idleness is leisure gone to seed.

ELI J. SCHLEIFER

———o———

Absence of occupation is not a rest;
A mind quite vacant is a mind distressed.

WILLIAM COWPER, *Retirement*

———o———

Idleness travels so slowly that poverty soon overtakes it.

———o———

Idleness is the parent of shame and poverty.

———o———

Idleness rusts the mind.

———o———

In works of labor, or of skill,
I would be busy too,
For Satan finds some mischief still
For idle hands to do.

ISAAC WATTS

Ignore, Ignorance

The only thing more expensive than education is ignorance.

———o———

Little can give you peace of mind like ignorance.

Independent-Review, Aztec, New Mexico

The person who doesn't know his own mind hasn't missed a thing.

———o———

Sometimes it would be better to be unborn than untaught or wrongly taught, for ignorance is the root of about every kind of misfortune that a person falls heir to.

———o———

Ignorance is a voluntary misfortune.

NICHOLAS LING

———o———

A man's ignorance is as much his private property, and as precious in his own eyes, as his family Bible.

OLIVER WENDELL HOLMES

———o———

What you don't know won't hurt you, but it may make you look pretty stupid.

———o———

Everyone is ignorant, only on different subjects.

WILL ROGERS

———o———

Ignorance of wrongdoing does not make one innocent for having done wrong.

———o———

If thou art wise, thou knowest thine own ignorance; and thou art ignorant if thou knowest not thyself.

MARTIN LUTHER

———o———

He that voluntarily continues to ignorance, is guilty of all the crimes which ignorance produces.

SAMUEL JOHNSON

———o———

Ignorance is not innocence but sin.

ROBERT BROWNING

———o———

The fool is happy that he knows no more.

ALEXANDER POPE,
Essay on Man, Epistle II

Illness

When Ma Is Sick

When Ma is sick, she pegs away,
She's quiet though, not much to say.
She goes right on adoin' things,
An' sometimes laughs, or even sings.
She says she don't feel extry well,
But then it's just a kind of spell.
She'll be all right tomorrow sure,
A good old sleep will be the cure.
An' Pa he sniffs, an' makes no kick,
For women folks is always sick.
And Ma she smiles, let's on she's glad;
When Ma is sick, it ain't so bad.

AUTHOR UNKNOWN

———o———

When Pa Is Sick

When Pa is sick, he's scared to death,
An' Ma and us just holds our breath.
He crawls in bed, and puffs and grunts
An' does all kinds of crazy stunts.
He wants "Doc" at once, an' mighty quick,
For when Pa's ill, he's awful sick.
He gasps an' groans, an' sort o' sighs,
He talks so queer, an' rolls his eyes.
Ma jumps an' runs, an' all of us,
Are plum worn out by all his fuss,
An' peace an' joy is mighty skeerce.
When Pa is sick, it's somethin' fierce.

AUTHOR UNKNOWN

———o———

Don't let us make imaginary ills when we know we have so many real ones to encounter.

OLIVER GOLDSMITH

———o———

For a sick man the world begins at his pillow and ends at the foot of his bed.

HONORÉ DE BALZAC

———o———

A little girl whose father was a minister was very sick. She asked to see her daddy but her mother explained that he was busy preparing his sermon.

A short time later the child asked a second time to see her daddy. She got the same answer.

After asking a third time and getting the same answer she said, "I'm a sick woman and I want to see my minister!"

———o———

Someone asked the church decorator what she did with the flowers after the services. She replied innocently,

"Oh, we take them to the people who are sick after the sermon."

———o———

Diseases enter by the mouth, misfortunes issue from it.

———o———

I'm so full of penicillin that if I sneeze in here I'm sure going to cure somebody.

———o———

The Presbyterian minister had been summoned to the bedside of a Methodist woman who was very ill. As he went up the walk, he met the little daughter and said to her, "I am very glad your mother remembered me in her illness. Is your minister out of town?"

"No," answered the child. "He's at home, but we thought it might be something contagious and we didn't want to expose him to it."

Imagination

Rife Imagination

Let tomorrow take care of tomorrow;
  Leave things of the future to fate;
What's the use to anticipate sorrow?
  Life's troubles come never too late.
If to hope overmuch be an error, 'tis
  One that the wise have preferred;
And how often have hearts been in terror
  Of evils that never occurred!

Let tomorrow take care of tomorrow;
  Short and dark as our life may appear,
We may make it still darker by sorrow,
  Still shorter by folly and fear!
Half our troubles are half our invention
  And often from blessings conferred
Have we shrunk, in the wild apprehension
  Of evils that never occurred.
                                    CHARLES SWAIN

———o———

It is wrong for any adult to impair the imagination of a child.

———o———

Several years ago when I was teaching kindergarten in a school for blind children, five-year-old John (who had sufficient sight to recognize color but not form) was finger-painting with bright red paint. When both of his hands were completely covered with the paint, he cupped them, turned to me and said:

"Look at my hands! They look as if they were . . ."

As he paused in the middle of his thought, I half expected him to say that they looked as if they were covered with blood. Instead he said: ". . . full of red roses!"

His charming imagination made such an impression on me that countless times since then, his lesson has helped me to "think beauty" and then see beauty when something unpleasant, either real or imagined, is more obvious. How much I owe to Johnny.
    FLORENCE S. ATKINSON in *Guideposts*

———o———

When I was a beggarly boy,
  And lived in a cellar damp,
I had not a friend nor a toy,
  But I had Aladdin's lamp;

When I could not sleep for cold
  I had fire enough in my brain,
And builded with roofs of gold
  My beautiful castles in Spain.
    JAMES RUSSELL LOWELL, *Aladdin*

———o———

Love is the triumph of imagination over intelligence.
                                    H. L. MENCKEN

Imitate

It has been well said, "Everyone is born an original and dies a copy."
                            Decision Magazine

———o———

Little boy to his sister: "Come on, let's play soldiers. I'll be a general, you be my secretary, and I'll dictate my memoirs."

    L'Orient, Beirut, Lebanon

———o———

Small boy in barber's chair: "I want my hair cut like daddy's – with a round hole on top."

The class was having a composition lesson. The teacher instructed: "Do not imitate what other people write. Simply be yourself and write what is in you."

Following this advice, Bobby turned in the following composition:

"We should not imitate others. We should write what is in us. In me there are my stomach, heart, liver, two apples, one piece of pie, a lemon drop, and my lunch."

Impossible

The actual is limited,
The impossible is immense.

ALPHONSE DE LAMARTINE

———o———

You do not test the resources of God until you try the impossible.

F. B. MEYER

———o———

Nothing is impossible to the man who doesn't have to do it himself.

———o———

God does not demand impossibilities.

ST. AUGUSTINE

———o———

God raises the level of the impossible.

CORRIE TEN BOOM

———o———

Nothing is impossible to a faithful and willing heart.

———o———

Nothing is impossible to a valiant heart.

Motto of JEANNE D'ALBERT, *mother of Henry IV*

———o———

You cannot have faith and tension at the same time.

GANDHI

———o———

What are Christians put into the world for except to do the impossible in the strength of God?

Ten Cannots

You cannot bring about prosperity by discouraging thrift.

You cannot help small men by tearing down big men.

You cannot strengthen the weak by weakening the strong.

You cannot lift the wage earner by pulling down the wage payer.

You cannot help the poor man by destroying the rich.

You cannot keep out of trouble by spending more than your income.

You cannot further the brotherhood of man by inciting class hatred.

You cannot establish security on borrowed money.

You cannot build character and courage by taking away man's initiative and independence.

You cannot help men permanently by doing for them what they could and should do for themselves.

ABRAHAM LINCOLN

———o———

A little boy was told to sit down in front.

"I can't," he replied. "I'm not made that way."

———o———

To the timid and hesitating everything is impossible because it seems so.

JOHN SCOTT

———o———

He who can see the invisible can do the impossible.

———o———

Few things are impossible to diligence and skill.

SAMUEL JOHNSON, *Rasselas*

———o———

Patient industry overcomes impossibilities.

BALTASAR GRACIÀN

Improve

People seldom improve when they have no other model but themselves to copy after.

OLIVER GOLDSMITH

The human race seems to have gone to a lot of trouble to improve everything but people.

———o———

Everyone can do something to make the world better. He can at least improve himself!

———o———

God has no self-improvement course for the flesh.

———o———

There is one person whom it is my duty to make good, and that is myself.

ROBERT LOUIS STEVENSON

———o———

If you don't keep becoming better, you will stop being good.

———o———

The improvement of the mind improves the heart and corrects the understanding.

AGATHON

———o———

Everything can be improved.

C. W. BARRON

Income

The reason many people don't live within their incomes is that they don't consider that living.

———o———

Our incomes should be like our shoes: if too small, they will gall and pinch us, but if too large they will cause us to stumble and to trip.

CHARLES CALEB COLTON

———o———

It is better to have a permanent income than to be fascinating.

OSCAR WILDE

———o———

If you live within your income you'll be without many things, the most important of which is worry.

WILLIAM WARD AYER

Individual

The modern world began with Christ's discovery of the individual.

JOHN MACMURRAY

———o———

Jesus Christ never met an unimportant person. That is why God sent His Son to die for us. If someone dies for you, you must be important.

DR. M. C. CLEVELAND

———o———

The worker is far more important to our Lord than the work.

MRS. CHARLES E. COWMAN

———o———

Everything of importance in the world was begun by one man or one woman.

CHANNING POLLOCK

———o———

Every great man is unique.

RALPH WALDO EMERSON

———o———

I fear uniformity. You cannot manufacture great men any more than you can manufacture gold.

JOHN RUSKIN

Industry

A. H. Smith, former president of the New York Central Railroad once defined his industry this way: "A railway is 95 percent man and 5 percent iron."

———o———

Poverty cannot overtake industry.

Japanese Proverb

———o———

The tree of industry bears golden fruit.

Japanese Proverb

———o———

God commends us to the ceaseless industry of the ant for noiseless eloquence.

———o———

The great end of all human industry is the attainment of happiness.

DAVID HUME

Andrew Carnegie was once asked which he considered to be the most important factor in industry: labor, capital, or brains? The canny Scot replied with a merry twinkle in his eye, "Which is the most important leg of a three-legged stool?"

Infidel

Replying to an infidel who had mailed him some literature, one Christian gave the following answer:
"My Dear Sir,
If you have anything better than the Sermon on the Mount, the story of the Prodigal Son; or if you have any code of morals superior to the Ten Commandments; if you can supply anything that will throw more light on the future and reveal to me a Father more merciful and kind than the New Testament does, please send it along."
There was no answer.

———o———

An infidel had just completed an eloquent address to a large audience. "And now, does anyone have any questions?" he asked.
An old man who had been a drunkard most of his life, but who had recently become a Christian, shuffled down the aisle and ascended the platform. Taking an orange from his pocket, he began to peel it.
The lecturer asked him to state his question, but the old man just went on — peeling his orange and eating it section by section.
Finally, wiping his hands on his pocket handkerchief, the old man turned to the lecturer and said: "No, here's my question. Can you tell me, was that orange sour or sweet?"
"Idiot!" retorted the lecturer in anger. "How do I know? I never tasted it!" To which the elderly man replied: "And how can you know anything about Christ, if you have never tasted Him?"

Influence

(See also Example)

Influence is the exhalation of character.

WILLIAM MACKERGO TAYLOR

We can foretell what our children will believe — what they will say and do, what they will praise and condemn — just by examining what is being planted in their minds by means of books, periodicals, television and radio.

FRANK C. LAUBACH

———o———

The proper time to influence the character of a child is about a hundred years before he is born.

WILLIAM RALPH INGE

———o———

A Father's Influence

An incident which impressed me deeply then and its impress has never faded happened when I was in the vicinity of ten years old. My father had told me to go to bed. I honestly thought he meant when I had finished a quite legitimate and proper occupation, for I was hobnobbing with a little crony of my age who had come to the house with an older person.
I remained talking with him. My father, later passing through the room and finding that I had not obeyed him, spoke with that directness of which he was capable, called brusqueness by some, and ordered me to bed at once. There was no standing on the order of my going after this.
I retreated, frightened and in tears, for such a tone of voice was a new experience in my life. I hurried to bed, but before I had time to fall asleep, he was at my bedside, kneeling and asking my forgiveness for the harsh way in which he had spoken to me, the tears falling down over his rugged, bearded face.
That was nearly half a century ago, but I would exchange any memory of life before I would surrender that. For all unknowing he was laying for me the consciousness of the Fatherhood of God, and the love of God. No sermon on the prodigal's father, and no words on the love of God have cast quite such a light as his huge figure kneeling in the twilight by my bed, asking the forgiveness of a child.

PAUL DWIGHT MOODY

"Who influenced you most toward Christ?" a friend once asked Henry Ward Beecher. "Was it some college professor, some great preacher, or a faithful Sunday School teacher?"

Beecher replied, "I doubt if the man knew at the time what an influence he was. He used to lie on his cot and read the New Testament, hardly aware that I was in the room. Then he'd talk to himself about what he read. Sometimes he would smile as he read. I never saw the Bible enjoyed like that. It challenged me more than any other thing."

"But you didn't tell me who this great man was."

"Oh, I'm sorry — that man was Charles Smith, a hired man on my father's farm."

———o———

SOME PARENTS SAY: "We will not influence our children in making choices and decisions in matters of religion!"
WHY NOT?
The ads will!
The press will!
The radio will!
The movies will!
The TV will!
Their neighbors will!
Their business will!
Their politicians will!
We can use our influence over flowers, vegetables, cattle.
Shall we ignore our children?

———o———

The length and breadth of our influence upon others depends upon the depth of our concern for others.

———o———

Had not Susannah Wesley been the mother of John Wesley, it is not likely that John Wesley would have been the founder of Methodism.

Susannah Wesley was the mother of John and Charles and seventeen other children. She was beautiful, energetic, devout. She knew Greek, Latin, French and theology.

In counsel to John she said, "Take this rule: Whatever weakens your reason, impairs the tenderness of your conscience, obscures your sense of God, or takes off the relish of spiritual things — in short, whatever increases the strength and authority of your body over your mind, that thing is sin so you, however innocent it may be in itself."

This Christian mother's counsel to her son John needs the attention of every mother and father and child today. If more parents would be Christian in character as Mrs. Wesley was, there would be less sabotaging of the children's lives with parental delinquency.

Gospel Banner

———o———

No man's actions stop with himself.

———o———

May every soul that touches mine,
Be it the slightest contact,
Get therefrom some good . . .
Some little grace . . . one kindly thought,
One aspiration yet unfelt,
One bit of courage from the darkening sky;
One gleam of faith
To brave the thickening ills of life;
One glimpse of brighter skies
Beyond the gathering mists
To make this life worth while.
GEORGE ELIOT (MARY ANN EVANS)

———o———

You cannot antagonize and influence at the same time.
JOHN KNOX

———o———

A Child Learns

If a child lives with hostility,
He learns to fight.
If a child lives with criticism,
He learns to condemn.
If a child lives with fear,
He learns to be apprehensive.
If a child lives with jealousy,
He learns to hate.
If a child lives with self-pity,
He learns to be sorry for himself.
If a child lives with encouragement,
He learns self-confidence and integrity.
If a child lives with praise,
He learns to be appreciative.

If a child lives with acceptance,
He learns to love.
If a child lives with approval,
He learns to like himself.
If a child lives with fairness,
He learns justice.
If a child lives with honesty,
He learns what truth is.
If a child lives with friendliness,
He learns that the world is a nice
place in which to live.

AUTHOR UNKNOWN

Ingratitude

I refuse to think that there is as much
ingratitude in the world as is commonly maintained. A great deal of water
is flowing underground which never
comes up as a spring.

ALBERT SCHWEITZER

———o———

Next to ingratitude, the most painful thing to bear is gratitude.

HENRY WARD BEECHER

———o———

A man is very apt to complain of
the ingratitude of those who have risen
far above him.

SAMUEL JOHNSON

Instruction

Instruction

Shape them, mold them, but leave
them whole,
Children with mind and thought and
soul.
Free to progress, inquire and soar
Far from the classroom's dusty core.

Light their genius! Give it wings
To overcome trite, mundane things.
Alert for the future's needs they rise
Children of God! His greatest prize.

BETH M. APPLEGATE in *This Day*

———o———

When you don't succeed after you've
tried again, you might read the instructions if they are still around.

Herald, Meeker, Oklahoma

———o———

Instruction enlarges the natural powers of the mind.

HORACE

The wise are instructed by reason;
ordinary minds, by experience; the
stupid, by necessity; and brutes by in-
stincts.

MARCUS TULLIUS CICERO

Integrity

Men Of Integrity

God give us men in times like these
With hope and courage strong;
Men like Daniel in days of old
Who'll stand against the wrong.

God give us men in times like these
With hearts and purpose true,
Who'll stand for right with all their
might
Despite what others do.

God give us men who will not swerve
From all that's fair and just,
With faith in Thee through war or
peace,
A steadfast perfect trust.

God give us men with vision keen,
Men of integrity,
Men who will put their hand in Thine,
Lead with humility.

War Cry

———o———

There is no better test for a man's
ultimate integrity than his behavior
when he is wrong.

———o———

Integrity without knowledge is weak
and useless.

Intellect, Intelligence

The intellect may acquire much information about how to live, but it is
the province of the will to make good.

———o———

It would be better to abandon our
over-rapid development of the intellect and to aim rather at training the
heart and the affections.

VICTOR HUGO

———o———

If we encounter a man of rare intellect, we should ask him what books
he reads.

RALPH WALDO EMERSON

Intelligence consists in recognizing opportunity.

Chinese Proverb

———o———

Your stock of intelligence is not so much what you can remember as what you can forget.

———o———

There are four aspects to intelligence: thinking, reflection, projection, and application.

THOMAS BLANDI

Intentions

Among the most commonly used paving materials in this country are concrete, macadam and good intentions.

FRANKLIN P. JONES

———o———

Unless good intentions are followed by deeds, they avail nothing.

———o———

Well intentioned persons who have never succeeded in managing their private affairs are ready to take over the destinies of worlds.

MANLY HALL

Interest

Few kindnesses are as warmly welcomed as sincere, objective interest.

NORMAN G. SHIDLE

———o———

It is easy to lose interest in a church in which you have nothing invested.

———o———

A pastor, calling in the luxurious office of one of his members who was a top executive, noticed that all of the man's drawers were labeled. He was not surprised. He knew the man had efficient habits. Left alone in the office for awhile, however, he grew curious. What would a man like this keep in his top drawer? He looked. The top drawer bore just one word: CHURCH.

Every man has his "top drawer" interest. The apostle Paul said: "For me to live is Christ." Jesus Himself taught His believers to "Seek . . . first the kingdom of God and His righteousness." Put Him first and you will rate your church high too. Higher than anything measurable by dollars and cents.

Today

———o———

It is the personal that interests mankind, that fires their imagination, and wins their hearts.

BENJAMIN DISRAELI

Intuition

Intuition is what enables a woman to contradict her husband before he says anything.

———o———

Let your intuitive powers, when developed, help you get the things in life you want.

HAROLD SHERMAN

———o———

All great men are gifted with intuition. They know without reasoning or analysis what they need to know.

Invitation

On church bulletin board: "You aren't too bad to come in. You aren't too good to stay out."

LOWELL NUSSBAUM in *Indianapolis Star*

———o———

The world says: "Come to me and I will fail you."
The flesh says: "Come to me and I will destroy you."
Christ says: "Come to Me and I will give you rest."

ST. BERNARD of Clairvaux

J

Jealousy

It is jealousy's peculiar nature,
To swell small things to great, nay, out
of nought,
To conjure much; and then to lose its
reason
Amid the hideous phantoms it has
formed.

EDWARD YOUNG, The Revenge

———o———

O jealousy thou magnifier of trifles!

JOHANN CHRISTOPH FRIEDRICH VON SCHILLER

———o———

Jealousy lives upon suspicion, and
it turns into fury or it ends as soon as
we pass from suspicion to certainty.

FRANÇOIS DUC DE LA ROCHEFOUCAULD
— Maxim 32

———o———

Jealousy dislikes the world to know
it.

LORD BYRON

———o———

Jealousy is a horse which the devil
likes to ride.

Job

The dreaded job takes more time
than the done job.

———o———

A veteran missionary to China was
approached by an American business-
man to accept a position with his corporation.
"You know the language and the culture of China very well," the business
executive said, "and for this knowledge
we will be happy to pay you well.
Let's begin with say — $10,000?"
"No," replied the missionary quickly.
"What about $15,000?" asked the ex-
ecutive.
Once more the missionary kindly
but firmly refused. Finally the offer
reached its ultimate — $25,000. But
still the missionary shook his head neg-
atively.

"Well, just how much would it take
to get you?" the executive asked in
desperation.
"Oh," replied the missionary, "your
first offer was more than enough. The
salary is fine, but your job is too small.
I have more important work to do."

———o———

It's a mistake to stop looking for
work as soon as you've landed a job.

———o———

One of life's hardest jobs is to keep
up the easy payments.

———o———

Doing nothing is the most tiresome
job in the world because you can't
quit and rest.

———o———

There is only one job in which you
can start at the top — and that's digging a hole.

Journey

A journey of a thousand steps begins with one.

Chinese Proverb

———o———

Good company in a journey makes
the way to seem the shorter.

Italian Proverb

———o———

We Go This Way But Once

We go this way but once, O heart of
mine,
So why not make the journey well
worthwhile,
Giving to those who travel on with us
A helping hand, a word of cheer, a
smile?

We go this way but once. Ah! never
more
Can we go back along the selfsame
way,
To get more out of life, undo the
wrongs,

Or speak love's words we knew, but
did not say.

We go this way but once. Then, let
us make
The road we travel blossomy and sweet
With helpful, kindly deeds and tender words,
Smoothing the path of bruised and
stumbling feet.

AUTHOR UNKNOWN

Joy

All who joy would win
Must share it, — happiness was born
a twin.

LORD BYRON, *Don Juan*

———o———

With trumpets and sound of the cornet
Be joyful before Him, the King.
Let the oceans burst forth with great
gladness,
The hills with His happiness ring.

NAOMI A. DALLAS

———o———

Joy is not gush; joy is not jolliness.
Joy is just perfect acquiescence in
God's will because the soul delights
itself in God Himself.

HAMMER WILLIAM WEBB-PEPLOE

———o———

Science cannot restore the joy of
life and help us laugh again. Joy and
laughter are the products of faith.
Men can laugh only when they believe.

GERALD KENNEDY

———o———

Joy is the standard that flies on the
battlements of the heart when the King
is in residence.

R. LEONARD SMALL

———o———

Jesus Christ can put joy into the joy-
less work of the twentieth century.

BERNARD RAMM

———o———

Great joy is only earned by great
exertion.

JOHANN WOLFGANG VON GOETHE

Without kindness there can be no
true joy.

THOMAS CARLYLE

———o———

Grief can take care of itself; but to
get the full value of joy you must have
somebody to divide it with.

MARK TWAIN

———o———

There is sweet joy in feeling that
God knows all and notwithstanding,
loves us still.

J. HUDSON TAYLOR

———o———

If you will but live up to your
privileges, you can rejoice with unspeakable joy.

———o———

The reflections on a day well spent
furnishes us with joys more pleasing
than ten thousand triumphs.

THOMAS À KEMPIS

———o———

Joy comes, grief goes, we know not
how.

JAMES RUSSELL LOWELL

Judge, Judgment

Great Spirit, help me never to judge
another until I have walked in his
moccasins for two weeks.

Sioux Indian Prayer

———o———

There is no fear of judgment for the
man who judges himself according to
the Word of God.

HOWARD G. HENDRICKS

———o———

We aren't judged by what we want
to do and can't, but by what we ought
to do and don't.

———o———

The habit of judging and condemn-
ing others can be a more serious blem-
ish than the things we so glibly point
out as others' faults.

———o———

God will judge us for what we retain.

J. HUDSON TAYLOR

Refuse to believe everything you hear, and you will rarely be embarrassed by your bad judgment.

———o———

We judge ourselves by what we feel capable of doing; others judge us by what we have done.

HENRY WADSWORTH LONGFELLOW

———o———

Judge of a tree from its fruit, not from its leaves.

PHAEDRUS

———o———

Be slow to judge but quick to forgive.

———o———

A fox should not be of the jury at a goose's trial.

THOMAS FULLER

———o———

The more one judges, the less one loves.

HONORÉ DE BALZAC

———o———

Be occupied with improving yourself and you will have little time to criticize and judge others.

———o———

Never judge a man's actions until you know his motives.

———o———

Others applaud your good judgment when you agree with them.

———o———

Better err on the side of charity than to misjudge anyone.

Just, Justice

Be just before you're generous.

RICHARD BRINSLEY SHERIDAN

Justice is the great interest of man on earth.

DANIEL WEBSTER

———o———

A man's vanity tells him what is honor, a man's conscience what is justice.

WALTER SAVAGE LANDOR

———o———

Justice discards party, friendship, and kindred, and is therefore, represented as blind.

JOSEPH ADDISON

———o———

Nothing can be honorable where justice is absent.

MARCUS TULLIUS CICERO

———o———

There is no virtue so truly great and godlike as justice.

JOSEPH ADDISON

Juvenile

Paul's exhortation to juveniles is timely: "To be subject to principalities and powers to obey magistrates, to be ready to every good work."

———o———

Perhaps the best antidote to juvenile delinquency is to stop trying to understand it, justify it, rationalize it; get old-fashioned and just punish it.

———o———

Juvenile delinquency is proving that some parents just are not getting at the seat of the problem.

KENNETH J. SHIVELY

K

Kind, Kindness

You have not lived a perfect day, even though you have earned your money, unless you have done something for someone who will never be able to repay you.

You cannot do a kindness too soon, because you never know how soon it will be too late.

Every right implies a responsibility, every opportunity an obligation, every possession a duty.

You'll never get hurt by the things you didn't say.

There are four things that will never come back: the spoken word, the sped arrow, the past life, the neglected opportunity.

From the Scrap Book of JOAN WINCHELL

————o————

If We Only Knew

If we only knew that the smiles we see
Often hide the tears that would fain be free,
Would we not more tender and loving be,
If we only knew?

If we only knew that the words we say
Oft may drive the peace from some heart away,
Would we speak those words in the selfsame way,
If we only knew?

If we only knew that some weary heart
Has been burdened more by our thoughtless art,
Would we cause the tears from those eyes to start,
If we only knew?

If we only knew, as we onward go,
Many things that here we can never know,
For more patient love we would often show,
If we only knew.

AUTHOR UNKNOWN

Let Me Be A Little Kinder

Let me be a little kinder,
Let me be a little blinder
To the faults of those about me;
Let me praise a little more;
Let me be, when I am weary,
Just a little bit more cheery;
Let me serve a little better
Those that I am striving for.

Let me be a little braver
When temptation bids we waver;
Let me strive a little harder
To be all that I should be;
Let me be a little meeker
With the brother that is weaker;
Let me think more of my neighbor
And a little less of me.

AUTHOR UNKNOWN

————o————

Kindness, if you show it to others, will radiate from you like the warmth of the sun over the hill tops.

————o————

Kindness, and courtesy, are infectious.

————o————

Guard within yourself that treasure, kindness. Know how to give without hesitation, how to lose without regret and how to acquire without meanness. Know how to replace in your heart by the happiness of those you love, the happiness that may be wanting to yourself.

GEORGE SAND

————o————

Seek to cultivate a buoyant, joyous sense of the crowded kindness of God in your daily life.

ALEXANDER MACLAREN

————o————

Shall we make a new rule of life . . . always to try to be a little kinder than is necessary.

SIR JAMES MATTHEW BARRIE,
The Little White Bird

The Day's Result

Is anybody happier because you passed
his way?
Does anyone remember that you spoke
to him today?
The day is almost over and its toiling
time is through;
Is there anyone to utter now a kindly
word of you?
Did you give a cheerful greeting to
the friend who came along,
Or a churlish sort of "Howdy"; then
vanish in the throng?
Were you selfish, pure and simple, as
you rushed along your way,
Or is someone mighty grateful for a
deed you did today?
Can you say tonight, in parting with
the day that's slipping fast,
That you helped a single brother of
the many that you passed?
Is a single heart rejoicing over what
you did or said?
Does the man whose hopes were fading now with courage look ahead?
Did you waste the day or lose it, was
it well or poorly spent?
Did you leave a trail of kindness, or a
scar of discontent?
As you close your eyes in slumber, do
you think that God would say,
"You have earned one more tomorrow
by the work you did today?"

                              AUTHOR UNKNOWN

———o———

Small kindnesses, small courtesies,
small considerations, habitually practiced in our social intercourse, give a
greater charm to the character than
the display of great talent and accomplishments.

                              MARY ANN KELTY

———o———

Kindness is a hard thing to give
away. It keeps coming back to the
giver.

                              RALPH SCOTT

———o———

Kindness is the kingpin of success
in life; it is the prime factor in overcoming friction and making the human
machinery run smoothly.

                              ANDREW CHAPMAN

I expect to pass through life but
once. If therefore, there be any kindness I can show, or any good thing I
can do to any fellow-being, let me
do it now, and not defer or neglect it,
as I shall not pass this way again.

                              WILLIAM PENN

———o———

Kindness is a language which the
deaf can hear and the blind can read.

                              MARK TWAIN

———o———

The best portion of a good man's life,
His little, nameless, unremembered
acts
Of kindness and of love.

                              WILLIAM WORDSWORTH, Tintern Abbey

———o———

A little word in kindness spoken,
A motion or a tear,
Has often healed a heart that's broken,
And made a friend sincere.

                              AUTHOR UNKNOWN

———o———

If you are not kind, you are the
wrong kind.

Kindergarten

Young Keith Flaniken reported
graphically on his first day at kindergarten:
"Well," he told his grandmother,
"we sang a while. Then we cried a
while. Then we sang a while."

                              Glendale News Press

———o———

The world is a great university.
From the cradle to the grave we are
always in God's great kindergarten,
where everything is trying to teach us
its lesson.

                              O. S. MARDEN

———o———

A kindergarten teacher is a smart
girl who knows how to make little
things count.

———o———

The five most important questions a
kindergarten child asks are:

1. Why?
2. Why?

3. Why?
4. Why?
5. Why?

———o———

A child's explanation of the kindergarten: "A garden full of children."

King, Kingdom

The king reigns but does not govern.

———o———

Kings are like stars — they rise and set,
they have
The worship of the world, but no repose.

PERCY BYSSHE SHELLEY, *Hellas*

———o———

There is no king who has not had a slave among his ancestors, and no slave who has not had a king among his.

HELEN KELLER

———o———

Though invisible, the kingdom of heaven is a reality among men.

———o———

Never does man enter the kingdom of heaven except as God, by the miracle of the new birth, make him a member of that kingdom.

Knowledge

Knowledge is awareness that fire will burn; wisdom is remembrance of the blister.

———o———

The only thing worse than a man who knows it all is a woman who hears it all.

———o———

Knowledge comes, but wisdom lingers.

ALFRED LORD TENNYSON, *Locksley Hall*

———o———

Some people know a lot more when you try to tell them something than when you ask them something.

———o———

Knowledge is of two kinds: we know a subject ourselves, or we know where we can find information upon it.

SAMUEL JOHNSON,
Boswell's *Life of Dr. Johnson*

None so dumb as he who knows all the facts of life and none of the paradoxes.

DON HEROLD

———o———

The Tree of Knowledge

The
Bible con-
tains 3,566,480
letters, 773,693
words, 31,102 verses,
1,189 chapters and
66 books. The long-
est chapter is the 119th
Psalm, the shortest and
middle chapter the 117th
Psalm. The middle verse is
8th of the 118th Psalm. The
longest name is in the 8th chapter of Isaiah. The word "and" occurs 46,227 times. The word "Je-
hovah" 6,855 times. The 37th chapter of Isaiah and the 19th chapter of
of the 2nd book of Kings are alike.
The longest verse is the 9th of the 8th
chapter of Esther; the shortest verse is
the 35th of the 11th chapter of John.
The 21st verse of the 7th chapter of
Ezra contains all the letters of the
alphabet except the letter J. The
finest piece of reading is
the 26th chapter of Acts.
The name of God is
not mentioned
in the
book of
Esther. The Bible
contains knowledge,
wisdom, holiness and love.

AUTHOR UNKNOWN

———o———

There is no knowledge which is not valuable.

EDMUND BURKE

———o———

If you have knowledge, let others light their candles by it.

THOMAS FULLER

———o———

Know Or Guess

The word "know" is found 200 times in the Bible. "Guess" is not found at all. Jesus said, "These things have I written unto you that believe on the name of the Son of God; that ye may *know* that ye have eternal life, and that ye may believe on the name of the Son of God" (I John 5:13).

———o———

Perhaps the greatest tragedy of man is that his knowledge increases so much faster than his wisdom.

———o———

He who does not increase his knowledge decreases it.

———o———

You do not need the acquirement of fresh knowledge half so much as to put in practice that which you already possess.

FRANCOIS DE SALIGNAC DE LA MOTHE FÉNELON

———o———

I may know, if I wish to know, all that I need to know.

———o———

Mere knowledge, apart from divine love, puffs one up with pride.

———o———

It is important to know what the Bible says before you try to figure out what it means.

———o———

To know is well; to do is better.

L

Labor

This is the gospel of labor, ring it, ye bells of the kirk!
The Lord of Love came down from above, to live with the men who work;
This is the rose that He planted, here is the thorn-curst soil:
Heaven is blest with perfect rest, but the blessing of Earth is toil.

HENRY VAN DYKE,
The Toiling of Felix. III, Envoy

———o———

Genius begins great works; labor alone finishes them.

JOSEPH JOUBERT

———o———

The end of labor is to gain leisure.

———o———

Life has granted nothing to mankind save through great labor.

HORACE

———o———

Toiling — rejoicing — sorrowing,
Onward through life he goes;
Each morning sees some task begin,
Each evening sees it close;
Something attempted, something done,
Has earned a night's repose.

HENRY WADSWORTH LONGFELLOW,
The Village Blacksmith

Language

Profanity is unreasonable and unmanly; it is an offense against God and man.

———o———

Language may be a vehicle of thought, but in some cases it is just an empty wagon.

———o———

Where God is concerned the only language open to us is prayer.

J. H. OLDHAM

———o———

Perhaps of all the creations of man language is the most astonishing.

LYTTON STRACHEY

———o———

Language Test Answers

A metaphor is a surprised simile.
To indicate an omission, insert a carrot.

LAURA A. NELSON in *NEA Journal*

She had cheeks like rose peddles.

SARA THOMASSON in *NEA Journal*

———o———

Language is the dress of thought.

SAMUEL JOHNSON

———o———

The finest command of language is often shown by saying nothing.

ROGER BABSON

Late

Troubled by latecomers to his church, Rowland Hill delivered this prayer: "O Lord, bless those mightily who are in their places; give grace to those who are on their way; and have mercy on those who are getting ready to come and will never arrive."

EDWIN WYLE in *Religious Digest*

———o———

The reason that some people come late is that we don't give them a reason for coming early.

———o———

He gets through too late who goes too fast.

PUBLILIUS SYRUS, *Maxim 767*

Laugh

When you laugh at your boss' joke, it may not prove you have a sense of humor, but it proves you have sense.

———o———

After a hard day's work in serious discussions, Theodore Cuyler and Charles H. Spurgeon went out into the country together for a holiday. They roamed the fields in high spirits like boys let loose from school, chatting and laughing and free from care. Dr. Cuyler had just told a story at which Pastor Spurgeon laughed uproariously. Then suddenly he turned to Dr. Cuyler and exclaimed:
"Theodore, let's kneel down and thank God for laughter!"
And there, on the green carpet of grass, under the trees, two of the world's greatest men knelt and thanked the dear Lord for the bright and joyous gift of laughter.
There is no antagonism between prayer and laughter. One is conclusive of spiritual health, the other of physical health.

The Sunday School World

———o———

A good laugh is sunshine in a house.

WILLIAM MAKEPEACE THACKERAY

Laugh and the world laughs with you. Cry and you simply get wet!

———o———

The fool will laugh though there be nought to laugh at.

MENANDER, *Monosticha 1081*

———o———

Men show their characters in nothing more clearly than in what they think laughable.

JOHANN WOLFGANG VON GOETHE

———o———

Laughter is the best medicine for a long and happy life. He who laughs — lasts.

WILFRED A. PETERSON

Law, Legal

The young lawyer was presenting his first case and wanted to be impressive. He began, "Long ago, before the world was created . . ." when the judge interrupted with: "We are very busy this morning; would you mind starting after the flood?"

———o———

Where law ends, tyranny begins.

WILLIAM PITT

———o———

Laws should be like clothes. They should be made to fit the people they are meant to serve.

CLARENCE DARROW

———o———

I sometimes wish that people would put a little more emphasis on the observance of the law than they do on its enforcement.

CALVIN COOLIDGE

———o———

The laws of God are for our guidance and perfecting.

———o———

The law — It has honored us; we may honor it.

DANIEL WEBSTER, *Speech at the Charleston Bar Dinner* [May 10, 1847]

———o———

Let a man keep the law — any law

— and his way will be strewn with satisfaction.

RALPH WALDO EMERSON

———o———

When a lawyer dies, he lies still.

———o———

While the legalist is severe with others and charitable with himself, the true saint is severe with himself and understanding and loving with others.

MYRON AUGSBURGER
in *From the Mennonite Pulpit*

———o———

The best use of good laws is to teach men to trample bad laws under their feet. One on God's side is a majority.

WENDELL PHILLIPS

Layman

It's The Laymen

Leave it only to the pastors, and soon
the church will die;
Leave it to the womenfolk, the young
will pass it by.
For the church is all that lifts us from
the coarse and selfish mob,
And the church that is to prosper
needs the layman on the job.
Now a layman has his business, and a
layman has his joys,
But he also has the training of all our
girls and boys;
And I wonder how he'd like it if
there were no churches here,
And he had to raise his children in a
godless atmosphere.
It's the church's special function to up-
hold the finer things,
To teach that way of living from
which all that's noble springs;
But the pastor can't do it single-hand-
ed and alone,
For the laymen of the country are the
church's buildingstones.
When you see a church that's empty,
though its doors are open wide,
It's not the church that's dying — it's
the laymen who have died.
It's not just by song or sermon that
the church's work is done,
It's the laymen of the country who for
God must carry on.

EDGAR A. GUEST

Lazy

The lazier a man is, the more he plans to do tomorrow.

Norwegian Proverb

———o———

Some men remind us of blisters. They don't show up until the work is done.

———o———

All good things will come to the other fellow if you will only sit down and wait!

———o———

Even if you are on the right track, you will get run over if you just sit there.

———o———

Too many people are ready to carry the stool when there's a piano to be moved.

———o———

He that rises late must trot all day, and shall scarce overtake his business at night, while laziness travels so slow-ly that poverty soon overtakes him.

BENJAMIN FRANKLIN,
Preface to Poor Richard Improved

Leader

The footsteps a boy follows in are apt to be those his father thought he'd covered up.

FRANKLIN P. JONES

———o———

Leaders must be readers.

DONALD LAIRD

———o———

A tactful leader must overlook as well as look over the work of his as-sociates.

LARRY WARD

———o———

One reason the big apples are al-ways on top of the basket is that there are always a lot of little ones holding them up there.

———o———

There are no bad soldiers, only bad officers!

NAPOLEON BONAPARTE

Reason and judgment are the qualities of a leader.

TACITUS

An efficient leader may, through his knowledge of his job and the magnetism of his personality, greatly increase the efficiency of others.

No matter what happens in this world there will always be room at the top and there will always be room for the pioneer.

He isn't a real boss until he has trained subordinates to shoulder most of his responsibilities.

Tomorrow's Christian leaders need Christian training today.

A strong leader knows that if he develops his associates he will be even stronger.

JAMES F. LINCOLN,
President Lincoln Electric Company

Any leader worth following gives credit easily where credit is due.

FRANKLIN J. LUNDBERG,
Chairman Jewel Tea Company

No man can lead who does not love the men he leads.

You can handle people more successfully by enlisting their feelings than by convincing their reason.

PAUL P. PARKER

Learn

We have learned to fly through the air like birds and to swim through the sea like fish. When will we learn to walk the earth like men?

R. W. HUGH JONES

It is better to learn late than never.

PUBLILIUS SYRUS, Maxim 864

A man learns only by two things: one is reading and the other is association with smarter people.

WILL ROGERS

What we have to learn to do we learn by doing.

ARISTOTLE

It is impossible for one to learn what he already thinks he knows.

We must unlearn some things before we can become truly learned.

To be proud of learning is a mark of great ignorance.

Better be ignorant of a matter than half know it.

PUBLILIUS SYRUS, Maxim 865

Learning without thought is labor lost; thought without learning is perilous.

CONFUCIUS

The bookful blockhead, ignorantly read,
With loads of learned lumber in his head,
With his own tongue still edifies his ears,
And always list'ning to himself appears.

ALEXANDER POPE,
Essay on Criticism, Part III

One pound of learning requires ten pounds of common sense to apply it.

Persian Proverb

Love of learning is seldom unrequited.

ARNOLD H. GLASOW in Quote

To learn to walk, the child must walk.
To learn to think, the child must think.

To learn to feel, the child must feel. To learn to live, the child must live. To make a life, the child must be free to make his own life. His activity is the molding influence which determines the nature of his attitudes and ideals. His own choices determine his destiny.

C. B. EAVEY

———o———

The test of a learned man is the ability to express himself so simply that the unlearned say, "He can't be so smart: I can understand him perfectly!"

The Banner

———o———

The light of learning does not have to burn brilliantly, but it must burn constantly.

———o———

Anyone who stops learning is old whether this happens at twenty or eighty. Anyone who keeps on learning not only remains young but becomes constantly more valuable, regardless of physical capacity.

HENRY FORD

———o———

We have learned no portion of Scripture until we have done what it teaches.

MALCOLM E. VAN ANTWERP

———o———

The end of learning is to know God, and out of that knowledge to love Him and imitate Him.

JOHN MILTON

———o———

If you get out of school today and stop learning tomorrow, you are uneducated the next day.

———o———

Learn the blessedness of the unoffended in the face of the unexplainable.

AMY CARMICHAEL

———o———

Seeing much, suffering much, and studying much, are the three pillars of learning.

BENJAMIN DISRAELI

Professor to class: If you get this in your head, you'll have it in a nutshell.

———o———

After his first day of school little Gary said, "I have to go back tomorrow because I haven't learned how to read or write yet."

Leisure

The advantage of leisure is mainly that we have the power of choosing our work; not certainly that it confers any privilege of idleness.

SIR JOHN LUBBOCK

———o———

Leisure time is when your wife can't find you.

———o———

Leisure is a beautiful garment, but it will not do for constant wear.

———o———

He hath no leisure who useth it not.

GEORGE HERBERT, *Jacula Prudentum*

———o———

Employ thy time well if thou meanest to gain leisure; and since thou art not sure of a minute, throw not away an hour.

BENJAMIN FRANKLIN

Letter

Dear letter, go upon your way,
O'er mountain, plain or sea;
God bless all who speed your flight
To where I wish you'd be.

And bless all those beneath the roof
Where I would bid you rest;
But bless even more the one
To whom this letter is addressed.

AUTHOR UNKNOWN

Liberty

Liberty without obedience is confusion, and obedience without liberty is slavery.

WILLIAM PENN

———o———

Liberty is the only thing you cannot

have unless you are willing to give it to others.

WILLIAM ALLEN WHITE

———o———

Experience teaches us to be most on our guard to protect liberty when the government's purposes are beneficent.

LOUIS DEMBITZ BRANDEIS

———o———

The real destroyer of the liberties of any people is he who spreads among them bounties, donations and largess.

PLUTARCH

———o———

There can be no such thing as liberty where there is not rational reflection and choice.

WILLIAM GRAHAM SUMNER

———o———

The God who gave us life gave us liberty at the same time.

THOMAS JEFFERSON

———o———

Our Heritage

Would that each true American, however great or small,
Might journey to that shrine of shrines, old Independence Hall.
And there within those sacred walls where those immortals met,
Renew our pledge to keep the faith, "Lest we forget — lest we forget."
Lest we forget that we must be
The keepers of our liberty.

JAMES WILLARD PARKS

———o———

Draw near and learn the faithful American lesson. Liberty is poorly served by those who are quelled by one failure or any number of failures, or from the casual indifference of the people, or from the sharp show of the tushes of power. Liberty relies on itself, invites no one, promises nothing, sits in calmness and light and knows no discouragement.

WALT WHITMAN

———o———

A day, an hour, of virtuous liberty
Is worth a whole eternity of bondage.

JOSEPH ADDISON

Liberty exists in proportion to wholesome restraining.

DANIEL WEBSTER

———o———

Is life so dear, or peace so sweet, as to be purchased at. the price of chains and slavery? Forbid it, Almighty God! I know not what course others may take, but as for me, give me liberty, or give me death!

PATRICK HENRY

Lie, Lying

White lies are but the ushers to black ones.

———o———

Parents who tell the bus driver that their fourteen-year-old son is too YOUNG to pay fare are the same ones who will tell the Department of Motor Vehicles that he is plenty OLD enough to get a driver's license.

———o———

A lie can be dressed up to look like the truth, but the dress will wear out.

———o———

An untruth a day old is called a lie; a year old it is called a falsehood; a century old it is called a legend. But the nature of a false statement is not altered by age.

CHARLES HADDON SPURGEON

———o———

Some persons profit by lying convincingly; I profit by telling the truth unconvincingly. It is not so difficult as you might suppose, for in this world, where actually nothing is commonplace, people believe only in the commonplace, in that which they are accustomed to see.

ROBERT L. RIPLEY

———o———

Figures don't lie, but liars figure.

———o———

A lie travels around the world while Truth is putting on her boots.

CHARLES HADDON SPURGEON

———o———

A truth that's told with bad intent
Beats all the lies you can invent.

WILLIAM BLAKE, *Auguries of Innocence*

The person who feels it is all right to tell white lies soon goes completely color-blind.

———o———

Once there was a mother who asked her young daughter, "Do you know what happens to little girls who tell lies?" To which the little girl replied, "Of course I do. They grow up and tell their little girls they'll get curly hair if they eat their spinach."

———o———

Exaggeration is a blood relation to falsehood, and nearly as blamable.
HOSEA BALLOU

———o———

Lie not, neither to thyself, nor man, nor God.
GEORGE HERBERT

———o———

If you tell the truth you don't have to remember anything.
MARK TWAIN

———o———

A liar should have a good memory.
QUINTILIAN, Institutiones Oratoriae

———o———

Some lie beneath the churchyard stone,
And some — before the speaker.
WINTHROP MACKWORTH PRAED

Life

Life leaps like a geyser for those who drill through the rock of inertia.
ALEXIS CARREL

———o———

The life of every man is a diary in which he means to write one story, and writes another; and his humblest hour is when he compares the volume as it is with what he hoped to make it.
SIR JAMES MATTHEW BARRIE

———o———

Since there is but a brief span between birth and death, learn to enjoy the span!

———o———

Up-hill

Does the road wind up-hill all the way?
Yes, to the very end.
Will the day's journey take the whole long day?
From morn to night my friend.

But is there for the night a resting place?
A roof for when the slow dark hours began.
May not the darkness hide it from my face?
You cannot miss that inn.

Shall I meet other wayfarers at night?
Those who have gone before.
Then must I knock, or call when just in sight?
They will not keep you standing at that door.

Shall I find comfort, travel-sore and weak?
Of labour you shall find the sum.
Will there be beds for me and all who seek?
Yea, beds for all who come.
CHRISTINA GEORGINA ROSSETT

———o———

Thirteen Progressions Of Life

At Five: "The stork brought us a new baby sister."
At Ten: "My Dad can lick any man twice his size."
At Fifteen: "Girls are just . . . blaaaah!"
At Twenty: "Just give me a chance. I'll show everybody!"
At Thirty: "In a few years, people will wake up and demand their rights."
At Thirty-five: "I'd be rich, if I'd stayed single."
At Forty: "I think I'd better have some more of those vitamin pills."
At Fifty-five: "Thank goodness I have a good bed."
At Sixty: "I was mighty fortunate to pick such a good wife."
At Sixty-five: "Why, I feel as young as I did twenty years ago."
At Seventy: "I don't know what these modern young people are coming to."
The King's Business

———o———

Life is fragile,
Handle with prayer.

Life is a mission. Every other definition of life is false, and leads all who accept it astray. Religion, science, philosophy, though still at variance upon many points, all agree in this, that every existence is an aim.

GIUSEPPE MAZZINE, *Life and Writings*

———o———

All of the animals except man know that the principle business of life is to enjoy it.

SAMUEL BUTLER

———o———

Life itself can't give you joy
Unless you really will it.
Life just gives you time of space —
It's up to you to fill it.

AUTHOR UNKNOWN

———o———

Life is like playing a violin solo in public and learning the instrument as one goes on.

SAMUEL BUTLER

———o———

Life is no brief candle to me. It is a sort of splendid torch which I have got hold of for the moment, and I want to make it burn as brightly as possible before handing it on to future generations.

GEORGE BERNARD SHAW

———o———

Someone's Bible

Thy life is someone's Bible, where
    Each day adds one new page;
Where chapters rise from little deeds
    That fill thy youth and age.

The friend who meets thee now and
        then
    Will read a line therein,
And find some cheer to strive anew,
    Or pretext for his sin.

Someday these speeding years —
    Their work of record done —
May show how often reading thee,
    His soul was lost or won.

Should Christ be grieved in him, thy
        Lord
    Thou mayest scarce requite,
If his resolve be framed from what
    Thy daily needs may write.

A godless act may fix his doom;
    Thy thoughtlessness he heeds;
Be careful friend, for where thou art,
    Someone his Bible reads.

E. C. KURTZ

———o———

Life is full of shadows but the sunshine makes them all.

———o———

Not only around our infancy
Doth heaven with all its splendors lie;
Daily, with souls that cringe and plot
We Sinais climb and know it not.

JAMES RUSSELL LOWELL,
Vision of Sir Launfal

———o———

Life's Melody

There is no music in a rest —
    Composers place it there
That we may pause and catch the note
    That follows, with more care;
God sends each life sometimes a "rest,"
    And we lament and grieve
That sickness, disappointing plans
    Give us unsought reprieve.
God writes the music of our lives,
    Our part to beat the time
And sing, and rest, pick up the tune —
    Go on with note sublime.

RUTH SMELTZER in *Sunshine Magazine*

———o———

True Life

Ah, life is lonely without God —
    A desert drear and wild;
One feels an exile far from home
    And like an orphan child.

Though weak and sinful, God is found
    By those who are sincere;
To hearts that hunger for His love
    He tenderly draws near.

To know the Father and the Son
    Is everlasting bliss;
Earth's fading joys cannot compare
    With joy as pure as this!

We leave earth's joys to seek in Him
    The good earth cannot give:
When fellowship with God is found,
    Then we begin to live.

MAX I. REICH

LIFE is built around:
Love
Integrity
Faith
Enthusiasm

———o———

Life is a hard, unceasing battle between man and his enemies, between woman and her friends.

———o———

Live your own life and you will die your own death.

Latin Proverb

———o———

I like trees because they seem more resigned to the way they have to live than other things do.

WILLA SIBERT CATHER, *O Pioneers!*

———o———

The best education in the world: struggling to get a living.

WENDELL PHILLIPS

———o———

Life is short and we have never too much time for gladdening the heart of those who are travelling the dark way with us.

HENRI-FRÉDÉRIC AMIEL

———o———

When my life
is past, how
glad I shall
Be that the
lamp of my
life has been shining for Thee.
I shall then not regret what I gave,
Of labor, or money for sinners
to save. I shall not mind that
the way has been rough. That my
Savior led me
— that will be
enough. When
I am dying
how glad I
shall be, that
the lamp of
my life has
been shin-
ing for THEE.

CLEAVER, *Missionary to Egypt*

———o———

Life is something that is happening to us while we are busy making other plans.

Life is short to the fortunate, long to the unfortunate.

APOLLONIUS of Tyana

———o———

Man always knows his life will shortly cease,
Yet madly lives as if he knew it not.

RICHARD BAXTER

———o———

I am drawing near to the close of my career; I am fast shuffling off the stage, I have been perhaps the most voluminous author of the day; and it is a comfort to me to think I have tried to unsettle no man's faith, to corrupt no man's principle, and that I have written nothing which on my deathbed I should wish blotted.

SIR WALTER SCOTT

———o———

In an old print shop there hangs a sign which reads: "Life is a grindstone and whether it grinds a man down or polishes him up depends on the stuff he's made of."

———o———

The hour which gives us life begins to take it away.

SENECA

———o———

Dost thou love life? Then do not squander time, for that is the stuff life is made of.

BENJAMIN FRANKLIN, *Almanac*

———o———

The life of man is a journey; a journey that must be travelled, however bad the roads or the accommodations.

OLIVER GOLDSMITH

Light

A group of tourists were visiting Carlsbad Caverns in New Mexico. Among those observing the wonders of the phenomenal underground labyrinth were a girl of twelve and her seven-year-old brother. When they had reached the deepest part of the caverns, as was customary, the guide turned off the lights for a moment's meditation and silence. The little boy became frightened and began to cry. And there in the pitch-black darkness and quietness of the cavern, many an adult received a moral lift from the clear whisper of the girl to her little brother, "Don't cry. Don't be afraid. There's someone here who knows where the lights are, and he can turn them on."

For many people there seems to be too much darkness in the world today. Yet, have you stopped to think of this: God knows where the lights are, and He can turn them on.

———o———

In darkness there is no choice. It is light that enables us to see the differences between things; and it is Christ who gives us light.

MRS. C. T. WHITMELL

———o———

God will never leave you without light enough to take one step; don't stop walking till the light gives out.

———o———

A traveler visiting the lighthouse at Calais said to the keeper, "But what if one of your lights should go out at night?"

"Never! Impossible!" he cried. "Yonder are ships sailing to all parts of the world. If tonight one of my burners were out, in six months I should hear from America and India, saying that on such a night the lights of Calais Lighthouse gave no warning and some vessel had been wrecked."

What a lesson to the people of God! Our lights must shine steadily and always, that other storm-tossed souls may be guided to Christ!

———o———

Lighthouses don't ring bells or fire guns to call attention to their light: they just shine.

———o———

We don't pretend to know anything about the speed of light, except that it gets here too early in the morning.

———o———

Whitewash always shows up blackest in the limelight.

———o———

When He came — there was no light; when He left — there was no darkness.

AUTHOR UNKNOWN

The man with time to burn never gave the world any light.

———o———

God sometimes puts us in the dark to prove to us that He is light.

Limit

Pull Me Out Of My Narrow Field

Lord, I confess unto Thee that I have lived in a narrow world. I have moved in the treadmill of my own thoughts, going around and around in the paralyzing circle of my restricted ideas.

I have kept myself dangerously confined to a small group of friends.

I have loved a few pictures, read a few books, touched the vast orbit of Thy truth and will at a few points.

Thrust me out of this small world into a large and expanding one, O Lord.

Transform me through ideas that come from the deep places of Thy plan and reach far into the distant confines of Thy unachieved will.

Enlarge and enrich my heart through many and varied and contagious friends.

Bring the islands of the sea next door to me through knowledge.

People my home and my heart with the mighty souls of all time through my sympathetic awareness of what they were and did. In His Name.

SOURCE UNKNOWN

———o———

We Limit God

Man's mind is small. We are, each day,
Concerned with things the eye can see,
With things to measure, count, or weigh;
Forgetting that, on bended knee,
The mind of God is ours to claim.
We limit God. We're halt and lame,
Though we might run, in His dear Name.

Unsearchable, God's wisdom, and
Unlimited, His wealth and might;
Yet worlds beneath His mighty Hand

Are seared and withered by the blight
Of unbelief. What loss! What shame!
Poor human clods: we fail to claim
Our riches in His precious Name!
VADYS MOTE VAUGHT

Listen

Nobody ever listened himself out of
a job.
CALVIN COOLIDGE

———o———

Some people are easily entertained
All you have to do is sit down and
listen to them.

———o———

You may wish to jot in the back of
your Bible these "hearing aids" to help
you get more from the pastor's mes-
sage. Listen —
Reverently — Habakkuk 2:20
Expectantly — Psalm 62:5
Prayerfully — I Samuel 3:10
Attentively — Acts 15:12
Understandingly — Nehemiah 8:8
Discerningly — Acts 17:11
Obediently — Matthew 7:24-27
ROY ROBERTSON

———o———

The best way to make a long story
short is to stop listening.

———o———

One way to be popular is to listen
to a lot of things you already know.

———o———

Let a man talk about himself and he
will think you're mighty interesting!

———o———

Train yourself to listen. You'll be
amazed at what you can learn when
your mouth is shut.

———o———

Some people think that God does
not speak to men today, but He does!
The trouble is that men refuse to listen.

———o———

A poor listener seldom hears a good
sermon.

We have two ears and only one
tongue in order that we may hear more
and speak less.
DIOGENES LAERTIUS

Literature

Grace Nies Fletcher in her book
Preacher's Kids says: "At ten I had
devoured Dickens; I had galloped with
Scott's armored knights, shivered
through the Paris sewers with Victor
Hugo. Cutting down a vocabulary to
fit the child's age as we do today always seem to me like cutting off the
baby to fit the crib. We offer our children Pablum instead of the red meat
of real literature."
Lutheran Education

———o———

No man but a blockhead ever wrote
except for money.
SAMUEL JOHNSON,
Boswell's *Life of Dr. Johnson*

———o———

In science, read, by preference, the
newest works; in literature, the oldest. The classic literature is always
modern.
EDWARD GEORGE BULWER- LYTTON,
Hints on Mental Culture

———o———

Literature is a very bad crutch, but
a very good walking-stick.
CHARLES LAMB

———o———

Literature is the thought of thinking
souls.
THOMAS CARLYLE

Little

Think not anything little, wherein we
may fulfill His commandments.
EDWARD B. PUSEY

———o———

Little Things

Lord, let me do the little things
Which may fall to my lot;
Those little inconspicuous ones
By others oft forgot.

A staff for age to lean upon,
  Strong hands to help the weak;
A loving heart with open door
  To all who solace seek.

To sit beside some silent bier
  And share their lonely grief;
To hold the palsied hand of care,
  Until there comes relief.

To hold my tongue when hot words
    rise,
  Speak kindly ones instead;
Nor harshly judge my fellow men
  In what they've done or said.

To share another's heavy load
  By word of courage given;
To help a fallen brother rise
  And bring him nearer Heaven.

If, like the Master, I can give
  Myself for those I love,
Rich joy and peace shall come to me,
  Sweet rest in Heaven above.

I know not when the day shall cease,
  But when life's curfew rings,
I want my Lord to find me then
  Still doing little things.
                           MRS. MORTON SIMS

——o——

Things insignificant to man may be
great in the sight of God.

——o——

He is a narrow-minded person who
despises little things.

——o——

Often the most useful Christians are
those who serve their Master in little
things. He never despises the day of
small things, or else He would not hide
His oaks in tiny acorns, or the wealth
of a wheat field in bags of little seeds.
            THEODORE LEDYARD CUYLER

——o——

Little Things

This is a world of little things. The
tallest mountain is only a gigantic mass
of little things. The sky-piercing office
buildings are composed of millions of
little things. Man's activities in every

field of endeavor are made up of trifles, little things that apparently count
for little.

If it had not rained the night before
Waterloo, Napoleon would have won
the battle. Rain was a little thing.

It was a little thing that led to the
discovery of America. Columbus was
about to turn his ships and go back to
Europe when a lookout saw seaweed
floating near the ship.

The lamp swinging in the cathedral
furnished the idea of the pendulum,
and from that idea we have our clocks.

Mankind has grown great and
strong, has subdued the earth, the water, and the air by a succession of little
victories.

We are building our lives of little
things. Habit is made up of countless
unnoticed actions. And from these we
weave our future. The veriest trifles
control our destinies.
                           Personality

——o——

Little things are great to little men.
                           OLIVER GOLDSMITH

Live, Living

Facing The Dawn

Sunrise and morning star,
  And one clear call to give;
And may there be no clouding of the
    skies
  When I set forth to live.
But such a glow as, shining, seems
    ablaze,
  Too full for shade or night,
When that which drew from out the
    sun's vast rays
  Bursts forth in light.

Daylight and morning bell,
  And after that to work;
And may there be no soft and subtle
    spell
  To make me shirk.
For though into the maze of toil and
    strife
  My tasks may set my way,
I hope to meet my Master life to life,
  As I shall live this day.
                           WILLIAM HIRAM FOULKES

Men will wrangle for Christianity, write for it, fight for it, die for it, anything but live for it.

———o———

Write your name in kindness, love, and mercy on the hearts of thousands you come in contact with year by year, and you will never be forgotten.

THOMAS CHALMERS

———o———

Let us live as people who are prepared to die, and die as people who are prepared to live.

JAMES S. STEWART

———o———

We must live our convictions and be willing to be misunderstood. Live in God.

W. B. MUSSELMAN

———o———

Nothing can get between God and me when I live close enough to Him.

———o———

A four-year-old boy was so quiet his mother wondered what he was up to. Looking for him, she found him sitting quietly on the steps. "What are you doing, Billy?" she asked.

He sighed and answered patiently, "Mother, can't you see I'm only living?"

———o———

Live each day as if it were thy last.

DRUMMOND of Hawthornden

———o———

Let us live in a great spirit, then we shall be ready for a great occasion.

GEORGE HODGES

———o———

To work fearlessly, to follow earnestly after truth, to rest with childlike confidence in God's guidance, to leave one's lot willingly and heartily to Him — this is my sermon to myself. If we could live more within sight of Heaven, we should care less for the turmoil of earth.

JOHN RICHARD GREEN

Take Time To Live

Take time to live;
The world has much to give
Of faith and hope and love:
Of faith, that life is good,
That human brotherhood
Shall no illusion prove;
Of hope, that future years
Shall bring the best in spite
Of those whose darkened sight
Would stir our doubts and fears;
Of love, that makes of life,
With all its griefs, a song;
A friend, of conquered wrong;
A symphony, of strife.
Take time to live,
Nor to vain mammon give
Your fruitful years.
Take time to live;
The world has much to give
Of sweet content; of joy
At duty bravely done;
Of hope, that every sun
Shall bring more fair employ.
Take time to live,
For life has much to give
Despite the cynic's sneer
That all's forever wrong;
There's much that calls for song.
To fate lend not your ear.
Take time to live;
The world has much to give.

THOMAS CURTIS CLARK

———o———

The man who lives by the Golden Rule today never has to apologize for his actions tomorrow.

Grit

———o———

The man who lives for Christ does not conform to his environment. He is drawn into a new one.

———o———

No one can live wrong and pray right. And no one who prays right can live wrong.

DAVID C. HALL

———o———

So live that when they check over your footprints on the sands of time, they won't find only the marks of a heel.

The only real way to "prepare to meet thy God" is to live with thy God so that to meet Him will be nothing strange.

PHILLIPS BROOKS

————o————

A child, hearing the minister shout when he prayed, said to his mother, "Don't you think that if he lived nearer to God he wouldn't have to talk so loud?"

————o————

Not everyone who wants to make a good living wants to earn it.

————o————

A man has to live with himself, and he should see to it that he always has good company.

CHARLES EVANS HUGHES

————o————

O Lord, let us not live to be useless.

JOHN WESLEY

————o————

To live with saints in heaven
  Will be eternal glory;
But to live with them on earth
  Is quite a different story!

————o————

Many who say "Our Father" on Sunday spend the rest of the week acting like orphans.

————o————

New Road Map

Proverbs 3:5-6 may well be labeled "The Road-Map for Christian Living." If we heed these directions not relying on our own insights alone, trusting the Lord with all our hearts, acknowledging the Lord in all we do and say each day, we will be sure to arrive safely at our destination, because the road will be made straight.

This age needs a road map for daily living. In God's Word, we have the master-plan and if we heed the Holy Spirit and obey the words of the wise man, we will have no regrets or fears — for we shall arrive home safely at eventide.

HARRY J. FISHER

I like to see a man proud of the place in which he lives; and so live that the place will be proud of him.

ABRAHAM LINCOLN

————o————

Live like Moses:

His first 40 years he was somebody.
His second 40 years he became nobody.
His third 40 years God became everybody.

————o————

It is not how many years we live, but what we do with them.

It is not what we receive, but what we give unto others.

GENERAL EVANGELINE BOOTH

————o————

Lessons In Living

Learn to laugh. A good laugh is better than medicine.
Learn to attend to your own business. Few men can handle their own well.
Learn to tell a story. A well-told story is like a sunbeam in a sick room.
Learn to say kind things. Nobody ever resents them.
Learn to avoid sarcastic remarks. They give neither the hearer nor the speaker any lasting satisfaction.
Learn to stop grumbling. If you can't see any good in the world, keep the bad to yourself.
Learn to hide aches with a smile. Nobody else is interested anyway.
Learn to keep troubles to yourself. Nobody wants to take them from you.
Above all, learn to smile. It pays!

————o————

Gracious living is when you have the house air-conditioned, and then load the yard with chairs, lounges and an outdoor oven so you can spend all your time in the hot sun.

Detroit News, Detroit, Michigan

————o————

The real art of living is beginning where you are.

————o————

Don't go around saying the world owes you a living. The world owes you nothing. It was here first.

MARK TWAIN

Live your life while you have it.
Life is a splendid gift —
There is nothing small about it.

FLORENCE NIGHTINGALE

———o———

At one time Edward Rijnders gave no indication that he would ever serve the Lord. At the age of 16, he said to his father, pastor of the Dutch Reformed Church in Doorn, "Do you believe what you are saying every Sunday?"

"Why, yes."

"Well, I don't."

"Then I forbid you to go to church. When you say there is no God, you stay at home Sunday morning. Now you have to live in the thought that God does not exist. You can come to the table after grace."

"It was a great experience," Rijnders said. "My father is a wise man. After three months I said to him, 'Father, I'm not able to live without God. It is impossible.'"

MARY SETH in *Presbyterian Life*

———o———

Upside-down Days

Some of my days fall into place
  Like soldiers on parade.
In half a jiffy — maybe less,
  My plans are wisely made.
No matter what I do, things go
  Like clockwork all day long,
And work out just as I desire,
  And things just can't go wrong.
But some days march in upside down,
  And simply won't be good;
So when I find things going wrong
  Instead of as they should,
I use a lot of extra care,
  And faith instead of doubting.
And extra effort now and then,
  And smiles instead of pouting,
And soon, I find, the day turns kind;
  Relenting, it rewards me.
And things I want, the way I want,
  It very soon accords me.

WILFRED T. COOKE in *Pilot*

———o———

Some wish to live within the sound
  Of church or chapel bell,

I want to run a rescue shop
  Within a yard of hell.

C. T. STUDD

———o———

Those who live with too much tension seldom live to enjoy a pension.

———o———

So live that you will have a good inside to show outside.

———o———

More people are reading the Bible which is bound in human skin than they are the one bound in leather.

Loan

Only Loaned

God didn't say that I might keep
This lovely autumn day,
Nor did He mean that through all time
The world could look this way.
He sent the beauty of the fall —
The changing autumn leaves,
And yet I know within my heart
God only loaned me these.

I marvelled at the reds and golds,
The mountains smiling fair,
And filled my mind with wondrous
  sights
I found most everywhere,
So much in beauty to behold
October's pleasantries,
And yet so soon will change, I know
God only loaned me these.

God only lends life's lovely things
However large or small.
He keeps them ever in His power
Then lends a share to all;
Old Mother Nature's golden days,
The mountains, plains and trees,
The joys and gladness they impart
God only lends us these.

GARNETT ANN SCHULTZ

Lonely

No man is lonely while eating spaghetti — it requires so much attention.

CHRISTOPHER MORLEY

A person isn't lonesome because he is alone but because he is not with some other person.

Breeze, Berlin, New Jersey

———o———

The Solitary Way

There is a mystery in human hearts,
And though we be encircled by a host
Of those who love us well, and are be-
  loved,
To every one of us, from time to time,
There comes a sense of utter loneliness;
Our dearest friend is "stranger" to our
  joy,
And cannot realize our bitterness.
"There is not one who really under-
  stands,
Not one to enter into all I feel;"
Such is the cry of each of us in turn.
We wander in a "solitary way,"
No matter what or where our lot may
  be;
Each heart, mysterious even to itself,
Must live its inner life in solitude.

And would you know the reason why
  this is?
It is because the Lord desires our love.
In every heart He wishes to be first;
He therefore keeps the secret-key Him-
  self,
To open all its chambers, and to bless,
With perfect sympathy and holy peace
Each solitary soul which comes to Him.
So when we feel this loneliness, it is
The voice of Jesus saying, "Come to
  me;"
And every time we are "not under-
  stood,"
It is a call to us to come again,
For Christ alone can satisfy the long-
  ing soul,
And those who walk with Him from
  day to day
Can never have a "Solitary Way."

And when beneath some heavy cross
  you faint
And say, "I cannot bear this load
  alone,"
You say the truth, Christ made it pur-
  posely
So heavy that you must return to Him.
The bitter grief that "no one understands"

Conveys a secret message from the
  King,
Entreating you to come to Him again;
The Man of Sorrows understands it
  well.
In all points tempted He can feel with
  you;
You cannot come too often or too near;
The Son of God is infinite in grace,
His presence satisfies the longing soul.
And those who walk with Him from
  day to day,
Can never have a "Solitary Way."

AUTHOR UNKNOWN

———o———

A young man once asked F. B. Meyer to help him find a new job, because
he was the only Christian in the entire
establishment, and found it so lonely
to stand by himself. "But," said Meyer,
"is not that one reason to hold your
ground? Surely the loneliness of a light
is the more reason why it should shine.
If there were more than one, it might
with some grace retire, but not if it is
alone."

———o———

He overcomes his lonely days who
walks with Christ, who walks with man.

JOHN HOWARD BLOUGH

———o———

Seldom can a heart be lonely
If it seek a lonelier still —
Self-forgetting, seeking only,
Emptier cups of love to fill.

FRANCES RIDLEY HAVERGAL

———o———

It is proper and beneficial sometimes
to be left to thyself.

THOMAS À KEMPIS

Look

In the Scriptures we are given four
commands to *look*:

1) *Look* into the Scriptures
  "Whosoever looketh into the perfect law of liberty and continueth
therein . . . shall be blessed in his
deed" (James 1:25).

2) *Look* unto Jesus
  "Looking unto Jesus the author

and finisher of our faith" (Hebrews 12:2).

3) *Look* on the fields
"Lift up your eyes and look on the fields for they are white unto harvest" (John 4:35).

4) *Look* for His coming
"Looking for that blessed hope and the glorious appearing of the great God and our Saviour Jesus Christ" (Titus 2:13).

T. J. BACH

———o———

If we are shut in by life's troubles, we can look to the open heaven above us.

JAMES M. CAMPBELL

———o———

Man is the only being God has created to look up.

———o———

Looking to self makes one miserable.

———o———

Look Up

Some people pass through this wonderful world
And never look up at the sky . . .
It's nothing to them that the lark sings there
While the great white clouds sail by.

It's nothing to them that the millions of stars
Weave a silver web at night . . .
They do not know of the hush that falls
When the dawn gives birth to light.

Oh, pity the people with all your heart,
Who never look up at the sky . . .
So many beautiful sights they miss
As the pageant of God goes by.

AUTHOR UNKNOWN

———o———

If we look around, like Moses,
  We will be afraid.
If we look down, like Peter,
  We will sink.
If we look on others, like Miriam,
  We will be envious.
If we look up to Jesus,
  We will be transformed.

AUTHOR UNKNOWN

Lose, Lost

Born To Lose

The expression: "I would give my right arm for it," has often been uttered.

One day it was unexpectedly fulfilled in New York.

A 22-year-old burglar gave his right arm for a television set he tried to steal.

He and two friends broke the window of a store in which the TV set was displayed. As he reached through the broken window to seize the set, a falling section of the plate glass fell on his right arm, almost severing it.

He was rushed to the hospital, where amputation above the elbow was completed.

His left arm was tattooed with the words, "Born to lose."

How mistaken can a person be? He was born to glorify God and to enjoy Him forever. He was not born to lose, but to win; for God is "long-suffering to usward, not willing that any should perish, but that all should come to repentance." (II Peter 3:9).

TOM OLSON in *Now*

———o———

The trouble with being a good sport is that you have to lose to prove it.

Times, Alamo, Tennessee

———o———

No man can lose what he never had.

IZAAK WALTON, *The Compleat Angler*

———o———

Prefer a loss to a dishonest gain. The one brings pain at the moment, the other for all time to come.

———o———

I left the tent where we were holding meetings one night, and among the number who left last was a young man to whom I was especially attracted by his fine looks. I walked down the street with him, and put to him the invariable question, "Are you a Christian?"

He said, "No sir; I am not."

Then I used every Scripture and every argument to get him to promise me to give his heart to God, but could not succeed. When about to separate, I asked him, "Are your father and mother alive?"

"Both alive," said he.

"Is your father a Christian?"

"Don't know; he has been a steward in the church for several years."

"Is your mother a Christian?"

"Don't know; she has been superintendent of the Sabbath school of the same church for some time."

"Do your father and mother ever ask the blessing at the table?"

"No sir."

"Did your father, mother, or sister ever ask you to be a Christian?"

"Mr. Sunday, as long as I can remember, my father or mother or sister never said a word to me about my soul. Do you believe they think I am lost?"

BILLY SUNDAY

———o———

For 'tis a truth well known to most,
That whatsoever thing is lost,
We seek it, ere it come to light,
In every cranny but the right.

WILLIAM COWPER

———o———

The loss of wealth is much; the loss of health is more; but the loss of Christ is such a loss that no man can restore.

E. W. P.

———o———

Sheep get lost, not because of the thicket, but because they wander away too far from the shepherd.

———o———

Sorrowfully, the little lost boy looked up and down the street, then went up to the policeman on the corner. "Sir," he asked hopefully, "did you see a lady go by without me?"

———o———

What Would It Profit?

If all the riches of this world were mine,
And all the lovely gems that brightly shine;
If I possessed a large estate and grand,
And choicest fruitful fields, and timber-land;

What would it profit me, if death should call,
And I should be compelled to leave it all?

If I could somehow win this world's applause,
And rise to lofty heights in some great cause;
If I could have my fondest hopes fulfilled,
And with the prestige won be greatly thrilled:
What would it profit if I reached my goal,
And then should die in sin, and lose my soul?

If I could boast myself of noble birth,
And consort with the greatest ones of earth;
If I could make some friends in every land,
And find in every place an outstretched hand:
How dreadful in the end would be my lot,
If Christ should then declare, "I know you not!"

Love

Love is a feeling of a feeling like a feeling we've never felt before.

———o———

To love oneself is the beginning of a lifelong romance.

OSCAR WILDE, *An Ideal Husband*

———o———

Love sacrifices all things
To bless the thing it loves.

EDWARD GEORGE BULWER-LYTTON

———o———

Let those love now who never loved before;
Let those who always loved, now love the more.

THOMAS PARNELL,
Translation of the Pervigilium Veneris

———o———

Love is a gift, take it, let it grow.
Love is a sign we should wear, let it show.
Love is an act, do it, let it go.

Love is indeed heaven upon earth; since heaven above would not be heaven without it.

WILLIAM PENN

If thou didst know the whole Bible by heart, and the sayings of all the philosophers, what would all that profit thee without the love of God, and without His grace? Vanity of vanities; all is vanity except to love God and to serve Him only.

THOMAS À KEMPIS

Love

There is a love that passeth understanding,
   A love whose greatness cannot measured be;
Like a vast ocean, without shore or landing;
   And that great love, it loveth you and me!

Nor height, nor depth, nor breadth, nor length can show it;
   No words of man can speak its tale to thee;
And yet thy poor weak heart may learn to know it —
   That wondrous love that loveth you and me!

For God so loved, He sent His Well-Beloved,
   His only Son, to die for you and me;
And thus His love to all the world He proved —
   Oh, proof divine; that cannot questioned be;
And Jesus died, and rose, and went to heaven,
   God's gift of love and life to you and me:
Oh, gift unspeakable! to be forgiven,
   And dwell with God and Christ eternally!

WILLIAM R. NEWELL

We hear a good deal about the power of love. If you really want to put it to the test, see what happens when it is applied to an enemy.

Those who deserve love least, need it most!

The Second Mile

Stern Duty said, "Go walk a mile
   And help thy brother bear his load."
I walked reluctant, but, meanwhile,
   My heart grew soft with help bestowed.
Then Love said, "Go another mile."
   I went, and Duty spake no more,
But Love arose and with a smile
   Took all the burden that I bore.
'Tis ever thus when Duty calls;
   If we spring quickly to obey,
Love comes, and whatso'er befalls,
   We're glad to help another day.
The second mile we walk with joy;
   Heaven's peace goes with us on the road,
So let us all our powers employ
   To help our brother bear life's load.

STEPHEN MOORE

If slighted, slight the slight, and love the slighter.

He loves not Christ at all who does not love Christ above all.

God and I have this in common — we both love His Son, Jesus Christ.

LANCE ZAVITZ

The law of love will keep us from doing a great many things which mere impulse would often do, and will make us very careful of every word and action.

A. B. SIMPSON

Before Christ, a man loves things and uses people. After Christ, he loves people and uses things.

HORACE WOOD

Love makes everything lovely; hate concentrates itself on the one thing hated.

GEORGE MACDONALD

Be persuaded, timid soul, that He has loved you too much to cease loving you.

FRANCOIS DE SALIGNAC DE LA MOTHE FÉNELON

———o———

One thing that we may have but which we cannot keep for ourselves is divine love. Love unexpressed will soon be love dispossessed.

———o———

Enjoying each other's good is heaven begun.

LUCY C. SMITH

———o———

The greatest happiness of life is the conviction that we are loved, loved for ourselves, or rather loved in spite of ourselves.

VICTOR HUGO, *Les Misérables*

———o———

On the whole, God's love for us is a much safer subject to think about than our love for Him.

C. S. LEWIS,
Mere Christianity, Christian Behaviour

———o———

What is love? It's when you don't give a thought for all the if's and want-to's in the world.

EUGENE O'NEILL

———o———

Love is the goal. Love is the way we wend.

CHRISTINA GEORGINA ROSSETTI

———o———

Though love is weak and hate is strong, Yet hate is short, and love is very long.

KENNETH BOULDING

———o———

You want to compete with His affection before you have understood it: that is your mistake. Show a little more deference to our Lord and allow Him to go first. Let Him love you a great deal before you have succeeded in loving Him even a little as you would wish to love Him. That is all that our Lord asks of you.

HENRI DE TOURVILLE

The Need And The Supply

O Love, my hunger is too deep
 For bread alone to still;
The void within too vast for aught
 Save deathless love to fill.

Where shall I find the nourishment
 That satisfied the soul?
Where is the potent remedy
 That makes the sin-sick whole?

O Love that died for me, Thou art
 My only resting place;
The answer to my deepest need
 I read in Jesus' face.

MAX I. REICH

———o———

Rooted In Love

Our strength and soul's integrity
Are deeper gifts of God's own grace:
As wind-bent branches of a tree
Return, in calm, to their own place,
We may be tossed by passing gales
Of sorrow, but our roots below
Hold to the love that never fails,
And in His peace we stand . . . and grow!

JEAN HOGAN DUDLEY

———o———

I look at her, somewhat resigned,
And guess the workings of her mind.
She's restless as a little wren,
And says that she's in love again.

Seems he has nice teeth, dark brown hair,
And wears his clothes with careless air.
Now I'm not jealous, y'understand,
But when he's here, I'm contraband.

I grin, and that she can't condone.
She waits for him to telephone.
It rings — she leaps — to hear him say,
"Gramma, I gotta 'A' today."

PAUL P. WENTZ in *Sunshine Magazine*

———o———

Are there some Christians that you just don't like? Remember that they are the Lord's possession, and then love them for *His* sake. To grasp this truth is to walk as the saints should walk.

Love feels no burden, thinks nothing of trouble, attempts what is above its strength, pleads no excuse of impractibility; for it thinks all things lawful for itself if possible.

THOMAS À KEMPIS

———o———

To be loved is better than to be famous.

———o———

Love is not soured by injustice; nor crushed by men's contempt.

A. S. LONDON

———o———

If thou neglectest thy love to thy neighbor, in vain thou professest thy love to God; for by thy love to God, the love to thy neighbor is begotten, and by the love to thy neighbor, thy love to God is nourished.

FRANCIS QUARLES

———o———

How shall we become lovely? By loving Him who is ever lovely.

ST. AUGUSTINE

———o———

There is in the world far more hunger for love and appreciation than there is for bread.

"Love is the fulfilling of the Law." It is the rule for fulfilling all rules, the new commandment for keeping all old commandments, Christ's one secret of the Christian life.

HENRY DRUMMOND

———o———

Love stops at nothing but possession.

THOMAS SOUTHERNE, *Oroonoko*

———o———

For the love of God is broader
Than the measure of man's mind,
And the heart of the Eternal
Is most wonderfully kind.

If our love were but more simple
We should take Him at His word:
And our lives would be all sunshine
In the sweetness of our Lord.

FREDERICK W. FABER,
Souls of Men Why Will Ye Scatter

———o———

Love is a wonder-worker, but it gets along better when it has brains to direct it.

BILLY SUNDAY

———o———

Love is life, and lovelessness is death.

FRANCES PAGET

M

Magic

Johnny came running home from school and announced excitedly, "They've got a magic record player at our school. It runs without anything!"

"A magic record player — it runs without anything?" asked his puzzled mother.

"Yes," explained Johnny, "you don't have to plug it into electricity — you don't even use electricity to make it play. All you have to do is wind it up with a crank!"

———o———

Grandfather Ba Te was a Baptist evangelist, and while he was preaching on the Burma-China border a Chinese chief, wishing to obstruct his work by devious means, sent a spy to a gospel session. Afterward the villagers lingered for a chat, and green tea was served. Grandfather declined, saying he preferred plain boiled water. "I regret that there is none ready," his host said apologetically. "Do you mind a short wait?"

"Oh, a glass of cold water will do — I'll boil it myself," replied Grandfather, who loved a practical joke. Surreptitiously taking a bottle of Eno's Fruit Salts from his bag, he poured a little into the water. Then he held the glass high for all to see the water bubbling, and drained it.

Later he learned that the spy had

hurried back across the border to warn his chief: "Do not try any tricks. Ba Te can boil water without fire. What is more, he can drink it while it is boiling!"

LOUISE PAW (Rangoon, Burma)
in *Reader's Digest*

Man, Mankind

Man is the greatest marvel in the universe. Not because his heart beats forty million times a year, driving the bloodstream a distance of over sixty thousand miles in that time; not because of the wonderful mechanism of eye and ear; not because of his conquest over disease and the lengthening of human life; not because of the unique quality of his mind, but because he may walk and talk with God.

The Nazarene Weekly

———o———

Man is the Only Animal that blushes. Or needs to.

MARK TWAIN, *Following the Equator*. Vol. I

———o———

Man is not truly man until he is God's man.

JOHN A. MACKAY

———o———

Man without God is a beast, and never more beastly than when he is most intelligent about his beastliness.

WHITTAKER CHAMBERS

———o———

For man is man and master of his fate.

ALFRED, LORD TENNYSON,
Idylls of the King

———o———

An old maid heard a rumor that she had found *the* man.

"Modesty and honesty," she said, "compel me to deny it, but thank God for the rumor."

———o———

Man is not the creature of circumstances. Circumstances are the creatures of men.

BENJAMIN DISRAELI, *Vivian Grey*. Book I

No man is more than another unless he does more than another.

MIGUEL DE CERVANTES

———o———

Man! thou pendulum betwixt a smile and a tear.

LORD BYRON

———o———

I mean to make myself a man, and if I succeed in that, I shall succeed in everything else.

JAMES A. GARFIELD

———o———

The man, whom I call deserving the name, is one whose thoughts and exertions are for others rather than himself.

SIR WALTER SCOTT

———o———

The bulk of mankind are schoolboys through life.

THOMAS JEFFERSON

———o———

Of all wonders, man himself is the most wonderful.

———o———

Man is but breath and shadow, nothing more.

SOPHOCLES

———o———

You Are Not Cheap

There is an old story of Muretus, a Christian scholar of the 16th century. One time he became ill while on a trip. The doctors who were called in to treat him did not know him. He looked so much like an ordinary individual that they said, "Let's try an experiment on him, for he looks of no importance." In the next room Muretus heard this remark, and he called to the doctors, "Call not any man cheap for whom Christ died."

It is so easy for us to downgrade individuals. Even Christian churches close their doors to people because their skin is of a different color. We are so prone to measure a man's importance according to the street on which he lives. It never bothers us that refugees continue to live in camps marked by squalor and poverty because, well, they are expendable. And then, too, we so often undervalue our own lives and willingly sell our birthright for a mess of pottage. For the cheapest price we sell our most precious heritage. Christ did not think of you that way. He believed you were worth the giving of His own life on the cross. Indeed, "call not any man cheap for whom Christ died." Not even yourself.

WILLIAM R. BUITENDORP in *Church Herald*

———o———

Someone knew what he was talking about when he said there are three states of man: "Yes, sir!" "No, sir!" and "Ulcer!"

———o———

It's a busy man who lives up to his wife's expectations.

———o———

Man is the head, but woman turns it.

Chinese Proverb

———o———

Every man is a volume, if you know how to read him.

WILLIAM ELLERY CHANNING

———o———

Women can resist a man's love, a man's fame, a man's personal appearance and a man's money, but they cannot resist a man's tongue when he knows how to use it.

WILKIE COLLINS

———o———

No man has an enemy worse than himself.

MARCUS TULLIUS CICERO

———o———

You can take my steel mills, my banks, my money, but leave me my men and I will build it all again.

ANDREW CARNEGIE

———o———

Gold is good in its place but living, brave, patriotic men are better than gold.

ABRAHAM LINCOLN

Rebellious Man

The plan and scheme of earth and
    heaven
By God's hands were devised,
While all the things that man may boast
    Are only improvised.
The sun, the moon and all the stars,
    The tides that ebb and flow,
Year after year return again,
    For God has willed it so.

Year after year come storms and rain
    The seasons come and go,
And in dark, island solitudes
    Some bright-hued blossoms grow.
The morning breaks on forests dark,
    Never traversed by man;
The sun beams on the desert wide
    According to God's plan;

But man, alone, defies the hand
    Of God that placed him here;
The most rebellious of all things
    Created on this sphere.
What, then, is man that he should
    boast?
Who is he to be proud?
Not one flower can he cause to bloom,
    Nor stem the smallest cloud.

CHARLES F. SMITH

———o———

The world needs fewer man-made goods and more God-made men and women.

SARAH ANNE JEPSON

Management

To handle yourself, use your head; to handle others, use your heart.

———o———

Good management is showing average people how to do the work of average people.

JOHN D. ROCKEFELLER, SR.

———o———

The job of management is to get the good out of a man without letting the bad interfere.

———o———

Management is the art of getting things done through people.

LAWRENCE APPLEY

Before we begin to manage the moon, it might be well to set our house in order here on earth.

Manners

Children are born mimics, so it is important that good manners should be the rule in the home. When you meet a youngster who is polite and thoughtful, you can be sure that he comes from a home where consideration for others' rights and feelings is taught and observed.

Tit-Bits

————o————

The test of good manners is to put up pleasantly with bad ones.

WENDELL WILKIE

————o————

Manners are noises you don't make when eating soup.

————o————

Good manners and soft words have brought many a difficult thing to pass.

SIR JOHN VANBRUGH, *Aesop*

————o————

Graciousness of manner is built upon very definite qualities of character, and chief among these is — adaptability, tact and poise.

Marriage

In married life no wife gets what she expected, and no husband expected what he's getting.

The Christian Parent

————o————

Lawyer: "But you can't marry again. If you do, your husband clearly specified in his will that his fortune will go to his brother."
Widow: "I know — it's the brother I'm marrying."

————o————

A woman must be a genius to create a good husband.

HONORÉ DE BALZAC

————o————

Men marry because they are tired, women because they are curious; both are disappointed.

OSCAR WILDE

You girls aspiring to get married — hearken to this voice of experience: a beautiful woman fascinates a man; a brilliant one interests him; a good one inspires him; but a sympathetic one gets him.

————o————

Any man who thinks he's more intelligent than his wife is married to a smart woman.

————o————

A truly happy marriage is one in which a woman gives the best years of her life to the man who has made them the best.

————o————

If there's any one thing a woman doesn't understand about marriage it's a husband.

————o————

"Does your husband live up to the promises he made during his courtship days?"
"Always. In those days he said he wasn't good enough for me."

————o————

Marriage starts with billing and cooing. The billing lasts.

————o————

When a man stops taking out a girl, it doesn't always mean they've broken up. He may have married her.

HERM ALBRIGHT in *Family Weekly*

————o————

A successful marriage requires falling in love many times, always with the same person.

MIGNON MCLAUGHLIN
in *The Atlantic Monthly*

————o————

Man's love is of man's life a thing apart;
'Tis a woman's whole existence.

LORD BYRON, *Don Juan*

————o————

Before marriage he talks and she listens. After marriage she talks and he listens. Later they both talk and the neighbors listen.

Common sense would avoid many divorces and also quite a few marriages.

———o———

The woman next door believes marriage is a give and take proposition. If her husband doesn't give her enough, she takes it out of his pocket.

———o———

The secret of happy marriage is simple: just keep on being as polite to each other as you are to your best friends.

ROBERT QUILLEN

———o———

A honeymoon is the vacation a man takes before starting to work for a new boss.

———o———

The main reason why some married folks don't pull together like a team is that one of them is just a nag.

———o———

Hasty marriage seldom proveth well.

WILLIAM SHAKESPEARE, *King Henry VI*

———o———

The one word above all others that makes marriage successful is "ours."

ROBERT QUILLEN

———o———

All marriages are happy — it's the living together afterwards that's tough.

———o———

Love is blind but marriage opens their eyes.

———o———

A real home is a picture of heaven on earth.

———o———

Success in marriage is more than finding the right person; it is a matter of being the right person.

———o———

Single women say they wouldn't marry the best man in the world. Married women know they didn't.

———o———

Make this agreement with your wife: if she will quit driving from the back seat, you will quit cooking from the dining room table.

Martyr

Blood of the martyrs is the seed of the Church.

TERTULLIAN, *Apologeticus*

———o———

Martyrdom is the only way in which a man can become famous without ability.

GEORGE BERNARD SHAW

———o———

Some ministers would make good martyrs; they are so dry they would burn well.

CHARLES HADDON SPURGEON

———o———

A death for love's no death but martyrdom.

C. CHAPMAN

Mathematics

To work out life's problems, we need to add love, subtract hate, multiply good, and divide between truth and error.

JANET T. COLEMAN

———o———

A schoolteacher was trying to explain subtraction to his young pupils.
"You have ten fingers," he said. "Suppose you had three less fingers, what would you have?"
A sweet little girl gave the quick answer, "I'd have no music lesson."

Sunshine Magazine

———o———

The greatest mathematician is he who daily counts his blessings.

DAVID PHELPS

———o———

A story has been written by Frederick Hall about the lad who played such an important role in the miracle of the loaves and fishes. It tells how the boy reported the exciting incident to his mother when he returned home that evening at sunset. When, with eyes still big with the wonder of it all, he had told how his five barley cakes and two dried lake fish had increased in the Master's hands until the vast crowd had been fed to a sufficiency, he added, "I wonder, Mother, if it would be that way with everything you gave Him?"

The Sunday School Times

Maturity

To be able to rejoice with another who succeeds when you have failed — that is a mark of real maturity!

———o———

Maturity: The capacity to endure uncertainty.

JOHN FINLEY, Harvard Professor

———o———

Maturity is the ability to live in someone else's world.

OREN ARNOLD in *The Kiwanis Magazine*

———o———

Maturity

If you can see a work which you have begun taken from you and given to another without feeling bitterness — that is maturity.

If you can listen to someone criticize you, even unkindly, and receive instruction from it without hard feelings — that is maturity.

If you can see others chosen for a job which you yourself are better qualified to do without feeling hurt — that is maturity.

If you can see a person do an act which is against your Christian standards and react without self-righteousness — that is maturity.

If you can hear a man argue a point of view which is contrary to your own and accept his right to his own opinion without a feeling of smugness — that is maturity.

If you can see someone you know deliberately snub you, and still make allowance for his actions — that is maturity.

If you can suffer nagging pain or ache, still singing and praising God, hiding your feelings for the sake of others — that is maturity.

If you can give yourself to help someone else who needs you, without having the idea that you are "a pretty good fellow" — that is maturity.

If you can crawl out of bed at an early hour to pray when you would rather sleep, because you realize that here lies your power with God — that is maturity.

If you can look upon every man as an object of God's yearning, so that you become burdened for his soul — that is maturity.

ANNE NUNEMAKER in *Moody Monthly*

Maxim

The winds and waves are always on the side of the ablest navigators.

EDWARD GIBBON, *Decline and Fall of the Roman Empire*

———o———

There are two things in the world that are only as big as the one who owns them: A dollar and a minute.

———o———

Do good by stealth, and blush to find it fame.

ALEXANDER POPE, *Satires, Epistles and Odes of Horace*

———o———

He who falls down gets up faster than he who lies down.

———o———

A hammer shatters glass but forges steel.

———o———

There is no right way to do a wrong thing.

———o———

Whitewashing the pump won't make the water pure.

DWIGHT L. MOODY

———o———

For, as I like a young man in whom there is something of the old, so I like an old man in whom there is something of the young; and he who follows this maxim, in body will possibly be an old man, but he will never be an old man in mind.

MARCUS TULLIUS CICERO, *De Senectute*

Pithy sentences are like sharp nails which force truth upon our memory.

DENIS DIDEROT

Memorial Day

The Dash Between The Dates

Memorial Day was over now,
All had left and I was alone.
I began to read the names and dates
Chiseled there on every stone.
The dates which showed whether it was Mom or Dad
Or daughter or baby son.
The dates were different but the amount the same,
There were two on every one.

It was then I noticed something,
It was but a simple line;
It was the dash between the dates
Placed there, it stood for time.
All at once it dawned on me
How important that little line.
The dates placed there belonged to God,
But that line is yours and mine.

It's God who gives this precious life
And God who takes away;
But that line between He gives to us
To do with what we may.
We know God's written the first date down
Of each and every one,
And we know those hands will write again,
For the last date has to come.

We know He'll write the last date down,
And soon, we know, for some.
But upon the line between my dates
I hope He'll write "well done."

LUCILLE BRITT
in *The Log of the Good Ship Grace*

Memory, Memorize

Strong Box

I have a treasured strong box,
Its contents are pure gold;
Where all these precious moments
Are mind to have and hold.

Inside I've put my baby's smile,
The sound of pattering feet;
My little girl's first childish song,
In babbling accent sweet.

There was a time when guests arrived.
My walls were scarred and marked;
I washed the handprints all away,
But framed them in my heart.

Now when my children both have grown,
And I am old and gray,
I'll turn the lock with mem'ry's key,
And while the hours away.

IRENE C. WALLIS

———o———

The true art of memory is the art of attention.

SAMUEL JOHNSON

———o———

A Bible stored in the mind is worth a dozen stored in the bottom of one's trunk.

———o———

The Chinese Christians, fearful that someday their precious Bibles might be taken away from them, hid the Word away in the most secure place possible, in their hearts. They memorized whole chapters of Scripture. In one district a missionary said that he knew of two hundred people who had memorized the entire New Testament. What strength and peace it must give them in the fiery trials they must endure under a Communist government.

F. S. DONNELSON

———o———

The good old days are the result of memory over misery.

Journal, Moro, Oregon

———o———

The memory is a treasurer to whom we must give funds, if we would draw the assistance we need.

NICHOLAS ROWE

———o———

In a Midwestern state, a newspaper reported that a local man had donated a loudspeaker to his church in memory of his wife.

———o———

Memory is a good thing if we learn to use it and do not let it use us.

EUGENIA PRICE

I remember your name perfectly, but I just can't think of your face.

———o———

No statue was ever erected to the memory of a man or woman who thought it was best to let well enough alone.

———o———

"It's a poor sort of memory that only works backwards."

LEWIS CARROLL,
Alice Through the Looking-Glass

———o———

Memory is the diary that we all carry about with us.

OSCAR WILDE,
The Importance of Being Earnest

———o———

For he lives twice who can at once employ
The present well, and ev'n the past enjoy.

ALEXANDER POPE, *Imitation of Martial*

———o———

I have a room whereinto no one enters
Save I myself alone:
There sits a blessed memory on a throne,
There my life centers.

CHRISTINA GEORGINA ROSSETTI,
Memory (II)

———o———

A Sunday School teacher had been teaching the Bible verse, "Draw nigh to God, and He will draw nigh to you" (James 4:8). By the time Charles got home he happily repeated his memory verse to Grandmother — his own version: "Draw a line unto me and I will draw a line unto you."

———o———

We commit the Golden Rule to memory and forget to commit it to life.

Mercy

A Tigress Saved By Mercy Gun

An angry tigress was saved from death by a "mercy gun" in Templar Park, near Kuala Lumpur, Malaya.

She was caught in an illegal wild boar trap; and she struggled for hours to free herself.

All conventional attempts to shoot the tigress out of the trap failed in the thick underbrush.

Five barbiturate capsules fired from Malaya's only "mercy gun" by Game Warden G. C. Metcalfe finally put the beast to sleep and into a coma that lasted four days!

It is mercy, but it is not in the shape of a gun, which the Lord uses to release human beings from the traps of sin and unbelief in which they are securely held — and from which their own efforts cannot extricate them.

TOM OLSON in *Now*

———o———

For Those Who Love

Have mercy always on the ones who love you.
Deny yourself the sharp impatient word.
When they are over-anxious, over-kind,
Your careless, hasty utterance is heard
Through all the lonely hollows of the heart
That loves, and loving, yearns.

Refrain! Refrain
In mercy from self-will, for those who love
Are desperately vulnerable to pain.

AUTHOR UNKNOWN

———o———

Teach me to feel another's woe,
To hide the fault I see;
That mercy I to others show,
That mercy show to me.

ALEXANDER POPE, *The Universal Prayer*

———o———

Mercy's indeed the attribute of heaven.

THOMAS OTWAY

———o———

Being all fashioned of the self-same dust,
Let us be merciful as well as just.

HENRY WADSWORTH LONGFELLOW,
Tales of a Wayside Inn

Merit

True merit, like a river, the deeper it is, the less noise it makes.

GEORGE SAVILE, LORD HALIFAX

———o———

Speak little and well if you wish to be considered as possessing merit.

French Proverb

———o———

Real merit of any kind, cannot long be concealed; it will be discovered, and nothing can depreciate it but a man exhibiting it himself. It may not always be rewarded as it ought; but it will always be known.

LORD CHESTERFIELD

Methods

Someone told Billy Sunday that they didn't like his methods. He answered, "How do you do it?" "Well, I don't try to preach," was the answer. "Then," said Billy, "I like the way I do it better than the way you don't do it."

———o———

We are looking for better methods; God is looking for better men.

JAMES WHITCOMB BROUGHER

Mind

It is easy to give another a "piece of your mind," but when you are through, you have lost your peace of mind.

———o———

Making up your mind is like making a bed; it usually helps to have someone on the other side.

———o———

Training the mind and overlooking the emotions may give us only monstrous machines long on thinking and short on feeling.

———o———

Most of us carry our own stumbling block around with us. We camouflage it with a hat.

Healthways

Most people take better care of their automobiles than their brains — they seldom put cheap fuel in their cars.

ROSCOE BROWN FISHER

———o———

A great many so-called open minds should be closed for repairs.

———o———

There are times when we need an open mind and a closed mouth, but there is never a time when we need a closed mind and an open mouth.

———o———

When a fellow ain't got much mind it don't take him long to make it up.

WILL ROGERS

———o———

I cannot put any price on that which I now value most — a mind.

———o———

As a field, however fertile, cannot be fruitful without cultivation, neither can a mind without learning.

MARCUS TULLIUS CICERO

———o———

The mind is not a vessel to be stuffed; it is a vessel made to transmute something.

———o———

Do not measure God's mind by your own.

GEORGE MACDONALD

———o———

Content is wealth, the riches of the mind;
And happy he who can such riches find.

JOHN DRYDEN

———o———

"Thou wilt keep him in perfect peace, whose mind is stayed on Thee: because he trusteth in Thee" (Isaiah 26:3).

An 86-year-old woman who has been a Christian for 79 years has tacked up in her room these words:

These things I have tried:

1. Laughing at difficulties, and found them disappearing.
2. Attempting heavy responsibility, and found it growing lighter.

3. Facing a bad situation and found it clearing up.
4. Telling the truth and found it most rewarding.
5. Believing men honest, and found them living up to expectation.
6. Trusting God each day, and found Him surprising me with His bountiful goodness.
7. Keeping my mind stayed on Him, and experiencing perfect peace.

———o———

When your mind goes blank, turn off the sound.

———o———

If you wish to know the mind of a man, listen to his words.
Chinese Proverb

———o———

As land is improved by sowing it with various seeds, so is the mind by exercising it with different studies.
PLINY THE ELDER

———o———

Were I so tall to reach the pole,
Or grasp the ocean with my span,
I must be measured by my soul:
The mind's the standard of the man.
ISAAC WATTS, *Horae Lyricae*

———o———

Measure your mind's height by the shade it casts!
ROBERT BROWNING, *Paracelsus*

———o———

The diseases of the mind are more destructive than those of the body.
MARCUS TULLIUS CICERO

———o———

Great minds have purposes, others have wishes. Little minds are tanned and subdued by misfortune; but great minds rise above them.
WASHINGTON IRVING

———o———

Cultivation of the mind is as necessary as food to the body.
MARCUS TULLIUS CICERO

———o———

Nurture your mind with great thoughts.
BENJAMIN DISRAELI

Minister

Minister's Moment

Here it is . . .
Saturday night.
Wonder what everyone's doing?
Me?
I'm waiting for another
wedding party to arrive.
Sermon's all done . . .
(Been working on it all week)
Bulletin is printed.
(Secretary has worked too).

I'm trying to relax a little . . .
store up my strength . . .
physical and spiritual for tomorrow.
Wonder how many will come to church?

A terrible responsibility . . .
(trying to speak of God)
Sometimes on Saturday night
I want to run.

But I pray . . .
and sweat a little too
(or is perspire nicer?)
thinking about Sunday.

What about you?
Do you ever think about Sunday?
ART MORGAN

———o———

The new Methodist minister was introducing his small son to a welcoming layman. "And this is my son John."
"Well," said the layman, "are you John the Baptist?"
"Oh, no," said the boy. "I'm John the Med'odist."
MRS. DAVID LETWAS in *Together*

———o———

Church member talking about her minister: "Six days of the week he's invisible and on the seventh he's incomprehensible."
News, Charlotte, North Carolina

———o———

The ministry of the Gospel is the poorest of trades and the noblest of callings.
THEODORE LEDYARD CUYLER

The world looks at ministers out of the pulpit to know what they mean in it.

RICHARD CECIL

———o———

A Methodist minister was found to have diabetes and while under treatment acted as hospital chaplain. His popularity in that post led to his retirement from the church, which made him a pastor emeritus. He was then hired by the hospital.

A woman in his former church, misunderstanding his honorary status, spread the word: "Poor Mr. Johnson — first he had diabetes, and now he has emeritus."

VIDA HOWARD in *Together*

———o———

We heard of a church service so solemn that a little girl whispered to her mother, "Does the minister live here or does he come down from Heaven every Sunday?"

———o———

Two ministers, given to arguing about their respective faiths, were in a very heated discussion. "That's all right," said one, calmly. "We'll just agree to disagree. After all, we're both doing the Lord's work — you in your way and I in His."

———o———

I would have every minister of the Gospel address his audience with the zeal of a friend, with the generous energy of a father, and with the exuberant affection of a mother.

FRANÇOIS DE SALIGNAC DE LA FÉNELON

———o———

A minister was called by the tax collector about a $500.00 church donation claimed by a parishioner.

"Did he give that amount?" asked the tax gatherer. The minister hesitated, then replied:

"No — but he will!"

MAXINE BARTLETT in *Together*

Miracles

The man for whom a miracle has been done never recognizes it as a miracle.

Miracles

The age of miracles is past,
    I hear the skeptic say;
How little does he understand
    Christ's miracles today.
His great and marv'lous works go on.
    How do I know, my friend?
He wrought His miracles in me,
    His wonders never end.

Did Jesus make the blind to see?
    My sight He has restored.
He caused the dumb to speak, you say?
    My lips now praise the Lord.
He also made the deaf to hear?
    But my ears too were sealed,
I could not hear His gentle voice
    'Til by His love He healed.

He passed through crowds and was
        not seen?
    Each day He walks with me
Through busy streets and thoroughfares
    And none but I can see.
He healed all manner of disease?
    With them I had my part;
He cured my sin-sick soul, you see,
    And healed my broken heart.

Did Peter walk upon the sea?
    When I'm cast down with care
He takes my hand — my spirit soars —
    And O, I walk on air.
No miracles today, you say?
    How wrong you are, my friend,
For what the Lord has done for me
    All human works transcend.

Yes — these are miracles to me —
    All blessings from above.
But, O, the greatest one of all —
    The wonder of His love.

LENA TRAAS

———o———

To have faith is to create; to have hope is to call down blessing; to have love is to work miracles.

———o———

Jesus was Himself the one convincing and permanent miracle.

IAN MACLAREN

———o———

Miracle Of Miracles!

My face is lined with living,
    My hair is touched with snow.

My hands are gnarled with giving,
  My feet are aged and slow.
The years are creeping on me
  As night descends on day,
Silently, like the shadows
  That steal the light away.
But when each night I kneel in faith
  At Jesus' feet to pray,
It's wonderful how young I feel,
  How peaceful and how gay!
My timid troubles disappear
  Before His throne, and then,
O miracle of miracles!
  I am a child again!

JESSIE CANNO ELDRIDGE

Misery

The comfort derived from the misery of others is slight.

MARCUS TULLIUS CICERO

———o———

There is no time so miserable but that a man may be true to himself.

———o———

Misery still delights to trace
Its semblance in another's vase.

WILLIAM COWPER

Missions, Missionary

First Missionaries

Was this the One the world had waited for?
Some thought He was. The woman at the well,
Astonished at the truth He dared to tell
Shared her conviction door to village door.
Was this the One? Mary and Martha swore
Not only by the awe He could compel
Or by the act of death that He could quell,
This was the Lord the people could adore.
But was He Saviour and the Son of God,
This carpenter of Nazareth, a man
So young to be so gently wise? Because

His touch held healing though He used no rod.
Was this Messiah sought since time began?
They changed our world who first belived He was.

DONNA DICKEY GUYER
in *Church Management*

———o———

Every heart with Christ is a missionary and every heart without Christ is a mission field.

DICK HILLIS

———o———

A colporteur missionary told the Christmas story to a group of people in a village in North India. Then he read the story from the Scriptures. "How long ago was this great day when God's Son was born?" one person asked. "About two thousand years ago," replied the missionary. "Then why has the news been so long in reaching us?" asked the villager in surprise. "Who has been hiding the Book all this time?"

CHARLES R. WOODSON

———o———

A missionary fell into the hands of cannibals.
"Going to eat me, I presume?" asked the missionary. The chief grunted. "Don't do it," he advised, "you won't like me." Thereupon the missionary took out a knife, sliced a piece from the calf of his leg and handed it to him. "Try this and see for yourself."
The chief took one bite and choked.
The missionary worked on the island for fifty years. He had a cork leg.

———o———

You cannot spell gospel without spelling GO.

———o———

The High Cost Of Missions

In 1839, John Williams, dubbed "The Apostle of the South Seas," and a missionary named Harris, sailed to the New Hebrides Islands and were clubbed to death by savages after a period of service for Christ.
Eighteen years later, G. N. Gordon and his wife took up the work on these islands and were killed in 1861.

Mr. Gordon's brother went to the same place and was killed in 1872.

A couple of missionaries named Turner and Nisbet later disembarked on the island of Tanna, stayed seven months, then fled for their lives by night in an open boat.

John G. Paton also heard the call of God to the New Hebrides. When he confided to a friend these plans, he was warned: "You will be eaten by cannibals!"

Paton replied, "Mr. Dickson, you are old . . . soon you will be put into the grave and eaten by worms. But if I can live and die serving the Lord Jesus Christ, it doesn't make any difference to me whether I'm eaten by cannibals or worms."

So Paton shoved off on his dangerous but God-appointed mission.

He learned the language, won for Christ many brute savages and held his first communion service in 1869 with twelve Christian natives partaking.

"I shall never taste a deeper bliss," he said, "until I gaze in the glorified face of Jesus Himself!"

Paton lived to see 16,000 South Sea islanders sing of God's love. And on the plains where savages once killed and ate each other, now stand Christian churches, schools and printing presses.

His life work behind him, John G. Paton is today enjoying his "deeper bliss" — gazing upon the glorified face of Him he served so well.

————o————

If I had a thousand lives to live, Africa should have them all.

BISHOP MACKENZIE

————o————

That land is henceforth my country which most needs the Gospel.

NIKOLAUS LUDWIG VON ZINZENDORF

————o————

A little girl just entering school said that she was from a missionary family.

"What is it like being a missionary?" the teacher asked.

"A barrel," the child replied.

It was a Jew who brought the Gospel to Rome, a Roman who took it to France, a Frenchman who took it to Scandinavia, a Scandinavian who took it to Scotland, a Scotsman who evangelized Ireland, and an Irishman who, in turn, made the missionary conquest of Scotland.

No country ever originally received the Gospel except at the hands of an alien.

Survey Bulletin

————o————

Your love has a broken wing if it cannot fly across the sea.

MALTBIE D. BABCOCK

————o————

You cannot do effective missionary work today without miracles.

ROBERT MCALISTER

————o————

A missionary is a person who never gets used to the thud of Christless feet on the way to eternity.

————o————

God had only one Son — and He was a missionary.

DAVID LIVINGSTONE

————o————

Unprayed for I feel like a diver at the bottom of a river with no connecting airline to the surface, or like a fireman wielding an empty hose on a burning building. With prayer I feel like David facing Goliath.

JAMES GILMOUR, Missionary to Mongolia

————o————

A one-legged school teacher from Scotland came to Hudson Taylor to offer himself for service in China.

"Why do you, with only one leg, think of going as a missionary?" asked Taylor.

"I do not see those with two legs going, so I must," replied George Stott.

He was accepted.

The Christian Beacon

————o————

The Voice Of One Who Wept

Today I heard the voice of one who wept in far-off lands,

Because of sin and misery, and begged
with outstretched hands
For one small lamp to light his dark.
Now fain I would have slept,
So stopped my ears, but in my heart
that sobbing voice still wept.

And then I heard the voice of One who
counted not the cost,
But left His ivory palaces to seek and
save the lost.
He said, "The sound of one who weeps
is coming up to Me.
Dost thou forget that last command
which I gave unto thee,

"To preach My Word to all the world?"
. . . O bitter be our shame!
Still hopeless millions walk the earth
who never heard His name,
And still the world spends lavishly in
every crowded mart,
And still the voice of Him who wept
is sobbing in my heart!

MARTHA SNELL NICHOLSON

Missions is taking the whole gospel
to the whole world by the whole
church.

I do not know that I shall live to see
a single convert, but I would not leave
my present field of labor to be made
king of the greatest empire on the
globe.

ADONIRAM JUDSON

Many of us will never reach the
mission field on our feet, but we can
reach them on our knees.

The only generation that can reach
this generation is our generation.

OSWALD SMITH

The funds of missionary societies depend not so much on the condition of
men's purses as on the state of their
soul. Unless a man cultivates a habit
of systematic giving when he had not
much to give, he will give little when
he is rich.

SAMUEL CHADWICK

Foreign missions are not an extra;
they are the acid test of whether or
not the Church believes the Gospel.

LESSLIE NEWBIGIN

In foreign missions, plant a tree;
don't import fruit.

LESTER SUMRALL

If God wants you on the mission
field, neither your money nor your
prayers will ever prove an acceptable
substitute.

When James Calvert went out as a
missionary to the cannibals of the Fiji
Islands, the captain of the ship sought
to turn him back. "You will lose your
life and the lives of those with you if
you go among such savages," he cried.
Calvert only replied, "We died before
we came here."

DAVID AUGSBURGER

Do we still want missionaries? Yes,
but we want missionaries who are God-
intoxicated men.

BISHOP ODUTOLA of Nigeria

A Missionary's Plea

Please pray for me, my friend — I need
your prayers
For there are burdens pressing hard
and many cares.
Pray, too, that Christ will make of me
The missionary that I ought to be.

Do pray for me, my friend, at morning
hour
That I may not be overcome by
Satan's power.
That mid the whirl and maze of things
My soul may drink of hidden springs.

And pray for me, my friend, when
night comes on alone,
God's stars look down upon us both,
apart.
Will you, dear friend, before you sleep,
Pray Him my soul with yours to
keep?

Cease not to pray for me — tho' sun-
dered far,

Come, meet me at the mercy seat
  from where you are;
Nor time nor distance can divide
  Our hearts that in His love abide.

AUTHOR UNKNOWN

———o———

Sophie had been praying for twelve
years to become a foreign missionary.
One day she had so prayed and the
heavenly Father seemed to say:
  "Sophie, stop! Where were you
born?" "In Holland, Father." "Where
are you now?" "In America, Father."
"Well, are you not a foreign missionary
already?"
  Then the Father said, "Who lives on
the floor above you?" "A family of
Swedes." "And who above them?"
"Why, some French." "And who in the
rear?" "Some Italians." "And a block
away?" "Some Chinese."
  "And you have never said a word
to these people about My Son? Do
you think I will send you thousands of
miles to the foreigner and the heathen
when you never care enough about
those at your own door to speak to
them about their souls?"

———o———

The Spirit of Christ is the spirit of
missions, and the nearer we get to Him
the more intensely missionary we must
become.

HENRY MARTYN

———o———

My son, if God has called you to be
a missionary, your Father in Heaven
would grieve to see you shrivel down
into a king.

CHARLES HADDON SPURGEON

———o———

Where Shall I Work?

"Master, where shall I work today?"
  And my love flowed warm and free.
Then He pointed out a tiny plot,
  And He said, "Work there for me."
But I answered quickly: "Oh, no, not
    there,
  Not anyone could see,
No matter how well my task is done —
  Not that small place for me!"
And His voice, when He spoke, it was
    so stern,

But He answered me tenderly:
  "Disciple, search that heart of thine.
Are you working for them, or for Me?
Nazareth was just a little place,
  And so was Galilee."

AUTHOR UNKNOWN

Mistakes

We recently heard about an editor
who explained away the mistakes that
crept into his publication with the
following notice: "If you find any mistakes, please consider that they appear
for the benefit of those readers who
always look for them. We try to print
something for everybody."

———o———

A story is told of the great Biblical
scholar, Bengel, as he lay on his deathbed. One of his friends quoted, or
rather misquoted, a well-known verse
of Scripture, adding the word "in"
where it did not belong: "I know in
whom I have believed."
  "No, no," said the dying believer,
"do not allow even a preposition to
come between my Savior and me: I
know whom I have believed!"

Gospel Witness

———o———

Among the floral displays received
by a new store on the occasion of its
opening was one that bore a card reading, "Deepest Sympathy."
  The manager immediately telephoned the florist.
  "But," the disturbed florist replied,
"what about the other party who received the card intended for you? It
read: 'Congratulations on your new lo-
cation'."

———o———

Admitting Mistakes

How often when we blunder, and are
  filled with guilty shame,
Do we invent excuses, and attempt to
  shift the blame!
But when we make mistakes, I find it's
  sensible and wise
To honestly admit them, and omit the
  alibis.

MARY HAMLETT GOODMAN

Nature DOES make mistakes. Sometimes she puts all the bones in the head and none in the back.

———o———

Nothing is opened by mistake as often as the mouth.

———o———

There is nothing final about a mistake, except its being taken as final.

PHYLLIS BOTTOME

———o———

I have made mistakes, but I have never made the mistake of saying that I never made one.

JAMES GORDON BENNETT

———o———

The quickest way to get a lot of undivided attention is to make a mistake.

Modern Life

Old-timers: Those who can remember when people were just people, instead of a bunch of numbers — Social Security, Zip Code, Area Code. . . .

———o———

Little Willie was in a store with his mother when he was given candy by one of the clerks.
"What must you say, Willie?"
"Charge it," he replied.

———o———

The materialistic age in which we live has blinded the eyes of many who fail to see that only what we do for, and through Christ, will live forever.

———o———

In this modern electric era, all a woman has to do to run her home is to keep on plugging.

Modesty

Modesty is the citadel of beauty and virtue.

DEMADES

———o———

Modesty is becoming to the great. What is difficult is to be modest when one is a nobody.

The Journal of Jules Renard

Modesty is a wonderful thing; it doesn't cost a cent and makes you look like a million.

———o———

Modesty: The gentle art of enhancing your charm by pretending not to be aware of it.

OLIVER HERFORD

Money

A dime is a dollar with the taxes taken out.

———o———

Why?

Why should we give money to save the heathen abroad when there are heathen in our own country?
Why should I give money to save those in other parts of the country when there are needy ones in my own town?
Why should I give to the poor of the town when my own church needs the money?
Why should I give to the church when my own family wants it?
Why should I give to my family what I want myself?
Why? Because I am a Christian; not a heathen.

A. P. UPHAM

———o———

One reason men's faces are put on money is that women are satisfied just to get their hands on it.

———o———

In presenting to his congregation the findings of the finance committee and explaining the need for more contributions, the minister sought to praise the laymen who have the best interests of the church at heart.
"You know," he said, "the preacher is the shepherd of his flock, and the finance committee acts as his crook."

MRS. ROBERT MOULTON in *Together*

———o———

He was not an outstanding Christian, as such. But he was very faithful. He seldom missed a service. Quietly he came and went each week, doing willingly whatever he could to help. Yes, there was something strange about him.

Each payday he made a special trip to the church office with his tithe from his modest income. One day the church secretary asked him why he made this special trip. Why not wait until Sunday? His answer: "I have a bad heart, and I don't want God's money in my pocket when I go."

———o———

It is good to check up once in a while, and make sure you have not lost the things that money cannot buy.
GEORGE HORACE LORIMER

———o———

Gold will be slave or master.
HORACE

———o———

A man's treatment of money is the most decisive test of his character, how he makes it and how he spends it.
JAMES MOFFATT

———o———

The poorest of all men is the one who has nothing but money.

———o———

The money you intend to save draws no interest.

———o———

A purse is doubly empty when it is full of borrowed money.

———o———

One day a certain old, rich man of a miserable disposition visited a rabbi, who took the rich man by the hand and led him to a window.
"Look out there," he said.
The rich man looked into the street.
"What do you see?" asked the rabbi.
"I see men, women, and children," answered the rich man.
Again the rabbi took him by the hand and this time led him to a mirror.
"Now what do you see?"
"Now I see myself," the rich man replied.
Then the rabbi said, "Behold, in the window there is glass, and in the mirror there is glass. But the glass of the mirror is covered with a little silver, and no sooner is the silver added than you cease to see others, but you see only yourself."
Moody Monthly

The kindergarten teacher was trying to teach her class to count money.
Placing a half dollar on her desk, she asked, "What is that?"
Said a small voice from the back row, "Tails."

———o———

Money is a form of power so intimately related to the possessor that one cannot consistently give money without giving self, nor can one give self without giving money. When a man gives money to a cause, he inevitably gives a part of himself, for his money is definitely a measure of his toil and talent. He supports with his money what he really values. Look at a man's budget, and you can quickly tell what matters most to him.
HENRY B. TRIMBLE

———o———

Earning maketh an industrious man; spending, a well-furnished man; saving, a prepared man; giving, a blessed man.
The Pentecostal Holiness Advocate

———o———

You will never win the world for Christ with your spare cash.

———o———

Money is like dynamite. It will destroy its possessor, according to the way it's handled.

———o———

Inflation is like putting on weight. It's easier to start than stop.

———o———

A budget is something that allows you to live within your means and without almost everything else.

———o———

One of the first things children learn at school is that other children get allowances.
Empire-Courier, Craig, Colorado

———o———

Often all it takes to start down the path to bankruptcy is a small raise in pay.

Having "money to burn" is a good way to start a fire which you can't put out.

———o———

Take care of your dollars and you will show more cents than your friends give you credit for.

———o———

Money never was made a fool of anybody; it only shows 'em up.

FRANK MCKINNEY HUBBARD

———o———

You can't take your money to heaven but you can send it on ahead.

Monument

The best monument is one with two legs going about the world witnessing for the Lord Jesus Christ to others.

DWIGHT L. MOODY

———o———

Those only deserve a monument who do not need one; that is, who have raised themselves a monument in the minds and memories of men.

WILLIAM HAZLITT

———o———

Who builds a church to God, and not to fame,
Will never mark the marble with his name.

ALEXANDER POPE, Moral Essays, Epistle III

Mother

Her Day

She cooked the breakfast first of all,
Washed the cups and plates,
Dressed the children and made sure
Stockings all were mates.
Combed their heads and made their beds,
Sent them out to play.
Gathered up their motley toys,
Put some books away.
Dusted chairs and mopped the stairs,
Ironed an hour or two,
Baked a jar of cookies and a pie,
Then made a stew.
The telephone rang constantly,
The doorbell did the same,
A youngster fell and stubbed his toe,
And then the laundry came.
She picked up blocks and mended socks
And then she polished up the stove.
(Gypsy folks were fortunate with carefree ways to rove!)
And when her husband came at six
He said: "I envy you!
It must be nice to sit at home
Without a thing to do!"

AUTHOR UNKNOWN

———o———

Mother's Love

Her love is like an island in life's ocean, vast and wide,
A peaceful, quiet shelter from the wind, and rain, and tide.

'Tis bound on the north by Hope, by Patience on the west,
By tender Counsel on the south, and on the east by Rest.

Above it like a beacon light shine Faith, and Truth, and Prayer;
And through the changing scenes of life,
I find a haven there.

AUTHOR UNKNOWN

———o———

Mother's Hands

What can be said of mother's hands can also not be said,
For who can count the vast drudgeries performed each day —
And who can surmise if drudgeries are really joys, because it is their pride . . .
And they also minister kindness.

LINDA CLARKE

———o———

Some mothers love their children selfishly: Their children exist for them.

Other mothers love their children slavishly: They exist for their children.

But some mothers love their children sacrificially: Their children and they exist for God.

JAMES SPRUNT

———o———

Maternal love: a miraculous substance which God multiplies as He divides it.

VICTOR HUGO

A Mother's Prayer

Lord, give me patience when wee hands
Tug at me with their small demands.
Give me gentle and smiling eyes;
Keep my lips from hasty replies.
Let not weariness, confusion, or noise
Obscure my vision of life's fleeting joys.
So, when in years to come, my house is still —
No bitter memories its rooms may fill.
Amen.

———o———

Sign on a supermarket bulletin: "Help a poor unwed mother. Take one of her kittens!"

———o———

Sign in a London maternity wear shop: "Two can look as chic as one."

———o———

Some men were discussing the various versions of the Bible. After they were finished giving the pros and cons of each Bible, a man who had been silent spoke up and said, "The best version of the Bible is the one my mother lived!"

———o———

One day a certain young mother was running on endlessly about the shortcomings of her children. Finally she paused long enough to ask, "What do you want out of life, anyway?" One child cautiously replied, "A quiet mother!"

The Christian Mother

———o———

A little boy, who was told by his mother that it was God who made people good, responded, "Yes, I know it is God, but Mothers help a lot."

Christian Guardian

———o———

A godly mother will point her children to God by the force of her example as much as by the power of her words.

———o———

You may have tangible wealth untold;
Caskets of jewels and coffins of gold,
Richer than I you can never be —
I had a mother who read to me.

STRICKLAND W. GILLILAN,
The Reading Mother

Motivation

Show me. Dare you. Prove it. If those words won't start you going, nothing will.

———o———

Man considereth the deeds, but God weigheth the intentions.

———o———

We only truly believe that which activates us.

DICK HILLIS

———o———

Triumphant father to mother watching teen-age son mow lawn: "I told him I lost the car keys in the grass."

DICK TURNER,
Newspaper Enterprise Association

Mottoes

A church in Kansas City has as its slogan:
"Wake up, sing up, preach up, pray up, but never give up, or let up, or back up, or shut up until the cause of Christ in this church and in the world is built up."

The Roundtable

———o———

A Good Motto

Talk less,
Pray more,
Obey God.
Rush less,
Love more,
Prove God.

———o———

Walk softly; speak tenderly; pray fervently.

T. J. BACH

———o———

If I falter — push me on.
If I stumble — pick me up.
If I retreat — shoot me.
Motto of the French Foreign Legion

Gentle in manner, strong in performance.

Motto of LORD NEWBOROUGH

Mouth

The mouth is the microphone of the heart.

ELEANOR L. DOAN

———o———

A lot of trouble in this world is caused by combining a narrow mind and wide mouth.

———o———

Mouth: The grocer's friend, the dentist's fortune, the orator's pride, and the fool's trap.

———o———

Nature did not make your ears so that they could be shut but did a perfect job on your mouth.

———o———

No man is so full of wisdom that he has to use his mouth as a safety valve.

Music

After teaching my second-graders "America the Beautiful," I listened while they sang it for me. And one voice rang out above the rest: "Oh, beautiful for space-ship skies . . ."

MARILYN KILBY in *NEA Journal*

———o———

The teacher played the "Star Spangled Banner" and asked her first-grade class to identify it. "That's easy," shouted a pupil. "It's what they play every Friday on television just before the fights."

———o———

Music, once admitted to the soul, becomes a sort of spirit, and never dies. It wanders perturbedly through the halls and galleries of the memory, and is often heard again, distinct and living, as when it first displaced the wavelets of the air.

EDWARD GEORGE BULWER-LYTTON

Sunday Nights

Some years ago within our small household
A simple formula my parents found
Whereby on Sunday nights, quite safe and sound,
We sang together — young as well as old.

The heat of Summer or king Winter cold
Lost their attractions when a jolly round
Or hymn or carol would indeed resound.
A choicer heritage all this than gold!

My mother, playing on the rare Rosewood
Was lovely in a flowing gown of blue:
And father, with his bass, was just the one
To harmonize the way a master should.

Such treasured nights I would bequeath to you
Who seek a sense of peace when day is done.

DORA FLICK FLOOD in *The Churchman*

———o———

Music should strike fire from the heart of man, and bring tears from the eyes of women.

LUDWIG VON BEETHOVEN

———o———

Music hath charms to soothe a savage breast,
To soften rocks, or bend a knotted oak.
I've read that things inanimate have moved,
And, as with living souls, have been informed
By magic numbers and persuasive sound.

WILLIAM CONGREVE, *The Mourning Bride*

———o———

Is there a heart that music cannot melt?
Alas! how is that rugged heart forlorn!

JAMES BEATTIE, *The Minstrel*

———o———

Music is nothing else but wild sounds civilized into time and tune.

THOMAS FULLER

Music is one of the fairest and most glorious gifts of God.

MARTIN LUTHER

———o———

Six-year-old Larry disagreed with his Sunday School teacher after the singing of the song, "The Light of the World Is Jesus."

"Jesus," Larry said, "is not the light of the world. The Sun and the Moon give the light."

———o———

Maybe the prayer hymn which was misprinted in the songbook wasn't too incongruous when, instead of "Land Me Safe On Canaan's Shore," it read, "Land My Safe On Canaan's Shore."

Mystery

Mystery Of Moods

Why are we whipped by our moods?
Why do we get the blues?
Why do we sigh and cry
Until we feel, "Oh, what's the use?"
Why after all this dejection,
Does our spirit soar like a breeze?
Why are we gay and blithesome and
    glad,
When a short while before,
We were lonely and sad?
Will somebody tell me . . . please?

BERNICE SMITH

———o———

A mystery is a fact every mind can see, but no one can explain. To reject an obvious fact because you cannot understand or explain it is childish.

———o———

One of the minor mysteries to many an angler is why fish decide to take their vacations at the same time the fisherman does.

N

Name

Many a man's name appears in the papers only three times: When he's too young to read, when he's too dazed to read, and when he's too dead to read.

———o———

Your Name

You got it from your father,
'Twas the best he had to give,
And right gladly bestowed it;
It is yours the while you live.
You may lose the watch he gave you
And another you may claim,
But remember, when you're tempted,
To be careful of his name.
It was fair the day you got it
And a worthy name to wear;
When he took it from his father
There was no dishonor there.

Through the years he proudly wore it,
To his father he was true,
And that name was clean and spotless
When he passed it on to you.

It is yours to wear forever,
Yours, perhaps, some distant morning,
To another boy to give,
And you'll smile as did your father
Smile above that baby there,
If a clean name and a good name
You are giving him to wear.

AUTHOR UNKNOWN

———o———

A census taker asked a woman how many children she had.

"Well," she began, "there's Billy, and Harry, and Martha, and —"

"Never mind the names," he interrupted, impatiently, "just give me the number."

The mother became indignant. "They haven't got numbers; they've all got names."

———o———

I know a life that is lost to God,
Bound down by the things of earth;
But I know a Name, a Name, a Name
That can bring that soul new birth.

AUTHOR UNKNOWN

I cannot love my lord, and not his name.

ALFRED, LORD TENNYSON

Narrow

Narrow-Minded

The preacher is sometimes accused of being narrow-minded because he insists upon the Christian's forsaking all to follow Christ.

But all of life is narrow, and success is to be found only by passing through the narrow gate and down the straight way.

There is no room for broad-mindedness in the chemical laboratory. Water is composed of two parts hydrogen and one part oxygen. The slightest deviation from that formula is forbidden.

There is no room for broad-mindedness in the mathematics classroom. Neither geometry, calculus, nor trigonometry allows any variation from exact accuracy, even for old times' sake. The solution of the problem is either right or it is wrong — no tolerance there.

There is no room for broad-mindedness in the garage. The mechanic there says that the piston rings must fit the cylinder walls within one-thousandth part of an inch. Even between friends there cannot be any variation if the motor is to run smoothly.

How, then, shall we expect that broad-mindedness shall rule in the realm of religion and morals?

The Log of the Good Ship Grace

Nature

Flowers are the poetry of earth, as stars are the poetry of heaven.

AUTHOR UNKNOWN

———o———

In a little church in the far south of Ireland, every window but one is of painted glass. Through that single exception may be seen a breathtaking view: a lake of deepest blue, studded with green islets, and backed by range after range of purple hills. Under the window is the inscription: "The heavens declare the glory of God, and the firmament showeth His handiwork."

ROBERT GIBBINGS

———o———

Invitation

Come and ride with me to the mountain side
Where the road leads up and the world is wide.

Come and bring your dreams that have gone astray,
You will find new ones on my tree-lined way.

Come and tour with me to the canyon's rim
And listen spellbound to nature's hymn.

Come and lift your eyes to the star-hushed night,
And release your soul for the wind's delight.

You will know at last that your heart is free
When you follow this path and ride with me.

AUTHOR UNKNOWN

———o———

He that follows nature is never out of his way. Nature is sometimes subdued, but seldom extinguished.

FRANCIS BACON

———o———

Nature gives to every time and season some beauties of its own; and from morning to night, as from the cradle to the grave, is but a succession of changes so gentle and easy that we can scarcely mark their progress.

CHARLES DICKENS

———o———

God's Gifts In Nature

We plow the fields and scatter
  The good seed on the land,
But it is fed and watered
  By God's almighty hand;
He sends the snow in winter,
  The warmth to swell the grain,
The breezes and the sunshine,
  And soft refreshing rain.

He only is the Maker
  Of all things near and far;

He paints the wayside flower,
  He lights the evening star;
The winds and waves obey Him,
  By Him the birds are fed;
Much more to us, His children,
  He gives our daily bread.

We thank Thee, then, O Father,
  For all things bright and good,
The seed-time and the harvest,
  Our life, our health, our food.
Accept the gifts we offer
  For all Thy love imparts,
And, what Thou most desirest,
  Our humble, thankful hearts.

              MATTHIAS CLAUDIUS

———o———

His eyes are dim who cannot see
A mountain's purple majesty.
His ears are deaf who cannot hear
Love songs of birds in spring of year.
His feet are numb who never seeks
A mountain breeze to cool his cheeks.
His soul is dead who gets no thrills
From rocks and woods and templed
  hills.
He who no wilderness has trod
Has missed a chance to walk with God.

———o———

Longing For The Mountains

There is a place where I long to be,
A place in the mountains high and
  free;

Away from the routine, procedures and
  strife,
Where one draws nearer to the beauties
  of life.

Where lonely streams plunge to depths
  below,
Churning from summits of sparkling
  snow;

Where the laurel, aspen and lofty pine
Remain untouched as in the beginning
  of time.

Where the eagle in his domain so ma-
  jestically fair,
Reels by the hour in the turbulent air.

Where at twilight is heard the voice
  of the thrush,
Which leaves me oblivious to the modern day rush.

             CARMON F. BECKER

Climb the mountains and get their
  good tidings.
Nature's peace will flow into you as
  sunshine flows into trees.
The winds will blow their own freshness into you,
And the storms their energy,
While cares will drop off like falling
  leaves.

             JOHN MUIR

———o———

A group of scientists in Chicago
were conducting an experiment. They
placed a female moth of a rare species
in a room. Four miles away a male
moth of the same species was released.
Despite the din and smoke of the city,
the distance, and the fact that the
female was in a CLOSED room, in a
few hours the male moth was found
beating its wings against the window
of the room in which the female was
confined! Can you explain such a phe-
nomenon? It's a miracle — a miracle
of nature. God made it so!

    The Log of the Good Ship Grace

———o———

There is a serene and settled majesty
to woodland scenery that enters into
the soul and delights and elevates it,
and fills it with noble inclinations.

             WASHINGTON IRVING

———o———

If you wish your children to think
deep thoughts, to know the holiest emotions, take them to the woods and hills,
and give them the freedom of the
meadows; the hills purify those who
walk upon them.

             RICHARD JEFFERIES

———o———

Walk with me a little mile down shimmering sunlit trails;
Listen with me a little while to nature's
  whispered tales.
If man could only understand the
  words that nature speaks,
He'd have the world at his command
  and find the truth he seeks.

             DEL BARTON

———o———

I saw two clouds at morning
  Tinged by the rising sun,

And in the dawn they floated on,
And mingled into one.
JOHN GARDINER CALKINS BRAINARD,
Epithalamium

———o———

The Voice Of Nature

A thousand sounds, and each a joy-
ous sound;
The dragon-flies are humming as they
please,
The humming birds are humming all
around,
The clithra all alive with buzzing bees,
Each playful leaf its separate whisper
found,
As laughing winds went rustling
through the grove;
And I saw thousands of such sights as
these
And heard a thousand sounds of joy
and love.
And yet so dull I was, I did not know
That He was there who all this love
displayed,
Shared all my joy, was glad that I
was glad;
And all because I did not hear the
word
In English accents say, "It is the Lord."
AUTHOR UNKNOWN

———o———

I can enjoy society in a room; but
out-of-doors, nature is company enough
for me.
WILLIAM HAZLITT

Needs, Necessity

I Must Go Shopping

One of these days I must go shopping. I am completely out of SELF-
RESPECT. I want to exchange the
SELF-RIGHTEOUSNESS I picked up
the other day for some HUMILITY,
which they say is less expensive and
wears better.

I want to look at some TOLERANCE
which is being used for wraps this
season; and someone showed me some
pretty samples of PEACE; we are so
low on that and we can never have
too much of it.

By the way, I must try to match
some PATIENCE that my neighbor

wears. It is very becoming to her and
I think would look equally good on me.
I might try that garment of LONG-
SUFFERING that they are displaying.
I never thought I would want to wear
it. And I must not forget to have my
SENSE OF HUMOR mended, and
look for some inexpensive EVERYDAY
GOODNESS.

It is surprising how quickly one's
stock of goods is depleted. Yes, I must
go shopping soon.
PATRICIA MUELLER

———o———

A great necessity is a great opportunity.
HENRY PARRY LIDDON

———o———

The world's most basic needs can be
summed up in four words: bread,
brains, belief, and brotherhood.
J. WALLACE HAMILTON
in *Tarbell's Teacher's Guide*

———o———

Necessity never made a good bargain.
BENJAMIN FRANKLIN

———o———

Many are our wants; few are our
needs.

———o———

Someone Needs You

If you're feeling low and worthless,
There seems nothing you can do,
Just take courage and remember
There is someone needing you.

You were created for a purpose,
For a part in God's great Plan;
Bear ye one another's burdens,
So fulfill Christ's law to man.

Are you Father, Son or Daughter?
You've a work, none else can do.
Are you Husband, Wife or Mother?
There is someone needing you.

If perhaps in bed you're lying,
You can smile or press the hand
Of the one who tells his story.
He will know you understand.

There are many sad and lonely,
And discouraged, not a few,
Who a little cheer are needing,
And there's someone needing you.

Someone needs your faith and courage,
Someone needs your love and prayer,
Someone needs your inspiration,
Thus to help their cross to bear.

Do not think your work is ended,
There is much that you can do,
And as long as you're on earth,
There is someone needing you.
                                    SUSIE B. MARR

Neighbor

Who Is My Neighbor?

Thy neighbor? It is he whom thou
  Hast the power to aid and bless —
Whose aching heart or burning brow
  Thy soothing hand may press.

Thy neighbor? 'Tis the fainting poor
  Whose eye with want is dim —
Whom hunger sends from door to door.
  Go thou and succor him.

Thy neighbor? 'Tis that weary man
  Whose years are at their brim —
Bent low with sickness, care and pain.
  Go thou and comfort him.

Thy neighbor? 'Tis the heart bereft
  Of every earthly gem —
Widow and orphan, helpless left,
  Go thou and shelter them.

When thou meetest a human form
  Less favored than thine own,
Remember, He thy neighbor is —
  Give bread instead of stone.

O, pass not, pass not heedless by,
  Perhaps thou canst redeem
The breaking heart from misery;
  Go — share thy lot with him.
                                    AUTHOR UNKNOWN

———o———

There's an ideal height for a back-
yard fence: just high enough to keep
the dogs out but low enough to shake
hands over.
———o———

Neighbors are good when they are
neighborly.

News, Newspaper

Pupils at a Canadian grade school
were asked why their families chose
the newspaper read in their homes.
One young fellow gave the following
reason: "Mom says she likes our paper
because when folded in two it exactly
fits the bottom of the bird cage."
                                    EDDIE OLYNUK in *Coronet*

———o———

In The News From The Headlines:

"Cemetery Site Is Approved By Body."
                        Manhattan, Kansas Mercury

"Ike Pledges Federal Aid in Lynching."
                        Harrisburg, Pennsylvania Patriot

"Beast Bites Bride, Harasses Trip."
                        Minot, North Dakota Daily News

"Writer Slaughter To Be At Fooley's."
                        Houston, Texas Post

———o———

A headline on the church page of a
California paper: "Church School
Women Want More Children."

———o———

On an October Sunday, an important eastern newspaper made the following listing in its radio schedule:
"1:00 — Back to God. (If no World
Series game.)"
                                    This Week Magazine

———o———

Let the greatest part of the news
thou hearest be the least part of what
thou believest, lest the greater part of
what thou believest be the least part
of what is true. Where lies are easily
admitted the father of lies will not
easily be excluded.
                                    FRANCIS QUARLES

———o———

The day the Rev. Smith took a turn
for the better after a long and serious
illness, the old church janitor decided
to give townspeople the good news.
They had been calling continuously to
ask about the minister. So on the bulletin board outside the church, the
janitor posted this announcement:
"God is good — Smith is better!"
                                    GLORIA FOSTER in *Together*

New Year

A New Year's Wish

To be of greater service, Lord,
A closer student of Thy Word;
To help to bear a brother's load
And cheer him on the heavenly road;
To tell the lost of Jesus' love,
And how to reach the home above;
To trust in God whate'er befall,
Be ready at the Master's call
For any task that He may give;
And thus through all the year to live
For Him who gave Himself for me
And taught me that my life should be
A life unselfish, not self-willed,
But with the Holy Spirit filled.

Selected

———o———

New Year's Thoughts

What is a year? A group of days
That may be used in many ways.
A year may be a priceless boon —
Alas, that it is gone so soon!
And yet we need not feel forlorn,
For now another year is born.
Our days and years are wisely planned.
They lie within the Master's hand.
So, with glad hope and right good cheer,
We welcome this, another year.

RALPH H. DUMONT

———o———

A New Year Wish

What shall I wish thee this New Year?
Health, wealth, prosperity, good cheer,
All sunshine — not a cloud or tear?
Nay! Only this:
That God may lead thee His own way,
That He may choose thy path each day,
That thou mayest feel Him near alway,
For this is bliss!

AUTHOR UNKNOWN

———o———

A Prayer Upon A Threshold

Here on my threshold, eager to start
Out through a New Year, Lord, I stand,
Waiting a moment, a prayer in my heart:

Go with me, Lord, and hold my hand.

There are such beautiful days ahead,
Blinding my eyes, Lord, may there be
Springs by the wayside, manna for bread,
And You, a companion, to walk with me.

Through any dark day, talk with me,
I am a small child, often afraid;
Lead through the darkness, let me see
Light ahead that Your lamp has made.

Here on the threshold, ready to start
Out through a year, untrod, unknown —
Now with a small child's trusting heart
I go, but I do not go alone.

GRACE NOLL CROWELL

———o———

The darkness hides the path ahead,
The stones we cannot see;
So many struggle on life's road
Complaining shamefully!
Fumbling, grumbling, stumbling on
Waiting for the light to dawn!

The light has dawned, for Christ has said:
"I am this dark world's Light."
Then why continue in the dark?
Without Him it is night!

So, as another New Year dawns,
May we walk close to Him;
The dazzling glory of His light
Will make all else grow dim;
His beaming, gleaming, streaming Light
Will shine, and make the pathway bright!

AUTHOR UNKNOWN

———o———

Still upward be thine onward course;
For this I pray today;
Still upward as the years go by
And seasons pass away.
Still upward in this coming year,
Thy path is all untried
Still upward may'st thou journey on,
Close by Thy Savior's side.

AUTHOR UNKNOWN

I Am The New Year

I am what you dreamed to be — but did not dare.

I am what you hoped to do — but did not will.

I am the distant country of achievement which you saw afar but the path to which you have not found.

I am the fellowships you have been too busy to form.

I am the books which, in spite of plans, you didn't take time to read.

I am the habits of yesterday crystallizing into the character of tomorrow.

I am the decisions of the old year, coming back into your life to empower or to imperil those of the new.

I am the vigor of a new purpose, putting life into your half-formed ambitions.

I am the Eternal Will of God at work within you.

I am the NEW YEAR!

PERCY R. HAYWARD

———o———

Seven Blessings For The New Year

May the Lord's presence this coming year be:

ABOVE YOU — to guard. "Know therefore this day . . . that the Lord He is God in heaven above" (Deuteronomy 4:39).

UNDERNEATH — to support. "The eternal God is thy refuge and underneath are the everlasting arms" (Deuteronomy 33:27).

BEHIND — as a rereward. "The God of Israel will be your rereward" (Isaiah 52:12).

AT YOUR RIGHT HAND — to protect. "Because He is at my right hand I shall not be moved" (Psalm 16:8).

BEFORE — to lead. "I will go before thee and make the crooked places straight" (Isaiah 45:2).

ROUND ABOUT — to shield from storms. "As the mountains are round about Jerusalem so the Lord is round about His people from henceforth even forever" (Psalm 125:2).

WITHIN — as Companion and Comforter. "And I will put my Spirit within you" (Ezekiel 36:27). "I am crucified with Christ nevertheless I live; yet not I, but Christ liveth in me" (Galatians 2:20).

MRS. JONATHAN GOFORTH
in The Sunday School Times

———o———

Correct Thou, Lord, for me
What ringeth harsh to Thee,
That heart and life may sing
Thy perfect song
The New Year long.

Night

Good Night

Some things go to sleep in such a funny way;
Little birds stand on one leg and tuck their heads away;
Chickens do the same, standing on their perch;
Little mice lie soft and still as if they were in church;
Kittens curl up close in such a funny ball;
Horses hang their sleepy heads and stand still in the stall;
Sometimes dogs stretch out, or curl up in a heap;
Cows lie down upon their sides when they would go to sleep.
But little babies dear are snugly tucked in beds,
Warm with blankets, all so soft and pillows for their heads.
Birds and beast and babe — I wonder which of all
Dream the dearest dreams that down from dreamland fall.

Child Lore

———o———

Night is the time to weep,
To wet with unseen tears
Those graves of memory where sleep
The joys of other years.

JAMES MONTGOMERY

Noble, Nobility

Be noble! and the nobleness that lies
In other men, sleeping, but never
dead,
Will rise in majesty to meet thine
own.

JAMES RUSSELL LOWELL

———o———

The beginning of true nobility comes
when a man ceases to be interested in
the judgment of men, and becomes interested in the judgment of God.

J. GRESHAM MACHEN

———o———

Better not to be at all than not be
noble.

ALFRED, LORD TENNYSON

Nothing

Since it is God's nature to make
something out of nothing, we must become nothing before He can make
something out of us.

MARTIN LUTHER

———o———

It's dangerous to try and be number
one because it's next to nothing.

———o———

Nothing can be obtained from nothing.

———o———

Nothing is cheap if you don't want
it.

Nothing is simpler than faith, and
nothing more sublime.

———o———

Man is as a circle whose circumfer-
ence has been erased.

Now

Life Is Too Short

To remember slights or insults.
To cherish grudges that rob me of
happiness.
To waste time in doing things that are
of no value.
To let past sins or mistakes cloud
future happiness.
To miss making friends because I am
too busy making money.
To give my youth to the devil and my
old age to God.
To dream of tomorrow when I may
never have one.
To put off making a confession of
Christ now.

CHARLES M. SHELDON

———o———

The only period of time you can
ever act upon is right now.

PAUL PARKER

———o———

"Now" is the watchword of the wise.

CHARLES HADDON SPURGEON

O

Obedience, Obey

Throughout the Bible . . . when God
asked a man to do something, methods,
means, materials and specific directions were always provided. The man
had one thing to do: obey.

ELISABETH ELLIOT

———o———

Obedience

I said, "Let me walk in the fields."
He said, "No, walk in the town."

I said, "There are no flowers there."
He said, "No flowers, but a crown."

I said, "But the skies are black;
"There is nothing but noise and din."

And He wept as He sent me back.
"There is more," He said; "there is
sin."

I said, "But the air is thick,
And fogs are veiling the sun."

He answered: "Yet souls are sick,
"And souls in the dark undone."

I said, "I shall miss the light
"And friends will miss me, they say."

He answered: "Choose ye tonight
"If I am to miss you, or they."

I pleaded for time to be given.
He said, "Is it hard to decide?

"It will not seem hard in heaven
"To have followed the steps of your
   Guide."

I cast one look at the fields,
   Then set my face to the town;

He said, "My child, do you yield?
Will you leave the flowers for the
   crown?"

Then into His hand went mine,
   And into my heart came He;

And I walk in a light divine
   The path I had feared to see.

                              GEORGE MACDONALD

———o———

The child who obeys without question is probably too young to talk.
                              JEANNE OPALACH

———o———

Have you learned that being obedient is better than being obstreperous?

———o———

In John 15, the secret of abounding
is abiding, the secret of abiding is obeying, and the secret of obeying is aban-
donment to Christ.
                              WILLIAM MIEROP

———o———

Cheerful obedience is the only kind
worth practicing.

———o———

The man who would lift others must
be uplifted himself, and he who would
command others must learn to obey.
                              CHARLES K. OBER

———o———

Where the need is greatest let us be
found gladly obeying the Master's command.
                              J. HUDSON TAYLOR

———o———

I believe that we get an answer to
our prayers when we are willing to
obey what is implicit in that answer.
I believe that we get a vision of God
when we are willing to accept what
that vision does to us.
                              ELSIE CHAMBERLAIN

———o———

The Breath Of God

May I in will and deed and word
   Obey Thee as a little child;
And keep me in Thy love, my Lord,
   For ever holy, undefiled;
Within me teach, and strive, and pray,
Lest I should choose my own wild way.

My spirit turns to Thee and clings,
   All else forsaking, unto Thee;
Forgetting all created things,
   Remembering only "God in me."
O living Stream; O gracious rain,
None wait for Thee, and wait in vain.
                              GERHARDT TER STEEGEN

———o———

"Mommy," said little Phil, "Tommy
never will learn to swim 'cause his
mommy won't let him go near the
water."
   "Yes? He is a good little boy to listen
to his mother."
   "Unhuh," agreed Phil, thoughtfully,
"and he'll go straight to Heaven the
first time he falls in."
                              TED DOUGLAS

———o———

A policeman noticed a boy with a
lot of stuff packed on his back riding a
tricycle around and around the block.
Finally he asked him where he was
going.
   "I'm running away from home," the
boy said.
   The policeman then asked him,
"Why do you keep going around and
around the block?"
   The boy answered, "My mother won't
let me cross the street."
                              Teach

———o———

Tom: "Did you know that Lot's wife
turned into a pillar of salt because she
did not obey God?"
   Charles: "That's nothing. My mother
turned into a telephone pole because
she didn't obey the traffic signal."

Obedience should be a child's first lesson.

BENJAMIN FRANKLIN

Obstacles

Obstacles are those frightful things you see when you take your eyes off the goal.

———o———

The block of granite which was an obstacle in the path of the weak, becomes a stepping-stone in the path of the strong.

THOMAS CARLYLE

———o———

The barriers of life may be ranked among its greatest benedictions.

FREDERICK B. MEYER

Offering

In a little parish church in Scotland one Sunday, so the story goes, a parishioner was horrified to discover that he had accidentally dropped a sovereign into the usher's basket, instead of the shilling he had intended.

After the service he went up to the head usher and, explaining, tried to get his money back. "Not on your life!" was the head usher's firm reply. "Money paid to the Lord is not returnable."

"Well," said the man, after reflection, "at least I'll get a sovereign's worth o' credit in heaven."

"That you weel not," announced the elder. "You'll get the shilling's worth you meant to drap in. The balance be just velvet for the Lord."

Onward, Canada, quoted in The Liguorian

———o———

If it weren't for parking meters and the church collection plates, the government could do away with nickels.

———o———

He dropped a quarter in the plate,
Then meekly raised his eyes;
Glad that his weekly rent was paid
To mansions in the skies.

———o———

There are many signs along the highways saying, "Keep the state green." It's a good idea to keep the offering the same way.

ELEANOR L. DOAN

———o———

When we place our offering in the plate, we are not really giving to God; we are simply taking our hands off of what belongs to Him.

———o———

A lady arriving at a church concert found two men at the door selling tickets.

"Oh," she said, "you're selling tickets! Why, I thought you were going to take up a collection, so I didn't bring any money along."

———o———

Does your religion stand up under the collection plate test?

———o———

A poor blind woman in Paris put twenty-seven francs into a plate at a missionary meeting. "You cannot afford so much," said one. "Yes, sir, I can," she answered.

On being pressed to explain, she said, "I am blind, and I said to my fellow straw-workers, 'How much money do you spend in a year for oil for your lamps when it is too dark to work nights?' They replied, 'Twenty-seven francs.'

"So," said the poor woman, "I found that I have so much in the year because I am blind and do not need a lamp, and I give it to shed light to the dark heathen lands."

Christian Endeavor World

Opinion

If you insist on sticking to your guns in any situation, be sure they are loaded.

———o———

"How well you and your wife get on," a friend remarked to a man whose marriage was very happy. "Don't you ever have differences of opinion?"

"Oh, yes," was the reply, "very often."

"You must get over them quickly."

"Ah, that's the secret," said the husband. "I never tell her about them."

Another person's good opinion of you is something to live up to, not to lean on.

———o———

One of the hardest secrets for a man to keep is his opinion of himself.

———o———

Public opinion in this country is everything.

ABRAHAM LINCOLN

———o———

Some men haven't any opinions but yours until they meet the next fellow.

Opportunity

Next to knowing when to seize an opportunity, the most important thing in life is to know when to forego an advantage.

BENJAMIN DISRAELI

———o———

Believe it or not, opportunity will look for you if you're worth finding.

———o———

No opportunity is ever lost — someone else picks up the ones you miss.

———o———

Why doesn't opportunity kick down the door instead of just knocking? Temptation does.

———o———

When opportunity knocks at the door some people are out in the yard looking for four-leaf clovers.

———o———

It's Up To Me

I get discouraged now and then
When there are clouds of gray,
Until I think about the things
That happened yesterday.
I do not mean the day before,
Or those of months ago.
But all the yesterdays in which
I had the chance to grow.
I think of opportunities
That I allowed to die
And those I took advantage of
Before they passed me by.

And I remember that the past
Presented quite a plight.
But somehow I endured it and
The future seemed all right.
And I remind myself that I
Am capable and free,
And my success and happiness
Are really up to me.

JAMES J. METCALFE

———o———

To see each morning a world made anew, as if it were the morning of the very first day; to treasure and use it, as if it were the final hour of the very last day.

FAY HARTZELL ARNOLD

———o———

Opportunity never comes — it's here.

———o———

God, teach us to take advantage of the opportunities offered us — not the people offering them.

———o———

The door of opportunity is so wide open that it's off its hinges.

ERNIE REB

———o———

Opportunities correspond with almost mathematical accuracy to the ability to use them.

———o———

An opportunist is a person who, finding himself in hot water, decides he needs a bath anyway.

———o———

When opportunity does knock,
By some uncanny quirk
It often goes unrecognized —
It so resembles work!

———o———

There are two kinds of opportunities, according to an old Japanese saying: those we chance upon and those we create. Either kind may represent the opportunity of a lifetime to any one individual but we are far more likely to recognize and take advantage of those we create.

With every rising of the sun
Think of your life as just begun.

AUTHOR UNKNOWN

———o———

A minister in a town is used to having his tiny daughter hustle up from Sunday School to help him shake hands with the congregation on the way out of church. He was a bit taken aback one Sunday, however, to notice that his eldest son had also joined the line and was busily collecting from customers on his paper route whom he had missed the day before on his regular rounds.

Maclean's Magazine

———o———

Opportunities are seldom labeled.

JOHN SHEDD

———o———

Opportunity often reveals great men in small places and small men in great places.

———o———

The hour of opportunity lies near the hours of prayer.

Opposite

Selfishness and service are at opposite poles. It is impossible to be characterized by both at the same time.

CAROL S. GISH

———o———

Our antagonist is our helper.

EDMOND BURKE,
Reflections on the Revolution in France

Optimism, Optimist

An optimist is one who thinks the good old days are yet to come!

———o———

An optimist is wrong as often as a pessimist, but he has a lot more fun.

———o———

The optimist proclaims that we live in the best of all possible worlds; and the pessimist fears this is true.

JAMES BRANCH CABELL, *The Silver Stallion*

———o———

Optimist: Happychondriac.

An optimist is a woman who starts hunting for her shoes when the guest speaker says "in conclusion . . ."

———o———

It would be interesting to know what an optimist and a pessimist see when both look into the same mirror at the same time.

———o———

Write in your heart that every day is the best day in the year.

RALPH WALDO EMERSON

———o———

Optimism is the content of small men in high places.

F. SCOTT FITZGERALD

———o———

An optimist laughs to forget, and a pessimist forgets to laugh.

———o———

The photographer had just taken a picture of an old man on his ninety-eighth birthday. He thanked the old gentleman, saying, "I hope I'll be around to take your picture when you're one hundred."

The old man replied: "Why not? You look healthy to me."

———o———

An optimist is a fisherman who brings along his camera.

———o———

Optimist: A man who can turn his car over to a parking lot attendant without looking back.

———o———

Optimist: A father who will let his son take the new car on a date.
Pessimist: One who won't.
Cynic: One who did.

———o———

An optimist is a bald-headed man who thinks his condition is only temporary.

———o———

No man ever impaired his eyesight by looking on the bright side of things!

The optimist says his glass is half full. The pessimist says his is half empty.

———o———

Optimism is one of the chief members of the faith family.

Organize

An organizer is the person who is the center of confusion.

———o———

Ninety percent of failure is due to lack of organization.

HENRIETTA C. MEARS

———o———

Well-arranged time is a mark of a well-arranged mind.

———o———

After forming a club, girls in my third-grade class gave me a list of their officers: the usual President, Vice-President, Roll Caller, Treasurer. But I was intrigued by the last officer listed — Decider!

ETHEL M. ANDERSON in *Reader's Digest*

Original, Originality

Originality is the act of forgetting where you read it.

———o———

If you want to be original, be yourself. God never made two people exactly alike.

Others

Plea For Others

You cannot pray the Lord's Prayer
  And even once say "I."
You cannot pray the Lord's Prayer
  And even once say "my."
Nor can you say the Lord's Prayer
  And not pray for another.
For when you ask for daily bread
  You must include your brother.
For others are included
  In each and every plea;
From the beginning to the end of it,
  It does not once say "me."

AUTHOR UNKNOWN

If a man be gracious and courteous to strangers, it shows he is a citizen of the world, and that his heart is no island cut off from other lands, but a continent that joins to them. If he be compassionate toward the afflictions of others, it shows that his heart is like the noble [myrrh] tree that is wounded itself when it gives the balm. If he easily pardons and remits offenses, it shows that his mind is planted above injuries. If he be thankful for small benefits, it shows that he weighs men's minds and not their trash. But above all, if he has St. Paul's wish to be *anathema* from Christ for the salvation of his brethren (Romans 9:3), it shows a nature that has a kind of conformity with Christ Himself.

FRANCIS BACON

———o———

To be subject to others is the worst kind of suffering for some people.

———o———

When you are good to others, you are best to yourself.

———o———

He who wishes to secure the good of others has already secured his own.

———o———

O merciful Father, who in compassion for Thy sinful children didst send Thy Son Jesus Christ to be the Savior of the world: Give us grace to serve one another in all lowliness, and to enter into the fellowship of His sufferings, who liveth and reigneth with Thee and the Holy Spirit, one God, world without end. Amen.

Book of Common Worship

———o———

As John Glenn orbited the earth, through those strange transitions from sunrise to sunset, men and instruments in marvelously sensitive attunement were keeping touch with him. Again and again, as messages came through from earth, he said, "I read you loud and clear."

We're given a strange, wonderful power for tuning in — at least to some extent — to one another as persons. Also, yet, how often we steel our thoughts against one another, or turn a cold shoulder to some other! God gives holy heart-ears for responding, for listening, and for turning to others with voluntary warmth, kindness, help. Only because He first loved us can we learn love. "Without us God will not, without Him we cannot!"

REV. A. C. FESSENDEN

P

Paradox

When a boy gets up at four o'clock in the morning to deliver papers, people say he is a go-getter. If the church should ask that same boy to get up at four to do some work for the Lord, they would say: "That's asking too much of a boy."

If a woman spends eight hours away from her home working in a factory or office or her garden, she is called an energetic wife. If, however, she is willing to do the same thing for the Lord, they say: "Religion has gone to her head."

———o———

If one ties himself down to making payments of $30 each week for some time on a item for personal enjoyment, he pays willingly. But if that same person is approached on tithing and asked to put the same amount in the offering plate, people say: "The preacher's crazy."

This is a crazy world indeed, where first things come last, and last things come first.

Evangelical Friend

———o———

A good many people soak up information like a blotter, but they seem to get it backward, also like a blotter.

———o———

One of the paradoxes of life is that the young are always wishing they were just a little older and the old are usually wishing they were a whole lot younger.

———o———

You can reach the top by staying on the level.

He enjoys much who is thankful for a little.

———o———

Paradox

With eight-year-old disdain, he balks
    At polishing his shoes;
Wears cowboy garb, and wants his shirts
    In bold, conflicting hues.
He likes odd caps, and every pair
    Of blue jeans sports a patch.
It's up to me to scrub his neck
    And see that both socks match.
But when it rains and I remind:
    "Now, wear your rubbers, dear,"
He argues back in all good faith —
    "But, Mom, I'll look so queer!"
MILDRED R. BENSMILLER

Pardon

How Far Is East From West?

How far is the East from the West?
It cannot be measured or proved;
But farther than this, so the Bible tells me,
My sins have fore'er been removed.

How high are the heavens above?
An infinite measureless space;
But higher than this is the gift of God's love,
So great is His mercy and grace.

How deep are the depths of the sea?
A fathomless measure, you say;
But farther than this, so my Saviour tells me,
My sins are fore'er cast away.

They're gone and forgotten by God,
And God has removed every doubt;

For covered by blood are my many transgressions,
My sins are fore'er blotted out.

"Return unto Me," saith the Lord,
For I have redeemed thee by blood,
Thy name is engraved on the palms of My hands,
And pardoned thou art, by thy God.

To Him we would joyfully sing,
Our praises to Him would ascend;
Our Saviour, our Shepherd, our Priest and our King,
Our true and unchangeable Friend.

AUTHOR UNKNOWN

———o———

He allowed no interval between assault and forgiveness; so that he was almost robbed of pain itself by the speed of pardon.

ST. GREGORY OF NAZIANZUS of his father

Parents

Child To Parent

1. Don't spoil me. I know quite well that I ought not to have all I ask for. I am only testing you.
2. Don't be afraid to be firm with me. I prefer it. It makes me feel more secure.
3. Don't let me form bad habits. I have to rely on you to detect them in the early stages.
4. Don't make me feel smaller than I am. It only makes me behave stupidly "big."
5. Don't correct me in front of people if you can avoid it. I'll take much more notice if you talk quietly with me in private.
6. Don't protect me from consequences. I need to learn the painful way sometimes.
7. Don't take too much notice of my small ailments. I am quite capable of trading on them.
8. Don't nag. If you do, I shall have to protect myself by appearing deaf.
9. Don't make rash promises. Remember that I feel badly let down when promises are broken.
10. Don't forget that I cannot explain myself as well as I should like. That is why I am not always very accurate.
11. Don't tax my honesty too much. I am easily frightened into telling lies.
12. Don't be inconsistent. That completely confuses me and makes me lose faith in you.
13. Don't put me off when I ask questions. If you do you will find I will stop asking and seek my information elsewhere.
14. Don't tell me my fears are silly. They are terribly real, and you can do much to reassure me if you try to understand.
15. Don't neglect me; I do not *want* to be a delinquent.

On And Off Duty

———o———

One trouble in raising a boy is that father always expects son to do exactly as much work as he never did.

———o———

In dealing with their children, many parents give in because they've given out.

———o———

Only fair but stern action against delinquent parents and snarling young thugs can bring a halt to the present plague of youthful lawlessness.

J. EDGAR HOOVER

———o———

Spare the rod when Junior is willful and disobedient — and when he grows up he'll probably carry one.

———o———

Parents are people who bear children, bore teen-agers and board newlyweds.

———o———

Small girl's essay on parents: "The trouble with parents is they are so old when we get them, it's hard to change their habits."

———o———

Some parents solve their toughest homework problems by sending their children to a boarding school.

Parents are just baby-sitters for God.

———o———

Too many parents expect strict obedience in other people's children.

———o———

As a gardener is dependent upon God to grow a plant, so a parent is dependent upon God to grow a life.

C. B. EAVEY

Past

We live in the present, we dream of the future, but we learn eternal truths from the past.

MADAME CHIANG KAI-SHEK

———o———

The past is never dead . . . it's not even past.

WILLIAM FAULKNER

———o———

It's never safe to be nostalgic about anything until you're absolutely sure there's no chance of its coming back.

———o———

What calls back the past, like the rich pumpkin pie?

JOHN GREENLEAF WHITTIER,
The Pumpkin

———o———

He who learns nothing from the past will be punished by the future.

———o———

You can't change the past, but you can ruin the present by worrying over the future.

Patience

Patience will do wonders, but it was not much help to the fellow who planted an orange grove in Maine.

———o———

Patience can accomplish much. It blunts the edge of misfortunes. By its steady exertion, success can be won a little bit at a time. Unfortunately, though, patience sometimes is confused with procrastination.

Be patient enough to live one day at a time as Jesus taught us, letting yesterday go, and leaving tomorrow till it arrives.

JOHN F. NEWTON

———o———

Living would be easier if men showed as much patience at home as they do when they're waiting for a fish to bite.

———o———

Patience on the road may often prevent patients in the hospital.

———o———

Patience is a quality most needed when it is exhausted.

———o———

Whenever our judgments and our feelings lack patience, they also lack wisdom and virtue.

JOSEPH JOUBERT

———o———

Beware the fury of a patient man.

JOHN DRYDEN, *Absalom and Achitophel*

———o———

Nothing is so full of victory as patience.

Chinese Proverb

———o———

Patience is the ability to keep your motor idling when you feel like stripping the gears.

———o———

All men commend patience, although few be willing to practice it.

THOMAS A KEMPIS

———o———

God sometimes permits us to be perplexed so that we may learn patience and better recognize our dependence upon Him.

Patriotism

There are no points of the compass on the chart of true patriotism.

ROBERT CHARLES WINTHROP

———o———

What a pity it is that we can die but once to save our country.

JOSEPH ADDISON

Patriotism is your conviction that this country is superior to all other countries because you were born in it.

GEORGE BERNARD SHAW

———o———

I only regret that I have but one life to lose for my country.

NATHAN HALE

———o———

He who loves not his country, can love nothing.

LORD BYRON

———o———

Far dearer, the grave or the prison,
Illumed by one patriot name,
Than the trophies of all who have risen
On Liberty's ruins to fame.

THOMAS MOORE

———o———

One who is a patriot is as willing to live sacrificially for his country as he is to die for it.

Peace

Peace with God helps mightily in living peaceably with men.

———o———

No man enjoys the serene calm of inner peace unless he has first known the harassing moments of a disquieted soul.

JOHN J. ZIER

———o———

Christ spells peace. When everything else in life fails Jesus draws near to support. He makes real, through His living Presence, that those whose minds are stayed on God shall be kept in perfect peace.

———o———

Drop thy still dews of quietness
Till all our striving cease;
Take from our souls the strain and stress,
And let our ordered lives confess
The beauty of thy Peace.

JOHN GREENLEAF WHITTIER

———o———

I never have found
Peace of mind
By giving folks a
Piece of mine.

LAURENCE C. SMITH

Peace, when "ruling" the heart and "ruling" the mind, opens in both every avenue of joy.

SARAH W. STEPHEN

———o———

Peace is not as much a goal to be achieved as a way to be walked.

———o———

Perfect Peace

I gazed into the storm-swept sky
Gray clouds piled high as eye could see.
A picture of my storm-swept soul
Not clouds, but troubles piled on me.

I fought – and struggled – planned and schemed
I'd solve each problem as it came,
And this I did for oh so long,
But trouble piled up just the same.

Now, all my time and strength were spent
As troubles piled up one by one,
But still my proud and stubborn heart
Refused to say – "God's will be done."

I would not fail – but still I did,
And then in utter anguish cried
For God to help me. Then I knew
Why I had failed, though I had tried.

Oh! Willful heart, you had to learn
How empty all our efforts, when
We trust in self, and not in God!
As empty as the world of men.

My storm-swept soul is calm at last.
These words of peace God spoke to me –
"Thou wilt keep him in perfect peace
Whose mind is stayed on Thee."

FLORA SORENSON

———o———

It is lamentable that peace does not come in capsules.

S. I. MCMILLEN

———o———

A little girl wrote an answer to a question in an examination: "Armistice was signed on November 11, 1918, and since then we have had two minutes of peace every year."

Before we can enjoy the peace of God we must know the God of peace.

———o———

We [do not] eschew concord and peace, but to have peace with man we will not be at war with God.

JOHN JEWELL

———o———

Peace is such a precious jewel that I would give anything for it but truth.

MATTHEW HENRY

———o———

Peace Today

Today Christ stilled a storm — not Galilee,
    But in my heart; I heard His "Peace, be still."
There raged a storm and tempest here, in me,
    And fear that I might perish made me ill.

The boat that is my life seemed tempest-tossed,
    And I forgot the Christ who knows our ships.
My heart sank low, I felt that all was lost,
    So that a cry of "Help me!" reached my lips.

I turned to Him and knew that He could save,
    That all my trials yield to His great will;
I felt the calming smoothness of the wave
    On which I rode, as Christ said, "Peace, be still."

HAZEL HARTWELL SIMON

People

There are three kinds of people: those who make things happen, those who watch things happen, and those who have no idea what happens.

Powergrams

———o———

I love mankind; it's people I can't stand.

He liked to like people, therefore people liked him.

MARK TWAIN

———o———

Two Kinds Of People

There are two kinds of people on earth today,
Just two kinds of people, no more, I say,
Not the good and the bad, for 'tis Well understood
The good are half bad and the bad Are half good.

Not the humble and proud, for in Life's busy span
Who puts on vain airs is not counted a man.
No! The two kinds of people on earth I mean,
Are the people who lift, and the People who lean.

Wherever you go, you will find The world's masses
Are ever divided in just these two classes.
And, strangely enough, you will Find, too, I wean,
There is only one lifter to twenty who lean.

This one question I ask. Are you Easing the load
Of overtaxed lifters who toil down the road?
Or are you a leaner who lets others bear
Your portion of worry and labor and care?

ELLA WHEELER WILCOX

———o———

You are not one person but three: the one you think you are, the one other people think you are and the person you really are.

———o———

I thought I heard the voice of God
    And climbed the highest steeple;
But God declared, "Go down again,
    I dwell among the people."

To get along with people and be successful in life, forget yourself and learn to love and be interested in other people.

NORMAN VINCENT PEALE

Perfect, Perfection

The nearest to perfection most people ever come is when filling out an employment application.

KEN KRAFT

——o——

Perfection consists not in doing extraordinary things, but in doing ordinary things extraordinarily well. Neglect nothing; the most trivial action may be performed to God.

ANGÉLIQUE ARNAULD

——o——

A man cannot have an idea of perfection in another, which he was never sensible of in himself.

SIR RICHARD STEELE

——o——

He who boasts of being perfect is perfect in folly. I never saw a perfect man.

CHARLES HADDON SPURGEON

——o——

Aim at perfection in everything, though in most things it is unattainable.

LORD CHESTERFIELD

——o——

This is the very perfection of a man, to find out his own imperfection.

ST. AUGUSTINE

Perseverance, Persistence

When you get into a tight place and everything goes against you, till it seems that you could not hold on a minute longer, never give up then, for that is just the place and time that the tide will turn.

HARRIET BEECHER STOWE

——o——

Perseverance is usually considered to be an admirable characteristic. Still it depends upon what it is at which one perseveres.

It's a wise person who knows how to draw the line between persistence and obstinance.

——o——

When a man has equipped himself by thought and study for a bigger job, it usually happens that promotion comes along even before it is expected.

P. G. WINNETT

——o——

Even a turtle gets nowhere until it sticks its neck out.

——o——

Consider the postage stamp: its usefulness consists in the ability to stick to one thing until it gets there.

"JOSH BILLINGS" (HENRY WHEELER SHAW)

——o——

Great works are performed, not by strength but by perseverance.

SAMUEL JOHNSON

——o——

Ninety thousand Norwegians stood for seven hours in biting cold weather to watch the ski jumpers in Oslo, Norway. The wind was so stiff the jumps had to be postponed several hours, but all ninety thousand braced themselves and stood fast. That's perseverance!

——o——

Thomas Edison made about 18,000 experiments before he perfected the arc light. Dr. Jonas Salk worked sixteen hours a day for three years to perfect the polio vaccine. A chemist, Paul Ehrlich worked day and night for years to perfect a chemical called "606" which would destroy the germ that causes syphilis. He had made 605 unsuccessful experiments, but the 606th was a success — thus the name: 606. Perseverance!

——o——

Do the best you can with what you possess,
Though it isn't much, yet it could be less.
He invites defeat who gives up to sighing,
But the battle is won if you keep on trying.

ISLA PASCHAL RICHARDSON

Persistent people begin their success where others end in failure.

EDWARD EGGLESTON

————o————

Neither snow, nor rain, nor heat, nor gloom of night stays these couriers from the swift completion of their appointed rounds.

Adaptation from HERODOTUS on the Main Post Office, New York City

————o————

An eight-year-old boy had been pestering his father for a watch. Finally his father said, "I don't want to hear about your wanting a watch again."

At dinner that night the family each gave a scripture verse at the dinner table and the boy repeated Mark 13:37: "And what I say unto you I say unto all, Watch."

————o————

Diamonds are pieces of coal that stuck to their jobs.

Personality

By a myriad observations we know of no effect greater than its corresponding cause — not even atomic chain reaction with its accompanying devastation. . . . On what rational grounds could we assume that an effect such as personality (the supreme distinction of mortal man in the animal world) was produced by a cause which lacked what it somehow managed to produce?

LEITH SAMUEL, *The Impossibility of Agnosticism*

————o————

Christ never *forces* the door of our personality. He gently knocks by circumstances, coincidences and providential leadings.

————o————

Life demands a great deal of sameness of all those who participate in living. But human differences are as precious as human conformity. Personality is the highest attribute of human life, and personality depends in major part on differences. But personality goes deeper than merely an outward show of differences. It is the mysterious spirit which can transform the tedium of sameness into spired differences.

Peabody Journal of Education

————o————

His personality is like a bent safety pin: it doesn't fit any place and is always sticking people in the wrong place.

————o————

The personality of the therapist is the most important human element in the therapeutic process.

THOMAS TYNDALL

————o————

Our possibilities of success are much more limited by our personality traits than by our intellect.

HENRY GREBER

Pessimist

A pessimist: If you give him an inch, he'd measure it.

————o————

A pessimist is one who feels bad when he feels good, for fear he'll feel worse when he feels better.

————o————

A pessimist is someone who likes to listen to the patter of little defeats.

————o————

It Can't Be Done

The man who misses all the fun
Is he who says, "It can't be done."
In solemn pride, he stands aloof
And greets each venture with reproof.
Had he the power, he would efface
The history of the human race.
We'd have no radio, no cars,
No streets lit by electric stars;
No telegraph, no telephone;
We'd linger in the age of stone.
The world would sleep if things were run
By folks who say, "It CAN'T be done."

AUTHOR UNKNOWN

Philosophy

A philosopher sees less on his tiptoes than a Christian on his knees.

A walk to the top of a hill at night to gaze at the stars may reveal more philosophy than the reading of many books.

———o———

Some people take everything philosophically. Like the man who slipped and fell on the ice one day in January. Gazing at the ice, he said: "I'm not angry. July will take care of you."

This Day

———o———

Philosophy is unintelligible answers to unsolvable problems.

HENRY ADAMS

———o———

Philosophy, rightly defined, is simply the love of wisdom.

MARCUS TULLIUS CICERO

———o———

A philosopher is one who desires to discern the truth.

PLATO

Picnic

The ideal place for a picnic is usually a little farther on.

———o———

Beach Picnic

The outing was really
A lulu, a dilly.
The fog was dense
And dank and chilly
But everyone tanned —
To third-degree burns —
And the kiddies fell over
The cliff by turns.

The hampers were bulging,
The menu faultless,
Though salads were sandy
And sandwiches saltless.
Some cutup went swimming
With Mother's new hat on,
And Gladys was nipped
By a crab that she sat on.

And then when the rains came —
They're sudden, you know —
We found all our things
As we started to go

Except Grandma's teeth,
Bill's swimming fins,
The keys to the car
And one of the twins.

ETHEL JACOBSON
in *New York Times Magazine*

Plans

There is no magic in little plans.

HENRIETTA C. MEARS

———o———

Some people who plan to get right with God at the eleventh hour, die at ten-thirty.

———o———

Plans get you into things, but you got to work your way out.

WILL ROGERS

Pleasure

The greatest pleasure I know is to do a good action by stealth, and to have it found out by accident.

CHARLES LAMB, *Table Talk*

———o———

We tire of those pleasures we take, but never of those we give.

———o———

The pleasantest thing in the world is to have pleasant thoughts, and the greatest art of living is to cultivate more pleasant thoughts.

———o———

Pleasure admitted in undue degree
Enslaves the will, nor leaves the judgment free.

WILLIAM COWPER

———o———

Your greatest pleasure is that which rebounds from hearts that you have made glad.

HENRY WARD BEECHER

Polite

Nothing is ever lost by politeness — except your seat on a bus.

———o———

Politeness comes from within, from the heart: but if the forms of politeness are dispensed with, the spirit and the thing itself soon die away.

JOHN HALL

———o———

Politeness to superiors is duty — to equals courtesy — to inferiors nobleness.

BENJAMIN FRANKLIN

———o———

Politeness costs nothing, and gains everything.

LADY MARY WORTLEY MONTAGU, *Letters*

———o———

Daddy and little son were repairing wire.

"Sing, 'Thank You, Lord, For Saving My Soul,'" said the little fellow. Daddy sang it twice.

"Do you think Jesus is saying, 'You're welcome'?"

Christian Living

Politics

An empty stomach is not a good political adviser.

ALBERT EINSTEIN

———o———

A politician is an animal who can sit on a fence and yet keep both ears to the ground.

———o———

Christopher Columbus was the world's greatest politician. He did not know where he was going, he went on borrowed money, and he did not know where he was when he got there.

YMCA Bulletin

———o———

The biggest trouble with political promises is that they go in one year and out the other.

Toastmaster

———o———

This country has gotten to where it is in spite of politics, not by the aid of it.

WILL ROGERS

———o———

He serves his party best who serves the country best.

RUTHERFORD BIRCHARD HAYES

Possess, Possessions

A wise man will desire no more than he may get justly, use soberly, distribute cheerfully, and leave contentedly.

———o———

Think About This . . .

Love that is hoarded moulds at last
Until we know some day
The only thing we ever have
Is what we give away.

And kindness that is never used
But hidden all alone
Will slowly harden till it is
As hard as any stone.

It is the things we always hold
That we will lose someday;
The only things we ever keep
Are what we give away.

LOUIS GINSBERG, *Song*

———o———

How To Possess

If you want to possess something, help create it. If you want to possess a landscape, try to reproduce it. To others it may seem very crude and ugly, but to you it will hold all the beauty of the original and more, for you have put your life into it. If you want to possess a flower, help it grow. If you want a share in the life of another, do something to make that life larger and better. So shall you become a part of the creative energy of God and share with Him as a son and heir a portion of His divine life.

FRANK O. HALL

———o———

He did not have a house where He could go
When it was night, — when other men went down
Small streets where children watched with eager eyes,
Each one assured of shelter in the town,
The Christ sought refuge anywhere at all.
A house, an inn, the roadside, or a stall.

HELEN WELSHEIMER, *The Transient*

It is not the possession of extraordinary gifts that makes extraordinary usefulness, but the dedication of what we have to the service of God.
FREDERICK WILLIAM ROBERTSON

———o———

The greatest possession is self-possession.

———o———

What you possess in the world will be found at the day of your death to belong to someone else, but what you are will be yours forever.
HENRY VAN DYKE

———o———

The more you have, the more you are in debt to God; and you have no reason to be proud of that which makes you a debtor.

———o———

What you have is God's; He has put you in charge of it for a time.

Poverty

Poverty is not dishonorable in itself, but only when it comes from idleness, intemperance, extravagance, and folly.
PLUTARCH

———o———

Poverty is a virtue greatly overrated by those who no longer practice it.
BARNABY C. KEENEY in Saturday Review

———o———

Poverty is usually the side-partner of laziness.

———o———

If you spend all your time collecting money for fear of poverty, you are practicing poverty already.

———o———

Poverty is very good in poems but very bad in the house; very good in maxims and sermons but very bad in practical life.
HENRY WARD BEECHER

———o———

Poverty is a state of being helpless to help the helpless!

I never feel sorry for poor boys. It is the children of wealth who deserve sympathy; too often they are starved for incentive to create success for themselves.
J. C. PENNEY

———o———

The poorest and most pitiable man is the one who has more than he needs but feels that he hasn't enough.

Power

The most efficient water power let
    loose through all the ages,
Is found in a married woman's tears,
    according to the sages.

———o———

The Lord Jesus said, "Ye shall find rest." Someone may say, "I had not thought of rest and peace: I want power." Please notice that peace and power are two sides of the same thing; peace is the inside, and power is the outgoing side. We are never promised the consciousness of power. We are promised power, but never the consciousness of it. We know the peace; others know the power.
S. D. GORDON

———o———

I can count on God to let power loose in my life when I am ready to let something loose — the hurtful habit, the crippling compromise, the unsurrendered ambition.
PAUL S. REES

———o———

Power with men proceeds from power with God.

———o———

Thinking we have some power of our own prevents our taking all power from Christ.

———o———

He is truly great in power who has power over himself.
CHARLES HADDON SPURGEON

———o———

Power tends to corrupt; absolute power corrupts absolutely.
LORD ACTON,
Letters to Bishop Mandell Creighton

Power is harder to handle than weakness.

———o———

Christ spells power. He is the power that releases us from death's hold. He is the power that keeps us true. He is the power that opens the door unto the Father's home for us. He is the power that guarantees life eternal and rich.

Practice

Practice makes perfect even when we are practicing a bad habit.

———o———

The more you practice what you know, the more you shall know what to practice.

———o———

Everything gets easier with practice — except getting up in the morning.

DAVE EASTMAN,
Los Angeles Times Syndicate

Praise

He who praises everybody praises nobody.

SAMUEL JOHNSON

———o———

What Shall I Render To My God?

What shall I render to my God
  For all His gifts to me?
Sing, heaven and earth, rejoice and praise
  In glorious majesty.

O let me praise Thee while I live,
  And praise Thee when I die,
And praise Thee when I rise again,
  And to eternity.

Mysterious depths of endless love
  Our admiration raise;
My God, Thy name exalted is
  Above our highest praise.

JOHN MASON

———o———

It's better to shout than to doubt,
  It's better to rise than to fall,
It's better to let the glory out
  Than to have no glory at all.

S. V. M. DOGGEREL

Praising and blessing God is work that is never out of season. Nothing better prepares the mind for receiving the Holy Ghost than holy joy and praise. Fears are silenced, sorrows sweetened, and hopes kept up.

MATTHEW HENRY

———o———

Matthew Henry said that he would not huddle up his praises in a corner. His sins had been open, God's mercy had been open, and he would make open profession and open payment.

JAMES BARR in *Lang Syne*

———o———

We often praise the evening clouds,
  And tints so gay and bold,
But seldom think upon our God,
  Who tinged these clouds with gold.

SIR WALTER SCOTT, *The Setting Sun*

———o———

A bit of praise goes far in giving confidence.

———o———

As the Greeks said, Many men know how to flatter, few know how to priase.

WENDELL PHILLIPS

———o———

If Christians praised God more, the world would doubt Him less.

CHARLES E. JEFFERSON

Prayer

When we work we work, when we pray, God works.

OSWALD SMITH

———o———

A Child's Prayer

Now I lay me down to sleep,
I pray Thee, Lord, the souls to keep
Of other children, far away
Who have no homes in which to stay,
Nor know where is their daily bread,
Nor where at night to lay their head,
But wander through a broken land
Alone and helpless —
Take their hand!

A German Prayer

The Place Of Power

There is a place where thou canst touch
  the eyes
Of blinded men to instant perfect
  sight,
There is a place where thou canst say
  "Arise"
To dying captives bound in chains
  of might.
There is a place where thou canst
  reach the store
Of hoarded gold and free it for the
  Lord,
There is a place upon some distant
  shore
Where thou canst send the worker
  or the Word.
There is a place where God's resistless
  power
Responsive moves to thine insistent
  plea,
There is a place — a simple trusting
  place
Where God Himself descends and
  fights for thee.
Where is that blessed place? Dost thou
  ask where?
O soul, it is the secret place of
  prayer.

ADELAIDE A. POLLARD

———o———

Five young college students, before
ordination, spent a Sunday in London,
and were anxious to hear some well-
known preachers in churches other than
their own. They found their way on a
hot Sunday to Spurgeon's Tabernacle.
While waiting for the doors to open a
stranger came up to them and said:
"Gentlemen, would you like to see the
heating apparatus of the church?"
They were not particularly anxious to
do so on a broiling day in July, but consented. They were taken down some
steps, and a door was thrown open,
and their guide whispered, "There,
Sirs, is our heating apparatus." They
saw before them 700 souls bowed in
prayer seeking a blessing on the service about to be held in the tabernacle
above. Their unknown guide was
Spurgeon himself. Are we surprised
that Spurgeon's sermons are still circulated?

Living Links

Prayer is not monologue, but dialogue.

ANDREW MURRAY

———o———

Talking to men for God is a great
thing, but talking to God for men is the
first thing.

———o———

Count it a blessing when God delays
the answer to your prayer in order to
enlarge your capacity to receive.

———o———

Many prayers go to the dead-letter
office of heaven for want of sufficient
direction.

———o———

Prayernik

From its launching pad of suff'ring
  Soars my missile through the air,
Past the sun and moon and planets
  Freighted heavily with prayer.

Faith divine is the propellant,
  (Faith, that God cannot deny)
Sending it a 'zillion light years
  To the city in the sky.

There, the Father hears the beeping,
  Knows the signal as His own;
Tunes in lovingly and listens
  As it orbits 'round the throne.

Back it zooms; the answers bearing
  From the One, whom I adore;
Balm and Blessing! . . . Peace and
  Power!
Praise His Name forevermore.

SARAH SMITH REED

———o———

Traveling On My Knees

Last night I took a journey
  To a land across the seas.
I didn't go by boat or plane,
  I traveled on my knees.

I saw so many people there
  In deepest depths of sin.
And Jesus told me I should go —
  That there were souls to win.

But I said, "Jesus, I can't go
  And work with such as these."
He answered quickly, "Yes, you can,
  By traveling on your knees."

He said, "You pray; I'll meet the need.
You call and I will hear.
Be anxious over all lost souls,
Of those both far and near."

And so I tried it, knelt in prayer,
Gave up some hours of ease;
I felt the Lord right by my side
While traveling on my knees.

As I prayed on and saw souls saved,
And twisted bodies healed,
I saw God's workers' strength renewed
While laboring in the field.

I said, "Yes Lord, I have a job,
'Tis Thee I'd ever please.
I'll gladly go and heed Thy call
By traveling on my knees."

SANDRA GOODWIN

———o———

The Power House
Is always there,
So push the button,
Labeled "Prayer."

RALPH H. DUMONT

———o———

Pray often, for prayer is a shield for
the soul, a sacrifice to God, and a
scourge for Satan.

Prayer is as the pitcher that fetcheth
water from the brook, therewith to
water the herbs. Break the pitcher and
it will fetch no water, and for want of
water the garden withers.

JOHN BUNYAN

———o———

If you can beat the devil in the matter of regular daily prayer, you can
beat him anywhere. If he can beat
you there, he can possibly beat you
anywhere.

PAUL RADER

———o———

Prayer is the highest use to which
speech can be put.

PETER TAYLOR FORSYTH

———o———

Prayer is not overcoming God's reluctance; it is laying hold of His highest willingness.

RICHARD CHENEVIX TRENCH

———o———

Satan trembles when he sees
A contrite nation on its knees.

Lord, we pray not for tranquility;
we pray that Thou grant us strength
and grace to overcome adversity.

SAVONARDLA

———o———

Gypsy Smith, when converted, immediately desired the conversion of his
uncle. Among gypsies it is not proper
for children to address their elders on
the subject of duty; so the boy just
prayed, and waited. One day his uncle
noticed a hole in his trousers, and said,
"Rodney, how is it that you have worn
the knees of your pants so much faster
than the rest of them?"
"Uncle, I have worn them out praying for you, that God would have you."
Then the tears came. The uncle put
his arm around the boy, drew him to
his side, and soon bent his knees to the
same Saviour.

Selected

———o———

Each prayer is answered,
That is so;
But for our good
It may be, "No!"

———o———

The spectacle of a nation praying is
more awe-inspiring than the explosion
of an atomic bomb.

J. EDGAR HOOVER

———o———

When praying, do not give God instructions — report for duty!

AUTHOR UNKNOWN

———o———

If your burdens seem great, remember this: "Daily prayers lessen daily
cares."

———o———

If we would have God hear what
we say to Him by prayer, we must be
ready to hear what He saith to us by
His Word.

MATTHEW HENRY

———o———

Prayer is a preparation for danger;
it is the armor for battle.

FREDERICK WILLIAM ROBERTSON

Certain thoughts are prayers. There are moments when, whatever be the attitude of the body, the soul is on its knees.

VICTOR HUGO

———o———

None can believe how powerful prayer is, and what it is able to effect, but those who have learned it by experience.

MARTIN LUTHER

———o———

The equipment for the inner life of prayer is simple. It consists of a quiet place, a quiet hour and a quiet heart.

Selected

———o———

Pray hardest when it is hardest to pray.

CHARLES H. BRENT

———o———

Lord, make me a channel of Thy peace,
That where there is hatred I may bring love;
That where there is wrong I may bring the spirit of forgiveness;
That where there is discord I may bring harmony;
That where there is error I may bring truth;
That where there is doubt I may bring faith;
That where there is despair I may bring hope;
And where there are shadows I may bring Thy light;
That where there is sadness I may bring joy;
Lord, grant that I may seek rather to comfort than be comforted,
To understand than be understood,
To love than be loved;
For it is by giving that one receives,
It is by self-forgetting that one finds,
It is by forgiving that one is forgiven,
It is by dying that one awakens to eternal life.

ST. FRANCIS OF ASSISI

Prayers of Children

A little boy prayed: "Lord, if you can't make me a better boy, don't worry about it. I'm having a real good time as it is."

A mother, interested in her son's learning some prayers, gave him a tract put out by the church board.

Some nights later she was pleased to hear him recite a prayer at dinner.

"Amen," he concluded. "This prayer is sponsored by the United Board of Churches."

E. RUTH ZIEGLER in *Together*

———o———

A little girl was overheard ending the Lord's Prayer thus: "For thine is the kingdom and the flowers that are growing. Amen."

OREN ARNOLD in *Home Life*

———o———

Five-year-old Jan likes long prayers, probably to forestall bedtime. She prays, "Jesus, bless Daddy and Mother. Bless everybody in the church. Bless everybody in the whole world."

The other night, however, after a moment's hesitation, she added, ". . . and everybody in outer space."

MRS. J. C. RAINEY in *Teach*

———o———

Five-year-old Kathie had a habit of making long drawn-out bedtime prayers. On one occasion her mother, thinking to shorten them, said, "Amen" during a slight pause. Kathie prayed on. Again her mother suggested, "Amen."

Then Kathie said, "God, don't pay any attention to her. She doesn't know when I'm done."

MRS. FREDA B. ELLIOTT in *Teach*

———o———

A tiny four-year-old was spending a night away from home. At bedtime, she knelt at her hostess' knee to say her prayers, expecting the usual prompting.

Finding the hostess unable to help her, concluded thus:

"Please, God, 'scuse me. I can't remember my prayers, and I'm staying with a lady who don't know any."

———o———

My children had been praying for a baby brother or sister and had been told to expect one. One week-end when we were camping out in the hills, young Herbert called out after bedtime that he had to get up and pray some more.

He got out of bed, knelt down, and said: "God you better not send the baby tonight. There isn't anyone home to take care of him."

MRS. M. NELLIE in *Teach*

———o———

A small boy knelt at his mother's knee and offered his evening prayer. When he had finished, he continued to speak softly while on his knees.

"What did you ask for?" his mother questioned.

"It isn't nice to always ask for things," replied the little fellow. "I just told God that I love Him."

Pentecostal Evangel

Preach, Preacher

Comment about a preacher: "He speaks very well, if he just had something to say!"

———o———

Any preacher who preaches beyond that which he has experienced is incapable of preaching with conviction.

BILLY GRAHAM

———o———

Inadvertent announcement by a pastor: "Next Sunday, I will preach my last sermon in this Lenten series. The choir will sing, 'Now All My Woes Are Over'."

MRS. LAURA JOHNSTON in *Together*

———o———

The pastor announced he was about to preach on "Christian Marriage and Family Life," but his choir got in a warning first by singing, "Turn Back, O Man, Foreswear Thy Foolish Ways."

———o———

A preacher tape-recorded his sermon, then sat down to listen to it and fell fast asleep.

———o———

Daniel Webster, the noted Senator and statesman, was once asked why he generally went to hear a poor country minister preach instead of one of the more brilliant clergymen of Washington.

"Well, you see," he explained, "in Washington they preach to Daniel Webster, the renowned individual, but this country preacher preaches to Daniel Webster, the sinner."

HAROLD HELFER in *Coronet*

———o———

A young man while preaching the Gospel in an open-air meeting heard this sarcastic remark: "Poor fellow, he's cracked." "Yes," he answered quickly, "thank God, that is where the light shone in."

———o———

A minister, but still a man.

ALEXANDER POPE, *Epistle to James Craggs*

———o———

The pastor was hoping to get a discount on the price of his suit. "I'm a poor preacher," he said.

"Yes, I know that," said the salesman, "I've heard you preach."

MARTIN P. SIMON, *Points for Parents*

———o———

My advice to pastors is to give up preaching for the next few months. Take an outline and spend time in prayer over it, and then enter the pulpit and tell the story of Jesus. People have had too much preaching.

J. WILBUR CHAPMAN

———o———

It often requires more courage to preach to one than to a thousand.

ADONIRAM J. GORDON

———o———

In order to preach aright take three looks before every sermon: one at thine own sinfulness; another at the depth of human wretchedness all around thee; and a third at the love of God in Christ Jesus, so that, empty of self and full of compassion toward thy fellowman, thou mayest be enabled to administer God's comfort to souls.

NIKOLAUS LUDWIG VON ZINZENDORF

———o———

"Did I preach too long?" asked Dr. H. C. Morrison, the great Methodist preacher, after one of his earliest sermons. "No, you did not preach too long," his friend answered, much to Morrison's relief; "but you talked too long after you stopped preaching."

———o———

Preachers can talk,
But never teach
Unless they practice
What they preach.
Defender

———o———

The preacher should tell people where to get on, not where to get off.

———o———

One preacher's calling cards had this sentence significantly printed on them: "What on earth are you doing for heaven's sake?"

———o———

None preaches better than the ant, and she says nothing.
BENJAMIN FRANKLIN, *Poor Richard*

———o———

I preached as never sure to preach again,
And as a dying man to dying men.
RICHARD BAXTER,
Love Breathing Thanks and Praise

———o———

To love to preach is one thing — to love those to whom we preach, quite another.
RICHARD CECIL

Prejudice

Opinions founded on prejudices are always sustained with the greatest violence.
SIR FRANCIS JEFFREY, LORD JEFFREY

———o———

Prejudice is the child of ignorance.
WILLIAM HAZLITT

———o———

Most of us have found by experience that it is a good thing to overhaul certain machinery. It would be a good thing for all of us to overhaul our prejudices once in awhile.

It is never too late to give up our prejudices.
HENRY DAVID THOREAU

———o———

Prejudice is a great timesaver; it enables us to form opinions without bothering to get the facts.

———o———

Beware of prejudices. They are like rats, and men's minds are like traps. Prejudices get in easily, but rarely do they get out. We cannot hold anyone in contempt without at the same time attracting contempt toward us. We cannot elevate a man without ourselves being elevated. Likewise, you cannot degrade another without falling into degradation yourself. Prejudice places you in bondage . . . it curtails your opportunities for success and happiness. Why not enjoy the freedom that calm reasoning and an understanding heart will give you! Human nature is so constituted that all see, and judge better, in the affairs of other men, than in our own.
TERENCE

———o———

Be careful that prejudice never closes its eyes to evidence.

Preparation

The great cry of our heart is that God will help us to be ready for whatever He has for us.
BOB PIERCE

———o———

Prepare today for tomorrow and forget about yesterday.
MARTIN VANBEE

———o———

God is preparing his heroes; and when the opportunity comes, he can fit them into their places in a moment, and the world will wonder where they came from.
A. B. SIMPSON

———o———

One who is not prepared today will be less so tomorrow.

I will study and get ready, and perhaps my chance will come.

ABRAHAM LINCOLN

Present

One of the devil's snares is so to occupy us with the past and the future as to weaken us for the present.

———o———

Historians explain the past, and economists the future. Thus only the present is confusing.

MRS. R. E. MILLARD
in *The Log of the Good Ship Grace*

———o———

Children have neither past nor future; they enjoy the present, which very few of us do.

JAMES ABRAM GARFIELD

———o———

Now and Then

NOW as through a glass, but darkly,
Future hopes by faith we trace;
THEN in realms of radiant glory
We shall see our Savior's face.

NOW by faith we see Him only,
Our reflections may be dim;
THEN when He appears to call us,
We shall really be like Him.

NOW, by scientific finds,
Men attempt to conquer space;
THEN, our mighty Lord will take us
Where He has prepared our place.

NOW, by His command, we're spreading
His great Gospel Truth abroad;
THEN, we'll see in His blest presence
Those we brought to Christ our Lord.

MABEL E. PALMER in *Now*

Pride

A crowd of people at the Franklin Park Zoo in Boston watched a peacock slowly spread its large tail and display its beautiful plumage. The bird held itself erect and strutted regally about the enclosure. Just then an old, drab-colored duck waddled slowly from a nearby pond and passed between the proud peacock and the admiring crowd. The peacock became enraged and drove the duck back into the water. The beautiful bird suddenly became ugly with anger. The plain and awkward duck, having returned to the pond, was no longer unattractive. He swam and dove gracefully in the pond, unaware that many eyes were watching him. The people who had admired the peacock loved the duck. They were reminded of the dangers of pride and that true happiness comes from being ourselves.

———o———

The Ashes Of Pride

Who was that man I saw today,
The one from whom I turned away
To hide the revulsion I felt inside?
That man in the gutter! Had he no pride?
A picture of weak-willed moral decay,
Such a sordid sight to spoil my day!

Who was that man? I can tell you tonight,
For the answer came like a flickering light
That grew until it enveloped me
In the ashes of pride — humility.
The answer came as I read God's Word
And it seemed as though His Voice I heard —

"Who was that man you saw today?
The one from whom you turned away
Was you, My son, had I let you race
The course of life without My Grace.
If left on your own, you would have been
Beside that man your pride condemns.

"Who was that man you saw today?
The one from whom you turned away
Is so loved by Me that I died for him!
Can you still in your foolish pride condemn?
That sordid sight was My child astray,
Did you stop to show him — and yourself —
    The Way?"

ART MOSSBERG

One feather in their cap and some persons topple over!

———o———

You can have no greater sign of a confirmed pride than when you think you are humble enough.

WILLIAM LAW

———o———

Most people spend money they don't have to buy things they don't want to impress people they don't like.

WILL ROGERS

———o———

Be not proud of race, face, place, or Grace.

CHARLES HADDON SPURGEON

———o———

A proud man is always looking down on things and people: and, of course, as long as you're looking down, you can't see something that's above you.

C. S. LEWIS,
Mere Christianity, Christian Behaviour

———o———

Pride was the sin of the angels in heaven.

———o———

A proud man is seldom a grateful man, for he never thinks he gets as much as he deserves.

HENRY WARD BEECHER

Problems

It is the first of all problems for a man to find out what kind of work he is to do in this universe.

THOMAS CARLYLE

———o———

If more problems were settled in the house of the Lord, fewer problems would be settled in the house of correction.

HENRIETTA C. MEARS

———o———

People are always trying to solve other people's problems and the world is full of wrong answers.

———o———

You're either helping solve the problem — or you're part of the problem.

BERNARD EDINGER

A sad looking character was shown into the office of a prominent psychiatrist. "I've lost all desire to go on, doctor. Life has become too hectic, too confused."

"Yes," said the doctor, clucking sympathetically. "I understand. We all have our problems. You'll need a year or two of treatments at fifty dollars a week."

There was a pause. "Well, that solves your problem, Doc. Now what about mine?"

———o———

Problems are the price of progress. Don't bring me anything but trouble. Good news weakens me.

CHARLES F. KETTERING

Procrastinate

If you put off until tomorrow what you should do today, someone may invent a machine to do it for you.

———o———

A successful procrastinator puts off his work so long that by the time it's finished, there's no time not to like what he's done.

JIM BULLOCK

———o———

Only two things come to him who waits: whiskers and bills.

———o———

Procrastination is not only the thief of time but it clutters up our lives with an appalling number of half-done things and with slovenly habits.

CLIFF COLE

———o———

He who waits to do a great deal of good at once will never do anything. Life is made up of little things.

———o———

Procrastination is the art of keeping up with yesterday.

DONALD MARQUIS, *Archy and Mehitabel*

———o———

Procrastination is the Thief of time;
Year after year it steals, till all are fled,
And to the mercies of a moment leaves
The vast concerns of an eternal scene.

EDWARD YOUNG, *Night Thoughts*

Procrastination is the thief of time. Collar him!

CHARLES DICKENS

Someday

Someday — I'm going down the street
And sit and chat with one whose feet
Have had to pause and rest awhile
Before they travel that last mile;
Well — someday.

Someday — A cake or pie I'll bake
And with a cheery smile I'll take
It to a home where there is need;
Just folks, of quite a different creed;
Well — someday.

Someday — a letter I will send
To that distant, lonely friend;
I'll tell her every little thing
That will joy and comfort bring;
Well — someday.

Someday — a quiet place I'll seek
Where I can hear my Father speak,
Where I can listen undisturbed
To His precious guiding Word;
Someday.

Someday — I'll surely take the time
To tell some soul of love divine,
Of salvation full and free,
Meant for them as well as me;
Someday.

Someday — I said it long ago.
The days slip by, and well I know
"Someday" will never come until
Today bends to my Father's will.
Why not today?

ROSELYN C. STEERE

It's surprising how many times some tasks have to be put off before they completely slip your mind.

Satan cares not how spiritual your intentions, or how holy your resolutions, if only they are fixed for Tomorrow!

J. C. RYLE

Progress

It's fine to be on the right track. But keep in mind the fact that you'll get run over if you just sit there.

OREN ARNOLD

All growth that is not toward God is growing to decay.

GEORGE MACDONALD

The best way to get from a lower position to a higher one is to be conspicuously efficient in the lower one.

What we call progress is the exchange of one nuisance for another nuisance.

HAVELOCK ELLIS

The time of day I do not tell as some
do by the clock,
Or by the distant chiming bell set on
some steepled rock,
But by the progress that I see in what
I have to do;
It's either 'Done O'Clock' for me, or
only 'Half-Past Through.'

Real progress sometimes means retracting our steps. Progress for Abraham meant going back to the place of an altar.

W. LYNN CROWDING

Progress always involves risks. You can't steal second base and keep your foot on first.

In our age of rapid advance, you have to run like mad to keep standing still.

The People Go

From bondage to spiritual faith
From spiritual faith to great courage
From courage to liberty
From liberty to selfishness
From selfishness to complacency
From complacency to apathy
From apathy to dependency
From dependency . . .
      Back into bondage.
      Where are we?

Promise

A promise: one thing you can and should keep after giving.

What many promising young men become is promising older men.
FRANKLIN P. JONES

———o———

The promises of God are just as good as ready money any day.
BILLY BRAY

———o———

God makes a promise.
Faith believes it.
Hope anticipates it.
Patience quietly awaits it.
AUTHOR UNKNOWN

———o———

Promise is most given when the least is said.
GEORGE CHAPMAN, *Hero and Leander*

———o———

Have you ever noticed how those who are the quickest with promises so often have the slowest memories for keeping them?

———o———

The prospect is as bright as the promises of God.
ADONIRAM JUDSON

———o———

The Promises

My Savior's grace is promised me,
His tender love and care,
His deep concern in every grief
Each burden He will share.

My Father's care is promised me,
His faithful, guiding hand
To lead me on and bear me up
To Heaven's golden strand.

My Father's wealth is promised me,
Supplying all my need;
He is a King, and I, His own,
Am rich, yes, rich indeed.

The Holy Ghost is promised me,
To in my heart abide,
To hold me steady, pray for me,
And keep me sanctified.
GEORGE H. TALBERT

Prosperity

Prosperity is only an instrument to be used, not a deity to be worshipped.
CALVIN COOLIDGE

Prosperity hides far more perils than does poverty.

———o———

Continued worldly prosperity is a fiery trial.
CHARLES HADDON SPURGEON

———o———

In prosperity men ask too little of God; in adversity they are likely to ask too much.

———o———

Prosperity has often proved more damaging to human character than adversity.

Proverbs

A proverb is one man's wit, and all men's wisdom.
LORD JOHN RUSSELL

———o———

A stitch on time costs plenty of carrying charges.

———o———

Angels rush in when fools fail to retread.

———o———

A man is judged by the finance companies he keeps.

———o———

A proverb is a short sentence based on long experience.
MIGUEL DE CERVANTES

———o———

Three things cannot be taught: generosity, poetry, and a singing voice.
Irish Proverb

———o———

There's a time to wink as well as to see.
BENJAMIN FRANKLIN

———o———

He gives twice who gives quickly.
Roman Proverb

———o———

Love does to us what life finds in us.
Old English Proverb

Psychiatrist, Psychology

A psychiatrist is a person who can tell you what everyone knows in terms that no one understands, and gets paid for it.

———o———

Woman to small child in store: "Behave! I have no time for psychology today."

———o———

The difference between a psychotic and a neurotic: The psychotic thinks two plus two is five. The neurotic knows two plus two is four, but he hates it!

———o———

A psychiatrist is a man who uses other people's heads to make money.

———o———

Anyone who goes to a psychiatrist must be out of his head.

———o———

A psychiatrist is "a mind-sweeper."

———o———

Modern psychology tells us that it's bad to be an orphan, terrible to be an only child, damaging to be the youngest, crushing to be in the middle, and taxing to be the oldest. There seems no way out except to be born an adult.

SIDNEY J. HARRIS in
Chicago Daily News

Pure, Purity

Visiting in a mining town, a young minister was being escorted through one of the coal mines. In one of the dark, dirty passageways, he spied a beautiful white flower growing out of the black mine earth. "How can there be a flower of such purity and beauty in this dirty mine?" the minister asked the miner. "Throw some of the coal dust on it and see," was the reply. He did and was surprised that as fast as the dirt touched those snowy petals, it slid right off to the ground, leaving the flower just as lovely as before. It was so smooth that the dirt could not cling to the flower.

Our hearts can be the same way. We cannot help it that we have to live in a world that is filled with sin, any more than that the flower could change the place where it was growing. But God can keep us so pure and clean that though we touch sin on every side, it will not cling to us. We can stand in the midst of it just as white and beautiful as that flower.

Hi Call

———o———

It is better to have clean hands and a pure heart than to have clever hands and a smooth tongue.

Purpose

At the age of nine Harry Dixon Loes was advised by his father not to waste time writing songs. But when he died at the age of seventy-two, he left the world with more than 3,000 gospel songs which he composed. Much of his work was published under pen names, as well as his own. Some of his best-known songs include, "Love Found A Way," "Blessed Redeemer" and "All Things in Jesus."

Alliance Witness

———o———

Men fail through lack of purpose rather than through lack of talent.

BILLY SUNDAY

———o———

Some time ago the tallest of HCJB's antenna towers in Quito, Ecuador came crumbling to the ground after lightning hit it, causing expensive damage and loss of air time. Staff members had varying interpretations. Some said, "Satan caused this." Others declared, "God is trying to say something to us." Perhaps the two viewpoints together expressed the whole truth. Whatever the final definition, we know this: the lightning bolt somehow stood within the circle of God's sovereignty. In His larger purpose the loss became gain.

ABE C. VAN DER PUY

———o———

We mostly spend our lives conjugating three verbs: "to want," "to have" and "to do," forgetting that these verbs have no significance except as they are included in the verb "to be."

EVELYN UNDERHILL

———o———

The world steps aside for the fellow who knows where he is going.

I go at what I have to do as if there were nothing else in the world for me to do.

CHARLES KINGSLEY

———o———

The secret of success is constancy to purpose.

BENJAMIN DISRAELI

Q

Quarrel

Most quarrels are inevitable at the time, incredible afterward.

FORSTER

———o———

But, children, you should never let
  Such angry passions rise;
Your little hands were never made
  To tear each other's eyes.

ISAAC WATTS, *Divine Songs*

———o———

The quarrel is a very pretty quarrel as it stands; we should only spoil it by trying to explain it.

RICHARD BRINSLEY SHERIDAN,
The Rivals

———o———

A little explained, a little endured,
A little forgiven, the quarrel's cured.

———o———

I hate a quarrel because it interrupts an argument.

GILBERT KEITH CHESTERTON

Questions

Everywhere in life, the true question is not what we gain, but what we do.

THOMAS CARLYLE

———o———

No question is ever settled
Until it is settled right.

ELLA WHEELER WILCOX,
Settle the Question Right

———o———

To a quick question, give a slow answer.

Italian Adage

It is better to debate a question without settling it than to settle a question without debating it.

JOSEPH JOUBERT

———o———

When a child was questioned about the Bible story he had heard in Sunday School, the following was his version of it:

"When Noah's Ark came to rest on the mountain, Noah said to all the animals, 'Go forth and multiply.'

"All of the creatures came out of the ark except the adders. When Noah called them to come, they said, 'We can't, we're adders, we can't multiply.'"

———o———

Teacher: "Which is the most popular cow in America?"

Pupil: "Magnesia. You can buy her milk in any drugstore."

Quiet

In times of quietness our hearts should
  be like trees,
Lifting their branches to the sky to
  draw down strength
Which they will need to face the storms
That will surely come.

TOYOHIKO KAGAWA

———o———

I Needed The Quiet

I needed the quiet so He drew me
  aside,
Into the shadows where we could confide.
Away from the bustle where all the day
  long

I hurried and worried when active and strong.

I needed the quiet tho' at first I rebelled
But gently, so gently, my cross He upheld
And whispered so sweetly of spiritual things
Tho weakened in body, my spirit took wings
To heights never dreamed of when active and gay.
He loved me so greatly He drew me away.

I needed the quiet. No prison my bed,
But a beautiful valley of blessings instead —
A place to grow richer in Jesus to hide.
I needed the quiet so He drew me aside.

ALICE HANSCHE MORTENSON

———o———

Quiet sleep feels no foul weather.

———o———

Slow Me Down!

Slow me down, Lord!
Ease the pounding of my heart by the quieting of my mind. Steady my hurried pace with a vision of the eternal reach of time. Give me, amidst the confusion of my day, the calmness of the everlasting hills. Break the tension of my nerves and muscles with the soothing music of the singing streams that live in my memory. Help me to know the magical restorative power of sleep.

Teach me the art of taking minute vacations — of slowing down to look at a flower, to chat with a friend, to pet a dog, to read from a good book. Remind me each day of the fable of the hare and the tortoise, that I may know that the race is not always to the swift; that there is more to life than increasing its speed. Let me look upward into the branches of the towering trees, and know that they grow tall because they grow slowly and well.

Slow me down, Lord, and inspire me to send my roots deep into the soil of life's ending values, that I may grow toward the stars of my greater destiny. Amen.

AUTHOR UNKNOWN

———o———

Quiet

"In quietness and confidence shall be your strength" (Isaiah 30:15).

"Quiet." What a strange old word
To use on this day's air!
'Tis many years since it was stressed
By humans anywhere.

Our very entertainment,
And the daily tools we need,
Either prattle, shriek, or roar,
To help our work succeed.

When some youngsters try to study,
Or type themes, or even think,
There must be a radio blaring,
(For mere quiet makes them shrink).

Hot impatience rules our living;
We can't wait for anything.
Things jump into place on order,
Or we rant instead of sing.

Our Bible bids us to be quiet;
— And our God proves values, too.
'Tis BELIEVING, that He asks for;
That's one thing that we can do.

MRS. F. MCQUAT

R

Race

A group of Negroes entered a classy restaurant.

"Sorry, it isn't our policy to serve members of the Negro race," the waitress said.

One of the visitors replied, "That's all right. We don't eat them anyway."

———o———

No race can prosper till it learns that there is as much dignity in tilling a field as in writing a poem.

BOOKER T. WASHINGTON,
Up From Slavery

———o———

If you hate me because I am ignorant I'll educate myself. If you hate me because I am dirty, I'll clean myself. If you hate me because I am pagan, I will become a Christian. But if you hate me because I am black, I can only refer you to God who made me black.

MILAN DAVID

Read

In the "good old days" it was a boy himself, rather than his teacher, who had to explain why he could not read.

CY N. PEACEL

———o———

The reading of good books is one of the most helpful ways in which young people can develop themselves. To read good books casually will not suffice. One must study every sentence and make sure of its full message. Good writers do not intend that we should get their full meaning without effort. They expect us to dig as one is compelled to dig for gold. Gold, you know, is not generally found in large openings, but in tiny veins. The ore must be subjected to a white heat in order to get the pure gold. Remember this when you read.

Young men and women who are seeking to learn all they can, have minds capable of receiving and retaining new impressions. There is nothing that will strengthen the mind, broaden the vision, enrich the soul more than the reading of good books.

J. C. PENNEY
in *Christian Herald*

———o———

Force yourself to reflect on what you read, paragraph by paragraph.

SAMUEL TAYLOR COLERIDGE

———o———

Learn to read slow: all other graces
Will follow in their proper places.

WILLIAM WALKER,
The Art of Reading

———o———

We learn six percent of what we hear but eighty-six percent of all we learn we learn from what we read.

———o———

Four-year-old Billy stood in awe of the great accomplishments of his six-year-old brother Johnny. "Can you really read?" Billy asked one day, admiration obvious in his voice.

"Sure," Johnny replied.

"What does that reading on the stove say?" Billy demanded.

Johnny regarded the brand name printed on the stove. For several seconds he tried to figure out the unfamiliar word. "I don't read stoves," he said at last. "I just read books."

———o———

Tell me what you read and I will tell you what you are.

———o———

Have you ever rightly considered what the mere ability to read means? That it is the key which admits us to the whole world of thought and fancy and imagination? To the company of saint and sage, of the wisest and the wittiest at their wisest and wittiest moment? That it enables us to see with the keenest eyes, hear with the finest ears, and listen to the sweetest voices of all time?

JAMES RUSSELL LOWELL

———o———

Reading maketh a full man, conference a ready man, and writing an exact man.

SIR FRANCIS BACON, *Of Studies*

———o———

To read without reflecting, is like eating without digesting.

EDMUND BURKE

Reason

Some reasons that sound good may not be sound reasons.

———o———

There are many reasons for doing a thing, but one of the most effective is the lack of an alternative; if you gotta do it, you gotta do it.

Transcript, Milton, Massachusetts

———o———

It is useless to attempt to reason a man out of a thing he was never reasoned into.

JONATHAN SWIFT

———o———

Where reason is most needed, usually it is not allowed to enter.

———o———

We don't want a thing because we have found a reason for it; we find a reason for it because we want it.

WILL DURANT

———o———

A four-year-old boy buckled on his new overshoes and went flippety-floppety down the street to visit his grandfather.

"You've got those overshoes on the wrong feet," grumbled Grandpa.

"But they're the only feet I have," said the grandson.

———o———

Reveal'd Religion first inform'd thy sight,

And Reason saw not, till Faith sprung the light.

JOHN DRYDEN, *Religio Laici*

———o———

Passion and prejudice govern the world; only under the name of reason.

JOHN WESLEY

Redemption

Humanitarian programs, though deep and sincere, are not enough. The world may be greatly blessed by them but not redeemed. As worthy as an act may be, simply painting the pump doesn't purify the water.

———o———

Two Hours

Two hours outshine upon the roll of
   Time
All other earthly hours as stars aloof;
One tells the moment, throbbing and
   sublime,
   When He was born beneath the stable roof,
Whose advent hosts of winging angels
   sang,
While all the sky with alleluias rang.

The other, when with glad unerring
   wing,
   The Easter Angel at command divine
Unsealed the stone and Love rose triumphing;
   (That tomb, were He unrisen, were mine and thine.)
For the first hour, all earthly hours
   are named,
But for the other's sake, a lost world
   is reclaimed.

LOUISE MANNING HODGKINS

———o———

When we say, "Something should be done about Skid Row," God is saying the same thing about us. That is why He sent His Son to help us.

J. VERNON MCGEE

Reflection

The world is a looking glass, and gives back to every man the reflection of his own face. Frown at it, and it will turn and look sourly upon you; laugh at it, and with it, and it is a jolly companion.

WILLIAM MAKEPEACE THACKERAY

————o————

You will find as you look back on your life that the moments that stand out above everything else are the moments when you have done things in a spirit of love.

HENRY DRUMMOND

————o————

A moment's insight is sometimes worth a life's experience.

OLIVER WENDELL HOLMES

————o————

The mirror always tells the truth, but the viewer interprets the reflection to suit himself.

————o————

There is one art which every man should be a master — the art of reflection.

SAMUEL TAYLOR COLERIDGE

Reform, Reformation

O Lord, reform thy world — beginning with me.

A Chinese Christian's Prayer

————o————

There's so much good in the worst of us, and so much bad in the best of us — that it's rather difficult to tell which of us ought to reform the rest of us.

————o————

Ah for a man to arise in me,
That the man I am may cease to be!

ALFRED, LORD TENNYSON

Regret

Might Have Been

The saddest words
Of tongue or pen
May well be
"It might have been,"
Especially silence
Left unbroken
And healing words
We might have spoken.

MAY RICHSTONE, adapted from
JOHN GREENLEAF WHITTIER, *Maud Muller*

Make the most of your regrets. To regret deeply is to live afresh.

HENRY DAVID THOREAU

Relatives

Small girl's definition of relatives: People who come to dinner who aren't friends.

————o————

He has more kinfolk than a microbe.

IRVIN SHREWSBURY COBB

————o————

Fate makes our relatives, choice makes our friends.

JACQUES DELILLE, *La Pitié*

Reliable

A small boy explained reliable this way: "A man lied once, then he lied again. He was reliable!"

————o————

Reliability is more important than ability; tackle-ability is really more to be commended than capability.

Religion

If we have an attack of real religion it will be contagious.

————o————

Religion is no more possible without prayer than poetry without language or music without atmosphere.

JAMES MARTINEAU

————o————

If your attitude toward religion were only a private matter you might take it as it comes without concerning yourself about it very seriously. But the trouble is it isn't private, it affects others.

————o————

He that has doctrinal knowledge and speculation only, without holy affection, never is engaged in the business of religion. True religion is a powerful thing . . . a ferment, a vigorous engagedness of the heart.

JONATHAN EDWARDS

We have just enough religion to make us hate, but not enough to make us love another.

JONATHAN SWIFT,
Thoughts on Various Subjects

———o———

To put more heart in your religion, you must have more religion in your heart.

———o———

When your religion gets into the past tense, it becomes pretense.

———o———

A seen religion is not always real, but a real religion is always seen.

———o———

To be furious in religion is to be irreligiously religious.

WILLIAM PENN

———o———

Too many people use religion like a spare tire – only in emergencies.

Banking

———o———

The aim of religion is not to get us into heaven, but to get heaven into us.

ULYSSES G. B. PIERCE

———o———

A near-sighted woman, called a "crank on religion," was once discovered talking religion to a wooden Indian in front of a cigar store. When chided for such "an undignified act," she said, "I would rather be a Christian and talk religion to a wooden Indian, than a wooden Christian who never talks religion to anyone."

———o———

Lord, let not my religion be a thing of selfish ecstacy;
But something warm with tender care and fellowship which I can share.
Let me not walk the other side of trouble's highway long and wide;
Make me a Good Samaritan, and neighbor unto every man.

CLARENCE M. BURKHOLDER

———o———

No one is dressed shabbier than he who uses his religion as a cloak.

DAVID YOUNG

Remedy

Our remedies oft in ourselves do lie,
Which we ascribe to Heaven.

WILLIAM SHAKESPEARE,
All's Well that Ends Well

———o———

There are some remedies worse than the disease.

PUBLILIUS SYRUS, *Maxim 301*

———o———

Extreme remedies are very appropriate for extreme diseases.

HIPPOCRATES, *Aphorisms*

———o———

He destroys his health by the pains he takes to preserve it.

VIRGIL

Remember

Things to remember: the value of time; the success of perseverance; the pleasure of working; the worth of character; the power of kindness; the influence of example; the obli..ation of duty; the wisdom of economy, the virtue of patience; the sound of laughter; the joy of originating; the thrill of accomplishing.

CARL YODER

———o———

Recollection is the only paradise from which we cannot be turned out.

JEAN PAUL RICHTER

———o———

To be a noble person it is a holy joy to remember.

ABRAHAM JOSHUA HESCHEL

———o———

Pleasure is the flower that fades; remembrance is the lasting perfume.

MARQUIS STANISLAS JEAN DE BOUFFLERS

———o———

Remembered
(Jeremiah 2:2)

Not forgotten, but remembered!
Child of God, trust on with cheer!
Thy great Father's help is promised
Every day throughout the year.

Not forsaken — but most precious
  Thou wilt ever to Him be;
Tenderly He whispers, "Fear not!
  I, the Lord, remember thee!"

Not forgotten, but remembered,
  Is the pledge of Love Divine!
He who loves and understands us,
  Best can plan thy path and mine.
His own Word cannot be broken,
  "As thy days thy strength shall be,"
He, Himself, the word hath spoken —
  "I, the Lord, remember thee!"

Not forgotten, but remembered —
  In His love for thee He planned,
Chosen, sealed, thy name engraven
  On His pierced and peerless hand.
When He calls thee, "Come up higher,"
  Thou shalt then His wonders see —
Wonders of His mighty promise —
  "I, the Lord, remember thee!"

L. C. HASLER

———o———

An old southerner, being questioned by a census taker, was having trouble remembering the birthdates of all his grandchildren. He asked his wife when one of the girls was born.

"Well," answered the wife, "I know she was born in 'tater time, but I'm blessed if I can remember if it was diggin' or plantin' time!"

Repentance

Real repentance thinks God's thoughts about sin and hates it; takes God's side against self and dies to it; turns to God Himself and serves Him.

———o———

For making a man repent his sins, there's nothing quite so convincing as catching him.

———o———

If we put off repentance another day, we have a day more to repent of and a day less to repent in.

MASON

———o———

Real repentance is sorrow for the deed, not for being caught.

Repentance is sorrow for sin converted into action, into change in manner of life.

Reputation

No man will ever bring out of the Presidency the reputation which carries him into it.

THOMAS JEFFERSON

———o———

When I devoted to God my ease, my time, my future, my life, I did not except my reputation.

JOHN WESLEY

———o———

Another way to get a reputation for enlightenment and wisdom is to say the things all men know, but which most of them have forgotten.

———o———

Lasting reputations are of slow growth; the man who wakes up famous some morning is very apt to go to bed some night and sleep it off.

"JOSH BILLINGS" (HENRY WHEELER SHAW)

———o———

What people say behind your back is your standing in the community.

EDGAR WATSON HOWE,
Country Town Sayings

———o———

Reputation is for time; character is for eternity.

JOHN B. GOFF

———o———

A good reputation is more valuable than money.

PUBLILIUS SYRUS, *Maxim 108*

———o———

Your reputation is the outcome of what you do; your character is determined by what you think.

———o———

A reputation for good judgment, fair dealing, truth, and rectitude, is itself a fortune.

HENRY WARD BEECHER

Credible Fable

Two brothers, convicted of stealing sheep, were branded on the forehead with the letters "S.T." meaning "Sheep Thief." One of the brothers was unable to bear the stigma, and tried to bury himself in a foreign land; but men asked him about the strange letters, so he kept on wandering restlessly, and at length, full of bitterness, died and was buried far from home.

The other brother said to himself, "I can't run away from the fact that I stole sheep. I will stay here and win back the respect of my neighbors and myself."

As years passed he built a reputation for integrity. Decades later, a stranger one day saw the old man with the letters on his forehead. He asked a native what they signified. "It happened a great while ago," said the villager. "I've forgotten the particulars, but I think the letters are an abbreviation of 'Saint'."

Rescue

A child was in a house in which a fire was raging away up in the fourth story. The child came to the window, and as the flames were shooting up higher and higher, she cried out for help. A fireman started up the ladder. The wind swept the flames near him, and it was getting so hot that he wavered. Thousands looked on, and their hearts quaked at the thought of the child having to perish. Someone in the crowd cried: "Give him a cheer!" Cheer after cheer went up, and as the man heard, he gathered fresh courage. Up he went into the midst of the smoke and the fire, and brought down the child in safety.

If you cannot go and rescue the perishing yourself, you can at least pray for those who do, and cheer them on. If you do, the Lord will bless the effort. Do not grumble and criticize; it takes neither heart nor brains to do that.

Daily Gems in *Moody Monthly*

He that turneth from the road to rescue another,
Turneth toward his goal:
He shall arrive by the foot-path of mercy,
God will be his Guide.

HENRY VAN DYKE,
The Tribe of the Helpers

Resolve, Resolutions

If it be my lot to crawl, I will crawl contentedly; if to fly, I will fly with alacrity; but, as long as I can avoid it, I will never be unhappy.

SYDNEY SMITH

———o———

Resolved, never to reprove another except I experience at the same time a peculiar contrition of heart.

HENRY MARTYN, in his diary

———o———

Beware of having too many resolutions and too little action.

———o———

I have never heard anything about the resolutions of the apostles, but a good deal about the *Acts* of the apostles.

HORACE MANN

———o———

January 2 is when most people find that it's easier to break a resolution than a habit.

Farm Journal

———o———

One reason we so often fail in our New Year's resolutions is that they are so often negative.

B. V. SEALS

———o———

The Backslider's Resolutions

January
"I hereby resolve to start to church this year. But I'll wait till February. Gotta get over the holidays. They take a lot out of a fellow, you know."
February
"Weather is terrible. I'll start when it warms up a bit. My blood is so thin this time of the year."
March
"Lots of sickness just now. Got to keep away from those bugs. A per-

son can't afford to take a chance."

April

"Easter . . . big crowds. You can't get a decent seat. Anyhow they won't miss me. It would look strange if I showed up only at Easter."

May

"I've been holed up all winter and now that the weather is getting pretty . . . It's time for reunions, too."

June

"I'll wait until the baby is older . . . how on earth do some folks bring their babies at two weeks of age and then never miss a Sunday?"

July

"Boy! Is the heat terrific! We've got that cabin that we still owe for . . . and that boat for Sunday pleasure."

August

"Preacher's on vacation. He'll never know if I miss this once. Never liked guest preachers anyhow . . . but when the preacher gets back . . ."

September

"School's started. Vacation threw me behind with my work. Gotta make one last visit to grandma's before the snow flies."

October

"Leaves are beautiful . . . I can worship God outdoors anyhow . . . and the kids will be cooped up all winter."

November

"My heart is bursting with gratitude and thanksgiving — the Christmas season will be a wonderful time to start back."

December

"What a madhouse . . . right after this is over my family and I will start back to church . . . the first Sunday in January. This next year I will resolve . . ."

ARNOLD PRATER in
The Miami Christian

———o———

Always bear in mind that your own resolution to succeed is more important than any other one thing.

Resources

One day an undergraduate came in to see me, blue in spirit because of the blue slip of those days which stated his indebtedness due that day in the college business office. So as to pray more intelligently with him I felt led to inquire as to his bill ($28.75, as I recall), and his resources ($.79).

Before we prayed I suggested he write an equation on the back of that bill. He wrote as I dictated:

$.79: $28.75 = 5$ loaves $+ 2$ small fishes: 5000 men $+$ women & children

"Which side of that equation is unbalanced?" I asked, but by that time his eyes had filled with tears. Together we prayed in faith to the Faithful One Who fed the multitude.

The next day unexpected money came in and the bill was paid.

And before you pray, take time to write down your resources and responsibilities and likewise learn anew our Lord's love and faithfulness.

V. RAYMOND EDMAN

———o———

Few men during their life-time come anywhere near exhausting the resources dwelling within them. There are deep wells of strength that are never used.

ADMIRAL RICHARD E. BYRD

Responsibility

Many are chosen, but they don't always accept.

———o———

The man who likes to shoulder his responsibilities never has room for a chip.

O. A. BATTISTA

———o———

Responsibility without accountability brings no result.

———o———

It is easy to dodge our responsibilities, but we cannot dodge the consequences of dodging our responsibilities.

SIR JOSIAH STAMP,
in The English Digest

———o———

Responsibilities move toward him who will shoulder them, and power flows to him who acts with energy.

I will go down, but remember that you must hold the ropes.

WILLIAM CAREY

———o———

Responsibility's like a string, we can only see the middle of. Both ends are out of sight.

WILLIAM MCFEE

———o———

You cannot escape the responsibility of tomorrow by evading it today.

ABRAHAM LINCOLN

Resurrection

The Gospels do not explain the resurrection; the resurrection explains Gospels.

JOHN S. WHALE

———o———

Christianity begins where religion ends, with the resurrection.

———o———

Song Of Resurrection

"Because Christ lives, I too shall live!"
O glorious truth divine!
To think that resurrection life was His
And shall be mine!

"Because Christ lives, I too shall live!"
I'll leave this lump of clay
And lift my wings to higher heights
On resurrection day!

"Because Christ lives, I too shall live!"
With Him I'll ever be
Rejoicing that He broke death's chains
And set my spirit free!

NAT OLSON

———o———

Simple markers are set upon the graves in the churchyard at Oberhofen, Switzerland. One who was too poor to purchase an engraved brass marker printed on a board the name and dates of birth and death of a departed loved one and placed it on the grave. Over this marker was put a little protective roof. In time a caterpillar fastened itself on the underside of the roof. There it passed through the death-like state of a chrysalis, and ultimately emerged as a beautiful butterfly, leaving its former corpse-like abode behind.

What a beautiful picture of the resurrection when Christ as His Second Coming "shall change our vile body, that it may be fashioned like unto His glorious body" (Philippians 3:21).

———o———

Belief in the resurrection is not an appendage to the Christian faith; it *is* the Christian faith.

JOHN S. WHALE

Retribution, Revenge

It was three o'clock in the morning when the telephone suddenly began to ring. Sleepily, Jones struggled out of bed and made his way across the room to answer it. "This is your neighbor," announced the angry voice on the other end. "Your dog has been barking all night, and I can't get to sleep. If you don't do something about it, I'm calling the police!"

The following night at three in the morning Jones phoned his neighbor. The sleepy man fumbled about for his slippers, then stumbled to the phone. "Listen, buster," Jones said, "I don't own a dog!"

———o———

Some people do odd things to get even!

———o———

Revenge proves its own executioner.

FORD

———o———

It costs more to revenge injuries than to bear them.

THOMAS WILSON

———o———

Revenge converts a little right into a great wrong.

Reverence, Reverently

Enter A Church Reverently

Enter a church reverently;
Leave it reverently, too,
Go alone, that the quiet
May strengthen you.

Each one alone — so it was meant —
Though a thousand are there;

Each heart emptied and waiting,
Each heart at prayer.

Then through the still sanctuary
Falls a communal peace,
God to each heart has spoken,
Each heart has peace.

CAROL M. RITCHIE

———o———

Oliver Wendell Holmes was once asked why he troubled to attend a small church where the preacher was a most ordinary man with no originality as a thinker. Dr. Holmes gave this fine reply:

"I go because I have a little plant called 'Reverence,' and I must needs water it once a week or it would die."

Revival

Revival is a renewing and a reformation of the church for action.

MAX WARREN

———o———

"How can we have revival?" someone asked the great evangelist, Gypsy Smith.

The wise, old preacher replied, "Take a piece of chalk, and draw a circle on the floor. Then step inside the circle and pray: 'Lord, send a revival inside this circle.'"

———o———

A native of India, writing to a friend about a great revival they were having, said, "We're having a rebible." Not a bad idea. The church needs to be "rebibled."

———o———

An old-fashioned minister asked the Lord to revive his church.

"You're asking the revival to start in the wrong place," the Lord told him. "Get the revival fires burning in your members' homes, and then your church will have a new glow."

———o———

In the hydraulics of evangelism, narrowness builds up pressure; that is to say, revivalism is still bringing in the sheaves.

GEORGE E. SWEAZEY

Reward

To receive a reward is a good thing; to deserve it is much better.

———o———

If we always have faith, hope and love,
Our reward is sure in heaven above.

———o———

The day is always his who worked in it with serenity and great aims.

RALPH WALDO EMERSON

———o———

The Day Of Rewards

I'm looking forward to a day, the day
    of eternal rewards
When Christians shall be given crowns
    from the hands of Christ, our Lord;
Oh, what a glorious sight to see the re-
    deemed ones all march past
With wonderful, heavenly dividends,
    the riches that will last.

I can see the pastors, those godly men
    who have guided and fed the flock,
I can see them there, with their crowns
    so fair, humbly and steadily walk
On the streets of gold, while their mem-
    bers behold the reward for faithful-
    ness;
And the missionaries, too, who've
    stayed pure and true, with their
    trophies of fruitfulness.

Yes, I'm looking forward to that day,
    the day of eternal rewards;
And I'm working, and praying, and giv-
    ing, that I might receive from Christ,
    the Lord
Some trophy, some crown, some divi-
    dend to show I've not lived in vain;
Right now, I'm rather pressed for time
    for soon He'll come again!

NAT OLSON

———o———

A man's better reward is what he becomes, not what he gets.

———o———

An award can pick up a good deal of prestige by being refused by the right person.

Herald-Journal, Clarinda, Iowa

"I think you're going to get an award at the end of the year," a first-grade teacher commented to a pupil for her perfect attendance.

A student excitedly spoke up from the back of the room: "I've got one of those on my hand — I think I got it playing with a frog."

Rich, Riches

It is better to live rich, than to die rich.

SAMUEL JOHNSON,
Boswell's *Life of Dr. Johnson, Vol. II*

———o———

A rich man is one who isn't afraid to ask the clerk to show him something cheaper.

———o———

We grow rich by depositing the Word of God in our hearts.

WILBUR SMITH

———o———

The futility of riches is stated very plainly in two places: the Bible and the income-tax form.

The Gilcrafter

———o———

A man is rich according to what he IS, not according to what he HAS.

———o———

Riches

How rich you may be, or how poor,
There is a way to tell for sure.
The method is a simple one,
And it is very quickly done.
How much or little is your part,
Your wealth is carried in your heart.
Your money, houses, bonds, and lands,
Slip easily from clutching hands.
The hours of happiness you share
With hands that cling and hearts that care,
The knowledge that you have a friend
Upon whose faith you can depend,
Love for your work, a sense of worth,
The joy and beauty of the earth,
Courage and confidence to meet
Whatever comes without defeat,
The worth you give on any day,
Nothing can take these things away.
Of riches this, friend, is your part,
All you can carry in your heart.

AUTHOR UNKNOWN

A tax collector one day came to a poor minister in order to assess the value of his property and to determine the amount of his taxes.

"I am a rich man," said the minister.

The official quickly sharpened his pencil and asked intently, "Well, what do you own?"

The pastor replied, "I am the possessor of a Saviour who earned for me everlasting life and who has prepared a place for me in the Eternal City."

"What else?"

"I have a brave, pious wife, and in the Bible it says, 'Who can find a virtuous woman? for her price is far above rubies.' "

"What else?"

"Healthy and obedient children."

"What else?"

"A merry heart which enables me to pass through life joyfully."

"What else?"

"That is all," replied the minister.

The official closed his book, arose, took his hat, and said, "You are indeed a rich man, Sir, but your property is not subject to taxation."

The King's Business

———o———

In this world, it is not what we take up, but what we give up, that makes us rich.

HENRY WARD BEECHER

———o———

We need not have riches in order to make life rich.

Right, Righteous

Better, though difficult, the right way to go,
Than wrong, 'tho easy, where the end is woe.

JOHN BUNYAN,
Pilgrim's Progress, Part I

———o———

Be sure you are right, then go ahead.

Motto of David Crockett in War of 1812

———o———

Sir, I would rather be right than be President.

HENRY CLAY, *Speech* (1850)

Rival

The best way to kill off a rival is to make him a friend.

———o———

He that falls in love with himself will have no rivals.

BENJAMIN FRANKLIN

Rule

No rule is so general, which admits not some exception.

ROBERT BURTON,
Anatomy of Melancholy

———o———

Don't blame the rule if you don't measure up.

———o———

Why is it that it's so much easier to make rules than to follow them?

———o———

We need to commit the Golden Rule to life as well as to memory.

S

Sacrifice

People talk of the sacrifice I have made in spending so much of my life in Africa. Can that be called a sacrifice which is simply paid back as a small part of a great debt owed to our God, which we can never repay? Is that a sacrifice which brings its own best reward in healthful activity, the consciousness of doing good, peace of mind, and the bright hope of a glorious destiny hereafter. I never made a sacrifice.

DAVID LIVINGSTONE

———o———

Once For All

Once into the holy place,
   Spotless, free from sin,
With His blood the sacrifice,
   Jesus entered in.
Once a year the high priest came
   Others' blood to bring,
But Christ suffered once for all,
   Himself sin's offering.
All the blood of bulls and goats
   Never could suffice:
Christ must offer once for all
   Perfect sacrifice.
Hanging there upon the cross,
   For lost men He pleaded;
"It is finished!" was His cry,
   Nothing more was needed.
No more daily sacrifice:
   Salvation's work complete,

Our High Priest at God's right hand
   Forever took His seat.
Can I add to such a work
   By my weak endeavor?
No! I rest secure in His
   Sacrifice forever.

BARBARA C. RYBERG

———o———

In a lonely valley in Switzerland a small band of patriots once marched against an invading force of ten times their strength. They found themselves one day at the head of a narrow pass, confronted by a solid wall of spears. They made assault after assault, but the bristling line remained unbroken. Time after time they were driven back decimated with hopeless slaughter. The forlorn hope rallied for the last time.

As they charged, their leader suddenly advanced before them with outstretched arms, and every spear for three or four yards of the line was buried in his body. He fell dead. But he prepared a place for his followers. Through the open breach, over his dead body, they rushed to victory and won the freedom of their country. So the Lord Jesus went before His people, the Captain of our salvation, sheathing the weapons of death and judgment to Himself, and preparing a place for us with His dead body.

HENRY DRUMMOND

Sacrifice is only that which is given after the heart has given all that it can spare. To sacrifice for Christ's sake brings joy unbounded and peace unmoved by the fleeting things of this life.

Saints

Every saint in heaven is as a flower in the garden of God, and every soul there is as a note in some concert of delightful music. All together blend in rapturous strains in praising God and the Lamb forever.

JONATHAN EDWARDS

———o———

A little child on a summer morning stood in a great cathedral. The sunlight streamed through the beautiful stained glass windows and the figures in them of the servants of God were bright with brilliant color. A little later the question was asked, "What is a saint?" The child replied, "A saint is a person who lets the light shine through."

———o———

Saints are persons who make it easier for others to believe in God.

NATHAN SÖDERBLOM

Sales

A woman who was taking her first plane ride was seated next to a minister. During some turbulence, the lady became fearful and turned to the minister, asking him if he couldn't do something.

"Lady," he replied, "I'm in sales, not management!"

———o———

A Bargain Sale

I'm offering for sale today
A lot of things I'll need no more;
Come, please, and take them all away,
I've piled them up outside my door.
I'll make the prices low enough,
And trust you, if it's trust you need;
Here I have listed all my stuff,
Make your selection as you read:

A lot of prejudices which
Have ceased to be of use to me;
A stock of envy of the rich,
Some slightly shopworn jealousy;
A large supply of gloom that I
Must not permit to clog my shelves;
I offer bargains — who will buy?
Name prices that will suit yourselves.

A lot of wishes I've outgrown,
A stock of silly old beliefs;
Some pride I once was proud to own,
A bulky line of dreads and griefs;
An old assortment of ill will,
A job lot of bad faith and doubt,
Harsh words that have their poison still;
Choose as you please — I'm closing out.

I need more room for kindliness,
For hope and courage and good cheer,
Take all the hatred I possess,
The superstitions and the fear;
A large supply of frailties I
Shall have no use for from today;
I offer bargains; who will buy?
The rubbish must be cleared away!

S. E. KISER in
The Log of the Good Ship Grace

———o———

Salesmanship consists of transferring a conviction by a seller to a buyer.

PAUL G. HOFFMAN

Salvation

There is not a child born into the world but that would go straight to Christ except that someone hinders him.

G. CAMPBELL MORGAN

———o———

As soon as a child is capable of being damned, it is capable of being saved.

CHARLES HADDON SPURGEON

———o———

Win the man, you win the family;
Win the family, you win the home;
Win the home and you win the community;
Win the community and you win the nation.

A Parent's Prayer

To us, we pray, Lord give the joy
Of leading our own girl and boy
To that most bless'd and holy place
Where they will meet Thee face to
face,
Confess their sins, see Christ's oblation,
Then in faith receive salvation.

We who have brought them, by Thy
help
Into this world of sin and pain
Would be the ones to lead their steps
Within th' eternal King's domain.

So guard our words and guide our
ways,
That in their very early days
Our little ones may grace receive
To see Christ dying — and believe.

While they are still beneath our wing
Accomplish, Lord, this holy thing.
This joy, more sweet than any other,
Belongs to Christian father and
mother.

AUTHOR UNKNOWN

———o———

E'er a child has reached to seven,
Teach him all the way to heaven,
Better still the work will thrive
If he learn before he's five.

———o———

Why should men pay such a high
price for damnation when salvation is
free?

———o———

The Man Next Door

Jesus died to bring salvation,
For the rich and for the poor;
Men of every tribe and nation —
He includes the man next door.

Millions are in heathen darkness
And with pleading hearts implore
For the gospel of salvation:
What about the man next door?

We are stewards of our possessions
And we bring from out our store
Means to spread abroad this gospel —
Don't forget the man next door.

"Go into all the world," said Jesus,
Tell them of my mighty power.
Bring your sheaves from every nation,
Bring with you the man next door.

When we stand before our Saviour
On that glad eternal shore,
Heaven's glory will be brighter
If we've brought the man next door.
SELECTED

———o———

God is the originating cause of salvation.
Jesus is the meritorious cause.
The Bible is the instrumental cause.
Faith is the conditional cause.
The Spirit is the efficient cause.
In other words:
God thought it.
Jesus bought it.
The Word taught it.
The mind caught it.
The soul sought it.
Faith brought it.
The Spirit wrought it.
The devil fought it.
But I've got it.
American Holiness Journal.

———o———

The elect are the "whosoever wills,"
the non-elect are the "whosoever
won'ts."
DWIGHT L. MOODY

———o———

An evangelist visited a man in a
pottery district who, in his younger
days, had been an infidel. The visitor
gazed upon two magnificent vases contained in a glass case. "What lovely
vases!" he remarked. "I suppose they
are very valuable?"
"Yes," was the reply.
"How much would you sell them
for?"
With a shake of the head, the man
turned to his questioner. "All the money in the world wouldn't tempt me to
part with either of them," he answered.
"Years ago I was a drunkard, a
gambler — one who sold his soul to the
devil. One day I was persuaded to
attend a revival meeting. I did so, and
on going home I passed a rubbish heap.
I saw there a piece of clay. Evidently

someone had thrown it away as being useless. I picked it up, took it home, kneaded it and molded it. Then I went to the wheel, and out of that worthless piece of clay I made those two vases. I thought to myself that if I could do such a thing as that, then God could do so with me. And thereafter I placed myself into His hands, and He has made me a new man."

————o————

The late Bishop Taylor Smith, the beloved evangelical of the Anglican faith, never lost an opportunity of introducing the subject of salvation to the ordinary people whom he met. On one occasion he sat in a barber's chair to have a shave, and ventured very courteously to mention the matter of salvation.

"I do my best," snapped the barber, "and that's enough for me."

The Bishop was silent until the shave was over, and when the next customer was seated the Bishop asked, "May I shave this man?"

"No, I'm afraid not," replied the barber, with a grin.

"But I would do my best," answered the Bishop.

"So you might, but your best would not be good enough for this gentleman."

"No," replied the Bishop quietly. "And neither is your best good enough for God."

————o————

We are saved by a Person, and only by a Person, and only by one Person.
WILLIAM F. MCDOWELL

————o————

He that will not be saved needs no preacher.

Satisfaction

A Good Day

To waken in the morning serene and quiet with the thought of His love and His strength — joyous in the thought of those whom He has given us to love and serve — humble in our weakness, and free from the shadow of self.

To care for our bodies as His temples and for our homes as His dwelling-place; striving to maintain in them that order, that beauty, and that law which He has ordained in His world.

To meet those who serve us with appreciation and sympathy, and those whom we serve with forethought and consideration.

To do the small duties with a sense that all faithful service ranks equally with God.

To pass over the rough places with joy, and through the dark places with peace.

To practice always His presence.

To see the beauty He has made.

To be where we are needed, and to make time for those who need us.

To pass on our way unhurried, without care, realizing that His is the Kingdom, the Power and the Glory.
SELECTED

————o————

Show me a thoroughly satisfied man — I will show you a failure.
THOMAS ALVA EDISON

————o————

If you are satisfied just to get by, step aside for the man who isn't.

Saving

The toughest part of putting something away for a rainy day is finding a clear day to do it.
Wall Street Journal

————o————

A man who both spends and saves has both enjoyments.
SAMUEL JOHNSON

————o————

When a man begins to think seriously of saving for a rainy day, it's probably a rainy day.
FRANKLIN P. JONES

————o————

At twenty a man thinks he can save the world;
At thirty he is happy if he can save part of his salary.

School

I feel so tired of school work, God, and
  every night it seems
That when I put away my books, I see
  them in my dreams.
Regardless of the many things that I
  would rather do,
I first must finish homework, God, and
  that is never through!
In spite of my complaining, though, I
  really can't deny
That I am very fortunate, because I
  know that I
Am learning things that I am sure will
  help me day by day
To meet whatever needs, O God, I
  have along the way.

GEORGE BILBY WALKER

———o———

Little Jerry's mother was crying when
he started for his first day at school.
"Aw, Mom, don't take it so hard," he
consoled her. "Just as soon as I learn
to write and read comics, I'll quit."

The Christian Science Monitor

———o———

School Days

The call to school it comes! It comes!
A muffler on the gypsy drums!
And birds and beasts and children sigh
While Summer murmurs soft, "Good-
  bye."
And gruff old Autumn paints his name
On leaves in shades of gold and flame.

Back to the classrooms and the books;
Back from vacation's cherished nooks;
Back with a sigh of deep regret;
Back to the cry of "Teacher's pet!"
Back to the place where pencils fly,
And love notes, too, upon the sly.

The call to school, it comes! It comes!
Recalling youth to maps and sums,
Athletic meets and frantic cheers,
But sad it falls on adult ears . . .
For hearts of grown-ups long in vain
To be a kid at school again!

NICK KENNY

———o———

Monday was the first day of school
for the little boy, and he enjoyed it
tremendously. Each day that followed,
he seemed to like it more. Then Friday came, and he returned home despondent. "Mom," he complained, "I've
been laid off for two days."

ANNA HERBERT in *Family Weekly*

Science

Everything science has taught me —
and continues to teach me — strengthens my belief in the continuity of our
spiritual existence after death.

WERNHER VON BRAUN

———o———

Science is but a mere heap of facts,
not a gold chain of truths, if we refuse
to link it to the throne of God.

FRANCES P. COBBE

———o———

There is something in man which
your science cannot satisfy.

THOMAS CARLYLE to Professor Tyndall

———o———

Science is a first-rate piece of furniture for a man's upper chamber, if
he has common sense on the ground
floor.

OLIVER WENDELL HOLMES

———o———

In this scientific age, the only impossible things are people.

———o———

Scientists are debating whether or not
splitting the atom was a wise crack.

———o———

Human science is an uncertain guess.

MATTHEW PRIOR

Scripture

It is very difficult for an individual
who knows the Scripture ever to get
away from it. It haunts him like an
old song. It follows him like the memory of his mother. It remains with him
like the word of a reverenced teacher.
It forms a part of the warp and woof
of his life.

WOODROW WILSON

Twenty-Third Psalm
(Vest-Pocket Edition)

Beneath me:	green pastures;
Beside me:	still waters;
With me:	my Shepherd;
Before me:	a table;
Around me:	my enemies,
After me:	goodness and mercy;
Beyond me:	the house of the Lord.

———o———

Two texts preachers ought to use for sermons more often than they do are: "Thou God seest me," and "The eyes of the Lord are in every place beholding the evil and the good."

———o———

A minister stood to read the Scripture at an evening camp meeting. As he opened his mouth and drew a deep breath, he sucked in a moth. Gulping but undaunted he said, "I was a stranger and ye took me in . . ."

Seasons

The seasons slip by and, before you know it, it's time for the bulbs you didn't get planted last fall not to come up.
Changing Times, The Kiplinger Magazine

———o———

To be interested in the changing seasons is a happier state of mind than to be hopelessly in love with spring.
GEORGE SANTAYANA

———o———

A few years ago in one of our first-grade classes, the teacher wanted to teach her students about the seasons of the year. One bright little lad waved his hand anxiously and said, "Teacher, I know what the four seasons are. They are squirrel season, quail season, duck season, and deer season."
MILDRED DANIELS in *Grade Teacher*

Secret

It's not so hard for a woman to keep a secret as it is for her to keep it a secret that she's keeping a secret.
SYDNEY J. HARRIS in *Coronet*

A secret is something you tell only one person at a time.

———o———

Some people have two ideas about a secret: it's either not worth keeping or it's too good to keep.

———o———

Let everyone carry his belongings in his own suitcase and his secrets in his own heart.

———o———

If you don't believe a ten-year-old boy can keep a secret, ask him where he left the family hammer.
Independent-Review, Aztec, New Mexico

———o———

One of the hardest secrets for a man to keep is his opinion of himself.

———o———

Secret sins seldom stay secret.

Security

Jesus Christ is no security against storms, but He is perfect security in storms.

———o———

God Holds The Key

God holds the key of all unknown
And I am glad;
If other hands should hold the key,
Or if He trusted it to me,
I might be sad.

The very dimness of my sight
Makes me secure;
For, groping my misty way,
I feel His hand: I hear Him say,
"My help is sure."

I cannot read His future plans;
But this I know:
I have the smiling of His face,
And all the refuge of His grace,
While here below.
J. PARKER

Self

God Pity Him!

God pity him who lives for self —
That one who does not share

The griefs and joys of other men,
That one who does not care.

God pity him who does not give
To others when in need;
God pity him who works and plans
For only selfish greed.

God pity him when sorrow comes
And no kind friend is there,
No one to grasp his trembling hand
And whisper low, "I care!"

God pity him when death shall come
And few stand by his bier;
So little missed by those he left,
They scarcely shed a tear!

God pity him who lives for self,
When the Master he shall see,
And Jesus says, "As you've done to
them,
You've done it unto Me."
MRS. EDNA B. HUGHES in
The Log of the Good Ship Grace

———o———

Sin has four characteristics:
  Self-sufficiency instead of faith;
  Self-will instead of submission;
  Self-seeking instead of benevolence;
  Self-righteousness instead of humility.

———o———

If you wish to know yourself, observe
how others act; if you wish to understand others, look into your own heart.
JOHANN CHRISTOPH FRIEDRICH VON SCHILLER

———o———

God hath entrusted me with myself.
EPICTETUS

———o———

We go on fancying that each man is
thinking of us, but he is not; he is like
us — he is thinking of himself.
CHARLES READE

———o———

It is the weight of self that overpowers;
Take up another's load, it carries ours.

———o———

Self-denial is an excellent guard of
virtue.
THOMAS TOWNSON

In the earlier years of my life I
studied the peculiarities of others.
Lately I am studying my own.
EDGAR WATSON HOWE

———o———

Nothing dies harder than the desire
to think well of oneself.
T. S. ELIOT,
Shakespeare and the Stoicism of Seneca

———o———

You can't be cheerful until you forget yourself. And you can't forget yourself until you remember others.

———o———

Selfishness aims for happiness but
always cheats itself out of it.

———o———

Lord, make me big enough to live
outside myself.
J. SHERMAN WALLACE

———o———

There's only one corner of the universe you can be certain of improving,
and that's your own self.
ALDOUS LEONARD HUXLEY

Serenity

To walk when others are running;
To whisper when others are shouting;
To sleep when others are restless;
To smile when others are angry;
To work when others are idle;
To pause when others are hurrying;
To pray when others are doubting;
To think when others are in confusion;
To face turmoil, yet feel composure;
To know inner calm in spite of everything —
This is the test of serenity.
DORIS LAGRASSE in *Sunshine Magazine*

Sermons

A sermon can help people in different ways. Some rise from it greatly
strengthened; others wake from it refreshed.

———o———

Parishioners' comments to their pastor upon leaving the church at the
close of services:

"Your sermons have been more meaningful ever since my husband lost his mind."

"Each of your sermons is better than the next one."

"I listened to every word you said and didn't understand any of them, but you have a nice face."

———o———

Child watching her father prepare his Sunday sermon: "Daddy, does God tell you what to say?"

Father: "He surely does. Why do you ask?"

Child: "Then, why do you scratch some of it out?"

Westminster Tidings

———o———

It warms the heart of a preacher to tell him how much you enjoyed his sermon, but if you want to pay him a real compliment tell him you will bring a friend to hear his next sermon.

———o———

You'd be surprised to know how many sermons are like blank cartridges, fired into the air just to hear a noise.

———o———

A sermon that gets only as far as the ear is like a dinner eaten in a dream.

CHARLES HADDON SPURGEON

———o———

An old Scottish woman said to her pastor, "That was a grand sermon you preached last Sabbath at the Kirk!"

Seeking to test her sincerity, he asked, "And what was the text?"

"Ah, meenister! I dinna ken the text or the words. But I came home and took the false bottom out o' my peck measure!"

Serve, Service

The story is told of a certain church in Europe which was bombed in World War II. In the explosion, a statue of Christ was mutilated by having the hands blown off. The statue has not been restored. It stands there today with the hands missing. But underneath has been put this well-known sentence: "Christ hath no hands but yours."

———o———

He has always chosen earthen vessels to be ambassadors of His grace. He proclaims His great Gospel through provincial dialects and He fills uncultured mouths with mighty arguments.

———o———

No man, no matter what may be his background can rise to the stature of spiritual manhood who has not found it nobler to serve somebody else than to serve himself.

———o———

It pays to serve the Lord; but don't serve the Lord because it pays — for if you serve the Lord because it pays, it then may not pay.

ROBERT G. LETOURNEAU

———o———

Have you been trying to serve God by halves or some other fraction? God asks total commitment.

———o———

O God, help us to be masters of ourselves that we may be servants of others.

SIR ALEC PATERSON

———o———

A New York City minister was pleased to have a churchgoer come to him to ask some questions about joining his church. After a long talk with the man the minister said, "One of the things that you will want to think about is the department of the church in which you would prefer to serve."

"Oh, I am not interested in anything like that," the man said. "I just want to join the church."

The minister was patient. "It is our custom to have all members divided into different service groups. Some work in the Sunday School, others in the music department, on the finance committee, the missionary emphasis group; many serve as church visitors. There are others who . . ."

"I didn't know that this was that kind of a church," the man interrupted. "I believe I will visit other churches before making a decision about joining."

The minister smiled kindly. "This church, you know, is known as 'The Church of the Saviour.' Maybe you are looking for 'The Church of the Heavenly Rest.'"

Adapted from *The Expositor*

———o———

Find out what God would have thee
   do,
Perform that service well;
For what is great and what is small,
'Tis only He can tell!

———o———

Some folks are bad spellers; they spell service "serve-us."

———o———

If you wish to be a leader you will be frustrated, for very few people wish to be led. If you aim to be a servant you will never be frustrated.

FRANK F. WARREN

Share

We cannot share what we do not possess.

———o———

We share our mutual woes,
Our mutual burdens bear,
And often for each other flows
The sympathizing tear.

JOHN FAWCETT,
Blest Be the Tie That Binds

———o———

About the only two things a child will share willingly are communicable diseases and his mother's age.

Wall Street Journal

———o———

Oh, many a shaft at random sent
Finds mark the archer little meant!
And many a word, at random spoken,
May soothe or wound a heart that's
   broken.

SIR WALTER SCOTT, *The Lord of the Isles*

There is a destiny that makes us brothers;
None goes his way alone.
All that we send into the lives of others
Comes back into our own.

EDWIN MARKHAM

Shut-Ins

God's Shut-Ins

A special glory seems to crown
The shut-in saint of God
A radiance of joy and peace
Bespeaks the way they've trod.

A patience and a yieldedness
To God's own precious will —
A steadfast faith and trust in Him
A purpose to fulfill.

Just like sweet flowers hidden there
Away from stress and strain,
They bloom in Christian loveliness
Midst loneliness and pain.

Shut out from Christian fellowship
They've loved and held most dear;
But now, shut in with Him alone
Who casts out every fear.

Within their quiet little room
Grow flowers of sweet content,
With fragrance of God's wondrous
   grace
And glory — heaven sent.

AUTHOR UNKNOWN

Signs

Sign on a new lawn in Alexandria, Virginia: "Please Don't Ruin The Gay Young Blades."

———o———

A New York bookstore, going out of business, had this sign in its window: "Words failed us."

———o———

No matter how clearly printed, "Keep Off The Grass" signs always seem to be illegible to two kinds of creatures: birds and some people.

———o———

Sign in the window of a vacant store: "We undersold everyone."

When a sign, "Stop for Pedestrians," was erected in a town square a near-sighted Baptist lady asked, "Why do we have to stop for Presbyterians?"

Silence

Well-timed silence hath more eloquence than speech.

MARTIN FARQUHAR TUPPER,
Proverbial Philosophy of Discretion

———o———

Silence is the unbearable repartee.

GILBERT KEITH CHESTERTON

———o———

Few men have ever repented of silence.

PATRICK HENRY

———o———

Silence

In silence comes all loveliness,
The dawn is ever still,
No noise accompanies the dew
That glistens on the hill.

The sunrise slips up quietly,
The moon is never heard,
And love that animates the eye
Surpasses any word.

So prayer is best in solitude,
It seems so very odd
That long ago, I did not know
In silence I'd find God.

JANE SAYRE

———o———

It does not mean that man has lost an argument when he is silent. He may be silent because he has won.

———o———

How can you expect God to speak to you in that gentle and inward voice which melts the soul, when you are making so much noise with your rapid reflections? Be silent, and God will speak again.

FRANÇOIS DE SALIGNAC DE LA MOTHE FÉNELON

———o———

Silence is the element in which great things fashion themselves.

THOMAS CARLYLE

Who is first silent in a quarrel springs from a good family.

———o———

The fact that silence is golden may explain why there's so little of it.

———o———

Silence is one of the hardest arguments to refute.

"JOSH BILLINGS" (HENRY WHEELER SHAW)

———o———

A man is known by the silence he keeps.

OLIVER HERFORD

———o———

Be silent or say something better than silence.

———o———

Silence is a better clue to intelligence than senseless chatter.

———o———

Think all you speak; but speak not all you think.

DELAUNE

———o———

Speech is great, but silence is greater.

THOMAS CARLYLE

Simplicity

Simplicity is an essential characteristic of greatness.

———o———

"The three greatest pieces in literature," observes an editor, "are the Lord's Prayer, the Twenty-Third Psalm and Lincoln's Gettysburg Address.
"Our Father which art in heaven, hallowed be Thy name . . . The Lord is my shepherd; I shall not want . . . Fourscore and seven years ago . . .
"Not a three-syllable word in them; hardly any two-syllable words. All the greatest things in human life are one-syllable things — love, joy, hope, home, wife, child, trust, faith, God. ALL great things are simple."

———o———

The simplicity which is in Christ is rarely found among us. In its stead are programs, methods, organizations, and a world of nervous activities which occupy time and attention, but can never satisfy the longing of the heart.

A. W. TOZER

---o---

A simple life is its own reward.

GEORGE SANTAYANA

---o---

God is not found in multiplicity, but in simplicity of thoughts and words.

MARGARET MARY HALLAHAN

Sin, Sinners

You can't put your sins behind you until you face them.

---o---

A small boy, fighting the town bully, was winning the battle. But while sitting astride the bully, he kept calling for help at the top of his voice. A passer-by asked him why he needed help. "I need help," answered the boy, because I can feel him starting to get up." So it is in our battle with sin. We constantly need God's help to win.

---o---

The Bible does not command sinners to go to church but it does tell the church to go out and seek the sinners.

---o---

One reason sin flourishes is that it is treated like a cream puff instead of a rattlesnake.

BILLY SUNDAY

---o---

Whenever a man is ready to uncover his sins, God is always ready to cover them with His blood.

---o---

A painstaking scientist discovered that the younger leaves of the compass plant, which grows in Texas, point north and south. By referring to them, one can find his direction even at night.

The younger leaves of the plant tilt edgewise to the ground and always point north and south. The older leaves, however, become weighted with dew and dust and point in all directions.

How tragic it is when a Christian becomes soiled and sullied by sin and worldliness and loses his power to effectively witness for Christ and point to "the Lamb of God, which taketh away the sin of the world" (John 1: 29).

WALTER B. KNIGHT

---o---

Remembered Sin

I made a lash of my remembered sins;
    I wove it firm and strong, with cruel tip,
And though my quivering flesh shrank from the scourge,
    With steady arm I plied the ruthless whip.

For surely I who had betrayed my Lord,
    Must needs endure this sting of memory.
But though my stripes grew sore, there came no peace,
    And so I looked again to Calvary.

His tender eyes beneath the crown of thorns
    Met mine, His sweet voice said, "My child, although
Those oft-remembered sins of thine have been
    Like crimson, scarlet, they are now like snow.

"My blood, shed here, has washed them all away,
    And there remaineth not the least dark spot,
Nor any memory of them, and so
    Should you remember sins which God forgot?"

I stood there trembling, bathed in light, though scarce
    My tired heart dared to hope. His voice went on,
"Look at thy feet, My child." I looked, and lo,
    The whip of my remembered sins was gone!

MARTHA SNELL NICHOLSON

---o---

Sin has many tools, but a lie is the handle which fits them all.

OLIVER WENDELL HOLMES,
The Autocrat of the Breakfast Table

The Law was broken in the people's hearts before it was broken by Moses' hand.

———o———

The ultimate proof of the sinner is that he does not recognize his own sin.

MARTIN LUTHER

———o———

A baker living in a small village bought his butter from a neighboring farmer. One day he became suspicious that the butter was not of the same weight as at first. For several days he weighed the butter, and concluded that the rolls of butter which the farmer brought were gradually diminishing in weight.

This angered the baker so that he had the farmer arrested. "I presume you have weights," said the judge. "No, sir," replied the farmer. "How then do you manage to weigh the butter that you sell?"

"That's easily explained," said the farmer. "When the baker began buying his butter from me, I thought I'd get my bread from him, and it's his one-pound loaf I've been using as a weight for the butter I sell. If the weight of the butter is wrong, he has himself to blame."

Sin is like that. If it becomes the rule of our lives, it turns upon us to betray us when we least expect it. The deceiver becomes the deceived.

Sincerity

Does Your Life Ring True?

You may testify in public
That you love the Lord,
You may sing aloud His praises
And proclaim His Word;
You may tell of sins forgiven
Just as others do;
But the question comes, my brother,
Does your life ring true?

How about your daily conduct
As you come and go?
Are you careless in your dealings?
Does your grocer know
He can trust you for the payment
When your bill comes due?
True religion bears this testing:
Does your life ring true?

Are you kind to those who hate you,
Helping when you can?
Are you patient and forgiving
Towards your fellow-man?
Are you doing unto others
As you'd have them do
Were they in your stead, my brother,
Does your life ring true?

People see as well as hear you:
More than words are deeds;
When your life and lips speak discord,
Who respects your creeds?
'Tis the faithful, daily witness
Of the blood-washed, who
Give to God the glory due Him,
For their lives ring true.

AUTHOR UNKNOWN

———o———

The first virtue of all really great men is that they are sincere. They eradicate hypocrisy from their hearts. They bravely unveil their weaknesses, their doubts, their defects. They are courageous. They boldly ride a-tilt against prejudices. No civil, moral, nor immoral power overawes them. They love their fellowmen profoundly. They are generous. They allow their hearts to expand. They have compassion for all forms of suffering. Pity is the very foundation-stone of genius.

ANATOLE FRANCE

Sing

He started to sing
As he tackled the thing
That couldn't be done,
And he did it.

EDGAR A. GUEST

———o———

During a song service the congregation was singing "Glad Day." On the second stanza the song leader suggested that the women sing the first phrase, "I may go home today," and the men sing the response, "Glad day, glad day."

———o———

Little boy: "Didn't God love Adam?"
Teacher: "Yes, of course. Why?"
Boy: "Well, we sing 'Jesus Loves Eve'n Me.'"

Teach

A Primary boy was enthusiastically singing "From fig tree unto fig tree" as he went from the departmental worship service to his Sunday School class. The dismayed superintendent, recognizing the tune, realized that he had not been careful in teaching these words to the song: "From victory unto victory."

———o———

"Who put the stars in the sky?" asked the Sunday School teacher in reviewing the previous week's lesson.
"I know," said Jimmy. "It was America!"
"How do you know it was America?" the teacher asked with interest.
"Well, for one thing, we sang about it in church," Jimmy explained. "You know, that song that goes, 'It took America to put the stars in place!'"

———o———

"What song would you like to sing today?" asked the Bible Club leader.
"The Andy song," quickly answered a little girl.
"But we don't know that song," the teacher said.
"Yes we do," answered the little girl. "We sing, 'Andy walks with me, Andy talks with me . . .'"

Skepticism

Skepticism can easily become the most fraudulant of all dogmatisms.

———o———

A laborer was asked by a skeptic, "Sam, how do you know you are saved?"
The laborer who was carrying a heavy sack of potatoes on his back took several steps, then suddenly dropped the bag. "How do I know I have dropped the bag?" he asked the skeptic. "I haven't looked around to see if it's gone from my back!"
"No," replied the skeptic. "But you can tell by the lessening of the weight."
"Yes," conceded the laborer. "And that is how I know I am saved. I lost the weight of sin and guilt I carried.

Instead I have found peace and satisfaction in the Lord Jesus Christ."

———o———

Most of the skepticism about the Bible arises from utter ignorance of it.

Sleep

Insomnia is what a person has when he lies awake all night for an hour.

———o———

Sweet are the slumbers of the virtuous man.

JOSEPH ADDISON, *Cato*

———o———

Sleep is the best cure for waking troubles.

MIGUEL DE CERVANTES

Smile

It takes seventy-two muscles to frown and only fourteen to smile. So, smile!

———o———

Keep smiling. It makes everybody wonder what you've been up to.

———o———

Smiles are the reflections of kindness, which the deaf can hear and the dumb can understand.

———o———

A smile is a wrinkle that shouldn't be removed.

Coast Federal Magazine

———o———

Smile And Smile

I gave a smile to one I met,
  She passed it to another;
He started running home to give
  It to his baby brother.

The baby smiled at its own dad,
  He passed it to his neighbor;
Next it slipped into a pit
  Where men were hard at labor.

So, on and on, from heart to heart,
  That smile kept ever spreading;
A light of life and cheerfulness
  It kept on ever shedding.

And when at night, as I sat down,
　All tired and warm from duty,
That smile came winging back to me —
　I marveled at its beauty!
GLADYS MELROSE GEARHART
in Log of the Good Ship Grace

———o———

A Smile

Let others cheer the winning man,
　There's one I hold worthwhile;
'Tis he who does the best he can.
　Then loses with a smile.

Beaten he is, but not to stay
　Down with the rank and file;
That man will win some other day
　Who loses with a smile.
AUTHOR UNKNOWN

———o———

Smiles give birth to smiles; "sour pusses" beget sour kittens.

———o———

A smile can add a great deal to one's face value.

———o———

A smile is a curve that can set lots of things straight.
Houston Bulletin

———o———

The world is like a mirror,
　Reflecting what you do.
And if your face is smiling,
　It smiles right back to you.
AUTHOR UNKNOWN

———o———

If a customer doesn't have a smile, give him one of yours.

Sorrow

Christ, who in the hour of sorrow
　Bore the curse alone;
I, who through the lonely desert
　Trod where He had gone.
He and I, in that bright glory
　One deep joy shall share;
Mine, to be forever with Him,
　His, that I am there.
PAUL GERHARDT

No sorrow touches man until it has been filtered through the heart of God.
JOE BLINCO

———o———

Sorrow leaves us good; it teaches us to know our friends.
HONORÉ DE BALZAC

———o———

Most of our sorrows spring from forgetfulness of God.

———o———

The remedy for sadness is prayer.
WILLIAM BERNARD ULLATHORNE

———o———

Only the soul that knows the mighty grief can know the mighty rapture. Sorrows come to stretch out spaces in the heart for joy.
EDWIN MARKHAM

Soul, Soul Winning

I Felt God Touch My Soul

I felt God touch my soul today —
　What holy, tranquil rest!
What blessed hope through faith in
　Him
　Came surging through my breast!
My mind was clear, my heart made
　pure,
　Touched by His sacred flame,
Plus every joy I could possess,
　Through faith in Jesus' name.

One touch from God, our Friend divine,
　Gives strength each trying hour,
And lends us courage, grace and love
　To foil the tempter's power.
Touch me again, dear Lord, I pray —
　I need Thee, oh, so much!
Please keep me zealous for Thy cause,
　Encouraged by Thy touch.
F. W. DAVIS

———o———

Your soul is eternal; feed it well.
DOUGLAS STIMERS

———o———

If your soul is hungry, don't quibble about the things you don't understand. Partake of the Bread of Life; then you'll live.

Sign on church bulletin board: "Be the soul support of your children."

———o———

Whenever the soul comes to itself and attains something of its natural soundness, it speaks of God.

TERTULLIAN

———o———

My soul is like a mirror in which the glory of God is reflected, but sin, however insignificant, covers the mirror with smoke.

ST. THERESA

———o———

As the flower turns to the sun, or the dog to his master, so the soul turns to God.

WILLIAM TEMPLE

———o———

When we reach for the souls of men, we touch Satan at his most sensitive spot.

CHARLES W. ANDERSON

———o———

Soul winners are not soul winners because of what they know, but because of Whom they know, and how well they know Him, and how much they long for others to know Him.

DAWSON TROTMAN

———o———

The soul in its highest sense is a vast capacity for God.

HENRY DRUMMOND

———o———

One can hardly think too little of oneself. One can hardly think too much of one's soul.

GILBERT KEITH CHESTERTON

———o———

Before any congregation can hope to excel in soul winning, the officers and members must first be at peace with each other.

ANDREW W. BLACKWOOD

———o———

The last thing the devil wants you to do is to win a soul definitely to Christ. If you don't believe it, try it.

The devil will let you go to prayer meeting, he will let you talk religious subjects and do "many mighty deeds," if only you will stop short of persuading men to accept Christ as Lord and openly confess Him before men.

CHARLES ALEXANDER

———o———

Said Dr. G. Campbell Morgan, "There was a time in my evangelistic work when I feared to talk to people of high position and culture in the inquiry room. Then one night I knelt beside an old man whom sin had all but wrecked. I spoke to him of the cleansing blood of Christ, and of the possibility of his becoming a new creature in Christ. Presently, someone asked, 'Please speak to the other man kneeling beside you.' I turned and recognized the mayor of the city, who six weeks before had sentenced the oldster to a month's hard labor. Both men were equally lost. Both accepted Christ. The mayor joyfully shook hands with the old man and said, 'Well, we didn't meet here the last time!'"

The old man recognized the mayor and said, "No, and we will never meet again as we did the last time! I'm a new man in Christ, and we are brothers!"

"That scene," said Dr. Morgan, "lingers with me yet. It removed my fear to speak to anyone about Christ."

WALTER B. KNIGHT

———o———

Evangelist Billy Sunday had returned to a city for a second series of meetings. One evening when the invitation was given for sinners to come forward, a man staggered up the aisle and stood before Sunday. "Do you remember me?" he asked.

"I don't believe I do," the evangelist answered.

"You should," the man said. "You saved me when you were here before."

"Yes," said Billy, "I imagine I did. You look like the kind of job I'd do. I know the Lord wouldn't do a job like that."

LULA M. OLDS in Reader's Digest

Space, Space Age

The true end in life is not to explore outer space for man's self-aggrandizement, but to prepare this inner space for God's glory.

————o————

The little boy's father was reading him nursery rhymes and doing quite well until he came to the account of the cow jumping over the moon. The boy thought a moment before asking: "That's interesting. Now tell me how the cow developed that much thrust."

F. G. KERNAN in *Family Weekly*

————o————

On bulletin board in front of the High Street Christian Church in Lexington, Kentucky: "Traveling to outer space? Instructions inside!"

————o————

A sign of our astronautical times occurred in the Kindergarten Department during prayer time for the pastor who was leaving on a world tour.
"Did you know Mr. Houk was going *around the world?*" asked the superintendent impressively.
To which one five-year-old replied, "How many times?"

Chimes, Glendale Presbyterian Church

————o————

The second graders' project on space travel hit a snag. One boy complained, "The girls want to put up curtains in our space ship."

Michigan Educational Journal

————o————

From Outer Space

He came — our God from outer space,
Became a man — to join our race;
But left His throne and glory there,
Our woes to take — our sins to bear.

In manger there — a little one,
'Twas known by few — this was God's Son;
The angels sang to shepherds lone,
The rest of men took ways their own.

This One from outer space was poor,
No pillow his — nor home secure;
On dusty paths with lesser speed,
As Roman guard each rode his steed.

The multitude He gladly fed —
Those lost in sin He homeward led;
The blind received their sight again,
And suff'ring ones — relief from pain.

He was not known — e'en by His kin,
His synagogue — He did not win;
His nation then received Him not,
And Pilate too joined in the plot.

At last the storm broke o'er His head,
No rest until they saw Him dead;
With seal and guard the tomb they close —
'Twas but three days — AND HE AROSE.

To outer space He now returned,
This One — the world had killed and spurned;
His promise is — "I'll come again" —
He's told us how but not the when.

If He's your Lord and Saviour — Friend
Your life on earth will safely end;
And you to outer space will go,
Your Glory Lord by face to know.

JOHN W. DUNLOP

Speak, Speakers, Speeches

Our speaker needs no introduction, just an early conclusion.

————o————

What You Say

What you say in a hurry
May cause you much worry;
So weight your words well —
What you'd say.

Ill-chosen expressions,
Oft give wrong impressions.
So think first, then speak;
It will pay.

W. LANGHORST

————o————

One critic of a speaker said, "He did not put enough fire in his speech."
A second critic replied, "He did not put enough of his speech in the fire!"

The best recipe for an after-dinner speech is to add a good portion of shortening.

———o———

Never rise to speak till you have something to say; and when you have said it, cease.

JOHN WITHERSPOON

———o———

The tire is as great as the length of the spoke.

———o———

World's best after-dinner speech: "Waiter, give me both checks."

———o———

Backward, turn backward, O Time, in thy flight,
I've just thought of a "come-back" I needed last night.

Sunshine Magazine

———o———

Briefly Speaking

We gave him thirty minutes,
He finished up in ten.
Oh, there's a prince of speakers
And a servant unto men.
His diction wasn't much as such,
He hemmed and hawed a bit,
And still he spoke a lot of sense
And after that — he quit.
At first we sat plumb paralyzed,
Then cheered and cheered again;
We gave him thirty minutes
And he finished up in ten!

From A Trade Magazine

———o———

Blessed is the man who, having nothing to say, abstains from giving in words evidence of the fact.

GEORGE ELIOT (MARY ANN EVANS),
Impressions of Theophrastus Such

———o———

"Our guest speaker needs no introduction — we don't have time for his speech!"

DALE MCFEATTERS

———o———

Generally speaking, preachers are.

Blessed are they that speak short for they shall be invited again.

———o———

Hint To Speakers:

Be brief,
Be bright,
Be gone.

———o———

There are two kinds of cleverness, and both are priceless. One consists of thinking of a bright remark in time to say it. The other consists of thinking of it in time not to say it.

The English Digest

———o———

What some public speakers lack in depth, they give you in length.

———o———

After the Sunday School Conference speaker had finished, the chairman said, "Now without wasting any more time we will go to our workshops."

———o———

A speaker's reply to a flowery introduction: "I appreciate those sweet words. They are like perfume: you can smell it but you can't swallow it."

———o———

The effective public speaker is one who forgets himself, looks at his audience, loves them, blesses them, gets the feel of their needs, and then seeks to fill those needs.

ERIC BUTTERWORTH in *Good Business*

———o———

Introduction of the last speaker at a banquet: "And he that is last, must be brief."

———o———

Some speakers who don't know what to do with their hands should try clamping them over their mouths.

G. NORMAN COLLIE
in *Saturday Evening Post*

———o———

Applause at the beginning of an address is faith, during the address is hope, at the end is charity.

He is considered the most graceful speaker who can say nothing in most words.

SAMUEL BUTLER

———o———

Lecturer: One with his hand in your pocket, his tongue in your ear, and his faith in your patience.

AMBROSE BIERCE

———o———

Why doesn't the fellow who says, "I'm no speech-maker," let it go at that instead of giving a demonstration.

FRANK MCKINNEY HUBBARD

———o———

"How long shall I speak?" asked the banquet speaker.

"As long as you wish," replied the master of ceremonies, "but the rest of us will leave about 8:30!"

———o———

A good many people can make a speech, but saying something is more difficult.

HERBERT V. PROCHNOW

———o———

Let us say what we feel, and feel what we say; let speech harmonize with life.

SENECA

———o———

Before we can speak God's message, we must learn to listen. The opened ear comes before the opened mouth.

A. B. SIMPSON

Guard Thy Lips

Words are things of little cost
Quickly spoken, quickly lost,
We forget them, but they stand
Witnesses at God's right hand
And their testimony bear
For us or against us there,
Oh how often ours have been
Idle words, and words of sin!
Words of anger, scorn and pride,
Or desire our faults to hide
Envious tales, or strife unkind
Leaving bitter thoughts behind.
Grant us, Lord, from day to day
Strength to watch and grace to pray;
May our lips from sin set free

Love to speak and sing of Thee
Till in Heaven we learn to raise
Hymns of everlasting praise.

AUTHOR UNKNOWN

———o———

Speech

Talk happiness. The world is sad enough
Without your woe. No path is wholly rough.
Look for the places that are smooth and clear,
And speak of them to rest the weary ear
Of earth, so hurt by one continuous strain
Of mortal discontent and grief and pain.

Talk faith. The world is better off without
Your uttered ignorance and morbid doubt.
If you have faith in God, or man, or self,
Say so; if not, push back upon the shelf
Of silence all your thoughts till faith shall come.
No one will grieve because your lips are dumb.

Talk health. The dreary, never-ending tale
Of mortal maladies is more than stale;
You cannot charm or interest or please
By harping on that minor chord, disease,
Say you are well, or all is well with you,
And God shall hear your words, and make them true.

ELLA WHEELER WILCOX

———o———

If you your lips would keep from slips,
Five things observe with care:
To whom you speak; of whom you speak;
And how, and when, and where.
If you your ears would save from jeers,
These things keep meekly hid:
Myself and I, and mine and my,
And how I do and did.

WILLIAM EDWARD NORRIS,
Nursery Rhyme, quoted in Thirlby Hall

God's great gift of speech abused
Makes thy memory confused.

ALFRED, LORD TENNYSON

Spirit, Spiritual

A solemn and religious regard to spiritual and eternal things is an indispensable element of all true greatness.

DANIEL WEBSTER

———o———

You can't win over the devil with physical force, with human influence, with scientific skill, with money, with arguments or threats or promises. It takes spiritual armor and weapons provided by God and Him alone.

———o———

Spiritual Bath

So you "already know" the Bible stories, and don't read the Good Book? A teenager answers: "Nobody has to bathe every day, but you'll smell if you don't. Reading the Bible a bit everyday is like taking a spiritual bath."

———o———

The spiritually successful person did the things that you intended to do.

———o———

Spiritual gifts are given, not for competition but for cooperation.

GERALD W. COX

Spring

Spring unlocks the flowers to paint the laughing soil.

REGINALD HEBER

———o———

Stately spring!
Whose robe-folds are valleys,
Whose breast-bouquet is gardens,
And whose blush is vernal evening.

JEAN PAUL RICHTER

———o———

It is always springtime in the heart that loves God.

JEAN-MARIE VIANNEY

———o———

Spring

Now Spring has passed my way again
And left me with a trace of loveliness
within her charm of tenderness and grace;
Calling forth the songs of birds, the flowers, and budding trees
And, with her warm and tender kiss, awakened memories.
To me she has been just as sweet as when, at ten,
I roamed the daisy fields of yore, and picked flowers in the glen.
I say that Spring has passed my way
And still it plays a part of all the lovely things of life I keep within my heart.

J. EVANS ANDERSON

———o———

Close to my heart I fold each lovely thing
The sweet day yields; and not disconsolate
With calm impatience of the woods, I wait
For leaf and blossom, when God gives us Spring.

JOHN GREENLEAF WHITTIER

———o———

Spring bursts today, for Christ is risen and all the earth's at play.

CHRISTINA GEORGINA ROSSETTI

———o———

Boy In Spring

He rolls his marbles, flies his kite,
And shares each day the fresh delight
Awakening across the land.
He has a baseball in his hand
When he goes out to join his friends.
So many happy hours he spends
Fishing beside a little stream
Where sunlight casts a shimmering gleam.
Oh, there is so much to enjoy
When beckoning Spring meets eager boy!

LOUISE DARCY

Stand

When pulling together means pulling away from God, a Christian must be willing to stand alone.

MAJOR MARGARET TROUTT

I'm standing, Lord.
There is a mist that blinds my sight.
Steep jagged rocks, front, left, and
    right,
Lower, dim, gigantic, in the night.
Where is the way?

I'm standing, Lord.
Since Thou hast spoken, Lord, I see
Thou hast beset — these rocks are Thee!
And since Thy love encloses me,
    I stand and sing.

                              BETTY STAM

Stand Close To All

Stand close to all, but lean on none,
    And if the crowd desert you,
Stand just as fearlessly alone,
    As if a throng begirt you;
And learn what long the wise have
    known
    Self-flight alone can hurt you.

                    WILLIAM S. SHURTLEFF

Stewardship

Stewardship: Keeping your hands off
that which belongs to God.

Stewardship

Steward I — and not possessor
Of the wealth entrusted me.
What, were God Himself the holder,
Would His disposition be?
This I ask myself each morning,
Every noon and night,
As I view His gentle goodness
With an ever new delight.

Steward only — never owner —
Of the time that He has lent.
How, were He my life's custodian,
Would my years on earth be spent?
Thus I ask myself each hour,
As I plod my pilgrim way,
Steeped in gratefulest amazement
At His mercy day by day.

Steward only — not possessor —
Of that part of Him that's I.
Clearer grows this truth and dearer,
As the years go slipping by.

May I softly go, and humbly,
Head and heart in reverence bent,
That I may not fear to show Him
How my stewardship was spent.
                    STRICKLAND W. GILLILAN

In stewardship no man can perform
the duty of another. No proxy is allowed or possible. Stewardship involves personal responsibility.
                              C. A. COOK

The story is told of a good farmer
who loved the Lord and believed in
stewardship. He was very generous indeed, and was asked by his friends why
he gave so much and yet remained so
prosperous? "We cannot understand
you," his friends said. "Why, you seem
to give more than the rest of us, and
yet you always seem to have greater
prosperity."
"Oh," said the farmer, "that is very
easy to explain. You see, I keep shoveling into God's bin and God keeps
shoveling more and more into mine,
and God has the bigger shovel."
                         HERBERT LOCKYER

What Is A Pledge?

A pledge is more than money or a
figure on a check.
It is the gift of a part of one's self to
Christ for His work.
It is a contribution to Christian edu-
cation.
It is an investment in a better com-
munity.
It is a gift of gratitude to God.
It is a vote for a Christian world.
It is an outreaching hand to other
nations in a ministry of health and
healing through missions.
It is a gesture of goodwill.
It is a service to those in sorrow.
It is an aid to our youth.
It is an expression of faith in the fu-
ture.
It is an effort to extend one's Chris-
tian influence.
A pledge is a holy thing, dedicated
to God for the service of all men.

Christmas Evans was hard pressed to make ends meet. This early nineteenth century pastor, beloved widely as the "Bunyan of Wales," preached to huge congregations which responded marvelously to his fervent eloquence. But his paydays were usually disappointing. Evans was often perplexed. He could not reconcile his hearers' insatiable appetite for sermons with their utter indifference to his material needs.

After an especially stirring message Christmas Evans was accosted by a leading woman of the congregation. "Well, Christmas Evans," she greeted, "I understand that we are again in arrears on your salary. I do hope you will be paid at the resurrection. You surely gave us a wonderful sermon today."

Evans eyed the woman closely. Her own prosperity was quite evident. "No doubt I will be rewarded at the resurrection," Evans answered, "but what am I to live on until that time? And what about my horse — what will she do? For her there will be no resurrection. But she does need to eat now!"

The pastor paused and the fashionable parishioner started to stammer an embarrassed apology. But Christmas Evans interrupted. "Moreover, what about people like you — what reward will you get at the resurrection for your unfaithfulness in stewardship? You get on so well in this world, are you not concerned lest it be hard with you at the resurrection?"

Adapted from *Gospel Herald*, printed in *The Sunday School World*

———o———

A man may decide to accept or reject Jesus Christ. But once he has accepted Christ, it is not for him to decide whether or not he will be a steward, for he becomes one when he becomes a Christian. He may be a poor steward, or a good steward, nevertheless, he is a steward. He has been entrusted with the gospel of Jesus Christ, and has been given the gift of eternal life, and it is his high calling to share this gift with others. The one requirement that is placed on a steward is that he be found faithful (I Corin-

thians 4:2). The ministry of Christian giving is fulfilled to the extent that a man is faithful in the stewardship of the gospel and of all that is his to share.

LUTHER POWELL in *Money and the Church*

———o———

In San Antonio, Texas, some church workers were soliciting contributions for the year. A woman said, "My husband lost his job, and we are on unemployment compensation for $28 per week. And so we are going to revise our contribution."

The workers expressed sympathy, and offered assistance to the family.

The woman said, "I said we would revise our contribution to the church. We will pay $2.80 per week."

A check of the church's congregation revealed that if the entire membership had been on unemployment compensation and given ten percent, the total contribution would have doubled.

Stranger

A stranger is a friend I have not yet met.

———o———

Not A Stranger

I shall not behold a stranger when I
    look upon the face
Of my own beloved Saviour, who re-
    deemed me by His grace;
He will be the same dear Jesus that I've
    known for many years,
Who has comforted in sorrow, cheered
    my heart and wiped my tears.

I shall not behold a stranger when
    some day I'll open wide
These mine eyes and in the glory find
    myself quite satisfied.
Then I'll be with Him forever, sins and
    fears and longings past,
In the house of many mansions I will
    be at home at last.

AUTHOR UNKNOWN

Strength

Dwight L. Moody tells the story of an Atlantic passenger who lay in his bunk in a storm, deathly seasick. A cry of "Man overboard!" was heard. "May God help the poor fellow," prayed the man, "there is nothing I can do." Then he thought, "At least I can put my lantern in the porthold," which he did. The man was rescued, and recounting the story the next day, said, "I was going down in the darkness for the last time when someone put a light in a porthole. It shone on my hand, and a sailor in the life boat grabbed it and pulled me in."

Weakness is no excuse for our not putting forth all the little strength we have, and who can tell how God will use it?

———o———

Our strength is shown in the things we stand for. Our weaknesses are shown in the things we fall for.

HUGH A. COWAN

———o———

"Look, Daddy, I pulled up this great big cornstalk all by myself."

"My, but you're strong, Dickie," said Daddy.

"I guess I am!" said Dickie. "The whole world had hold of the other end of it."

———o———

Little Johnny (his eyes filled with tears, to mother peeling onions): "Those onions are strong, Mom; I can smell them with my eyes!"

———o———

Prayer For Strength

This is my prayer to Thee, my Lord — Strike, strike at the root of penury in my heart.

Give me the strength lightly to bear my joys and sorrows.

Give me the strength to make my love fruitful in service.

Give me the strength never to disown the poor or bend my knees before insolent might.

Give me the strength to raise my mind above daily trifles.

And give me the strength to surrender my strength to Thy will with love.

RABINDRANATH TAGORE

Do not pray for an easy task. Pray to be stronger!

Strikes

Strikes

Strikes are quite proper, but mind you strike right:
Strike at your vices at once with your might.
Strike off the fetters of fashion and pride,
Strike at the follies which swarm at your side.
Strike at the customs which lead men to drink,
Strike for the freedom to think and let think.
Strike for your friend and be thoughtful and kind,
Strike for the truth and speak out your own mind.
Strike in the strength which comes from above,
Strike for the cause of peace and of love.
Strike not with the fist, and give no man a blow.
Strike in the spirit which blesses the foe.
Strike in that fashion, strike home and strike straight,
Strike now, my good friends, there's no reason to wait.

CHARLES HADDON SPURGEON

Study

There are more men ennobled by study than by nature.

MARCUS TULLIUS CICERO

———o———

There is no study that is not capable of delighting us after a little application to it.

ALEXANDER POPE

———o———

In cheerfulness is the success of our studies.

PLINY

———o———

Let the great book of the world be your principal study.

LORD CHESTERFIELD

Success

Success is the fine art of making mistakes when nobody is looking.

———o———

The measure of success is not whether you have a tough problem to deal with, but whether it's the same problem you had last year.

JOHN FOSTER DULLES

———o———

Success formula: Think up a product that costs a dime to make, sells for a dollar and is habit-forming.

———o———

Success comes in cans. Failure comes in can'ts.

FRED SEELEY

———o———

Only in dictionaries does success come before work.

———o———

If you wish to succeed in life, make perseverance your bosom friend, experience your wise counselor, caution your elder brother, and hope your guardian genius.

JOSEPH ADDISON

———o———

To succeed in the world, you must assert yourself;
To succeed in God's sight, you must deny yourself.

———o———

I would rather fail in a cause that will someday succeed than to succeed in a cause that will someday fail.

WOODROW WILSON

———o———

To laugh often and much; to win the respect of intelligent people and the affection of children; to earn the appreciation of honest critics and endure the betrayal of false friends; to appreciate beauty, to find the best in others; to leave the world a bit better, whether by a healthy child, a garden patch, or a redeemed social condition; to know even one life has breathed easier because you lived. This is to have succeeded.

RALPH WALDO EMERSON

Success is the ability to get along with some people — and ahead of others.

———o———

Some people got to the top just by being stuck in the back of the elevator.

———o———

There is so much I have learned, I sometimes wonder whether I have been a success at all.

ABRAHAM LINCOLN

———o———

Success measured merely by money is too cheap.

———o———

If success made the heart swell the way the head does, this would be a great deal better world.

———o———

To succeed, work your tongue little, your hands much, and your brains most.

———o———

Our successes we ascribe to ourselves; our failures to destiny.

———o———

The man who wakes up and finds himself successful in God's work has not been asleep.

———o———

If at first you don't succeed, you are running about average.

The Lion

———o———

Self-trust is the first secret of success.

RALPH WALDO EMERSON

———o———

If at first you don't succeed, don't succumb.

ARNOLD H. GLASGOW

———o———

If you think you cannot succeed you are probably right!

———o———

If success turns your head, you're facing in the wrong direction.

———o———

You're on the road to success when

you realize that failure is merely a detour.

WILLIAM G. MILNES, JR.

———o———

Success is to be measured not so much by the position that one has reached in life as by the obstacles which he has overcome while trying to succeed.

BOOKER T. WASHINGTON

———o———

Success is never final and failure never fatal. It's courage that counts.

GEORGE F. TILTON

Suffering

No pain, no palm; no thorns, no throne; no gall, no glory; no cross, no crown.

WILLIAM PENN

———o———

My mind is absorbed with the sufferings of man. Since I was twenty-four there never [has been] any vagueness in my plans or ideas as to what God's work was for me.

FLORENCE NIGHTINGALE

———o———

It is suffering and then glory. Not to have the suffering means not to have the glory.

ROBERT C. MCQUILKIN

———o———

We that are sick
Must suffer pain,
Yes, that may be —
But this our comfort,
That it leaves us free
To look up quietly
At Calvary.

HIROMI

———o———

We learn from the things we suffer.

AESOP

———o———

Suffering for Christ is not when we are buffeted for our faults, or when we are busybodies in other men's matters, but when we are straight for God, not men-pleasers. Have convictions for God and obey them.

Pain is no evil unless it conquers us.

GEORGE ELIOT (MARY ANN EVANS)

Summer

Summer is the topsy-turvy season when the goldfish have to be boarded out while the family goes on a fishing trip.

The English Digest

———o———

Summertime is the time when it's too hot to do the things it was too cold to do during the winter.

———o———

If I Could

If I could take my brush and paint
    heaven's azure blue,
Or could I etch the hush of early morn-
    ing dew;

If I could set the fleecy white of every
    drifting cloud,
Or capture glowing, golden tones with
    autumn hues endowed;

But I can only watch the tender hand
    of God
Pull back each summer's curtain from
    off this changing sod!

Upon earth's mighty easel God paints
    His pictures rare,
And grants His humble creatures a
    sanctuary there.

JANET MILLER

———o———

Summer Gold

The hills are decked with gold nuggets
As summer puts on her display.
Bright dandelions break through the
    earth
And seem to appear in a day.

Roadsides glisten with yellow
Like a million suns in the grass,
And children can have all the gold
By gathering when they pass.

A few short weeks and the gold is gone
And silver has taken its place
As little seeds wing their way in the
    air . . .
Parachutes of delicate lace.

NORMA REESER

Sunday

Sunday Morning

If I could turn life's pages back and
from its golden store
Could take some precious moments
and make them mine once more,
I would not ask for wealth or fame,
not far-flung fields to roam,
But just for Sunday morning on the old
farm home.

Those were the days of toil and hardship, care that could not be denied,
But the Sabbath brought a respite —
worldly tasks were laid aside.
House all shining, quiet, peaceful,
mother's face so dear, so blest,
Father's voice in prayer uplifted, "Lord,
we thank Thee for Thy rest."

Clean white cloth upon the table, silver
gleaming, china gay,
With a place laid for the preacher,
should he honor us today;
On the spare bed little garments, dainty
ruffles snowy white,
All that mother love could compass to
make Sunday a delight.

No stained windows, no grand organ
made that little church so fair;
Plain the people were and humble, but
'twas love that brought them there.
And the awe and holy quiet, emblem
of the heavenly grace,
God was near and very precious as we
met Him in His place.

                                    MABEL TACKABURY

———o———

I feel as if God had, by giving the
Sabbath, given fifty-two springs in every year.

                    SAMUEL TAYLOR COLERIDGE

———o———

Sunday used to be the day of rest
but in recent years it seems that far
too many of us have to spend the
other six days resting up from Sunday.

———o———

Dismissed, But Promoted

Stephen Girard, the late Philadelphia
millionaire, one Saturday bade his
clerks come the next day and unload
a vessel which had just arrived. One
young man stepped up to the desk
and said, as he turned pale, "Mr.
Girard, I cannot work tomorrow."

"Well, sir, if you cannot do as I wish,
we can separate."

"I know that, sir," said the young
man. "I also know that I have a
widowed mother to care for, but I cannot work on Sunday."

"Very well, sir," said the proprietor,
"go to the cashier's desk and he will
settle with you."

For three weeks the young man
tramped the streets of Philadelphia
looking for work. One day a bank
president asked Mr. Girard to name a
suitable person for cashier of a new
bank about to be started. After reflection Mr. Girard named this young
man.

"But I thought you discharged him?"

"I did," was the answer, "because he
would not work on Sunday; and the
man who will lose his situation from
principle is the man to whom you can
entrust your money."

                                    Fellowship News

———o———

In answer to a query about working
on Sunday, Billy Graham said, "It
should not detract from a man's reverence to do what is required. Even Jesus spoke about the ox in the ditch on
the Sabbath. But if your ox gets in
the ditch every Sabbath, you should
either get rid of the ox or fill up the
ditch."

Chicago Tribune-New York News Snydicate

Sunday School

Everybody who believes that Sunday School ought to be, ought to be in
Sunday School.

Everybody who comes to Sunday
School ought to stay for church. Everybody who comes to church ought
to come in time for Sunday School.

There's a place for both. There's a
place for both in both, and if both are
not in both there's something wrong
with both.

                                    CLATE RISLEY

A young minister had been asked quite unexpectedly to address a Sunday School class. To give himself time to collect his thoughts, he said to the class, "Well, children, what shall I speak about?"

One little girl, who had herself memorized several declamations, called out: "What do you know?"

———o———

The Sunday School is perpetuated by its own products.

HENRIETTA C. MEARS

———o———

It Is

If the gospel of Jesus Christ is the hope of the world —
And it is.

If the church is the divinely appointed agency for the dissemination of the gospel —
And it is.

If the church school is the recruiting station and training camp of the church —
And it is.

Then the church school is the hope of the world.

JAMES DE FOREST MURCH,
Christian Education And The Local Church

———o———

Labor Not In Vain

My dishes went unwashed today,
    I didn't make the bed,
I took God's hand and followed
    To Bible School instead.

O yes, we went adventuring,
    My young people and I,
Explaining in the Bible,
    The truths none can deny.

That my house was neglected,
    That I didn't sweep the stair,
In twenty years no one on earth
    Will know, or even care.

But that I've helped a girl or boy,
    In Christian witness grow,
In twenty years, the whole wide world
    May look, and see, and know.

AUTHOR UNKNOWN

Did You Know That . . .

1. One out of every three unsaved people enrolled in Sunday School is won to Christ, but one out of 250 unsaved people not enrolled in the Sunday School is won to Christ.

2. Church members who are enrolled in Sunday School give twenty times as much per capita as members not in Sunday School.

3. Every church member is equally responsible for winning the lost, attending Sunday School, and supporting the church in prayer, participation and giving.

First Baptist Reminder

———o———

Someone asks how we can get rid of the trend toward increased moral delinquencies. The sustained, wholesome moral atmosphere imparted through habitual attendance upon Sunday School and church will do it.

———o———

A young friend, who attended Sunday School for the first time, was asked how she liked it. "What did your teacher tell you?" her mother inquired.

The little girl replied, "To be quiet."

HELEN GAINES in *Together*

———o———

One of the great Sunday School leaders of our time has quoted some figures to prove that an older person seldom accepts Christianity who hasn't been taught at his mother's knee or in the Sunday School.

———o———

If pupils are not here in Sunday School, they won't hear.

———o———

What I See

His trousers were torn, rolled up at
    the knees,
A hole in his shirt, which he caught on
    a tree.
But I see a soul for whom Jesus died,
Clothed in righteousness, pressed to
    His side.

I see not the labour and hours of prayer,
Spent for that freckled face boy over there.
But I see a Saviour with arms opened wide,
Waiting in heaven to take him inside.

I see not the freckles, but a man fully grown,
A heart filled with God's Word, that I've carefully sown,
A life speaking forth, for the Saviour each day,
O Lord, for this boy, I earnestly pray.

I see not his energy in mischief bent,
But put to the task where the Lord meant it spent.
Oh Lord, make this little mischievous boy,
A power for Thee, to Thy heart a great joy.

WILLIAM E. KIRSCHKE
in The Sunday School News

———o———

Our Sunday School lessons need to be up-to-date and down-to-earth.

CLATE RISLEY

———o———

A little four-year-old suddenly lost interest in Sunday School. When her mother asked her why she no longer wanted to go, the child replied, "I just don't want to go anymore since Moses died."

———o———

A little girl in Sunday School was drawing something on her paper. The pastor happened by and asked her what it was. She said it was a picture of God. Gently he explained that nobody really knows what God looks like. Said she, "They will when I finish this picture."

Sunday School Superintendent

Every Sunday School superintendent should have two schools in mind: the one he has and the one he wants to have.

———o———

A successful Sunday School superin-tendent is one who is maladjusted to the status quo.

Sunday School Journal

Surrender

We learn from Saul's failure that the surrendered life is the only secure and truly successful life.

HENRIETTA C. MEARS

———o———

Surrendering one's will to the divine will may seem to be a negative procedure, but it gives positive dividends.

S. I. MCMILLEN

———o———

One who will not surrender cannot be permanently overcome.

Suspicion

Suspicion is about the only thing that can feed on itself and grow larger all the while.

———o———

There is nothing makes a man suspect much, more than to know little, and therefore men should remedy suspicion by procuring to know more, and not keep their suspicions in smother.

FRANCIS BACON

———o———

If you have no confidence in man, you are to be suspected.

Sympathy

A woman working in a greeting card shop asked a teenager who had been looking through the selection of cards, if she needed help. The girl answered, "Yes, do you have a sympathy card for a girl whose telephone is out of order?"

Chicago Tribune

———o———

Being myself no stranger to suffering, I have learned to relieve the suffering of others.

VIRGIL

It is reported that a sympathy note to a parson injured on a ski slope read in part: "It is my understanding that while Methodists fall from grace, Presbyterians fall from awkwardness."

We have lived and loved together
Through many changing years;
We have shared each other's gladness,
And wept each other's tears.

CHARLES JEFFERYS

T

Tact

Tact is the art of saying nothing when there is nothing to say.

———o———

Tact is the art of making other people think they know more than you do.

———o———

Tact is the ability to shut your mouth before someone else wants to.

Talent

The Talent

God gave me a talent;
And I threw it away;
Into the winds of yesterday.
I had no time to work for God;
Nor follow the paths my dear Saviour had trod.
So He gave it again to this unworthy soul;
Taking me humbly into His fold.
He said, "My child, what will you do with
This talent I have twice given you?"
I cried, "Oh Lord, forgive me I pray,
I'll take the talent and use it today.
I'll teach others that they might see
The wonderful life that's found in Thee."

DEANE CHARLTON

———o———

The Hidden Talent

My vessel is almost empty,
My lamp is burning low;
The day is fast approaching
When I must surely go

To stand before the Saviour
A strict account to give

Of how I've used my talent
While in this world I lived.

Shall I hear His words of welcome
As He bids me enter in?
Or His words of condemnation
Because I lived in sin?

Then I pray Thee, Lord, have mercy
And I shall ever faithful be
To use the precious talent
That Thou hast given me,

So when my work is finished
And the victory has been won
May I stand before Thee unashamed
And hear Thee say, "Well done,

"Thou hast improved thy talent
And faithful thou hast been;
So good and faithful servant
Come thou and enter in."

What have you done with your talent?
Are you using it today?
Or is it in a napkin
Wrapped and hidden away?

GLENNA CORDELL

———o———

Talent is built in solitude; character in the stream of the world.

JOHANN WOLFGANG VON GOETHE

———o———

Buried seeds may grow but buried talents never.

ROGER BABSON

———o———

Use what talents you possess: the woods would be very silent if no birds sang there except those that sang best.

HENRY VAN DYKE

———o———

Your unused talents give you no advantage over one who has no talents at all.

Talk

Tommy: "Mommy, canIgooutsideand playwithmyballandbat?"
Mommy: "Tommy, slow down! You talk so fast no one can understand you!"
Tommy: "You just don't LISTEN fast enough!"

———o———

A henpecked weatherman claims: "My wife speaks 150 words a minute with gusts up to 180."

———o———

You cannot learn and talk at the same time.

———o———

Monopoly Note

To hold conversations
Is normal, I know,
But there are some people
Who hate to let go!

F. G. KERNAN

———o———

Those who have nothing to say generally take the longest to say it.

———o———

"I am afraid, doctor," said a woman to her physician, "that my husband has some terrible mental affliction. Sometimes I talk to him for hours and then discover that he literally hasn't heard a word I said."
"That isn't an affliction," was the reply; "that's a divine gift."

———o———

He who talks without thinking runs more risks than he who thinks without talking.

———o———

Two women were just ready to board a big airliner. One of them turned to the pilot and commented: "Now, please don't go faster than sound. We want to talk."

———o———

To those who talk and talk and talk,
This adage doth appeal:
The steam that toots the whistle
Will never turn a wheel.

JOSEPH LINWOOD

A Bore talks mostly in the first person, a Gossip in the third and a Brilliant Conversationalist in the second.

———o———

If God intended that we should talk more than we listen, He would have given us two mouths and one ear.

———o———

Children live in a world of sound. Perhaps because there is so much of it, many children learn to ignore talk.

DAVID AND ELIZABETH RUSSEL
in *Listening Aids Through the Grades*

———o———

If All That We Say

If all that we say in a single day,
With never a word left out,
Were printed each night in clear black and white,
'Twould prove queer reading, no doubt.
And then just suppose, ere our eyes we could close
We must read the whole record through;
Then wouldn't we sigh and wouldn't we try
A great deal less talking to do?
And I more than half think
That many a kink
Would be smoother in life's tangled thread,
If half that we say in a single day were left forever unsaid.

AUTHOR UNKNOWN

———o———

Man can read some people like a book, but cannot shut them up so easily.

———o———

The average woman talks twenty-five percent faster than her husband — listens.

———o———

Take a lesson from the whale: The only time he gets harpooned is when he comes up to spout.

The Liguorian

———o———

I don't care how much a man talks, if he only says it in a few words.

"JOSH BILLINGS" (HENRY WHEELER SHAW)

He that thinketh by the inch
And talketh by the yard
Deserveth to be kicked by the foot.

———o———

Wise men talk because they have something to say; fools, because they have to say something.

PLATO

———o———

No longer talk at all about the kind of man a good man ought to be — but be such.

———o———

Our deeds and our conversation usually resemble each other like twins. If we like what we are doing, we are inclined to talk about it; and if we like very much to talk about something, we shall probably become involved with it.

DELBERT R. GISH

———o———

The little boy was taking his baby sister for a walk when a neighbor stopped them. "What an adorable child," she gushed. "Does she talk yet?"

"No," the boy replied. "She has her teeth, but her words haven't come in yet."

FRANK BENNING

———o———

Those who have but little business to attend to, are great talkers. The less men think, the more they talk.

CHARLES DE SECONDAT MONTESQUIEU

———o———

Talking to men about God is a great thing, but talking to God for men is greater still.

———o———

Talk little and do much, without caring to be seen.

FRANÇOIS DE SALIGNAC DE LA MOTHE FÉNELON

———o———

One way to keep people from jumping down your throat is to keep your mouth shut.

———o———

Trying to get a word in edgewise with some people is like trying to thread a sewing machine with the motor running.

A famous publisher declares, "If you are an articulate person, you utter some thirty thousand words each day." If put in print, this would mean enough books to fill an entire college library. How many pages of these volumes you are constantly writing will be denounced by God as "worthless speech"?

We read in Matthew 12:36, 37: "Every idle word that men shall speak, they shall give account thereof in the day of judgment. For by thy words thou shalt be justified, and by thy words thou shalt be condemned." Words are so dangerous. We utter them so frequently without thought or consideration, little realizing that every word we speak either curses or blesses.

J. ALLEN BLAIR

———o———

There's only one rule for being a good talker: learn to listen.

CHRISTOPHER MORLEY

———o———

Blessed are they who have nothing to say, and who can be persuaded to say it.

JAMES RUSSELL LOWELL

Task

If you find yourself face to face with an impossible task, regard it as a compliment God has paid you. He knows you are the person who can do that task.

———o———

The task of life is not to be engaged in perpetual rebellion, but to find and serve our true Master.

E. L. ALLEN

———o———

No unwelcome tasks become any the less unwelcome by putting them off till tomorrow.

ALEXANDER MACLAREN

———o———

You are not required to complete the task; neither are you permitted to lay it down.

The Talmud

Taxes

Taxpayers: Those who don't have to pass a civil service examination to work for the government.

———o———

It seems a little silly now, but this country was founded as a protest against taxation.

———o———

Go ahead and be thrilled when you sign the check for your income tax. What you write may not be history, but it provides the stuff that makes the making of history possible.

Advocate, Manawa, Wisconsin

———o———

One of my eighth-graders listed these as local, state, and federal taxes: Gas tax, income tax, and thumb tax.

ETHEL KAISER in *NEA Journal*

———o———

There are said to be 112 hidden taxes in a pair of shoes. No wonder a lot of shoes pinch.

Grit

———o———

In this world nothing is certain but death and taxes.

BENJAMIN FRANKLIN, *Letter to M. Leroy*

Teacher, Teaching

It is easier to teach the book of Matthew to a boy than it is to teach a boy the book of Matthew.

ESTHER ELLINGHUSEN

———o———

The teacher was having her trials and finally wrote the mother: "Your son is the brightest boy in my class, but he is also the most mischievous. What shall I do?"
The reply came duly: "Do as you please. I am having my own troubles with his father."

———o———

Problem For Parents

Most any family secret
This lady soon gets word of,
And most domestic squabbles
She certain has heard of!

But is she just a gossip
Who has no moral scruples? . . .
No, she's the first-grade teacher
With confiding little pupils!

MARGARET SCHUMACHER

———o———

To teach something you don't know is like coming back from somewhere you haven't been.

———o———

If, instructing a child, you are vexed with it for want of adroitness, try, if you have never tried before, to write with your left hand, and then remember that a child is all left hand.

JOHN FREDERICK BOYES

———o———

The only way we can teach the Word of God is to live the Word of God.

HENRIETTA C. MEARS

———o———

There are two classes of teachers: those who say it can't be done, and those who are doing it.

———o———

In a way, the great teacher does not teach anything quantitatively measurable. He performs certain actions, says certain things that create another teacher. This other teacher is the one hidden inside the student. When the master teacher is finished, the newborn professor inside the youngster takes over, and with any luck the process of education continues till death.

CLIFTON FADIMAN in *Holiday*

———o———

To The Beginning Teacher

One bleak fact will confront you
And, briefly, shred plans to rubble.
For each student sparked with genius,
There'll be ten with ignition trouble.

BETH BLUE in *NEA Journal*

———o———

What Is A Teacher?

To a child thrust into a strange world, a teacher is the best thing that can happen.
A teacher is courage with Kleenex

in her pocket, Sympathy struggling with a snowsuit, and Patience with papers to grade.

Teachers spend twelve hours a day searching for truth and the other twelve searching for error.

A teacher does not really mind sniffles, squirmings, stomach-aches, and spills. Neither does she disintegrate before tears, fights, futility, excuses, parents who spout, little boys who shout and little girls who pout.

——o——

Most of all, a teacher is somebody who likes somebody else's children — and has strength left to go to the PTA meeting.

AUTHOR UNKNOWN

——o——

Re: Teacher Merit Rating

In days gone by
When friends I met
Asked, "How are you?"
I would reply,
"I'm fine, thank you!"
(I meant it, too!)
But I've been Rated,
And Berated,
Investigated,
Evaluated,
Annotated,
And Tabulated.
Now when I'm asked,
"How are you?"
I may reply,
"You're fine, thank you,
But how am I?"
(I wonder, too!)

JUSTA TEECHER in Montana Education

——o——

One teacher plus a piece of chalk equals two teachers.

——o——

A Teacher Speaks

Thank you, dear Lord, for giving me
Life's greatest opportunity;
Though I'm not worthy, Lord, to teach,
I pray that thro' me Thou shalt reach
The heart of each small girl and boy
Ere Satan comes to rob, destroy.

I pray that my whole aim might be
To lead each child to Calvary;
To make Thy Word live in his heart,
And warn him never to depart;
I know when I have done my best
That Thou art there to do the rest.

Forever conscious may I be
Of such responsibility;
Help me fore'er to keep in mind
That I must show them how to find
The One Who waits so patiently,
And says to them, "Come unto Me."

When from my class I am away,
Still keep me true, dear Lord, I pray;
If anywhere by chance I pass
A member of my little class,
May he see Christ the Crucified
And Him in me exemplified.

MATILDA CLOER

——o——

You sit still while I instill.

A. V. WASHBURN

——o——

First grade teacher: "Dickie, what am I going to do with you? The closing bell has rung already and your picture isn't colored, and you don't know your memory verse. I don't suppose you learned a thing today. Now why is that, Dickie?"

Dickie: "Well, you made me sit down and be still and listen, and you *teached* me and *teached* me and *teached* me 'till I couldn't learn anything!"

Teach Magazine

——o——

The main idea in Sunday School teaching is to drive home the point, not the class.

Sunday School Promoter

——o——

The mayor met the principal of the toughest school in town. The principal was obviously downcast and the mayor asked him why.

"School's been open only a short time," the educator explained, "and already we've had thirty-nine dropouts."

"It's that bad?" the mayor said. "After all, you're in the roughest section of town.

"That's the trouble," replied the principal, "thirty-eight of the thirty-nine dropouts were teachers."

How to tell students what to look for without telling them what to see is the dilemma of teaching.

LASCELLES ABERCROMBIE

———o———

Begin early to teach children, for they begin early to sin. What is learned young is learned for life. What we hear at the first, we remember to the last. A child's first lesson should be obedience, and after that you may teach it what you please. Yet the young mind must not be laced too tight, or you may hurt its growth and hinder its strength. A child's back must be made to bend, but not be broken. He must be ruled, but not with a rod of iron. His spirit must be conquered, but not crushed.

Ere your boy has reached to seven,
Teach him well the way to heaven;
Better still the work will thrive
If he learns before he's five.

CHARLES HADDON SPURGEON

———o———

A child promoted to a new class said to a dearly beloved teacher: "I wish you knew enough to teach me next year."

———o———

A Plea For Junior

Teacher, teacher, shed a tear,
Junior comes to school this year.
He has never known restraint,
He, in short, is not a saint!

You will sprout some new gray hair
Teaching Junior to be fair,
Since his Mama let him do
Just what Junior wanted to.

Now he is a problem child,
Selfish, stubborn, cruel, wild.
Gentle teacher, need I say,
Mama should be spanked today?

AUTHUR UNKNOWN
printed in *Christian Parents*

———o———

The Teacher

Leader, educator, counselor of youth
    who will tomorrow lead the nation
    and the world.

Object of the hero worship of those
    who need and seek a mentor and
    friend.
Giver of courage to him who would
    falter;
Strength to him who would despair;
Faith to him who is afraid;
Understanding to him who is con-
    fused;
Confidence to him who feels inade-
    quate;
Inspiration to him whose toil seems
    pointless;
Guidance to him whose path is un-
    clear;
Friendship to him who feels alone;
Direction through discipline to him
    whose feet would stray from the
    path of duty.
Slow to anger, quick to forgive, eager
    to heal.
Teacher — in whose ranks are found
    the best that history of mankind
    offers;
Mohammed, Socrates, Moses, Jesus of
    Nazareth —
Teacher — hold your head proudly,
    though heart and soul and mind
    be humble,
Humble in the humility that prepares
    the way for wisdom:
For you are the symbol of the quest
    for knowledge that recognizes no
    goal —
The mountain with no top, the path
    without an end.
You are the seeker after the ever elu-
    sive truth,
And the leader of others who will pick
    up and continue the quest,
The unending quest that leads man
    out of the darkness of ignorance,
And into the light that God has pre-
    pared
For His supreme creation, mankind.

NORMA LUCE JUNE in *The Instructor*

Teen-Agers

Teen-Ager . . .

She uses my nail polish, wears my hose;
Swipes my make-up to powder her nose;

Borrows my lipstick, the sweater I
  knitted
(A trifle too large, but she said it just
  fitted!);
She reads all my magazines, samples
  my books,
Commandeers my compact to check
  on her looks;
Talks me out of that hat that I'd only
  worn twice.
She takes all that I give all — except
  my advice!

JEAN CONDER SOULE

———o———

To a teen-ager, walking distance is
that between the telephone and the
garage.

IVERN BOYETT

———o———

The father of a rapidly growing teen-
ager was asked by a friend how the
boy was.
"Okay," grumbled the parent, "but
he's getting too smart to out-argue and
too big to spank. I can hardly wait for
him to fall in love so's some little girl
will take him down a notch or two!"

F. G. KERNAN

———o———

There's no getting around it. The
chief difference between teen-agers
and middle-agers is simply thirty
pounds and thirty years.

———o———

The trouble with teen-agers and
transistors is that they're both portable.

Changing Times, The Kiplinger Magazine

———o———

Too Young

He drops in on our daughter daily
To spend the evening munching gaily.

And while I do not hit the ceiling,
Lately I have started feeling

As our bills for food grow greater
That maybe our refrigerator

Is too young to be already
Going steady!

THOMAS USK

———o———

Adolescence is when children start
bringing up their parents.

You can always tell a teen-age boy,
and odds are he'll argue.

———o———

A teen-age fad is something the
grown-ups find out about three months
after it is out of date.

———o———

A teen-ager said he'd rather be dead
than be different.

———o———

The best way to tie down a teen-
ager is with a telephone cord.

ROBERT S. WILLETT

———o———

The basic trouble with teen-agers is
that they are forever acting like a
bunch of adolescents.

———o———

One way to keep your teen-age
daughter out of hot water is to put
dirty dishes in it.

———o———

When the teacher discovered that
one of her ninth-graders was well stuck
up with bubble gum, she reproved him
and sent him out to remedy the situation. As he left the class, came a voice
from the rear: "Have gum. Will travel."

Telephone

The man who said one half of the
world does not know how the other
half lives never was on a rural phone
line!

———o———

"Well," the father congratulated his
teen-age daughter, "you usually talk on
the phone two hours. This time only
forty-five minutes. What happened?"
"Wrong number," replied the girl.

———o———

One day a man telephoned his
butcher but mis-dialed and, without
knowing it, reached his pastor.
"Do you have any brains today?" the
caller asked.
"No," the pastor replied, "but I do
have some heart."

Temper

Evangelist Billy Sunday once said, "You say that you have a bad temper but it's over in a minute. So's a shotgun, but it blows everything to pieces."

BILLY GRAHAM

———o———

We must interpret a bad temper as the sign of an inferiority complex.

ALFRED ADLER

———o———

While there may be some things that don't improve the longer you keep them, there are others that do. One is your temper.

———o———

Hitting the ceiling is the wrong way to get up in the world.

War Cry

———o———

Bad temper is murder in the heart, whether it be hot anger or the cold acid of sarcasm.

J. EDWIN ORR

———o———

Temper

When I have lost my temper
   I have lost my reason too.
I'm never proud of anything
   Which angrily I do.

When I have talked in anger,
   And my cheeks were flaming red,
I have always uttered something
   Which I wish I had not said.

In anger I have never
   Done a kindly deed or wise,
But many things for which I felt
   I should apologize.

In looking back across my life,
   And all I've lost or made,
I can't recall a single time
   When fury ever paid.

So I struggle to be patient,
   For I've reached a wiser age;
I do not want to do a thing
   Or speak a word in rage.

I have learned by sad experience
   That when my temper flies
I never do a worthy deed,
   A decent deed or wise.

AUTHOR UNKNOWN

Bad temper is its own scourge. Few things are more bitter than to feel bitter. A man's venom poisons himself more than his victim.

CHARLES BUXTON

Temperance

The teacher was presenting a lesson on temperance, telling his Junior boys that it was harmful to smoke. As a review he asked the question, "Where do boys go who learn to smoke?"
One boy replied, "Up the alley."

———o———

One misses, by abstaining, no enjoyment at parties he must attend as a part of his official duties; rather, his faculties are completely at his command if his alertness is not numbed, if his decisions — social, domestic, governmental — are uninfluenced by that which brings tragedy, heartaches, headache, embarrassment, illness, and loss of touch with reality.

SENATOR MARK HATFIELD

———o———

Temperance means the abstinence from all that is evil, and the moderate use of all that is good.

NED H. HOLMGREN

Temptation

When you flee temptation, be sure you don't leave a forwarding address.

———o———

To avoid unnecessary temptations is half of the battle in overcoming evil.

———o———

Temptations need not be hindrances. As we put them beneath our feet, they lift us to higher ground.

LOIS F. BLANCHARD

———o———

Temptation is the stuff of which Christians are made. If the devil never tempts you, you can't develop your resistance to sin.

BILLY SUNDAY

———o———

When you meet temptation, turn to the right!

Many men have too much will power. It's won't power they lack.

JOHN A. SHEDD

———o———

Most of us keep one eye on the temptation we pray not to be led into.

MARY H. WALDRIP in *Advertiser and News*

———o———

I have found in all my experience that in every temptation the victory depends on resisting the first attack. To stop and reason for a moment is dangerous. Is the object or gratification forbidden? That is enough if we truly love the Lord our God. But when we deliberate, we throw ourselves into the arms of Satan.

Neither ought consequences to be considered. God will see to them; better suffer anything than His frown. Oh, may I ever walk by this rule, and live to please my God alone!

WILLIAM CARVOSSO

———o———

Three great temptations which face us all:

The temptation to recline;
The temptation to shine;
The temptation to whine.

DAVID CHRISTIE

Ten Commandments

A high school senior was trying out for a summer job on the small town newspaper. "Would you be any good at rewrite?" the editor asked him.

"Sure," said the teen-ager brashly.

"Okay. Let's see you rewrite this and make it short and to the point." With that, the editor handed the boy a copy of the Ten Commandments.

The boy looked at them, scratched his head, and then in a burst of inspiration scribbled something across the top of the paper, which he then handed back.

The editor took one look and said, "You're hired, boy!"

The teen-ager had written the word "Don't!"

———o———

The Ten Commandments still cover all human relations and all spiritual relations.

RALPH BREWER

———o———

When the editor of a small newspaper was short of material to fill his columns one week, he asked his typesetter to fill in with the Ten Commandments.

After that week's issue had been circulated, the editor received a letter from one reader saying, "Cancel my subscription. You are getting too personal."

Testimony

Dim eyes cannot read fine print. Let your testimony for Christ be written in large letters that the world may see.

WILLIAM WARD AYER

———o———

An ounce of testimony is worth a ton of propaganda.

———o———

Listening to a group of people talking one day about the fine testimony meetings which were held in their church, a lawyer quietly remarked, "To a lawyer there is a vast difference between testimony and evidence."

———o———

A woman testifying at a prayer meeting: "I ain't what I ought to be; and I ain't what I'm going to be; but anyway, I ain't what I was."

Northern Lights

———o———

It is one thing to testify in a church service surrounded by people who agree and appreciate the testimony; but it is an entirely different matter to testify to the person outside of Christ who is ignorant of the Gospel or in opposition to its truth.

LORA LEE PARROTT

Testing

Faithful Is He Who Has Promised

Are you passing through a testing?
Is your pillow wet with tears?

Do you wonder what the reason,
  Why it seems God never hears?
Why it is you have no answer
  To your oft-repeated plea?
Why the heaven still is leaden
  As you wait on bended knee?

Do you wonder as you suffer,
  Whether God does understand?
And if so, why He ignores you,
  Fails to hold you in His hand?
Do black doubts creep in, assail you,
  Fears without, and fears within
Till your brave heart almost falters
  And gives way to deadly sin?

All God's testings have a purpose —
  Some day you will see the light.
All He asks is that you trust Him,
  Walk by faith and not by sight.
Do not fear when doubts beset you,
  Just remember — He is near.
He will never, never leave you.
  He will always, always hear.

When the darkened veil is lifted,
  Then, dear heart, you'll understand
Why it is you had to suffer,
  Why you could not feel His hand
Giving strength when it was needed,
  Giving power and peace within.
Giving joy through tears and trial,
  Giving victory over sin.
                        JOHN E. ZOLLER

The test of love is not feeling, but
obedience.
          WILLIAM BERNARD ULLATHORNE

Seventh-graders' answers on a quiz:
  Three types of clouds are cumulus,
nimbus, and stimulus.
  Ku Klux Klan was a relative of
Kublai Khan.
        JANE WOODWORTH in *NEA Journal*

Thankfulness, Thanksgiving
(See also Gratitude)

He enjoys much who is thankful for
a little.
                    WILLIAM SECKER

Thanksgiving is possible only for
those who take time to remember.

No one can give thanks who has a
short memory.

Our despondent moods are, for the
most part, moods of ingratitude.

I Give Thee Humble Thanks

For all the gifts that Thou dost send,
For every kind and loyal friend,
For prompt supply of all my need,
For all that's good in word or deed,
For gift of health along life's way,
For strength to work from day to day,
  I give Thee humble thanks.

For ready hands to help and cheer,
For listening ears Thy voice to hear,
For yielded tongue Thy love to talk,
For willing feet Thy paths to walk,
For open eyes Thy Word to read,
For loving heart Thy will to heed,
  I give Thee humble thanks.

For Christ who came from Heaven
  above,
For the Cross and His redeeming love,
For His mighty power to seek and
  save,
For His glorious triumph o'er the
  grave,
For the lovely mansions in the sky,
For His blessed coming by-and-by,
  I give Thee humble thanks.
                        CLIFFORD LEWIS

During a harvest festival in India, an
old widow arrived at her church with
an extraordinarily large offering of rice
— far more than the poor woman could
be expected to afford.
  The itinerant pastor of the church
did not know the widow well. But he
did know that she was very poor and
so he asked her if she were making the
offering in gratitude for some unusual
blessing.
  "Yes," replied the woman. "My son
was sick and I promised a large gift to
God if he got well."

"And your son has recovered?" asked the pastor.

The widow paused. "No," she said. "He died last week. But I know that he is in God's care; for that I am especially thankful."

———o———

If one should give me a dish of sand, and tell me there were particles of iron in it, I might look for them with my eyes and search for them with my clumsy fingers, and be unable to detect them; but let me take a magnet and sweep through it, and how would it draw to itself the almost invisible particles by the mere power of attraction.

The unthankful heart, like my finger in the sand, discovers no mercies; but let the thankful heart sweep through the day, and as the magnet finds the iron, so it will find, in every hour, some heavenly blessings, only the iron in God's sand is gold!

HENRY WARD BEECHER

———o———

Thanksgiving Day

The snow is flying and trees are bare;
The birds have left us . . . Thanksgiving is here!
There's laughter outside and stomping of feet,
The children, all nine, have come home to eat.

With the ice thick and glassy on the pond down the lane,
There is skating and merriment since Thanksgiving came.
There's even a sled ride for the fearless and daring
While the women are busy the meal preparing.

The turkey's full of stuffing and is baked a golden brown,
The tantalizing odor brings the hungry children round.
There's a hush and a silence as the blessing is said . . .
In deepest reverence each bows his head
And offers a prayer of gratitude and praise

For bountiful blessings these Thanksgiving days.

MRS. PAUL E. KING

———o———

A thankful heart is not only the greatest virtue, but the parent of all other virtues.

MARCUS TULLIUS CICERO,
Oratio Pro Caeno Plancio, XXXIII

———o———

I Thank God

For the glorious sunshine;
For the gentle showers;
For the fields and mountains;
For the birds and flowers;
For my home and parents;
For Thy care of me;
All my heart, dear Father,
Now I give to Thee.
Amen.
Little Folks

———o———

Matthew Henry, the famous Bible scholar, was once accosted by thieves and robbed of his purse. He wrote these words in his diary:

"Let me be thankful first because I was never robbed before; second, although they took my purse, they did not take my life; third, because, although they took my all, it was not much; and fourth, because it was I who was robbed, not I who robbed."

———o———

He scurried down the gnarled old tree
While two sharp eyes peered out at me,
A bushy tail wagged to-and-fro,
I found a hazelnut to throw.

And on his two hind legs he rose
To catch it; then, in comic pose
He entertained with cunning pranks
Squirrel talk denoting "Many thanks!"

LORRAINE GOOD

Theology

It's about time we gave up all this theological grand opera and went back to practicing the scales.

VANCE HAVNER

Brethren, if you are not theologians, you in your pastorates are just nothing at all.

CHARLES HADDON SPURGEON

———o———

We are not interested in armchair theology but rather that every pastor should be a theologian.

BRUCE D. NICHOLAS, Yeotmal

———o———

Your theology may be as clear as ice, but unless you put it into practice it will leave you just as cold.

Think, Thought

Great thought is no longer the privilege of the few. It is given to all men but for the price of concentration and dedication.

———o———

Be careful of your thoughts. They may break into words at any time.

———o———

Think It Through

Are you worried or depressed?
Think it through.
Feel unequal to the test?
Think it through.
Concentrate your heart and mind,
Get right down to facts and grind,
A solution you can find —
Think it through.

Are you out of luck and work?
Think it through.
Face your problem, do not shirk,
Think it through.
Seek and find your proper place,
Persevere with smiling face,
Be a hero in the race —
Think it through.

Do you feel like giving up?
Think it through.
Is your share a bitter cup?
Think it through.
God gives you the power to do,
He will make it clear to you,
You must do something too —
Think it through.

GRENVILLE KLEISER

God's Thoughts And Mine

(Isaiah 55:8; Philippians 4:8)

The Hammer thoughts
That pound and shatter peace;
The Rodent thoughts
That gnaw and will not cease;

The Briar thoughts
That pull and prick and scratch;
The Rover thoughts
That I can never catch;

The Serpent thoughts
That leave their lairs at night;
The Shadow thoughts
That dim the new day's light;

These are my thoughts.
Oh, take them, Lord, I pray,
Out of my heart
And cast them far away;

And in their stead
Give me those thoughts of Thine
So crystal-clear,
So holy, high and fine,

That I shall grow,
By their pure grace enticed,
Worthy to think
The lovely thoughts of Christ.

AUTHOR UNKNOWN

———o———

The Scriptures remind us that "As a man thinketh in his heart, so is he." This Biblical admonition tells us that we cannot think in terms of failure, and then succeed . . . in terms of weakness, and then be strong . . . in terms of fear, and then be courageous . . . in terms of doubt, and then have faith.

W. G. VOLLMER

———o———

The mind is a garden
Where thought flowers grow,
The thoughts that we think
Are seeds that we sow.

AUTHOR UNKNOWN

———o———

Make not your thoughts your prison.

———o———

We often make our duties harder by thinking them hard.

FREDERICK TEMPLE

A man's life is what his thoughts make it.

MARCUS AURELIUS

————o————

A man is what he thinks about all day long.

RALPH WALDO EMERSON

————o————

You become what you allow yourself to think — even when you don't think so.

————o————

Some people are like automatic elevators; they can remember but they don't think.

Southern California Presbyterian

————o————

Take time to deliberate; but when the time for action arrives, stop thinking and go in.

ANDREW JACKSON

————o————

A group of children first visited a planetarium, then looked at tiny flowers. Afterward they drew on paper some of the things they had seen. One boy put a dot in the corner of the drawing. "This is me," he wrote, then added thoughtfully, "but I am bigger than the stars because I can think."

Quote

————o————

Think Right

Think smiles, and smiles shall be;
Think doubt, and hope will flee;
Think love, and love will grow;
Think hate, and hate you'll know.
Think good, and good is here;
Think vice — its jaws appear!
Think joy, and joy ne'er ends;
Think gloom, and dusk descends.
Think faith, and strength's at hand;
Think ill — it stalks the land.
Think peace, sublime and sweet,
And you that peace will meet;
Think fear, with brooding mind,
And failure's close behind.
Think this: "I'm going to win."
Think not on what has been,
Think victory; think "I can!"
Then you're a winning man!

DAVID V. BUSH

He is the rich man, and enjoys the fruit of his riches, who summer and winter forever can find delight in his own thoughts.

HENRY DAVID THOREAU

————o————

An eight-year-old's definition of thinking: When you keep your mouth shut and your head keeps on talking to itself.

————o————

We probably wouldn't care so much what people think of us if we only knew how seldom they do!

————o————

People who have no time, don't think. The more you think, the more time you have.

HENRY FORD

————o————

Thought begets the will to create.

THOMAS J. WATSON

————o————

The ancestor of every action is a thought.

RALPH WALDO EMERSON

————o————

He who has slight thoughts of sin never had great thoughts of God.

JOHN OWEN

————o————

The greatest thought that can occupy a man's mind is his accountability to God.

DANIEL WEBSTER

————o————

The thoughts you think will irradiate you as though you are a transparent vase.

MAURICE MAETERLINCK

Time

If you have work to do — do it now.
If you have a witness to give — give it now.
If you have a soul to win — win him now.
If you have an obligation to discharge — discharge it now.
If you have a debt to pay — pay it now.

If you have a wrong to right — right it now.

If you have a confession to make — make it now.

If you have a preparation to make — make it now.

If you have children to train — train them now.

AUTHOR UNKNOWN

———o———

Time is passing and you are passing out of time.

ROY L. LAURIN

———o———

Take care of the minutes, for the hours will take care of themselves.

ALEXANDER POPE

———o———

Little drops of water, little grains of sand,
Make the mighty ocean and the pleasant land.
Thus the little minutes, humble though they be,
Make the mighty ages of eternity.

JULIA A. FLETCHER CARNEY

———o———

You will never "find" time for anything. If you want time, you must make it.

CHARLES BUXTON

———o———

Lose an hour in the morning and you will be looking for it the rest of the day.

LORD CHESTERFIELD

———o———

Every year it takes less time to fly across the ocean and longer to drive to the office.

RAYMOND DUNCAN
in *The Saturday Evening Post*

———o———

Years — nothing goes swifter than the years.

OVID

———o———

The years teach much which the days never know.

RALPH WALDO EMERSON

———o———

Kenneth Smith had seven minutes to spare between trips as motorman-

conductor on a trolley line in Baltimore. The half-acre loop where his run ended was covered with a dense underbrush and a thicket. He decided to put his seven minutes to work. At the end of each trip he worked at cleaning out the brush and weeds. Eventually he turned the loop that had been an eyesore into a garden.

JAMES KELLER, *One Moment, Please*

———o———

Time Is

Too Slow for those who Wait,
Too Swift for those who Fear,
Too Long for those who Grieve,
Too Short for those who Rejoice;
But for those who love,
Time is not.

HENRY VAN DYKE, *For Katrina's Sun-Dial*

———o———

If you want to become a man of the hour, learn first to make every minute count.

———o———

One of the illusions of life is to think that the present hour is not the critical and decisive hour. Write it on your heart that every day is the best day of the year.

RALPH WALDO EMERSON

———o———

Great men never complain about the lack of time. Alexander the Great and John Wesley accomplished everything they did in 24-hour days.

FRED SMITH

———o———

The real secret of how to use time is to pack it as you would your luggage, filling up the small spaces with small things.

HENRY HADDOW

———o———

You wake up in the morning, and lo! your purse is magically filled with twenty-four hours of the magic tissue of the universe of your life. No one can take it from you. It is uneatable. No one receives either more or less than you receive. Waste your infinitely precious commodity as much as you will, and the supply will never be withheld from you. Moreover, you cannot draw on the future. Impossible to get into debt. You can only waste the passing moment. You cannot waste tomorrow; it is kept for you.

ARNOLD BENNETT

————o————

If you spend most of the time dreaming of tomorrow and regretting yesterday, you won't find a great deal of time left for doing anything today.

————o————

No Time For Him?

What! No time for Him today?
For Him who traveled all the way
From that solemn Upper Room
To the Garden's stony tomb?

See Him in Gethsemane,
Where great drops of agony
From His brow fall, one by one,
As He prays, "Thy will be done."

Follow Him to Pilate's hall —
Thence to Calvary's bitter gall.
See Him suffer hell's own pangs
While upon the Cross He hangs.

Hear His words — do they decry
Those who led Him there to die?
He prays for those who hate Him most
As He renders up the ghost.

Well I know He willingly
Lived and died — and all for me.
How then can I ever say,
"I've no time for Him today!"

LOUISE E. SCHILLINGER

————o————

Don't fret over what you'd do with your time if you could live it over again . . . get busy with what you have left.

MARTIN VANBEE

————o————

So valuable is time that God gives only a moment of it at once, and He gives that moment but once in all eternity.

————o————

People who cannot find time for recreation are obliged sooner or later to find time for illness.

JOHN WANAMAKER

Mother (explaining the keeping of time): "Here are the hours, these are the minutes, and these are the seconds."

Little daughter: "Where are the jiffies?"

ROSANN MOELLER in My Chum

————o————

An inch of gold will not buy an inch of time.

————o————

A person does the things he really wants to do, but complains about not having time to do the things he pretends he wants to do.

————o————

Well-arranged time is a sure mark of a well-arranged mind.

————o————

Timing is the chief ingredient in judgment.

WILLIAM FEATHER

————o————

Ease Up A Bit

I say, my lad, what's your hurry?
    You can't catch up with time.
No matter how fast you travel,
    You'll always be behind.
So, ease up on the gas a bit,
    Enjoy the trees and sod;
You can't catch up with time, my lad,
    It's in the hand of God.

GARRETT NUVEN

————o————

Take Time

Take time to hear their prayers at night,
And cuddle them a bit.
Tell them a story now and then,
And steal a little time to sit
And listen to their childish talk,
Or take them for a walk.

We little know it now — but soon
They will be gone (the years are swift).
For life just marches on and on;
And heaven holds no sweeter gift
Than shouting boys with tousled hair,
Who leave their joys just anywhere.

Take time to laugh and sing and play,
To really cherish and enjoy
A little girl with flaxen curls
And the small wonder of a boy.
They ask so little when they're small,
Just love and tenderness — that's all.
                    AUTHOR UNKNOWN

Tithing

The Tither's Surprises

The Christian who begins to tithe
will have at least six surprises. He will
be surprised:
1. At the amount of money he has
   for the Lord's work.
2. At the deepening of his spiritual
   life in paying the tithe.
3. At the ease in meeting his own
   obligations with the nine-tenths.
4. At the ease of going from one-
   tenth to a larger giving.
5. At the prudent disposal afforded
   to a faithful and wise steward over
   the nine-tenths that remain.
6. At himself in not adopting the
   plan sooner!

——o——

The Tithe

Ah, when I look up at the cross
Where God's great steward suffered
      loss
Of life and shed His blood for me,
A trifling thing it seems to be
To pay a tithe, dear Lord, to Thee,
Of time or talent, wealth or store —
Full well I know I owe Thee more!
But that is just the reason why
I lift my heart to God on high
And pledge, my love, my all in all.
This holy token at Thy cross
I know as gold, must seem but dross,
But in my heart, Lord, Thou dost see
How it has pledged my all to Thee,
That I a steward true may be.
                    AUTHOR UNKNOWN

——o——

Thy Tithe

My pay-check barely reaching 'round,
In fact, it's sometimes short;
Takes all that I can rake and scrape
To keep up this old fort.

I've doctor bills for aches and ills
And car insurance due.
This traffic ticket must be paid;
The plumber says he'll sue.

I have to get new license tags,
There's income tax to pay,
And then you say give ten percent —
Just show me how, I pray.

Well, here is what the Bible says,
And it is proven true,
"You're putting money in a bag
That has holes thru and thru."

You're paying great "devourers,"
Whom God says He'll rebuke,
Just hold Him to His promise
In six, thirty-eight of Luke.

Right when the hour is darkest
Is time to start this test,
For God can then best show us
Nine-tenths will reach, when blest.
                    CLESSON K. SCOLES

Today

All the flowers of all the tomorrows
are in the seeds of today.
                    Chinese Proverb

——o——

Perhaps Today!

Perhaps today shall sound the mystic
      summons,
The shout, the voice, the trump, not
      by all heard;
And, from their scattered silent resting
      places,
The dead in Christ will rise to meet
      the Lord;
While we, the ransomed, living in a
      moment
Shall be caught up — according to His
      Word.

Perhaps today, from every clime and
      nation,
Shall souls redeemed ascend to meet
      the Lord;
To suffering ones — great, glad eman-
      cipation;
To those who toil for Him, a sure re-
      ward;
We look not down a track of unknown
      years;

It may be that today our Lord appears.

Perhaps today, with problems fresh out-breaking,
With growing evils rampant o'er the earth,
When sore distress, nigh every land is shaking, —
Perhaps today the Saviour may come forth.
Earth's leaders fail; the forces are too great;
But — lift your heads, the Lord is at the gate!

AUTHOR UNKNOWN

———o———

One to-day is worth two to-morrows.

FRANCIS QUARLES

———o———

Today And Time

Today is here. I will start with a smile and resolve to be agreeable. I will not criticize. I refuse to waste my valuable time.

Today in one thing I know I am equal with all others — time. All of us draw the same salary in seconds, minutes, and hours.

Today I will not waste my time because the minutes I wasted yesterday are as lost as a vanished thought.

Today I refuse to spend time worrying about what might happen — it usually doesn't. I am going to spend time making things happen.

Today I am determined to study to improve myself, for tomorrow I may be wanted, and I must not be found lacking.

Today I am determined to do the things that I should do. I firmly determine to stop doing the things I should not do.

Today I begin by doing and not wasting my time. In one week I will be miles beyond the person I am to-day.

Today I will not imagine what I would do if things were different. They are not different. I will make success with what material I have.

Today I will stop saying, "If I had

time —" I know I never will "find time" for anything. If I want time, I must make it.

Today I will act toward other people as though this might be my last day on earth. I will not wait for tomorrow. Tomorrow never comes.

GERALD B. KLEIN

———o———

Our todays and yesterdays are the blocks with which we build.

HENRY WADSWORTH LONGFELLOW

———o———

You are younger today than you ever will be; make use of it for the sake of tomorrow.

———o———

Today well-lived, makes every yesterday a dream of happiness and every tomorrow a vision of hope.

OLIVER WENDELL HOLMES

———o———

Begin Today

Dream not too much of what you'll do tomorrow,
How well you'll work perhaps another year;
Tomorrow's chance you do not need to borrow —
Today is here.

Boast not too much of mountains you will master,
The while you linger in the vale below;
To dream is well, but plodding brings us faster
To where we go.

Talk not too much about some new endeavor
You mean to make a little later on;
Who idles now will idle on forever
Till life is done.

Swear not some day to break some habit's fetter,
When this old year is dead and passed away;
If you have need of living wiser, better,
Begin today!

AUTHOR UNKNOWN

Two Care-Free Days

There are two days of the week about which I never worry.

One of these days is *yesterday*. Yesterday, with all its cares and frets, with all its pains and aches, its mistakes and blunders, has passed forever beyond the reach of my recall. I cannot undo any act that I wrought; I cannot unsay a word that I said on yesterday. All that it holds of my life — of wrongs, regret and sorrow is in the hands of the Mighty Love that can bring honey out of the rock, turn weeping into laughter and give beauty for ashes.

And the other day that I do not worry about is *tomorrow*. Tomorrow, with all its possible adversities, its burdens, its perils, its large promise and poor performance, its failures and mistakes . . . is as far beyond the reach of *my* mastery as its dead sister — yesterday. It is a day of God's. It will be mine.

There is left for myself, then, but one day of the week — today. And any man can fight the battles of today. Any woman can carry the burdens of just one day. Any one of us can resist the temptation of the few moments we call today. It is when we willfully add the burden of those two awful eternities — yesterday and tomorrow — to the burdens and cares of today, that we break down.

Only the mighty God Himself can sustain such burdens. And so, in His infinite wisdom, He has carefully measured out to us our "each day's portion" — and gives the promise "As thy day, so shall thy strength be."

W. J. JEFFERS in *New Horizons*

Tolerance

Tolerance is the only real test of civilization.

SIR ARTHUR HELPS

————o————

I believe with all my heart that civilization has produced nothing finer than a man or woman who thinks and practices true tolerance.

FRANK KNOX

Tolerance is the eternal virtue through which good conquers evil and truth vanquishes untruth.

J. EDGAR HOOVER

————o————

Be quick to always spread a little cloak
Of tolerance on faults of other folk.
Remember that if ALL the truth were known,
A circus tent won't cover up your own!

————o————

The most lovable quality that any human being can possess is tolerance. Tolerance is the vision that enables one to see things from any other's viewpoint. It is the generosity that concedes to others the right to their own opinion and their own peculiarities. It is the bigness that enables us to let people be happy in their own way instead of our way.

AUTHOR UNKNOWN

————o————

Tolerance is the ability to let other people be happy in their own way!

EARLEY

Tomorrow

Satan cares not how spiritual your intentions, or how holy your resolutions, if only they are fixed for tomorrow.

J. C. RYLE

————o————

If you want a life of power in your tomorrows you will need to have been obedient to God in your yesterdays.

CARL E. BRAND

————o————

Jimmy, age four, asked his mother, "Is this tomorrow?"

For ten minutes or so she explained the difference between yesterday, today, tomorrow, and he listened intently.

Then he said, "All I asked was 'is this tomorrow!'"

————o————

The only preparation for tomorrow is the right use of today.

Tomorrows

Don't worry 'bout the yesterdays which
have already gone,
But plan about tomorrows which are
just beyond the dawn.

Events that happen'd yesterday we
never can correct,
While those to come tomorrow, we
can possibly select.

There are so many things to plan for
days which lie ahead,
That time is wasted when we think of
yesterdays instead.

Unpleasant memories which clog the
peacefulness of mind,
Can, with tomorrow's projects, be completely cast behind.

No matter what has taken place upon
the day before,
It soon will be discarded if the morrow
we explore.

FRED TOOTHAKER

Tomorrow Will Not Do

The story is told of a man who
dreamed one night that he was carried to a conference of evil spirits.
They were discussing the best means
of destroying men. One rose and said,
"I will go to earth and tell them the
Bible is a fable, and not God's Word."
Said another, "Persuade them that
Christ was only a man." Still another
said, "Let me go; I will tell them there
is no God, no Saviour, no heaven, no
hell." "No, that will not do," they said.
"We could never make men believe
that."
Finally one old devil, wise as a serpent but not as harmless as a dove,
rose and said: "Let me go; I will tell
them that there is a God, there is a
Saviour, there is a heaven and a hell,
too. But I will tell them there is no
hurry; tomorrow will do; tomorrow will
be even as today!" And he was the
devil they sent!
The story is fiction, but its message
is a fact. The devil is among us today,
now; but the wise are not deceived by
his lies. "What will you do with Jesus
who is called the Christ?" The man

who thinks that tomorrow will do even
as today is of all men the most deceived.

J. H. MARION, JR.

Faith in tomorrow makes today beautiful.

REX MOBLEY

Tongue

The tongue being in a wet place is
prone to slip!

A loose tongue often gets its owner
into tight places.

Even though the tongue weighs
practically nothing, it's surprising how
few people are able to hold it.

If you can hold your tongue you can
hold your temper.

Some can't help having false teeth,
but everyone can have a true tongue.

The examination was complete. The
surgeon assured the young man that
the only hope of saving his life was
the removal of his tongue. The young
man was already in surgery when he
learned the full story. Tenderly the
surgeon told him that even though the
operation should be successful, he
would never again be able to speak.
He was asked if there was anything
he wished to say before the operation
began.
The young man on the operating
table was a Christian. When he realized he would never again be able to
testify in song and word for His Lord,
a shadow crossed his face. But soon
the shadow passed and sitting up he
lifted his voice and sang, "There Is A
Fountain Filled With Blood."
How he sang! His heart was in the
song. Then he came to the last stanza:
"Then in a nobler, sweeter song
I'll sing Thy power to save,

When this poor, lisping, stammering
  tongue
Lies silent in the grave."
The operation was performed, but
the patient never regained consciousness. His last song on earth was prophetic of his first song in heaven.

———o———

On Guard

You have a little prisoner;
  He's nimble, and he's clever;
He's sure to get away from you
  Unless you watch him ever.

And when he once gets out, he makes
  More trouble in an hour
Than you can stop in many a day,
  Working with all your power.

He gets your playmates by the ears;
  He says what isn't so,
And uses many ugly words
  Not good for you to know.

Quick, fasten tight the ivory gates,
  And chain him while he's young!
For this most dangerous prisoner
  Is just — your little tongue.
                    P. L. in *The Young Soldier*

———o———

Prayer For My Tongue

Lord, grant this one request, I pray:
Guide Thou my tongue! The words I
  say
Can never be called back again;
Should they cause anger, sorrow, pain,
Then in an ever wid'ning sphere
They spread their havoc far and near.
So guide my tongue in ev'ry word,
That it may bless where it is heard.
                    EUGENE LINCOLN

———o———

Better to slip with the foot than with
the tongue.
                    English Proverb

———o———

The tongue of slander slays three:
the speaker, the spoken to, and the
spoken of.

———o———

The human tongue is a deadly weapon, whether it be sharp or blunt.

The old-fashioned doctor used to
diagnose the condition of his patient by
his tongue. The same method might
still be used to determine a person's
moral and spiritual health.

Travel

Two matronly ladies to travel agent:
"We'd like to get completely away from
civilization, near some nice shopping
district."
                    FRANKLIN FOLGER, *Newspaper Features*

———o———

To travel is to possess the world.
                    BURTON HOLMES

———o———

If you really look like your passport
photo, chances are you're really not
well enough to travel.
                    General Features Corporation

———o———

Too often travel, instead of broaden-
ing the mind, merely lengthens the conversation.
                    DREW

———o———

If you have some hard bumps, you
are probably traveling out of the rut.

Treasure

Opened Treasures

They opened their treasures, the wise
  men of old,
And prostrate they fell on the ground,
Exultant in spirit, they worshiped the
  Lord,
For Jesus, the Savior, they'd found!

The Treasure of Heaven in Bethlehem
  lay,
Incarnate was God from above;
No wonder their treasures they opened
  to Him —
Their feeble expressions of love!

We may not have treasures of glory or
  gold,
Or perfumes to pour at His feet;
Though if we but knew of the worth
  of the Christ,
We would give Him our homage complete.

Our treasured desires we'd open anew,
Our secrets, our dreams and our all —
We would offer as incense our praises to Him,
Adoring before Him we'd fall!

This Savior from Heaven is worthy indeed;
And treasures of earth become dim!
But joys everlasting in Jesus are found;
Oh, open your treasures to Him!

MARIE L. OLSON in *Now*

———o———

Treasures

One by one He took them from me,
  All the things I valued most,
Until I was empty-handed;
  Every glittering toy was lost,

And I walked earth's highways, griev-
    ing,
  In my rags and poverty,
Till I heard His voice inviting,
  "Lift your empty hands to Me!"

So I held my hands toward Heaven,
  And He filled them with a store
Of His own transcendent riches,
  Till they could contain no more.

And at last I comprehended
  With my stupid mind and dull,
That God could not pour His riches
  Into hands already full!

MARTHA SNELL NICHOLSON

———o———

Borrowed Treasures

I thank you, God —
For all you've given me.
Your sun,
Your beach,
Your ocean's roar;
Your trees upon the cool
Green shore.
I thank You for the rose
Within my garden;
That is Yours.
The starlit skies,
The twinkle in my infant's
Eyes —
The world.

EVALENA FISHER

Trial

If your cup of trial is sometimes bitter, put in more of the sugar of faith. If you feel chilled by the disappointments of your plans or the unkindness of others, get into the sunshine of Christ's love. If income runs down, invest more in God's precious promises. A good, stout, healthy faith will sweeten your affections, and sweeten your toils, and sweeten your home, and sweeten the darkest hours that may lie between this and heaven. Adherence will bring assurance.

THEODORE LEDYARD CUYLER

———o———

God does not take away trials or carry us over them, but strengthens us through them.

EDWARD B. PUSEY

———o———

Nothing will show more accurately what we are, than the way we meet trials and difficulties.

———o———

Trials and temptations do not weaken us, but they do show us where we are weak, that we may become strong.

———o———

Every trial that we pass through is capable of being the seed of a noble character. Every temptation that we meet in the path of duty is another chance of filling our souls with the power of Heaven.

FREDERICK TEMPLE

———o———

Dr. Paul Carlson in his last tape-recorded message before his death at Stanleyville, Congo, said: "Pray that through the trials we face here we may be an effective witness for Christ, and that we may see growth in the church."

———o———

A blacksmith, about eight years after he had given his heart to God, was approached by an intelligent unbeliever with the question: "Why is it you have so much trouble? I have been watching you. Since you joined the Church and began to 'walk square,' and seem to love everybody, you have had twice as many trials and accidents as you had before. I thought that when a man gave himself to God his troubles were over. Isn't that what the parsons tell us?"

With a thoughtful, but glowing face, the blacksmith replied:

"Do you see this piece of iron? It is for the springs of a carriage. I have been 'tempering' it for some time. To do this I heat it red-hot, and then plunge it into a tub of ice-cold water. This I do many times. If I find it taking 'temper,' I heat and hammer it unmercifully. In getting the right piece of iron I found several that were too brittle. So I threw them in the scrap-pile. Those scraps are worth about a cent a pound; this carriage spring is very valuable."

He paused, and his listener nodded. The blacksmith continued:

"God saves us for something more than to have a good time — that's the way I see it. We have the good time all right, for God's smile means heaven. But he wants us for service just as I want this piece of iron. And he has put the 'temper' of Christ in us by testing us with trial. Ever since I saw this I have been saying to him, "Test me in any way you choose, Lord; only don't throw me in the scrap-pile."

——o——

To Be Called A Brick

A brick is made of clay;
    So is man.
A brick is square and plumb and true;
    So a man ought to be.
A brick is useless until it has been
        through the fire;
    So is man.
A brick is not so showy as marble, but
        it is more useful;
    Man is not made for show, but for
        service.
A brick fulfills its purpose only by be-
        coming a part of something greater
        than itself;
    The same is true of a man.
When a man fulfills this description,
    he has a right to be called a brick.
                          AUTHOR UNKNOWN

Trouble

The easiest way to get into trouble is to be right at the wrong time.

——o——

The fellow who's really in trouble is one who's in bad company when he's alone.

——o——

The man was complaining glumly to a friend that family trouble had him down. His friend suggested that perhaps he was taking it too seriously — that there were two sides to every question. "That's right," agreed the morose one, "but in my house the two sides are always my wife's and her mother's."

——o——

It's much easier to borrow trouble than it is to give it away.

——o——

During the First World War, a disastrous fire broke out in the Greek city of Salonica. The historic church of St. Demetrius suffered considerably from the fire. The scorching heat destroyed the plaster covering of the west wall, and exposed a seventh century painting of St. Demetrius fighting a ravaging fire in Salonica in his own day. One of the things that the flames through which we pass do for us is to break through the surface of the years and reveal the souls of the saints and heroes of old who fought similar fires in their own day.

——o——

The person who looks for trouble should have his eyes examined.

——o——

Some people bear three kinds of trouble:
    All they ever had,
    All they have now,
    All they expect to have.
                    EDWARD EVERETT HALE

——o——

A good way to forget your troubles is to help others out of theirs.

A lot of trouble in this world is caused by combining a narrow mind with a wide mouth.

———o———

I have never met a man who has given me as much trouble as myself.

DWIGHT L. MOODY

———o———

When a neighbor once asked a mother of twelve if she had a lot of trouble with so many children, she replied: "Never trouble. Bother at times, maybe. Bother is in the hands. Trouble is in the heart."

———o———

You don't need help to get into trouble, but usually you have it.

Journal-Enquirer, Grayson, Kentucky

———o———

You don't need references to borrow trouble.

———o———

If you must talk about your troubles, don't bore your friends with them — tell them to your enemies, who will be delighted to hear about them.

OLIN MILLER
in Chicago Sun-Times Syndicate

———o———

Borrow trouble for yourself, if that's your nature, but don't lend it to your neighbors.

RUDYARD KIPLING

———o———

All the troubles of life come upon us because we refuse to sit quietly for a while each day in our rooms.

BLAISE PASCAL

———o———

I am an old man and have known a great many troubles, but most of them have never happened.

MARK TWAIN

———o———

When you help out a man in trouble, you can be sure of one thing: he won't forget you — next time he's in trouble.

Illinois General News

———o———

Let us give up our work, our thoughts, our plans, our selves, our

lives, our loved ones, over all into His hands. When you have given all unto God, there will be nothing left for you to be troubled about.

J. HUDSON TAYLOR

———o———

Troubles

I've got a heap of troubles
 And I've got to work them out.
But I look around and see
 There's trouble all about.
And when I see my troubles,
 I just look up and grin
And count all the trouble
 That I'm not in.

True, Truth

It is not hard to find the truth; what is hard is not to run away from it once you have found it.

ETIENNE GILSON in Ladies' Home Journal

———o———

Truth is the hardest missile one can be pelted with.

GEORGE ELIOT (MARY ANN EVANS)

———o———

In any emergency in life there is nothing so strong and safe as the simple truth.

CHARLES DICKENS

———o———

I do not ask that He must prove
His Word is true to me;
And that before I can believe
He first must let me see.
It is enough for me to know
'Tis true because He says 'tis so.
On His unchanging Word I'll stand,
And trust till I can understand.

AUTHOR UNKNOWN

———o———

Truth does not hurt unless it ought to.

———o———

God requires us to give credit to the truths which He reveals, not because we can prove them, but because He reveals them.

DANIEL WEBSTER

———o———

Truth is tough. It will not break,

like a bubble, at a touch; nay, you may kick it about all day, like a football, and it will be round and full at evening.

———o———

It does not require a long lesson to present a great truth.

———o———

Truth is the secret of eloquence and of virtue, the basis of moral authority; it is the highest summit of art and life.
HENRI-FRÉDÉRIC AMIEL, *Journal*

———o———

The New Testament does not say, "You shall know the rules, and by them you shall be bound," but "You shall know the truth, and the truth shall make you free."
JOHN BAILLIE

———o———

The reason some people arrive at the truth a good deal more quickly than others is not because of their intuition or superior brain power. They simply ask more questions.

———o———

Our world is so exceedingly rich in delusions that a truth is priceless.
CARL GUSTAV JUNG

———o———

There is nothing so powerful as truth, — and often nothing so strange.
DANIEL WEBSTER,
Argument on the Murder of Captain White

———o———

Truth is the most valuable thing we have. Let us economize it.
MARK TWAIN
Following the Equator, Vol. I

———o———

We search the world for truth. We cull
The good, the true, the beautiful,
From graven stone and written scroll,
From all old flower-fields of the soul;
And, weary seekers of the best,
We come back laden from the quest,
To find that all the sages said
Is in the Book our mothers read.
JOHN GREENLEAF WHITTIER, *Miriam*

———o———

If you tell the truth, you have in-

finite power supporting you; but if not, you have infinite power against you.
CHARLES GEORGE GORDON

———o———

Truth sits upon the lips of dying men.
MATTHEW ARNOLD, *Sohrab and Rustum*

———o———

No pleasure is comparable to the standing upon the vantage-ground of truth.
FRANCIS BACON, *Of Truth*

———o———

This above all: to thine own self be true,
And it must follow, as the night the day,
Thou canst not then be false to any man.
WILLIAM SHAKESPEARE, *Hamlet*

———o———

Being True

Think truly and thy thought
Shall the world's famine feed;
Speak truly and thy word
Shall be a fruitful seed;
Live truly and thy life
Shall be a great and noble creed.
HORATIUS BONAR

Trust

Trust in God is an antidote for fear of men.

———o———

Trust is the chief conqueror of difficulties.

———o———

They greatly dare who greatly trust. If our faith were greater, our deeds would be larger.

———o———

God has never been able to use any man in a large way who could not be trusted in an emergency.

———o———

You can trust the man who died for you.
MRS. CHARLES E. COWMAN

We were crowded in the cabin;
  Not a soul would dare to sleep;
It was midnight on the waters
  And the storm was in the deep.

'Tis a fearful thing in winter
  To be shattered by the blast,
And hear the rattling trumpet
  Thunder, "Cut away the mast!"

So we shuddered there in silence,
  For the stoutest held his breath
While the hungry sea was roaring
  And the breakers threatened death.

And as thus we sat in darkness,
  Each one busy in his prayers,
"We are lost!" the captain shouted
  As he staggered down the stairs.

But his little daughter whispered,
  As she took his icy hand,
"Isn't God upon the ocean
  Just the same as on the land?"

Then we kissed the little maiden
  And we spoke in better cheer;
And we anchored safe in harbor
  When the morn was shining clear.
                    JAMES T. FIELDS
            from a *McGuffey Fourth Reader*

———o———

Sure, it takes a lot of courage
  To put things in God's hands,
To give ourselves completely,
  Our lives, our hopes, our plans;
To follow where He leads us
  And make His will our own,
But all it takes is foolishness
  To go the way alone.
                       BETSEY KLINE

———o———

I have no answer for myself or thee,
Save that I learned beside my mother's
    knee:
"All is of God that is, and is to be;
And God is good." Let this suffice us
    still,
Resting in childlike trust upon His will
Who moves to His great ends un-
    thwarted by the ill.
                   WILLIAM COWPER

———o———

When I try I fail; when I trust, He
succeeds.

When you cannot trust God you
cannot trust anything; and when you
cannot trust anything you get the condition of the world as it is today.
                        BASIL KING

———o———

Trusting

You ask how you learn to trust Him?
Dear child, you must just let go!

Let go of your frantic worry,
And the fears which plague you so;

Let go of each black tomorrow
Which you try to live today;

Let go of your fevered planning,
He knoweth all your way.

Fear not lest your slipping fingers
Let go of your Saviour too, —

Trusting is only knowing
He'll not let go of you!
            MARTHA SNELL NICHOLSON

———o———

Trust him little who praises all, him
less who censures all, and him least
who is indifferent about all.
                    JOHANN LARATER

———o———

What does a child do whose mother
or father allows something to be done
which it cannot understand? There is
only one way of peace. The loving
child trusts.
                    AMY CARMICHAEL

———o———

It is an equal failing to trust everybody, and to trust nobody.

Try

Try, Try Again

'Tis a lesson you should heed,
  Try, try again;
If at first you don't succeed,
  Try, try again;
Then your courage should appear,
For, if you will persevere,
You will conquer, never fear;
  Try, try again.

Once or twice though you should fail,
  Try, try again;

If you would at last prevail,
  Try, try again;
If we strive, 'tis no disgrace
Though we do not win the race;
What should you do in the case?
  Try, try again.

If you find your task is hard,
  Try, try again;
Time will bring you your reward,
  Try, try again;
All that other folks can do,
Why, with patience, should not you?
Only keep this rule in view:
  Try, try, again.
                              T. H. PALMER

————o————

Triumph is just UMPH added to
TRY!
                         Sunshine Magazine

————o————

You Haven't Tried Yet!

I was busy in my basement worshop
when four-year-old Mike came and
stood at my elbow. "Daddy, will you
fix my scooter?" he asked.

Guiltily, I looked down at the completely wrecked scooter which he held
in his hand. I had backed over it with
the car earlier that day. I couldn't
possibly fix it; it was too badly dam-
aged. Irritated, I said, "Mike, I told
you before that I can't fix your scooter.
I'm sorry."

A troubled expression came over
Mike's face. "But Daddy, you haven't
tried yet!"

How could a father resist such an
appeal? I set to work and, to my
surprise, I discovered that I could fix
the scooter.

Later, I wondered how often we
excuse ourselves from attempting a difficult assignment or taking a new step
in faith by saying, "I can't," when the
truth is we haven't tried yet.
                           HERBERT GIBSON

U

Unbelief

Unbelief is giving God the lie.
          CHARLES HADDON SPURGEON

————o————

Unbelief is something of which the
devils are not guilty.

————o————

God does not think so lightly of our
doubt and unbelief as we do.

Understand, Understanding

The Fifth Commandment

An old schoolmaster said one day to
a clergyman, who came to examine his
school, "I believe the children know the
catchism word for word."

"But do they understand it? That is
the question," said the clergyman.

The schoolmaster bowed respectful-
ly, and the examination began. A little
boy had repeated the fifth commandment, "Honor thy father and thy
mother," and he was asked to explain
it. Instead of trying to do so, the little
boy, with his face covered with blushes, said, almost in a whisper, "Yesterday I showed some strange man over
the mountain, and the sharp stones cut
my feet. The man saw they were
bleeding, and gave me some money
to buy shoes. I gave it to my mother,
for she had no shoes either, and I
thought I could go barefooted better
than she could."
                               Selected

————o————

Teacher: "Johnny, are your folks
diplomats?"
Johnny: "No, they are Lutherans."

————o————

Man to young boy: "Does your dog
have a pedigree?"
Boy: "No, we cut that off."

The story is told of a young theological student who one day came to the great preacher, Charles H. Spurgeon, telling him that the Bible contained some verses which he could not understand about which he was very much worried. To this Spurgeon replied, "Young man, allow me to give you this word of advice: You must expect to let God know some things which you do not understand."

The Sunday School Times

———o———

It is man's mission to learn to understand.

VANNEVAR BUSH

———o———

O God, help us not to despise or oppose what we do not understand.

WILLIAM PENN

———o———

Seeing may be believing, but it isn't necessarily understanding.

Tribune-News, Cartersville, Georgia

———o———

God — let me be aware.
Stab my soul fiercely with others' pain,
Let me walk seeing horror and stain.
Let my hands, groping, find other hands.
Give me the heart that divines, understands.

MIRIAM TEICHNER

———o———

Whoever would fully and feelingly understand the words of Christ, must endeavor to conform his life wholly to the life of Christ.

THOMAS À KEMPIS

———o———

By comparison with God's perfect understanding, we are like a man inside a barrel looking through a bunghole.

R. R. BROWN

Unhappy, Unhappiness

The worst kind of unhappiness, as well as the greatest amount of it, comes from our conduct to each other.

FREDERICK WILLIAM FABER

Whoever does not regard what he has as most ample wealth, is unhappy, though he be master of the world.

EPICURUS

———o———

A perverse temper, and a discontented, fretful disposition, wherever they prevail, render any state of life unhappy.

MARCUS TULLIUS CICERO

Unknown

The world knows nothing of its greatest men.

SIR HENRY TAYLOR

———o———

Everything unknown is taken to be magnificent.

TACITUS

———o———

Unknown, unmissed.

Urgent

Later Than You Think

A young boy awakened at midnight. He listened to the old grandfather's clock strike out the melody of midnight — one, two, three, four . . . and on to twelve. But something went wrong with the old clock and it kept on striking . . . thirteen . . . fourteen . . . fifteen . . . sixteen. The boy became alarmed and ran into his father's bedroom.

He startled his father with these words, "Daddy, I just heard the old clock strike sixteen! It must be later than it's ever been before!"

There's no time to waste. No time for frivolity, or worldly pursuits. It's time to seek the Lord. It's later than it's ever been before!

The Log of the Good Ship Grace

———o———

We have all eternity to tell of victories won for Christ but we have only a few hours before sunset in which to win them.

JONATHAN GOFORTH

Use, Useful, Useless

Square yourself for use. A stone that may fit in the wall is not left in the way.
Persian Proverb

———o———

Let's quit trying to use God and ask God to use us.

———o———

The really useful worker is so busy being useful that he hasn't time to consider how useful he is.

———o———

Use what you have, that you may have more to use.
CHARLES HADDON SPURGEON

Use is the best estimate of value.

———o———

Use pastime so as to save time.

———o———

A Christian girl who was saved from shipwreck by getting into a lifeboat said, "I was not afraid to die, for Christ is my Savior. But I was ashamed to die, for my life had been so useless."

———o———

We lose what we don't use.
ALFRED ARMAND MONTAPERT

———o———

No one is useless in this world who lightens the burden of another.
CHARLES DICKENS

V

Vacation

A vacation should be just long enough for the boss to miss you, and not long enough for him to discover how well he can get along without you.

———o———

There is no vacation from godliness.

———o———

If all the year were playing holidays, To sport would be as tedious as to work.
WILLIAM SHAKESPEARE, *King Henry IV*

———o———

"You didn't take a vacation this year, did you?"
"No, I thought I needed a rest."

———o———

No man needs a vacation so much as the person who just had one.
ELBERT HUBBARD

———o———

Every now and then go away, have a little relaxation, for when you come back to your work your judgment will be surer, since to remain constantly at work will cause you to lose power of judgment. Go some distance away, because then the work appears smaller, and more of it can be taken in at a glance, and lack of harmony and proportion is more readily seen.
LEONARDO DA VINCI

———o———

Isn't it wonderful how school vacation runs out at about the same time as your patience?

———o———

If a person looks tired and careworn, don't suggest a vacation. He has probably just had one.

Valentine

First Time

The wee man held in one chubby hand
A valentine message so true,
A small red heart and written inside
Those three magic words, "I love you."

This moment both shall long remember,

For nothing is ever so fine
As when a lad gives his first sweet-
heart
Her very first gay valentine.
VIRGINIA K. OLIVER

———o———

Oh! if it be to choose and call thee
mine,
Love, thou art everyday my Valentine.
THOMAS HOOD

———o———

Valentine To A School Teacher:

The bees do the work
  And the bees get the honey;
But we do the work
  And you get the money!

Value, Values

Sound Values

Marshall Field once indicated the
following twelve reminders that can
be helpful in obtaining a sound sense
of values:

The value of time.
The success of perseverance.
The pleasure of working.
The dignity of simplicity.
The worth of character.
The power of kindness.
The influence of example.
The obligation of duty.
The wisdom of economy.
The virtue of patience.
The improvement of talent.
The joy of originating.
MARSHALL FIELD

———o———

What we obtain too cheaply, we esteem too lightly. It is dearness, that
gives everything its value.
THOMAS PAINE

———o———

A sense of values is the most important single element in human personality.

———o———

No inferior form of energy can be
simply converted into a superior form
unless at the same time a source of
higher value lends it support.
CARL GUSTAV JUNG

Treasures

I was standing in Tiffany's great
store in New York, and I heard the
salesman say to a lady who had asked
him about some pearls, "Madam, this
pearl is worth $17,000."

As I looked around that beautiful
store, I imagined them bringing all
their stock up to my house, and saying,
"We want you to take care of this tonight." What do you think I would do?
I would go as quickly as I could to the
telephone and call up the Chief of
Police and say, "I have all Tiffany's
stock in my house, and it is too great a
responsibility. Will you send some of
your most trusted officers to help me?"

But I have a little boy in my home,
and for him I am responsible. I have
had him for nine years, and some of
you may have just such another little
boy. I turn to this old Book and I read
this word: "What shall it profit a man if
he gain the whole world and lose his
own soul?" It is as if he had all the
diamonds and rubies and pearls in the
world, and held them in one hand, and
just put a little boy in the other, and
the boy would be worth more than all
the jewels. If you would tremble because you had $17,000 worth of jewels
in the house one night, how shall you
go up to your Father and your son be
not with you?
J. WILBUR CHAPMAN

———o———

The chemical analysis of the human
body is:

Sulphur	Enough to rid a dog of fleas.
Lime	Enough to whitewash a chicken coop.
Fat	Enough for six bars of soap.
Iron	Enough for a 6-penny nail.
Phosphorus	Enough for twenty boxes of matches.
Sugar	Enough for ten cups of coffee.
Potassium	Enough to explode a toy cannon.

Total value, ninety-eight cents!
Scientists of Northwestern University

have re-estimated the value of the basic elements in the human body, formerly placed at ninety-eight cents, and consider them now worth $31.04.

———o———

The parent who gives his child seventy-five cents for a movie and a dime for Sunday School is teaching him a set of values that could carry through a lifetime.

———o———

We can only be valued as we make ourselves valuable.

RALPH WALDO EMERSON

Victory

It was Paul who had malaria and poor eyesight, who was whipped, imprisoned, stoned and shipwrecked who said, "God has turned my life into a pageant of triumph."

A. BONNINGRAM

———o———

The first and best victory is to conquer self; to be conquered by self is, of all things, the most shameful and vile.

PLATO

———o———

God will give us the victory if we will go to the fight.

———o———

There is no victory without the stench and heat of battle; there is no shining without burning. But when we finish our spiritual campaign in the battlefield of earth, we will stand before our Lord Jesus Christ and be pleasing to Him.

LIEUTENANT ROBERT C. HOLLAND, JR.

———o———

Christ spells victory. Even though we have trials and tribulations, we experience defeats and frustrations, we can be of good cheer because we know that the One in whom we have placed our confidence has overcome the world.

———o———

Before the winds that blow do cease,
  Teach me to dwell within Thy calm;
Before the pain has passed in peace,

Give me, my God, to sing a psalm,
Let me not lose the chance to prove
The fulness of enabling love.
O Love of God, do this for me:
Maintain a constant victory.

AMY CARMICHAEL

———o———

On the day of victory, no fatigue is felt.

Arab Proverb

———o———

The first step on the way to victory is to recognize the enemy.

CORRIE TEN BOOM

———o———

The way to get the most out of a victory is to follow it up with another which makes it look small.

HENRY S. HASKINS

———o———

Victory

Keep on trying, forego sighing,
God will help us do our best.
It's by working, not by shirking,
We find comfort, joy and rest.
It's by loving, not by hating,
That we build the life sublime;
It's our blessing, not our cursing,
That brings victory, every time.

BERNICE SMITH

———o———

To be effective one must be unaffected. Outward defeat often spells inward victory.

———o———

A life of victory hinges upon three things: an act, a purpose, and a habit: an initial act, a fixed purpose, a daily habit.

The initial act is that of personal surrender to the Lord Jesus as Master.

The fixed purpose is that of doing what will please Him, and only that, at every turn, in every matter, regardless of consequences.

The daily habit is that of spending a quiet time daily in prayer alone with the Lord over His Word. After the initial act of surrender, the secret of a strong, winsome Christian life is in spending time daily alone with God over His Word in prayer.

S. D. GORDON

———o———

Victory is a thing of the will.

MARSHAL FERDINAND FOCH

———o———

Victories that are easy are cheap. Those only are worth having which come as the result of hard fighting.

HENRY WARD BEECHER

———o———

If there be no enemy, no fight;
If no fight, no victory;
If no victory, no crown.

SAVONAROLA

Virtue, Virtuous

Sincerity and truth are the basis of every virtue.

CONFUCIUS

———o———

When men grow virtuous in their old age, they only make a sacrifice to God of the devil's leavings.

ALEXANDER POPE,
Thoughts on Various Subjects

———o———

The [Christian] Puritan held, incredible as it may seem, that morals are more important than athletics, business or art; that the good life must be founded on virtue.

RALPH BARTON PERRY

———o———

Virtue has many preachers, but few martyrs.

CLAUDE ADRIEN HELVETIUS

———o———

A large part of virtue consists in good habits.

WILLIAM PALEY

———o———

Virtue can see the duty regardless of how great the darkness be.

———o———

Riches adorn the dwelling; virtue adorns the person.

Chinese Proverb

Virtue herself is her own fairest reward.

SILIUS ITALICUS, *Punica*

———o———

Rarely do we like the virtues we do not have.

———o———

Virtue is a jewel of great price.

———o———

Virtue consists in doing our duty in the various relations we sustain to ourselves, to our fellowmen, and to God, as it is made known by reason, revelation, and Providence.

ARCHIBALD ALEXANDER

———o———

The greatest offense against virtue is to speak ill of it.

WILLIAM HAZLITT

———o———

We value great men by their virtue and not their success.

CORNELIUS NEPOS

Vision

Poor eyes limit your sight; poor vision limits your deeds.

FRANKLIN FIELD

———o———

Vision is the art of seeing things invisible.

JONATHAN SWIFT,
Thoughts on Various Subjects

———o———

Vision is of God. A vision comes in advance of any task well done.

KATHERINE LOGAN

———o———

The vision of God is the transfiguration of the world; communion with God is the inspiration of the life.

BROOKE FOSS WESTCOTT

Visit, Visitation

Visit neighbors, kith, and kin,
But don't always be about.
Often too much dropping in
Causes falling out.

JANE MERCHANT

One day I rang a door bell,
In a casual sort of way.
'Twas not a formal visit,
And there wasn't much to say.
I don't remember what I said —
It matters not, I guess —
I found a heart in hunger,
A soul in deep distress . . .
It meant so little to me
To knock at a stranger's door,
But it meant heaven to him
And God's peace forever more.

AUTHOR UNKNOWN

———o———

Visits always give pleasure — if not
the coming, then the going.

Portuguese Proverb

Vocation
Vocation

By the way I do my job —
  keep a ledger,
  till the soil,
  prepare a meal,
  advise a client,
  love my child,
  serve a customer —
I witness to my faith, and win on
behalf of the church a good reputation
  before the world.

FRED C. HOLDER

———o———

Teen-ager to vocational counselor:
"How do I know what I want to be
when I get out of school? Maybe
they haven't even invented my job yet."

The Improvement Era

W

Wait

All things come to him who waits —
provided he knows what he is waiting
for.

WOODROW WILSON

———o———

Satan has many wiles. His favorite
is "Wait a while."

———o———

I Must Wait

I know I am impatient, Lord,
I want to run ahead;
Speak to my heart and make me
Willing to be led.
Your clock is always right, Lord
It never does run late;
Your schedule can't be hurried
So teach me, Lord, to wait.

Your time is never my time —
Oh, make this plain to me
And give me patience so to wait
And Thy fulfillment see.
I see through a glass darkly
And in this earthly state
I only know impatience,
So teach me, Lord, to wait.

I pray for Thy anointing,
I need Thy holy touch;
Oh, send me a full measure —
I need it, oh, so much.
Please keep me calm and trusting
In this world of strife and hate;
And 'mid the hurrying, worrying throng
Oh, teach me, Lord, to wait.

RETA BELLE LYLE

———o———

Waiting for a phone call frets him,
Waiting on his wife upsets him.
Almost any kind of waiting
Starts his temper activating.
He's the guy who finds delight
Waiting for the fish to bite!

S. OMAR BARKER in *Capper's Weekly*

———o———

They Wait Too Long

Some people wait too long in life
To use their clever brains.
And then they find it is too late
To make impressive gains.
They will not take the time to get
The knowledge they require
To reach the glorious success
To which their hearts aspire.

For they would rather have their fun
And play around today,
Than try to reach a certain goal
That seems so far away.
The value of their dreams in life
Is something that they measure
In terms of idle wanderings
And moments made for pleasure.

And strange as it may seem, they have
The nerve to weep and wail
And wonder why with all their brains
Their feeble efforts fail.

JAMES J. METCALFE

———o———

Wait Upon The Lord

Wait thou, my soul, upon the Lord —
  He is thy strength and life:
Lift up thy heart — mount up and fly
  Above the stress and strife;
For there thy strength shall be re-
    newed
  In that celestial sphere;
Then through the valley thou canst
    walk
  By faith and not by fear.

Wait thou, my soul, upon the Lord,
  And with the wings of faith,
Rise up to mountain tops of truth
  Where each reviving breath
Shall fill thy soul with songs of joy;
  And on the sacred height,
Renew thy strength to walk the plain,
  Amid the gloom of night.

Thou art too weak to walk the paths
  Where days seem dark and long?
Then wait on Him, thy gracious Lord,
  Until the victor's song
Thou, too, hast heard amid the heights
  And cherished as thine own —
Until on mountain tops of faith
  The triumph has been won.

Wait then upon the Lord; yea, wait
  Till earthly doubts grow dim;
Yea, mount above the clouds of care
  And fellowship with Him.
There He will train thee for the task
  Where common duties call,
And in the strength renewed by Him
  Thou shalt not faint or fall.

AUTHOR UNKNOWN

The man who waits for things to
turn up, usually finds that his toes do
it first.

———o———

While you wait for great things, the
door to the little ones may close.

American Friend

———o———

Patient waiting is often the highest
way of doing God's will.

———o———

All good abides with him who wait-
eth wisely.

HENRY DAVID THOREAU

Walk

It is better to walk straight, even
though alone, than to stagger in the
"best" of circles.

———o———

I'm a slow walker, but I never walk
back.

ABRAHAM LINCOLN

———o———

Men think of a fifty-mile hike as
training in physical fitness. Women
call it shopping.

———o———

The one who walks with God always gets to his destination.

———o———

One who walks with God always
knows in what direction he is going.

———o———

I like long walks, especially when
they are taken by people who annoy
me.

FRED ALLEN

Want

A Man Must Want

It's wanting keeps us young and fit;
It's wanting something just ahead
And striving hard to come to it,
That brightens every road we tread.

The man is old before his time
Who is supremely satisfied,

And does not want some hill to climb
Or something life has still denied.

A man must want from day to day,
Must want to reach a distant goal
Or claim some treasure far away,
For want's the builder of the soul.

He who has ceased to want has
    dropped
The working tools of life, and stands
Much like an old-time clock has
    stopped,
While time is moldering his hands.

Want is the spur that drives us on
And oft its praises should be sung,
For man is old when want is gone —
It's what we want that keeps us young.
AUTHOR UNKNOWN

———o———

It's impossible to have everything
you want because if this were so you'd
always be missing the fun of wanting
something.

———o———

Some people think they are poor
just because they do not have everything they want.
ROY L. SMITH

———o———

God is waiting to be wanted.
A. W. TOZER

War

The tragedy of war is that it uses
man's best to do man's worst.
HARRY EMERSON FOSDICK

———o———

I bet you that history don't record
any two nations ever having a war
with each other unless they had a conference first.
WILL ROGERS

———o———

The only way to make war impossible
is to stop getting ready for war.
FRANK CRANE

———o———

War is death's feast.

———o———

War! that mad game the world so
loves to play.
JONATHAN SWIFT,
Ode to Sir William Temple

Waste

Waste of Muscle, waste of Brain,
Waste of Patience, waste of Pain,
Waste of Manhood, waste of Health,
Waste of Beauty, waste of Wealth,
Waste of Blood, waste of Tears,
Waste of Youth's most precious years,
Waste of Ways the Saints have trod,
Waste of Glory, waste of God — War!
G. A. STUDDERT-KENNEDY

———o———

There never was a good war, or a
bad peace.
BENJAMIN FRANKLIN

———o———

War is the business of barbarians.
NAPOLEON BONAPARTE

———o———

Take my word for it, if you had seen
but one day of war, you would pray to
Almighty God, that you might never
see such a thing again.
THE DUKE OF WELLINGTON

Watch

In the children's meeting we sang
with the smallest children:
"Be careful, little eyes, what you see.
Be careful, little ears, what you hear.
Be careful, little mouth, what you
say . . .
For the Father up above
Is looking down on you in love,
So be careful . . ."
Little almost four-year-old Hans
broke out in tears. "No!" he shouted,
"I don't want to have a father who
watches over me so carefully."
Had he not uttered from his heart
that which we sometimes feel? We
want a loving God who helps us out
of all our difficulties, but not One who
sees the wrong things we do.
HEDWIG GUT, in *Gospel Call*

———o———

A man becomes wise by watching
what happens to him when he isn't!

———o———

Teacher: "Jimmy, what are you doing?"

Jimmy: "Nothing! With you and Mom and God and Santa Claus watching all the time, what can I do?"

———o———

Watching man as our ideal does not make us spiritual.

———o———

No one ever falls into sin as the result of being too watchful.

Water

A crew shipwrecked in the Atlantic had been drifting for days in a small lifeboat, suffering from extreme thirst. When all hope had been abandoned, smoke was discerned on the horizon and a vessel bore down upon them. With all their strength they mustered a pitiful shout, "Water! Water!" From the bridge came what seemed to be a mocking answer, "Dip your bucket over the side!" Without knowing it, they had drifted into the area where the mighty Amazon River bears its fresh waters out to sea. Unaware, they were floating in an ocean of plenty. "Ho, every one that thirsteth, come . . ." says God's Word.

———o———

Water: A liquid that freezes slippery side up.

Way

You Know The Way

Shortly after 1918, when the Soviets came to power in western Russia, a young baroness of German parentage was thrown into prison and condemned to death. While waiting for execution, Marion Von Klodt, a devout Christian, wrote a hymn, which was immediately taken up by other prisoners and swept through camps across Russia. Today it is sung in many languages in churches across the communist world. Marion Von Klodt sang the hymn as she went before the firing squad.

You know the way,
  Though I myself do not,

This thought gives me
  A peace beyond compare.
What shall I fear
  What terrors fill with anguish,
By night and day,
  Although my soul does languish?

You know the way;
  You also know the time.
Your plan for me
  Has long since been prepared.
I praise you, Lord,
  With all my deepest feeling
For all your care,
  Your love to me revealing.

You know all things:
  From whence the wind doth blow.
The storm of life
  You can alone subdue.
I am at peace,
  Content, though still not knowing,
For you have planned
  The way I am now going.
                              MARION VON KLODT

Weakness

Although men are accused of not knowing their own weakness, yet perhaps as few know their own strength. It is in men as in soils, where sometimes there is a vein of gold which the owner knows not of.
                              JONATHAN SWIFT

———o———

The acknowledgement of our weakness is the first step toward repairing our loss.
                              THOMAS A KEMPIS

———o———

You cannot run away from a weakness; you must some time fight it out or perish; and if that be so, why not now, and where you stand?
                              ROBERT LOUIS STEVENSON,
                              The Amateur Emigrant

Wealth

You can use the wealth of this world in the service of the Master. To gain is not wrong. It is only wrong when grasping becomes the main object of life.
                              CHARLES HADDON SPURGEON

Wealth makes worship.
Old Proverb

If we command our wealth, we shall be rich and free. If our wealth commands us, we are poor indeed.
EDMUND BURKE

A thousand times God called his name,
A thousand times God touched his hand;
He turned aside for wealth and fame;
And built his house upon the sand.
FRANKLIN PIERCE RENO

Wealth consists not in having great possessions, but in having few wants.
EPICURUS

Weddings

The kindest and the happiest pair
Will find occasion to forbear,
And something every day they live
To pity, and perhaps forgive.
WILLIAM COWPER

Dad gets the worst of it, no doubt,
With daughter's wedding frills:
At first the wedding BELLS ring out
Then come the wedding BILLS.

A golden wedding is when the couple has gone fifty-fifty!

There's nothin' like a weddin'
To make a feller learn;
At first he thinks she's his'n,
But later finds he's her'n.
AUTHOR UNKNOWN

Weight

The difference between a career girl and a housewife is twenty pounds.

It's not the minutes you take at the table that make you overweight — it's the seconds.

A little girl was describing a set of scales: "It's something you stand on and then get really mad."

Paunch Lines

Hey diddle, diddle,
I'm watching my middle,
I'm hoping to whittle it soon;
But eating's such fun
I may not get it done,
Till my dish runs away with my spoon!
Printed from *The Owl* in the *Hi-Desert Star*

One Weigh

I lost five pounds;
No one said a word.
I gained back three —
And that's all I've heard!
LUCY LOLLI RANKIN in *Family Weekly*

A larger-than-average woman stepped on the scales, not knowing they were out of order. The indicator stopped at seventy-five pounds.
A little boy standing by watched her intently. "Whaddaya know," he marveled. "She's hollow!"

Wicked

There is a method in man's wickedness, —
It grows up by degrees.
FRANCIS BEAUMONT and JOHN FLETCHER,
A King and No King

No man ever became extremely wicked all at once.
JUVENAL, *Satires*

For never, never, wicked man was wise.
ALEXANDER POPE, *Odyssey of Homer*

Wife

Nothing lovelier can be found
In woman, than to study household good,
And in good works her husband to promote.
JOHN MILTON

Thy wife is a constellation of virtues; she's the moon, and thou art the man in the moon.

WILLIAM CONGREVE, *Love for Love*

———o———

How much the wife is dearer than the bride.

GEORGE, LORD LYTTELTON

———o———

Ten Commandments For Wives

I. Honor thy own womanhood, that thy days may be long in the house which thy husband provideth for thee.

II. Expect not thy husband to give thee as many luxuries as thy father hath given thee after many years of hard labor and economies.

III. Forget not the virtue of good humor, for verily all that a man hath will he give for a woman's smile.

IV. Thou shalt not nag.

V. Thou shalt coddle thy husband, for verily every man loveth to be fussed over.

VI. Remember that the frank approval of thy husband is worth more to thee than the sidelong glances of many strangers.

VII. Forget not the grace of cleanliness and good dressing.

VIII. Permit no one to assure thee that thou art having a hard time of it; neither thy mother, nor thy sister, nor thy maiden aunt, nor any of thy kinfolk, for the judge will not hold her guiltless who letteth another disparage her husband.

IX. Keep thy home with all diligence, for out of it cometh the joys of thine old age.

X. Commit thy ways unto the Lord thy God and thy children shall rise up and call thee blessed.

———o———

A successful wife knows how much to believe of what she hears about her husband.

Pioneer-Times, Houlton, Maine

———o———

All other good by fortune's hand are given,
A wife is the peculiar gift of heaven.

ALEXANDER POPE

What is there in the vale of life
Half so delightful as a wife,
When friendship, love, and peace combine
To stamp the marriage-bond divine?

WILLIAM COWPER

———o———

His house she enters, there to be a light,
Shining within, when all without is night;
A guardian angel o'er his life presiding,
Doubling his pleasures, and his cares dividing!

SAMUEL ROGERS, *Human Life*

———o———

The world well tried — the sweetest thing in life
Is the unclouded welcome of a wife.

NATHANIEL PARKER WILLIS, *The Lady Jane*

———o———

While the true wife clings and leans, she also helps and inspires.

O. G. WILSON

———o———

An ideal wife is any woman who has an ideal husband.

BOOTH TARKINGTON

———o———

The ideal wife is one who knows when her husband wants to be forced to do something against his will.

SYDNEY J. HARRIS

———o———

A constantly nagging wife had a momentary change of heart and bought her husband two neckties for his birthday. Finding them on his dresser, the surprised husband put one on and went down to the dining room for breakfast.

"Humph!" the wife snorted. "So you don't like the other one?"

Watchman-Examiner

———o———

A perfect wife does not expect a perfect husband.

Courier, Houma, Louisiana

———o———

A wife is one who remodels your funny stories as you tell them.

Will, Willing

He that complies against his will
Is of the same opinion still.
Which he may adhere to, yet disown
For reasons to himself best known.
SAMUEL BUTLER, *Hudibras*

———o———

He is a fool who thinks by force or
skill
To turn the current of a woman's will.
SIR SAMUEL TUKE, *Adventures of Five Hours*

———o———

Where is the man who has the power
and skill
To stem the torrent of a woman's will?
For if she will, she will, you may depend on't;
And if she won't, she won't; so there's
an end on't.
*Inscribed on a pillar on the mount in
the Dane John Field, Canterbury*

———o———

Our wills are ours, we know not how,
Our wills are ours, to make them
thine.
ALFRED, LORD TENNYSON,
In Memoriam

———o———

Where there's a will there's a lawsuit.

———o———

Most parents know from experience
that where there's a will, there's a
won't.
FRANCIS O. WALSH

———o———

If a mother could mix the willingness
of a two-year-old with the brawn of a
sixteen-year-old, she'd have a real
helper.
Journal-Transcript, Franklin, New Hampshire

———o———

All lay hold on the willing horse.

———o———

The secret of an unsettled life lies
too often in an unsurrendered will.

———o———

People do not lack strength; they
lack will.
VICTOR HUGO

Don't make the mistake of taking
your will for God's will.

Winter

I love thee, all unlovely as thou seem'st,
And dreaded as thou art.
WILLIAM COWPER, *The Task*

———o———

God gave us our memories so that
we might have roses in December.
SIR JAMES MATTHEW BARRIE

———o———

Winter lingered so long in the lap of
Spring that it occasioned a great deal
of talk.
EDGAR WILSON NYE

———o———

I crowned thee king of intimate de-
lights,
Fireside enjoyments, home-born happi-
ness,
And all the comforts that the lowly
roof
Of undisturb'd Retirement, and the
hours
Of long uninterrupted evening, know.
WILLIAM COWPER, *The Task*

———o———

Winter Viewpoints

Restful time when the earth slumbers
'neath the snow,
Hiding all her treasures while frosty
north winds blow.

A time when woodland creatures have
need of bounty store,
And yet God watches over them while
winter's at their door.

Enchanted time for children, as crystal
flakes of white
Descend to make a wonderland and
fill hearts with delight.

A fireside time for grown-ups when
home is best of all,
And golden memories of the past are
pleasant to recall.
LAVERNE P. LARSON

The Lovely Days Of Winter

The lovely days of winter come,
The wind is like a muffled drum.
I did not miss this pastel sky
When summer roses bloomed near-
by;
I did not know that on this hill
There was such beauty, chaste and
still;
That mirrored ice in frozen stream
Could catch and hold a vagrant
dream;
That tall bare trees so hard and brown
Could sing though leaves had fluttered
down —
But now with new-found joy I see
All that summer hid from me.

AUTHOR UNKNOWN

Wise, Wisdom

The only person less popular than
a wise guy is a wise guy who's right.

———o———

What this country needs is a special
encyclopedia with blank pages for
those who know everything.

———o———

The wise man appreciates the good
points of the worst things that happen
to him.

———o———

It is what we find out after we know
it all, that counts.

———o———

There is nothing so like a wise man
as a fool who holds his tongue.

ST. FRANCIS DE SALES

———o———

Nine tenths of wisdom consists of
being wise in time.

THEODORE ROOSEVELT

———o———

I recall the advice given to me when
as a young, green editor I joined the
staff of a New York book publishing
house. I asked the publisher in just
what line he thought I should specialize. His reply was interesting.
"The successful editor may know a
little about many things or much about
a few things, but one thing is absolutely
necessary: He must know how to use
the wisdom and experience of others."

WILLIAM H. LEACH in Church Management

———o———

The lesson of wisdom is, be not dismayed by soul-trouble. Count it no
strange thing, but a part of ordinary
Christian experience. Should the power of depression be more than ordinary,
think not that all is over with your
usefulness. Cast not away your confidence, for it hath great recompense of
reward. Even if the enemy's foot be on
your neck, expect to rise and overthrow
him. Cast the burden of the present,
along with the sin of the past and the
fear of the future, upon the Lord. Live
by the day — aye, by the hour.

CHARLES HADDON SPURGEON

———o———

The wise man doesn't expect to find
life worth living; he makes it that way.

———o———

Wisdom doesn't always mean knowing what to do. It can be just as important to know what not to do.

———o———

Wise people believe only half of
what they hear — wiser ones know
which half to believe.

———o———

Many might attain to wisdom, if
they were not assured that they already possessed it.

SENECA

———o———

The wisdom of today is the fruit of
the education of all past centuries. We
are heirs to the accomplishments of
forgotten ages. The knowledge we possess is as a tree which draws its life
from the debris of forests that have
crumpled into dust.

HENRY WARD BEECHER

———o———

He is a wise man who does not
grieve for the things which he has not,
but rejoices for those which he has.

EPICTETUS

The clouds may drop down titles and
   estates;
Wealth may seek us; but wisdom must
   be sought;
Sought before all; (but how unlike all
   else
We seek on earth!) 'tis never sought
   in vain.
       EDWARD YOUNG, *Night Thoughts*

———o———

Knowledge is proud that he has learned
   so much;
Wisdom is humble that he knows no
   more.
       WILLIAM COWPER, *The Task*

———o———

It is more easy to be wise for others
than for ourselves.
       FRANÇOIS, DUC DE LA ROCHEFOUCAULD

———o———

Burt, Jr., was one of the Three Wise
Men in the Sunday School pageant,
and so was his father, one Christmas
long ago. "Well, Dad," he said, "wisdom must run in the family."

———o———

Wisdom

When I have ceased to break my wings
Against the faultiness of things,
And learned that compromises wait
Behind each hardly opened gate,
When I can look Life in the eyes,
Grown calm and very coldly wise,
Life will have given me the Truth,
And taken in exchange – my youth.
       SARA TEASDALE, *Wisdom*

———o———

Wisdom is knowing when to speak
your mind and when to mind your
speech.

———o———

He is wise who has endured all the
pains of mankind – and still smiles in
serenity.

———o———

Wisdom is ofttimes nearer when we
   stoop
Than when we soar.
       WILLIAM WORDSWORTH

The wise man must be wise before,
not after the event.
       EPICHARMUS

———o———

"Tommy," said his Uncle John, "do
you have a girl?"
"I should say not," shouted the ten-
year-old and ran off to his baseball
game.
   The little girl next door smiled
wisely at Uncle John and said, "They're
always the last ones to know."
       FRANK HOLLAND

———o———

Be wiser than other people if you
can; but do not tell them so.
       LORD CHESTERFIELD, *Letter to His Son*

Wish

My Daily Wish

My daily wish is that we may
See good in those who pass our way:
Find in each a worthy trait
That we shall gladly cultivate;
See in each one passing by
The better things that beautify –
A softly spoken word of cheer,
A kindly face, a smile sincere.

I pray each day that we may view
The things that warm one's heart
   anew:
The kindly deeds that can't be
   bought –
That only from the good are wrought,
A burden lightened here and there,
A brother lifted from despair,
The aged ones freed from distress;
The lame, the sick brought happiness.

Grant that before each sun has set
We'll witness deeds we can't forget:
A soothing hand to one in pain,
A sacrifice for love – not gain;
A word to ease the troubled mind
Of one whom fate has dealt unkind.
So, friend, my wish is that we may
See good in all who pass our way.
       PHIL PERKINS

———o———

For every person who wishes dreams
came true, there are at least ten who
thank heaven that they don't.

Many of us spend half our time wishing for things we could have if we didn't spend half our time wishing.

Talelights

Witness

Who builds a church within his heart
And takes it with him everywhere
Is holier far than he whose church
Is but a one-day house of prayer.

MORRIS ABEL BEER,
The Church in the Heart

————o————

Witnessing is first by being and then by doing.

————o————

They witness best for Christ who say least about themselves.

————o————

Billy Sunday's choir leader, Homer Rodeheaver, told the following touching story about a boy who sang in his choir:

Joey was not quite bright. He would never leave the tabernacle at night till he could shake my hand. He would stand right next to me until the last man had gone in order to say good-bye. It was embarrassing at times. One evening a man came forward to speak to me. He said, "I want to thank you for being so kind to Joey. He isn't quite bright and has never had anything he enjoyed so much as coming here and singing in the choir. He has worked hard during the day in order to be ready in time to come here at night. He has coaxed us to come too, and it is through him that my wife and our five children have been led to the Lord. His grandfather, seventy-five years old and an infidel all his life, and his grandmother have come tonight, and now the whole family is converted."

————o————

Witnessing is not just something a Christian says, but what a Christian is!

Of course words are important — but they are no substitute for Christ-like demeanor. Pious language cannot camouflage profane practice.

Indeed, words constitute an indictment against the man whose actions contradict what he professes.

The world will listen if the life manifests Christian character . . . the world will scoff at the emptiness of words, however pious, if the witness of the life is wanting.

Conditioned to demonstration, modern man awaits the confirmation of the claims by the consistent conduct of the claimant.

Let every serious-minded Christian who would be an effective witness for Christ live as though he had to earn the right to be heard.

RICHARD C. HALVERSON

————o————

Witnessing is the unfulfilled part of man's devotion.

MARK LEE

————o————

Resolution

Could I but dip a brush of flame
Into a pot of gold,
Across the sky I'd write His name
In letters brilliant, bold.
Had I a voice of thunder,
Or the lightning's brilliant flash,
Could I make use of ocean's roar —
The angry waves that dash,
Of these and more I would avail
To make His wonders known,
To cause all mankind to cry "Hail!"
And worship at His throne.
But since I can't make use of these,
I'll faithful witness give
To draw men's hearts,
My God to please —
By how I daily live!

CHARSTEN CHRISTENSEN

————o————

Every called soul is to be a herald and a witness; and we are to aim at nothing less than this, to make every nation, and every creature in every nation, acquainted with the Gospel tidings.

A. T. PIERSON

————o————

Christ did not tell His disciples to sit still and let sinners come to them.

Woman, Women

What a strange thing is man! And
what a stranger
Is woman! What a whirlwind is her
head,
And what a whirlpool full of depth
and danger
Is all the rest about her! Whether
wed,
Or widow, maid or mother, she can
change her
Mind like the wind; whatever she has
said
Or done, is light to what she'll say or
do; —
The oldest thing on record, and yet
new!

LORD BYRON

———o———

Woman, they say, was only made of
man;
Methinks 'tis strange they should be so
unlike!
It may be all the best was cut away,
To make the woman, and the naught
was left
Behind with him.

FRANCIS BEAUMONT and JOHN FLETCHER

———o———

If the heart of a man is depress'd
with cares,
The mist is dispell'd when a woman
appears.

JOHN GAY, The Beggar's Opera

———o———

Earth's noblest thing, a Woman perfected.

JAMES RUSSELL LOWELL, Irene

———o———

O woman! lovely woman! Nature
made thee
To temper man; we had been brutes
without you;
Angels are painted fair, to look like
you;
There is in you all that we believe
of heaven,
Amazing brightness, purity, and truth,
Eternal joy, and everlasting love.

THOMAS OTWAY, Venice Preserved

With women the heart argues, not
the mind.

MATTHEW ARNOLD

———o———

An explorer says an Eskimo woman
is old at forty. An American woman
is not so old at forty. In fact, she's
not even forty!

———o———

Not all women give most of their
waking thoughts to the problem of
pleasing men. Some are married.

———o———

As soon as you cannot keep anything from a woman, you love her.

PAUL GERALDY

———o———

A woman will wear a swim suit
when she doesn't swim, a tennis outfit when she doesn't play tennis, and
ski pants when she doesn't ski. But
when she puts on a wedding dress —
she means business.

———o———

Women can never be as successful
as men; they have no wives to advise
them.

———o———

No wonder women live longer than
men — see how long they're girls.

———o———

Women are very loyal. When they
reach an age they like, they stick to it.

———o———

Women are unpredictable. You never know how they're going to manage
to get their own way.

BEATRICE MANN in Buck Bits

———o———

A woman needs no eulogy, she
speaks for herself.

———o———

Woman was last at the cross and
first at the grave of Christ.

———o———

Anyone can recognize a nagging
woman except when that woman is
looking in a mirror.

A woman's whole life is a history of the affections.

WASHINGTON IRVING,
Rip Van Winkle. The Broken Heart

———o———

The difference between a beautiful woman and a charming woman: A beautiful woman is a woman you notice, while a charming woman is one who notices you.

Sunshine Magazine

———o———

The only way to understand a woman is to love her — and then it isn't necessary to understand her.

SYDNEY J. HARRIS

———o———

It does not take a very bright woman to dazzle some men.

Wonder

We Wonder

We all have wondered, more or less,
Why this or that must be.
Why some of us find happiness
That others fail to see.
Why some of us are lifted high
And lead throughout life's role,
While others even though they try
Can never reach their goal.

Why some can meet the tempter's wrath
And find the strength to stay
Upon the straight and narrow path
And never lose their way;
While others walking by their side
Will try to beat life's game,
And wander off where paths are wide
That lead to sin and shame.

And oftentimes when death draws near,
With sickle grim and cold,
To reap the life of someone dear,
The young as well as old;
We'll hear the question asked by some,
If all of this is just;
If life is worth the struggle from
The embryo to the dust.

We ponder over many things,
But here we'll never know

The reason for the happenings
That mystify us so;
But when earth's scenes recede and we
Respond to Heaven's call,
We'll see things then as God doth see
And understand them all.

DONALD LAVERN WALKER

———o———

Wonder is the feeling of a philosopher, and philosophy begins in wonder.

PLATO

Words

The oldest, shortest words — "yes" and "no" — are those which require the most thought.

PYTHAGORAS

———o———

Good words are worth much, and cost little.

GEORGE HERBERT, *Jacula Prudentum*

———o———

Many a blunt word has a sharp edge.

———o———

I'm careful of the words I say
To keep them soft and sweet.
I never know from day to day,
Which ones I'll have to eat.

———o———

The knowledge of words is the gate of scholarship.

JOHN WILSON

———o———

If you insist upon having the last word, make it your first.

———o———

Our words have wings, but fly not where we would.

GEORGE ELIOT (MARY ANN EVANS)

———o———

High praise and honour to the bard is due
Whose dexterous setting makes an old word new.

HORACE

———o———

A word to the wise is enough.

PLAUTUS

Some by old words to fame have made
  pretence,
Ancients in phrase, mere moderns in
  their sense;
Such labored nothings, in so strange a
  style,
Amaze the unlearned, and make the
  learned smile.
ALEXANDER POPE,
Essay on Criticism, Part II

———o———

A blow with a word strikes deeper
than a blow with a sword.
ROBERT BURTON, Anatomy of Melancholy

———o———

Harsh words, though pertinent, un-
  couth appear;
None please the fancy who offend the
  ear.
SIR SAMUEL GARTH, The Dispensary

———o———

O, many a shaft at random sent
Finds mark the archer little meant!
And many a word, at random spoken,
May soothe or wound a heart that's
  broken!
SIR WALTER SCOTT,
The Lord of the Isles. Canto V

———o———

He draweth out the thread of his
verbosity finer than the staple of his
argument.
WILLIAM SHAKESPEARE,
Love's Labour's Lost

———o———

Most Important Words

Five most important words: I am
  proud of you.
Four most important words: What is
  your opinion?
Three most important words: If you
  please.
Two most important words: Thank you.
The least important: I.
This Day

———o———

Boy: "Father, may I have an encyclopedia?"
Father: "No, I bought you a bicy-
cle, use it."

One good thing you can give and
still keep is your word.

———o———

How much can you say in a three-
minute phone call? A lot. Slow talkers
can get in about 450 words, while
people who talk fast can whiz through
about 750 words.
Many important ideas can be expressed in three minutes. Consider:
  Lincoln needed only 267 words for
the Gettysburg Address.
  Shakespeare used just 363 for Hamlet's famous soliloquy, "To Be Or Not
To Be."
  The Lord's Prayer has 56 words.
  The Ten Commandments, which set
a whole moral code for mankind, 297.
  In contrast, the words used in a Federal order dealing with the price of
cabbage totaled 26,911.

———o———

About Words

Never be afraid of big words.
Most big words name little things,
Like microscopical, and mosquito, and
  pediculosis.
Most small words name big things,
Like sky, and land and air and sun,
And man and wife and love and life
  and God.

Try to use small words.
It is hard to do, but they say what
  you mean.
If you don't know what you mean, use
  big words.
They will confuse little people.
AUTHOR UNKNOWN

———o———

Don't stop to pick up the kind words
you drop.

———o———

A timely word may lessen stress, but
a loving word may heal and bless.

———o———

Words

A careless word may kindle strife;
A cruel word may wreck a life.

A bitter word may hate instill;
A brutal word may smite or kill.

A gracious word may smooth the way;
A joyous word may light the day.

A timely word may lessen stress;
A loving word may heal and bless.

MILDRED HOUSTON

———o———

The difference between the right word and the almost right word is the difference between lightning and the lightning bug.

MARK TWAIN

———o———

Words that sound wise to certain people sound ridiculous to others; for some people value only the speaker, others what is said.

Work

A noble life is not a blaze
Of sudden glory won,
But just an adding up of days
In which good work is done.

AUTHOR UNKNOWN

———o———

If you owned the company, would you want someone to do the job you're doing the way you're doing it?

BREE SMITH

———o———

Work hard — the job you save may be your own.

———o———

Get your spindle and your distaff ready, and God will send you the flax.

English Proverb

———o———

Be glad for work that's difficult,
For tasks that challenge you;
Workers find a thousand joys
The idle never do.

———o———

Put work into your life and life into your work.

———o———

I began by working with my own hands for my daily bread.

HERBERT HOOVER

A *Working Prescription*

Seldom do physicians of the various medical schools agree in the diagnosis and treatment of diseases, but the following prescription is one that is unanimously recommended and accepted:
If health is threatened — work.
If disappointments come — work.
If you are rich — continue to work.
If faith falters and reason begins to fail — work.
If dreams are shattered and hope seems dead — work.
If sorrow overwhelms you and loved ones are untrue — work.
If you are burdened with seemingly unfair responsibilities — work.
If you are happy — keep right on working. For where there is idleness there is room for doubt and fear.
No matter what ails you — work. Work as if your life were in peril, for it is!

War Cry

———o———

All work and no play makes Jack a big tax bill.

———o———

Too often we attempt to work for God to the limit of our incompetency, rather than to the limit of God's omnipotency.

J. HUDSON TAYLOR

———o———

I learned to work mornings, when I could skim the cream off the day and use the rest for cheese-making.

JOHANN WOLFGANG VON GOETHE

———o———

If He has work for me to do I cannot die.

HENRY MARTYN

———o———

It is better to burn the candle at both ends, and in the middle, too, than to put it away in the closet and let the mice eat it.

HENRY VAN DYKE

———o———

If you must choose between getting a job done and getting credit for it, get it done.

No man is born into the world whose
work
Is not born with him; there is always
work,
And tools to work withal, for those who
will;
And blessed are the horny hands of
toil!

JAMES RUSSELL LOWELL,
A Glance Behind the Curtain

———o———

The tendency to work is born in us,
but laziness is acquired.

———o———

Absence of occupation is not rest,
A mind quite vacant is a mind distress'd.

WILLIAM COWPER, *Retirement*

———o———

Every community has at least one
poor soul who will do all the work if
given a few chairmanships.

———o———

An employee entered the manager's
office to ask for a raise: "I've been
here nearly ten years doing three men's
work for one man's pay," he said.
"I'm sorry we can't give you a raise,"
said the manager, "but if you'll tell
me who the other two men are I'll fire
them."

———o———

Personnel manager of applicant:
"What we're after is a man of vision,
a man with drive, determination, fire;
a man who never quits; a man who
can inspire others; a man who can pull
the company's bowling team out of
last place!"

———o———

An employment office was checking
on an applicant's list of references:
"How long did this man work for you?"
a former employer was asked.
"About four hours," was the quick
reply.
"Why, he told us he'd been there a
long time," said the astonished caller.
"Oh, yes," answered the ex-employ-
er, "he's been here two years."

Wall Street Journal

Most people like hard work. Particularly when they are paying for it.

FRANKLIN P. JONES
in *The Saturday Evening Post*

———o———

Lord, temper with tranquillity
My manifold activity,
That I may do my work for Thee
In very great simplicity.

AUTHOR UNKNOWN

———o———

Thank God every morning when you
get up that you have something to do
that day which must be done, whether
you like it or not. Being forced to
work, and forced to do your best, will
breed in you temperance and self-control, diligence and strength of will,
cheerfulness and content, and a hundred virtues which the idle never
know.

CHARLES KINGSLEY,
Town and Country Sermons

———o———

Everyone admires a worker. Even
a mosquito gets a pat on the back
when he starts working.

———o———

Very often we are half out of our
predicament the moment we get up
and start working.

———o———

I've Often Found

I've often found that working with my
hands
Has eased my heart when I have been
distressed;
Despair has yielded to a straight, white
hem,
A sock to mend, a crumpled gown
I've pressed.

And once or twice when hope was
strangely lost
The hurt was lessened when I baked
a pie,
And I felt gayer when I washed the
towels
In crisp, bright suds and hung them
out to dry.

There is a rhythm of relief, dear God,
In quiet toil, and so I ask of you
Then when life brings me disappoint-
ment, grief,
My hands may find some humble
task to do.

HELEN WELSHIMER

A Psalm Of Life

Let us, then, be up and doing,
With a heart for any fate;
Still achieving, still pursuing,
Learn to labour and to wait.

HENRY WADSWORTH LONGFELLOW

If the power to do hard work is not
a talent, it is the best possible substitute for it.

JAMES ABRAM GARFIELD

Your work should be a challenge,
not a chore; a blessing, not a bore.

HAL STEBBINS

Waste not your Hour, nor in the vain
pursuit
Of This and That endeavour and dispute.

EDWARD FITZGERALD,
Rubáiyát of Omar Khayyám

Things are never so much appreciated as when, like a chicken, we must
do a certain amount of scratching for
what we get.

EPICTETUS

Folks who never do any more than
they get paid for, never get paid for
any more than they do.

I never did anything worth doing
by accident, nor did any of my in-
ventions come by accident.

THOMAS ALVA EDISON

If you have built castles in the air,
your work need not be lost. Now put
the foundations under them.

HENRY DAVID THOREAU

The best preparation for tomorrow's
work is to do your work as well as you
can today.

ELBERT HUBBARD

When Henry Ward Beecher expressed his admiration for a horse he
was hiring, the liveryman responded
enthusiastically. "He'll work any place
you put him and will do all that any
horse can do."

Beecher regarded the horse with
greater appreciation than before and
said wistfully, "I wish he were a member of my church! How we need
workers like him!"

LEO POLMAN in *Christian Life*

Nothing makes a man work like being "debt propelled."

Let me but find it in my heart to say,
This is my work; my blessing, not my
doom;
Of all who live, I am the one by whom
This work can best be done in the
right way.

HENRY VAN DYKE, *The Three Best Things*

The Christian cannot have his God
without being willing to work in His
service. Even Adam was not allowed
to be idle in the Garden, but was given
something by God to do (Genesis 2:
15).

MARTIN LUTHER

No rule of success will work if you
don't.

If you want work well done, select
a busy man — the other kind has no
time.

The man who does not do more work
than he's paid for isn't worth what he
gets.

ABRAHAM LINCOLN

World

Attachment to Christ is the only secret of detachment from the world.

Carol Willis, eight, was writing hard, and her lawyer-father sat down to look over her shoulder. "I'm writing a report on the world," she said. Mr. Willis wondered if that wasn't a pretty big order. "It's okay," she said. "Three of us in my class are working on it."

NEIL MORGAN in *San Diego Tribune*

———o———

Ever see a world so fine
As this world of yours and mine?
Sun and moist from end to middle,
Just as sweet as song and fiddle;
Dust and dew, and rest and dream,
Country roads and rippling stream,
Town and city, mill and street —
Ever see a world so sweet?

Baltimore Sun

———o———

A Strip Of Blue

I do not own an inch of land,
  But all I see is mine —
The orchards and the mowing fields,
  The lawns and gardens fine.
The winds my tax collectors are,
  They bring me tithes divine —
Wild scents and subtle essences,
  A tribute rare and free;
And, more magnificent than all,
  My window keeps for me
A glimpse of blue immensity,
  A little strip of sea.

Here I sit as a little child
  The threshold of God's door
Is that clear band of chrysoprase;
  Now the vast temple floor,
The blinding glory of the dome
  I bow my head before.
Thy universe, O God, is home,
  In height or depth to me;
Yet here upon Thy footstool green
  Content I am to be.
Glad when is opened unto my need
  Some sea-like glimpse of Thee.

LUCY LARCOM

———o———

The Bible shows how the world progresses. It begins with a garden, but ends with a holy city.

PHILLIPS BROOKS

———o———

The world is too much with us. Late and soon,

Getting and spending, we lay waste our powers.

WILLIAM WORDSWORTH, *Sonnet*

———o———

The devil will promise you the whole world, but he doesn't own a grain of sand.

———o———

The Christian is not ruined by living in the world, but by the world living in him.

———o———

The world today needs reality, not formality.

LESTER SUMRALL

———o———

Take the world as it is, not as it should be.

German Proverb

Worry

An unusual woman was being interviewed by a reporter. Although a widow for years, she had reared six children of her own and twelve adopted children. In spite of her busy and useful life, she was noted for her poise and charm.

The reporter asked how she had managed.

"You see, I'm in a partnership."

"What kind of partnership?"

She replied, "One day, a long time ago, I said, 'Lord, I'll do the work, and you do the worrying,' and I haven't had a worry since."

War Cry

———o———

Did you know that when you are worrying, you are literally choking yourself to death? The very word "worry" comes from an old Anglo-Saxon word which means "to choke!"

———o———

Worry and faith are incompatible. If your faith is strong, you need not worry. If it is weak, worrying won't help it.

S. T. LUDWIG

———o———

Daily Dozen For Worriers

1. Believe in yourself — you are marvelously endowed.

2. Believe in your job — all honest work is sacred.
3. Believe in this day — every minute contains an opportunity to do good.
4. Believe in your family — create harmony by trust and cooperation.
5. Believe in your neighbor — the more friends you can make the happier you will be.
6. Believe in uprightness — you cannot go wrong doing right.
7. Believe in your decisions — consult God first, then go ahead.
8. Belive in your health — stop taking your pulse . . .
9. Believe in your church — you encourage others to attend by attending yourself.
10. Believe in the now — yesterday is past recall; tomorrow may never come.
11. Believe in God's promises — "I am with you always." He meant it!
12. Believe in God's mercy — if God forgives you, you can forgive yourself. Try again tomorrow.

ALASTAIR MACODRUM in *Christian Herald*

———o———

When Peter Marshall was chaplain of the U.S. Senate he once shocked that dignified body in his opening prayer by saying:

"Help us to do our very best this day and be content with today's troubles, so that we shall not borrow the troubles of tomorrow. Save us from the sin of worrying, lest stomach ulcers be the badge of our lack of faith. Amen."

———o———

It is not the work, but the worry
That drives all sleep away,
As we toss and turn and wonder
About the cares of the day.
Do we think of the hands' hard labor
Or the steps of the tired feet?
Ah, no! But we plan and wonder
How to make both ends meet.

———o———

Green Pastures

Last night I started counting sheep
When I had gone to bed,

For I had worries large and small
Which drove sleep from my head.
The sheep had many little lambs
And these I counted too,
Thus through the flock I went until
The Shepherd came in view.
And then I thought, "Why spend the time
In simply counting sheep
When I can walk with Him and pray
For folk who cannot sleep?"
I walked with Him awhile, and then
He smiled, and said to me —
"Look back, where are your worries now?"
But not one could I see!

MILDRED ALLEN JEFFERY

———o———

Worry empties a day of its strength, not of its trouble.

———o———

When you feel down at the mouth, think of Jonah. He came out all right.

———o———

Worry has nowhere to go, and it gets nowhere.

———o———

Our fatigue is often caused not by work, but by worry, frustration and resentment.

DALE CARNEGIE

———o———

Worry Or Pray?

Worry? Why worry? What can worry do?
It never keeps a trouble from overtaking you.
It gives you indigestion, and wakeful hours at night,
And fills with gloom the days, however fair and bright.

It puts a frown upon the face, and sharpness in the tone,
We're unfit to live with others, and unfit to live alone.
Worry? Why worry? What can worry do?
It never keeps a trouble from overtaking you.

Pray? Why pray? What can praying do?

Praying really changes things, arranges
life anew.
It's good for your digestion, gives
peaceful sleep at night,
And fills the grayest, gloomiest day
with rays of glowing light.

It puts a smile upon your face, the
love note in your tone,
Makes you fit to live with others, and
fit to live alone.
Pray? Why pray? What can praying
do?
It brings God down from Heaven, to
live and work with you.

AUTHOR UNKNOWN

———o———

When you are worried, read:
The Upholding Verses Isaiah 41:10, 13
The Optimism Verse   Romans 8:28
The Waiting Verse   Psalm 27:14

Worship

To worship the Holy Trinity is an
art taught by the Holy Spirit. He uses
various schools: the school of suffering,
the school of experience, the school of
knowledge. He uses people to teach
this art, and one of them is you.

M. L. K. in *Lutheran Education*

———o———

When a fellow claims that he can
worship as well out in the open country, in a mountain resort or at the
beach as he can at church, it seems
that he probably feels no particular
urge to worship at all.

———o———

Worship is more than words, and
communion is deeper than conversation.

NORMAN R. OKE

———o———

True worship doesn't depend on
preacher or place, but on the attitude
of the heart.

———o———

What Is Worship?

It is the exposure of what man is
to what he ought to become.

It is the knife of conscience re-
moving that which offends.
It is the medicine of the Great
Physician for tired bodies and weary
souls.
It is the door into the abundant
life.
It is the hand of a small child seeking the hand of his Father.
It is permitting our bodies to rest
while our souls catch up.
It is the book of memories and aspirations.
It is our little soul seeking the bigness of God.

———o———

What greater calamity can fall upon
a nation than the loss of worship.

THOMAS CARLYLE

———o———

One who knows God, worships God.

———o———

We become like that which we worship — God, self, or anything else.

———o———

As you worship, so you serve.

THOMAS LATHERN JOHNS

———o———

"What do you think about when you
see church doors open to everyone
who wants to worship God there?" a
teacher asked her Sunday School class
in an integrated Washington, D.C.,
church. A Negro junior replied, "It
is like walking into the heart of God."

———o———

True worship is not lip service but
life service.

———o———

Worship refreshes the soul as sleep
refreshes the body.

Worth

To realize the worth of the anchor,
we need to feel the storm.

———o———

So much is a man worth as he es-
teems himself.

FRANCOIS RABELAIS, *Works. Book II*

If one could buy some people at their real worth and sell them for what they think they are worth, he would soon become rich.

———o———

What you are determines your worth.

———o———

The unexamined life is not worth living.

PLATO

———o———

Any worth found in man is the worth of One who was more than man.

Wound

What wound did ever heal but by degrees?

WILLIAM SHAKESPEARE

———o———

Love On, O Heart, Love On!

If wounded by some critic's word,
  Or hurt by tongues that utter lies;
If false reports on you are heard
  By those who watch with faithless
    eyes,
Don't seek revenge and rise to strike
  And think your foes will soon be
    gone,
Or hope that God your pluck will like,
  But love, O heart, love on, love on!

Love on in spite of wounding darts,
  In spite of what the critics say;
Love men through grace that God im-
    parts
  When at the feet of Christ you pray.
The way of love will bring you out,
  Though dark the night before the
    dawn;
Then keep in faith and shun the doubt,
  And love, O heart, love on, love on!

WALTER E. ISENHOUR

Write

In The Dark

I keep a little memo pad
Beside my bed, to write
The multitude of thoughts and things
Which come to me at night;
Ideas rare are written there,

Reminders — how I need them —
The only trouble is, of course,
Comes morning, I can't read them.

STEPHEN SCHLITZER

———o———

The fellow who can recognize the handwriting on the wall probably has a child who writes legibly.

———o———

A good writer is one who knows that little words never hurt a really big idea.

———o———

A journalism student, while visiting a newspaper plant, came to the editorial room and asked the City Editor: "If you please, sir, could you give me a few pointers on how to run a newspaper?"

"Sorry, son, but you've come to the wrong person," replied the Editor. "Just ask any one of our subscribers."

———o———

"Professor, what is this you wrote at the end of my paper?"

"I only suggested that you write plainer next time."

———o———

The budding author sent a poem to an editor and wrote: "Please let me know at once if you can use it for I have other irons in the fire."

The editor wrote back: "Remove irons and insert poem."

———o———

Editors call themselves "we" so the person who doesn't like an article will think there are too many for him to lick.

———o———

Anybody can make history; only a great man can write it.

OSCAR WILDE

———o———

"Do you think any of your writings will live on after you are gone?"

"Oh, that doesn't worry me at all. What I am anxious about is that my writings keep me living on before I go."

When I started out to write and mispelled a few words, people said I was just plain ignerant. But when I got all the words wrong, they declared I was a humorist and said I was quaint.

WILL ROGERS

———o———

How easy is pen-and-paper piety! I will not say it costs nothing; but it is far cheaper to work one's head than one's heart to goodness. I can write a hundred meditations sooner than subdue the least sin in my soul.

THOMAS FULLER

———o———

He who wields the pen shapes the future.

LUTHER WESLEY SMITH

———o———

The one thing that most men can do better than anyone else is read their own handwriting.

———o———

A Junior High English class, assigned a composition on "My Family" got this classic essay turned in:
"My father is an insurance man and my mother is a tired housewife."

———o———

The only real problem the writer has found since the discovery of papyrus is to write.

HAL G. EVARTS in The Writer

———o———

For men use, if they have an evil turn, to write it in marble: and whoso doth us a good turn we write it in dust.

THOMAS MORE,
Richard III and his Miserable End

———o———

Of writing many books there is no end.

ELIZABETH BARRETT BROWNING

———o———

By a long habit of writing one acquires a greatness of thinking and a mastery of manner which holiday writers, with ten times the genius, may vainly attempt to equal.

OLIVER GOLDSMITH

———o———

Never write what you dare not sign.

I'll make thee glorious by my pen,
And famous by my sword.

JAMES GRAHAM MONTROSE,
My Dear and Only Love

———o———

Beneath the rule of men entirely great,
The pen is mightier than the sword.

EDWARD GEORGE BULWER-LYTTON, Richelieu

Wrong

It may make a difference to all eternity whether we do right or wrong today.

JAMES F. CLARKE

———o———

One wrong action can cause a lifelong regret.

———o———

There's nothing shameful about being wrong. Nobody can be right all the time.

———o———

It is better to suffer wrong than to do it, and happier to be sometimes cheated than not to trust.

SAMUEL JOHNSON

———o———

Many three-word phrases in our language are powerful or significant or informative; but the one that probably gives the greatest over-all peace of mind is "I was wrong."

Advocate, Allen, Oklahoma

———o———

It is easy to tell when you're on the wrong road. You hardly ever see any detour signs.

———o———

It is a wicked thing to be neutral between right and wrong.

THEODORE ROOSEVELT

———o———

A wrong-doer is often a man that has left something undone, not always he that has done something.

MARCUS AURELIUS, Meditations. VIII

———o———

If things go wrong don't go with them.

ROGER BABSON

Y

Yesterday

Don't let yesterday use up too much of today.

WILL ROGERS

———o———

Live in the sunshine of today and not in the shadows of yesterday.

———o———

Striking from the Calendar
Unborn Tomorrow and dead Yesterday.

EDWARD FITZGERALD,
The Rubáiyát of Omar Khayyám

Yield

We make ourselves the servants of that one to whom we yield.

———o———

It is no virtue to be so unyielding that you cannot consider any position other than your own.

———o———

The willow which bends to the tempest often escapes better than the oak which resists it.

SIR WALTER SCOTT

Yoke

Yokes are good for youthful shoulders.

———o———

Christ has a yoke for our necks as well as a crown for our heads.

———o———

Christ's yoke is lined with love.

———o———

He who said, "My yoke is easy," did not live an easy life.

You, Yourself

You will not be loved yourself if you love none but yourself.

———o———

Be yourself. Ape no greatness. Be willing to pass for what you are. A good farthing is better than a bad sovereign. Affect no oddness; but dare to be right, though you have to be singular.

SAMUEL COLEY

———o———

Be yourself. It is an impossibility to be otherwise, though thousands attempt it.

A. PURNELL BAILEY

———o———

Believe in yourself, and what others think won't matter.

RALPH WALDO EMERSON

———o———

You

"Your task — to build a better world," God said.
I answered, "How?
This world is such a large, vast place,
So complicated now!
And I so small and useless am —
There's nothing I can do!"
But God, in all His wisdom, said,
"Just build a better you!"

DOROTHY R. JONES

Young, Youth

If you want to keep young, work with young people. If you want to grow old, try to keep up with them.

———o———

In America, the young are always ready to give those who are older than themselves the full benefit of their inexperience.

OSCAR WILDE

———o———

"Hello, George! You have changed; what's making you look so old?"
"Trying to keep young," was the reply.
"Trying to keep young?" queried the other.
"Yes — nine of them," was the gloomy response.

There's probably nothing wrong with the younger generation that the older generation didn't outgrow.

———o———

Blessed are the young, for they shall inherit the national debt.

HERBERT HOOVER

———o———

Young people are our most priceless national asset.

J. EDGAR HOOVER

———o———

A boy's voice changes when he reaches fourteen; a girl's when she reaches a telephone.

———o———

Young people are alike these days in many disrespects.

———o———

Young people, like soft wax, soon take an impression.

———o———

Youth is not a time of life — it is a state of mind. You are as young as your faith, as old as your doubt; as young as your self-confidence, as old as your fear; as young as your hope, as old as your despair.

J. C. BRASWELL

———o———

Don't say that modern youth is wild,
Just exercise forbearance;
The faults within each problem child
May come from problem parents.

———o———

The problem of youth is not youth — it is the spirit of the age.

———o———

We need to train youth for action but educate them for speech and thought.

———o———

In youth we run into difficulties, in old age difficulties run into us.

"JOSH BILLINGS" (HENRY WHEELER SHAW)

———o———

Happy will he be in old age who learns to trust God in the days of his youth.

Never forget or prove false the dreams of your youth.

———o———

Youth

You see youth as a joyous thing
About which love and laughter cling;
You see youth as a joyous elf
Who sings sweet songs to please himself.
You see his laughing, sparkling eyes
To take earth's wonders with surprise,
You think him free from cares and woes,
And naught of fears you think he knows,
You see him tall, naively bold,
You glimpse these things, for you are old.

———o———

A group of high school girls was practicing the anthem for the Sunday morning service. They lacked breath when they came to the long "A-a-a-men." The leader, a highly trained musician, said: "Now, girls, if you don't hold that 'A' so long you will have more time for the 'men'."

———o———

Youth needs more to learn how to think than what to think.

———o———

The follies of youth become the vices of mankind and the disgrace of old age.

———o———

Wise is the youth who does not employ his first years so as to make his last miserable.

———o———

Don't laugh at a youth for his affectations; he is only trying on one face after another to find his own.

L. P. SMITH

———o———

One young person showing the family album to a friend: "I threw away all my comic books when I found this!"

Z

Zeal, Zealous

Zeal is like fire; it needs both feeding and watching.

———o———

Zeal without knowledge is like haste to a man in the dark.

Zeal that is spiritual is also charitable.

———o———

Zeal without knowledge is fire without light.

JOHN RAY

———o———

INDEX

(Capital letters indicate the main listing of a heading which is a separate subject in the Sourcebook.)